Theorizing
COMMUNICATION

*To Heidi's Dad—whose patience with
problems seemed nearly endless and*

To Karen Tracy—Bob's partner in life

Theorizing
COMMUNICATION

Readings
Across
Traditions

Edited by

Robert T. Craig
University of Colorado at Boulder

Heidi L. Muller
University of Northern Colorado

SAGE Publications
Los Angeles • London • New Delhi • Singapore

For information:

Sage Publications, Inc.
2455 Teller Road
Thousand Oaks, California 91320
E-mail: order@sagepub.com

Sage Publications India Pvt. Ltd.
B 1/I 1 Mohan Cooperative Industrial Area
Mathura Road, New Delhi 110 044
India

Sage Publications Ltd.
1 Oliver's Yard
55 City Road
London EC1Y 1SP
United Kingdom

Sage Publications Asia-Pacific Pte. Ltd.
33 Pekin Street #02-01
Far East Square
Singapore 048763

Printed in the United States of America.

Library of Congress Cataloging-in-Publication Data

Theorizing communication: readings across traditions/edited by Robert
T. Craig and Heidi L. Muller.
    p. cm.
Includes bibliographical references and index.
ISBN 978-1-4129-5237-8 (pbk.)
  1. Communication—Research. 2. Communication—Research—History. I. Craig, Robert T.
II. Muller, Heidi L.

P91.3.T49 2007
302.207′2—dc22   2006034021

This book is printed on acid-free paper.

07   08   09   10   11   10 9 8 7 6 5 4 3 2 1

Acquiring Editor:	Todd R. Armstrong
Editorial Assistant:	Sarah K. Quesenberry
Project Editor:	Astrid Virding
Copyeditor:	Renee Willers
Typesetter:	C&M Digitals (P) Ltd.
Proofreader:	Scott Oney
Indexer:	Juniee Oneida
Cover Designer:	Candice Harman
Marketing Associate:	Amberlyn M. Erzinger

CONTENTS

INTRODUCTION

HEIDI L. MULLER AND ROBERT T. CRAIG

Theorizing Communication: Readings Across Traditions, a new introduction to communication theory based on an integrative model for the field, is designed to engage readers in a very practical project of theorizing communication. Craig (1999) envisioned communication theory as a field of study that integrates seven distinct traditions of thought with a shared focus on practical communication problems (see unit II, reading 5). Leading textbooks have adopted the seven traditions model as an overview perspective of the field. Because communication theory actually encompasses hundreds of different theories that approach communication from various, seemingly unrelated points of view, the subject is notoriously confusing for beginning students. Making sense of communication theory is further complicated by the diversity of intellectual styles within the communication discipline. Because different theories are in essence written in different languages, assembling a coherent picture of communication theory often seems like an unwieldy if not overwhelming task. Brief textbook overviews of the integrative model are therefore helpful for giving the field some initial unity and structure, thus helping students to make sense of it.

Our purpose in this book is to provide a deeper background for understanding and using that integrative approach to communication theory. For that purpose we have assembled a reference collection of primary source readings along with introductory notes and suggestions for further research. The readings include both classic texts from the traditions of communication theory and newer selections reflecting current trends. The book creates a more fully developed structure for making sense of the varied and constantly evolving ideas that compose the field of communication theory. It also highlights the possibility, practicality, and usefulness of the project of theorizing communication for everyone ranging from advanced scholars to curious general readers.

THE PROJECT OF THEORIZING COMMUNICATION

Communication theory is more than just an expansive litany of abstract concepts formulated by accomplished scholars for others to understand, apply, and investigate. For us, to study communication theory means to become actively engaged in the project of theorizing communication. This is not a project that is somehow removed from ordinary life. Theorizing is a formalized extension of everyday sense-making and problem solving. Theorizing begins with a heightened awareness of our own communication experiences and expands that awareness to engage with communication problems and practices in the social world. Theories are not just intellectual abstractions; they are ways of thinking and talking that arise from different interests, and they are useful for addressing different kinds of practical problems. Over time, specific avenues of thought have been surveyed and cleared (and sometimes paved) as scholars and others have participated in these specialized forms of discourse. These established, cultivated ways of thinking and talking are what we call traditions of communication theory. Learning communication theory means learning these traditions, learning how to use them as lenses for examining communication problems in different ways, and learning how to participate in the specialized forms of discourse by which the traditions of communication theory constantly grow, develop, and change.

To summarize in a different way, learning to engage in the project of theorizing communication as we approach it in this book has four key requirements. First, we must understand the close connection between theoretical ways of thinking and talking about communication and our ways of thinking and talking about communication in everyday life. Second, we must understand the logic of practical theory—how theories can be explicitly designed and used to address practical problems. Third, we must understand the traditions of communication theory and their usefulness as a way of integrating the field. Fourth, however, we must also understand that traditions should not be reified or taken for granted, and that the project of theorizing requires questioning and rethinking theoretical traditions as we use them. These four points are explained in more detail in the following sections.

UNDERSTANDING METADISCOURSE: COMMUNICATION THEORY AND EVERYDAY TALK

In some sense, everyone is already a communication theorist. That is, throughout society there is an ongoing conversation about communication and communication theory in which everyone is already engaged to some extent. Cameron (reading 30) points out that *metadiscourse*— everyday talk about communication—has become a major preoccupation of people in modern

societies. Although the widespread awareness of the importance of communication that Cameron describes is a fairly new phenomenon, the readings in unit I reveal that our commonplace ideas and ways of talking about communication have evolved over many centuries. Communication theory, in essence, extends those commonplace ideas to enable a more sophisticated, insightful level of conversation about communication problems and practices.

Ideas in communication theory are often intellectually refined versions of ordinary practical concepts. For example, certain elements of what is now called the transmission or source-message-receiver model of communication were already present in the ancient culture of Homeric Greece (see reading 1). Other ideas about communication as transmission emerged with Christian speculation about the communication of angels (reading 2), bureaucratic discourse about the construction of roads and canals in early modern France (reading 3), and innovations in electronic media from the telegraph in the mid-19th century to the present (reading 4). Semiotic and cybernetic theories of communication (see units IV and VI) have modified and systematized these now commonplace ideas about communication between minds, flow and circulation through networks, and have modified and systematized ways of using information to achieve influence and control at a distance.

As the process of theorizing reflects on ordinary ideas about communication, it also criticizes those ideas and generates alternative, more carefully thought out designs for thinking and talking. Semiotics (the theory of communication through signs and symbols) is not just an elaboration of commonplace ideas about the use of words to communicate. From the 17th-century philosopher John Locke's critique of the abuses of language (reading 10) to the most recent deconstruction of popular ideas about communication with extraterrestrial aliens (reading 14), theorists in this tradition have challenged the conventional wisdom about communication in enlightening and sometimes disturbing ways.

The theorizing process is creative as well as critical. Locke's remedies for the abuse of language still continue to echo several centuries later in teachings and popular advice about effective communication. Plato's devastating critique of the unprincipled nature of rhetoric (reading 6) was soon followed by Aristotle's effort to put the art of rhetoric on a sounder theoretical foundation (reading 7), which in turn has been both extended and challenged by later theorists (for examples, see readings 8 and 9). Phenomenological writings about genuine dialogue (unit V) have both questioned the possibility of authentic human contact and articulated the conditions for achieving it. Research in social psychology (unit VII) has corrected naive assumptions about the psychological processes involved in communication while also providing a wealth of experimentally tested hypotheses. Sociocultural theorists (unit VIII) have shown how communication makes human society possible while critical theorists (unit IX) have both unmasked the ideologies and power structures that distort communication and envisioned the possibility of more genuinely democratic forms of social life.

As we become more deeply involved in these theoretical and everyday discourses on communication, we gain a fuller understanding of communication scholarship and become more aware of our own perspectives on communication, more discerning in our observations of communication in the society around us, more articulate critics of communication theory, and more thoughtful participants in the communication process. This is the practicality of the project of theorizing communication.

UNDERSTANDING THE LOGIC OF PRACTICAL THEORY

Thinking practically, when is it that we become aware of our communication? It could be argued that most of the time we do not think about our communication. We simply communicate, whether by talking with people, watching TV, or browsing the Web. However, we often think about our communication when something goes wrong, when a problem of communication becomes apparent. Why did members of the group show up in two different meeting places? What did I say that made my friend angry with me? How do I know if this news on TV is just "spin"? Can I trust this information I found on the Web? We also think about our communication when we find ourselves faced with particularly problematic situations and need to decide what to do. How do I tell my boss about what went wrong in the meeting today without affecting my chances of promotion? As a journalist, how can I remain objective while reporting a nasty and misleading political campaign? That we think about communication at these points is in keeping with the logic of practice. As Craig and Tracy (1995) pointed out, "When ongoing action is blocked, we think: and in thinking we reinterpret the problematic situation so as to continue action" (p. 252). Such is the nature of communication practice.

A practical approach says that there is no way to devise or apply a theory that would provide the right answer that would eliminate these problems. Rather, communication is inherently problematic. What worked this time in communicating with this boss may not be what works next time with another or even the same boss. "The underlying philosophy is not realism (theory describes the world) or idealism (theory constitutes the world) but rather a reflective pragmatism (theory informs praxis)" (Craig & Tracy, 1995, p. 252). The way we think and talk about communication affects how we communicate, and the way we communicate affects how we think about communication; as noted above, we tend to think about communication when we encounter communication problems.

Communication theory and theorizing, as well as the communication discipline as a whole, can be undertaken from such a practical perspective (Craig, 1989). In a practical theory, theory is informative to communication practitioners. Additionally, the actual practices of communication (the way people in fact do communicate) and the communities of practice (those who engage in a specific way of communicating) inform communication theory. Finally, the process of communication theorizing is a practical response to experienced communication problems. Rather than seeking to develop a theory that enables communicators to eradicate communication problems, practical theorizing allows us to engage in discourses through which we can examine and name problems and can provide us with new ways of thinking and talking about communication as well as tools to strategically manage problems in our communication.

This is not, of course, the only possible approach to communication theory. One interesting contrast to a practical approach is an empirical social scientific approach. In an empirical approach, the goal of theory is to explain communication phenomena. Theory construction is done within the parameters of scientific methods. Theories are constructed to be testable and to provide illumination into the underlying workings of communication in a way that allows for prediction of communicative actions. In this book there are examples of theories constructed within this empirical paradigm. Some of these include readings by Berger and Calabrese and Bandura (unit VII) and Lang (unit VI).

Another interesting contrast is philosophically based normative theories. In this kind of theorizing, abstract principles are constructed to provide ideal models for how things could or should occur. This theorizing is done in adherence to rational principles, and the results of this theorizing provide a basis for evaluating communication as it actually occurs. Again, in this book there are examples of theories constructed from a normative philosophical approach. Some of these include readings by Plato (unit III), Buber and Gadamer (unit V), and Habermas (unit IX).

When taking a practical perspective, there are at least two ways in which practical theory can be developed. One is inductively: empirically studying and analyzing communication problems and the ways people think about and address them. Craig and Tracy (1995) provide an example of this kind of theorizing in which ethnographically informed discourse analysis was used to reconstruct the dilemmas, ideals, and techniques used by participants in academic discussions. Through participation in discussions, analysis of taped interaction, and interviews, the researchers were able to identify (1) the problems participants faced as well as (2) the principles they used to guide their decision making about how to deal with these problems, and finally (3) the communication techniques they used to manage these problems in their actual interaction. Critical reflection on these findings allowed the researchers to construct a practical theory of intellectual discussion that was grounded in the actual practices of such discussions. Other examples of this kind of theoretical work can be seen in Ashcraft's (2001) examination of a women's safe-house and in Muller's (2002) exploration of collegiate classroom discussion.

The other way of constructing practical theory is deductively: conceptualizing already existing theories—including scientific and philosophical theories—in terms of their practical applications and applying them to particular communication problems. This second approach is the one for which this book is particularly useful. It allows multiple theories to be applied, increasing the richness and flexibility of our thinking as we consider a practical problem from various points of view.

This approach is what Tracy and Muller (2001) used with school board meetings that participants experienced as difficult. The study called into question the naming of the problem by many local participants and media outlets as due to the nasty personalities of the board members and sought to address the nature of problem formulation. By looking through multiple theoretical lenses, different aspects of the interaction were found to be problematic, leading to different diagnoses of the school board's interactional trouble. Was the problem due to the structure and organization of the meetings, the "thin skin" of participants, or their lack of skill in making arguments? As is seen in this study, different theoretical lenses can lead to different diagnoses, which can each lead to a different potential solution of the problem. Additionally, these diagnoses can be used to reflexively critique the practicality of the established theories.

This second approach to constructing practical theory begins to answer the question, Why are theories included in this volume that were not constructed from a practical perspective? These theories can be applied practically, and through following the logic of practice, they can be applied to particular problems and critiqued with regard to their usefulness. Craig (reading 5) argues that all communication theories have practical implications. Every theory implies a practical orientation to communication that can be useful for addressing some range of problems and undoubtedly is biased toward some interests and segments of society over others. Issues of gender, for example, are highlighted by some theories while being ignored by most other theories. Some theories conceptualize problems from a more social or cultural point of view; others from a more individualistic point of view. The diversity of theories allows us to consider the advantages and disadvantages of approaching problems in different ways. Debate in the field should focus on the practical interests served by theories and the biases, gaps, and areas of agreement and disagreement among those different practical approaches. This form of dialogue among diverse theories is what Craig calls "dialogical-dialectical coherence" (reading 5). Within the project of theorizing, the logic of practical theory highlights that the more familiar we become with communication theorizing, the more aware we will become of a wider range of communication problems, the more facile we will become with ways to think and talk about these problems, and the more options we will perceive for managing problematic situations. The more thoroughly we understand established ways of thinking and talking about communication (communication theories), the more lenses we will have available through which to identify and diagnose communication problems.

THEORIZING TRADITIONS: THE USEFULNESS OF HISTORY

A third aspect of the project of theorizing is that of understanding and using *traditions* of theory. To make sense of the differences among theories,

it helps to understand that every theory follows certain traditions and not others. A tradition is something handed down from the past, but no living tradition is static. Traditions are constantly changing. Outside of some tradition, in fact, change and innovation would have little meaning. Even just applying traditional ideas to a new situation typically requires some creativity and involves changing the ideas in some way. Theorists invent new ideas to solve problems they perceive in existing ideas in a particular tradition. Gadamer (see reading 17), one of the greatest philosophers of tradition, pointed out that every new work in a tradition stands as an answer to some question it poses about the tradition, and that every work will, in turn, be questioned by later works that continue the tradition (Gadamer, 1984, pp. 333–341). Later works in a tradition build upon earlier works, which is why in this book we have organized the readings in each tradition chronologically.

It would be impossible to live a meaningful human life outside of all traditions. Traditions have shaped our identities and thereby have a certain unavoidable authority over us. As Gadamer explained, "The validity of morals, for example, is based on tradition. They are freely taken over, but by no means created by a free insight or justified by themselves. This is precisely what we call tradition: the ground of their validity" (1984, p. 249). Gadamer also used the example of legal interpretation. When the courts interpret a law they consider legal precedent and case law—a tradition of legal interpretation—along with the wording of the statutes themselves. The meaning of a law changes over time as new cases bring up new issues and circumstances change, revealing biases and gaps in older interpretations of the law. Judges of course frequently disagree about the meaning of the law, and this state of disagreement is also characteristic of traditions. Traditions are not homogeneous. Every tradition is characterized by a history of argument about beliefs and values that are important to the tradition. "Traditions, when vital, embody continuities of conflict," wrote MacIntyre (1981, p. 206), another important theorist of tradition and social practices. "A living tradition then is an historically extended, socially embodied argument, and an argument precisely in part about the goods which constitute that tradition" (MacIntyre, 1981, p. 207). Critical theorists (see unit IX) rightly question the authority of traditions, but as Gadamer would point out, in doing so they are following the traditions of critical theory.

Placing theories within traditions thus highlights the innovativeness of theories by showing how each one carries forward certain ideas and assumptions from a particular history of arguments while also departing from that tradition to contribute something new and different. Even a theory that rebels against its tradition and rejects major parts of it can still belong to the tradition in significant ways. The feminist rhetorical theory of Foss and Griffin (reading 9) is a good example. While rejecting the idea that persuasion is the purpose of rhetoric—an idea deeply embedded in the tradition of rhetorical theory— Foss and Griffin continue to assume that the basic format of communication is that of a speaker and of an audience. As a feminist critical theorist, Jansen (reading 35) shares parts of the feminist tradition with Foss and Griffin, yet she writes about communication from a very different point of view, reflecting essential differences between the tradition of critical communication theory in which she primarily writes and the rhetorical tradition of Foss and Griffin.

The field of communication theory, considered as a tradition in its own right, is both quite new and very old. The term *communication theory* was not widely used until the 1940s, when it primarily referred to certain fields of electrical engineering that included information theory and cybernetics (and it still has that meaning for engineers). Social science courses in communication theory, which began to be taught around 1950, brought together an eclectic set of ideas from existing traditions such as semiotics, social psychology, and cybernetics. The field of communication theory, in a very real sense, grew backward in time as it grew forward in time. Over time, several traditions of thought, such as rhetoric, which existed long before there was ever a field called

communication theory, were incorporated into the field. Retrospectively, they came to be seen as traditions of communication theory, which is how the field came to include the multiple traditions that it now does. The problem we now face in the project of theorizing is how to use these multiple traditions most productively for the betterment of human communication.

Each of the seven traditions has different things to say about society as well as about the nature of communication. The rhetorical tradition is the oldest of the seven traditions, in this volume traced back to Plato and Aristotle, and within it communication is conceptualized as the art of discourse. The semiotic tradition conceptualizes communication as intersubjectivity mediated by signs and also has a lengthy history beginning here with Locke's notion of the imperfection of words. The other five traditions have more modern origins of theorization, as will be discussed in the introductions to each unit; they arise as scholars theorize around problems in their sociohistorical contexts. Husserl laid the initial theorizing foundation for the phenomenological tradition in which communication is conceptualized as the experience of the other. Hermeneutics and dialogue are key ideas within this tradition. Cybernetics, traced back to Wiener and including a variety of intersecting approaches and ideas, conceptualizes communication as information processing. The sociopsychological approach conceptualizes communication as social interaction. Chosen as a first reading here is a piece by Hovland in which he sets out a framework for the empirical study of communication by social scientists. The sociocultural tradition conceptualizes communication as a symbolic process that produces and reproduces shared sociocultural patterns. Mead was one of the first scholars to theorize how communication forms, reflects, and maintains the structure of society. The critical tradition conceptualizes communication as discursive reflection overcoming the distortion of truth by power. Within this volume, this tradition is traced back to Marx and Engels.

When looking at each of these traditions within a historical progression of theorizing, interesting differences are seen in the development of thought. Differences in trajectory, pace, variation in voices, and coherence speak to the idea that these traditions are alive, that in the ongoing project of theorizing there have been different paths, and that these pathways have distinct shapes and routes that differently map out the changing ideas about the nature of communication.

Although each tradition provides communication theorists with a particular discourse within which to think, talk, and write about communication phenomena, it is important to note that these traditions are not like distinct canal channels levied off from each other. Rather, they are more like free-flowing rivers on relatively level bottomlands where the main course is usually distinguishable, but the braided channels often intersect and it takes relatively little environmental change to bring about a mixture of the waters and even reconfiguration of the channels. This intermingling of ideas is ever present and is especially palpable in some of the contemporary readings in which, as one reads, it becomes clear that, although the piece adds something to its primary tradition, it also seems to connect to ideas from one or more other traditions as well. For instance, the reading by Poster in unit VIII has been included in the sociocultural unit, but as a post-structuralist piece might it not also have a home in the semiotic or critical tradition? Some of the interwoven nature of readings will be addressed in the introductory sections to several units and in some of the suggested projects for additional theorizing.

A straightforward benefit of the traditions approach is that by being able to follow the development of a line of thinking, one can more deeply understand that perspective by placing it within its sociohistorical and intellectual context. Additionally, through reading conceptualizations from different eras, one can get a glimpse into the aspects of interaction that were experienced as problematic at that time. There are also nonhistorical benefits of a traditions approach. One is that each tradition provides a different lens through which to examine a communication practice. In essence, the traditions approach allows one to take a multi-perspective exploration into understanding a communication practice.

QUESTIONING AND RETHINKING THE TRADITIONS

How well do the seven traditions work as a framework for organizing the various conceptions of communication theory? Why did we select these particular readings? What has been left out? Are there some readings that *must* be included if one is to understand a specific tradition? Are there just seven main traditions, or there are others? Should there be a separate feminist tradition? Should Asian or other non-Western writings on communication be included as one or more separate traditions? If the goal of communication theorizing is to lead to better communication practices, is it likely that what are considered to be good communication practices today will be considered good communication in a decade or a century? Similarly, does the nature of what are experienced as communication problems change across time? Does communication itself change over time? These are all great questions that may come into varying degrees of focus as one reads this book and that hopefully will enliven the ongoing communication theory conversation. Within this volume, questions such as these that seem especially relevant to a particular tradition are posed at the end of the introduction to that unit. Questions for further exploration are also raised in the suggested projects at the end of each unit. The conclusion of the volume returns to address some areas of concern and inquiry surrounding the idea of traditions.

While it is important to understand and use the traditions of communication theory in the project of theorizing, it is equally important to understand that the seven traditions presented in this book have been constructed through acts of interpretation and are not cast in stone. Some theorists may interpret the traditions differently than we do. Some may prefer to cut the theoretical pie differently, producing fewer, or more, or xvi • THEORIZING COMMUNICATION

just a different set of traditions. These differences should be acknowledged and discussed as they emerge, but this is not a reason to reject the idea of theoretical traditions.

As we have noted, all theories respond to problems and reflect biases specific to particular cultures, social groups, and times in history. Our own scheme of communication theory as a field is no exception. Although it is not possible to escape our own sociohistorical context or to eliminate all biases, an awareness of history at least sensitizes us to the possibility of discovering and revising our biases through dialogue with others and in response to changing circumstances. This is an advantage of taking a historical approach to theory. Traditions are characterized by change as well as continuity. Full engagement in the project of theorizing requires reflexive questioning and a willingness to revise our understanding of the field.

The communication theory course still is not yet highly standardized. It varies quite a bit between speech and media-oriented communication programs, between programs with an empirical social science orientation versus those more oriented to interpretive social science or humanities approaches, and between institutions where communication is now established as an academic discipline versus universities around the world where its institutional identity is more variable or unclear. This is one of the problems to which our approach to the field is a practical response. The widespread interest in Craig's (1999) integrative model seems to reflect an impulse toward standardization, but the continuing diversity of the field guarantees that not everyone will find the model equally suitable. It may not appeal to those who follow a strictly empirical social science approach, or to those who view communication theory primarily as media theory or critical cultural studies, or from within a particular tradition such as semiotics, rhetoric, or social psychology. Because it tries to construct a center to the field that connects all of those different approaches, it necessarily seems biased and unbalanced from a standpoint within any one of them. However, for those wanting a catholic approach to the field, it provides a way

to organize their own understandings and may allow thinkers who work primarily in different traditions a way to communicate with each other.

SUMMARY AND OVERVIEW OF THE BOOK

One way to become a reflective, engaged, and active participant in the conversation about communication theory is to approach this volume as a part of an ongoing project of theorizing one's own sociohistorical context. One key to doing so is to understand the close connection between theoretical ways of thinking and talking about communication and our everyday ways of thinking and talking. It is also important to understand the logic of practical theory and what it means to reflexively link theory and practical problems of communication. Finally, it is important to understanding the traditions of communication theory and their potential usefulness as an integrative framework without reifying them. Rather, one must engage the traditions of communication theory as a critical inquirer seeking to further one's theoretical scholarship and improve one's ability to observe, analyze, and participate as an informed communicator. To facilitate engagement in the project of theorizing, this volume has been structured in the following way.

Unit I traces the history of the idea of communication, emphasizing the concept's historicity and cultural embeddedness. It contextualizes the volume by addressing the historical origins of the very idea of communication. These selections show that what is understood as communication is not static. Rather, the idea of communication is interwoven with the sociohistorical context of the time; as the context changes, so does the idea of communication. These four readings highlight four different conceptions of communication in their specific sociohistorical contexts. This historical perspective embraces a fluidity that is consistent with the identifiably different and yet permeable seven traditions; it is also consistent with the idea that what is gained through each tradition is a particular discourse for understanding communication phenomena and a particular set of conceptual tools for tackling communication problems.

Unit II introduces the metatheoretical perspective of the book and invites debate on its assumptions. The section contains Craig's (1999) piece in which the idea of communication theory as a field including the seven traditions was introduced.

Units III through IX focus on the seven traditions. The core of each of the seven units on specific traditions of communication theory is a set of four or five readings. The readings are full or excerpted original texts, each holding a place of importance in its respective tradition. The progression of readings in each unit is similar. The first one or two are early texts representing "classic" statements of the tradition's distinctive way of conceptualizing communication. The next one or two readings present some specific concepts or approaches that are linchpins in defining the tradition and are integral to theorizing within it. The last one or two readings represent current statements of the tradition, in some cases radical new departures from the tradition or hybrids incorporating ideas from other traditions.

Also, each unit begins with a unit introduction and ends with a section on projects for theorizing. Although the introductions to units I and II are somewhat different in that they are not centered on one of the seven traditions, they are the same in spirit as those for units III through IX. In each introduction the background, central assumptions, and range of perspectives of the relevant field of theory are discussed. These introductions contextualize the readings and, especially for some of the longer or more difficult readings, provide access by highlighting some of the key ideas in each reading. The questions included in the introductions to each unit certainly might be used for class discussion, class projects, or papers. The projects for additional theorizing at the end of each unit contain three segments. The first is a set of additional readings broken down by the subsection of the tradition, which should enable further exploration into existing theory within the tradition. The second component is an application exercise designed as a way to experientially explore key ideas, ways of thinking, and/or ways of talking within the tradition. These are intended as introductory exercises that could be used by a class or an individual to initially engage in practicing communication in a particular traditional fashion. The final segment of each of these sections consists of projects. These are provided as ideas for theoretically informed research projects that, if actualized, would extend, mix with other traditions, or critique a tradition. We intend these projects to be more advanced than the questions in the introductions or the application exercises, and yet they are constructed often through laying out a series of questions that could again be fodder for discussion, projects, or papers at various levels. There are five of these projects in each unit. These projects are often linked directly to readings in the unit and also include ideas for related additional reading.

While the progression of readings is similar across the units on the seven traditions, they were not designed to mimic or mirror each other. Rather, they were designed to illustrate the progression of thought in each tradition—to highlight developing strands of thought while allowing some insight into the diversity of each tradition. Scholars who are experts in a particular tradition can readily point out other readings that could or even must be included in order to fully understand the historical heritage and/or current thinking of that tradition. We hope, however, each reading we have selected provides a piece—a particular conceptualization that is linked and yet different from those in the other included pieces—of the conceptual puzzle that makes up a tradition. In keeping with the idea of conversation, each piece should allow some insight into a tradition but should also raise some questions about the tradition; in fact, while the readings are intended to provide grounding in key concepts necessary to the exploration of particular traditions, they have also been chosen to stimulate discussion about the very idea of theoretical traditions. The readings in each unit are not meant to be exhaustive, nor are they meant to be uniquely definitive. They are meant to introduce readers to significant lines of thought that contribute to the scholarship of communication theory. The discussions that emerge from this encounter with the traditions of communication theory will participate in the construction of the idea of communication in our contemporary sociohistorical context. And as readers propose alternative texts that could or should have been included in each unit, the discourse of each tradition will be continued.

In our Concluding Reflections, we step back and reflect on the state of the field of communication theory and address some problems that seem to hold the potential for fruitful theorizing, especially at the metatheoretical level. We also reexamine the seven traditions framework and highlight some critiques of this framework. The essay ends with thoughts about the future of the field of communication theory.

This book provides a foundation for ongoing work in the field of communication theory. As readers work to understand, discuss, apply, and critique these texts, their engagement in the practical discipline of communication, the project of theorizing communication, and the cultivation of communication practices in society will continue.

REFERENCES

Ashcraft, K. L. (2001). Feminist organizing and the construction of "alternative" community. In G. J. Shepherd & E. W. Rothenbuhler (Eds.), *Communication and community* (pp. 79–110). Mahwah, NJ: Lawrence Erlbaum.

Craig, R. T. (1989). Communication as a practical discipline. In B. Dervin, L. Grossberg, B. J. O'Keefe, & E. Wartella (Eds.), *Rethinking communication: Vol. 1. Paradigm issues* (pp. 97–122). Newbury Park, CA: Sage.

Craig, R. T. (1999). Communication theory as a field. *Communication Theory, 9*, 119–161.

Craig, R. T., & Tracy, K. (1995). Grounded practical theory: The case of intellectual discussion. *Communication Theory, 5*, 248–272.

Gadamer, H.-G. (1984). *Truth and method* (2nd ed.; G. Barden & J. Comming, Trans.). New York: Crossroad.

MacIntyre, A. (1981). *After virtue: A study in moral theory*. Notre Dame, IN: University of Notre Dame Press.

Muller, H. L. (2002). *Navigating the dilemmas of collegiate classroom discussion*. Unpublished doctoral dissertation, University of Colorado at Boulder.

Tracy, K., & Muller, H. (2001). Diagnosing a school board's interactional trouble: Theorizing problem formulating. *Communication Theory, 11*, 84–104.

ACKNOWLEDGMENTS

The editors would like to thank a wide range of people who were involved in bringing this book to completion. We are grateful to the authors and publishers who granted permission for their readings to be included. We would like to recognize the efforts of Todd Armstrong, Sarah Quesenberry, Camille Herrera, Deya Saoud, and Astrid Virding at SAGE Publications. We appreciate the insightful and rigorous feedback from reviewers of both the proposal and manuscript phases of this project: Kenneth N. Cissna, University of South Florida; Marianne Dainton, La Salle University; Stephen W. Littlejohn, Domenici Littlejohn, Inc.; Robert D. McPhee, Arizona State University; Peter Oehlkers, Salem State College; Gerry Philipsen, University of Washington; Rodney A. Reynolds, Pepperdine University; and Wallace V. Schmidt, Rollins College.

We thank the Department of Communication, University of Colorado at Boulder, and the department staff for support and for assisting in various ways. We also thank Maria Hegbloom and Michael Vicaro for assistance in selecting, scanning, and editing the readings; librarian Deborah Creamer for assistance in locating and obtaining permissions; and Priscilla Brown for assistance in formatting and proofreading the scanned readings.

UNIT I   INTRODUCTION

Historical and Cultural Sources of Communication Theory

The four readings in this first unit examine the idea of communication in selected historical eras ranging from the archaic Greece of Homer's *Iliad* and *Odyssey* to the present. As noted in the general introduction, formal theories of communication elaborate, refine, and often intend to reform everyday ways of thinking and talking about communication that are current in the theorist's own time, but those current everyday ideas may be ingrained in cultural patterns that have evolved over many centuries. Understanding the idea of communication historically, we can come to see the taken-for-granted assumptions about communication of our own time in a different, more critical perspective. Examining specific historical ideas also provides a common set of reference points for understanding how the traditions of communication theory presented in later units have interacted with practical metadiscourse over time.

Highlighting, as an example, one particularly important such concept, contemporary theorists have criticized the current dominance of a transmission (sender-message-receiver) model of communication in everyday thinking. For instance, Reddy's (1979) widely cited study of metaphors in English found an overwhelming preponderance of what he called conduit metaphors for communication. Typical examples included phrases such as "try to get your *thoughts across* better," "none of Mary's feelings *came through to me*," and "you have to *put* each concept *into words* very carefully" (pp. 286–287). Implicitly, we seem to think of communication as a process of packaging our thoughts and feelings into words and sending them through a conduit (a communication channel) to recipients who unpack them and receive the meanings intended—unless, of course, some of those little packets of meaning were lost or damaged in transit! The readings in this unit reveal that similar ways of talking about communication have existed in European languages and cultures since ancient times and have changed through the centuries with changes in other aspects of social life such as religion, economics, and technology.

In the first reading, Rob Wiseman gives a fascinating glimpse into communication as it may have been understood and experienced in the distant world of archaic Greece (around 600 BCE, when Homer's great epic poems, the *Iliad* and the *Odyssey*, were first recorded in writing). The method of metaphor analysis Wiseman uses is particularly interesting because it can be compared with research such as Reddy's (1979) on metaphors in later times. Like Reddy, but with radical differences, Wiseman finds a transmission model of communication implied by an abundance of metaphors in the Homeric epics. The radical difference is that the Homeric Greek, unlike modern European languages, had no concept of mind as a place where private thoughts and emotions existed independently of the words or actions that expressed them. Those ancient Greeks did not talk about putting their thoughts into words because they saw no difference between thoughts and words. They did not think the brain had anything to do with thought or perception. All the action was in other parts of the body, especially the heart and lungs, with various body parts sometimes acting as independent agents. Communication was a process of breathing words out of one person's lungs and placing them directly into another's lungs. There was no conduit or channel and no message or meaning distinct from the words transmitted.

This model of communication, however bizarre it may seem, is interesting to contemplate in light of recent postmodern theories in semiotics, cybernetics, and phenomenology that have called into question the modern picture of communication as a process of transmitting ideas and feelings from one mind to another. For various examples, see Peters on communication with aliens (reading 14), Chang on the impossibility of communication (reading 18), and Luhmann on the idea that only communication communicates (reading 22). The power of words continued to be a central theme of ancient Greek culture, from which emerged the rhetorical tradition of communication theory in the writings of Plato and Aristotle (unit III). Modern social psychology (unit VII) is based on very different assumptions about the mind and behavior, but like the ancient Greeks, social psychologists still picture communication as a process of influence from person to person.

The second reading, "The Spiritualist Tradition" by John Durham Peters, is excerpted from his book *Speaking Into the Air: A History of the Idea of Communication* (1999), a title that may suggest that communication is something like the archaic Greek model of transmission from the lungs. Peters, however, in this excerpt traces a very different spiritual concept of transmission through developments in Christian thought during the Roman Empire and Middle Ages and through the beginnings of modern physics in 17th-century Europe.

In this spiritualist tradition—the deep background from which modern semiotic and phenomenological theories emerged (see units IV and V)—words are merely the outward physical signs of mental or spiritual experiences within a person. The problem of communication is how those interior experiences can be transmitted and shared with others. Ancient and medieval Christian sources (especially the Gospel of John and the writings of Augustine and Thomas Aquinas), Peters finds, "establish spirit-to-spirit linkage as a normative vision of how intercourse ought to work" (1999, p. 63). Speculation about communication with angels in the Christian tradition was echoed in 17th-century physical speculation on action at a distance and the transmission of invisible forces such as gravity through the ether of space. Peters concludes, "The concept of communication as we know it originates from an application of physical processes such as magnetism, convection, and gravitation to occurrences between minds" (reading 2). The ideal of communication became some kind of spiritual or mental telepathy in which meanings are transmitted from one mind to another. Ordinary linguistic communication always falls short of this spiritualist ideal, but Locke's semiotic theory (unit IV, reading 10) tried to show how the ideal could be approximated through the careful use of language. Peters takes up some practical implications of the fact that our real communication always falls short of the spiritualist ideal in a later section of his book on the problem of communicating with aliens (reading 14).

The next reading, combining two excerpts from *The Invention of Communication* by Armand Mattelart (1996), takes us to France in the 17th and 18th centuries and uses a different historical methodology to show how the idea of communication has been influenced by seemingly unrelated practical activities including scientific studies of blood circulation and projects for building roads, canals, and bridges. The opening section amusingly contrasts the premodern mentality portrayed in the classic Spanish novel *Don Quixote* against the modern, rational, scientific outlook that was beginning to emerge in the 1600s, a century during which the kingdom of France began ambitious projects for improving internal "communication" by constructing roads, bridges, and canals. In the policy debates surrounding those projects, communication was discussed using metaphors drawn from the recent scientific discovery of blood circulation. The efficient circulation of people and goods among all parts of the country was compared to the circulation of blood in a living body, with the capital city of Paris being the powerful, centrally located "heart" through which everything would flow. Improvements to the communication "network" (a term that also first appeared around this time) would facilitate national unity, economic development, and central political control. By-products included scientific engineering techniques and modern forms of industrial and military organization. "In France under the Old Regime," Mattelart concludes, "the basis of a body of ideas on 'communications' began to be formed, that is, a proper mode of thinking about the relations between movement, the economy, and society, between 'networks,' the state, and national unity" (reading 3). In a process that continued through the modern era, the idea of communication was increasingly associated with ideals of rationality, progress, and universal community. Concepts that evolved in this period formed the basis for later cybernetic, sociocultural, and critical theories of communication.

The Carey piece, a chapter from his book *Communication as Culture: Essays on Media and Society* (1989), shows how the religious and spiritual connotations of communication, the tradition of identifying communication with transportation, and the ideas spawned by the introduction of new electronic media beginning with the telegraph in the 19th century all merged to form the now familiar transmission model. Commenting in a critical vein that "the transmission view of communication has dominated American thought since the 1920s," Carey offers contemporary communication theorists an alternative, ritual model that he argues is just as deeply rooted in the history of popular, especially American, religious and social ideas (reading 4). "If the archetypal case of communication under a transmission view is the extension of messages across geography for the purpose of control," he writes, "the archetypal case under a ritual view is the sacred ceremony that draws persons together in fellowship and commonality" (reading 4).

The second part of Carey's chapter moves from the history of ideas to the questions of communication theory and metatheory. This reading would fit as well in unit II on metatheory or unit VIII on the sociocultural tradition as it does in this unit. Carey's discussion of symbols also substantially adds to semiotic theory (unit IV). We have placed the reading in this unit to highlight Carey's views on the historical and cultural sources of communication theory and because his historical account of the transmission and ritual models complements the previous readings. However, we should not neglect his theoretical and metatheoretical contributions.

Carey's theoretical purpose is to show how communication can be theorized from a ritual view, and his metatheoretical purpose is to show that communication theory itself is a form of ritual communication. Defining communication as "a symbolic process whereby reality is produced, maintained, repaired, and transformed," Carey argues that we produce reality by creating symbolic models or representations that give our collective experience of the world a meaningful form. Just as the reality of a sacred ceremony is produced by those who participate together in performing the ritual, the reality of a child's way of walking home from school can be produced by creating a symbolic model that might take the form of verbal directions, a map, or even a dance or a song that can guide the child through the streets between school and home. Symbolic communication has this creative power because systems of abstract symbols, such as language, music, or conventions for drawing maps, are characterized by *displacement* (they can refer to things that are not physically present) and *productivity* (they can be used to create an infinite number of different representations). The realities that we produce in communication must be maintained and repaired in further communication or may be transformed into different realities (for example, communication transforms a stranger into a friend and then maintains the friendship through shared rituals, repairing it as needed). A key point is that models *of* reality also become models *for* reality. (Having plotted a route to somewhere, we then use it to produce the reality of our trip.) Carey concludes by applying the same logic to communication theory. Models of communication are symbolic representations that produce the reality of communication. If we represent communication as a transmission process, then that becomes the model we use to guide our practice of communication. A ritual model of communication produces a different reality. Communication theory is a reflexive ethically significant science because, in constructing theoretical models of and for communication, we help to produce the very reality that we study.

This unit on historical and cultural sources of the idea of communication sets the stage for subsequent units on metatheory and on the seven intellectual traditions of communication theory. With that in mind, you may come up with many questions while reading these selections. To what extent do ideas about communication discussed in these readings still influence popular thinking and practices? Listening carefully to the talk that goes on around us, do everyday ways of talking about communication show traces of Homer? Of spiritualism? Of ideas like network, flow, and circulation? Of transmission and ritual models? What common ways of thinking and talking about communication are *not* reflected in these readings? Are new media and technologies influencing how we think and talk about communication? How about modern political discourse and the growth of industries like media, marketing, and advertising? How will the idea of communication evolve as the world continues to change in these and other ways?

While reading Wiseman's piece, you may find yourself imagining what it would be like to experience communication as a process of breathing words from lung to lung. Is it true that thinking and perceiving happen in the chest as much as they do in the brain? When you are thinking to yourself, for example, can you feel words being formed somewhere in the general region of your lungs and heart? When someone says something that has a strong impact on you, do you feel the impact more in your chest than in your head? Does our modern knowledge of anatomy and physiology make such experiences irrelevant? Where and how *does* communication actually happen?

Peters describes a tradition of thought in which perfect communication can only occur on a spiritual level. How useful is this idea? Does it apply to our daily experience? (The answer may depend in part on your religious beliefs and practices or your attitude toward psychic phenomena.) Does the spiritualist tradition provide a helpful ideal that can guide our efforts to communicate? On the other hand, does it create unrealistic expectations that can never be satisfied in practice?

Mattelart shows how ways of talking about communication can be related to certain practical activities. Road building and telecommunications engineering may lend themselves to talk about networks and circulation. Do teachers, therapists, and salespeople have other ways of discussing communication related to their particular activities? Mattelart also shows how the idea of communication became associated with rationality and progress. Does communication still have an aura of modernity that vaguely associates it with scientific and progressive ideals? How do these connotations affect rhetorical uses of the word *communication,* for example in advertising? What may be some practical aspects of the current sociohistorical context that are continuing to link the idea of communication with modern rationality and progress or perhaps are changing the meaning of communication in certain ways?

As you read in the Carey piece about the transmission and ritual views, you may wonder about the practical consequences of taking one or the other view as a model for communication. Do we tend to take a transmission view in some situations and a ritual view in others? What would we do differently if those views were reversed? Do Carey's comments on the public and social nature of symbols return us to something almost like the archaic Greek model described by Wiseman that made no distinction between message and meaning? How does it matter, how does one determine, what view of communication is taken by participants in a communication practice?

REFERENCES

Carey, J. W. (1989). *Communication as culture: Essays on media and society.* Winchester, MA: Unwin Hyman.

Mattelart, A. (1996). *The invention of communication* (S. Emanuel, Trans.). Minneapolis: University of Minnesota Press.

Peters, J. D. (1999). *Speaking into the air: A history of the idea of communication.* Chicago: University of Chicago Press.

Reddy, M. J. (1979). The conduit metaphor: A case of frame conflict in our language about language. In A. Ortony (Ed.), *Metaphor and thought* (pp. 284–324). Cambridge, UK: Cambridge University Press.

1

Metaphors Concerning Speech in Homer

Rob Wiseman

The oldest texts in the Western tradition large enough for detailed analysis are the *Iliad* and the *Odyssey*.[1] Neither, of course, is a text on communication. But we can glean from them how the archaic Greeks understood communication by looking at the ways in which Homeric poets described speaking, how people used it and were affected by it, as well as at the metaphors they used to explain it.[2] In this chapter, I have used examples from the longer and older of the two, the *Iliad,* except where the *Odyssey* provides clearer examples.[3]

We need to be aware, when looking at Homer, that the conceptual world of the archaic Greeks is very different from our own. In particular, there was not really a category for "mental stuff": no words that translate naturally as 'mind', 'thought', 'thinking', 'idea' or 'concept'. Emotional life is also curiously limited from our perspective. While there are terms for immediate feelings, such as anger, delight, rage, hate, joy, and lust, there are no corresponding abstract terms, such as 'sadness' or 'anticipation'. Everything we describe as 'mental' and most of what we call 'emotional', the *Iliad* describes physiologically: either as sensations and hypostases, or by relating them to organs of the body. In the *Iliad* and *Odyssey,* the important organs and physiological sensations are, in order of frequency:

[1] thumos

[2] phrenes, usually plural, but occasionally singular, phrēn

[3] kradiē, which is equivalent to the heart

[4] kēr, heart

[5] ētor

[6] noos[4]

[7] psukhē.[5]

SOURCE: Wiseman, R. D. (2003). Metaphors concerning speech in Homer. In *The development of ideas about communication in European thought from ancient Greece to the early modern age* (pp. 33–54). Unpublished doctoral dissertation. Canberra, Australia: Australian National University. Reprinted by permission.

In this chapter, I have focused on the two most frequent terms, *thumos* and the *phrenes,* because together they cover almost all aspects of communication in Homer. Their functions however are not limited to communication. In particular they relate to the development of what would later become understood as emotion, mind and thought—all of which became highly problematic in the later history of ideas about communication. Consequently, in this chapter, I discuss the entire system of concepts concerning *thumos* and the *phrenes* within which ideas about communication developed. This chapter begins with a summary of what their physiological roles were in Homer, then describes how what we understand as emotional and mental life is explained metaphorically using these terms. At the end, I have reconstructed the system of communication-as-transmission implicit in Homer.

THUMOS AND THE PHRENES

The most commonly mentioned organs in both the *Iliad* and the *Odyssey* are the *phrenes* (or sometimes *prapides).* They appear directly 180 times in the *Iliad* and in a number of derived terms, such as *metaphrenes.*

As most translators note, *phrenes* is difficult to render in English, and even the Greeks of the classical age found it perplexing. After Hippocrates and the establishment of systematic medicine in the early fourth century BC, the term *phrenes* acquired a specialized medical sense meaning 'mind' or 'diaphragm'. This is how Plato uses the word in the *Timaeus,*[6] and most translators do likewise when the organ is being described. But usually this does not make sense in Homer. For instance, the *phrenes* are plural,[7] which the midriff and diaphragm clearly are not. They are described as *melainai,* 'blackish' or 'dark-coloured',[8] whereas the diaphragm is pink. The *phrenes* are repeatedly described as being 'filled up with' *thumos* and *menos,* and *thumos* being 'contained in' or 'moving within' the *phrenes,*[9] which implies that they have some space within them—hardly a characteristic of a

thin muscular sheet. Furthermore, the *phrenes* are said to 'shut in the heart'[10] or to surround it at the front. Homer repeatedly points to the *phrenes* being in the chest, not the abdomen.[11] Even the most elementary understanding of anatomy would not confuse the position of the diaphragm this badly. Another useful source of information about the nature of the *phrenes* are the descriptions of battle wounds in the *Iliad.* When Patroklos pulls his spear out of Sarpedon's chest, the *phrenes* came out with it,[12] not what would happen if a spear was thrust to the diaphragm, firmly attached to the ribs as it is. Nor would we expect the diaphragm to be damaged as the result of a chest wound. Wounds to the liver do not entail any mention of damage to the far more important *phrenes,*[13] yet if the *phrenes* is the diaphragm or midriff, it must have been pierced by sword or spear. Soldiers stabbed between the shoulder-blades are said to have been pierced 'in the *metaphrenes*', literally 'behind the *phrenes*',[14] an odd term if the *phrenes* means 'diaphragm'.

Onians[15] presents a powerful argument that, in Homer, the *phrenes* were the lungs. This would amply explain their position in the chest, in front of or surrounding the heart;[16] their 'dark' grey-blue colour; their hollow nature; and the fact that they are not damaged in abdominal wounds but are in chest wounds.

Closely associated with the *phrenes* is *thumos.*[17] *Thumos* is the most important of the physiological terms in Homer: it appears over 430 times in the *Iliad* alone, nearly three times as often as any other term. *Thumos* gives translators even more trouble than the *phrenes;* some describe it as 'untranslatable'. Etymologically, it seems related to smoke and vapour. It is a substance frequently 'poured' into the *phrenes.* It is no great leap to guess that if the *phrenes* are the lungs, then *thumos* is breath. *Thumos* however also has associations with blood, is frequently hot, and is distinguished from normal air, *aêr.*

This interpretation of *thumos* as breath fits neatly with many passages in the *Iliad.* For instance, when Hector is recovering from a blow to the chest from Ajax's stone, Apollo finds him:

. . . sitting now, no longer sprawled, as he gathered *thumos* back into him and recognised his companions about him. The sweat and hard breathing began to stop . . . [18]

In other words, he is recovering from being winded and stunned, and is getting his breath back. Similarly, when Odysseus revives from near drowning, his *thumos* returns to his *phrenes*.[19]

It would be a mistake however to believe that *thumos* and *phrenes* are identical to our modern English words *breath* and *lungs*. In our modern age, we see our lungs as parts of an integrated whole we call a 'body'. In Homer, there is neither a term for, nor concept of, the body as a whole; all we see is an aggregate of organs and limbs. All of the organs are autonomous of the character to some extent and some, like the *phrenes* and *thumos,* are quite independent, credited with agency of their own. (This lack of cohesion will be crucial for explaining thought in Homer.)

THE FUNCTION OF *THUMOS* AND *PHRENES* IN HOMER

Thumos as Life Substance

Most of the time in the *Iliad,* the *phrenes* or *thumos* do not refer to organs of the body. Rather, they are the basis for metaphors of a great number of activities. For instance, when someone dies, their *thumos* 'flies' from their limbs or bones:

[hit by a stone] Epikles dropped like a diver from the high bastion, and the thumos left his bones.[20]

. . . but the spear fixed in the right shoulder of Pedaros the horse, who screamed as he blew his *thumos* away, and went down in the noise in the dust, and the *thumos* flitted from him.[21]

Thumos, literally interpreted as 'breath', obviously is not a property of bones or limbs. But used metaphorically to mean 'life', 'spirit', or 'life-activity', then it makes sense to talk of *thumos* going out of a person or an animal as they die and their limbs cease to move.

Breathing is an obvious sign of life, so it should not be surprising that people let breath stand for 'life' or attribute to it the properties that animate otherwise inert flesh.[22] Modern English has a few metaphorical expressions consistent with the idea of life ending when breathing stops: "He *breathed* his last", "She *gasped* out her life", "With her last *breath* . . ." or simply "He's stopped *breathing*." It is metaphors on *thumos* and the *phrenes* that are the key to understanding how people communicate in Homer.

Emotion and Feelings

Emotion in the *Iliad* is described quite differently from the way we talk about it today. We usually think of emotions as internal events which are prior to, and the cause of, 'displays' of emotions. When we say "I cried because I was sad" or "I laughed because I was happy", we imply the emotion 'happy' or 'sad' preceded and precipitated the outward sign, 'laughing' or 'crying'. By contrast, people in Homer have no 'insides' where emotions can reside.[23] There is only laughing, crying, and so on. They are not the signs of emotion—they *are* the emotion. For instance, at the beginning of the last book of the *Iliad*, Achilles mourns for the dead Patroklus:

. . . nor did sleep who subdues all come over him, but he tossed and turned from one side to the other . . . he let fall the swelling tears, lying sometimes on his side, sometimes on his back, now again prone on his face; then he would stand upright, and pace turning in distraction along the beach of the sea . . . [24]

This is not grief as an internal event, but a description of what someone looking on would see. Nonetheless, we are left in no doubt about how Achilles feels as he tosses and turns in his bed, weeps, and paces the beach. This is the way that people's grief, rage, fear and envy are usually described in Homer—as what can be seen from the perspective of an onlooker. Idomeneus describes the characteristics of cowards and brave men:

the skin of the coward changes colour one way and
another, and the heart inside him has no control to
make him sit steady, but he shifts his weight from
one foot to another, then settles firmly on both feet,
and the heart inside his chest pounds violent as
he thinks of the death spirits ['seeks death gods'],
and his teeth chatter together: but the brave man's
skin will not change colour, nor is he too much
frightened . . . [25]

There are times in the *Iliad* when the perspective shifts to describe the feelings that characters
themselves experience. When this happens
though, what we are given is a description of the
physical sensations—'feelings' in the most literal sense. Sometimes we still explain emotional
states this way in modern English. An actor with
stage-fright may say "I feel sick" rather than "I
am frightened". Some other expressions we have
for describing fear are:

A hair-raising flight. A stomach-churning experience. I had butterflies in my stomach. The film gave
me goose bumps. He makes my skin crawl. He broke
out in a cold sweat. I went weak at the knees.

Modern English has hundreds of similar
expressions, particularly for strong feelings like
fear. We describe what we 'feel' without naming
an emotion. Describing the physical sensations—
'feelings'—is the normal way in the *Iliad* and the
Odyssey of describing what we would call 'emotions', although both poems do use a few terms
for strong emotions such as fear, anger, fury, and
grief.

In Homer, there is also an association made
between the feeling and the organ where the feeling is experienced. The organs are frequently
said to be responsible for the feeling or are the
source of it. There are many examples in modern
English of this type of association. The most
important organ associated with the feelings in
English is, of course, the heart.

His *heart* leapt. Her *heart* sank. His *heart* swelled
with pride. He's her sweet-*heart*. She's *heart*-
broken. He's hard-*hearted*. She's *heartless* . . .

Thumos, *Phrenes*, and Emotion

In Homer, the *phrenes* take the leading role in
what we call emotional life. For instance, when
Agamemnon weeps with fear, the picture in the
Iliad is physiological, not emotional:

In close succession came the cries in his breast . . .
from the heart, and his *phrenes* quivered within
him.[26]

More often, the *phrenes* are not merely the
site of feelings. Homer repeatedly speaks of the
phrenes being 'filled up' with strength *(menos)*
or anger *(kholos).*[27]

[. . . and among them stood up Agamemnon rag-
ing], the *phrenes* within filled black to the brim
with anger . . . [28]

Given the close association of *thumos* with
the *phrenes,* we might expect similar expressions
linking *thumos* with *feelings.* We do, and far
more commonly than with the *phrenes.* Just as
the *phrenes* of the sailors were shaken when they
were afraid,[29] Odysseus clears corpses out of the
way of a chariot so that the horses will "not be
shaken within [their *thumos*], at stepping on dead
men."[30] Like the *phrenes,* the *thumos* may also
be 'filled' with anger or hate.

Just as the *thumos* is related to the breath, so
breath in turn is used to refer to a person's emotional state. Different emotional states are associated with different breathing patterns: in rage
breathing is rough, fast and shallow; when
people are calm, their breathing is deep, slow
and regular. Different breathing cycles are quite
easy to see, so it is not surprising that people
associate different types of breathing with a
person's (imputed) emotional state. Modern
English has many expressions associating breath
and different ways of breathing with emotion:

She *caught her breath* with surprise. He *panted*
with lust. She *gasped* in horror. We *held our breaths*
in suspense. You can all *breathe more easy when*
the exam is over. There was a *sigh* of relief. The
audience yawned with boredom.[31]

Although the treatment of *thumos* and *phrenes* in describing emotion is often parallel in Homer, they are not entirely interchangeable. In particular, *thumos* is far more independent of a person than are their *phrenes,* and often has agency of its own. Sometimes *thumos* is the instigator of action or emotion, and the character themselves seems little more than an onlooker. For instance below, it is not Ajax but his *thumos* that wants to fight:

mine own *thumos* also within my breast is the more eager to war and do battle . . . [32]

Similarly, it is not Aeneas, but his *thumos* that is glad:

even so the *thumos* of Aeneas was glad in his breast when he saw the throng of his host[33]

We can summarize all of these expressions with three metaphors:

[1] THUMOS AND THE PHRENES ARE THE ORGANS THAT FEEL

[2] THUMOS AND THE PHRENES ARE WHERE PEOPLE FEEL

[3] FEELING IS BREATHING (although obviously, not all kinds of feeling involve breathing, and not every kind of breathing involves a feeling.)

THE HOMERIC CONCEPT OF MIND AND THOUGHT

Mind

In the examples above, the *phrenes* and *thumos* might appear to behave somewhat like what we call 'the mind', and *thumos* also like 'thought' or 'thoughts'. Here is another apparently consistent example, where Agamemnon praises a captured girl above his wife, Clytemnestra:

. . . for she is in no way inferior, neither in build, nor stature, nor *phrenes,* nor in accomplishment.[34]

Phrenes translated as 'lungs' here makes no sense, but in the context, it would translate well as 'wits' or 'intelligence'. Elsewhere in Homer, the *phrenes* and *thumos* may also take delight listening to music or speeches. More unusually, the *phrenes* may also take delight in sight: an unusual activity, it might seem, for the lungs.

When he had satisfied his *phrenes* with looking at the intricate armour . . . [35]

I shall stay here upon the fold of Olympus still, watching, to please my *phrenes.*[36]

There are many examples of the *phrenes* knowing and perceiving things. When Hector becomes separated from the other Trojans in battle, it is not he but his *phrenes* that recognizes this:

And Hector knew the truth within his *phrenes.*[37]

Or when Achilles recognises the disguised King Priam, he says:

I know you, Priam, in my *phrenes.*[38]

Thumos may also be involved in knowing and seeing, either in conjunction with the *phrenes,* or by itself.

I know this thing well in my *phrenes* and my *thumos* knows it.[39]

Memory too is a function of speaking, and hence of *thumos* and the *phrenes.*[40] After reciting a list of warriors' names, Homer finishes by saying:

But what man could tell forth from his *phrenes* the names of others.[41]

In understanding the role of the *phrenes* and *thumos,* we need to avoid an anachronism. In these examples, the *phrenes* and *thumos* may appear to be equivalent to 'the mind' or 'mental activity', but the concept of 'mind' is a much later one, for which there is no parallel in

Homer.[42] The *phrenes* are not 'the mind', although they are where a person feels. Nor is *thumos* 'the mind' or 'thought' or any kind of 'mental stuff'. We have to understand each of the examples above as primarily a physical experience in some part of the body. This might appear impossible in some of the examples, such as where sight is experienced in the chest. However, while it is physically impossible, it is nonetheless quite plausible that people did genuinely experience this sensation. Compare this situation to the modern location of the mind, where most modern people 'feel' themselves thinking 'inside' their head. At a physical level, this is just as impossible as experiencing sight in the chest, because there are no nerves inside the cranium capable of physical stimulation. What appears to happen in both cases is that people experience what they expect to experience.

Thinking

Just as there is no 'mind' or 'mental stuff' in Homer, characters in the *Iliad* do not appear to be conscious of thinking. They do not deliberate privately; they do not make conscious choices; they do not reason with themselves. This is not to say that Homer's characters are thoughtless or automatons, but rather that what we understand as 'thinking' is treated quite differently.

To understand how Homer deals with thought, we have to shed several modern assumptions. To do this, I need to construct several anachronistic metaphors, that do not occur in Homer, but which will help explain the concepts used in the poems.

In the previous section, I showed that a person's *thumos* and *phrenes* could be delighted in speech or music or sights, as well as be the site of strong feelings, such as anger or hate or lust. In Homer, there is no significant difference in the treatment between what we would see as 'emotional' and 'intellectual' activities. If the two domains are treated the same, and if we were discussing metaphors in modern English, then we might expect three metaphors for thinking which parallel those I discussed earlier for feeling:

[1] THINKING IS BREATHING

[2] THUMOS AND THE PHRENES ARE WHERE PEOPLE THINK

[3] THUMOS AND THE PHRENES ARE ORGANS THAT THINK

From a modern point of view, all three appear absurd. We associate thinking with the brain, not the lungs, and breath and breathing have no connection with thinking. There are no expressions in ordinary modern English consistent with any of these metaphors. In the *Iliad* and *Odyssey* however, there are many expressions that we can understand as consistent with all three metaphors (remembering that 'thinking' does not occur literally in Homer, and that this is an exercise to help us understand, not a literal rendering.)

Expressions consistent with the THINKING IS BREATHING metaphor are rare. But we can understand it as a concatenation of two others; both of which appear commonly:

[4] SPEAKING IS BREATHING

[5] THINKING IS SPEAKING

The first metaphor, SPEAKING IS BREATHING, is obvious: speaking *always* involves breathing; it is impossible to speak without exhaling so it would be perfectly natural to conceive of one in terms of the other. In modern English, we have many expressions implying just this:

> We're just *gasbagging*. He's full of *hot air*. Don't *breathe* a word. She yelled at the top of her *lungs*. The speaker was *long-winded*. Save your *breath*. He *choked* on his words.

In Homer, one word used for the verb 'to speak' is *aīsthein,* meaning more literally 'to breathe' or 'to wheeze'.[43]

> The hero [Achilles] spoke like this and bent [persuaded] the *phrenes* of his brother, since he urged [aisima] wisely. And Menelaos obeyed him . . .[44]

Adjectives of speech are also another useful insight into how the metaphor SPEAKING IS BREATHING is used in Homer. *Pepnueín,* meaning 'to breathe' is often used in the context of knowledge or wisdom being breathed into or out of a person.[45] So, for instance, in the *Odyssey,* Penelope's strategy to avoid her unwelcome suitors is breathed into her:

> Some god breathed into my *phrenes* to set up a great loom and weave a robe[46]

The second metaphor, THINKING IS SPEAKING, would arise easily in a culture without writing, such as the one the *Iliad* and *Odyssey* are composed in. Imagine people in such a community trying to decide whether a person is wise or not. In the *Iliad,* there are basically three tests by which a person is judged: by the excellence of their advice, by how well they handle themselves in debates and councils, and the extent to which they can persuade others. For a culture without a term for (or apparently concept of) 'thinking', what could be more natural than to treat wisdom as good speaking?

> It is a naive recognition of the importance of words in thinking . . . We today may regard [words] as sounds of auditory images, symbols, but it was natural to identify them with the breath with which they were uttered.[47]

But it is not only the activity of what we would call 'thinking' that is described in terms of speech: so are 'thoughts'. In the following example, the jealous Hera has found out that Zeus and the goddess Thetis have been conspiring together, and she demands to know what he is up to:

> "Treacherous one, what god has been planning counsels with you? Always it is dear to your *phrenes* in my absence to think of secret things and decide on them. Never have you patience frankly to speak forth to me the thing you purpose."

> Then to her the father of gods and men made answer:

> "Hera, do not go on hoping that you will hear all my thoughts, since these will be too hard for you,

though you are my wife. Any thought that is right for you to listen to, no one neither man nor any immortal shall hear it before you . . ."[48]

In this translation, Lattimore—a modern translator writing for modern English readers with modern expectations—has naturally used words 'think' and 'thoughts'. But in Homeric Greek, the entire scene is cast in terms of speech. The expression "hear my thoughts" indicates that what Lattimore has translated as 'thoughts' *can* be spoken. The words that Lattimore has translated as 'thought'—*muthos* and *epos*—are not properly mental terms, but related to speaking also: *muthos* is the source of our word *myth; epos* the source of *epic.* In Homeric Greek they mean roughly, 'speech', 'spoken words' or 'that which is uttered'; the related verb *eipein* means broadly 'to speak' or 'to utter'. So the phrase *emous epielpeo muthous eidesein* translates more literally as "Hear all of my *words*". Similarly, *epieikes akouemen ou tis epeita* would be more closely rendered "*words* that are right for you to hear." (To make one more anachronistic metaphor: what we see here is a metaphor, THOUGHTS ARE WORDS, which is consistent with the metaphor THINKING IS SPEAKING.)

Even when Zeus will not say what he is 'thinking', his *muthoi* are not 'mental things' with an existence in the mind before they are uttered in speech—the way modern thinkers conceive of thoughts. They exist simply as words that have not been said, 'trapped within the *phrenes*'. This image appears several times elsewhere in Homer, for instance, when Achilles says how he hates liars:

> detest the man, who hides one thing in [his] *phrenes,* and speaks forth another[49]

The logic of the metaphor allows us to make complete sense of this concept. To cast the metaphors in modern English: if THOUGHTS ARE WORDS, and WORDS ARE BREATH, and in speech words are breathed out of the *phrenes,* then an 'unsaid thought' (as we might call it) is for Homer an 'unsaid word' and thus an 'unbreathed word'. And if a breath has not been breathed out, then it must still be within the *phrenes.*

This cycle of metaphors brings us closer to understanding the other metaphors I suggested at the beginning of this section: THUMOS AND PHERENES ARE THE ORGANS THAT THINK and THUMOS AND THE PHRENES ARE WHERE PEOPLE THINK. But we can also see how both need modifying. While the *phrenes* are certainly where *muthoi* and *epoi* come from, we cannot move directly to the metaphor that people think in their *phrenes* or *thumos* or even create words in them. The problem of whether and how people deliberate remains.

Deliberation and Reflection

If we make the same assumptions about physiology as Homer, then the metaphors on breath and speaking discussed above will explain all aspects of what we call 'thinking' as we observe it in other people—after all, what we call thinking we actually impute to other people: all we actually observe are their actions and what they say. But they will not do to explain our personal *experience* of thinking. Nowadays, we treat thinking as an 'internal' experience, in which we make decisions in the 'privacy of our own mind'. There is no parallel in Homer. People do not have 'minds' with 'insides' in which they may 'think privately'.[50] While the *thumos* and *phrenes*—where *muthoi* and *epoi* come from— may be said to be 'filled up' there is no implication in the *Iliad* that they are ever 'empty' or have space within them.

There is a second impediment to reflective thought in Homer. I noted earlier that the Homeric Greeks do not describe the human body as a unit, a whole, but rather as an aggregate of limbs and organs. Without a notion of a unified, integrated body, it seems impossible that the physiologically-minded Homeric Greeks could conceive of a unified *self*—and scholars agree that there is no self in Homer.[51] Consequently, there would be no way that Homeric Greeks could conceive of thinking to my self. But rather than apparently prohibiting the idea of self-thinking, this lack of integration may be the key to how the archaic Greeks understood decision-making.

Imagine someone trying to work out the solution to some problem. Now, a person who is unsure about what to do, trying to reach a decision, is someone in search of wise advice. As we have seen, the source of wisdom—which is understood as a type of speech—was the *phrenes,* and by association, *thumos.* Because the Homeric Greeks apparently conceived of both the *phrenes* and *thumos* as autonomous agents like another person, a character might ask them for advice in the same way that they might discuss the problem with another person. This is precisely how deep reflection is described in Homer: as debating with the *phrenes* or *thumos.* When Menelaos is unsure what to do:

> deeply disturbed, he spoke with his own great-hearted *thumos.*[52]

And in case we should have any doubts that it is his *thumos* he is addressing, rather than him simply 'talking to himself', he asks:

> Yet still, why does the *thumos* within me debate on these things?[53]

There are many occasions where someone ponders different courses of action with their *phrenes,*[54] or their *thumos,*[55] or both.[56] There are also expressions where someone "breathes in two ways", which might be consistent with the metaphor—analogous to the situation when we say "I am in two minds about. . . ." Other types of self-reflective thought, such as believing and holding opinions, are also described in terms of speech. For instance, Zeus sends Agamemnon a false dream, so that the king "thought that on that very day he would take Priam's city."[57] The word Lattimore translates as 'thought', *phē,* means literally 'said'.[58]

Nobody thinks to themselves in the *Iliad;* everyone speaks to their *thumos* or *phrenes.* So despite appearing an odd concept to us, the metaphor REFLECTING IS SPEAKING WITH

THE PHRENES OR THUMOS does provide a coherent framework for explaining reflective thought. Not that much reflection goes on in the *Iliad*. Mostly, 'thoughts' come from outside the person themselves—either from a god, or from their *phrenes* or *thumos*.

> . . . on the tenth day of [the plague] Achilles called the people to assembly [to say] a thing put into his *phrenes* by the goddess of the white arms, Hera.[59]

There are of course times when people do not know how they came up with a solution, they just know what to do. In these cases, the *thumos* is the source of the solution, or demands something be done or said. (The *phrenes* are rarely the source of this kind of independent advice—presumably reflecting the fact that *thumos* is more independent than the *phrenes,* and so a more plausible source for 'outside' advice.)

> Listen to me, you Trojans and strong-greaved Acheans, while I speak what the *thumos* within my breast urges . . . [60]

To summarize, much of what we understand as thinking and reflecting in Homer can be understood as part of a single consistent system organised around speaking.

[1] SPEAKING IS BREATHING

[2] WISDOM IS GOOD SPEAKING

[3] WISE PEOPLE HAVE GOOD WORDS

[4] THUMOS AND THE PHRENES ARE THE SOURCE OF WORDS

[5] WISE PEOPLE HAVE GOOD PHRENES

[6] THUMOS AND THE PHRENES ARE INDEPENDENT AGENTS

[7] SOLVING PROBLEMS IS DEBATING WITH OTHERS

[8] SOLVING PROBLEMS IS SPEAKING TO ONE'S THUMOS OR PHRENES

A DESCRIPTION OF COMMUNICATION

With these metaphors relating speaking, breathing, feeling and deciding, we are now in a position to understand how communication is implicitly structured in Homer.

Speaking happens when words (*muthoi, epoi*) are breathed (*aīsthai*) or blown (*epnei*) out of the *phrenes*. Listening is simply the reverse process.[61] For instance, when Nestor calls to Achilles, sleeping in his hut:

> Quickly the sound [breath] came inside [Achilles'] *phrenes* and [waking] he went forth from the hut.[62]

Communication takes place when one person breathes their words into the *phrenes* of another—just as in the examples earlier, a god or goddess may place an 'idea' in someone's *phrenes*.[63] An expression that appears repeatedly is:

> . . . put away in your *phrenes* this other thing I tell you . . . [64]

> Father Zeus of the shining bolt, I will tell you a message [word] and put it in your *phrenes*.[65]

Persuasion can also be explained as the influence of one person's words on the *phrenes* of another. When Achilles tries to dissuade his brother from fighting Hector, he speaks to him at length:

> The hero spoke like this and bent the *phrenes* of his brother since he urged [breathed] justice.[66]

> So he spoke, and stirred the *thumos* and strength in each man.[67]

There are obvious similarities between this model and the basic parts of modern communication-as-transmission: the presence of a 'sender' and a 'receiver', and the passage of words physically—bodily—from one person to another. It is also worth noting that the modern conduit metaphor[68] makes no more distinction between the passage of thoughts and emotions than Homer does.

But there is an important difference between this ancient 'Homeric model' and the modern transmission model. In the transmission model, there is a 'message' with an existence outside of any person reading or speaking it. There is no corresponding portion in the Homeric model. In Homer, words are never separate from a person. If we think of words as breath-from-the-*phrenes,* the reason for this is obvious: there can be no speaking separate from the person that speaks them, nor breath without someone to breathe it.[69] The *Iliad* and the *Odyssey* are told from the perspective of a world where all communication is spoken. How the message comes to be seen as independent of both speakers and hearers, I discuss elsewhere.[70]

We have no other Greek texts from before the fifth century BC large enough to check how widespread this model is, but a very similar description was in widespread use during the fifth century BC. Moreover, when we compare the basic physiological architecture of the Homeric model with the beliefs of other cultures of the same period, there are many similarities.[71] Together, this suggests that some variation of communication-as-transmission is one of the most basic explanations of human communication, and would help to explain why it remains so pervasive.

One final observation: in Homer we find a complete if simple description of human communication. It is not an explicit theory, but an aspect of a larger, integrated set of beliefs about the make-up of the human body, the way it functions, and the life-substances supposed to animate it. What we do not find in Homer is a theory of mind. The organs that eventually evolve into the mind and the soul in classical Greek thought—*thumos* and *phrenes*—are primarily associated with speech and breath, not cognition and reflection. What we understand as 'thinking' is dealt with largely in terms of speaking, debating and persuading, and is subject to the organs of breathing and speech. In Homer, what we would call 'mind' is largely dependent upon speech and communication—completely the opposite of the mainstream modern view, which gives priority to the mind.

REFERENCES

Adkins, A. D. H. (1960). *From the many to the one.* Ithaca, NY: Cornell University Press.

Homer. (translation, 1961). *The Iliad of Homer* (R. Lattimore, Trans.). Chicago and London: The University of Chicago Press.

Homer. (translation, 1991). *The Odyssey of Homer* (R. Lattimore, Trans.). New York: HarperPerennial.

Jaynes, J. (1976). *The origins of consciousness in the breakdown of the bicameral mind.* Harmondsworth, Middlesex: Penguin.

Onians, R. B. (1954, 2nd edition). *The origins of European thought about the body, the mind, the soul, the world, time, and fate.* Cambridge: Cambridge University Press.

Reddy, M. J. (1979). The conduit metaphor: A case of frame conflict in our language about language. In A. Ortony (Ed.), *Metaphor and thought* (pp. 284–324). Cambridge: Cambridge University Press.

Snell, B. (1953). *The discovery of the mind* (T. G. Rosenmeyer, Trans.). Cambridge, MA: Harvard University Press.

Wiseman, R. D. (2003). *The development of ideas about communication in European thought from ancient Greece to the early modern age.* Unpublished doctoral dissertation. Canberra, Australia: Australian National University.

NOTES

1. Internal evidence suggests that the *Iliad* and the *Odyssey* date from around the early eighth century BC. They were preserved in oral recitation and, according to Greek tradition, were first transcribed around 600 BC in Athens, although the earliest surviving papyri and quotations from classical authors suggest there were many variations on both tales.

2. The *Iliad* and the *Odyssey* are not products of poets in the modern sense, but of oral bards, *aoidoi.* A key feature of oral poetry is that it is not memorized verbatim but, in each performance, the poem is constructed anew—literally 're-told'—out of a vast stock of stock phrases and themes. This stock is not the possession of any individual: to be preserved over the long periods we know these poems survived, the *aoidoi* had to draw on the language and idioms of the communities they lived in, and be intelligible to those communities: an unintelligible bard was unlikely to

survive, much less be regarded as a genius as Homer was. Consequently, we can take the description of communication presented in the Homeric poems to be representative not only of the individual bards from whom the *Iliad* and the *Odyssey* were first transcribed, but also of the wider Greek-speaking communities of the eighth to sixth centuries BC.

3. There is a limit to the amount of 'gleaning' the *Iliad* and the *Odyssey* can survive before being distorted from their true nature as tales describing the siege of Troy and the journey of Odysseus home again. I have included only expressions and formulas that occur at least four times, omitting one-off words and phrases unless they can be clearly linked to already accepted formulas. This approach excludes subtleties and also some of the idiosyncrasies of the bard from whom the epics were transcribed, and allows us to focus on what, by their frequency, are probably core expressions used by Greeks of the seventh century BC to describe communication.

4. From the Homeric *noos* evolved the important, but quite different term of the fifth and fourth centuries BC, *nous,* mind.

5. *Psukhē* evolved into the important term for soul and mind of the Greek philosophers, which usually appears spelt *psyche* in English texts.

6. Plato *Timaeus* 70a

7. The singular *phren* is used very occasionally, but for metrical reasons only.

8. *Iliad* 1:103, 17:499, 17:573

9. *Iliad* 8:202, 9:458

10. *Iliad* 16:481

11. *Iliad* 10:9, 16:503

12. *Iliad* 16:503

13. *Iliad* 20:470

14. *Iliad* 2:265, 5:40

15. Onians 1954, Chapter 2.

16. The Latin equivalent, *praecordia,* preserves rather more transparently the position of this organ in front of *(prae)* the heart *(cordis)*.

17. *Iliad* 1:193, 8:169, 11:411, 15:163, 16:435, 17:106, 18:15 amongst many other examples.

18. *Iliad* 15:239–242. Unless I have noted otherwise, I have used Lattimore's translation of the *Iliad* (1951) throughout.

19. *Odyssey* 5:456–458

20. *Iliad* 12:385–386

21. *Iliad* 16:467–469. See also *Iliad* 23:880, 12:386 and 16:743.

22. Our word *spirit* has *spiro,* meaning 'breath', as its etymological root. The other obvious sign of life

is warmth. We find *thumos* described as hot and so is presumably responsible for the body's heat.

23. Jaynes 1976, particularly pp. 257–281

24. *Iliad* 24:4–6, 9–12

25. *Iliad* 13:279–285. Lattimore has translated *kēras oïomenōi* as "thinks of the death spirits", but *menos* in Homer is physical strength or a wish experienced as physical desire; it is not mental.

26. *Iliad* 10:9–10 (translated by Onians 1954).

27. Physiologically, people in deep rage or exercising all their strength take large, deep breaths, filling their lungs with oxygen to fuel the exertion. The flush of oxygen is also associated with a release of adrenalin, causing a rush of energy and strength. It is easy to see how people could feel as though they were being 'filled up' with strength through the lungs.

28. *Iliad* 1:101–104. Describing rage as 'black' or 'dark', *melainai,* may be from association with the lungs which are usually either splotched with dark patches or else completely black.

29. *Iliad* 15:627–628

30. *Iliad* 10:491–493

31. These expressions are different from Homeric metaphors because in each case the emotion or feeling (surprise, lust, horror, expectation, relief, boredom) causes the particular type of breathing: That is, there is a separation drawn between the two. In Homer, all we have is the description of breathing. People in Homer do not 'sigh with relief'—they just 'breathe easier'.

32. *Iliad* 13:73–74

33. *Iliad* 13:494–495. See also *Iliad* 14:156.

34. *Iliad* 1:114–115

35. *Iliad* 19:19

36. *Iliad* 20:23. For further examples of the *phrenes* and sight, see *Iliad* 9:186 and 19:172–174.

37. *Iliad* 22:296

38. *Iliad* 24:563. For similar formulas where the *phrenes* knows, see *Iliad* 1:333, 5:406, 6:447 and 21:61.

39. *Iliad* 4:163

40. The association of memory with speech is a normal one in oral communities.

41. *Iliad* 17:260

42. Jaynes (1976), Snell (1953), Adkins (1960)

43. *Aïsthein* is related to the Latin words *asthma* 'gasp, wheeze' and *aspere* 'to breathe', and the Sanskrit *asmi,* 'to breathe'.

44. *Iliad* 7:120

45. There are other interpretations on the use of *pepnueín* amongst different translators. Onians however devotes considerable space, supported by dozens of examples, to show that it must relate to the activity

of breathing, and options offered by other translators make neither etymological nor contextual sense. See Onians 1954, pp. 56–59, for this complex argument.

46. *Odyssey* 19:138–139 (translated by Murray)
47. Onians 1954, p. 14
48. *Iliad* 1:541–548
49. *Iliad* 9:312–313
50. Jaynes 1976, pp. 259–272. There are a handful of exceptions where people do hold things 'inside', but literary evidence suggests that they are later additions to the poems.
51. See Snell 1953, p. 6
52. *Iliad* 17:90
53. *Iliad* 17:97. Homer uses precisely the same expressions when Agenor and Hector work out what to do (*Iliad* 21:552 and 22:98), and when they both ask why their *thumos* is debating (*Iliad* 21:562 and 22:122).
54. *Iliad* 2:3, 9:434, 14:264, 16:435, 20:310
55. *Iliad* 10:506, 14:20, 21:137, 24:680
56. *Iliad* 1:193, 5:671, 11:411, 15:163, 17:106, 18:15, 20:264
57. *Iliad* 2:37
58. Onians 1954, p. 13
59. *Iliad* 1:54–55
60. *Iliad* 7:67–68, and also *Iliad* 8:5–6

61. The ears are not mentioned in relation to listening in either the *Iliad* or *Odyssey* so there is no explicit mention made of how words enter into the listener.
62. *Iliad* 10:139–140, translated by Onians 1954, p. 69
63. *Iliad* 1:54–55
64. *Iliad* 1:297, 4:39, and many other places.
65. *Iliad* 19:121
66. *Iliad* 6:61–62. There are other examples of persuasion in the *Iliad* although the formulas are different. *Iliad* 4:104, 7:120–121, 12:173, 13:788, 6:842 and obliquely 22:357.
67. *Iliad* 15:500
68. Reddy 1979.
69. There is one minor exception to this lack of separation between speakers and their words. Homer repeatedly uses the expression 'winged words'. Exactly what he means is unclear, but the favoured theories are either a metaphor on arrows fletched with feathers, or a metaphor of bird in flight. In either case however, the idea of words 'flying' between one person and another is preserved.
70. Wiseman 2003, Chapter 4.
71. A full comparison of Homer with contemporary poets lies outside the scope of this thesis. . . .

2

THE SPIRITUALIST TRADITION

JOHN DURHAM PETERS

CHRISTIAN SOURCES

Although, as I argued in chapter 1, some strains in the Christian tradition emphasize imperfection and asymmetry as conditions of compassion, the mainstream of doctrine solidifying in later antiquity calls for those who love to be "in" each other in a decidedly unphysical way. The Gospel of John is perhaps the first Christian source for the characteristically double mixture of tragicomic breakdown and soulful unity that still informs communication theory. John, compared with the synoptic Gospels, is rich in face-to-face dialogue, and much of it consists of more or less spectacular misfires: the woman at the well, mistaking Jesus' teaching about living water, asks for water that will never run out; Nicodemus, puzzled at being told he has to reenter the womb, fails to understand the command to be born anew; the disciples are as dopey in their inability to "get it" as the tendentiously portrayed

Pharisees are willful in their misunderstanding. The Gospel of John is structured in many ways by dialogic mishaps. The hearers of Jesus consistently mistake the body of the metaphor for the spirit (to use John's language). And often, just when the dialogue has collapsed, there comes the moment of recognition. Something larger breaks through. John is thus, to be sure, no booster of dialogism—the faith that conversation leads to mutual clarification. The book shows how often dialogue is motivated by misunderstanding in the first place. When higher powers burst onto the scene—the wind, the light, the other world—dialogue vanishes into something else: prayer, loss, bafflement, faith.

John paints on a cosmic canvas. The whole book is about the revelation of light and resistance to it.[1] Conversational collisions are everyday mirrors of the larger battle between light and darkness. As the call finds no response, so the light is often ignored. The witness of truth is taken as a

SOURCE: Peters, J. D. (1999). *Speaking into the air: A history of the idea of communication* (pp. 66–80). Chicago, IL: University of Chicago Press. Reprinted by permission.

scandal. At the end of Jesus' long and highly metaphorical bread of life sermon, which climaxes in the shocking command to eat his flesh and drink his blood, he says: "It is the Spirit that quickeneth; the flesh profiteth nothing: the words that I speak unto you, they are spirit, and they are life."[2] The priority of the spirit over the flesh is here not only a metaphysical and moral admonition, but an interpretive principle that resonates in later Christian hermeneutics.[3] Right understanding, for the Gospel of John, comes from catching the tenor without tripping on the vehicle. We are to dwell in the metaphor's meaning, not its mechanics to discover the *logos* within the flesh. But such apprehension is hidden from most.

The fourth Gospel dramatizes the antinomy of transparency and obstruction in communication. Perhaps most intensely, in the farewell speech of chapters 14–17, especially in the climactic intercessory prayer of chapter 17, Jesus is portrayed as advocating shared being on a spiritual plane as the highest state his disciples can attain with each other, him, and the Father, perhaps almost as if in compensation for the dialogue follies in the rest of the book. The Gospel of John makes frequent use of the grammatical case called "the ontological dative," a form that makes it possible to speak of one person's being "in" another, as God is in Christ, or Christ is in his disciples. The ontological dative opens up thinking about how persons can share spiritual substance, something important in the theology of the Trinity, as well as angelology and communication theory. The Gospel of John does not, of course, offer an account of communication as the symbolic modes of connections among minds. It does provide both a vision of consubstantiality that is attained only in spirit and a sharp sense for all the obstacles to seeing. John gives us the combination of blocked understandings and wished for unions characteristic of "communication" as a concept.

Augustine: The Spirit Over the Letter

Augustine is in many ways a fountainhead of the concept of communication and a key figure in the history of linguistic theory. Tzvetan Todorov regards him as the key figure in semiotic theory between Plato and Saussure.[4] Whatever the originality of his thinking on language and signs, no one can dispute its thoroughness or its subsequent influence. As the intellectual architect of Latin Christianity, Augustine (354–430) exerted a massive influence on European life from the fifth century through the Renaissance and, via his influence on Luther and the Puritans, on modern intellectual life as well.[5] The literary genre he made famous in the *Confessions* has never been more alive. This formidable man may not have used the word "communication" as we do, but he certainly set up conditions for its flourishing. Forging neo-Platonist currents and Christian doctrine, Augustine saw the soul as immaterial and developed the full armor of oppositions that communication is still designed to overcome and reproduce, such as soul and body, intellect and sense, eternity and time, and inside and outside. Augustine helped build both the interior self and the dream of overcoming it in communication.[6] If communication is what makes the privacy of the self accessible to others, the concept presupposes—even needs—the principle of interiority.[7]

Augustine's theory of the sign is elaborated in many works, but his early dialogue *De Magistro* (On the teacher) articulates many of his key positions, but with few of the larger theological ramifications that come later. A sign is a marker of interior and exterior realities. It points to and shows things that antedate it, but it has no legitimate role as an agent of imagination or invention. "Words possess only sufficient efficacy to remind us in order that we may see things, but not to exhibit the things that we may know them." A teacher may use signs to draw the learner's attention to certain aspects of a topic, but ultimately there "is nothing which is learned by means of signs." Nothing can be ultimately learned from a teacher in any case: instruction comes not from words "but by means of the things themselves which God reveals within the soul." The things themselves are all but infinitely superior to words. In sum, "we should not attribute to words more than is proper." Words are like cue cards, pointers to things mental and material, but their value lies outside them.[8] Augustine is here quite far from Saussure (for whom words acquire significance in their mutual semiotic relationships) or Wittgenstein (for whom words behave in language games, interwoven with concrete forms of life).

For Augustine, the sign is a passive vessel that suppresses itself for the sake of what it carries. In one sense, Augustine may be the inventor of the concept of "medium."[9] Communication happens both because of and in spite of the medium, a term he uses in a broad sense to refer alike to the body, a means to an end, and a means of conveyance. Means are to be used (*uti*), and ends are to be enjoyed (*frui*). Throughout *De Doctrina Christiana* Augustine argues for the legitimacy of the sign as an interpretive help as long as it does not usurp the all-important spirit it is supposed to point to. Scripture can be read with any aid available including knowledge of Hebrew or Greek or the pagan arts of grammar, rhetoric, history, science, and philosophy—so long as one does not conflate the aid with the end. The hermeneutic "as" is fine, substituting one thing for another, so long as we arrive at the underlying meaning and kick away the ladder once we get there. Augustine wants interpreters not to get caught in technical difficulties or interference in transmission. Such is servitude to the letter rather than liberty in the spirit.

Augustine's examples of means are often in fact what we would call media of transport and communication (the same word, after all, is used for both in Latin). His metaphors of traveling in fact capture much about both his view of interpretation and of the human sojourn more generally. Our self-love, he writes, we ought to treat "not with such love and delight as if it were a good to rest in, but with a transient feeling rather, such as we have toward the road, or carriages, or other things that are merely means."[10] Media are not to be loved, only to be used. The danger for us pilgrims is in confusing things to use and to enjoy: "The beauty of the country through which we pass, and the very pleasure of the motion, charm our hearts, and turning these things which

we ought to use into objects of enjoyment, we become unwilling to hasten the end of our journey; and becoming engrossed in factitious delight, our thoughts are diverted from that home whose delights would make us truly happy. Such is a picture of our condition in this life of mortality."[11] Such is also a picture of the plight that awaits those who linger too long in the letter.

Augustine uses the contrast of flesh and spirit to explain signs. The sound of a word is material; the significance of a word is mental. Like human beings, the word is split into a body (sound) and spirit (meaning). To explain the word, Augustine often resorts to the Word, the *logos* of the Gospel of John, "the Word made flesh," the second member of the Trinity; it is remarkable how consistently discussions of the work of language accompany his discussions of the Incarnation. Just as the "incarnate Word" took a body of clay to be sensible to a fallen humanity, so our inner thoughts must assume the acoustic tabernacles of articulate speech in order to be sensible to other people. In both cases embodiment serves as a means of communication or manifestation.

> Just as when we speak, in order that what we have in our minds may enter through the ear into the mind of the hearer, the word which we have in our hearts becomes an outward sound and is called speech; and yet our thought does not lose itself in the sound, but remains complete in itself, and takes the form of speech without being modified in its own nature by the change: so the Divine Word, though suffering no change in nature, yet became flesh, that He might dwell among us.[12]

This remarkable analogy speaks volumes. Neither the thought nor the Word loses itself in its descent into sensible form. The nature remains constant in a new carrier. Embodiment is at best an expedient of exhibition, not of ontological importance. This is the program of communication as the meeting of two inner ideas, unperturbed by their materialities. The content remains identical across all its embodiments.

Indeed, the inner word in the human heart has little to do with body, culture, or history. It is not

Latin, Greek, or Hebrew but only employs such perceptible carriers. In a meditation in the *City of God* on the tower of Babel and the angels, the two great archetypes of failed and perfect communication in the Western tradition, Augustine argues that divine speech needs no such carriage. God speaks to the angels "in an ineffable manner of His own . . . [which] has no noisy and passing sound," since God can evoke the inner word immediately, without recourse to mediation. In contrast, when God speaks to us he must adapt to the grossness of our instruments. Sensible signifiers are concessions to our carnal state. If we are especially open, however, God's words can circumvent the mediation of physical signs and be perceived (not heard) within. Generally, however, humans grasp each other's thoughts only via acoustic or visual means. "For either the unchangeable Truth speaks directly to the mind of the rational creature in some indescribable way, or speaks through the changeable creature, either presenting spiritual images to our spirit, or bodily voices to our bodily sense."[13] Augustine leaves no doubt that the indescribable speaking of truth to spirit is preferred over the audiovisual stimulation of bodily sense.

For Augustine, the appearance of God to humans is essentially a media problem. For how could God, he asks, "appear" to the patriarchs and prophets when God has no appearance or physical form? If God appeared to appear, he was resorting to deception, donning a disguise to meet the crudity of human sense organs. Theophany is either deception (of humans) or debasement (of God). Augustine's notion of communication solves the riddle: "For as the sound which communicates the thought conceived in the silence of the mind is not the thought itself, so the form by which God, invisible in his own nature, became visible, was not God himself." Both God's appearance and the movement of words between people involve what we might call the principle of bodily indifference. "Nevertheless it is He Himself who was seen under that form, as that thought itself is heard in the sound of the voice; and the patriarchs recognized that, though the bodily form

was not God, they saw the invisible God."[14] To borrow a Johannine distinction, God was in the appearance, but not of the appearance. In the interior lies the truth.

God in Augustine's account is thus willing to stage a tête-à-tête for a human audience, putting on a ventriloquist show of sorts for human consumption—even, as Augustine says, making his voice obey the laws of resonance in real space. "For God speaks with a man not by means of some audible creature dinning in his ears, so that atmospheric vibrations connect Him that makes with him that hears the sound." Though humans may experience such vibrations, they are not direct tokens of God's presence. Such contact is not possible between mortals and eternal beings, since "it is by means of a semblance of a body that He speaks, and with the appearance of a real interval of space."[15] Communications from God are effects designed for the capacities of human senses. Since God is supposedly nowhere and no-when, he must create effects of presence for his children. Augustine's account of divine communication with mortals foreshadows modern communications and the problem of how to conjure the credible presence of an absent body for an audience remote in time, space, or degree.

In sum, for Augustine the word is a marker that points to external and internal realities. It has the crucial job of revealing interiors, the world of thought and spirit. Just as we humans are encased in flesh, words are as well. God and angels may occasionally circumvent our bodies but in general must condescend to them. For him, to bypass language is to foretaste redemption from our bodies and to emulate the angels, who dispense with outer signs and traffic solely in inner meanings. Communication without words is, in his view, a legitimate aspiration for humans, an ideal that might help us rise out of the Babel of the earthly city. When "we hear with the inner ear some part of the speech of God, we approximate to the angels."[16] Or as R. A. Markus writes, "For Augustine semantic activity—understanding and communicating through language—was the index of the human need for transcendence in the most general terms: for union with other minds in the very act of understanding a shared world."[17] Nothing less than spiritual liberation is at stake in our relation to the sign: "And nothing is more fittingly called the death of the soul than when that in it which raises it above the brutes, the intelligence namely, is put in subjection to the flesh by a blind adherence to the letter . . . it is surely a miserable slavery of the soul to take signs for things, and to be unable to lift the eye of the mind above what is corporeal and created, that it may drink in eternal light."[18] Our struggle with communication is an index of our fallenness, one portion of our lot as immersed in a world of lights and colors trying to find our way back to God. Augustine exhorts us to overcome our deficiencies—our opaque flesh and obstreperous wills—and become like angels whose relationships with others are unlimited by the barriers of skin and skull.

Augustine's theology of the incarnate Word, metaphysics of flesh and spirit, and psychology of inner and outer, all sustain his vision of communication as coordinated interiorities. His sense that the human lot is to be moved by desire, often for the wrong things, resonates with the vision of eros from Plato to Freud. Even language for Augustine is moved by passion. Though I have barely sounded the subtleties of his thought, it should be clear enough why Augustine is such a ready target for recent critics. His theory of language was an explicit foil in Wittgenstein's *Philosophical Investigations,* since Augustine (in Wittgenstein's version) argues that the meaning of words consists in their reference to things rather than springing from their place in ecosystems of lived practices.[19] Though Derrida has spent more effort tracking ontotheological clues in Rousseau, Hegel, or Heidegger, could there be a better example of a "logocentrist," a devotee of the transcendental signified, an ontotheologian, than Augustine?[20] He ranks writing below speech, exemplifying the grammatological regime that Derrida has taken such pains to dismantle: "But whereas we exhibit . . . bodily signs either to ears or eyes of persons present to whom we speak, letters have been invented that we might be able

to converse also with the absent; but these are signs of words, as words themselves are signs in our conversations of those things which we think."[21] It does not take much squinting, here or elsewhere, to see Augustine as a proponent of the metaphysics of presence.[22]

Augustine's theory of communication, as well as Christian hermeneutics more generally, has still greater political and ethical stakes. Derrida's larger aim may be not only to redeem writing from its subservience to speech, but to rescue the people of the book from their oppression by a hermeneutics that equates liberty with the spirit and bondage with the letter, a hermeneutics that Augustine upholds.[23] He singles out the Jews as the people most captive to the letter. The Gentiles take literal truths figuratively, he argues, as the Jews take figurative truths literally.[24] Either is a grave spiritual error (though he thinks the Jews have it more right than the Gentiles, since their service to the letter is at least motivated by devotion to God). Modes of interpretation, again, are not just spectacles through which to view the world; they are symptoms of one's spiritual condition. Augustine agrees on both moral and interpretive grounds with Paul's formula: "The letter killeth, but the spirit giveth life."[25]

Recent critiques of communication as spirit-to-spirit concourse, then, are often motivated not only by a sense of the descriptive inadequacy of that vision, but by its felt legacy of persecution, its long entanglement with a policy that denigrates the letter. As Susan Handelman argues, such thinkers as Freud, Harold Bloom, Jacques Lacan, Gershom Scholem, and Jacques Derrida all stem from a heretical tradition of rabbinical interpretation that has long resisted the Christian privilege of the spirit over the letter as a regime in which difference is outlawed.[26] The resistance to communication as spiritual transportation has a moral and political motive: the defense of difference over—or within—identity. Derrida and his compatriots invoke a world in which texts do not have outsides, interiority is a feature not of psychology but of discourse, and strange exchanges take place between the living and the dead. John and Augustine are both advocates of interiority whose texts are laced with anti-Semitism in intricate ways, and this fact will have to inform any responsible reading of their calls for oneness in soul or transparency in interpretation.[27] For my part, I do not take the sublimities of Christian romantic hermeneutics as a *simple* product of sublimation or the yearning for spiritual unity as *reducible* to hatred of the world. The Christian tradition, if one can speak of such, invites us not to abandon the possibility of a community unsullied by scapegoating. Its utopia is a solidarity in which no Other is expelled. The Jewish tradition, in counterpoint, reminds us of the otherness that crops up everywhere, even—or most especially—where we wish it absent in our communions with other texts like ourselves. The one tradition brings the tidings that the reconciliation has taken place; the other reminds us that it hasn't happened yet. Suspended between the hope of an atonement that enables solidarity with all creatures and the keen awareness of its recurrent absence may be the place to abide. (This may be, by the way, the neighborhood of the Gospel of John.)

Angels: The Principle of Bodily Indifference

Speculation about the angels has been one dominant form of considering communication in the history of European thought.[28] Since they have no carnal bodies, they are quite capable of fusing together in the bliss of pure intelligence. Though traditions of angelology are diverse, both orthodox and esoteric, ranging across such traditions as Christian Gnosticism, Sufism, and Kabbalah, angels present a model for communication as it should be. They provide us a lasting vision of the ideal speech situation, one without distortion or interference. Angels—a term that comes from the Greek *angelos,* messenger—are unhindered by distance, are exempt from the supposed limitations of embodiment, and effortlessly couple the psychical and the physical, the signified and the signifier, the divine and the human. They are pure bodies of meaning.

The angels are highly relevant, not just forgotten creatures from the childhood of the race. It is a cliché to disparage medieval Scholasticism for calculating how many angels could dance on the head of a pin, but this question is of some moment for communication theory, since it concerns the physical basis of significant differences. Is the sign material? Is information? What is the physical status of a just noticeable difference? Does the carrier of the message occupy space or not? Is the "spirit" of meaning separable from the "flesh" of the sign? With a little transposition, the question of the capacity of the angels' dance hall takes us to the heart of semiotic theory, the coupling of signifier and signified. If an infinity of angels can dance on the head of a pin, then angelic bodies and souls are consubstantial in a way that Plato's lovers could only dream of. Unrestricted communication would then be possible. If the head of the pin gets at all crowded, however, clearly angelic bodies occupy space, however infinitesimal. A principle of finitude arises. Invitations to the ball must then be restricted. If the floor space is in fact scarce, things intellectual do indeed have a corporeal correlate—thoughts might have weight and extension—which troubles the dream of communication, reminding us again of the body and the letter.

Ghosts and angels haunt modern media, with their common ability to spirit voice, image, and word across vast distances without death or decay. The logo of Deutsche Grammophon was long an angel with a stylus inscribing sound directly onto the phonograph disk; AT&T bragged of the speed and extent of its system with images of cherubically plump angels adorning the telephone wires.[29] Angels carry dispatches that are never lost or misdelivered or garbled in transit, at least not by the good angels. Though angels have been a chief target of enlightened mockery—Hobbes, Voltaire, Gibbon, and Freud all made both sport and theory from them—they preside over some of the high points of Western literature (Dante's *Paradiso,* Milton's *Paradise Lost,* Goethe's *Faust*) and hover over modernist literature and art (Rilke,

Klee, Chagall, Benjamin, Wallace Stevens) and over more recent works (Rushdie's *Satanic Verses,* Wenders's *Wings of Desire,* Kushner's *Angels in America*). Images of childhood purity, feminine long-suffering, ethnicity, and cyberspace all borrow from the mother lode of angelology. Above all, the angels embody our worries about communication, forming the horizon of our upward possibility. Since Augustine at least, angels have been the epitome of perfect communication, a model of how we would talk if we had no obstructions. Even since the earliest dreams in the seventeenth century of instantaneous long-distance communication among humans, angelic swiftness has been the standard against which human capacities were measured. The angels are our communicative betters.

As Stuart Schneiderman suggests, angelology can be read as semiotics by other means. The bodies of angels and their couplings are allegories of signs and their syntax. But in the dominant Thomistic tradition, angels stand for communication as if bodies did not matter. Mortimer Adler, a leading student of the angels, suggests that one lesson the angels teach us is what love would be in a world without sex or gender.[30] Adler takes the adoration of universals stripped of any personal content as love in its most noble form. But his angels lack the organs of eros. Even more fatally, they lack the bodies whose vulnerability might stir a fellow creature's bowels of mercy. It's unclear how real either eros or *agape* could be to them. Adler's gutless angels exemplify the aridness of much hankering after "communication" that persists to this day. There are of course countertraditions of fallen or meddling angels, some of them quite naughty, making all kinds of mischief, sexual and otherwise, with mortals, gods, and creation itself.

Saint Thomas Aquinas, the Doctor Angelicus and Adler's inspiration, is a high point in Scholastic angelology and offers a beautiful example of the dream of communication. He is more explicit than Augustine on how the speech of angels, who themselves are hierarchically arranged into angel species or "choirs," works.

The need to communicate, Aquinas argues, is not only a product of the deficiencies of earthly knowledge and vision. Since diverse orders of angels each enjoy a varying degree of knowledge of God and his works, a motive for talk remains among them.[31] Like Augustine and Plato, Aquinas contrasts inner and outer speech. Inner speech among mortals can be cloaked by two things: by the density of our bodies and by our wills. This cloaking can be either devious or proper depending on the situation. Since his angels have no fleshly bodies, nothing to hide, and no reason to conceal anything, the external speech of the voice "does not befit an angel, but only interior speech belongs to him." Since the purpose of mortal speech is to manifest what is hidden, what use would speech be among such lucidly intelligible beings? Angels speak by directing their "concept" or mind "in such a way that it becomes known to the other." Aquinas's vision of angelic contact is similar to what psychical research called "thought-transference" or telepathy. The speech of angels "is interior, but perceived, nevertheless, by another."[32] The interiority of one angel is transmitted to an other without loss or remainder. Since angels, as pure form, lack material bodies, "neither difference of time nor local distance has any influence whatsoever." Angels commune through a noiseless rustle of intelligence without the ministry of language or matter. In just this way, Aquinas adds, human minds, after the Resurrection, will no longer be hidden from each other, to the delight of the righteous and the horror of the wicked. For Aquinas, angels understand others in an instantaneous unfurling of interiorities. The self and the other would both be transparent to behold.

The angels, in sum, are supposed to show us the way out of the flybottle of our ineluctable privacy. They, of all beings, know no communication breakdown, for they are not encased within a shell of flesh or subject to an obstreperous will. Their selfhood is both individual and collective. Since their bodies have no matter, which is the principle of individuation, they are simultaneously themselves and their entire species.[33] Compared with such "connaturality" (a Thomistic term that gives us the French verb for being acquainted with, *connaître*), our lowly attempts at "communication" appear woefully deficient!

FROM MATTER TO MIND: "COMMUNICATION" IN THE SEVENTEENTH CENTURY

The angelology of Augustine, Aquinas, and others gives us the intellectual basis for the dream of shared interiors in communication. But their language was Latin, and the term *communicatio* itself did not have a privileged role in such discussions. *Communicare* in Latin meant to share or make common and had no special reference to sharing thoughts.[34] It is largely in the seventeenth century that the new sense of "communication" first begins to emerge in modern English, and we can see the development of the concept by briefly examining such central figures of British science in the seventeenth century as Bacon, Glanvill, Wilkins, and Newton. The concept of communication as we know it originates from an application of physical processes such as magnetism, convection, and gravitation to occurrences between minds. In the seventeenth century the term was consistently used to refer to what the Scholastics called *actio in distans*—action at a distance. Since at least the Scholastics, action at a distance has been a problem in natural philosophy: How can one body influence another without palpably touching it?[35] It is speculations about such action, including between minds—what Francis Bacon called "the transmission of immateriate virtues"—that sets "communication" on its modern course. Ideal relations between souls have long been understood as a question of action at a distance—Plato's lovers who do not touch or Aquinas's angels for whom no distance matters—and this notion gets recapitulated in the quasi-physical dreams of communication by scientists in the seventeenth century and spiritualists in the nineteenth.

The semantic history of "communication" owes much to psychophysical speculations. Francis Bacon, for instance, the founding spokesman for modern science, thought it "agreeable to reason, that there are at the least some light effluxions from spirit to spirit, when men are in presence one with another, as well as from body to body."[36] His list of "operations by transmission" that "work at a distance, and not at touch" includes light, sound, heat, gravity (pre-Newtonian), and magnetism; odors, infections, and "the affections"; and sympathetic transmission, as between amulets and actions, or a sword and the wounds it caused, however distant the victim. This uneasy mix for later thinkers does not respect the interdependent separation of nature and society in what Bruno Latour calls the "modern constitution."[37]

Bacon's inclusion of psychological phenomena among remote processes, not unlike the approach of his later heirs in psychical research, is echoed by his disciple Sir Joseph Glanvill, who used the phenomenon of sympathetic vibration in acoustics to explain how one mind may "bind" (secretly control) another. Imagination consisted of cerebral motions that agitated the "Aether" and propagated through this "liquid medium" to other minds, just as plucking a lute's string "causeth a proportionable motion in the sympathizing consort, which is distant from it and not sensibly touched." Such vibration at a distance also explained, Glanvill added, how "Angels inject thoughts into our minds, and know our cogitations."[38] Imaginative empathy or acoustic action: the notion of sympathy has inhabited moral and physical universes since Pythagoras. Here with the fusion of mental and material processes occurring through a subtle ether, Glanvill articulates the framework within which communication would be thought about for well over two centuries.[39]

Angelic alacrity also inspired a striking seventeenth-century anticipation of telecommunications. Bishop John Wilkins, like Glanvill both a Baconian and a founder of the Royal Society, wrote a book in 1641 called *Mercury, or The Secret and Swift Messenger: Shewing How a*

Man May with Privacy and Speed Communicate His Thoughts to a Friend at a Distance, whose title expresses the enduring ambitions of privacy and speed in long-distance communication. Angels, he argues (like Aquinas), discourse *per insinuationem spederum*—by "an unveiling of their own Natures in the knowledge of such Particulars as they would discover to another." Humans, having "Organical Bodies," however, "cannot communicate their thoughts [in] so easie and immediate a way. And therefore have need of some Corporeal Instruments, both for the Receiving and Conveying of Knowledge."[40] Our instruments—ear, eye, tongue, and feet—are tortoiselike compared with those of the angels, whose speed matches that of the "Primum Mobile", the outermost sphere of the Ptolemaic universe. Our bodies, then, are multiply handicapped. Wilkins's proposed compensation for our handicaps was a binary coding of the alphabet in visible or audible media, such as trumpets, bells, cannons, drums, flame, or smoke. Unlike the nineteenth century, Wilkins had no idea of physical means such as the telegraph to send signals themselves; he relied on the eyes and ears, these being the only senses that "are of quick Perception, when their objects are remote."[41] The distances Wilkins could cover are limited by the acuity of the eyes and ears and the curvature of the earth. He did not yet know the quicksilver status of the electrical signal.

Newtonian physics, the capital fact of science and philosophy in eighteenth-century Europe, gave new energy to speculation about action at a distance and hence boosted the fortunes of communication as well. Newton's description in his 1687 *Principia* of universal gravitation and its operation was first and foremost an account of action at a distance. Like magnetism, light, and heat, he thought gravity traveled via an "imponderable" or insensible fluid. The word Newton used for this fluid, in both his English and Latin writings, was "medium."[42] Newton called this "universal and subtle" medium the *sensorium dei* (sensorium of God). He saw the cosmos as bathed in a cosmic intelligence communicating at a distance through a marvelous, intangible

essence. This force or intelligence prevented us from flying off into space and kept the moon in orbit and the tides ebbing and flowing. Like his late nineteenth-century British successors in physics, Newton took this medium not simply as a sterile physical fact but as full of spiritual suggestion. In Newton "communication" and "medium" have much of their modern senses without their modern spheres of use. One means the transmission of immaterial forces or entities at a distance, the other the mechanism or vehicle of such transmission.

Bacon, Glanvill, Wilkins, Newton–these are not crackpots, but the cream of English science in the seventeenth century and founders of modern scientific culture. Their interest in angels and the ether, and in natural and cultural communicative action at a distance, was not retrograde but transitional. These examples show that "communication" mainly referred to physical processes of transmission and metaphysical processes of consubstantiation, the boundary between subject and object being quite ragged. Tangibles such as robes, fortunes, plants, and commodities and intangibles such as light, heat, blessings, praise, secrets, vices, thoughts, and ideas could all be "communicated."[43] In the process of remaking Scholastic categories into scientific ones, "communication" took a new turn.

NOTES

1. For the argument that the medium *and* message of John are revelation, see John Ashton, *Understanding the Fourth Gospel* (Oxford: Clarendon Press, 1991), chap. 14.

2. John 6:63 KJV.

3. For example, Augustine, *The City of God,* Great Books of the Western World, ed. Robert Maynard Hutchins, vol. 18 (Chicago: Encyclopaedia Britannica, 1952), 313 (10.24).

4. Tzvetan Todorov, *Theories of the Symbol,* trans. Catherine Porter (Ithaca: Cornell University Press, 1982), 15; Giovanni Manetti, *Theories of the Sign in Classical Antiquity,* trans. Christine Richardson (Bloomington: Indiana University Press, 1993), 157; Ake Bergvall, "The Theology of the

Sign: St. Augustine and Spenser's Legend of Holiness," *Studies in English Literature 33* (1993): 22–42, at 24.

5. For instance, Schelling, Kierkegaard, Freud, Heidegger, and Wittgenstein.

6. Charles Taylor, *Sources of the Self: The Making of the Modern Identity* (Cambridge: Harvard University Press, 1989), chap. 7.

7. See Briankle G. Chang, *Deconstructing Communication: Representation, Subject, and Economies of Exchange* (Minneapolis: University of Minnesota Press, 1996), chap. 2.

8. St. Augustine, *De Magistro,* trans. George G. Leckie (New York: Appleton-Century, 1938), 46, 43, 50, 55 (from chaps. 10, 11, 12, 14).

9. See Paul A. Soukup, "Thinking, Talking, and Trinitarian Theology: From Augustine to Aquinas on Communication," paper presented at seventy-second annual conference of the Speech Communication Association, Chicago, 1986.

10. Augustine, *On Christian Doctrine,* Great Books of the Western World, ed. Robert Maynard Hutchins, vol. 18 (Chicago: Encyclopaedia Britannica, 1952), 634 (1.35).

11. Augustine, *On Christian Doctrine,* 625 (1.4).

12. Augustine, *On Christian Doctrine,* 627 (1.13).

13. Augustine, *City of God,* 426 (16.6).

14. Augustine, *City of God,* 307 (10.13).

15. Augustine, *City of God,* 323 (11.2).

16. Augustine, *City of God,* 426 (16.6).

17. R. A. Markus, "Signs, Communication, and Communities in Augustine's De Doctrina Christiana," in *De Doctrina Christiana: A Classic of Western Culture,* ed. Duane W. H. Arnold and Pamela Bright (Notre Dame: University of Notre Dame Press, 1995), 100.

18. Augustine, *On Christian Doctrine,* 660 (3.5).

19. Ludwig Wittgenstein, *Philosophical Investigations,* trans. G. E. M. Anscombe (Oxford: Basil Blackwell, 1953), secs. 1–4.

20. Susan Handelman, *The Slayers of Moses: The Emergence of Rabbinic Interpretation in Modern Literary Theory* (Albany: SUNY Press, 1982), 118; see 107–20.

21. Augustine, *On the Trinity,* trans. Arthur West Hadden, in *The Works of Aurelius Augustine,* ed. Marcus Dods (Edinburgh: Clark, 1873), 7:399 (15.10.19).

22. Jacques Derrida, *De la grammatologie* (Paris: Minuit, 1967).

23. Allan Megill, *Prophets of Extremity: Nietzsche, Heidegger, Foucault, Derrida* (Berkeley: University of California Press, 1985), chap. 8.

24. See *De Doctrina Cristiana,* book 3.

25. 2 Cor. 3:6 KJV.

26. Handelman, *Slayers of Moses.*

27. Daniel Boyarin's treatment of the intertwined universalism and racism of Paul's thinking is a model of how to confront such intricacy: *A Radical Jew: Paul and the Politics of Identity* (Berkeley: University of California Press, 1994).

28. See Stuart Schneiderman's neglected but brilliantly deadpan book, *An Angel Passes: How the Sexes Became Undivided* (New York: New York University Press, 1988).

29. *The Magic of Communication: A Tell-You-How Story* (N.p.: AT&T Information Department, 1932).

30. Mortimer Jerome Adler, *The Angels and Us* (New York Macmillan, 1982).

31. Thomas Aquinas, *Summa Theologica.* Great Books of the Western World, ed. Robert Maynard Hutchins, vol. 19 (Chicago: Encyclopaedia Britannica, 1952), 546.

32. Thomas Aquinas, *Summa Theologica,* 549–51.

33. Frederick Copleston, *A History of Philosophy* (1948; Garden City, N.Y.: Image Books, 1985), 2:330–31.

34. *Oxford Latin Dictionary* (Oxford: Clarendon Press, 1968), 369.

35. Mary B. Hesse, *Forces and Fields: The Concept of Action at a Distance in the History of Physics* (Westport, Conn.: Greenwood, 1970).

36. Francis Bacon, *Sylva Sylvarum, or A Natural History* (1605), in *The Works of Francis Bacon,* ed. Basil Montagu (Philadelphia: Carey and Hart, 1848), 2:129.

37. Bruno Latour, *We Have Never Been Modern,* trans. Catherine Porter (Cambridge: Harvard University Press, 1993).

38. Joseph Glanvill, *The Vanity of Dogmatizing* (New York: Columbia University Press, 1931), 199–200.

39. On Renaissance notions of natural sympathy, see Michel Foucault, *The Order of Things* (New York: Pantheon, 1970), 17–44, and François Jacob, *The Logic of Life: A History of Heredity,* trans. Betty E. Spillman (New York: Pantheon, 1974), 20–32.

40. John Wilkins, *Mercury, or The Secret and Swift Messenger: Shewing How a Man May with Privacy and Speed Communicate His Thoughts to a Friend at a Distance,* 3d ed. (1641: London, 1707), 1–2.

41. Wilkins, *Mercury,* 69.

42. Leo Spitzer, "Milieu and Ambiance," in *Essays in Historical Semantics* (New York: S. F. Vanni, 1948), 179–225.

43. *Oxford English Dictionary,* s.v. "communicate."

3

THE INVENTION OF COMMUNICATION

ARMAND MATTELART

THE PATHS OF REASON

In the course of the seventeenth century, intellectual reform placed on the agenda a program for a science both useful and factual, from which emerged the representation of a world in movement and open to change.

The advent of communication as a project and a realization of reason descended directly from the ideal of the perfectibility of human societies. A first constellation of ideas took shape around the communication routes and the link that united them to the formation of a national space. Its principal home was France in the seventeenth and eighteenth centuries, where the transport of people, goods, and messages and the formation of a unified domestic market both faltered on the poor development of canals and roads.

Revealing the new criteria of knowledge and action, metaphors of the organism and of mechanics, of the living and the machine, were mobilized by economic and political thought to represent the new modes of regulation and organization of society.

Philosophers of Doubt and Motion

The seventeenth century dawned under the sign of the ingenious Don Quixote of La Mancha, and it waned under that of the engineer Vauban (1633–1707). The former fought in bare fields against windmills, while the latter built strongholds and directed sieges. The errant knight, whose epitaph says "He . . . whose courser, Rosinante hight / Long bore him many a way," is the symbol of nomadic communication. By

SOURCE: Mattelart, A. (1996). *The invention of communication* (S. Emanuel, Trans.). Minneapolis, MN: University of Minnesota Press. ("The Paths of Reason," pp. 3–12 and 15–17). Originally published as L'invention de la communication © 1994 Éditions la Découverte. English translation copyright 1996 by the Regents of the University of Minnesota. Reprinted by permission.

contrast, Vauban, the architect of fortifications, who also commissioned the drawing of maps, undertook population surveys, and inventoried the different means of circulation, embodies one of the first attempts to master communication. Both prepared the way for the Age of Enlightenment.

What a striking contrast between Rosinante, the horse whose "bones stuck out like the corners of a *real*," and who proves, like her rider, always ready to succumb to enchantments, and the culture of the horse that then prevailed entirely under the aegis of Mars! The equestrian culture, which dated from far back, still had much time ahead of it. One hundred and forty years after the death of Miguel de Cervantes Saavedra, the *Encyclopédie* would still speak of the horse as an "animal gifted for war" and explain with a wealth of details how, since the book of Job, the *Iliad*, and the *Aeniad*, it has always been so. In the article on "Equitation," one could read that "the horse in a sense stimulates the man in the moment of combat; its movements and its agitation calm the natural palpitation that the bravest of warriors has difficulty preventing as the first apparatus of battle appears."

Despite appearances, we are indeed embarked on a history of communication. Let us recall the analysis by Paul Virilio, the theoretician of speed, on the invention of the animal as vehicle. "Man attains one of the very first forms of relativity," he writes, "his territory will no longer be what it has been, now that the swiftness of the courser has gradually detached him from it. Places will become points of departure and arrival, shores one leaves or approaches, and surface area will be merely the limits of equestrian navigation."[1]

From the steed to the iron horse appearing at the end of the nineteenth century, the true ancestor of the tank, a long history leads up to scientific equitation, hippology, the exact science of a horse's movements. The analytical geometry of a horse's gallop leads to the mechanical art of the motor. The translation into mathematics of the movements of a horse will accompany a great change in military strategy: the gradual emergence of the idea of mobility and the mobilization of armies in the field.

Descartes, who was twenty years old when Cervantes (1547–1616) died, liked to repeat: "Give me matter and movement, and I will make you a world." The author of *Don Quixote* might have replaced the word "matter" with "imagination." Both men were former soldiers, but more especially they were philosophers of doubt, as has been magnificently analyzed by a specialist in Cervantes studies, Jean Cassou. Cervantian doubt is both a "successor to the doubt of Montaigne, cousin to the doubt of Hamlet, older brother to the doubt of Sigismond, the hero of Calderón's *Life Is a Dream,* and forerunner of the methodical doubt of Descartes."[2]

In the second part of his *Don Quixote,* published in 1615, the Spanish author dramatizes an "enchanted head" made of bronze, which is said to have been invented by a Polish disciple of a Scottish astrologer, and which, fixed to a table, answers the questions posed to it. This experiment reminds us that Spain at the time was fond of those android automatons, distant ancestors of the computer, which will come into vogue in the eighteenth century. But it is not the technical aspect of the inventions of his day that captures Cervantes's attention. What interests him is the literary myth of Pygmalion. He was, after all, the author of *Galatea,* a pastoral romance in the taste of the time, written in 1584, twenty-one years before the publication of the first part of *Don Quixote.* Galatea was the "artificial woman" of Greek mythology to whom Aphrodite, not wishing to yield to Pygmalion, gives life by penetrating into an ivory statue that he had laid in his bed, begging her to have pity on him. What fascinates the Hidalgo in these "wonderful machines" that were hunted down by the Inquisition—"the always watchful sentinels of our faith"—are their powers of illusion. Moreover, the *Quixote* episode ends with the unmasking of the ruse. It is in fact the nephew of the innkeeper who answers the guests' questions, thanks to a brass pipe linking the bronze head to the chamber underneath. "Nevertheless," notes Cervantes, "in the opinion of Don Quixote and Sancho Panza, the head continued to be enchanted."[3]

If Cervantes had lived at the end of the nineteenth century, he would probably have belonged to that line of magicians and mediums of the Academy of prestidigitators who, from Jean-Eugène Robert-Houdin (1805–71) to Georges Méliès (1861–1938), brought about the shift from the theater of illusions to the magic lantern. Inversely, too, if Méliès had lived at the beginning of the seventeenth century, the scenario of his *Voyage à travers l'impossible,* that "unlikely venture by a group of scientists from the incoherent Geographical Society" going off to discover the King of the Stars (the Sun), would not have been outshone by the knight-errant.[4] Nor should we forget that the French pioneer of special effects also had borrowed a story from ancient myth when he filmed *Pygmalion and Galatea* in 1898 (a work that had been thought lost, until a copy was found in a Barcelona attic in 1993!).

On the other hand, Descartes, in his search for universal truth and for an order of knowledge analogous to mathematics, exercised his imagination by conceiving automata in order to prove that animals do not have a soul, feelings, or thought, and are therefore merely machines, "animal machines," which function by automatic response. His view contrasted with that of Montaigne, who thought that animals made better use of reason than did human beings.

In this light, the expression "disenchantment of the world," coined by Max Weber (1864–1920) to designate the advent of scientific and rational thought in the West, acquires a very particular resonance.

Vauban and River Topography

In Vauban's time, the absence of a fluid and coherent system of communication was still a major obstacle to the organization of a French national space.

At about the same time as Cervantes was writing *Don Quixote,* the minister of Henri IV, the Duke of Sully (1560–1641), an advocate of the free circulation of grains, had no doubt tried to develop the bases of a policy. But the basis of a policy of communication at the level of the entire country appeared only in the 1660s with Louis XIV's comptroller-general of finances, Jean-Baptiste Colbert (1619–83). Moreover, this was the era when another minister, Louvois (1641–91), effected two other essential reforms: as secretary of state for war, he reorganized the army from top to bottom by introducing discipline, creating a corps of engineers, and restructuring the military transport service; as superintendent general of the post office, he instituted the full monopoly over the conveyance of correspondence, up until then divided between the state and private institutions such as the university. Colbert completed the reform of means of transport by taking measures to ameliorate the equine stock so as to counteract the increasing dependence of the kingdom at war on foreign horses. Three edicts organized the construction and administration of the national stud farms and created the label "royal stallion."

Cartographic surveys of the kingdom began when Colbert hired Jean Dominique Cassini (1625–1712), the first in a family dynasty of astronomers and geographers. The production of maps had been dominated since the second half of the sixteenth century by Amsterdam publishers and geographers. Vauban created the corps of geographical engineers and took stock of the need for and progress of communication routes, in particular waterways. Navigation projects were at that time the nearly exclusive responsibility of the military engineering corps.

In 1699, Vauban composed a memorandum on "river navigation"—he enumerated more than 190 routes—in which he evaluated case by case the possibilities for rendering navigable those rivers that were not yet so, by means of canals "to communicate the navigation of rivers one with another." This project was the crowning effort in his unceasing labors to improve river navigation, which, according to his estimates, was potentially twenty-five times more economical than land transportation.

Vauban insisted on the importance of better management of taxes with a view to providing the resources necessary for these large-scale projects, indispensable for commerce. He concluded:

> If the king should take a liking for it and put some effort into it, the greatest good that could ever happen to this kingdom would ensue, thanks to easier circulation of foodstuffs, which would procure a considerable increase in them, and consequently a rise in well-being and convenience, and a very great ease for the provinces in helping each other in expensive years and in times of war.[5]

This idea of interprovincial solidarity had been in the air since its formulation by Antoine de Montchrestien at the start of the century. In his *Traité d'Œconomie Politique* (1615)—it was the first time this term "political economy" appeared—this mercantilist author advanced the necessity of an "intranational division of labor" (while refusing the idea of an international division).

As for the older and more general idea of reciprocal dependence, which one finds in Vauban and many others, it is by no means foreign to the meaning that for a long time was conferred on the word "communication" by reducing it to "commerce." In the article that the *Encyclopédie* devoted to this topic in 1753, we read:

> By commerce we mean in a general sense a *reciprocal communication*. It applies more particularly to the communication that men have with each other in the productions of their lands and their industry. Infinite Providence, whose creation is nature, has willed, by the variety that It spreads, putting men into dependence on each other: the Supreme Being has formed links in order to bring peoples to preserve peace among themselves and to love each other . . . This reciprocal dependence of men, by the variety of commodities that they can furnish each other, extends to real needs and to the needs of opinion.

Did not Montesquieu also say that "the history of commerce is that of communication"?

Colbert's policy was in harmony with Vauban's judgments. It grants priority to inland navigation routes. The invention of locks by two Italian engineers from Viterbo, in the sixteenth century, had made possible the creation of canals. The first test of a lock—the idea of which had been brought to France by Leonardo da Vinci—took place on the Vilaine River in Brittany in the period 1538–75. The first great canal, running from Briare on the Loire, the foremost French river, was to Buges on Seine, a distance of fifty-nine kilometers. Although its construction began at the start of the century under the auspices of Sully, it would not be inaugurated until 1642.

The first stroke of the pickax in the building of the Midi canal was struck in 1663; this "canal for the junction of seas" was completed in 1684. It ran 240 kilometers, with a width of thirty-eight meters. It was the first canal of such a magnitude constructed in Europe. To achieve it the supervisor of the project, Pierre Paul Riquet (1604–80), applied for the first time a complex hydraulic mechanics. Another innovation was the use by civil engineering of gunpowder to dig a tunnel. These great projects could not have been carried out without a meticulous method of personnel management. In contrast with the usual labor situation of the time, under Riquet fixed wages, benefits, and even retirement plans ensured a spirit of emulation. At the origin of this great royal project was a strategic aim: the navy had to be able to move from the Atlantic to the Mediterranean while avoiding Gibraltar. Ultimately, however, the canal would not prove wide enough to allow warships through and it could only transport equipment, arms, and troops.[6]

Vauban himself drew up the plans for four other canals, notably that of Orléans (begun in 1679 and finished in 1690). Nevertheless, all this work amounted to little with respect to the infrastructural needs of a domestic market. But it was enough for the German historian of transportation, Richard von Kaufmann, in a book published in the last years of the nineteenth century, to see in it, retrospectively, the birth of the star-shaped network that will mark networks that come later:

> The examination of the configuration of France, which would later suggest to the government the best plan for the establishment of a network of

railways, already indicated to [Vauban] the importance of the country's natural navigable waterways, their extension, and their junction by canals. And thus a network of interior navigation was established, radiating from the center of the country just as the great railway lines were to do.[7]

Whether or not it was a structuring effect of a natural configuration, Paris for Vauban could only be the "true heart of the kingdom," the "common mother of Frenchmen and the summation of France." "If the Prince is to the state what the head is to the human body, which cannot be doubted," he wrote in 1689,

one could say that the capital city of this state is what the heart is to this same body, since the heart is considered the first organ to be alive and the last to die; the principle of life, the source and seat of natural warmth, from whence it spreads to all the parts of the body, which it animates and sustains until the body has totally ceased to live.[8]

The Bridge Engineers

Meanwhile, the construction of roads throughout the national territory met with abundant administrative resistance. Colbert created the Ponts et Chaussées, which was entrusted in 1669 with the building and maintenance of "bridges, roads, canals, rivers, and ports." The engineering corps of Ponts et Chaussées, organized in the form of a pyramid as civil servants of the state, would be definitively constituted in 1716.

Since the beginning of the sixteenth century, jurists had recognized the public character of routes, bringing them into the "domain of the sovereign." But it was only in 1705 that a royal writ began to lay the foundations of a normalization of the layout and traffic (via expropriation, alignments, duties and obligations of bordering residents, weights, and types of means of transportation, etc.). In 1720, another ruling fixed the width of routes and the planting of their banks. In 1731, road police became necessary

to prohibit all rubble collectors, plowmen, wine growers, gardeners, and others from filling in the

ditches and cutting down the embankments that line the major routes, and along this distance to prevent them, in their plowing or otherwise, from dumping any rubble, dung, refuse, and other impediments to public passage, . . . from digging up the cobblestones from Paris streets, and likewise from the roadways of the faubourgs, suburbs, and public lanes.[9]

It was not until 1738 that the century's great founding document for the policy of road systems was formulated (the equivalent of which in the following century would be the 1842 law on the construction of the railway network). These instructions from the comptroller-general, Jean Orry, also established the use of forced labor [*corvée*] for the "building of roads." But the introduction of this use of forced labor, in fact, dated back further, that is, to the last years of Louis XIV's reign (1661–1715), when it was necessary to make the routes practicable for the transport of munitions in the provinces affected by war. Certain intendants drew lessons from this experience and extended it to peacetime. But the first road administrations were not able to shield their management from the control of treasurers. This would not occur until 1743, with the creation of the Détail des Ponts et Chaussées, entrusted to Daniel Trudaine (1703–69), who maintained the separation of technical services from financial services.

In 1744 began a systematic charting of the national territory, as large-scale topography made its appearance. A central bureau of draftsmen, the embryo of the future École des Ponts et Chaussées, was created by Trudaine "for the supervision and inspection by geographers and draftsmen of maps for the routes and great avenues of the kingdom."[10] The grandson of Colbert's geographer, César Cassini de Thury (1714–84), relying on a vast triangulation of the country, made the first large-scale map (at 1/86,400). This effort was achieved thanks to voluntary contributions and under the auspices of the Académie des Sciences. The gradual replacement of Cassini's atlas by the map of the general staff of armies was not complete until 1831, when the corps of geographical engineers founded by Vauban was in fact incorporated into the general staff. (The publication of this topographical map, with a scale of 1/80,000, would last from 1832 to 1880.)

In 1747, Trudaine presided over the creation of the École des Ponts et Chaussées (which did not, in fact, take this name until the early 1770s). Seventy to eighty students were trained there at a time. The most advanced ones taught the others skills including arithmetic, hydraulics, drafting, stonecutting, and the calculation of the pavement area. All students learned architecture, physics, chemistry, and mineralogy from the foreign professors at the school. Then they were all sent into the field to "become educated in the practice of constructions: drafting of plans, surveying, and so on."[11]

In their actual practice, these engineers, in attempting to master the different phases in the development of a construction project, questioned the old mode of labor organization through corporations and guilds. At the same time as an "esprit de corps" was formed, the foundations of a new ideal were developed, guided by technical and economic rationality and an ideology of the relation of communication with Nature and Reason.

Communication had the mission of bringing about a rational and "good" nature—since there was also such a thing as irrational and "bad" nature, a nature that separates, interposes itself between men, and lies at the root of prejudices. This point is clearly explained by Yves Chicoteau and Antoine Picon, historians of the École, in the conclusion to a groundbreaking study of the dissertations ("the style competition") organized for the bridge-building pupils under the Old Regime:

> By introducing a distance between terms that Reason nevertheless ought to bring together, this fundamentally bad nature ought to be combated. This is the whole meaning of an engineer's deeds, establishing communication routes, building bridges across precipices to bring men together. To illustrate this viewpoint, the metaphor of famine was very frequently used by engineers of the Ponts et Chaussées. By separating men, nature creates

the conditions of scarcity, since it allows one province to overflow with grain while another lacks everything. The engineer is therefore invested with a mission to "correct" these inequalities by allowing the circulation of commodities. Transposed, this conception makes the engineer the privileged servant of Reason since he combats prejudices by making men communicate. The eighteenth century considered, in effect, that prejudices were born of isolation, whereas Reason fought them by making possible the coming together of individuals.[12]

For these engineers, this coming together, which corresponds to an ideal nature, becomes identical with the map as a projection of a rational system in which everything should communicate.

Thus, in France under the Old Regime the basis of a body of ideas on "communications" began to be formed, that is, a proper mode of thinking about the relations between movement, the economy, and society, between "networks," the state, and national unity. As Fernand Braudel would point out at the end of the 1970s:

> Given the huge dimensions of France, it is clear that progress in transportation was crucial to the unification of the country, though it was by no means adequate at this stage, as has been pointed out with reference to periods closer to our own time by the historian Jean Bouvier (who maintains that the national market did not exist in France before the completion of the railway network) and the economist Pierre Uri (who goes even further, claiming categorically that present-day France will only be a true economic unit when the telephone system has reached "American-style perfection"). They are no doubt right. But the admirable engineers of the Ponts et Chaussées who built the eighteenth-century roads were certainly responsible for progress towards a French national market.[13]

In contrast, in England at the beginning of the eighteenth century, the question of circulation and communication was no longer the subject of theoretical debate. It was already anchored in the reality of a domestic market, generator of exchanges and ties, whose formation had been accelerated by the Irish expedition and the victory over Scotland. The kingdom rid itself very early of many of its tolls and other internal barriers, and its system of communication was national. The attraction of the capital, a sole and enormous head (with 10 percent of the population), and a network of coastal navigation and waterways were combined in the establishment of the national space. Substantial investments in the first quarter of the eighteenth century brought to completion a network of navigable rivers extending 1,160 miles, which put the greater part of the country at no more than fifteen miles from water transportation.[14] This was facilitated by considerable advantages: not only a more compact territory and, unlike the continent, a nobility of gentlemen-entrepreneurs experienced in pecuniary rationality, but also very regular rivers, easy to deepen, which did not wash along alluvial deposits and which were separated by level surfaces that were easily cut through by junction canals.

France, on the other hand, was a giant divided against itself, always torn between Lyons and Paris, and was still in search of its unification via the market. Five-sixths of its population lived in the countryside, and the other sixth originated from it or lived off it. England, strengthened by its conquest of its domestic market, and whose cities contained about 30 percent of the population, had already begun to dream of making itself the center of a new "world-economy." But she would still have to wait until the 1780s to supplant Amsterdam.

[. . .]

Discovery of Circulatory Movement

The philosopher and Lord Chancellor of England, Francis Bacon (1561–1626), established the principles of a science based on facts. His *Novum Organum* (1620) is a plea for a theory of scientific progress, and for progress itself through science—a science founded on experiments and observation and capable of inventing the means of "making us better and more happy" and "making human life gentler."

In this era, the secular inertia of dogma was challenged and people began to believe in the virtue of movement. The world came to be seen as perfectible.

The idea of circulation, to which the genesis of the modern concept of communication was indissolubly linked, saw the light of day in the laboratories of this scientific Reformation. It was the "first biological revolution" that caused it to flourish.[15] The method of microscopic observation contributed to the constitution of human anatomy and comparative anatomy as well as early physiology.

In 1628, the work of William Harvey (1578–1657), *Exercitatio anatomica de motu cordis et sanguinis in animalibus,* overturned millenarian ideas about blood circulation. The ancient theory of Claude Galien (131–201) asserted that only the veins contained blood, product of a transformation of the chyle formed from digested food. The English doctor discovered the mechanism of circulation and described the heart's movements: blood arrives in the heart by the veins and leaves by the arteries, with heartbeats producing a perpetual movement in the closed circuit. This was the first representation of the mechanism of an organic function.

Some forty years later, the Italian naturalist and physician Marcello Malpighi (1628–94) completed this physiological discovery by showing how the passage of the blood from the arteries to the veins takes place. This founder of microscopic anatomy, the future histology, performed the first complete anatomical study of an invertebrate (the silkworm) and proceeded to a systematic and comparative study of different animal and vegetable tissues. On this occasion he imported into science the word "network," which until then had been reserved for lace making. Malpighi's "network" was at first the "reticulated matter of the skin," only observable thanks to the new microoptics. The microscopes that appeared around 1615 in fact remained prototypical until around 1660.

To express his discovery of the blood's circulatory movement, it is true that Harvey drew on the mechanical image of the lift and force pump.

But he also had recourse to an astronomical image in which he compared the heart to the sun as that which occupies the central place in the water cycle, with its evaporation and its condensation into clouds and rain, and then the return of water to the earth, renewing the cycle. This metaphor indicates that before this revolution in knowledge affecting physical bodies, there had been another that had changed the understanding of celestial bodies. In 1543, Nicholas Copernicus's essay *De revolutionibus orbium coelestium* had undermined the scholastic dogma of geocentrism, the belief in a cosmos formed around the earth, with the latter at the summit of the celestial hierarchy. In less than a century and a half, an epistemological upheaval took place: from the closed world to an infinite universe. This shift began with Copernicus, and it continued with Johannes Kepler (1571–1630), author of *Mysterium cosmographicum* (The secret of the world) (1596), who in 1611 perfected an astronomical telescope.[16] It culminated with Isaac Newton (1642–1727), who in 1687 assembled into a coherent whole the vision of a homogeneous and infinite universe. It was through its application to Copernican cosmology that the term "system" would make its breakthrough at the end of the seventeenth century, and become common in the philosophical discourse of the eighteenth century.[17] It was also via this science that the term "revolution" would make its entry into political vocabulary.

Meanwhile, we owe to the discovery of blood circulation the paradigm of bodily mechanics, with its law of functional physiological necessity from which the discourses on communication and society would never cease to draw metaphors.

Notes

1. P. Virilio, "L'Empire de l'emprisem," *Traverses,* no. 13 (December 1978).

2. J. Cassou, "Cervantes," *Encyclopaedia Universalis.* See also his introduction to the work of the Spanish writer in *Cervantes, Don Quichotte, Nouvelles Exemplaires* (Paris: La Pléiade, 1949).

3. M. Cervantes, *The Ingenious Gentleman Quixote of La Mancha,* trans. C. Jarvis, ed. E. C. Riley (Oxford and New York: Oxford University Press, 1992), Part II, chapter 62, "Which treats of the adventure of the enchanted head with other trifles that must not be omitted," 977–78.

4. M. Malthête-Méliès, *Méliès l'enchanteur* (Paris: Hachette, 1973).

5. S. de Vauban, *Oisivetés de M. de Vauban* (Paris: J. Corréard, 1843), 139. On Vauban's initiatives with respect to canals, see J. Mesqui, *Vauban et le projet de transport fluvial* (Paris: Association Vauban, 1983).

6. J.-L. Marfaing et al., *Canal royal de Languedoc. Le partage des eaux* (Éditions Loubatière, published by the Conseil d'Architecture, d'Urbanisme et de l'Environnement [CAVE] de la Haute-Garonne, 1992).

7. R. von Kaufmann, *La Politique française en matière de chemins de fer* (Paris: Librairie Polytechnique, C. Béranger, 1900), 803.

8. *Oisivetés de M. de Vauban,* 45.

9. M. Gautier (architect, engineer, and inspector of the kingdom's routes, bridges, and roadways), *Traité de la construction des chemins* (Paris: Chez Laporte, 1778).

10. Quoted in G. Reverdy, *Atlas historique des routes de France* (Paris: Presses de l'École des Ponts et Chaussées, 1986), 89.

11. See J. Langins, "La préhistoire de l'École polytechnique," *Revue d'histoire des sciences,* vol. 44 (1991).

12. Y. Chicoteau and A. Picon, "Forme, technique et ideologie, les ingénieurs des Ponts et Chaussées à la fin du XVIIIᵉ siècle," *Culture technique,* no. 7 (March 1982): 193–94.

13. F. Braudel, *Civilisation and Capitalism: 15th-18th Century,* trans. revised by Sian Reynolds (London: Collins, 1981–84), vol. 3, *The Perspective of the World,* 322.

14. Ibid., 367.

15. M. Grmek, *La première révolution biologique* (Paris: Payot, 1990).

16. J. Kepler, *The Secret of the Universe,* trans. A. M. Duncan (New York: Abaris Books, 1981). On this evolution, see A. Koyré, *The Astronomical Revolution: Copernicus, Kepler, Borelli,* trans. R. E. W. Madison (Ithaca, N.Y.: Cornell University Press, 1973).

17. R. Sasso, "Système et discours philosophique," in *Recherches sur le XVIIᵉ siècle* (Paris: CNRS, 1978).

4

A CULTURAL APPROACH TO COMMUNICATION

JAMES W. CAREY

I.

When I decided some years ago to read seriously the literature of communications, a wise man suggested I begin with John Dewey. It was advice I have never regretted accepting. Although there are limitations to Dewey—his literary style was described by William James as damnable—there is a depth to his work, a natural excess common to seminal minds, that offers permanent complexities, and paradoxes over which to puzzle—surely something absent from most of our literature.

Dewey opens an important chapter in *Experience and Nature* with the seemingly preposterous claim that "of all things communication is the most wonderful" (1939: 385). What could he have meant by that? If we interpret the sentence literally, it must be either false or mundane. Surely most of the news and entertainment we receive through the mass media are of the order that Thoreau predicted for the international telegraph: "the intelligence that Princess Adelaide had the whooping cough." A daily visit with the New York *Times* is not quite so trivial, though it is an experience more depressing than wonderful. Moreover, most of one's encounters with others are wonderful only in moments of excessive masochism. Dewey's sentence, by any reasonable interpretation, is either false to everyday experience or simply mundane if he means only that on some occasions communication is satisfying and rewarding.

SOURCE: Carey, J. W. (1989). *Communication as culture: Essays on media and society* (pp. 13–36). Winchester, MA: Unwin Hyman. Copyright 1989 from *Communication as Culture: Essays on Media and Society* by J. W. Carey. Reproduced by permission of Routledge/Taylor & Francis Group, LLC.

In another place Dewey offers an equally enigmatic comment on communication: "Society exists not only by transmission, by communication, but it may fairly be said to exist in transmission, in communication" (Dewey, 1916: 5). What is the significance of the shift in prepositions?[1] Is Dewey claiming that societies distribute information, to speak rather too anthropomorphically, and that by such transactions and the channels of communication peculiar to them society is made possible? That is certainly a reasonable claim, but we hardly need social scientists and philosophers to tell us so. It reminds me of Robert Nisbet's acid remark that if you need sociologists to inform you whether or not you have a ruling class, you surely don't. But if this transparent interpretation is rejected, are there any guarantees that after peeling away layers of semantic complexity anything more substantial will be revealed?

I think there are, for the body of Dewey's work reveals a substantial rather than a pedestrian intelligence. Rather than quoting him ritualistically (for the lines I have cited regularly appear without comment or interpretation in the literature of communications), we would be better advised to untangle this underlying complexity for the light it might cast upon contemporary studies. I think this complexity derives from Dewey's use of communication in two quite different senses. He understood better than most of us that communication has had two contrasting definitions in the history of Western thought, and he used the conflict between these definitions as a source of creative tension in his work. This same conflict led him, not surprisingly, into some of his characteristic errors. Rather than blissfully repeating his insights or unconsciously duplicating his errors, we might extend his thought by seizing upon the same contradiction he perceived in our use of the term "communication" and use it in turn as a device for vivifying our studies.

Two alternative conceptions of communication have been alive in American culture since this term entered common discourse in the nineteenth century. Both definitions derive, as with much in secular culture, from religious origins, though they refer to somewhat different regions of religious experience. We might label these descriptions, if only to provide handy pegs upon which to hang our thought, a transmission view of communication and a ritual view of communication.

The transmission view of communication is the commonest in our culture—perhaps in all industrial cultures—and dominates contemporary dictionary entries under the term. It is defined by terms such as "imparting," "sending," "transmitting," or "giving information to others." It is formed from a metaphor of geography or transportation. In the nineteenth century but to a lesser extent today, the movement of goods or people and the movement of information were seen as essentially identical processes and both were described by the common noun "communication." The center of this idea of communication is the transmission of signals or messages over distance for the purpose of control. It is a view of communication that derives from one of the most ancient of human dreams: the desire to increase the speed and effect of messages as they travel in space. From the time upper and lower Egypt were unified under the First Dynasty down through the invention of the telegraph, transportation and communication were inseparably linked. Although messages might be centrally produced and controlled through monopolization of writing or the rapid production of print, these messages, carried in the hands of a messenger or between the bindings of a book, still had to be distributed, if they were to have their desired effect, by rapid transportation. The telegraph ended the identity but did not destroy the metaphor. Our basic orientation to communication remains grounded, at the deepest roots of our thinking, in the idea of transmission: communication is a process whereby messages are transmitted and distributed in space for the control of distance and people.[2]

I said this view originated in religion, though the foregoing sentences seem more indebted to politics, economics, and technology. Nonetheless, the roots of the transmission view of communication, in our culture at least, lie in essentially religious attitudes. I can illustrate this by a devious though, in detail, inadequate path.

In its modern dress the transmission view of communication arises, as the *Oxford English Dictionary* will attest, at the onset of the age of exploration and discovery. We have been reminded rather too often that the motives behind this vast movement in space were political and mercantilistic. Certainly those motives were present, but their importance should not obscure the equally compelling fact that a major motive behind this movement in space, particularly as evidenced by the Dutch Reformed Church in South Africa or the Puritans in New England, was religious. The desire to escape the boundaries of Europe, to create a new life, to found new communities, to carve a New Jerusalem out of the woods of Massachusetts, were primary motives behind the unprecedented movement of white European civilization over virtually the entire globe. The vast and, for the first time, democratic migration in space was above all an attempt to trade an old world for a new and represented the profound belief that movement in space could be in itself a redemptive act. It is a belief Americans have never quite escaped.

Transportation, particularly when it brought the Christian community of Europe into contact with the heathen community of the Americas, was seen as a form of communication with profoundly religious implications. This movement in space was an attempt to establish and extend the kingdom of God, to create the conditions under which godly understanding might be realized, to produce a heavenly though still terrestrial city.

The moral meaning of transportation, then, was the establishment and extension of God's kingdom on earth. The moral meaning of communication was the same. By the middle of the nineteenth century the telegraph broke the identity of communication and transportation but also led a preacher of the era, Gardner Spring, to exclaim that we were on the "border of a spiritual harvest because thought now travels by steam and magnetic wires" (Miller, 1965: 48). Similarly, in 1848 "James L. Batchelder could declare that the Almighty himself had constructed the railroad for missionary purposes and, as Samuel Morse prophesied with the first telegraphic message, the purpose of the invention was not to spread the price of pork but to ask the question 'What Hath God Wrought?'" (Miller, 1965: 52). This new technology entered American discussions not as a mundane fact but as divinely inspired for the purposes of spreading the Christian message farther and faster, eclipsing time and transcending space, saving the heathen, bringing closer and making more probable the day of salvation. As the century wore on and religious thought was increasingly tied to applied science, the new technology of communication came to be seen as the ideal device for the conquest of space and populations. Our most distinguished student of these matters, Perry Miller, has commented:

> The unanimity (among Protestant sects), which might at first sight seem wholly supernatural, was wrought by the telegraph and the press. These conveyed and published "the thrill of Christian sympathy, with the tidings of abounding grace, from multitudes in every city simultaneously assembled, in effect almost bringing a nation together in one praying intercourse." Nor could it be only fortuitous that the movement should coincide with the Atlantic Cable, for both were harbingers "of that which is the forerunner of ultimate spiritual victory. . . ." The awakening of 1858 first made vital for the American imagination a realizable program of a Christianized technology. (Miller, 1965: 91)

Soon, as the forces of science and secularization gained ground, the obvious religious metaphors fell away and the technology of communication itself moved to the center of thought. Moreover, the superiority of communication over transportation was assured by the observation of one nineteenth century commentator that the telegraph was important because it involved not the mere "modification of matter but the transmission of thought." Communication was viewed as a process and a technology that would, sometimes for religious purposes, spread, transmit, and disseminate knowledge, ideas, and information farther and faster with the goal of controlling space and people.

There were dissenters, of course, and I have already quoted Thoreau's disenchanted remark on the telegraph. More pessimistically, John C. Calhoun saw the "subjugation of electricity to the mechanical necessities of man . . . (as) the last era in human civilization" (quoted in Miller, 1965: 307). But the dissenters were few, and the transmission view of communication, albeit in increasingly secularized and scientific form, has dominated our thought and culture since that time. Moreover, as can be seen in contemporary popular commentary and even in technical discussions of new communications technology, the historic religious undercurrent has never been eliminated from our thought. From the telegraph to the computer the same sense of profound possibility for moral improvement is present whenever these machines are invoked. And we need not be reminded of the regularity with which improved communication is invoked by an army of teachers, preachers, and columnists as the talisman of all our troubles. More controversially, the same root attitudes, as I can only assert here rather than demonstrate, are at work in most of our scientifically sophisticated views of communication.

The ritual view of communication, though a minor thread in our national thought, is by far the older of those views—old enough in fact for dictionaries to list it under "Archaic." In a ritual definition, communication is linked to terms such as "sharing," "participation," "association," "fellowship," and "the possession of a common faith." This definition exploits the ancient identity and common roots of the terms "commonness," "communion," "community," and "communication." A ritual view of communication is directed not toward the extension of messages in space but toward the maintenance of society in time; not the act of imparting information but the representation of shared beliefs.

If the archetypal case of communication under a transmission view is the extension of messages across geography for the purpose of control, the archetypal case under a ritual view is the sacred ceremony that draws persons together in fellowship and commonality.

The indebtedness of the ritual view of communication to religion is apparent in the name chosen to label it. Moreover, it derives from a view of religion that downplays the role of the sermon, the instruction and admonition, in order to highlight the role of the prayer, the chant, and the ceremony. It sees the original or highest manifestation of communication not in the transmission of intelligent information but in the construction and maintenance of an ordered, meaningful cultural world that can serve as a control and container for human action.

This view has also been shorn of its explicitly religious origins, but it has never completely escaped its metaphoric root. Writers in this tradition often trace their heritage, in part, to Durkheim's *Elementary Forms of Religious Life* and to the argument stated elsewhere that "society substitutes for the world revealed to our senses a different world that is a projection of the ideals created by the community" (1953: 95). This projection of community ideals and their embodiment in material form—dance, plays, architecture, news stories, strings of speech—creates an artificial though nonetheless real symbolic order that operates to provide not information but confirmation, not to alter attitudes or change minds but to represent an underlying order of things, not to perform functions but to manifest an ongoing and fragile social process.

The ritual view of communication has not been a dominant motif in American scholarship. Our thought and work have been glued to a transmission view of communication because this view is congenial with the underlying wellsprings of American culture, sources that feed into our scientific life as well as our common, public understandings. There is an irony in this. We have not explored the ritual view of communication because the concept of culture is such a weak and evanescent notion in American social thought. We understand that other people have culture in the anthropological sense and we regularly record it—often mischievously and patronizingly. But when we turn critical attention to American culture the concept dissolves into a residual category useful only when psychological and sociological data are exhausted. We realize that the underprivileged live in a culture of poverty, use the notion of middle-class culture as an epithet, and occasionally applaud our high and generally scientific culture. But the notion of culture is not a hard-edged term of intellectual discourse for domestic purposes. This intellectual aversion to the idea of culture derives in part from our obsessive individualism, which makes psychological life the paramount reality; from our Puritanism, which leads to disdain for the significance of human activity that is not practical and work oriented; and from our isolation of science from culture: science provides culture-free truth whereas culture provides ethnocentric error.

Consequently, when looking for scholarship that emphasizes the central role of culture and a ritual view of communication, one must rely heavily on European sources or upon Americans deeply influenced by European scholarship. As a result the opportunities for misunderstanding are great. Perhaps, then, some of the difference between a transmission and a ritual view of communication can be grasped by briefly looking at alternative conceptions of the role of the newspaper in social life.

If one examines a newspaper under a transmission view of communication, one sees the medium as an instrument for disseminating news and knowledge, sometimes *divertissement,* in larger and larger packages over greater distances. Questions arise as to the effects of this on audiences: news as enlightening or obscuring reality, as changing or hardening attitudes, as breeding credibility or doubt. Questions also are raised concerning the functions of news and the newspaper: Does it maintain the integration of society or its maladaptation? Does it function or misfunction to maintain stability or promote the instability of personalities? Some such mechanical analysis normally accompanies a "transmission" argument.

A ritual view of communication will focus on a different range of problems in examining a

newspaper. It will, for example, view reading a newspaper less as sending or gaining information and more as attending a mass, a situation in which nothing new is learned but in which a particular view of the world is portrayed and confirmed. News reading, and writing, is a ritual act and moreover a dramatic one. What is arrayed before the reader is not pure information but a portrayal of the contending forces in the world. Moreover, as readers make their way through the paper, they engage in a continual shift of roles or of dramatic focus. A story on the monetary crisis salutes them as American patriots fighting those ancient enemies Germany and Japan; a story on the meeting of a women's political caucus casts them into the liberation movement as supporter or opponent; a tale of violence on the campus evokes their class antagonisms and resentments. The model here is not that of information acquisition, though such acquisition occurs, but of dramatic action in which the reader joins a world of contending forces as an observer at a play. We do not encounter questions about the effect or functions of messages as such, but the role of presentation and involvement in the structuring of the reader's life and time. We recognize, as with religious rituals, that news changes little and yet is intrinsically satisfying; it performs few functions yet is habitually consumed. Newspapers do not operate as a source of effects or functions but as dramatically satisfying, which is not to say pleasing, presentations of what the world at root is. And it is in this role—that of a text—that a newspaper is seen; like a Balinese cockfight, a Dickens novel, an Elizabethan drama, a student rally, it is a presentation of reality that gives life an overall form, order, and tone.

Moreover, news is a historic reality. It is a form of culture invented by a particular class at a particular point of history—in this case by the middle class largely in the eighteenth century. Like any invented cultural form, news both forms and reflects a particular "hunger for experience," a desire to do away with the epic, heroic, and traditional in favor of the unique, original, novel, new—news. This "hunger" itself has a history grounded in the changing style and fortunes of the middle class and as such does not represent a universal taste or necessarily legitimate form of knowledge (Park, 1955: 71–88) but an invention in historical time that, like most other human inventions, will dissolve when the class that sponsors it and its possibility of having significance for us evaporates.

Under a ritual view, then, news is not information but drama. It does not describe the world but portrays an arena of dramatic forces and action; it exists solely in historical time; and it invites our participation on the basis of our assuming, often vicariously, social roles within it.[3]

Neither of these counterposed views of communication necessarily denies what the other affirms. A ritual view does not exclude the processes of information transmission or attitude change. It merely contends that one cannot understand these processes aright except insofar as they are cast within an essentially ritualistic view of communication and social order. Similarly, even writers indissolubly wedded to the transmission view of communication must include some notion, such as Malinowski's phatic communion, to attest however tardily to the place of ritual action in social life. Nonetheless, in intellectual matters origins determine endings, and the exact point at which one attempts to unhinge the problem of communication largely determines the path the analysis can follow.

The power of Dewey's work derives from his working over these counterposed views of communication. Communication is "the most wonderful" because it is the basis of human fellowship; it produces the social bonds, bogus or not, that tie men together and make associated life possible. Society is possible because of the binding forces of shared information circulating in an organic system. The following quotation reveals this tension and Dewey's final emphasis on a ritual view of communication:

> There is more than a verbal tie between the words common, community, and communication. Men live in a community in virtue of the things which they have in common; and communication is the way in which they come to possess things in common. What they must have in common . . . are aims, beliefs, aspirations, knowledge—a common understanding—likemindedness as sociologists say. Such things cannot be passed physically from one to another like bricks; they cannot be shared as persons would share a pie by dividing it into physical pieces. . . . Consensus demands communication. (Dewey, 1916: 5–6)

Dewey was, like the rest of us, often untrue to his own thought. His hopes for the future often overwhelmed the impact of his analysis. Ah! "the wish is father to the thought." He came to overvalue scientific information and communication technology as a solvent to social problems and a source of social bonds. Nonetheless, the tension between these views can still open a range of significant problems in communication for they not only represent different conceptions of communication but correspond to particular historical periods, technologies, and forms of social order.[4]

The transmission view of communication has dominated American thought since the 1920s. When I first came into this field I felt that this view of communication, expressed in behavioral and functional terms, was exhausted. It had become academic: a repetition of past achievement, a demonstration of the indubitable. Although it led to solid achievement, it could no longer go forward without disastrous intellectual and social consequences. I felt it was necessary to reopen the analysis, to reinvigorate it with the tension found in Dewey's work and, above all, to go elsewhere into biology, theology, anthropology, and literature for some intellectual material with which we might escape the treadmill we were running.

II.

But where does one turn, even provisionally, for the resources with which to get a fresh perspective on communication? For me at least the resources were found by going back to the work of Weber, Durkheim, de Tocqueville, and

Huizinga, as well as by utilizing contemporaries such as Kenneth Burke, Hugh Duncan, Adolph Portman, Thomas Kuhn, Peter Berger, and Clifford Geertz. Basically, however, the most viable though still inadequate tradition of social thought on communication comes from those colleagues and descendants of Dewey in the Chicago School: from Mead and Cooley through Robert Park and on to Erving Goffman.

From such sources, one can draw a definition of communication of disarming simplicity yet, I think, of some intellectual power and scope: communication is a symbolic process whereby reality is produced, maintained, repaired, and transformed.

Let me attempt to unpack that long first clause emphasizing the symbolic production of reality.

One of the major problems one encounters in talking about communication is that the noun refers to the most common, mundane human experience. There is truth in Marshall McLuhan's assertion that the one thing of which the fish is unaware is water, the very medium that forms its ambience and supports its existence. Similarly, communication, through language and other symbolic forms, comprises the ambience of human existence. The activities we collectively call communication—having conversations, giving instructions, imparting knowledge, sharing significant ideas, seeking information, entertaining and being entertained—are so ordinary and mundane that it is difficult for them to arrest our attention. Moreover, when we intellectually visit this process, we often focus on the trivial and unproblematic, so inured are we to the mysterious and awesome in communication.

A wise man once defined the purpose of art as "making the phenomenon strange." Things can become so familiar that we no longer perceive them at all. Art, however, can take the sound of the sea, the intonation of a voice, the texture of a fabric, the design of a face, the play of light upon a landscape, and wrench these ordinary phenomena out of the backdrop of existence and force them into the foreground of consideration. When Scott Fitzgerald described Daisy Buchanan as having "a voice full of money" he moves us, if

we are open to the experience, to hear again that ordinary thing, the sound of a voice, and to contemplate what it portends. He arrests our apprehension and focuses it on the mystery of character as revealed in sound.

Similarly, the social sciences can take the most obvious yet background facts of social life and force them into the foreground of wonderment. They can make us contemplate the particular miracles of social life that have become for us just there, plain and unproblematic for the eye to see. When he comments that communication is the most wonderful among things, surely Dewey is trying just that: to induce in us a capacity for wonder and awe regarding this commonplace activity. Dewey knew that knowledge most effectively grew at the point when things became problematic, when we experience an "information gap" between what circumstances impelled us toward doing and what we needed to know in order to act at all. This information gap, this sense of the problematic, often can be induced only by divesting life of its mundane trappings and exposing our common sense or scientific assumptions to an ironic light that makes the phenomenon strange.

To a certain though inadequate degree, my first clause attempts just that. Both our common sense and scientific realism attest to the fact that there is, first, a real world of objects, events, and processes that we observe. Second, there is language or symbols that name these events in the real world and create more or less adequate descriptions of them. There is reality and then, after the fact, our accounts of it. We insist there is a distinction between reality and fantasy; we insist that our terms stand in relation to this world as shadow and substance. While language often distorts, obfuscates, and confuses our perception of this external world, we rarely dispute this matter-of-fact realism. We peel away semantic layers of terms and meanings to uncover this more substantial domain of existence. Language stands to reality as secondary stands to primary in the old Galilean paradigm from which this view derives.

By the first clause I mean to invert this relationship, not to make any large metaphysical claims but rather, by reordering the relation of communication to reality, to render communication a far more problematic activity than it ordinarily seems.

I want to suggest, to play on the Gospel of St. John, that in the beginning was the word; words are not the names for things but, to steal a line from Kenneth Burke, things are the signs of words. Reality is not given, not humanly existent, independent of language and toward which language stands as a pale refraction. Rather, reality is brought into existence, is produced, by communication—by, in short, the construction, apprehension, and utilization of symbolic forms.[5] Reality, while not a mere function of symbolic forms, is produced by terministic systems—or by humans who produce such systems—that focus its existence in specific terms.

Under the sway of realism we ordinarily assume there is an order to existence that the human mind through some faculty may discover and describe. I am suggesting that reality is not there to discover in any significant detail. The world is entropic—that is, not strictly ordered—though its variety is constrained enough that the mind can grasp its outline and implant an order over and within the broad and elastic constraints of nature. To put it colloquially, there are no lines of latitude and longitude in nature, but by overlaying the globe with this particular, though not exclusively correct, symbolic organization, order is imposed on spatial organization and certain, limited human purposes served.

Whatever reality might be on the mind of Bishop Berkeley's God, whatever it might be for other animals, it is for us a vast production, a staged creation—something humanly produced and humanly maintained. Whatever order is in the world is not given in our genes or exclusively supplied by nature. As the biologist J. Z. Young puts it, "the brain of each one of us does literally create his or her own world" (1951: 61); the order of history is, as Eric Vogelin puts it, "the history of order"—the myriad forms in which people have endowed significance, order, and meaning in the world by the agency of their own intellectual processes.

Ernst Cassirer said it, and others have repeated it to the point of deadening its significance: man lives in a new dimension of reality, symbolic reality, and it is through the agency of this capacity that existence is produced. However, though it is often said, it is rarely investigated. More than repeat it, we have to take it seriously, follow it to the end of the line, to assess its capacity to vivify our studies. What Cassirer is contending is that one must examine communication, even scientific communication, even mathematical expression, as the primary phenomena of experience and not as something "softer" and derivative from a "realer" existent nature.

Lest someone think this obscure, allow me to illustrate with an example, an example at once so artless and transparent that the meaning will be clear even if engaging complexities are sacrificed. Let us suppose one had to teach a child of six or seven how to get from home to school. The child has been driven by the school, which is some six or seven blocks away, so he recognizes it, but he has no idea of the relation between his house and school. The space between these points might as well be, as the saying goes, a trackless desert. What does one do in such a situation?

There are a number of options. One might let the child discover the route by trial and error, correcting him as he goes, in faithful imitation of a conditioning experiment. One might have the child follow an adult, as I'm told the Apaches do, "imprinting" the route on the child. However, the ordinary method is simply to draw the child a map. By arranging lines, angles, names, squares denoting streets and buildings in a pattern on paper, one transforms vacant space into a featured environment. Although some environments are easier to feature than others—hence trackless deserts—space is understood and manageable when it is represented in symbolic form.

The map stands as a representation of an environment capable of clarifying a problematic situation. It is capable of guiding behavior and simultaneously transforming undifferentiated space into configured—that is, known, apprehended, understood—space.

Note also that an environment, any given space, can be mapped in a number of different modes. For example, we might map a particularly important space by producing a poetic or musical description. As in the song that goes, in part, "first you turn it to the left, then you turn it to the right," a space can be mapped by a stream of poetic speech that expresses a spatial essence and that also ensures, by exploiting the mnemonic devices of song and poetry, that the "map" can be retained in memory. By recalling the poem at appropriate moments, space can be effectively configured.

A third means of mapping space is danced ritual. The movements of the dance can parallel appropriate movements through space. By learning the dance the child acquires a representation of the space that on another occasion can guide behavior.

Space can be mapped, then, in different modes—utilizing lines on a page, sounds in air, movements in a dance. All three are symbolic forms, though the symbols differ; visual, oral, and kinesthetic. Moreover, each of the symbolic forms possesses two distinguishing characteristics: displacement and productivity. Like ordinary language, each mode allows one to speak about or represent some thing when the thing in question is not present. This capacity of displacement, of producing a complicated act when the "real" stimulus is not physically present, is another often noted though not fully explored capacity. Second, each of these symbolic forms is productive, for a person in command of the symbols is capable of producing an infinite number of representations on the basis of a finite number of symbolic elements. As with language, so with other symbolic forms: a finite set of words or a finite set of phonemes can produce, through grammatical combination, an infinite set of sentences.

We often argue that a map represents a simplification of or an abstraction from an environment. Not all the features of an environment are modeled, for the purpose of the representation is to express not the possible complexity of things but their simplicity. Space is made manageable by the reduction of information. By doing this, however, different maps bring the same environment alive in different ways; they produce quite different realities. Therefore, to live within the purview of different maps is to live within different realities. Consequently, maps not only constitute the activity known as mapmaking; they constitute nature itself.

A further implication concerns the nature of thought. In our predominantly individualistic tradition, we are accustomed to think of thought as essentially private, an activity that occurs in the head—graphically represented by Rodin's "The Thinker." I wish to suggest, in contradistinction, that thought is predominantly public and social. It occurs primarily on blackboards, in dances, and in recited poems. The capacity of private thought is a derived and secondary talent, one that appears biographically later in the person and historically later in the species. Thought is public because it depends on a publicly available stock of symbols. It is public in a second and stronger sense. Thinking consists of building maps of environments. Thought involves constructing a model of an environment and then running the model faster than the environment to see if nature can be coerced to perform as the model does. In the earlier example, the map of the neighborhood and the path from home to school represent the environment; the finger one lays on the map and traces the path is a representation of the child, the walker. "Running" the map is faster than walking the route and constitutes the "experiment" or "test."

Thought is the construction and utilization of such maps, models, templates: football plays diagrammed on a blackboard, equations on paper, ritual dances charting the nature of ancestors, or streams of prose like this attempting, out in the bright-lit world in which we all live, to present the nature of communication.

This particular miracle we perform daily and hourly—the miracle of producing reality and then living within and under the fact of our own productions—rests upon a particular quality of symbols: their ability to be both representations "of" and "for" reality.[6]

A blueprint of a house in one mode is a representation "for" reality: under its guidance and control a reality, a house, is produced that expresses the relations contained in reduced and simplified form in the blueprint. There is a second use of a blueprint, however. If someone asks for a description of a particular house, one can simply point to a blueprint and say, "That's the house." Here the blueprint stands as a representation or symbol of reality: it expresses or represents in an alternative medium a synoptic formulation of the nature of a particular reality. While these are merely two sides of the same coin, they point to the dual capacity of symbolic forms: as "symbols of" they present reality; as "symbols for" they create the very reality they present.

In my earlier example the map of the neighborhood in one mode is a symbol of, a representation that can be pointed to when someone asks about the relation between home and school. Ultimately, the map becomes a representation for reality when, under its guidance, the child makes his way from home to school and, by the particular blinders as well as the particular observations the map induces, experiences space in the way it is synoptically formulated in the map.

It is no different with a religious ritual. In one mode it represents the nature of human life, its condition and meaning, and in another mode— its "for" mode—it induces the dispositions it pretends merely to portray.

All human activity is such an exercise (can one resist the word "ritual"?) in squaring the circle. We first produce the world by symbolic work and then take up residence in the world we have produced. Alas, there is magic in our self deceptions.[7]

We not only produce reality but we must likewise maintain what we have produced, for there are always new generations coming along for whom our productions are incipiently problematic and for whom reality must be regenerated and made authoritative. Reality must be repaired for it consistently breaks down: people get lost physically and spiritually, experiments fail, evidence counter to the representation is produced,

mental derangement sets in—all threats to our models of and for reality that lead to intense repair work. Finally, we must, often with fear and regret, toss away our authoritative representations of reality and begin to build the world anew. We go to bed, to choose an example not quite at random, convinced behaviorists who view language, under the influence of Skinner, as a matter of operant conditioning and wake up, for mysterious reasons, convinced rationalists, rebuilding our mode of language, under the influence of Chomsky, along the lines of deep structures, transformations, and surface appearances. These are two different intellectual worlds in which to live, and we may find that the anomalies of one lead us to transform it into another.[8]

To study communication is to examine the actual social process wherein significant symbolic forms are created, apprehended, and used. When described this way some scholars would dismiss it as insufficiently empirical. My own view is the opposite, for I see it as an attempt to sweep away our existing notions concerning communication that serve only to devitalize our data. Our attempts to construct, maintain, repair, and transform reality are publicly observable activities that occur in historical time. We create, express, and convey our knowledge of and attitudes toward reality through the construction of a variety of symbol systems: art, science, journalism, religion, common sense, mythology. How do we do this? What are the differences between these forms? What are the historical and comparative variations in them? How do changes in communication technology influence what we can concretely create and apprehend? How do groups in society struggle over the definition of what is real? These are some of the questions, rather too simply put, that communication studies must answer.

Finally, let me emphasize an ironic aspect to the study of communication, a way in which our subject matter doubles back on itself and presents us with a host of ethical problems. One of the activities in which we characteristically engage, as in this essay, is communication about communication itself. However, communication is not some pure phenomenon we can discover; there is no such thing as communication to be revealed in nature through some objective method free from the corruption of culture. We understand communication insofar as we are able to build models or representations of this process. But our models of communication, like all models, have this dual aspect—an "of" aspect and a "for" aspect. In one mode communication models tell us what the process is; in their second mode they produce the behavior they have described. Communication can be modeled in several empirically adequate ways, but these several models have different ethical implications for they produce different forms of social relations.

Let us face this dilemma directly. There is nothing in our genes that tells us how to create and execute those activities we summarize under the term "communication." If we are to engage in this activity—writing an essay, making a film, entertaining an audience, imparting information and advice—we must discover models in our culture that tell us how this particular miracle is achieved. Such models are found in common sense, law, religious traditions, increasingly in scientific theories themselves. Traditionally, models of communication were found in religious thought. For example, in describing the roots of the transmission view of communication in nineteenth century American religious thought I meant to imply the following: religious thought not only described communication; it also presented a model for the appropriate uses of language, the permissible forms of human contact, the ends communication should serve, the motives it should manifest. It taught what it meant to display.

Today models of communication are found less in religion than in science, but their implications are the same. For example, American social science generally has represented communication, within an overarching transmission view, in terms of either a power or an anxiety model. These correspond roughly to what is found in information theory, learning theory, and influence theory (power) and dissonance, balance

theory, and functionalism or uses and gratifications analysis (anxiety). I cannot adequately explicate these views here, but they reduce the extraordinary phenomenological diversity of communication into an arena in which people alternatively pursue power or flee anxiety. And one need only monitor the behavior of modern institutions to see the degree to which these models create, through policy and program, the abstract motives and relations they portray.

Models of communication are, then, not merely representations of communication but representations *for* communication: templates that guide, unavailing or not, concrete processes of human interaction, mass and interpersonal. Therefore, to study communication involves examining the construction, apprehension, and use of models of communication themselves—their construction in common sense, art, and science, their historically specific creation and use: in encounters between parent and child, advertisers and consumer, welfare worker and supplicant, teacher and student. Behind and within these encounters lie models of human contact and interaction.

Our models of communication, consequently, create what we disingenuously pretend they merely describe. As a result our science is, to use a term of Alvin Gouldner's, a reflexive one. We not only describe behavior; we create a particular corner of culture—culture that determines, in part, the kind of communicative world we inhabit.

Raymond Williams, whose analysis I shall follow in conclusion, speaks to the point:

> Communication begins in the struggle to learn and to describe. To start this process in our minds and to pass on its results to others, we depend on certain communication models, certain rules or conventions through which we can make contact. We can change these models when they become inadequate or we can modify and extend them. Our efforts to do so, and to use the existing models successfully, take up a large part of our living energy. . . . Moreover, many of our communication models become, in themselves, social institutions. Certain attitudes to others, certain forms of address, certain

tones and styles become embodied in institutions which are then very powerful in social effect. . . . These arguable assumptions are often embodied in solid, practical institutions which then teach the models from which they start. (1966: 19–20)

This relation between science and society described by Williams has not been altogether missed by the public and accounts for some of the widespread interest in communication. I am not speaking merely of the contemporary habit of reducing all human problems to problems or failures in communication. Let us recognize the habit for what it is: an attempt to coat reality with clichés, to provide a semantic crucifix to ward off modern vampires. But our appropriate cynicism should not deflect us from discovering the kernel of truth in such phrases.

If we follow Dewey, it will occur to us that problems of communication are linked to problems of community, to problems surrounding the kinds of communities we create and in which we live.[9] For the ordinary person communication consists merely of a set of daily activities: having conversations, conveying instructions, being entertained, sustaining debate and discussion, acquiring information. The felt quality of our lives is bound up with these activities and how they are carried out within communities.

Our minds and lives are shaped by our total experience—or, better, by representations of experience and, as Williams has argued, a name for this experience is communication. If one tries to examine society as a form of communication, one sees it as a process whereby reality is created, shared, modified, and preserved. When this process becomes opaque, when we lack models of and for reality that make the world apprehensible, when we are unable to describe and share it; when because of a failure in our models of communication we are unable to connect with others, we encounter problems of communication in their most potent form.

The widespread social interest in communication derives from a derangement in our models of communication and community. This derangement derives, in turn, from an obsessive commitment to a transmission view of communication and the derivative representation of communication in complementary models of power and anxiety. As a result, when we think about society, we are almost always coerced by our traditions into seeing it as a network of power, administration, decision, and control—as a political order. Alternatively, we have seen society essentially as relations of property, production, and trade—an economic order. But social life is more than power and trade (and it is more than therapy as well). As Williams has argued, it also includes the sharing of aesthetic experience, religious ideas, personal values and sentiments, and intellectual notions—a ritual order.

Our existing models of communication are less an analysis than a contribution to the chaos of modern culture, and in important ways we are paying the penalty for the long abuse of fundamental communicative processes in the service of politics, trade, and therapy. Three examples. Because we have looked at each new advance in communications technology as an opportunity for politics and economics, we have devoted it, almost exclusively, to matters of government and trade. We have rarely seen these advances as opportunities to expand people's powers to learn and exchange ideas and experience. Because we have looked at education principally in terms of its potential for economics and politics, we have turned it into a form of citizenship, professionalism and consumerism, and increasingly therapy. Because we have seen our cities as the domain of politics and economics, they have become the residence of technology and bureaucracy. Our streets are designed to accommodate the automobile, our sidewalks to facilitate trade, our land and houses to satisfy the economy and the real estate speculator.

The object, then, of recasting our studies of communication in terms of a ritual model is not only to more firmly grasp the essence of this "wonderful" process but to give us a way in which to rebuild a model of and for communication of some restorative value in reshaping our common culture.

NOTES

1. For further elaboration on these matters, see chapter 4.

2. For an interesting exposition of this view, see Lewis Mumford (1967).

3. The only treatment of news that parallels the description offered here is William Stephenson's *The Play Theory of Mass Communication* (1967). While Stephenson's treatment leaves much to be desired, particularly because it gets involved in some largely irrelevant methodological questions, it is nonetheless a genuine attempt to offer an alternative to our views of communication.

4. These contrasting views of communication also link, I believe, with contrasting views of the nature of language, thought, and symbolism. The transmission view of communication leads to an emphasis on language as an instrument of practical action and discursive reasoning, of thought as essentially conceptual and individual or reflective, and of symbolism as being preeminently analytic. A ritual view of communication, on the other hand, sees language as an instrument of dramatic action, of thought as essentially situational and social, and symbolism as fundamentally fiduciary.

5. This is not to suggest that language constitutes the real world as Ernst Cassirer often seems to argue. I wish to suggest that the world is apprehensible for humans only through language or some other symbolic form.

6. This formulation, as with many other aspects of this essay, is heavily dependent on the work of Clifford Geertz (see Geertz, 1973).

7. We, of course, not only produce a world; we produce as many as we can, and we live in easy or painful transit between them. This is the problem Alfred Schutz (1967) analyzed as the phenomenon of "multiple realities." I cannot treat this problem here, but I must add that some such perspective on the multiple nature of produced reality is necessary in order to make any sense of the rather dismal area of communicative "effects."

8. The example and language are not fortuitous. Thomas Kuhn's *The Structure of Scientific Revolutions* (1962) can be seen as a description of how a scientific world is produced (paradigm creation), maintained (paradigm articulation, training, through exemplars, of

a new generation of scientists), repaired (by dismissing anomalous phenomena, discounting counter-evidence, forcing nature more strenuously into conceptual boxes), and transformed (in revolutions and their institutionalization in textbooks and scientific societies).

9. See Dewey (1927). To maintain continuity in the argument, let me stress, by wrenching a line of Thomas Kuhn's out of context, the relation between model building and community: "The choice . . . between competing paradigms proves to be a choice between incompatible modes of community life" (1962: 92).

WORKS CITED

Dewey, John (1916). *Democracy and Education.* New York: Macmillan.

———. (1927). *The Public and Its Problems.* New York: Henry Holt and Co.

———. (1939). *Intelligence in the Modern World* (collected works). New York: Modern Library.

Durkheim, Emile (1953). *Sociology and Philosophy.* New York: Free Press.

Geertz, Clifford (1973). *The Interpretation of Cultures.* New York: Basic Books.

Kuhn, Thomas S. (1962). *The Structure of Scientific Revolutions.* Chicago: University of Chicago Press.

Miller, Perry (1965). *The Life of the Mind in America.* New York: Harcourt, Brace and World.

Mumford, Lewis (1967). *Technics and Human Development.* New York: Harcourt Brace Jovanovich.

Park, Robert Evans (1955). "News as a Form of Knowledge." In *Society* (pp. 71–88). New York: Free Press.

Schutz, Alfred (1967). *Collected Papers, Vol. 1. The Problem of Social Reality.* The Hague: Martinus Nijhoff.

Stephenson, William (1967). *The Play Theory of Mass Communication.* Chicago: University of Chicago Press.

Williams, Raymond (1966). *Communications.* London: Chatto and Windus.

Young, J. Z. (1951). *Doubt and Certainty in Science.* Oxford, England: Clarendon Press.

Projects for Theorizing the Historical and Cultural Sources of Communication Theory

Additional Readings on Historical and Cultural Sources

To learn more about the history of communication theory: Hardt (1992); Mattelart (1996); Peters (1999); Rogers (1994); Schiller (1996).

Application Exercise

In keeping with the theme of this unit, which looks at communication theory in history, look around at what is going on in the world today. Imagine fifty years from now: What sorts of things (e.g., media, politics, social values, communication media, social issues, popular culture, discussion forums, etc.) might people point to and say these are the things that were influencing communication theory at this time? Prepare an argument to support your conclusions about what will be seen as most influential.

Projects

1. The question of ideological bias often comes up in writings on the history of communication theory. Has the idea of communication been used to support ideologies of liberal individualism, capitalism, and imperialism? Has it promoted unrealistic expectations about human understanding and progress or the devaluation of manual labor? Has it been associated with gender stereotypes? To learn more about these and related issues read Cameron (2000), Chapters 5 and 6; Carey (1989); Grossberg (1982); Hardt (1992); Mattelart (1996); Peters (1999); Schiller (1996).

2. Communication theory has also been criticized for cultural bias. All of the readings in this unit focus on the idea of communication as it has developed in a Western (primarily European and Euro-American) civilization that traces its origins to ancient Greece and Rome. Although the explicit concept of communication and formal theories of communication may have originated in the Western tradition, should communication theory be restricted to that tradition? People everywhere communicate regardless of whatever words they may use to describe what we now call the communication process. Critics have argued, however, that Western theories do not always apply to people in non-Western cultures. To learn more about non-Western communication theory read Chen and Miike (2003), Ito (1989), Jia (2001), Kim (2002), Kincaid (1987), and Miike (2006). How has communication been theorized in various non-Western cultural

traditions? What are the main similarities and differences? Aside from these primarily Asian examples, do other world cultures, or groups within modern multicultural societies such as African Americans, have distinct ideas about communication that should be theorized? Do all cultures have specific ways of thinking and talking about human interaction that can be formally articulated as theories of communication? Can the cultural biases of communication theory be overcome? Can there be universal theories of communication that transcend cultures?

3. The evolution of media technologies has been widely considered a key factor in the history of communication. The invention of writing, the spread of the printing press and literate culture, the development of electronic communication beginning with the telegraph, the growth of mass media, and most recently the introduction of new digital technologies including the Internet have all been noted as watersheds in communication. New media, it has been argued, not only change how we communicate but also change how we think. The Homeric Greece described in the Wiseman reading was a preliterate culture based on oral communication. How does the concept of communication in that culture differ from concepts that emerged in the more literate culture of the early Christian thinkers described by Peters? How did those concepts change with developments in modern science and engineering as described by Peters, Mattelart, and Carey? To learn more about the history of media and the idea of communication, read Carey (1989), Chesebro and Bertelsen (1996), Havelock (1986), Innis (1951), McLuhan (1964), Ong (1982), and Peters (1999).

4. Cameron (2000; see also reading 30 in this volume) argues that communication under current social conditions described by the terms "reflexive modernity" and "enterprise culture" is increasingly regarded in many sectors of society (such as business, education, therapy, and self-help literatures) as a set of technical skills that can be improved through training and expert knowledge. In later sections of her book (see

especially Chapters 2 and 3), she further elaborates these ideas about communication skills. Read these sections of Cameron (2000) and compare the popular ideas about communication skills she describes to current academic theories on communication skills (Greene & Burleson, 2003; Hargie, 1997). What does this comparison suggest about the role that academic communication theory is now, can be, or should be playing in the expert systems that are currently informing popular understandings of communication? What are the practical advantages and disadvantages of theorizing communication as a set of skills?

5. A project to consider as one moves further into this volume and reads the units on each of the seven traditions of communication theorizing is to look across sections at contemporary theorists within different traditions. In doing so, one could examine whether they are theorizing similar problems or if they share certain conceptions of communication that seem to be a part of practices of their times even though they are theorizing in different traditions. One way to think about this project is that it addresses a general question: What can the communication theorizing of a time tell us about the sociocultural context of that time?

REFERENCES

Cameron, D. (2000). *Good to talk? Living and working in a communication culture*. London: Sage.

Carey, J. W. (1989). *Communication as culture: Essays on media and society*. Winchester, MA: Unwin Hyman.

Chen, G.-M., & Miike, Y. (Eds.). (2003). Asian approaches to human communication [Special issue]. *Intercultural Communication Studies, 12*(4), 1–218.

Chesebro, J. W., & Bertelsen, D. A. (1996). *Analyzing media: Communication technologies as symbolic and cognitive systems*. New York: Guilford.

Greene, J. O., & Burleson, B. R. (Eds.). (2003). *Handbook of communication and social interaction skills*. Mahwah, NJ: Lawrence Erlbaum.

Grossberg, L. (1982). The ideology of communication: Post-structuralism and the limits of communication. *Man and World, 15*(1), 83–102.

Hardt, H. (1992). *Critical communication studies: Communication, history, and theory in America.* London and New York: Routledge.

Hargie, O. D. W. (Ed.). (1997). *The handbook of communication skills* (2nd ed.). New York: Routledge.

Havelock, E. (1986). *The muse learns to write: Reflections on orality and literacy from antiquity to the present.* New Haven, CT: Yale University Press.

Innis, H. A. (1951). *The bias of communication.* Toronto, Ontario, Canada: University of Toronto Press.

Ito, Y. (1989). A non-Western view of the paradigm dialogues. In B. Dervin, L. Grossberg, B. J. O'Keefe, & E. Wartella (Eds.), *Rethinking communication: Vol. 1. Paradigm issues* (pp. 173–177). Newbury Park, CA: Sage.

Jia, W. (2001). *The remaking of the Chinese character and identity in the 21st century: The Chinese face practices.* Westport, CT: Ablex.

Kim, M.-S. (2002). *Non-Western perspectives on human communication.* Thousand Oaks, CA: Sage.

Kincaid, L. D. (Ed.). (1987). *Communication theory: Eastern and Western perspectives.* San Diego, CA: Academic Press.

Mattelart, A. (1996). *The invention of communication* (S. Emanuel, Trans.). Minneapolis: University of Minnesota Press.

McLuhan, M. (1964). *Understanding media: The extensions of man.* New York: McGraw-Hill.

Miike, Y. (2006). Non-Western theory in Western research? An Asiacentric agenda for Asian communication studies. *Review of Communication, 6*(1–2), 4–31.

Ong, W. J. (1982). *Orality and literacy: The technologizing of the word.* London: Methuen.

Peters, J. D. (1999). *Speaking into the air: A history of the idea of communication.* Chicago: University of Chicago Press.

Rogers, E. M. (1994). *A history of communication study: A biographical approach.* New York: Free Press.

Schiller, D. (1996). *Theorizing communication: A history.* New York: Oxford University Press.

UNIT II   INTRODUCTION

METATHEORY

What is theory? What are the goals of theorizing? How are theories made? How are they used? How can I tell a better theory from a weaker or less valid one? Anyone who engages thoughtfully in the project of theorizing communication needs to reflect on these fundamental, metatheoretical questions. An explicitly articulated way of answering such questions is a *metatheory,* a theory of theory.

This book is based on a metatheory that we outlined briefly in the Introduction, where we presented four key elements of the project of theorizing: the interaction between communication theory and ordinary metadiscourse, the logic of practical theory, the traditions of communication theory, and the need to question and rethink theoretical traditions even as we work within them. These metatheoretical principles derive from Craig's (1999) article, "Communication Theory as a Field," which is reprinted in full in this unit (reading 5). In addition to presenting this fuller statement of the metatheory behind this book, our purpose in unit II is to open up the larger debate about metatheory in communication studies, inviting readers to engage in the project of metatheorizing.

Not all communication theorists see eye to eye on theory. In fact, they approach theory from a variety of metatheoretical standpoints. Anderson (1996; Anderson & Baym, 2004) has described the differences with reference to four types of metatheoretical assumptions that underlie any theoretical claim:

- *Ontology:* assumptions about existence such as the nature of the human individual and how we relate to the world around us. For example, theorists disagree about whether the phenomena we study exist objectively, independent of our theories, or whether they exist only as socially interpreted, a process that can be influenced by theories—in which case the objects we study do not exist independently of our theories.

- *Epistemology:* assumptions about knowledge such as what it means to know something and how knowledge claims can be proven. For example, empiricists assume that knowledge must be grounded in empirical observation whereas idealists and rationalists locate the basis of knowledge in ideas or innate forms of reasoning.

- *Praxeology:* assumptions about the practice of theory such as how a theory should be structured and presented, precedents that should be cited to establish a theory's relevance and originality, how a theory should be used, and other common expectations within the particular intellectual community that is the theory's primary audience. As you browse from unit to unit in this book, you will notice that each theoretical tradition has certain distinctive writing styles, touchstone authors, ways of referring to other theory and research, and reasoning patterns.

• *Axiology:* assumptions about the values that determine the worth of a theory, how a theory should contribute to society. For example, there is a great divide between so-called value-free scientific theorizing that is intended only to provide society with carefully tested, objective knowledge and normative or value-based theorizing that is explicitly intended to evaluate and influence communication practices.

Because it is impossible to theorize communication without making some assumptions of these kinds, at least implicitly, every theory can be said to have an underlying metatheory or at least some underlying metatheoretical assumptions. For example, here is how Anderson (1996) summarized the metatheoretical assumptions of Berger and Calabrese's uncertainty reduction theory (reading 24):

> Thus, it is marked by the material criterion and its complement in scientific realism, as well as by determinism, reductionism, the attribute model, the absence of agency, foundational empiricism and formal logic underlying the social science genre of writing, and an expected silence on questions of value. (p. 205)

A clear contrast to uncertainty reduction theory is provided by Foss and Griffin's theory of invitational rhetoric (reading 9), which assumes that communicators are responsible agents, that our practice of communication can be shaped by theory, that theoretical knowledge claims can take the form of value-based principles, that theoretical writing need not rely on formal logic, and that a key purpose of theorizing communication is to influence how we communicate and evaluate communication. Most of these assumptions

are not stated explicitly by the theorists but can be detected by reading between the lines for what is taken for granted as true.

The purpose of explicit metatheorizing is to articulate and defend a coherent set of metatheoretical assumptions to guide the practice of theorizing. Social scientists and philosophers have debated extensively on metatheory without reaching any final consensus, and communication theorists have also been actively engaged in these debates. In the Introduction we contrasted our own *practical theory* approach against two alternatives: *empirical scientific theory,* the goal of which is to provide empirically well-supported explanations that increase our capacity to predict and control communication processes, and *philosophical normative theory,* which articulates ideal principles by which to evaluate and practice communication. Other currently prominent metatheoretical stances include *hermeneutics* or *interpretive social science, critical theory,* and *postmodernism.* There are, of course, important differences within each of these schools of thought, and the whole range of metatheoretical positions can be mapped in various ways by highlighting different distinctions. We will touch on some of these complexities in a brief overview of current approaches.

Scientific metatheorists argue that communication should be studied as an empirical science in which theories are constructed and validated by scientific methods. Theories in this volume representing the sociopsychological tradition (unit VII) are good exemplars of the empirical scientific approach. Scientific theories are usually presented in the form of explicitly defined concepts and logically linked sets of propositions intended to explain a specific range of empirical phenomena and are constructed with close attention to programs of empirical research. A good scientific theory builds on existing research and provides a systematic basis for deriving hypotheses that can be tested in further research.

All scientific metatheorists agree on this general picture of theory but differ about certain metatheoretical assumptions.

Recent discussions of empirical scientific theory in communication studies have focused on *postpositivism* and *scientific realism.* Postpositivism (Miller, 2000; Corman, 2005) rejects certain assumptions of a strict positivist epistemology while holding a more limited stance on "realism, objectivity, and the scientific *goal* of value-free inquiry" (Miller, 2000, p. 58). Scientific realism (Greene, 1994; Pavitt, 1999, 2000, 2001) defends the stronger ontological and epistemological claim that theories should refer to real existing entities with discoverable causal powers. It opposes more skeptical views known as instrumentalism (scientific concepts are merely instruments for explaining empirical data and do not necessarily correspond to real entities) and perspectivism (phenomena are theory-laden because the perspective or paradigm from which a theory is constructed determines how empirical observations will be interpreted). For example, the concept of uncertainty (see reading 24) for a realist must refer to a real psychological state with the power to cause certain effects. For an instrumentalist, uncertainty is merely a convenient scientific fiction that is valid if it helps to make accurate predictions of independent experimental results. For a perspectivist, even the experimental results are largely (though not entirely) determined by the theory of uncertainty reduction. Pavitt (1999) argues that realism requires communication scientists to be more careful in defining concepts, but Pavitt fails to explain how researchers can tell the difference between real entities and merely useful scientific fictions in practice. From our standpoint as practical theorists, it is especially important to notice how different metatheories construe the relationship between communication theory and practice, a relationship that depends on all four types of metatheoretical assumptions but especially the axiology or purposes of theory.

Craig (1989, extending the work of Bochner, 1985, and Habermas, 1971, among other scholars) argued that empiricism, hermeneutics, and critical theory connect theory to practice in fundamentally different ways. Empirical scientific theory connects theory to practice primarily by trying to identify generalizable causal mechanisms that determine the outcomes of communication processes, thus making it possible to predict and control results. Theories of human social behavior, from this point of view, are not essentially different from theories in the physical and natural sciences. For example, a good scientific theory of persuasion should make it possible to increase the effectiveness of persuasive messages by manipulating the social and psychological processes that cause persuasion to happen. This technological or instrumental way of relating theory to practice "is value-neutral and objective in the sense that it plays no explicit role in the choice of ends but only attempts to provide effective and efficient means to achieve human goals" (Craig, 1989, p. 107).

Hermeneutical-interpretive approaches argue that the social sciences, including communication studies, are essentially different from the physical and natural sciences because human social action is ontologically different from natural processes. Humans, in short, are self-interpreting beings. Atoms and flowers may do wonderful things but *they never mean anything by what they do.* Humans, in contrast, usually act on the basis of some understanding of what they are doing, and life in human society depends on our ability to interpret the meanings of our own and other people's actions. Of course, this is what we do in everyday communication, but those everyday understandings are usually limited to our immediate practical needs. The purpose of ethnographic, historical, and other forms of interpretive inquiry is to broaden and deepen our understanding of social life by interpreting the specific meanings that are shared in various cultural groups, social situations, art forms, and so on, including the rich heritage of historical records and artifacts that have come down to us from the past.

Although it may be possible to identify some generalizable causal mechanisms that influence human behavior, interpretive metatheories assume that the practical potential for this kind of empirical scientific theory is not very great. Interpretive metatheories, in fact, often downplay the value and importance of theory. The relationship of theory to practice is quite modest and limited from their point of view: Theories merely offer possible interpretive themes or frameworks that can be helpful for understanding particular situations. For example, Carey's theory of communication as culture (reading 4) can sensitize us to the historical roots and the range of cultural meanings associated with the transmission and ritual views of communication, but Carey provides no scientifically testable explanation of communication processes that can be used to predict and control outcomes. On the other hand, his theory may be more useful than scientific theories in providing a richer understanding of the values (such as influence or community) that we might seek to achieve in communication.

Critical theory, like hermeneutic-interpretive approaches, rejects scientific theory's value-neutral, technological way of relating theory and practice. In contrast to hermeneutics, however, critical theory envisions a larger role for theory as a conceptual foundation for questioning, challenging, and potentially transforming common everyday understandings and practices, especially by unmasking ideological illusions and hidden relations of power (for example, in feminism's critical questioning of traditional gender roles).

Critical theory is further explained and illustrated in unit IX of this volume. In that unit we also mention newer approaches, such as feminist and postcolonial theory, whose metatheoretical assumptions differ from classic critical theory in some respects. In feminist communication theory, for example, Kramarae (1989) argues that feminists reject the tendency of traditional male critical theory "to construct divisions between those 'who know' and those who don't" (p. 157); Allen (1996) illustrates the application of a distinct approach to feminist standpoint theory and Rakow and Wackwitz (2004) identify key themes of difference, voice, and representation in feminist theory. The question of a distinct feminist tradition of communication theory will be taken up again in the Concluding Reflections of this volume. In the following paragraphs we focus briefly on two other current metatheoretical positions that also may or may not be considered to fall within the scope of critical metatheory: postmodernism and practical theory.

Mumby (1997) distinguishes four current metatheoretical positions, all of which he regards as discourses that respond in different ways to what he calls the Enlightenment project, a tradition of European thought that goes back to the 18th century. He writes, "The basic goal of [the Enlightenment project] is to enable human beings to develop systems of reason that enable them to transcend oppression in its various forms" (Mumby, 1997, p. 3). This statement implies the important insight that all modern and postmodern metatheories, even including so-called value-neutral scientific theory, express a critical axiological impulse with clearly political implications: to liberate society from blind traditionalism, authoritarianism, and irrationality. However, different metatheories approach this common emancipatory task in radically different ways. (Empirical scientific theorists tend to think the best way to emancipate society is by providing objective knowledge.) Mumby considers all three of Craig's (1989) main branches of metatheory to be forms of modernism, which he calls positivistic modernism, interpretive modernism, and critical modernism; his main point is to argue that *postmodernism* is a fourth tradition, essentially different from the other three.

Postmodernism, which includes poststructuralist theory, rejects modernist assumptions such as the ontology of the autonomous rational mind, the epistemological separation between truth and power, and the idea that language can express stable meanings and personal identities. For postmodernists, reality exists only "in the complexly articulated systems of discourse in which people are always situated" (Mumby, 1997, p. 21). Examples of postmodernist theory in this volume include Chang (reading 18), Poster (reading 28), and aspects of Deetz (reading 34), among others. The fact that these readings occur in different units representing different traditions of communication theory seems to support Mumby's contention that postmodernism is not a form of critical theory. On the other hand, Deetz and even Mumby himself both integrate postmodernist ideas within an essentially critical approach. Postmodernism can be regarded as an extension of critical theory's radical questioning of ideological illusions to include even the most fundamental assumptions about meaning, truth, reason, and personhood. The debatable question is whether the critical project itself is undermined in this process of extending it.

After distinguishing empiricism, hermeneutics, and critical theory with regard to their ways of relating theory to practice, Craig (1989) went on to argue that *practical discipline* should be distinguished as an approach that departs from mainstream critical theory while sharing its central commitment of relating theory to practice dialectically through a process of critical reflection. Critical theory's exclusive focus on power relations and ideological critique, Craig argued, ignores the numerous ways that "communicative practices make universalistic claims on us quite apart from their role in any particular social order" (1989, p. 110). Practical discipline is a critical enterprise devoted to cultivating communication arts such as rhetoric, interpersonal conversation, and democratic decision making on their own terms. The practical problems that need to be addressed theoretically are not restricted to

the unmasking of ideological illusions, but rather include such mundane considerations as how to balance competing communicative requirements in leading a group discussion. On the other hand, a practical discipline should not ignore the kinds of social concerns raised by critical theory. "To question whether a communicative practice serves dominant interests to the detriment of broader interests, or whether a practice is consistent with a defensible social or political philosophy—these kinds of questions are always possible; they are among the 'stock issues' of debate in any discipline concerned with the cultivation of *praxis*" (Craig, 1989, p. 111). The extent to which practical theory is distinct from critical theory then depends on the degree to which ordinary practical questions about communication can legitimately be addressed without constant attention to questions of power and ideology in society and by the same token, the degree to which questions of power and ideology can be effectively addressed without first understanding everyday communication practices in their own terms. We favor a practical theory approach that begins with everyday practices and applies the insights of critical theory when relevant.

Craig and Tracy (1995) elaborated the idea of practical theory by distinguishing it from both empirical scientific theory and normative philosophical theory (see our discussion of these distinctions in the Introduction). Practical theory, they argued, is a way of reconstructing communicative practices:

"Theoretical reconstruction" of a practice means that the practice is typified or *idealized* such that particular instances are redescribed in less context-specific, more universalized terms. In idealizing a practice, a theoretical reconstruction also *rationalizes* it so that values and principles implicit in the practice are made explicit and a reasoned basis for "good practice" and reasoned judgments of practice is constructed. Practical theory can thus be thought of as a *rational reconstruction* of practice. (p. 252)

Craig and Tracy (1995) went on to show how a communication practice such as the intellectual discussion that goes on in academic seminars can be reconstructed by observing and critically reflecting on the *problems*, *techniques,* and *situated ideals* that constitute the normative basis for the practice. (For reviews of more recent work applying this method of grounded practical theory, see Barge & Craig, in press, and Tracy, 2005).

Practical theory itself is not a unified metatheory. Writings on practical theory now compose a substantial body of literature, in which Barge (2001; Barge & Craig, in press) has identified three broad approaches that he describes as mapping, engaged reflection, and transformative practice. Our practical discipline approach to practical theory falls under Barge's category of engaged reflection. The key differences are that the mapping approach describes communication problems and practices objectively, whereas engaged reflection reconstructs them critically; and that transformative practice develops theory in the process of direct professional intervention to change practices, whereas engaged reflection takes a less direct approach of engaging with societal discourses about communication problems.

Perhaps the most important point to be gleaned from the preceding quick overview of metatheory is that the metatheoretical assumptions behind this book do not represent a consensus of communication theorists. Our metatheory is one of many that are debated in the field. It is, however, a position we believe to be supported by strong arguments as we have shown here and will elaborate further in the following article by Craig.

Craig presents our metatheory as a response to *the problem of incoherence in the field of communication theory*. Communication theory developed independently in various disciplines and traditions of thought and has not formed a coherent field of study because there has been no awareness of common goals or issues across traditions. Theories in different traditions are perceived to have no relevance to each other because they are based on such disparate metatheoretical assumptions, all of which make perfect sense within the respective traditions but little sense to thinkers in other traditions. This state of fragmentation is unfortunate, he argues, because a field of communication theory, if properly conceived, would have the potential to make important intellectual and social contributions.

His proposal is to organize the field around the idea that every theoretical tradition offers a potentially useful perspective on practical communication problems. Arguably, thinkers in various disciplines became interested in communication theory precisely because they wanted to address what has been widely regarded as an important problem in society, the problem of communication. They found ways to address communication from within their particular intellectual traditions, and the task now is to bring those perspectives together to investigate and debate socially important issues. What we need is not a unified theory of communication, which would be impossible to achieve anyway, but rather a way of seeing how different traditions of communication theory are relevant to each other and have interesting issues to debate in common. This is what Craig refers to as dialogical-dialectical coherence.

As a basis for dialogical-dialectical coherence, Craig proposes a model for the field based on two key principles. The first, called the *constitutive metamodel,* maintains that there can be no one objectively true theory of communication but that the idea of communication can be constituted in different ways for different practical purposes. Theorists have recently argued that communication is the primary social process that constitutes our common world. The constitutive metamodel recognizes the paradox that communication itself, as an element of our common world, is therefore constituted in communication, and what communication becomes for us therefore depends on how we communicate about it.

This leads to Craig's second principle of *communication theory as metadiscourse,* which is the key to establishing a productive relationship between communication theory and practice. Everyday talk about communication conducted for practical purposes is called *practical metadiscourse.* Communication theory is also a way of talking about communication for practical purposes, or rather a series of different ways of talking in different traditions. This *theoretical metadiscourse* differs from practical metadiscourse by virtue of being more systematic and intellectually sophisticated, yet it is deeply related to practical metadiscourse in ways that we need to understand better than we now do. Theories can be *relevant* to practice in two complementary ways. First, they are *plausible* if consistent with commonplace ideas about communication (called metadiscursive commonplaces). Second, they are *interesting* if they challenge other commonplace ideas. Because different theories define communication in different ways that appeal to and challenge different commonplaces, different theories may be plausible and interesting for opposite reasons. Metadiscursive commonplaces that one theory supports, other theories may challenge. These are the key points on which debate across the field of communication theory is needed. They are also the points on which communication theory can be imported into everyday practical metadiscourse to provide new and stimulating ways for people to discuss communication problems. This is the practicality of communication theory.

Craig goes on to define an open-ended set of seven main traditions of communication theory and array them in a matrix to display both the uniqueness of each tradition as a form of metadiscourse and points of disagreement (*topoi* or places for argument) between traditions that may stimulate debate in the field. No more will be said here about the seven traditions; they are discussed and illustrated throughout this book. What Craig's model of the field especially contributes is a framework for thinking about the traditions in relation to each other as alternative points of view for addressing practical communication problems. Readers will be challenged to apply and reflect upon the usefulness of this mode of thinking as we survey the traditions.

Other questions may come to mind while you read this chapter: What are your own metatheoretical commitments? Do you believe in the possibility and value of objective scientific knowledge as the best way for scholars to contribute to the betterment of society? How important is theory? Does theory have only a modest role to play in understanding communication, as interpretive scholars claim, or does it have an important role to play, as both scientific and critical scholars maintain, although for different reasons? Can theory change the world? Should it? How could this actually happen? If postmodernists are correct, what basis can we have for even knowing how we would want to change the world? Does the constitutive view of communication lead to an unacceptable relativism? If Craig is right that there can be no one true theory of communication, what is the point of trying to theorize communication? Why have a field of communication theory if the various traditions are already practically relevant in their own different ways? What practical problems can communication theory address? What interesting problems does Craig's matrix representation of the field suggest? What possibilities for future theorizing seem most promising, and which ones are you most motivated to pursue? Reflection on this model of the field will continue with projects for theorizing at the conclusion of this unit.

REFERENCES

Allen, B. J. (1996). Feminist standpoint theory: A black woman's (re)view of organizational socialization. *Communication Studies, 47,* 257–271.

Anderson, J. A. (1996). *Communication theory: Epistemological foundations.* New York: The Guilford Press.

Anderson, J. A., & Baym, G. (2004). Philosophies and philosophic issues in communication, 1995–2004. *Journal of Communication, 54*(4), 589–615.

Barge, J. K. (2001). Practical theory as mapping, engaged reflection, and transformative practice. *Communication Theory, 11,* 5–13.

Barge, K. J., & Craig, R. T. (in press). Practical theory. In L. R. Frey & K. N. Cissna (Eds.), *Handbook of applied communication research.* Mahwah, NJ: Lawrence Erlbaum.

Bochner, A. P. (1985). Perspectives on inquiry: Representation, conversation, and reflection. In M. L. Knapp & G. R. Miller (Eds.), *Handbook of interpersonal communication* (pp. 27–58). Beverly Hills, CA: Sage.

Corman, S. R. (2005). Postpositivism. In S. May & D. K. Mumby (Eds.), *Engaging organizational communication theory and research: Multiple perspectives* (pp. 15–34). Thousand Oaks, CA: Sage.

Craig, R. T. (1989). Communication as a practical discipline. In B. Dervin, L. Grossberg, B. J. O'Keefe, & E. Wartella (Eds.), *Rethinking communication: Vol. 1. Paradigm issues* (pp. 97–122). Newbury Park, CA: Sage.

Craig, R. T. (1999). Communication theory as a field. *Communication Theory, 9,* 119–161.

Craig, R. T., & Tracy, K. (1995). Grounded practical theory: The case of intellectual discussion. *Communication Theory, 5,* 248–272.

Greene, J. O. (1994). What sort of terms ought theories of human action incorporate? *Communication Studies, 45,* 187–211.

Habermas, J. (1971). *Knowledge and human interests* (J. J. Shapiro, Trans.). Boston: Beacon Press.

Kramarae, C. (1989). Feminist theories of communication. In E. Barnouw, G. Gerbner, W. Schramm, T. L. Worth, & L. Gross (Eds.), *International encyclopedia of communications* (Vol. 2, pp. 157–160). New York: Oxford University Press.

Miller, K. I. (2000). Common ground from the post-positivist perspective: From "straw person" argument to collaborative coexistence. In S. R. Corman & M. S. Poole (Eds.), *Perspectives on organizational communication: Finding common ground* (pp. 46–67). New York: Guilford.

Mumby, D. K. (1997). Modernism, postmodernism, and communication studies: A rereading of an ongoing debate. *Communication Theory, 7,* 1–28.

Pavitt, C. (1999). The third way: Scientific realism and communication theory. *Communication Theory, 9,* 162–188.

Pavitt, C. (2000). Answering questions requesting scientific explanations for communication. *Communication Theory, 10,* 379–404.

Pavitt, C. (2001). *The philosophy of science and communication theory.* Huntington, NY: Nova Science.

Rakow, L. F., & Wackwitz, L. A. (2004). *Feminist communication theory: Selections in context.* Thousand Oaks, CA: Sage.

Tracy, K. (2005). Reconstructing communicative practices: Action-implicative discourse analysis. In K. L. Fitch & R. E. Sanders (Eds.), *Handbook of language and social interaction* (pp. 301–319). Mahwah, NJ: Lawrence Erlbaum.

5

COMMUNICATION THEORY AS A FIELD

ROBERT T. CRAIG

Communication theory is enormously rich in the range of ideas that fall within its nominal scope, and new theoretical work on communication has recently been flourishing.[1] Nevertheless, despite the ancient roots and growing profusion of theories about communication, I argue that communication theory as an identifiable field of study does not yet exist.[2]

Rather than addressing a field of theory, we appear to be operating primarily in separate domains. Books and articles on communication theory seldom mention other works on communication theory except within narrow (inter)disciplinary specialties and schools of thought.[3] Except within these little groups, communication theorists apparently neither agree nor disagree about much of anything. There is no canon of general theory to which they all refer. There are no common goals that unite them, no contentious issues that divide them. For the most part, they simply ignore each other.[4]

College courses in communication theory are increasingly offered at all levels, and numerous textbooks are being published. However, a closer look at their contents only further demonstrates that, although there exist many theories of communication—indeed, way too many different theories to teach effectively in any one course—there is no consensus on the *field*.

Anderson (1996) analyzed the contents of seven communication theory textbooks and identified 249 distinct "theories," 195 of which appeared in only one of the seven books. That is, just 22% of the theories appeared in more than one of the seven books, and only 18 of the 249 theories (7%) were included in more than three books. If communication theory were really a field, it seems likely that more than half of the

SOURCE: From Robert T. Craig (1999), Communication Theory as a Field. *Communication Theory, 9,* pp. 119–161, used by permission of the International Communication Association.

introductory textbooks would agree on something more than 7% of the field's essential contents. The conclusion that communication theory is not yet a coherent field of study seems inescapable.[5]

Although communication theory is not yet a coherent field, I believe it can and should become one. A field will emerge to the extent that we increasingly engage as communication theorists with socially important goals, questions, and controversies that cut across the various disciplinary traditions, substantive specialties, methodologies, and schools of thought that presently divide us.

In this essay I argue that all communication theories are relevant to a common practical life-world in which *communication* is already a richly meaningful term. Communication theory, in this view, is a coherent field of metadiscursive practice, a field of discourse about discourse with implications for the practice of communication. The various traditions of communication theory each offer distinct ways of conceptualizing and discussing communication problems and practices. These ways derive from and appeal to certain commonplace beliefs about communication while problematizing other beliefs. It is in the dialogue among these traditions that communication theory can fully engage with the ongoing practical discourse (or metadiscourse) about communication in society (Craig, 1989; Craig & Tracy, 1995).

Succeeding sections of the essay develop the following points:

1. Communication theory has not yet emerged as a coherent field of study because communication theorists have not yet found a way beyond the disabling disciplinary practices that separate them.

2. The potential of communication theory as a field can best be realized, however, not in a unified theory of communication but in a dialogical-dialectical disciplinary matrix, a commonly understood (though always contestable) set of assumptions that would enable productive argumentation across the diverse traditions of communication theory.

3. A disciplinary matrix can be developed using a constitutive metamodel of communication that opens up a conceptual space in which diverse first-order models can interact, and a conception of communication theory as theoretical metadiscourse productively engaged with the practical metadiscourse of everyday life.

4. Based on these principles, a tentative reconstruction of the multidisciplinary traditions of communication theory can appear as seven alternative vocabularies for theorizing communication as a social practice.

In conclusion, I suggest applications and extensions of the matrix and implications for disciplinary practice in the field of communication theory.

ROOTS OF INCOHERENCE

The incoherence of communication theory as a field can be explained by communication theory's multidisciplinary origins and by the particular ways in which communication scholars have used and too often misused the intellectual fruits that continue to pour from this multidisciplinary horn of plenty.

Multidisciplinary Origins

One of the most interesting facts about communication theory is that it has cropped up more or less independently in so many different academic disciplines. Littlejohn (1982), in what may be still the closest thing we have to a comprehensive schematic overview, traced contributions to communication theory from disciplines as diverse as literature, mathematics and engineering, sociology, and psychology.[6] Budd and Ruben's (1972) anthology of communication theory included chapters representing 24 disciplinary approaches in alphabetical order from Anthropology to Zoology.

The communication discipline initially tried to set itself up as a kind of interdisciplinary clearinghouse for all of these disciplinary approaches. This spirit of interdisciplinarity is still with us and deserves to be cultivated as one of our more meritorious qualities. The incorporation of so many different disciplinary approaches has made it very hard, however, to envision communication theory as a coherent field. What, if anything, do all of these approaches have to do with each other? Developed within various disciplines to address various intellectual problems, they are, in Kuhn's (1970) sense of the term, incommensurable: They neither agree or disagree about anything but effectively bypass each other because they conceive of their nominally shared topic, communication, in such fundamentally different ways.

Dance (1970) reviewed 95 published definitions of communication that had appeared in the 50s and 60s.[7] He concluded that the definitions differed in so many ways (he distinguished fifteen conceptual components) that communication might better be theorized as a "family" of related concepts rather than a unitary concept in order to avoid "dissension, academic sniping, and theoretical divisiveness" (p. 210). Working in a positivist tradition that at least held the concept of theory stable, Dance perhaps underestimated the difficulty of integrating definitions derived eclectically from disciplines with incommensurable intellectual agendas, now often involving radically different conceptions of "theory" (Craig, 1993). Given a plethora of definitions of communication and the difficulty of integrating or deciding among them in any satisfactory way, it became conventional wisdom among communication scholars (e.g. Fisher, 1978; Murphy, 1991) that to argue over definitions of communication was pointless. What, then, is it *not* pointless for communication theorists to argue over, if not the primary concept that constitutes their common field of study?

From Sterile Eclecticism to Productive Fragmentation

According to Peters (1986), communication research has been intellectually impoverished in part because of the peculiar way in which the discipline was institutionalized in U.S.

universities. The term communication, he argues, was used by Wilbur Schramm and others as an institutional legitimizing device in ways that precluded any coherent definition of "the field, its intellectual focus, and its mission" (p. 527). In establishing itself under the banner of communication, the discipline staked an academic claim to the entire field of communication theory and research—a very big claim indeed, since communication had already been widely studied and theorized. Peters writes that communication research became "an intellectual Taiwan—claiming to be all of China when, in fact, it was isolated on a small island" (p. 545). Perhaps the most egregious case involved Shannon's mathematical theory of information (Shannon & Weaver, 1948), which communication scholars touted as evidence of their field's potential scientific status even though they had nothing whatever to do with creating it, often poorly understood it, and seldom found any real use for it in their research. The sterile eclecticism of communication theory in this mode is evident in the cataloguing traditions still appearing in most of our recent communication theory textbooks. The "field" of communication theory came to resemble in some ways a pest control device called the Roach Motel that used to be advertised on TV: Theories check in, but they never check out. Communication scholars seized upon every idea about communication, whatever its provenance, but accomplished little with most of them—entombed them, you might say, after removing them from the disciplinary environments in which they had thrived and were capable of propagating—and communication scholars contributed few original ideas of their own.

Peters (1986) also points to a related phenomenon that I may interpret somewhat differently than he. Leading communication scholars were quite aware of the problem I am calling "sterile eclecticism" and sought to overcome it by developing systematic, theoretically based research programs. Since most of their theories and research paradigms were borrowed from other disciplines, this meant, in effect, initiating communication research programs closely based upon research programs in those other disciplines, so that much political communication research, for example, was little more than "political science as practiced in the field of communication" (Peters, 1986, p. 548), and, similarly, much interpersonal communication research was, and continues to be, little more than experimental social psychology as practiced in the field of communication.

Interdisciplinarity and cross-disciplinary borrowing are, of course, useful practices in themselves and ought to be encouraged in order to mitigate the fragmentation of knowledge among disciplines. The problem, as Peters (1986) suggested, is that mostly borrowed goods were leveraged to sustain institutional claims to disciplinary status without articulating any coherent, distinctive focus or mission for this putative communication discipline.

Communication research became productive by importing fragments of various other disciplines into its own culture, but the fragments did not and never could, in the ways they were used, cohere as a self-sustaining whole that was something more than the sum of its parts. This condition further explains why communication theory has not yet emerged as a coherent field. Each of the fragments of communication research has been productive within its own domain, hence my term "productive fragmentation." As long as the research discipline is thus fragmented, the textbooks will continue to be mired in sterile eclecticism and there will continue to be more and more communication theories but still no *field* of communication theory.

RECONSTRUCTING COMMUNICATION THEORY AS A FIELD

The Goal: Dialogical-Dialectical Coherence

In considering remedies for incoherence, the goal should not be some chimerical unified theory of communication, just over the rainbow. Such a unified theory will always be out of reach, and we probably should not want one even if it were attainable. No active field of inquiry has a fully unified theory. A perfectly coherent field would be a static field, a dead field, but the practice of communication itself is very much alive and endlessly evolving in a worldly scene of contingency and conflict. Communication theory, the theory of this practice, in all likelihood will never, therefore, achieve a final, unified form. The goal, indeed, should be the very condition that Dance (1970) was so keen to avoid: theoretical diversity, argument, debate, even at the cost of occasional lapses into academic sniping. The goal should not be a state in which we have nothing to argue about but one in which we better understand that we all have something very important to argue about.

If, however, we should not chase after the chimera of a unified theory, neither should we be distracted from the path of inquiry by the red herring of antidisciplinarity. Productive theoretical arguments most readily occur within an interpretive community sustained by a disciplinary matrix, a background of assumptions shared in common. But disciplinarity does not require that diversity and interdisciplinarity be suppressed.[8] To be a discipline means only, at a minimum, that many of us agree that we disagree about certain matters that are consequential in certain ways and therefore worth discussing. A discipline in this sense is nothing more nor less than "a conversational community with a tradition of argumentation" (Shotter, 1997).

The goal, in short, should be dialogical-dialectical coherence: a common awareness of certain complementarities and tensions among different types of communication theory, so it is commonly understood that these different types of theory cannot legitimately develop in total isolation from each other but must engage each other in argument. My purpose here is to explore how communication theory might be reconstructed within a practical discipline to reveal such complementarities and tensions and thereby constitute a coherent field. For this purpose I will propose a tentative theoretical matrix constructed on the basis of two principles. The first of these principles derives from the "constitutive" model of communication that has been featured in other recent efforts to conceptualize a field of communication theory but puts the constitutive model through a reflexive turn from which it emerges looking quite different.

Principle One:
The Constitutive Model of
Communication as Metamodel

Although the earlier debate over defining communication largely ceased after Dance (1970), the concept of communication has once again, roughly since the late 1980s, become a subject of serious discussion among communication theorists. Amidst a general flourishing of communication theory, this renewed focus on the concept of communication reflects a growing conviction among at least some scholars that communication theory *can* become a coherent field of inquiry, a field of central importance to social thought. In conceptualizing communication, we construct, in effect, a "communicational" perspective on social reality and so define the scope and purpose of a communication discipline distinct from other social disciplines.[9]

Among the most interesting of these field-defining proposals have been several versions of a constitutive or ritual model of communication. Typically, the proposed model is defined largely by contrast with its dialectical opposite, a transmission, or informational, model of communication that, it is claimed, continues to dominate lay and much academic thought (Carey, 1989; Cronen, 1995; Deetz, 1994; Pearce, 1989; Peters, 1989; Rothenbuhler, 1998; Shepherd, 1993; Sigman, 1992, 1995b). According to the conventional transmission concept, communication is a process of sending and receiving messages or transferring information from one mind to another.

This transmission model of communication has come under heavy attack in recent years. Peters (1989) has traced its origins to 18th-century empiricism with its individualistic and ultimately solipsistic assumptions (also see Taylor, 1992, 1997). Carey (1989), Deetz (1994), Pearce (1989), and Shepherd (1993), among others, have variously argued that the transmission model is philosophically flawed, fraught with paradox, and ideologically backward, and that it should at least be supplemented, if not entirely supplanted, by a model that conceptualizes communication as a constitutive process that produces and reproduces shared meaning. The constitutive model offers the discipline of communication a focus, a central intellectual role, and a cultural mission (i.e., to critique cultural manifestations of the transmission model).

Several important themes run through this literature. One is that ideas about communication have evolved historically and are best understood in a broader context of cultural and intellectual history. A second is that communication theories are reflexive: Formal theories, that is, often draw from ordinary, culturally based ways of thinking about communication but these theories, once formulated, can also influence, either to reinforce or to change, everyday thinking and practice. The relationship between theory and culture is thus reflexive, or mutually constitutive. Communication theories help to create the very phenomena that they purport to explain (Carey, 1989; Krippendorff, 1997).

This leads to a third theme, which is that theories of communication, because they are historically and culturally rooted and reflexive, have practical implications, including political ones. Because they influence society, theories always serve some interests—often, unsurprisingly, interests of the more privileged and powerful strata of society—more than others. For example, a transmission model of communication can serve the interests of technical experts, such as scientists and engineers, when it is used to reinforce cultural beliefs that highlight the value of experts as reliable sources of information.

A fourth theme is that the communication can be a legitimate intellectual discipline, but only if it embraces a communicational perspective on social reality that is radically distinct from, but at least equal in status to, such established disciplinary perspectives as those of psychology, sociology, economics, linguistics, and so on. Each of these disciplinary perspectives has its own ways of explaining certain aspects of communication.

Psychological theories explain, for example, the cognitive processes by which people are able to create messages (Berger, 1997). But a communicational perspective completely turns the explanatory tables. Communication, from a communicational perspective, is not a secondary phenomenon that can be explained by antecedent psychological, sociological, cultural, or economic factors; rather, communication itself is the primary, constitutive social process that explains all these other factors. Theories about communication from other disciplinary perspectives are not, in the strict sense, within the field of communication theory since they are not based on a communicational perspective. All genuine communication theory acknowledges the consequentiality of communication (Sigman, 1995b); it acknowledges communication itself as a fundamental mode of explanation (Deetz, 1994).[10]

Deetz points out that new disciplines (in the sense of fundamentally new modes of explanation) "arise when existing modes of explanation fail to provide compelling guidance for responses to a central set of new social issues" (1994, p. 568). Today, the central social issues have to do with who participates in what ways in the social processes that construct personal identities, the social order, and codes of communication. Against the traditional informational view of communication that takes these elements for granted as a fixed framework that must be in place in order for communication to occur, Deetz endorses an emerging "communication perspective" that focuses on "describing how the inner world, outer world, social relations, and means of expression are reciprocally constituted with the interactional process as its own best explanation" (1994, p. 577).

Especially noteworthy is that the arguments advanced in support of a constitutive model of communication, as the passages just quoted from Deetz (1994) illustrate, most often are not purely theoretical. The changing social situation in which communication is theorized, it is said, calls for new ways of thinking about communication. The constitutive model is presented as a practical response to contemporary social problems such as those arising from the erosion of the cultural foundations of traditional ideas and institutions, increasing cultural diversity and interdependence, and widespread demands for democratic participation in the construction of social reality. Just as a transmission model can be used to bolster the authority of technical experts, a constitutive model can hopefully serve the causes of freedom, toleration, and democracy.[11]

Although I largely agree with these arguments for a constitutive model of communication, I favor a pragmatic interpretation that does not necessarily reject other models, such as the transmission model, for practical purposes. That is, I take the constitutive model to be a metamodel that opens up a conceptual space in which many different theoretical models of communication can interact. Logically, a first-order model of communication is a perspective on communication that highlights certain aspects of the process. Thus, for example, a transmission model pictures communication as a process in which messages flow from sources to receivers. A second-order model, or metamodel, is a perspective on models that highlights certain aspects of models. A constitutive metamodel of communication pictures models of communication as different ways of constituting the communication process symbolically for particular purposes. The failure to distinguish logically between first-order models of communication and the constitutive metamodel is, I believe, a category mistake that produces at least two sorts of confusion.

First, a paradox lurks in the dialectical opposition between constitutive and transmission models. Since the constitutive model typically denies that any concept has a true essence except as constituted within the communication process, to assert that the constitutive model is the "true" model of communication would seem self-contradictory. Despite the impression one might get from a superficial reading of the literature, the definition of communication is not a binary choice between two competing models, transmission versus constitutive which in fact is no choice at all because the transmission model, as usually presented, is scarcely more than a straw figure set up to represent a simplistic view. A transmission model, regarded as one way of constituting communication symbolically for pragmatic purposes, is perfectly consistent with the constitutive model. That is, the constitutive model does not tell us what communication really is but rather implies that communication can be constituted symbolically (in and through communication, of course) in many different ways, including (why not, if it is useful to do so for some purposes?) as a transmission process.[12] Transmission-like notions of communication, whatever their philosophical flaws, continue to have cultural currency.[13] We may find, moreover, upon critical reflection, that there are often good reasons for using a transmission model: that it can be useful to distinguish pragmatically between communication sources and receivers, to map the flow of information through systems, or to think of messages as containers of meaning or of communication as an intentional act performed in order to achieve some anticipated outcome. Transmission models can be defended, for example, on grounds that they cultivate a particular kind of alertness to the diversity and relativity of perspectives and the ever-present dangers of distortion and misunderstanding in communication.[14]

Second, and more generally, the constitutive model, unless clearly distinguished as a metamodel, may tend to confuse communication itself with communication as theorized within certain limited traditions and thus, by excluding other useful traditions, unduly restrict the field of communication theory. The constitutive model is perhaps most easily confused with what I will define later in this essay as a sociocultural tradition of communication theory. In this tradition, communication is theorized as a process that produces and reproduces—and in that way constitutes—social order. Confusing the constitutive metamodel with this first-order sociocultural model of communication can lead to the false impression that other traditions of communication theory—such as those I will call the cybernetic and sociopsychological traditions—are not genuine communication theories because they

do not take a communicational perspective on social reality. To the contrary, as I will show, these other traditions can be reconstructed according to the constitutive metamodel as alternative types of communication explanations—not just explanations of communication based on noncommunication factors. In short, there are many different ways in which communication can be theorized, or constituted symbolically, within a constitutive metamodel. The sociocultural tradition of communication theory is just one of those ways.

The mere fact that communication can be theorized in various ways within a constitutive metamodel does not, however, give us any good reason to do so, nor does it give us any good reason to expect that a coherent field of communication theory would result from such a proliferation of theories. Does this "pragmatic" line of thinking—the more theories the better—put us right back in the same old pickle of sterile eclecticism or, at best, productive fragmentation? I shall argue that communication theory in all its open-ended diversity can be a coherent field, and useful too, if we understand it in a certain way as metadiscourse, a discourse about discourse, in the context of a practical discipline. This is the second principle for constructing a dialogical-dialectical disciplinary matrix.

Principle Two: Communication Theory as Metadiscourse

My reading of Taylor (1992) sparked a key insight that led to this essay on communication theory as a field. In a critique of language theory from Locke to the present, Taylor "represents the technical practice of theorizing language, interpretation, communication, and understanding . . . as derived from . . . our ordinary, everyday practices of talking about what we say and do with language" (1992, p. 10). Formal linguistic theory, he claims, can be, and in effect has been, derived by transforming commonplaces of *practical metadiscourse*—such as the commonplace belief that people ordinarily understand each other's utterances—into theoretical axioms or empirical hypotheses. Each language theory establishes its plausibility by appealing rhetorically to the taken-for-granted validity of some of these metadiscursive commonplaces while subjecting others to skeptical challenge. As each language theory questions metadiscursive commonplaces that other theories take for granted, language theory as a whole becomes an *intellectual metadiscourse* structured as a closed, self-referential game. The only way out of this self-contained rhetorical game of intellectual metadiscourse, Taylor (1992) suggests, is to set aside the pseudo-problem on which it is based—that of explaining how communication is possible—and to turn instead to the empirical study of practical metadiscourse—how communication is reflexively accomplished in practice.

Practical metadiscourse is intrinsic to communicative practice. That is, communication is not only something we do but also something we refer to reflexively in ways that are practically entwined with our doing of it. When Ann says to Bill, for example, "you can't possibly know what I'm talking about," Ann appeals, in the form of a metadiscursive remark, to certain commonplace beliefs about meaning and reference (such as the belief that true understanding comes only from personal experience), probably in order to undermine some assertion of Bill's. Practical discourse abounds in such metadiscursive commonplaces, which are important in everyday life for all sorts of pragmatic functions.

Taylor's (1992) deconstruction of language theory sparked the insight that *all* communication theory, not just language theory, is a kind of metadiscourse, a way of talking about talk, that derives much of its plausibility and interest by appealing rhetorically to commonplaces of everyday practical metadiscourse. Sociopsychological trait theories of communication, for example, seem plausible because they appeal to the commonplace notion that people's communication styles reflect their personalities. *Communication apprehension* theory is just a more sophisticated version of everyday metadiscourse about shyness, as in "she was afraid to talk to him because she's so shy."

My working assumption, then, to paraphrase Taylor (1992), is that the technical practice of communication theory largely derives from our ordinary, everyday practices of talking about communication, and my analysis of the broader, more heterogeneous field of communication theory follows Taylor's narrower, more tightly structured analysis of language theory in some respects. There is, however, an important difference. Whereas Taylor (1992) portrays language theory as a closed, self-referential game, completely divorced from the pragmatic functions that animate practical metadiscourse, I envision communication theory as an open field of discourse engaged with the problems of communication as a social practice, a theoretical metadiscourse that emerges from, extends, and informs practical metadiscourse.

In this vision, our task is not to *de*construct communication theory. (What would be the point? It's already a mess.) Rather, we must *re*construct communication theory as a theoretical metadiscourse engaged in dialogue with the practical metadiscourse of everyday life. This conception of theoretical metadiscourse embraces the implications and commitments that flow from a constitutive metamodel of communication. It acknowledges the reflexivity of communication theory and our consequent obligation, as theorists of communication, to address our theoretical work to the cultural situation that has given rise to our discipline. It acknowledges, in other words, the potential for communication theory to assist in the cultivation of communication as a social practice, and so for communication to develop as a practical discipline (Craig, 1989, 1995, 1996a, 1996b; Craig & Tracy, 1995).

In a practical discipline of communication, theory is designed to provide conceptual resources for reflecting on communication problems. It does this by theorizing (conceptually reconstructing) communicative practices within relatively abstract, explicitly reasoned, normative idealizations of communication (Craig, 1996b; Craig & Tracy, 1995). Communication can be theorized, of course, from many different perspectives, so the field of communication theory becomes a forum in which to discuss the relative merits of alternative practical theories. This discussion about alternative theories constitutes what I am calling theoretical metadiscourse.

Communication has the potential to be a practical discipline in the first place because "communication" is already a richly meaningful concept in our lifeworld. If ours is a culture in which we tend to think that all problems are fundamentally problems of communication (McKeon, 1957), in which we often find that we need to "sit down and talk" in order "to work out problems" in our relationships (Katriel & Philipsen, 1981), in which we ritually avow that communication is the only tie that can hold together a diverse society across the vast spatial and cultural gaps that divide us (Carey, 1989), then communication is already a topic much discussed throughout society, and everyone already knows that communication is important and worth studying in order to improve. Because communication is already so much talked about in society, communication theory can be constructed inductively through critical studies of everyday practice, in part by transcribing and theoretically reconstructing the "situated ideals" articulated by people themselves in their everyday metadiscourse. This critical-inductive way of constructing communication theory has been explored in earlier work on "grounded practical theory" (Craig & Tracy, 1995).

Communication also has the potential to be a practical discipline in part because communication is already an important theoretical category within a wide range of established disciplines, from which we can derive a rich array of conceptual resources for reflecting on the practice of communication. These already-established traditions of communication theory offer distinct, alternative vocabularies that can be critically reconstructed as alternative ways of conceptualizing communication problems and practices. The rich intellectual heritage of communication theory constitutes, then, a second starting point for constructing a field of communication theory. Communication theory can be constructed deductively, starting from theory, as well as inductively,

starting from practice. This critical-deductive way of constructing communication theory is the one we are exploring in the present essay.

Although theoretical ideas about communication have been developed in various disciplines with incommensurable intellectual agendas, it is nevertheless a reasonable working assumption that every one of those ideas is potentially relevant to practice. One interesting, although admittedly speculative, reason for thinking so is that communication may have been theorized in all these different disciplines during the 20th century in part just *because* it has become such a culturally important category of social practice. This assumption is consistent with the reflexivity, or mutual influence, between communication theory and cultural practice as suggested by Carey (1989), Deetz (1994), and other writers. From a rhetorical perspective, one way for an academic discipline to legitimize itself in the culture is to establish its social relevance by showing that it has something interesting to say about culturally salient themes and practical problems—such as, in our culture, communication.

If this is true that the widespread theorization of communication in so many different academic disciplines has arisen in part from an impulse toward practical relevance, then the multidisciplinary heritage of communication theory is ready-made, to some extent, for the purposes of a practical discipline. My goal in the remainder of this essay is to show how the potential practical relevance of all communication theories, whatever their disciplinary origins, can be exploited to construct a field, a common ground, a common (meta)discursive space, in which all communication theories can interact productively with each other and, through the medium of practical metadiscourse, with communication practice.

My method for reconstructing the traditions of communication theory to highlight their practical relevance loosely follows Taylor (1992). I assume that theoretical metadiscourse (that is, communication theory) derives from and theorizes practical metadiscourse (everyday ways of talking about communication), and in so doing both (a) appeals rhetorically to certain metadiscursive commonplaces, which is what makes a theory seem plausible and common-sensical from a lay point of view, and (b) skeptically challenges other metadiscursive commonplaces, which is what makes a theory seem interesting, insightful, or maybe absurdly nonsensical from a lay point of view. This combination of plausibility and interestingness constitutes the presumptive practical relevance of a theory. Because different theories turn out to be relevant in significantly different and often conflicting ways, theoretical metadiscourse turns back on itself to debate the differences and thereby constitutes itself as a dialogical-dialectical field. Our present task, then, is to jump-start that self-reflexive process in the field of communication theory.

A SKETCH OF THE FIELD: SEVEN TRADITIONS

So far, I have argued that communication theory is not yet a coherent field but has the potential to become a dialogical-dialectical field based on two principles: (a) a constitutive metamodel of communication, and (b) a conception of communication theory as metadiscursive practice within a practical discipline. To see where this approach might take us, I will sketch seven reconstructed traditions of communication theory, arrayed in a matrix that highlights practically relevant complementarities and tensions among them.

Tables 5.1 and 5.2 summarize the seven traditional standpoints, which are further discussed in the following pages. In Table 5.1, each tradition is identified by its characteristic definition of communication and its associated definition of communication problems, metadiscursive vocabulary, taken-for-granted metadiscursive commonplaces that make the tradition plausible, and metadiscursive commonplaces that the tradition interestingly reinterprets or challenges.

Table 5.2 continues the analysis by suggesting topoi (that is, dialectical commonplaces or stock arguments) for argumentation across the traditions. The purpose of Table 5.2 is to indicate distinctive critical objections that each tradition would typically raise against each tradition's typical way of analyzing communication practices.[15]

The traditions are briefly discussed in the following sections. The discussions generally follow and supplement Tables 5.1 and 5.2 but without commenting in detail on each cell. In order to illustrate the traditions, including blends of different traditions, I do cite recent literature on communication theory as appropriate. Without question, these are instrumental constructions rather than essential categories, but they represent recognizable communities of scholarship. While attempting to be inclusive, in selecting and defining the traditions I have made decisions that undoubtedly reflect my own intellectual biases and limitations. Other scholars are invited to point these out.

The contents of the seven traditions, I hope, will resonate with any reader who is moderately well acquainted with the broad range of communication theory. Several of the seven correspond fairly closely to certain chapters in Littlejohn's (1996b) influential textbook, for example. Despite the familiarity of the contents, however (these are, after all, *traditions* of communication theory), the structure of the matrix differs radically from conventional ways of dividing up the field. Communication theories have traditionally been classified by disciplinary origin (e.g. psychology, sociology, rhetoric), level of organization (e.g. interpersonal, organizational, mass), type of explanation (e.g. trait, cognitive, system-theoretic), or underlying epistemology (e.g. empiricist, interpretive, critical). By contrast, the scheme I am proposing divides the field according to underlying conceptions of communicative practice. A startling effect of this shift in perspective is that communication theories no longer bypass each other in their different paradigms or on their different levels. Communication theories suddenly now have something to agree and disagree about—and that "something" is communication, not epistemology.

The Rhetorical Tradition: Communication as a Practical Art of Discourse

> Formally speaking, rhetoric is the collaborative art of addressing and guiding decision and judgment—usually public judgment that cannot be decided by force or expertise. Rhetorical inquiry, more commonly known as the study of public communication, is one of the few areas of research that is still actively informed by its own traditions. . . . (Farrell, 1993, p. 1)

> The primary source of ideas about communication prior to this century, dating back to ancient times, was rhetoric. (Littlejohn, 1996a, p. 117)

In the tradition of rhetorical theory that originated with the ancient Greek sophists and runs through a long and varied history down to the present, communication has typically been theorized as *a practical art of discourse.*[16] This way of theorizing communication is useful for explaining why our participation in discourse, especially public discourse, is important and how it occurs, and holds forth the possibility that the practice of communication can be cultivated and improved through critical study and education. Problems of communication in the rhetorical tradition are conceived as social exigencies that can be resolved through the artful use of discourse to persuade audiences (Bitzer, 1968).

Rhetorical theory seems plausible and useful because it appeals to certain commonplace beliefs about communication. We all know that rhetoric is a powerful force in society. Most will readily agree that in matters of opinion it is good to hear about different sides of a question before reaching our own judgment, so rhetoric seems to be basically necessary and useful even though it is too often poorly done, annoying, or even seriously harmful. For such reasons it is important for us to understand how rhetoric works and to cultivate our abilities as critical consumers as well as effective producers of rhetoric. We know that some people are better communicators than others and that the best examples of rhetoric can

rise to the level of great art. Since we know that communicators vary in wisdom and skill and that skill, if not wisdom, can often be improved through instruction and practice, it is reasonable to think that people can become better communicators by learning and practicing methods of communication that can be invented or discovered through research and systematically taught. Moreover, once we understand that public advocacy is just one of many areas of communicative practice, such as interpersonal conversation, news reporting, CD-ROM design, and so on, it becomes obvious that all communication can be theorized as practical art and studied in much the same ways as rhetoric has traditionally been studied. This is why it now comports with common sense to think of communication as a practical discipline.

But, if the rhetorical tradition seems plausible and useful because it appeals to many commonplace beliefs about communication, it is also interesting because it challenges other commonplace beliefs and reveals some of the deepest paradoxes of communication. It challenges the commonplaces that mere words are less important than actions, that true knowledge is more than just a matter of opinion, and that telling the plain truth is something other than the strategic adaptation of a message to an audience. For over two millennia rhetorical theorists have disputed about the relative places of emotion and logic in persuasion, whether rhetoric is inherently good or bad or just a neutral tool, whether the art of rhetoric has any special subject matter of its own, and whether theory has any useful role to play in the improvement of practice. These are interesting questions—or can be made so by a skillful teacher—in part because they are deeply puzzling intellectually and in part because they can be connected to real problems that all of us face in our everyday lives. We really should reflect, for example, on how we are swayed by the emotional appeals that pervade political and commercial advertising, and rhetorical theory provides a useful vocabulary with which to conceptualize and discuss this common experience.

(Text continues on page 78)

Table 5.1 Seven Traditions of Communication Theory

	Rhetorical	Semiotic	Phenomenological	Cybernetic	Sociopsychological	Sociocultural	Critical
Communication theorized as:	The practical art of discourse	Intersubjective mediation by signs	Experience of otherness; dialogue	Information processing	Expression, interaction, and influence	(Re)production of social order	Discursive reflection
Problems of communication theorized as:	Social exigency requiring collective deliberation and judgment	Misunderstanding or gap between subjective viewpoints	Absence of, or failure to sustain, authentic human relationship	Noise; overload; underload; a malfunction or "bug" in a system	Situation requiring manipulation of causes of behavior to achieve specified outcomes	Conflict; alienation; misalignment; failure of coordination	Hegemonic ideology; systematically distorted speech situation
Metadiscursive vocabulary such as:	Art, method, communicator, audience, strategy, commonplace, logic, emotion	Sign, symbol, icon, index, meaning, referent, code, language, medium, (mis)understanding	Experience, self and other, dialogue, genuineness, supportiveness, openness	Source, receiver, signal, information, noise, feedback, redundancy, network, function	Behavior, variable, effect, personality, emotion, perception, cognition, attitude, interaction	Society, structure, practice, ritual, rule, socialization, culture, identity, coconstruction	Ideology, dialectic, oppression, consciousness-raising, resistance, emancipation

(Continued)

Table 5.1 (Continued)

	Rhetorical	Semiotic	Phenomenological	Cybernetic	Sociopsychological	Sociocultural	Critical
Plausible when appeals to metadiscursive commonplaces such as:	Power of words; value of informed judgment; improvability of practice	Understanding requires common language; omnipresent danger of miscommunication	All need human contact, should treat others as persons, respect differences, seek common ground	Identity of mind and brain; value of information and logic; complex systems can be unpredictable	Communication reflects personality; beliefs and feelings bias judgments; people in groups affect one another	The individual is a product of society; every society has a distinct culture; social actions have unintended effects	Self-perpetuation of power and wealth; values of freedom, equality, and reason; discussion produces awareness, insight
Interesting when challenges metadiscursive commonplaces such as:	Mere words are not actions; appearance is not reality; style is not substance; opinion is not truth	Words have correct meanings and stand for thoughts; codes and media are neutral channels	Communication is skill; the word is not the thing; facts are objective and values subjective	Humans and machines differ; emotion is not logical; linear order of cause and effect	Humans are rational beings; we know our own minds; we know what we see	Individual agency and responsibility; absolute identity of self; naturalness of the social order	Naturalness and rationality of traditional social order; objectivity of science and technology

Table 5.2 Topoi for Argumentation Across Traditions

	Rhetorical	Semiotic	Phenomenological	Cybernetic	Sociopsychological	Sociocultural	Critical
Against rhetoric	The art of rhetoric can be learned only by practice; theory merely distracts	We do not use signs; rather they use us	Strategic communication is inherently inauthentic and often counterproductive	Intervention in complex systems involves technical problems rhetoric fails to grasp	Rhetoric lacks good empirical evidence that its persuasive techniques actually work as intended	Rhetorical theory is culture bound and overemphasizes individual agency vs. social structure	Rhetoric reflects traditionalist, instrumentalist, and individualist ideologies
Against semiotics	All use of signs is rhetorical	Langue is a fiction; meaning and intersubjectivity are indeterminate	Langue-parole and signifier-signified are false distinctions. Languaging constitutes world	"Meaning" consists of functional relationships within dynamic information systems	Semiotics fails to explain factors that influence the production and interpretation of messages	Sign systems are not autonomous; they exist only in the shared practices of actual communities	Meaning is not fixed by a code; it is a site of social conflict
Against phenomenology	Authenticity is a dangerous myth; good communication must be artful, hence strategic	Self and other are semiotically determined subject positions and exist only in/as signs	Other's experience is not experienced directly but only as constituted in ego's consciousness	Phenomenological "experience" must occur in the brain as information processing	Phenomenological introspection falsely assumes self-awareness of cognitive processes	Intersubjectivity is produced by social processes that phenomenology fails to explain	Individual consciousness is socially constituted, thus ideologically distorted

(Continued)

Table 5.2 (Continued)

	Rhetorical	Semiotic	Phenomenological	Cybernetic	Sociopsychological	Sociocultural	Critical
Against cybernetics	Practical reason cannot (or should not) be reduced to formal calculation	Functionalist explanations ignore subtleties of sign systems	Functionalism fails to explain meaning as embodied, conscious experience	The observer must be included in the system, rendering it indeterminate	Cybernetics is too rationalistic; e.g. it underestimates the role of emotion	Cybernetic models fail to explain how meaning emerges in social interaction	Cybernetics reflects the dominance of instrumental reason
Against socio-psychology	Effects are situational and cannot be precisely predicted	Sociopsychological "effects" are internal properties of sign systems	The subject-object dichotomy of sociopsychology must be transcended	Communication involves circular causation, not linear causation	Sociopsychological theories have limited predictive power, even in laboratory	Sociopsychological "laws" are culture bound and biased by individualism	Sociopsychology reflects ideologies of individualism, instrumentalism
Against sociocultural theory	Sociocultural rules etc. are contexts and resources for rhetorical discourse	Sociocultural rules etc. are all systems of signs	The social lifeworld has a phenomenological foundation	The functional organization of any social system can be modeled formally	Sociocultural theory is vague, untestable, ignores psychological processes that underlie all social order	Sociocultural order is particular and locally negotiated but theory must be abstract and general	Sociocultural theory privileges consensus over conflict and change
Against critical theory	Practical reason is based in particular situations, not universal principles	There is nothing outside the text	Critique is immanent in every authentic encounter with tradition	Self-organizing systems models account for social conflict and change	Critical theory confuses facts and values, imposes a dogmatic ideology	Critical theory imposes an interpretive frame, fails to appreciate local meanings	Critical theory is elitist and without real influence on social change

The Semiotic Tradition: Communication as Intersubjective Mediation by Signs

[S]emiotics has paid a great deal of attention to how people convey meanings and thus has developed a vocabulary we can borrow for our own uses. (Leeds-Hurwitz, 1993, p. xv)

Miscommunication . . . is the scandal that motivates the concept of communication. (Peters, 1989, p. 397)

Semiotics, the study of signs, like rhetoric, has ancient roots (Manetti, 1993), but semiotics as a distinct tradition of communication theory can be said to have originated in the language theory of John Locke (the much neglected Book III).[17] This tradition runs through Peirce and Saussure, whose seminal works founded two quite different disciplines of semiotics, and continues down to current theories of language, discourse, interpretation, nonverbal communication, culture, and media. In the semiotic tradition, communication is typically theorized as *intersubjective mediation by signs.* Communication theorized in this way explains and cultivates the use of language and other sign systems to mediate between different perspectives. Problems of communication in the semiotic tradition are primarily problems of (re)presentation and transmission of meaning, of gaps between subjectivities that can be bridged, if only imperfectly, by the use of shared systems of signs.

Locke (1690/1979) argued that we cannot take it for granted that people ordinarily understand each other. Taylor (1992), as I mentioned earlier, shows how all language theories since Locke can be construed as a series of replies to Locke's skeptical argument against the commonplace assumption of intersubjective understanding. Semiotic theory now commonly asserts that signs construct their users (or "subject-positions"), that meanings are public and ultimately indeterminate, that understanding is a practical gesture rather than an intersubjective psychological state, and that codes and media of communication are not merely neutral structures or channels for the transmission of meanings but have sign-like properties of their own (the code shapes the content and the medium itself becomes a message, or even *the* message [McLuhan, 1964]).

Semiotic communication theory seems plausible and practical when it appeals to the common-sense beliefs that communication is easiest when we share a common language, that words can mean different things to different people so miscommunication is a constant danger, that meanings are often conveyed indirectly or by subtle aspects of behavior that may go unnoticed, and that certain ideas are easier to express in certain media (a picture is worth a thousand words; email should not be used for delicate business negotiations). On the other hand, semiotics can seem interesting, insightful, or even absurdly implausible to ordinary people when it challenges other commonplace beliefs such as that ideas exist in people's minds, that words have correct meanings, that meanings can be made explicit, that communication is a voluntary act, and that we use signs and media of communication as tools to represent and share our thoughts.

As distinct traditions within the field of communication theory, rhetoric and semiotics are closely akin in some ways and hybrids of the two are not uncommon (e.g. Burke, 1966; Kaufer & Carley, 1993a, 1993b). Rhetoric can be thought of as the branch of semiotics that studies the structures of language and argument that mediate between communicators and audiences. Semiotics can also be thought of as a particular theory of rhetoric that studies the resources that are available for conveying meanings in rhetorical messages.

But semiotics and rhetoric also have sharp differences with important practical implications. Peters points out that "Locke understood communication not as a kind of speech, rhetoric, or discourse, but an alternative to them" (1989, p. 394). In modernist thought, rhetoric has often been cast as the enemy of communication. Communication for modernists is all about reason, truth, clarity, and understanding; rhetoric is all about traditionalism, artifice, obfuscation, and manipulation. Communication marks the new way of science and enlightenment; rhetoric the old way of obscurantism and reaction.

In postmodernist thought, of course, all of this has largely been turned on its head. For poststructuralist semioticians all communication *is* rhetoric—if by rhetoric we mean uses of language for which reason, truth, clarity, and understanding can no longer be upheld as normative criteria. In the rhetorical tradition of communication theory, however, rhetoric typically means something quite different and arguably more useful (see above). It means communication designed to appeal to an audience and inform their judgment on important matters of opinion and decision. In short, the theoretical debate between rhetoric and semiotics is practically important because it is ultimately about the normative basis for our everyday use of concepts like judgment, meaning, and truth in practical metadiscourse.

The Phenomenological Tradition: Communication as the Experience of Otherness

> Phenomenological understanding of dialogue is not a theory imposed from above by some autocratic reason, but rather it is an exposition of the communicative process as it takes place in experience. (Pilotta & Mickunas, 1990, p. 81)

> Communication thus implies noncomprehension, for I am most firmly placed in a situation of communication with the other when I recognize that someone has come to me but do not understand why and do not quite understand what he, she, or it says. (Chang, 1996, p. 225)

In the mainly 20th-century tradition of phenomenology that runs from Husserl through the existential and hermeneutic phenomenologists and broadly includes such different sorts of thinkers as Martin Buber, Hans-Georg Gadamer, and Carl Rogers, communication is theorized as *dialogue* or *experience of otherness*. Communication theorized in this way explains the interplay of identity and difference in authentic human relationships and cultivates communication

practices that enable and sustain authentic relationships.

Authentic communication, or dialogue, is founded on the experience of direct, unmediated contact with others. Communicative understanding begins in prereflective experience arising from our bodily existence in a shared lifeworld. Once we set aside the dualisms of mind and body, subject and object, as phenomenologists argue, we see that direct, unmediated contact with others is a very real and utterly necessary human experience, although it may be a fleeting experience that easily degrades into some form of inauthenticity. For example, when I feel a cold or angry glance from another person, I first experience the glance as a direct expression of the other's coldness or anger directed to me, not as an external sign of an internal, mental state of the other that can be interpreted in different ways (see Pilotta & Mickunas, 1990, pp. 111–114). In thus experiencing the other's expression toward me, I directly experience our commonality and also our difference, not only the other as other to me but myself as other to the other.

Hence, phenomenology challenges the semiotic notion that intersubjective understanding can only be mediated by signs (Stewart, 1995, 1996) as well as the rhetorical notion that communication involves artful or strategic uses of signs. Although "dialogue does not just happen" (except as a fleeting experience) neither can it be "planned, pronounced, or willed" (Anderson, Cissna, & Arnett, 1994, p. xxi). My experience of the other's anger may be sustained in a dialogue that deepens our mutual understanding, but no conscious effort on my part can ensure such a happy outcome to an experience that, in the normal course of events, is more likely to alienate us. Among the paradoxes of communication that phenomenology brings to light is that conscious goal-seeking, however benevolent one's intentions may be, annihilates dialogue by interposing one's own goals and strategies as a barrier against one's direct experience of self and other. Problems of communication as conceived within the phenomenological tradition of communication theory thus arise from the necessity and yet the inherent difficulty—even, arguably, the practical impossibility—of sustained, authentic communication between persons.

The phenomenological tradition, despite the arcane language in which it is so often couched, can be made plausible to ordinary people through rhetorical appeals to the commonplace beliefs that we can and should treat each other as persons (I-Thou) not as things (I-It), and that it is important to acknowledge and respect differences, to learn from others, to seek common ground, and to avoid polarization and strategic dishonesty in human relations. We have all experienced encounters with others in which we seemed to discover an immediate understanding beyond words. We all know, as phenomenologists variously affirm, that honesty is the best policy, that supportive relationships are essential to our healthy development as human beings, and that the most satisfactory human relationships are characterized by reciprocity and nondomination.

Phenomenology, however, is not only plausible but also interesting from a practical standpoint because it both upholds dialogue as an ideal form of communication yet also demonstrates the inherent difficulty of sustaining dialogue. It challenges our commonsense faith in the reliability of techniques for achieving good communication. It problematizes such commonsense distinctions as those between mind and body, facts and values, words and things.

Phenomenology shares with rhetorical theory an impulse to search for common ground among people with differing points of view and with semiotics the assumption that what is fundamentally problematic in communication has to do with intersubjective understanding. Phenomenology differs sharply from rhetoric, though, on questions of authenticity versus artifice and just as radically from semiotics on the relation between language and meaning. Phenomenology, from a rhetorical point of view, can seem hopelessly naive or unhelpfully idealistic in approaching the practical dilemmas that real communicators must face whereas rhetoric, from a phenomenological point of view, can seem unduly cynical or pessimistic about the potential for authentic human contact. When rhetoric and phenomenology are combined the result is typically an antirhetorical rhetoric in which persuasion and strategic action are replaced by dialogue and openness to the other (e.g. Brent, 1996; Foss & Griffin, 1995; Freeman, Littlejohn, & Pearce, 1992), or else a hermeneutical rhetoric in which the roles of theory and method in communicative practice are downplayed (Gadamer, 1981; Leff, 1996).

Vis-à-vis semiotics, as Stewart (1995, 1996) has shown, the phenomenological tradition, with its doctrine of communication as direct contact, fundamentally questions the distinction between words and things and the assumption that communication can occur only through the mediation of signs. Thus, mixtures of semiotics and phenomenology can produce a theoretical compound that is deconstructively explosive if not impenetrably dense (e.g. Chang, 1996; Lanigan, 1992). In reply to this poststructuralist challenge, the traditional semiotician argues that signs must have stable meanings in order for communication to occur in practice (Ellis, 1991, 1995), whereas the traditional phenomenologist reiterates that the communicative use of language is a form of direct, unmediated contact between persons (Stewart, 1995).

What is at stake pragmatically in the debate between semiotics and phenomenology is obliquely illustrated by Peters (1994). It is commonly asserted that interpersonal interaction is the basic form of human communication and that mass or technologically mediated communication is at best a poor substitute for direct human contact. Peters (1994), who elsewhere has severely criticized Lockean semiotics (Peters, 1989), here relies on the semiotic assumption of an inherent "gap" between transmission and reception of messages in order to argue that mass communication is actually more basic than interpersonal. "No distance," he now argues, "is so great as that between two minds," and "Dialogue conceals general features of discourse that are more evident in texts, especially the fact of distanciation" (p. 130). In the end, however, Peters acknowledges that both dialogue and mediated communication are important, but difficult to combine because of "an enduring tension between specific and general modes of address" (p. 136). Only dialogue satisfies the basic human needs for "companionship, friendship and love," but mass communication expresses an "equally noble impulse" toward normative universality that often conflicts with the demands of intimacy (p. 136). "The distinction, then, between interpersonal and mass communication has hidden utopian energies" (p. 136) and potentially illuminates "our plight as creatures who belong both to a family and to a polis" (p. 137).

The Cybernetic Tradition: Communication as Information Processing

> We have decided to call the entire field of control and communication theory, whether in the machine or in the animal, by the name of Cybernetics. (Wiener, 1948, p. 19)

> Modern communication theory arose out of the cybernetic marriage of statistics and control theory. (Krippendorff, 1989, p. 444)

> Communication theory, the study and statement of the principles and methods by which information is conveyed . . . (Oxford English Dictionary, 1987)

> Communication theory. See INFORMATION THEORY. (Audi, 1995)

Modern communication theory originated with the cybernetic tradition and the work of such mid-20th-century thinkers as Shannon, Wiener, von Neumann, and Turing (Heims, 1991; Krippendorff, 1989). This cybernetic tradition extends to current theories in areas as diverse as systems and information science, cognitive science and artificial intelligence, functionalist social theory, network analysis, and the Batesonian school of interpersonal communication (e.g., Watzlawick, Beavin, & Jackson, 1967). Communication in the cybernetic tradition is theorized as *information processing* and explains

how all kinds of complex systems, whether living or nonliving, macro or micro, are able to function and why they often malfunction. Epitomizing the transmission model, cybernetics conceives of communication problems as breakdowns in the flow of information resulting from noise, information overload, or mismatch between structure and function and, as resources for solving communication problems, offers various information-processing technologies and related methods of systems design and analysis, management and, on the "softer" side, therapeutic intervention.

Cybernetics has plausibility as a way of theorizing communication in part because it appeals rhetorically to the commonplace assumptions of everyday materialism, functionalism, and rationalism. For cybernetics, the distinction between mind and matter is only a functional distinction like that between software and hardware. Thought is nothing more than information processing and so it makes perfect sense to say that individual thought is "intrapersonal" communication and that groups and organizations also think, whole societies think, robots and artificial organisms will eventually think.[18] Cybernetics thus evokes the plausibility of a world in which Commander Data might be truly the most "human" member of the *Enterprise* crew: To assert otherwise is merely soft-headed sentimentality (a two-edged criticism in this case). Cybernetics, then, is also interesting and sometimes implausible from a commonsense view because it points out surprising analogies between living and nonliving systems, challenges commonplace beliefs about the significance of consciousness and emotion, and questions our usual distinctions between mind and matter, form and content, the real and the artificial.

Cybernetics also challenges simplistic notions of linear cause and effect by appealing to our commonsense understanding that communication processes can be enormously complex and subtle. Although rooted in technological functionalist thought, it emphasizes the problems of technological control, the perverse complexity and unpredictability of feedback processes, and the pervasive likelihood that communicative acts will have unintended consequences despite our best intentions. A great practical lesson of cybernetics is that the whole is greater than the sum of the parts, so it is important for us as communicators to transcend our individual perspectives, to look at the communication process from a broader, systemic viewpoint, and not to hold individuals responsible for systemic outcomes that no individual can control.

In valorizing technique and artifice, cybernetics shares common ground with rhetoric;[19] in collapsing human agency into underlying or overarching symbol-processing systems it resembles semiotics;[20] in stressing the emergence of meaning in the interactions among elements of a system it is like phenomenology.[21] Cybernetics, however, also has sharp differences with each of these other traditions. Communication as rhetoric is artful discourse that informs practical judgment, but communication as information processing is merely a mechanism that performs certain functions. Semiotics has problems with the cybernetic notion of "information," which reduces semantic content (*what* a message means) to mere function (such as feedback or reduction of uncertainty). For the phenomenologist, authentic communication requires congruency between experience and expression, so sincerity is essential to the I-thou relationship of dialogue. But the cybernetician (like the semiotician) points out that we can never really know if another person, or even oneself, is being sincere in this way. From a cybernetic view, there are probably better ways to evaluate the reliability of information, rather than trying to figure out if someone is being sincere.

In general, then, cybernetics, in contrast to other traditions of communication theory, cultivates a practical attitude that appreciates the complexity of communication problems and questions many of our usual assumptions about the differences between human and non-human information processing systems.

The Sociopsychological Tradition: Communication as Expression, Interaction, and Influence

> [In the 1950s] the study of communication found its greatest exemplars in the voting studies of Lazarsfeld and Berelson and the experimental persuasion studies of Hovland. By the mid-1950s, theoretically-focused communication study was concerned with issues of effects. This work recreated the general mediational framework in social psychology that was already evident in the 1930s . . . the mediating roles in communication of recipient predispositions and social processes, and . . . the possibility of differential effects. (Delia, 1987, p. 63)

> [T]he kinds of "why" questions communication scholars choose to answer may differ from those that intrigue psychologists. . . . As communication theorists, we also need to understand when, how, and why interaction alters sender behavior patterns and receiver judgments. (Burgoon & Buller, 1996, pp. 316–317)

The 20th-century tradition of experimental social psychology, which continues to predominate in much of what is called "communication science" (Berger & Chaffee, 1987), theorizes communication as *a process of expression, interaction, and influence,* a process in which the behavior of humans or other complex organisms expresses psychological mechanisms, states, and traits and, through interaction with the similar expressions of other individuals, produces a range of cognitive, emotional, and behavioral effects.

Communication, in short, is the process by which individuals interact and influence each other. Communication may occur face-to-face or through technological media and may flow from one to one, one to many, or many to many, but in all formats it involves (contrary to the phenomenological view) interposed elements that mediate between individuals. Whereas for semiotics communication is mediated by signs and sign systems, for social psychology it is mediated by psychological predispositions (attitudes, emotional states, personality traits, unconscious conflicts, social cognitions, etc.) as modified by the emergent effects of social interaction (which may include the effects of media technologies and institutions as well as interpersonal influence).

Communication theorized in this way explains the causes and effects of social behavior and cultivates practices that attempt to exert intentional control over those behavioral causes and effects. Communication problems in the sociopsychological tradition are thus thought of as situations that call for the effective manipulation of the causes of behavior in order to produce objectively defined and measured outcomes.

Social psychology seems plausible and practically useful because it appeals to our commonsense beliefs and our everyday practical concerns about the causes and effects of communication. We readily believe that our ways of communicating and our reactions to the communications of others vary according to our individual personalities. Human nature being what it is, we are not surprised to learn that our judgments can be influenced by the immediate social context and are often biased in predicable ways by our strong beliefs, attitudes, and emotional states. We know too that interactional processes in groups, such as those involving leadership and conflict, can affect group outcomes, so it is important to understand these causal relations in order to manage the processes effectively.

While appealing to these commonplace beliefs, sociopsychological theory deeply challenges the equally commonsensical premise that humans are rational beings. Its recurrent demonstrations of human weakness and irrationality challenge our commonsense faith in our own personal autonomy.[22] Moreover, social psychology skeptically questions all unproven assumptions about causal influences on human behavior, for which it requires—and attempts to provide—rigorous experimental evidence. It criticizes rhetoric, for example, for lacking proof that its persuasive techniques really work, and cybernetics for reducing all communication to information

processing algorithms that ignore the vagaries of motivation, personality, and emotion. As a mode of social practice, social psychology, like cybernetics, valorizes technique; it holds forth the promise that our lives can be improved through the self-conscious application by experts of techniques of psychological manipulation and therapy. Thus, a sociopsychological theory of rhetoric tends to view rhetoric more as a technology of psychological manipulation rather than an art of discourse that informs the receiver's judgment. Social psychology is not, however, without its own moral view: It implies a strong moral imperative that we as individual communicators should make responsible choices based on scientific evidence concerning the likely consequences of our messages.

The Sociocultural Tradition: Communication as the (Re)Production of Social Order

> Communication is a symbolic process whereby reality is produced, maintained, repaired, and transformed. (Carey, 1989, p. 23)

> Wherever activities or artifacts have symbolic values that articulate individuals into positions vis-à-vis each other or their collectivities, the communicative is present. (Rothenbuhler, 1993, p. 162)

> A communication practice—or discursive practice—is, then, an actual means of expression in a community, given that community's specific scenes and historical circumstances (in the broadest sense). (Carbaugh, 1996, p. 14)

Sociocultural communication theory represents the "discovery" of communication, largely since the 19th century and partly under the influence of semiotic thought, within the intellectual traditions of sociology and anthropology. Communication in these traditions is typically theorized as *a symbolic process that produces and reproduces shared sociocultural patterns.* So conceived, communication explains how social order (a macro-level phenomenon) is created, realized, sustained, and transformed in micro-level interaction processes. We exist in a sociocultural environment that is constituted and maintained in large part by symbolic codes and media of communication.[23] The term "(re)production" suggests the paradoxical reflexivity of this process. Our everyday interactions with others depend heavily on preexisting, shared cultural patterns and social structures. From this point of view, our everyday interactions largely "reproduce" the existing sociocultural order. But, social interaction is also a creative process that permits and even requires a good deal of improvisation that, albeit collectively and in the long run, "produces" the very social order that makes interaction possible in the first place. A central problem of sociocultural theory is thus to find the right balance, to sort out the complex relations between, production and reproduction, micro and macro, agency and structure, particular local culture and universal natural law, in social life. A primary axis of debate is between structural theories that give explanatory priority to relatively stable, macro-level patterns and interpretive or interactionist theories that give priority to micro-level processes in which social order is locally cocreated and negotiated by members.[24]

Communication problems in the sociocultural tradition are thought of as gaps across space (sociocultural diversity and relativity) and across time (sociocultural change) that disable interaction by depleting the stock of shared patterns on which interaction depends. Conflicts, misunderstandings, and difficulties in coordination increase when social conditions afford a scarcity of shared rituals, rules, and expectations among members. Sociocultural theory thus has much to say about problems arising from technological change, breakdown of traditional social orders, urbanization and mass society, bureaucratic rationalization and, more recently, postmodern cultural fragmentation and globalization. Such perturbations in the ecology of codes and media disrupt interaction but at the same time enable the creative production of new meanings and new means of communication.

Hybrids of sociocultural and other traditions of communication theory are quite common, so common indeed that relatively "pure" exemplars of sociocultural communication theory may be hard to come by. Social action media theory, for example, melds a range of sociocultural, phenomenological, and semiotic perspectives (Schoening & Anderson, 1995). CMM (Coordination Management of Meaning) theory melds interactionist social theory with cybernetic and dialogical concepts (Cronen, 1995; Pearce, 1989). Conversation analysis has interactionist, phenomenological, and semiotic roots (Heritage, 1984).

Rhetorical theory in the 20th century has also taken a strongly sociocultural turn in which rhetoric has quite often been conceptualized as an instrument for improving human relations (Ehninger, 1968), and "some have argued that acculturation to the forms and practices of organizations, social groups, sciences, technologies, subcultures, and cultures is significantly rhetorical learning . . . [of] what is communicatively appropriate to particular bodies of content in particular situations" (Arnold, 1989, p. 464). Sociocultural order thus constitutes the materials of rhetoric while rhetoric becomes a method, whether consciously or unconsciously applied, for the constitution of social order.

In all of these hybrid traditions, however, a distinct sociocultural "voice" can be heard. It is the voice, for example, that criticizes social psychology for its excessive individualism, inattention to macro-social forces, and insensitivity to cultural differences and calls, again and again, for sociopsychologically dominated communication research to adopt a more "cultural" or "social" approach.[25] Likewise it criticizes classical rhetoric for its naive assumptions about agency (in portraying great orators as shapers of history, for example), and semiotics for abstracting signs and sign processes from the larger sociocultural context in which they function.

This sociocultural voice has also worked its way into everyday practical metadiscourse. Sociocultural theory is plausible from a lay point of view in part because it appeals rhetorically to the commonplace beliefs that individuals are products of their social environments, that groups develop particular norms, rituals, and world views, that social change can be difficult and disruptive, and that attempts to intervene actively in social processes often have unintended consequences. But sociocultural theory also challenges many commonplace assumptions, especially our tendencies to take for granted the absolute reality of our own and others' personal identities, to think of social institutions as if they were inevitable natural phenomena, to be ethnocentric or insensitive to cultural differences, and to overattribute moral responsibility to individuals for problems, like poverty and crime, that are largely societal in origin. Sociocultural theory cultivates communicative practices that acknowledge cultural diversity and relativity, value tolerance and understanding, and emphasize collective more than individual responsibility. The everyday practical discourse of blame and responsibility, for example, has clearly been influenced by theoretical discourses on "society" in the sociocultural tradition (Bowers & Iwi, 1993).

The Critical Tradition: Communication as Discursive Reflection

> For the communicative model of action, language is relevant only from the pragmatic viewpoint that speakers, in employing sentences with an orientation to reaching understanding, take up relations to the world, not only directly as in teleological, normatively regulated or dramaturgical action, but in a reflective way. . . . They no longer relate straightaway to something in the objective, social, or subjective worlds; instead they relativize their utterances against the possibility that their validity will be contested by other actors. (Habermas, 1984, p. 98)

> When we see the constraints that limit our choices we are aware of power relations; when we see only choices we live in and reproduce power. (Lannamann, 1991, p. 198)

> Systematically distorted communication, then, is an ongoing process within particular systems as they strategically (though latently) work to reproduce, rather than produce, themselves. (Deetz, 1992, p. 187)

> Undoability is the ultimate consequence of the adage that power becomes slippery when reflected upon. (Krippendorff, 1995, p. 113)

The origins of critical communication theory can be traced to Plato's conception of Socratic dialectic as a method for attaining truth in the give and take of disputative interaction by asking questions that provoke critical reflection upon the contradictions that come to light in the process. Critical communication theory emphasizes a certain instability that inheres, according to Habermas (1984), in every act of communication oriented to the achievement of mutual understanding, a built-in telos towards articulating, questioning, and transcending presuppositions that are judged to be untrue, dishonest, or unjust. Communication that involves only the transmission-reception or ritual sharing of meanings is inherently faulty, distorted, incomplete. Authentic communication occurs only in a process of *discursive reflection* that moves towards a transcendence that can never be fully and finally achieved—but the reflective process itself is progressively emancipatory.

The tradition of critical social theory (broadly construed) runs from Marx through the Frankfurt School to Habermas, or alternatively through other strands of late Marxism and post-Marxism to current theories of political economy, critical cultural studies, feminist theory, and related schools of theory associated with new social movements (such as postcolonial theory and queer theory).[26] For critical communication theory, the basic "problem of communication" in society arises from material and ideological forces that preclude or distort discursive reflection. Communication conceived in this way explains how social injustice is perpetuated by ideological distortions and how justice can potentially be restored through communicative practices that enable critical reflection or consciousness-raising in order to unmask those distortions and thereby enable political action to liberate the participants from them.

The critical tradition is plausible from a lay point of view when it appeals to commonplace beliefs about the omnipresence of injustice and conflict in society, the ways in which power and domination can overcome truth and reason, and the potential for discourse with others to produce liberating insight, demystification, perhaps even the realization that one has been "had." Critical theory appeals to commonplace values of freedom, equality, and reason, yet it challenges many of our commonplace assumptions about what is reasonable. It challenges the naturalness of the social order and questions the rational validity of all authority, tradition, and conventional belief—including traditional beliefs about the nature of reason itself which, it claims, have distorted reason in the service of capitalism, racism, and patriarchy. It challenges commonplace assumptions about the objectivity and moral-political neutrality of science and technology. It challenges the pervasive individualism of our culture and the ideological dominance of instrumental reason, the assumption that rationality consists entirely in means-ends calculations where the ends in question can only be voluntaristically chosen based on individual interests. It is, or at least tries to be, the most deeply practical kind of theory, although its notion of what is practical often clashes sharply with commonsense notions of practicality. Fundamentally, in the tradition of Marx, its point is not to understand the world—and certainly not to teach students how to get along successfully in the world as it is. Its point is to change the world through praxis, or theoretically reflective social action.

Any mode of communication theory can take a self-reflexive, critical turn and so produce a hybrid variety such as critical rhetoric (McKerrow, 1989) or critical semiotics (Hodge & Kress, 1993; Fairclough, 1995). Most interesting, from the standpoint of dialogical-dialectical coherence, are efforts to acknowledge and work through the contradictions between critical theory and other traditions of communication

theory as, for example, Condit (1989) and Farrell (1993) have done in rhetorical theory. The literature on critical theory vis-à-vis sociocultural theory is, of course, vast, indeed nearly coextensive with the entire body of recent social theory, for critical theory is inherently a critique of the reproduction of social order that is sociocultural theory's central theme.

Yet, critical theory offers, I believe, a model for communication practice that differs radically from the sociocultural model of communication as (re)production. For the critical theorist, an activity that merely reproduces existing social order, or even one that produces new social order, is not yet authentic communication. In order for social order to be based on genuine mutual understanding (as distinct from strategic manipulation, oppressive conformity, or empty ritual), it recurrently becomes necessary for communicators to articulate, question, and openly discuss their differing assumptions about the objective world, moral norms, and inner experience (Habermas, 1984, pp. 75–101; also see Deetz, 1992, 1994).

The critical-theoretic model of communication as discursive reflection thus resembles the phenomenological concept of dialogue, to which it adds, however, a distinctly dialectical aspect. In a critical perspective, phenomenological dialogue represents an ideal form of communication but one that existing sociocultural conditions may render unlikely. A model of dialogue is defective, therefore, that fails to move participants towards reflection on the sociocultural conditions that potentially disable dialogue. It is the dialectical questioning of presuppositions that unmasks those conditions and thereby points the way to social changes that would render genuine dialogue possible. A similar pattern of communication characterizes various forms of ideology critique and feminist or identity-based consciousness-raising. It also clearly applies to Krippendorff's (1995) recent theory of "undoing" power, a work that draws upon cybernetic and phenomenological modes of communication theory to create a hybrid critical theory that seems considerably more sanguine than most other critical theories about the potential for insight alone (in the absence of concerted political action) to change the world.

Critical theory is criticized from other theoretical traditions for politicizing science and scholarship, and for asserting a universal normative standard for communication based on a priori ideology. Some critics of critical theory believe that science should have nothing to say about normative standards; others that normative standards should be based on objective empirical criteria; still others that normative standards can only be relative to local cultures and particular communication practices. In response to its critics, critical theory criticizes other theoretical traditions for their blindness to their own ideological presuppositions and their false pretensions to political neutrality. For critical theorists, local practices and empirical outcomes of communication cannot be taken at face value but must always be judged in light of a reflective analysis of the distorting effects of power and ideology in society.

As these arguments go on, perhaps the most useful contribution of critical theory, aside from its obvious relevance to the discourse of social injustice and change, may be to cultivate a deeper appreciation of discursive reflection as a practical possibility intrinsic to all communication. Communication, as I pointed out earlier, is not only something we do, it is something we recurrently talk about in ways that are practically entwined with our doing of it. This practical metadiscourse always has the potential to develop into a truly reflective discourse that engages communication theory with practice (Craig, 1996b). A critical tradition of communication theory thus confirms that reflective discourse and, therefore, communication theory itself, have important roles to play in our everyday understanding and practice of communication.

WORKING THE FIELD:
CONCLUDING REFLECTIONS

This preliminary sketch of communication theory as a field presents much to think about

and leaves much to do. I conclude with brief reflections on the agenda for future work and implications for disciplinary practice in communication studies.

The Work Ahead: Exploration, Creation, Application

The work ahead involves *exploring* the field to discover key issues and map the complex topography of the traditions; *creating* new traditions of communication theory and new ways of schematizing the field; and *applying* communication theory by engaging it with practical metadiscourse on communication problems.

Exploring the field involves both traversing the traditions to explore the complementarities and tensions among them and spelunking the traditions to explore their internal complexity.

The theoretical matrix invites us to locate points of agreement and disagreement among the traditions of communication theory. In so doing, we will articulate central themes and problems of communication theory as a field. Notions of communication strategy and technique, for example, are salient in several traditions. But thinking across these traditions, including rhetoric, phenomenology, cybernetics, social psychology, and critical theory, problematizes these notions in theoretically and practically interesting ways. The problem of strategy versus authenticity (rhetoric or social psychology versus phenomenology), the problem of intentionality versus functionality (rhetoric or phenomenology versus cybernetics), the problem of proving the effectiveness of techniques (social psychology versus rhetoric), the problem of instrumental reason as ideological distortion (critical theory versus cybernetics or social psychology)—these problems can now be recognized and addressed as central, field-defining problems of communication theory.

As we further explore the traditions it will be important to bear in mind that each tradition is internally complex and open to multiple interpretations. The traditions of communication theory can be redefined, recombined, hybridized, and subdivided in various ways. The rhetorical tradition includes many proliferating and contending schools of thought as do semiotics, phenomenology, and so on. Theoretical fields may appear like fractals—graphic functions that have the same formal properties at every level of granularity. Each tradition of communication theory itself is a complex field which, when magnified, displays a dialogical-dialectical field structure of multiple traditions much like that of communication theory as a whole. If we zoom out to a coarser level of granularity, the field of communication theory collapses into one tradition of thought within a complex mega-field of the human sciences. Perhaps an ideal, "user-friendly" way of representing communication theory would be in the form of an interactive hypertext that would allow us to pursue the subject on a myriad of paths through hyperlinks within and across levels to hybrid traditions and alternative schematizations, cognate disciplines, and multimedia recordings of communication practices linking theory to practical metadiscourse.[27]

Creating new theory is a task that our efforts to explore the field will inevitably necessitate and inspire as we stumble over conceptual gaps, new ideas, and new forms and practices of communication.

Each of the seven traditions is based on a unique model of communicative practice, essentially different from all others in the matrix. They compose, therefore, a distinguishable set of alternatives, but not a logically exhaustive set. The field of communication theory is logically open to new traditions, subject only to the limitation that each new tradition must be based on a unique model of communicative practice that, when integrated into the field (which may involve redefining other traditions) is not logically redundant with any other model.

Any of the following traditions, for example, might potentially be reconstructed to create distinct theorizations of communicative practice:

• A feminist tradition in which communication might be theorized as *connectedness to others,* thus giving voice to "the distinctive emphasis that many women put on contextual thinking and decision-making, a focus on the importance and usefulness of talk, connectedness, and relationships" (Kramarae, 1989, p. 157; also see Foss & Griffin, 1995). How would this model of communication differ from the phenomenological model of dialogue? How would it resituate feminism vis-à-vis critical theory?

• An aesthetic tradition in which communication might be theorized as *embodied performance,* thus highlighting the "poetic" aspect of communication in the creation of rituals, relationships, meanings, and truths (e.g. Conquergood, 1992; Hopper, 1993). How would this differ from semiotic and sociocultural models of communication? How would it reposition rhetoric and critical theory in the field (Conquergood, 1992; Laffoon, 1995)?

• An economic tradition in which communication might be theorized as *exchange,* thus emphasizing that every message (anything transferable from one agent to another) has an exchange value that equates to its meaning. What would this tradition look like, reconstructed after extracting it from its several entanglements with other traditions such as critical theory (Schiller, 1994), phenomenology (Chang, 1996), and social psychology (Roloff, 1981)?

• A spiritual tradition in which communication might be theorized as *communion on a non-material or mystical plane of existence,* thus revealing the ultimately ineffable roots of community—and its practical dependency on faith—in a realm of experience that transcends history and all human differences (e.g. Cooper, 1994; Crawford, 1996; Goodall, 1996; Pym, 1997; Ramsey, 1997). How does this transcendent community intersect with other kinds of transcendence posited by phenomenology (in dialogue), sociocultural theory (in culture), and critical theory (in reflection)?

If these examples seem facile, consider the rigorous standard imposed by the requirement that every new tradition must contribute a unique theorization of communicative practice. For example, the idea of a biological tradition of communication theory might seem plausible given the recent interest in biological approaches to communication (e.g. Cappella, 1996), but I am not aware of any distinct biological way of theorizing communicative practice that would not be better described as semiotic (e.g. Liska, 1993), sociopsychological (e.g. Cappella, 1991, 1995), or cybernetic (as in studies of genetic information processing or feedback loops in ecosystems). Communication practice, theorized as mediation by signs (semiotics), interaction (social psychology), or information processing (cybernetics), can perhaps be explained by biological principles such as those of organismic development or evolution by natural selection (Cappella, 1991, 1995, 1996; Hauser, 1996; Horvath, 1995), but I am unaware of any unique biological conceptualization of communicative practice itself. A tradition that does not meet this rigorous standard is logically outside the field of communication theory.

This does not, of course, rule out the possibility that someone will discover or invent a biological theorization of communication. New ideas are always emerging in academic discourse and may suggest new ways of theorizing communication. New theorizations of communication can also emerge from grounded practical theory, through the critical study and conceptual reconstruction of communicative practices in any cultural tradition or local setting (Craig & Tracy, 1995). In principle, then, we have every reason to assume that new traditions of communication theory and new views on old traditions will continue to be discovered or invented, so we should not hope, nor need we worry, that the work of creating communication theory will ever be completed.

Applying communication theory involves engaging the traditions of theoretical metadiscourse with practical metadiscourse on real communication problems. It is in this process of application that communication theory can most logically be tested to establish its relevance and usefulness for guiding the conduct and criticism of practice.[28] Each tradition provides a metadiscursive vocabulary in which communication problems and practices can be conceptualized and discussed. Mastering multiple vocabularies of communication theory makes it possible to examine communication problems from various points of view and to apply vocabularies that seem appropriate and helpful in each case.[29] Because each tradition appeals to some metadiscursive commonplaces while challenging others, each vocabulary has the potential to provoke and inform metacommunicative reflection. Discussions about whether someone is being overly "strategic" in their communication, for example, might apply the vocabularies of rhetoric and phenomenology and provoke reflection on the paradoxes of radically authentic communication. Such a reflective discourse can move along a continuum between theory and practice and, in its more theoretical moments, can become indistinguishable from the theoretical metadiscourse of communication theory itself (Craig, 1996b). In these moments of intersection between theoretical and practical metadiscourse, the work of exploring, creating, and applying communication theory merges in one activity.

Implications for Disciplinary Practice in Communication Studies

The main implication for our disciplinary practice is that we communication theorists all now have something very important to argue about—the social practice of communication—so we should stop ignoring each other and start addressing our work to the field of communication theory. As a result of our doing so, there will be a field of communication theory.

What exactly is involved in addressing our work to the field? Three things, I suggest (along with Anderson, 1996): (a) orienting to the field as a broad disciplinary audience; (b) giving voice to the field's distinctive concerns in interdisciplinary research; and (c) educating our students in the field. To elaborate:

1. Communication theorists should address their writing, even though usually on specialized topics, to the field as a whole. This means they should show an awareness of relevant traditions of communication theory, engage central themes and issues in the field, highlight practical implications, and respond to interests and criticisms anticipated from other traditions. Given the realities of academic specialization, individual scholars cannot be expected to understand every area of the field in depth. Arguments directed across traditions will not always, then, be very innovative and may be technically naïve in some respects. But still they will signal the field-relevance of the work and provide entry points (and motivating irritants) for other scholars, more deeply involved at the intersections between certain theoretical traditions, to correct errors, clarify issues, and carry the discussion to deeper levels. That is what dialogical-dialectical coherence might look like in practice.

2. The theoretical matrix suggests both the interdisciplinary centrality as well as the disciplinary focus of communication studies. Every tradition refers to interdisciplinary research areas (in political communication, semiotics and cultural studies, philosophy, information science, and so on) that can be enriched by other perspectives from communication theory. Tracy (1990, 2001), for example, has asserted a distinct communication approach to interdisciplinary discourse studies, characterized by its normative and applied interests, awareness of audience, and focus on problems and strategies. These characteristics bespeak a blend of rhetorical, sociopsychological, and other influences from communication theory. Communication scholars informed by the traditions of their field have opportunities to move beyond productive fragmentation and contribute something more to interdisciplinary studies.

3. Those of us who teach communication theory face unique challenges. Undergraduates come to communication classes for something practical and we offer them theory. They come for something comprehensible and we offer them fragments of a subject no one can comprehend—up to 249 theories and still counting. The analysis in Tables 5.1 and 5.2 invites a pedagogy that treats the entire field as a resource for reflecting on practical problems and, in moving from a sketchy overview more deeply into the field, moves not away from practical concerns but more deeply into them.

Advanced students must also learn to use communication theory in other ways. Students wanting to do original research "cannot ignore the need to specialize methodologically, and hence theoretically" (Reeves, 1992, p. 238). Still, a broad overview of the field can enable them to address the implications of specialized work to wider disciplinary, interdisciplinary, and lay audiences. The "job" of learning communication theory at an advanced level becomes a little easier for specialists in each tradition who can focus primarily on "their own" row and column of Table 5.2—that is, on issues between their own tradition of communication theory and other traditions. Other cells in the matrix can largely be left to specialists in other traditions.

Drawing on one tradition of communication theory, we might think of Tables 5.1 and 5.2 as a scaffold for building a scheme of rhetorical invention—a scheme of commonplaces and stock arguments—that can assist in preparing students of communication to participate in the discourse of the discipline at large, just as the traditional art of rhetoric prepares citizens to participate in the discourse of general public affairs. The art of rhetoric appeals to "commonplace" or "public" or "social" knowledge—knowledge already shared in common by members of an audience. Similarly, the field of communication theory marks out a common discursive space—a space for theoretical metadiscourse—in which more specialized theoretical discourses can engage with each other and with practical metadiscourse on questions of communication as a social practice. This field of communication theory is not a repository of absolute truth. It claims no more than to be useful.

Notes

1. For a far from complete sample of recent books presenting original work explicitly on general communication theory, without regard to disciplinary origin but excluding work on more specific topics like media effects or interpersonal relationships, see Altheide (1995), Anderson (1996), Angus & Langsdorf (1992), Carey (1989), Chang (1996), Deetz (1992), Goodall (1996), Greene (1997), Harris (1996), Hauser (1996), Kaufer & Carley (1993a), Leeds-Hurwitz (1995), Mantovani (1996), Mortensen (1994, 1997), Norton & Brenders (1995), Pearce (1989), Pilotta & Mickunas (1990), Rothenbuhler (1998), Sigman (1995b), Stewart (1995), J. Taylor (1993), T. Taylor (1992), Theall (1995).

2. There are some indicators of a field (see Anderson, 1996; Craig, 1989). Further, histories of communication theory are beginning to appear (Mattelart, 1996; Schiller, 1996); and collective works (handbooks, encyclopedias, anthologies) of varying currency, inclusiveness, and usefulness can be found (e.g. Arnold & Bowers, 1984; Barnouw et al., 1989; Casmir, 1994; Cobley, 1996; Crowley & Mitchell, 1994; Cushman & Kovacic, 1995; Kovacic, 1997; Philipsen & Albrecht, 1997).

3. Communication theory comes from many different academic disciplines, and scholars notoriously ignore work published outside of their own disciplines. Hence, they tend to write about communication while paying no attention to work being done anywhere else, most especially within the communication discipline proper. To their credit, communication scholars themselves have tended to deviate from this pattern. They frequently cite work from other disciplines. Indeed, often they are more likely to cite work from outside than inside their own discipline. Hence, they tend not to cite each other, beyond their own little cliques, which has the unintended consequence that communication scholars are relatively little cited by anyone either inside *or* outside of their own discipline (Myers, Brashers, Center, Beck, & Wert-Gray, 1992; Paisley, 1984; Reeves & Borgman, 1983; Rice, Borgman, & Reeves, 1988; So, 1988).

4. "It is as if the field of communication research were punctuated by a number of isolated frog ponds—with no friendly croaking between the ponds, very little productive intercourse at all, few cases of successful cross-fertilization" (Rosengren, 1993, p. 9).

5. Hence, it is not surprising that one writer asks why there are so few communication theories (Berger, 1991) while another asks why there are so many (Craig, 1993). They disagree not only on what to count as a theory but on the size and shape of the field in which they are counting theories.

6. General histories of communication studies (Delia, 1987; Rogers, 1994) have also emphasized the field's multidisciplinary origins.

7. Dance & Larson (1976) extended the list to 126 definitions, a number that, in the nature of things, can only have increased with time.

8. For a critique that emphasizes the more oppressive, exclusionary tendencies of traditional disciplines, see McLaughlin (1995), Sholle (1995), and Streeter (1995). Although these critics are against the "discipline" of communication, they are for the "field" of communication, which they describe as a "postdiscipline." Despite the difference in terminology, we seem to agree that communication studies should aspire to some (nonoppressive, nonexclusionary) sort of coherence. Other critics have attacked the very idea of coherence, citing important institutional and intellectual benefits that flow from disciplinary fragmentation (e.g. O'Keefe, 1993; Newcomb, 1993; Peters, 1993; Swanson, 1993). I hope to address these arguments in detail in another essay. Here I can only respond by offering a different, but not necessarily incompatible, perspective.

9. See, for versions of this argument, Beniger (1993); Berger & Chaffee (1987, p. 894); Cronkhite (1986); Deetz (1994); Luhmann (1992); Motley (1991); Pearce (1989); Rothenbuhler (1993, 1996, 1998); Shepherd (1993); Sigman (1992, 1995a, 1995b).

10. Might communication studies even claim to be the fundamental discipline that explains all other disciplines, since disciplines themselves are social constructs that, like all social constructs, are constituted symbolically through communication? Yes, of course, but only as a joke! Virtually any discipline can claim to be the "fundamental" social discipline based on some tortured argument in which all social processes become fundamentally cognitive, economic, political, cultural—or indeed, why not chemical or subatomic? The irony that makes the joke funny is that every discipline occupies the precise center of the universe in its own perspective. Communication is no exception, but communication as a metaperspective—a perspective on perspectives—may help us to appreciate the irony of our situation.

11. See especially Deetz (1994); also see Carey (1989), Pearce (1989), and Shepherd (1993). The idea that communication has an essential role in the

formation of democratic community has philosophical roots in American pragmatism. For classic statements of this view see Dewey (1916, 1927) and McKeon (1957).

12. This logical paradox, that communication exists only as constituted by communication (but gee, what constitutes the communication that constitutes communication?), has been well explored within the cybernetic tradition of communication theory (e.g., Bateson, 1972; Krippendorff, 1997; Luhmann, 1992). It is but one manifestation of the paradoxical reflexivity between meaning and context, or message and meta-message, that characterizes all communication.

13. Carey (1989), McKinzie (1994), Reddy (1979), and Taylor (1992) all suggest that communication, in Euro-American cultures at least, is commonly thought of as a transmission process.

14. Although proponents of a constitutive model do not always reject the transmission model completely, they seldom sing its virtues. Peters (1994) is perhaps an exception.

15. Notice that reflexive self-criticisms of each tradition from its own standpoint are indicated in the diagonal cells from upper left to lower right of Table 5.2. These might be taken as fissures or points of instability for deconstructing the traditions, but I prefer to think of them as zones of self-questioning that potentiate dialogue and innovation.

16. Arnold defines rhetoric as the "study and teaching of practical, usually persuasive communication" and notes the underlying "hypothesis that the influence and significance of communication depend on the methods chosen in conceiving, composing, and presenting messages" (1989, p. 461).

17. The classic text is Locke (1690/1979); see Peters (1989), Steiner (1989), Taylor (1992).

18. For classic statements of this functionalist view of mind, see Bateson (1972) and Dennett (1979).

19. Kaufer & Butler (1996) can be regarded as a hybrid of rhetoric and cybernetics.

20. For various blends of the two see Cherry (1966); Eco (1976); Wilden (1972).

21. Krippendorff's recent work (e.g. 1993) represents a movement from cybernetics towards phenomenology that retains significant traces of the former. Several chapters in Steier's (1991) anthology on reflexivity display similar tendencies.

22. As Herman points out, the rise of psychology as a cultural worldview during the 20th century was fueled in part by a series of wars and other terrible events that "called rationality and autonomy into question" (1995, p. 7).

23. Meyrowitz claims "that virtually all the specific questions and arguments about a particular medium, or media in general, can be linked to one of three underlying metaphors for what a medium is . . . media as conduits, media as languages, media as environments" (1993, p. 56). In the sociopsychological tradition media are conduits; in the semiotic tradition they are languages; in the sociocultural tradition they are environments.

24. Recent attempts to strike a balance between the two poles include, for example, structuration theory (Giddens, 1984), practice theory (Bourdieu, 1992), and ecological models (e.g. Altheide, 1995; Mantovani, 1996).

25. Recent calls for a "constitutive" or "communicational" communication theory have often followed this line of argument; see, for example, Carey (1989), Sigman (1992, 1995a, 1995b), and several chapters in Leeds-Hurwitz (1995). Also see Sigman (1987); Thomas (1980).

26. For a recent symposium illustrating the current centrality of Habermas in this tradition, see Huspek (1997).

27. On cybernetic principles of good communication, a user-friendly representation of communication theory should be structured so as to facilitate efficient cognitive processing. Based on Miller's (1956) classic theory of human information processing capacity, this would limit the number of distinct "traditions" (or "chunks") of theory that could be included at any one level of the theoretical scheme to about seven, which happens to be the precise number of traditions in the present matrix.

28. Methods and standards for testing or critically assessing practical communication theory raise complex issues beyond the scope of the present essay. See Craig (1995, 1996b) and Craig & Tracy (1995) for work that broaches discussion on these issues.

29. This is consistent with Jonsen and Toulmin's view that the application of theory in practice is inherently rhetorical and perspectival rather than "geometrical" (formally deductive) (1988, p. 293). Alternative theories are not mutually exclusive but offer limited, complementary perspectives on practical problems (Craig, 1996b).

REFERENCES

Altheide, D. L. (1995). *An ecology of communication: Cultural formats of control.* New York: Aldine de Gruyter.

Anderson, J. A. (1996). *Communication theory: Epistemological foundations.* New York: Guilford Press.

Anderson, R., Cissna, K. N., & Arnett, R. C. (Eds.). (1994). *The reach of dialogue: Confirmation, voice and community.* Cresskill, NJ: Hampton Press.

Angus, I., & Langsdorf, L. (Eds.). (1992). *The critical turn: Rhetoric and philosophy in postmodern discourse.* Carbondale: Southern Illinois University Press.

Arnold, C. C. (1989). Rhetoric. In E. Barnouw, G. Gerbner, W. Schramm, T. L. Worth, & L. Gross (Eds.), *International encyclopedia of communications* (Volume 3, pp. 461–465). New York: Oxford University Press.

Arnold, C. C., & Bowers, J. W. (Eds.). (1984). *Handbook of rhetorical and communication theory.* Boston: Allyn & Bacon.

Audi, R. (Ed.). (1995). *The Cambridge dictionary of philosophy.* New York: Cambridge University Press.

Barnouw, E., Gerbner, G., Schramm, W., Worth, T. L., & Gross, L. (Eds.). (1989). *International encyclopedia of communications* (4 volumes). New York: Oxford University Press.

Bateson, G. (1972). *Steps to an ecology of mind.* New York: Ballantine Books.

Beniger, J. R. (1993). Communication—Embrace the subject, not the field. *Journal of Communication, 43*(3), 18–25.

Berger, C. R. (1991). Communication theories and other curios. *Communication Monographs, 58,* 101–113.

Berger, C. R. (1997). *Planning strategic interaction: Attaining goals through communicative action.* Mahwah, NJ: Erlbaum.

Berger, C. R., & Chaffee, S. H. (Eds.). (1987). *Handbook of communication science.* Newbury Park, CA: Sage.

Bitzer, L. F. (1968). The rhetorical situation. *Philosophy and Rhetoric, 1,* 1–14.

Bourdieu, P. (1992). *The logic of practice.* Stanford, CA: Stanford University Press.

Bowers, J., & Iwi, K. (1993). The discursive construction of society. *Discourse & Society, 4,* 357–393.

Brent, D. (1996). Rogerian rhetoric: Ethical growth through alternative forms of argumentation. In B. Emmel, P. Resch, & D. Tenney (Eds.), *Argument revisited; argument redefined: Negotiating meaning in the composition classroom* (pp. 73–96). Thousand Oaks, CA: Sage.

Budd, R. W., & Ruben, B. D. (Eds.). (1972). *Approaches to human communication.* Rochelle Park, NJ: Hayden.

Burgoon, J. K., & Buller, D. B. (1996). Interpersonal deception theory: Reflections on the nature of theory building and the theoretical status of interpersonal deception theory. *Communication Theory, 6,* 310–328.

Burke, K. (1966). *Language as symbolic action: Essays on life, literature, and method.* Berkeley, CA: University of California Press.

Cappella, J. N. (1991). The biological origins of automated patterns of human interaction. *Communication Theory, 1,* 4–35.

Cappella, J. N. (1995). An evolutionary psychology of Gricean cooperation. *Journal of Language and Social Psychology, 14,* 167–181.

Cappella, J. N. (Ed.). (1996). Symposium: Biology and communication. *Journal of Communication, 46*(3), 4–84.

Carbaugh, D. (1996). *Situating selves: The communication of social identities in American scenes.* Albany, NY: SUNY Press.

Carey, J. W. (1989). *Communication as culture: Essays on media and society.* Winchester, MA: Unwin Hyman.

Casmir, F. L. (Ed.). (1994). *Building communication theories: A socio/cultural approach.* Hillsdale, NJ: Erlbaum.

Chang, B. G. (1996). *Deconstructing communication: Representation, subject, and economies of exchange.* Minneapolis: University of Minnesota Press.

Cherry, C. (1966). *On human communication: A review, a survey, and a criticism* (2nd ed.). Cambridge, MA: MIT Press.

Cobley, P. (Ed.). (1996). *The communication theory reader.* New York: Routledge.

Condit, C. M. (1989). The rhetorical limits of polysemy. *Critical Studies in Mass Communication, 6,* 103–122.

Conquergood, D. (1992). Ethnography, rhetoric, and performance. *Quarterly Journal of Speech, 78,* 80–97.

Cooper, T. W. (1994). Communion and communication: Learning from the Shuswap. *Critical Studies in Mass Communication, 11,* 327–345.

Craig, R. T. (1989). Communication as a practical discipline. In B. Dervin, L. Grossberg, B. J. O'Keefe, & E. Wartella (Eds.), *Rethinking communication; Volume 1: Paradigm issues* (pp. 97–122). Newbury Park, CA: Sage.

Craig, R. T. (1993). Why are there so *many* communication theories? *Journal of Communication, 43*(3), 26–33.

Craig, R. T. (1995). Applied communication research in a practical discipline. In K. N. Cissna (Ed.), *Applied communication in the 21st century* (pp. 147–155). Mahwah, NJ: Erlbaum.

Craig, R. T. (1996a). Practical theory: A reply to Sandelands. *Journal for the Theory of Social Behaviour, 26,* 65–79.

Craig, R. T. (1996b). Practical-theoretical argumentation. *Argumentation, 10,* 461–474.

Craig, R. T., & Tracy, K. (1995). Grounded practical theory: The case of intellectual discussion. *Communication Theory, 5,* 248–272.

Crawford, L. (1996). Everyday tao: Conversation and contemplation. *Communication Studies, 47,* 25–34.

Cronen, V. E. (1995). Coordinated management of meaning: The consequentiality of communication and the recapturing of experience. In S. J. Sigman (Ed.). *The consequentiality of communication* (pp. 17–65). Hillsdale, NJ: Erlbaum.

Cronkhite, G. (1986). On the focus, scope, and coherence of the study of human symbolic activity. *Quarterly Journal of Speech, 72,* 231–246.

Crowley, D., & Mitchell, D. (Eds.). (1994). *Communication theory today.* Stanford, CA: Stanford University Press.

Cushman, D. P., & Kovacic, B. (Eds.). (1995). *Watershed research traditions in human communication theory.* Albany, NY: SUNY Press.

Dance, F. E. X. (1970). The "concept" of communication. *Journal of Communication, 20,* 201–210.

Dance, F. E. X., & Larson, C. E. (1976). *The functions of communication: A Theoretical Approach.* New York: Holt, Rinehart & Winston.

Deetz, S. A. (1992). *Democracy in an age of corporate colonization: Developments in communication and the politics of everyday life.* Albany, NY: SUNY Press.

Deetz, S. A. (1994). Future of the discipline: The challenges, the research, and the social contribution. In S. A. Deetz (Ed.), *Communication yearbook 17* (pp. 565–600). Thousand Oaks, CA: Sage.

Delia, J. G. (1987). Communication research: A history. In C. R. Berger and S. H. Chaffee (Eds.), *Handbook of communication science* (pp. 20–98). Newbury Park, CA: Sage.

Dennett, D. C. (1979). *Brainstorms: Philosophical essays on mind and psychology.* Montgomery, VT: Bradford.

Dewey, J. (1916). *Democracy and education: An introduction to the philosophy of education.* New York: Macmillan.

Dewey, J. (1927). *The public and its problems.* Chicago: Swallow Press.

Eco, U. (1976). *A theory of semiotics.* Bloomington: Indiana University Press.

Ehninger, D. (1968). On systems of rhetoric. *Philosophy and Rhetoric, 1,* 131–144.

Ellis, D. G. (1991). Post-structuralism and language: Non-sense. *Communication Monographs, 58,* 213–224.

Ellis, D. G. (1995). Fixing communicative meaning. *Communication Research, 22*(5), 515–544.

Fairclough, N. (1995). *Critical discourse analysis: The critical study of language.* New York: Longman.

Farrell, T. B. (1993). *Norms of rhetorical culture.* New Haven, CT: Yale University Press.

Fisher, B. A. (1978). *Perspectives on human communication.* New York: Macmillan.

Foss, S. K., & Griffin, C. L. (1995). Beyond persuasion: A proposal for an invitational rhetoric. *Communication Monographs, 62,* 2–18.

Freeman, S. A., Littlejohn, S. W., & Pearce, W. B. (1992). Communication and moral conflict. *Western Journal of Communication, 56,* 311–329.

Gadamer, H.-G. (1981). *Reason in the age of science* (F. G. Lawrence, Trans.). Cambridge, MA: MIT Press.

Giddens, A. (1984). *The constitution of society: Outline of the theory of structuration.* Berkeley: University of California Press.

Giddens, A. (1991). *Modernity and self-identity: Self and society in the late modern age.* Cambridge, UK: Polity Press.

Goodall, H. L., Jr. (1996). *Devine signs: Connecting spirit to community.* Carbondale: Southern Illinois University Press.

Greene, J. O. (Ed.). (1997). *Message production: Advances in communication theory.* Mahwah, NJ: Erlbaum.

Habermas, J. (1984). *The theory of communicative action; Volume 1: Reason and the rationalization of society* (T. McCarthy, Trans.). Boston: Beacon Press.

Harris, R. (1996). *Signs, language and communication.* New York: Routledge.

Hauser, M. D. (1996). *The evolution of communication.* Cambridge, MA: MIT Press.

Heims, S. J. (1991). *The cybernetics group.* Cambridge, MA: MIT Press.

Heritage, J. (1984). *Garfinkel and ethnomethodology.* Cambridge, UK: Polity Press.

Herman, E. (1995). *The romance of American psychology: Political culture in the age of experts.* Berkeley: University of California Press.

Hodge, R., & Kress, G. (1993). *Language as ideology* (2nd ed.). London: Routledge.

Hopper, R. (Ed.). (1993). Performance and conversation [Special issue]. *Text and Performance Quarterly, 13,* 113–211.

Horvath, C. W. (1995). Biological origins of communicator style. *Communication Quarterly, 43,* 394–407.

Huspek, M. (Ed.). (1997). Special issue: Toward normative theories of communication: The Frankfurt School [Special Issue]. *Communication Theory, 7,* 265–381.

Jonsen, A. R., & Toulmin, S. (1988). *The abuse of casuistry: A history of moral argument.* Berkeley: University of California Press.

Katriel, T., & Philipsen, G. (1981). "What we need is communication": "Communication" as a cultural category in some American speech. *Communication Monographs, 48,* 301–317.

Kaufer, D. S., & Butler, B. S. (1996). *Rhetoric and the arts of design.* Mahwah, NJ: Erlbaum.

Kaufer, D. S., & Carley, K. M. (1993a). *Communication at a distance: The influence of print on sociocultural organization and change.* Hillsdale, NJ: Erlbaum.

Kaufer, D. S., & Carley, K. M. (1993b). Condensation symbols: Their variety and rhetorical function in political discourse. *Philosophy and Rhetoric, 26,* 201–226.

Kovacic, B. (Ed.). (1997). *Emerging theories of human communication.* Albany, NY: SUNY Press.

Kramarae, C. (1989). Feminist theories of communication. In E. Barnouw, G. Gerbner, W. Schramm, T. L. Worth, & L. Gross (Eds.), *International encyclopedia of communications* (Volume 2, pp. 157–160). New York: Oxford University Press.

Krippendorff, K. (1989). Cybernetics. In E. Barnouw, G. Gerbner, W. Schramm, T. L. Worth, & L. Gross (Eds.), *International encyclopedia of communications* (Volume 1, pp. 443–446). New York: Oxford University Press.

Krippendorff, K. (1993). Conversation or intellectual imperialism in comparing communication (theories). *Communication Theory, 3,* 252–266.

Krippendorff, K. (1995). Undoing power. *Critical Studies in Mass Communication, 12,* 101–132.

Krippendorff, K. (1997). Seeing oneself through others' eyes in social inquiry. In M. Huspek & G. P. Radford (Eds.), *Transgressing discourses: Communication and the voice of other* (pp. 47–72). Albany, NY: SUNY Press.

Kuhn, T. S. (1970). *The structure of scientific revolutions* (2nd ed.). Chicago: University of Chicago Press.

Laffoon, E. A. (1995). Reconsidering Habermas' conception of performance. In S. Jackson (Ed.), *Argumentation and values; Proceedings of the ninth SCA/AFA conference on argumentation* (pp. 267–273). Annandale, VA: Speech Communication Association.

Lanigan, R. L. (1992). *The human science of communicology: A phenomenology of discourse in Foucault and Merleau-Ponty.* Pittsburgh, PA: Duquesne University Press.

Lannamann, J. W. (1991). Interpersonal communication research as ideological practice. *Communication Theory, 1,* 179–203.

Leeds-Hurwitz, W. (1993). *Semiotics and communication: Signs, codes, cultures.* Hillsdale, NJ: Erlbaum.

Leeds-Hurwitz, W. (Ed.). (1995). *Social approaches to communication.* New York: Guilford.

Leff, M. (1996). The idea of rhetoric as interpretive practice: A humanist's response to Gaonkar. In A. C. Gross & W. M. Keith (Eds.), *Rhetorical hermeneutics: Invention and interpretation in the age of science* (pp. 89–100). Albany, NY: SUNY Press.

Liska, J. (1993). Bee dances, bird songs, monkey calls, and cetacean sonar: Is speech unique? *Western Journal of Communication, 57,* 1–26.

Littlejohn, S. W. (1982). An overview of contributions to human communication theory from other disciplines. In F. E. X. Dance (Ed.), *Human communication theory: Comparative essays* (pp. 243–285). New York: Harper & Row.

Littlejohn, S. W. (1996a). Communication theory. In T. Enos (Ed.), *Encyclopedia of rhetoric and composition: Communication from ancient times to the information age* (pp. 117–121). New York: Garland.

Littlejohn, S. W. (1996b). *Theories of human communication* (5th ed.). Belmont, CA: Wadsworth.

Locke, J. (1979). *An essay concerning human understanding* (P. H. Nidditch, Ed.). New York: Oxford University Press. (Original publication 1690)

Luhmann, N. (1992). What is communication? *Communication Theory, 2,* 251–259.

Manetti, G. (1993). *Theories of the sign in classical antiquity.* Bloomington: Indiana University Press.

Mantovani, G. (1996). *New communication environments: From everyday to virtual.* London, UK: Taylor & Francis.

Mattelart, A. (1996). *The invention of communication* (S. Emanuel, Trans.). Minneapolis: University of Minnesota Press.

McKeon, R. (1957). Communication, truth, and society. *Ethics, 67,* 89–99.

McKerrow, R. E. (1989). Critical rhetoric: Theory and praxis. *Communication Monographs, 56,* 91–111.

McKinzie, B. W. (1994). *Objectivity, communication, and the foundation of understanding.* Lanham, MD: University Press of America.

McLaughlin, L. (1995). No respect? Disciplinarity and media studies in communication. Feminist communication scholarship and "the woman question" in the academy. *Communication Theory, 5,* 144–161.

McLuhan, M. (1964). *Understanding media: The extensions of man.* New York: McGraw-Hill.

Meyrowitz, J. (1993). Images of media: Hidden ferment—and harmony—in the field. *Journal of Communication, 43*(3), 55–66.

Miller, G. A. (1956). The magical number seven, plus or minus two: Some limits on our capacity for processing information. *Psychological Review, 63,* 81–97.

Mortensen, C. D. (1994). *Problematic communication: The construction of invisible walls.* Westport, CT: Greenwood.

Mortensen, C. D., with Ayres, C. M. (1997). *Miscommunication.* Thousand Oaks, CA: Sage.

Motley, M. T. (1991). How one may not communicate: A reply to Andersen. *Communication Studies, 42,* 326–340.

Murphy, M. A. (1991). No more "What is communication?" *Communication Research, 18,* 825–833.

Myers, R. A., Brashers, D., Center, C., Beck, C., & Wert-Gray, S. (1992). A citation analysis of organizational communication research. *Southern Communication Journal, 57,* 241–246.

Newcomb, H. (1993). Target practice: A Batesonian "field" guide for communication studies. *Journal of Communication, 43*(3), 127–132.

Norton, R., & Brenders, D. (1995). *Communication and consequences: Laws of interaction.* Mahwah, NJ: Erlbaum.

O'Keefe, B. (1993). Against theory. *Journal of Communication, 43*(3), 75–82.

Paisley, W. (1984). Communication in the communication sciences. In B. Dervin & M. J. Voigt (Eds.), *Progress in communication sciences* (Vol. 5, pp. 1–43). Norwood, NJ: Ablex.

Pearce, W. B. (1989). *Communication and the human condition.* Carbondale: Southern Illinois University Press.

Peters, J. D. (1986). Institutional sources of intellectual poverty in communication research. *Communication Research, 13,* 527–559.

Peters, J. D. (1989). John Locke, the individual, and the origin of communication. *Quarterly Journal of Speech, 75,* 387–399.

Peters, J. D. (1993). Genealogical notes on "the field." *Journal of Communication, 43*(4), 132–139.

Peters, J. D. (1994). The gaps of which communication is made. *Critical Studies in Mass Communication, 11,* 117–140.

Philipsen, G., & Albrecht, T. L. (Eds.). (1997). *Developing communication theories.* Albany, NY: SUNY Press.

Pilotta, J. J., & Mickunas, A. (1990). *Science of communication: Its phenomenological foundation.* Hillsdale, NJ: Erlbaum.

Pym, A. (1997). Beyond postmodernity: Grounding ethics in spirit. *Electronic Journal of Communication, 7*(1). [Online: http://www.cios.org/getfile\Pym_V7N197].

Ramsey, R. E. (1997). Communication and eschatology: The work of waiting, an ethics of relief, and areligious religiosity. *Communication Theory, 7,* 343–361.

Reddy, M. J. (1979). The conduit metaphor: A case of frame conflict in our language about language. In A. Ortony (Ed.), *Metaphor and thought* (pp. 284–324). Cambridge, UK: Cambridge University Press.

Reeves, B. (1992). Standpoint: On how we study and what we study. *Journal of Broadcasting and Electronic Media, 36,* 235–238.

Reeves, B., & Borgman, C. L. (1983). A bibliometric evaluation of core journals in communication research. *Human Communication Research, 10,* 119–136.

Rice, R. E., Borgman, C. L., & Reeves, B. (1988). Citation networks of communication journals, 1977–1985: Cliques and positions, citations made and citations received. *Human Communication Research, 15,* 256–283.

Rogers, E. M. (1994). *A history of communication study: A biographical approach.* New York: Free Press.

Roloff, M. E. (1981). *Interpersonal communication: The social exchange approach.* Beverly Hills, CA: Sage.

Rosengren, K. E. (1993). From field to frog ponds. *Journal of Communication, 43*(3), 6–17.

Rothenbuhler, E. W. (1993). Argument for a Durkheimian theory of the communicative. *Journal of Communication, 43*(3), 158–163.

Rothenbuhler, E. W. (1996). Commercial radio as communication. *Journal of Communication, 46*(1), 125–143.

Rothenbuhler, E. W. (1998). *Ritual communication: From everyday conversation to mediated ceremony.* Thousand Oaks, CA: Sage.

Schiller, D. (1994). From culture to information and back again: Commoditization as a route to knowledge. *Critical Studies in Mass Communication, 11,* 93–115.

Schiller, D. (1996). *Theorizing communication: A history.* New York: Oxford University Press.

Schoening, G. T., & Anderson, J. A. (1995). Social action media studies: Foundational arguments and common premises. *Communication Theory, 5,* 93–116.

Shannon, C., & Weaver, W. (1948). *The mathematical theory of communication.* Urbana: University of Illinois Press.

Shepherd, G. J. (1993). Building a discipline of communication. *Journal of Communication, 43*(3), 83–91.

Sholle, D. (1995). No respect? Disciplinarity and media studies in communication. Resisting disciplines: Repositioning media studies in the university. *Communication Theory, 5,* 130–143.

Shotter, J. (1997). Textual violence in acadame: On writing with respect for one's others. In M. Huspek & G. P. Radford (Eds.), *Transgessing discourses: Communication and the voice of other* (pp. 17–46). Albany, NY: SUNY Press.

Sigman, S. J. (1987). *A perspective on social communication.* Lexington, MA: Lexington Books.

Sigman, S. J. (1992). Do social approaches to interpersonal communication constitute a contribution to communication theory? *Communication Theory, 2,* 347–356.

Sigman, S. J. (1995a). Question: Evidence of what? Answer: Communication. *Western Journal of Communication, 59,* 79–84.

Sigman, S. J. (Ed.). (1995b). *The consequentiality of communication.* Hillsdale, NJ: Erlbaum.

So, C. Y. K. (1988). Citation patterns of core communication journals: An assessment of the developmental status of communication. *Human Communication Research, 15,* 236–255.

Steier, F. (Ed.). (1991). *Research and reflexivity.* Newbury Park, CA: Sage.

Steiner, P. (1989). Semiotics. In E. Barnouw, G. Gerbner, W. Schramm, T. L. Worth, & L. Gross (Eds.), *International encyclopedia of communications* (Volume 4, pp. 46–50). New York: Oxford University Press.

Stewart, J. (1995). *Language as articulate contact: Toward a post-semiotic philosophy of communication.* Albany, NY: SUNY Press.

Stewart, J. (Ed.). (1996). *Beyond the symbol model: Reflections on the representational nature of language.* Albany, NY: SUNY Press.

Streeter, T. (1995). No respect? Disciplinarity and media studies in communication. Introduction: For the study of communication and against the discipline of communication. *Communication Theory, 5,* 117–129.

Swanson, D. L. (1993). Fragmentation, the field, and the future. *Journal of Communication, 43*(4), 163–172.

Taylor, J. R. (1993). *Rethinking the theory of organizational communication: How to read an organization.* Norwood, NJ: Ablex.

Taylor, T. J. (1992). *Mutual misunderstanding: Scepticism and the theorizing of language and interpretation.* Durham, NC: Duke University Press.

Taylor, T. J. (1997). *Theorizing language.* New York: Pergamon.

Theall, D. F. (1995). *Beyond the word: Reconstructing sense in the Joyce era of technology, culture, and communication.* Buffalo, NY: University of Toronto Press.

Thomas, S. I. (1980). Some problems of the paradigm in communication theory. *Philosophy of the Social Sciences, 10,* 427–444.

Tracy, K. (1990). Framing discourse research to speak to issues of communicative practice. *Text, 10,* 117–120.

Tracy, K. (2001). Discourse analysis in communication. In D. Schiffrin, D. Tannen, & H. Hamilton (Eds.), *Handbook of discourse analysis.* (pp. 725–749). Oxford: Blackwell.

Watzlawick, P., Beavin, J. H., & Jackson, D. D. (1967). *The pragmatics of human communication: A study of interactional patterns, pathologies, and paradoxes.* New York: W. W. Norton.

Wiener, N. (1948). *Cybernetics.* New York: John Wiley.

Wilden, A. (1972). *System and structure: Essays in communication and exchange.* London: Tavistock.

PROJECTS FOR METATHEORIZING

ADDITIONAL READINGS ON METATHEORY

A. To learn more about comparing different metatheoretical approaches: Anderson (1996); Anderson and Baym (2004); Benson and Pearce (1977); Corman and Poole (2000); May and Mumby (2005); Shepherd, St. John, and Striphas (2006).

B. To learn more about scientific realism: Greene (1994); Pavitt (1999, 2000, 2001).

C. To learn more about postmodern and critical approaches: Mumby (1997); Huspek (1997); also see unit IX of this book.

D. To learn more about practical theory: Barge (2001); Barge and Craig (in press); Craig and Tracy (1995); Cronen (2001); Penman (2000).

APPLICATION EXERCISE

Decide on a specific phenomenon or practice (e.g., why this was a wet winter, why men talk the way they do, why a particular celebrity is popular) and ask three people for their theories (to explain why things are the way they are). Then, think metatheoretically about these theories and answer the following questions: What is the value-usefulness of each of these theories? Is one more valuable than another? How would you determine which is the best theory? Do these theories have shared underlying assumptions, or different assumptions, about how the world works? Are these theories fundamentally different theories or are they different articulations of essentially the same theory? Do these

theories link to any theories you have encountered in your experience or education?

PROJECTS

1. Based on the additional readings listed above or other readings on metatheory, summarize the principles of several different metatheoretical stances and attempt to articulate your own position with respect to those different views. Which metatheories do you find most acceptable or unacceptable? What is the best approach? What should be the goals of communication theory? What are the most important elements of a good theory? By what criteria should theories be evaluated?

2. If every theory is based on metatheoretical assumptions that may be implicit or explicit, then any theory presented in this book can be analyzed to discover its underlying metatheory. What metatheoretical views do the readings we have selected for this book represent? Read several chapters in various parts of the book, articulate the implicit or explicit metatheoretical assumptions of each, and compare them to other metatheoretical stances. How easy is it to determine the underlying metatheory? What metatheories are represented in this book?

3. Myers (2001) criticized Craig's model of the field from a social scientific point of view. Read Myers's critique and Craig's (2001) reply. What other metatheoretical views are most closely aligned with their two positions? Assess the Myers-Craig exchange and argue for your own position on the issues they raise.

4. This book organizes the field of communication theory according to the seven traditions identified by Craig. How does this compare with other ways of classifying and organizing theories of communication? Review several general textbooks or reference works on communication theory and compare their organization (e.g., Cobley, 1996; Crowley & Mitchell, 1994; Griffin, 2006; Infante, Rancer, & Womack, 2003; Lederman, 1998; Littlejohn & Foss, 2005; Mattelart & Mattelart, 1998; Miller, 2005; Mortensen, 1973; West & Turner, 2004). What are the main different approaches? If traditions of communication theory are identified, how are they defined and how are they used to interpret and organize theories? Do different ways of organizing the field seem related to different metatheoretical stances? What is the point of classifying theories, anyway? Do all of these schemes, including the seven traditions, oversimplify the field? If many theories do not fall neatly into one tradition, as Craig admits, and if the traditions are constantly changing, what is the usefulness of defining traditions?

5. Craig states that new traditions of communication theory are possible and mentions several likely candidates (feminist, aesthetic, economic, spiritual) and one candidate that he argues is unlikely (biology). Select a possible new tradition of communication theory (one of those discussed by Craig or some other tradition), read the literature of that tradition, and try to conceptualize it as a tradition of communication theory by adding a new column to Craig's Table 5.1 and a new column and row to Table 5.2. (That is, try to define the tradition in terms of its distinct definition of communication and communication problems, metadiscursive vocabulary, commonplace ideas about communication that it supports or challenges, and points of controversy between the proposed tradition and other traditions.) Having attempted to define this new tradition and to incorporate it into the field, consider reasons for and against including the new tradition. Does the new tradition offer a distinct way of theorizing communication? Does it raise interesting practical issues in comparison with other traditions? What are the strengths and weaknesses of the tradition?

REFERENCES

Anderson, J. A. (1996). *Communication theory: Epistemological foundations*. New York: Guilford.

Anderson, J. A., & Baym, G. (2004). Philosophies and philosophic issues in communication, 1995–2004. *Journal of Communication, 54*(4), 589–615.

Barge, K. J. (Ed.). (2001). Practical theory [Special issue]. *Communication Theory, 11*(1), 5–123.

Barge, K. J., & Craig, R. T. (in press). Practical theory. In L. R. Frey & K. N. Cissna (Eds.), *Handbook of applied communication research*. Mahwah, NJ: Lawrence Erlbaum.

Benson, T. W., & Pearce, W. B. (Eds.). (1977, Winter). Alternative theoretical bases for the study of human communication: A symposium. *Communication Quarterly, 25*(1), 1–73.

Cobley, P. (Ed.). (1996). *The communication theory reader*. New York: Routledge.

Corman, S. R., & Poole, M. S. (Eds.). (2000). *Perspectives on organizational communication: Finding common ground*. New York: Guilford.

Craig, R. T. (1993). Why are there so many communication theories? *Journal of Communication, 43*(3), 26–33.

Craig, R. T. (2001). Minding my metamodel, mending Myers. *Communication Theory, 11*, 133–142.

Craig, R. T., & Tracy, K. (1995). Grounded practical theory: The case of intellectual discussion. *Communication Theory, 5*, 248–272.

Cronen, V. E. (2001). Practical theory, practical art, and the pragmatic-systemic account of inquiry. *Communication Theory, 11*, 14–35.

Crowley, D., & Mitchell, D. (Eds.). (1994). *Communication theory today*. Stanford, CA: Stanford University Press.

Greene, J. O. (1994). What sort of terms ought theories of human action incorporate? *Communication Studies, 45*, 187–211.

Griffin, E. (2006). *A first look at communication theory* (6th ed.). Boston: McGraw-Hill.

Huspek, M. (Ed.). (1997). Toward normative theories of communication: The Frankfurt School [Special issue]. *Communication Theory, 7*, 265–381.

Infante, D. A., Rancer, A. S., & Womack, D. F. (2003). *Building communication theory* (4th ed.). Prospect Heights, IL: Waveland Press.

Lederman, L. C. (Ed.). (1998). *Communication theory: A reader*. Dubuque, IA: Kendall/Hunt.

Littlejohn, S. W., & Foss, K. (2005). *Theories of human communication* (8th ed.). Belmont, CA: Thomson Wadsworth.

Mattelart, A., & Mattelart, M. (1998). *Theories of communication: A short introduction* (J. A. Cohen & S. G. Taponier, Trans.). Thousand Oaks, CA: Sage.

May, S., & Mumby, D. K. (Eds.). (2005). *Engaging organizational communication theory and research: Multiple perspectives*. Thousand Oaks, CA: Sage.

Miller, K. (2005). *Communication theories: Perspectives, processes, and contexts* (2nd ed.). Boston: McGraw-Hill.

Mortensen, C. D. (Ed.). (1973). *Basic readings in communication theory*. New York: Harper & Row.

Mumby, D. K. (1997). Modernism, postmodernism, and communication studies: A rereading of an ongoing debate. *Communication Theory, 7*, 1–28.

Myers, D. (2001). A pox on all compromises: Reply to Craig (1999). *Communication Theory, 11*, 231–240.

Pavitt, C. (1999). The third way: Scientific realism and communication theory. *Communication Theory, 9*, 162–188.

Pavitt, C. (2000). Answering questions requesting scientific explanations for communication. *Communication Theory, 10*, 379–404.

Pavitt, C. (2001). *The philosophy of science and communication theory*. Huntington, NY: Nova Science.

Penman, R. (2000). *Reconstructing communicating: Looking to a future*. Mahwah, NJ: Lawrence Erlbaum.

Shepherd, G. J., St. John, J., & Striphas, T. (Eds.). (2006). *Communication as . . . : Perspectives on theory*. Thousand Oaks, CA: Sage.

West, R., and Turner, L. H. (2004). *Introducing communication theory: Analysis and application*. (2nd ed.). New York: McGraw Hill.

UNIT III   INTRODUCTION

THE RHETORICAL TRADITION

Rhetoric is a word of many connotations. No wonder, in that it has been studied since the study of communication began and still there persists the question: Is rhetoric a part of communication theory or is it a way of thinking distinct from communication theory? Often the answer to this question hinges on whether one thinks social scientific and humanistic studies should be placed under one umbrella of communication theory or whether the communication discipline should be divided into two separate camps. In the approach taken in this reader, the answer is that rhetoric is an identifiable tradition of thinking and talking about communication. Rather than seeing two main traditions within the communication discipline, this view sees rhetoric as one of seven traditions of communication theory. It is the tradition in which topics and ideas such as audience, enthymeme, agency, argument, identification, and persuasion are discussed and theorized. As a tradition, rhetoric is a humanistic, interpretive way of thinking about communication, and thus the pieces included in this section all have that flavor. Rhetoric also has a very deep and rich history that could never be captured in a select few readings. As such, the four pieces included here serve as a small sample of the range and variety of ideas in this field, yet they also illustrate shared strands of thought that are found within the rhetorical communication theory tradition.

Although there are many possible ways to delineate a rhetorical perspective, the distinguishing characteristic taken as central here is that the rhetorical tradition conceptualizes communication as an art of discourse. People act as rhetors (persuasive speakers) and engage in an artistic practice of discourse. A notion of rhetoric as an art is what led to the first critique of rhetoric. As was discussed in the Introduction, communication theorists theorize in response to communication problems they experience in their sociohistorical context. As such, Plato theorized in response to what he considered the problematic nature of the rhetors and rhetoric in Athens. Stated simply, the problem Plato encountered was the *problem of rhetoric.* His theorizing about this problem led him to write the first philosophical critique of rhetoric (in which he followed lines of thought derived from his mentor, Socrates, who did not write down his philosophy). In the dialogue *Gorgias,* Socrates questions whether rhetoric is a true art or merely a knack for flattery. For Plato, rhetoric, as it was practiced by the Sophists, was not an art and therefore, according to Plato, scholars should not pursue rhetoric but rather should pursue the art of dialectic, which engages in the pursuit of truth. Thus Plato elevated philosophy to the most worthy of endeavors while relegating rhetoric to a suspect undertaking.

Including this dialogue as one of the four rhetoric readings highlights that to be a critic is a central part of theorizing in the rhetorical tradition. Plato's image and treatment of rhetoric as seen in this dialogue has made an indelible impression on the rhetorical landscape, as has the kind of interaction portrayed in all of his dialogues. The idea of an active interchange of interlocutors provides one model for how to grow in one's understanding of the ideas in any and all the readings to follow.

The second piece in this unit is excerpted from Aristotle's *Rhetoric*. The problem he encountered can be described, perhaps a bit playfully, as the *problem of Plato*. Plato's searing critique of rhetoric placed it as a non-theoretical as well as a fruitless (or deceitful) endeavor. From another angle, Aristotle could be seen as responding to the problem of the need for the interchange of ideas if there were to be democracy in the Greek *polis*, or city-state. In other words, Aristotle theorized around the necessity of reasoned public deliberation. If there were to be this kind of interchange in Athens, rhetoric would be the mode of popular discourse. One could simply not take Plato's approach and throw away rhetoric in favor of dialectic. Rather, if public deliberation were to be undertaken by the social and political animal, it needed to be done in a principled fashion. Thus, responding implicitly to Plato's critique of rhetoric in our excerpt, Aristotle undertakes a systematic exploration of *logos*, or persuasion by means of logical arguments. As part of such, he defines rhetoric as the faculty of observing in any given case the available means of persuasion and distinguishes the main kinds of persuasion and their specific principles. Although other writers such as Isocrates responded to this same problem, as rhetoric's first systematic theorist, Aristotle introduced many of the analytic concepts still used by rhetorical scholars such as the enthymeme, topoi, and ethos. Much of the ensuing work in the rhetorical tradition is either a descendent of or a reaction to Aristotle's rhetorical typologies.

The third reading is from Burke, a key 20th-century thinker who broadened the scope of the rhetorical tradition. During the years of World War II and the ensuing Cold War, the problem Burke encountered was the *problem of propaganda*. Stated in other words, this problem is the problem of the pervasiveness of persuasion. Although the visibility of the rhetorical nature of language varies from text to text and although not all texts are overtly and preparedly designed to persuade in a strictly argumentative fashion and others purposefully veil their persuasion, in the excerpts included here Burke explores the idea that all language use is rhetorical—that is, aimed at moving people. The symbol-using animal uses language strategically. In making this claim, Burke does not seek to replace the established tradition of taking persuasion as the central rhetorical pursuit. Rather, he seeks to carve out a niche for rhetoric that cannot be taken over by aesthetics and can be seen as of at least equal importance to the emerging scientific theorizing of his day.

For Burke, texts need to be analyzed rhetorically, and the rhetorical nature of things like scientific talk and religious talk need to be examined. Centering on the idea of identification, and incorporating ideas such as the scapegoat and pentadic criticism, Burke proposes that the rhetorical nature of and the motives within speech can be theorized. All texts are open to rhetorical critique, and theorizing about the use of language by the symbolizing animal should be a central pursuit. Not that it was exclusively so prior to Burke, but with the incorporation of Burke's ideas, rhetoricians were clearly not limited to studying public speeches; and as future thinkers build on Burke's ideas, the texts open to rhetorical critique continue to expand, as does the theorizing about the range of strategies people use in moving their audiences.

Foss and Griffin's essay on invitational rhetoric provides a new set of concepts as well as comparisons and contrasts to the ideas of

Plato, Aristotle, and Burke. The problem encountered by these theorists is the *problem of persuasion*. Unlike Burke, who continued in the tradition of understanding persuasion as the central pursuit of rhetorical study in a time when critical and feminist scholars have taken on the challenge of rewriting the standards within traditions, these authors respond to the dominant model by proposing a contrasting view of the possibility of rhetoric. According to Foss and Griffin, rhetorical study should not focus on evaluating and developing rhetors as speakers who persuade their audiences. Rather, the goal of rhetors and rhetorical study should be presentation as invitation. Debate and presentation designed to show the strength of one's position through defensible support of claims does not good rhetoric make. In this new model, based on the goal of inviting transformation, the speaker does not try to force a change of belief on the audience as one would do when persuading; rather, the speaker presents in a way that will enable transformation if the listener chooses to engage in such an alteration. This model leads not only to new ways of speaking but also to a distinct set of standards for evaluating rhetors and rhetoric.

Although this piece is certainly not definitive of all future directions in rhetoric, one aspect of traditions in general that it illustrates very nicely is how thought can change over time and yet still be part of a tradition. Through both introducing new analytical tools and indicating how these tools are connected to prior ideas, these authors provide an example of the continued development of thought within the rhetorical tradition. Thought within a tradition does not need to follow in a lockstep fashion from existing ideas; rather, scholars within a tradition can use existing ideas as a springboard to go in new directions, and they can incorporate ideas from other traditions into a tradition just as they can continue to apply existing ideas to new contexts or find new uses for older ideas.

The foundational ideas in these readings can be discussed separately or in conjunction with each other. While there are certainly many significant rhetorical ideas that have not been included in this section and this section is not designed to provide an in-depth exploration of rhetoric, the four pieces included do provide a sketch of the kinds of things highlighted when theorizing communication from a rhetorical perspective. The idea that communication can be theorized as an art of discourse is one tradition of thought within communication theory. Rhetors speak so as to influence audiences. It is significant, too, that the intermixed nature of the traditions can be seen within these four readings. For example, Plato's text, his critique of rhetoric and its place and acceptance in Greek society, might be considered as foundational to the critical tradition of communication theory as it is to the rhetorical tradition. Similarly, the feminist approach in Foss and Griffin builds on ideas within the critical tradition as well as those of the rhetorical tradition.

Looking through the lens provided by the rhetorical tradition, we are drawn to focus on strategic language use. The pieces included here provide some of the ideas that those who specialize in the rhetorical tradition use in their theorizing of the strategic use of language. In reading these four pieces, one can begin to ascertain for oneself the nature of the thought and the talk that is the rhetorical tradition of communication theory. As you read, you may find yourself pondering some of these kinds of questions: What exactly is the rhetorical communication theory tradition? What are some of the key ideas and concepts within this tradition? These basic questions, along with many others, can be explored as one views one's own experiences, the texts one encounters, and other formulations of communication through the lens of the ideas found in these readings.

In keeping with the general approach of the project of theorizing, some of the following questions also may be informed through discussion of these readings: What communication problems does the lens of rhetorical theory illuminate? How tightly does the tradition hold together? Is the Foss and Griffin reading an extension of rhetoric or is it a better example of a different perspective on communication? What is the difference between invitation and persuasion? How much do you align with rhetorical thought? How does it inform your own theories of communication? What techniques does rhetoric provide to manage the communication difficulties you experience? What new ideas and vocabulary do you now have to talk about communication? What aspects of life do you now see as strategic communication (rhetoric) that you didn't previously? All of these questions and more are the inquiries that communication theorists may ask as they delve into these readings.

6

GORGIAS

PLATO

Persons of the Dialogue: Callicles, Socrates, Chaerephon, Gorgias, Polus

Scene: The house of Callicles.

Callicles. The wise man, as the proverb says, is late for a fray, but not for a feast.

Socrates. And are we late for a feast?

Cal. Yes, and a delightful feast; for Gorgias has just been exhibiting to us many fine things.

Soc. It is not my fault, Callicles; our friend Chaerephon is to blame; for he would keep us loitering in the Agora.

Chaerephon. Never mind, Socrates; the misfortune of which I have been the cause I will also repair; for Gorgias is a friend of mine, and I will make him give the exhibition again either now, or, if you prefer, at some other time.

Cal. What is the matter, Chaerephon—does Socrates want to hear Gorgias?

Chaer. Yes, that was our intention in coming.

Cal. Come into my house, then; for Gorgias is staying with me, and he shall exhibit to you.

Soc. Very good, Callicles; but will he answer our questions? for I want to hear from him what is the nature of his art, and what it is which he professes and teaches; he may, as you [Chaerephon] suggest, defer the exhibition to some other time.

Cal. There is nothing like asking him, Socrates; and indeed to answer questions is a part of his exhibition, for he was saying only just now, that any one in my house might put any question to him, and that he would answer.

Soc. How fortunate! will you ask him, Chaerephon—?

Chaer. What shall I ask him?

Soc. Ask him who he is.

SOURCE: Plato. (c. 380 BC). *Gorgias* (Benjamin Jowett, Trans.; excerpts). Retrieved May 23, 2005, from http://infomotions .com/etexts/philosophy/400BC-301BC/plato-gorgias-343.txt. (This document is in the public domain.)

Chaer.	What do you mean?
Soc.	I mean such a question as would elicit from him, if he had been a maker of shoes, the answer that he is a cobbler. Do you understand?
Chaer.	I understand, and will ask him: Tell me, Gorgias, is our friend Callicles right in saying that you undertake to answer any questions which you are asked?
Gorgias.	Quite right, Chaerephon: I was saying as much only just now; and I may add, that many years have elapsed since any one has asked me a new one.
Chaer.	Then you must be very ready, Gorgias.
Gor.	Of that, Chaerephon, you can make trial.
Polus.	Yes, indeed, and if you like, Chaerephon, you may make trial of me too, for I think that Gorgias, who has been talking a long time, is tired.
Chaer.	And do you, Polus, think that you can answer better than Gorgias?
Pol.	What does that matter if I answer well enough for you?
Chaer.	Not at all: —and you shall answer if you like.
Pol.	Ask:—
Chaer.	My question is this: If Gorgias had the skill of his brother Herodicus, what ought we to call him? Ought he not to have the name which is given to his brother?
Pol.	Certainly.
Chaer.	Then we should be right in calling him a physician?
Pol.	Yes.
Chaer.	And if he had the skill of Aristophon the son of Aglaophon, or of his brother Polygnotus, what ought we to call him?
Pol.	Clearly, a painter.
Chaer.	But now what shall we call him—what is the art in which he is skilled.
Pol.	O Chaerephon, there are many arts among mankind which are experimental, and have their origin in experience, for experience makes the days of men to proceed according to art, and inexperience according to chance, and different persons in different ways are proficient in different arts, and the best persons in the best arts. And our friend Gorgias is one of the best, and the art in which he is a proficient is the noblest.
Soc.	Polus has been taught how to make a capital speech, Gorgias; but he is not fulfilling the promise which he made to Chaerephon.
Gor.	What do you mean, Socrates?
Soc.	I mean that he has not exactly answered the question which he was asked.
Gor.	Then why not ask him yourself?
Soc.	But I would much rather ask you, if you are disposed to answer: for I see, from the few words which Polus has uttered, that he has attended more to the art which is called rhetoric than to dialectic.
Pol.	What makes you say so, Socrates?
Soc.	Because, Polus, when Chaerephon asked you what was the art which Gorgias knows, you praised it as if you were answering some one who found fault with it, but you never said what the art was.
Pol.	Why, did I not say that it was the noblest of arts?
Soc.	Yes, indeed, but that was no answer to the question: nobody asked what was the quality, but what was the nature, of the art, and by what name we were to describe Gorgias. And I would still beg you briefly and clearly, as you answered Chaerephon when he asked you at first, to say what this art is, and what we ought to call Gorgias: Or rather, Gorgias, let me turn to you, and ask the same question: what are we to call you, and what is the art which you profess?
Gor.	Rhetoric, Socrates, is my art.
Soc.	Then I am to call you a rhetorician?

Gor. Yes, Socrates, and a good one too, if you would call me that which, in Homeric language, "I boast myself to be."

Soc. I should wish to do so.

Gor. Then pray do.

Soc. And are we to say that you are able to make other men rhetoricians?

Gor. Yes, that is exactly what I profess to make them, not only at Athens, but in all places.

Soc. And will you continue to ask and answer questions, Gorgias, as we are at present doing and reserve for another occasion the longer mode of speech which Polus was attempting? Will you keep your promise, and answer shortly the questions which are asked of you?

Gor. Some answers, Socrates, are of necessity longer; but I will do my best to make them as short as possible; for a part of my profession is that I can be as short as any one.

Soc. That is what is wanted, Gorgias; exhibit the shorter method now, and the longer one at some other time.

Gor. Well, I will; and you will certainly say, that you never heard a man use fewer words.

Soc. Very good then; as you profess to be a rhetorician, and a maker of rhetoricians, let me ask you, with what is rhetoric concerned: I might ask with what is weaving concerned, and you would reply (would you not?), with the making of garments?

Gor. Yes.

Soc. And music is concerned with the composition of melodies?

Gor. It is.

Soc. By Here, Gorgias, I admire the surpassing brevity of your answers.

Gor. Yes, Socrates, I do think myself good at that.

Soc. I am glad to hear it; answer me in like manner about rhetoric: with what is rhetoric concerned?

Gor. With discourse.

Soc. What sort of discourse, Gorgias?—such discourse as would teach the sick under what treatment they might get well?

Gor. No.

Soc. Then rhetoric does not treat of all kinds of discourse?

Gor. Certainly not.

Soc. And yet rhetoric makes men able to speak?

Gor. Yes.

Soc. And to understand that about which they speak?

Gor. Of course.

Soc. But does not the art of medicine, which we were just now mentioning, also make men able to understand and speak about the sick?

Gor. Certainly.

Soc. Then medicine also treats of discourse?

Gor. Yes.

Soc. Of discourse concerning diseases?

Gor. Just so.

Soc. And does not gymnastic also treat of discourse concerning the good or evil condition of the body?

Gor. Very true.

Soc. And the same, Gorgias, is true of the other arts:—all of them treat of discourse concerning the subjects with which they severally have to do.

Gor. Clearly.

Soc. Then why, if you call rhetoric the art which treats of discourse, and all the other arts treat of discourse, do you not call them arts of rhetoric?

Gor. Because, Socrates, the knowledge of the other arts has only to do with some sort of external action, as of the hand; but there is no such action of the hand in rhetoric which works and takes effect only through the medium of discourse. And therefore I am justified in saying that rhetoric treats of discourse.

Soc. I am not sure whether I entirely understand you, but I dare say I shall soon know better; please to answer me a question:—you would allow that there are arts?

Gor. Yes.

Soc. As to the arts generally, they are for the most part concerned with doing, and require little or no speaking; in painting, and statuary, and many other arts, the work may proceed in silence; and of such arts I suppose you would say that they do not come within the province of rhetoric.

Gor. You perfectly conceive my meaning, Socrates.

Soc. But there are other arts which work wholly through the medium of language, and require either no action or very little, as, for example, the arts of arithmetic, of calculation, of geometry, and of playing draughts; in some of these speech is pretty nearly co-extensive with action, but in most of them the verbal element is greater—they depend wholly on words for their efficacy and power: and I take your meaning to be that rhetoric is an art of this latter sort?

Gor. Exactly.

Soc. And yet I do not believe that you really mean to call any of these arts rhetoric; although the precise expression which you used was, that rhetoric is an art which works and takes effect only through the medium of discourse; and an adversary who wished to be captious might say, "And so, Gorgias, you call arithmetic rhetoric." But I do not think that you really call arithmetic rhetoric any more than geometry would be so called by you.

Gor. You are quite right, Socrates, in your apprehension of my meaning.

Soc. Well, then, let me now have the rest of my answer:—seeing that rhetoric is one of those arts which works mainly by the use of words, and there are other arts which also use words, tell me what is that quality in words with which rhetoric is concerned:—Suppose that a person asks me about some of the arts which I was mentioning just now; he might say, "Socrates, what is arithmetic?" and I should reply to him, as you replied to me, that arithmetic is one of those arts which take effect through words. And then he would proceed to ask: "Words about what?" and I should reply, Words about [odd] and even numbers, and how many there are of each. And if he asked again: "What is the art of calculation?" I should say, That also is one of the arts which is concerned wholly with words. And if he further said, "Concerned with what?" I should say, like the clerks in the assembly, "as aforesaid" of arithmetic, but with a difference, the difference being that the art of calculation considers not only the quantities of odd and even numbers, but also their numerical relations to themselves and to one another. And suppose, again, I were to say that astronomy is only [words]—he would ask, "Words about what, Socrates?" and I should answer, that astronomy tells us about the motions of the stars and sun and moon, and their relative swiftness.

Gor. You would be quite right, Socrates.

Soc. And now let us have from you, Gorgias, the truth about rhetoric: which you would admit (would you not?) to be one of those arts which act always and fulfil all their ends through the medium of words?

Gor. True.

Soc. Words which do what? I should ask. To what class of things do the words which rhetoric uses relate?

Gor. To the greatest, Socrates, and the best of human things.

Soc. That again, Gorgias, is ambiguous; I am still in the dark: for which are the greatest and best of human things? I dare say that you have heard men singing at feasts the old drinking song, in which the singers enumerate the goods of life, first health, beauty next, thirdly, as the writer of the song says, wealth [honestly] obtained.

Gor. Yes, I know the song; but what is your drift?

Soc. I mean to say, that the producers of those things which the author of the song praises, that is to say, the physician, the trainer, the money-maker, will at once come to you, and first the physician will say: "O Socrates, Gorgias is deceiving you, for my art is concerned with the greatest good of men and not his." And when

I ask, Who are you? he will reply, "I am a physician." What do you mean? I shall say. Do you mean that your art produces the greatest good? "Certainly," he will answer, "for is not health the greatest good? What greater good can men have, Socrates?" And after him the trainer will come and say, "I too, Socrates, shall be greatly surprised if Gorgias can show more good of his art than I can show of mine." To him again I shall say, Who are you, honest friend, and what is your business? "I am a trainer," he will reply, "and my business is to make men beautiful and strong in body." When I have done with the trainer, there arrives the money-maker, and he, as I expect, utterly [despises] them all. "Consider Socrates," he will say, "whether Gorgias or any one-else can produce any greater good than wealth." Well, you and I say to him, and are you a creator of wealth? "Yes," he replies. And who are you? "A money-maker." And do you consider wealth to be the greatest good of man? "Of course," will be his reply. And we shall rejoin: Yes; but our friend Gorgias contends that his art produces a greater good than yours. And then he will be sure to go on and ask, "What good? Let Gorgias answer." Now I want you, Gorgias, to imagine that this question is asked of you by them and by me; What is that which, as you say, is the greatest good of man, and of which you are the creator? Answer us.

Gor. That good, Socrates, which is truly the greatest, being that which gives to men freedom in their own persons, and to individuals the power of ruling over others in their several states.

Soc. And what would you consider this to be?

Gor. What is there greater than the word which persuades the judges in the courts, or the senators in the council, or the citizens in the assembly, or at any other political meeting?—if you have the power of uttering this word, you will have the physician your slave, and the trainer your slave, and the money-maker of whom you talk will be found to gather treasures, not for himself, but for you who are able to speak and to persuade the multitude.

Soc. Now I think, Gorgias, that you have very accurately explained what you conceive to be the art of rhetoric; and you mean to say, if I am not

mistaken, that rhetoric is the artificer of persuasion, having this and no other business, and that this is her crown and end. Do you know any other effect of rhetoric over and above that of producing persuasion?

Gor. No: the definition seems to me very fair, Socrates; for persuasion is the chief end of rhetoric.

Soc. Then hear me, Gorgias, for I am quite sure that if there ever was a man who—entered on the discussion of a matter from a pure love of knowing the truth, I am such a one, and I should say the same of you.

Gor. What is coming, Socrates?

Soc. I will tell you: I am very well aware that [I] do not know what, according to you, is the exact nature, or what are the topics of that persuasion of which you speak, and which is given by rhetoric; although I have a suspicion about both the one and the other. And I am going to ask—what is this power of persuasion which is given by rhetoric, and about what? But why, if I have a suspicion, do I ask instead of telling you? Not for your sake, but in order that the argument may proceed in such a manner as is most likely to set forth the truth. And I would have you observe, that I am right in asking this further question: If I asked, "What sort of a painter is Zeuxis?" and you said, "The painter of figures," should I not be right in asking, "What kind of figures, and where do you find them?"

Gor. Certainly.

Soc. And the reason for asking this second question would be, that there are other painters besides, who paint many other figures?

Gor. True.

Soc. But if there had been no one but Zeuxis who painted them, then you would have answered very well?

Gor. Quite so.

Soc. Now I want to know about rhetoric in the same way;—is rhetoric the only art which brings persuasion, or do other arts have the same effect? I mean to say—Does he who teaches anything persuade men of that which he teaches or not?

Gor. He persuades, Socrates,—there can be no mistake about that.

Soc. Again, if we take the arts of which we were just now speaking:—do not arithmetic and the arithmeticians teach us the properties of number?

Gor. Certainly.

Soc. And therefore persuade us of them?

Gor. Yes.

Soc. Then arithmetic as well as rhetoric is an artificer of persuasion?

Gor. Clearly.

Soc. And if any one asks us what sort of persuasion, and about what,—we shall answer, persuasion which teaches the quantity of odd and even; and we shall be able to show that all the other arts of which we were just now speaking are artificers of persuasion, and of what sort, and about what.

Gor. Very true.

Soc. Then rhetoric is not the only artificer of persuasion?

Gor. True.

Soc. Seeing, then, that not only rhetoric works by persuasion, but that other arts do the same, as in the case of the painter, a question has arisen which is a very fair one: Of what persuasion is rhetoric the artificer, and about what?—is not that a fair way of putting the question?

Gor. I think so.

Soc. Then, if you approve the question, Gorgias, what is the answer?

Gor. I answer, Socrates, that rhetoric is the art of persuasion in courts of law and other assemblies, as I was just now saying, and about the just and unjust.

Soc. And that, Gorgias, was what I was suspecting to be your notion; yet I would not have you wonder if by-and-by I am found repeating a seemingly plain question; for I ask not in order to confute you, but as I was saying that the argument may proceed consecutively, and that we may not get the habit of anticipating and suspecting the meaning of one another's words; I would have you develop your own views in your own way, whatever may be your hypothesis.

Gor. I think that you are quite right, Socrates.

Soc. Then let me raise another question; there is such a thing as "having learned"?

Gor. Yes.

Soc. And there is also "having believed"?

Gor. Yes.

Soc. And is the "having learned" the same [as] "having believed," and are learning and belief the same things?

Gor. In my judgment, Socrates, they are not the same.

Soc. And your judgment is right, as you may ascertain in this way:—If a person were to say to you, "Is there, Gorgias, a false belief as well as a true?" —you would reply, if I am not mistaken, that there is.

Gor. Yes.

Soc. Well, but is there a false knowledge as well as a true?

Gor. No.

Soc. No, indeed; and this again proves that knowledge and belief differ.

Gor. Very true.

Soc. And yet those who have learned as well as those who have believed are persuaded?

Gor. Just so.

Soc. Shall we then assume two sorts of persuasion, —one which is the source of belief without knowledge, as the other is of knowledge?

Gor. By all means.

Soc. And which sort of persuasion does rhetoric create in courts of law and other assemblies about the just and unjust, the sort of persuasion which gives belief without knowledge, or that which gives knowledge?

Gor. Clearly, Socrates, that which only gives belief.

Soc. Then rhetoric, as would appear, is the artificer of a persuasion which creates belief about the just and unjust, but gives no instruction about them?

Gor. True.

Soc. And the rhetorician does not instruct the courts of law or other assemblies about things just and unjust, but he creates belief about them; for no one can be supposed to instruct such a vast multitude about such high matters in a short time?

Gor. Certainly not.

Soc. Come, then, and let us see what we really mean about rhetoric; for I do not know what my own meaning is as yet. When the assembly meets to elect a physician or a shipwright or any other craftsman, will the rhetorician be taken into counsel? Surely not. For at every election he ought to be chosen who is most skilled; and, again, when walls have to be built or harbours or docks to be constructed, not the rhetorician but the master workman will advise; or when generals have to be chosen and an order of battle arranged, or a proposition taken, then the military will advise and not the rhetoricians: what do you say, Gorgias? Since you profess to be a rhetorician and a maker of rhetoricians, I cannot do better than learn the nature of your art from you. And here let me assure you that I have your interest in view as well as my own. For likely enough some one or other of the young men present might desire to become your pupil, and in fact I see some, and a good many too, who have this wish, but they would be too modest to question you. And therefore when you are interrogated by me, I would have you imagine that you are interrogated by them. "What is the use of coming to you, Gorgias? [. . . What] you teach us to advise the state?— about the just and unjust only, or about those other things also which Socrates has just mentioned?" How will you answer them?

Gor. I like your way of leading us on, Socrates, and I will endeavour to reveal to you the whole nature of rhetoric. You must have heard, I think, that the docks and the walls of the Athenians and the plan of the harbour were devised in accordance with the counsels, partly of Themistocles, and partly of Pericles, and not at the suggestion of the builders.

Soc. Such is the tradition, Gorgias, about Themistocles; and I myself heard the speech of Pericles when he advised us about the middle wall.

Gor. And you will observe, Socrates, that when a decision has to be given in such matters the rhetoricians are the advisers; they are the men who win their point.

Soc. I had that in my admiring mind, Gorgias, when I asked what is the nature of rhetoric, which always appears to me, when I look at the matter in this way, to be a marvel of greatness.

Gor. A marvel, indeed, Socrates, if you only knew how rhetoric comprehends and holds under her sway all the inferior arts. Let me offer you a striking example of this. On several occasions I have been with my brother Herodicus or some other physician to see one of his patients, who would not allow the physician to give him medicine, or apply a knife or hot iron to him; and I have persuaded him to do for me what he would not do for the physician just by the use of rhetoric. And I say that if a rhetorician and a physician were to go to any city, and had there to argue in the Ecclesia or any other assembly as to which of them should be elected state-physician, the physician would have no chance; but he who could speak would be chosen if he wished; and in a contest with a man of any other profession the rhetorician more than any one would have the power of getting himself chosen, for he can speak more persuasively to the multitude than any of them, and on any subject. Such is the nature and power of the art of rhetoric And yet, Socrates, rhetoric should be used like any other competitive art, not against everybody— the rhetorician ought not to abuse his strength any more than a pugilist or pancratiast or other master of fence; because he has powers which are more than a match either for friend or enemy, he ought not therefore to strike, stab, or slay his friends. Suppose a man to have been trained in the palestra and to be a skilful boxer—he in the fulness of his strength goes and strikes his father or mother or one of his familiars or friends; but that is no reason why the trainers or fencing-masters should be held in detestation or banished from the city—surely not. For they taught their art for a good purpose, to be used against enemies and evil-doers, in self-defence not in aggression, and others have perverted their instructions, and turned to a bad use their own strength and skill. But not on this account are the teachers bad, neither is the art in fault, or bad in itself; I should rather say that those who make a bad use of the art are to blame. And the same argument holds good of rhetoric; for the rhetorician can speak against all men and upon any subject—in short, he can persuade the multitude better than any other man of anything which he pleases, but he should not therefore seek to defraud the physician or any other artist of his reputation merely because he has the power; he ought to use rhetoric fairly, as he would also use his athletic powers. And if after having become a rhetorician he makes a bad use of his strength and skill, his instructor surely ought not on that account to be held in detestation or banished. For he was intended by his teacher to make a good use of his instructions, but he abuses them. And therefore he is the person who ought to be held in detestation, banished, and put to death, and not his instructor.

Soc.   You, Gorgias, like myself, have had great experience of disputations, and you must have observed, I think, that they do not always terminate in mutual edification, or in the definition by either party of the subjects which they are discussing; but disagreements are apt to arise—somebody says that another has not spoken truly or clearly; and then they get into a passion and begin to quarrel, both parties conceiving that their opponents are arguing from personal feeling only and jealousy of themselves, not from any interest in the question at issue. And sometimes they will go on abusing one another until the company at last are quite vexed at themselves for ever listening to such fellows. Why do I say this? Why, because I cannot help feeling that you are now saying what is not quite consistent or accordant with what you were saying at first about rhetoric. And I am afraid to point this out to you, lest you should think that I have some animosity against you, and that I speak, not for the sake of discovering the truth, but from jealousy of you. Now if you are one of my sort, I should like to cross-examine you, but if not I will let you alone. And what is my sort? you will ask. I am one of those who are very willing to be refuted if I say anything which is not true, and very willing to refute any one else who says what is not true, and quite as ready to be

refuted as to refute— [. . .] I for I hold that this is the greater gain of the two, just as the gain is greater of being cured of a very great evil than of curing another. For I imagine that there is no evil which a man can endure so great as an erroneous opinion about the matters of which we are speaking and if you claim to be one of my sort, let us have the discussion out, but if you would rather have done, no matter—let us make an end of it.

Gor.   I should say, Socrates, that I am quite the man whom you indicate; but, perhaps, we ought to consider the audience, for, before you came, I had already given a long exhibition, and if we proceed the argument may run on to a great length. And therefore I think that we should consider whether we, may not be detaining some part of the company when they are wanting to do something else.

Chaer.   You hear the audience cheering, Gorgias and Socrates, which shows their desire to listen to you; and for myself, Heaven forbid that I should have any business on hand which would take me [away] from a discussion so interesting and so ably maintained.

Cal.   By the gods, Chaerephon, although I have been present at many discussions, I doubt whether I was ever so much delighted before, and therefore if you go on discoursing all day I shall be the better pleased.

Soc.   I may truly say, Callicles, that I am willing, if Gorgias is.

Gor.   After all this, Socrates, I should be disgraced if I refused, especially as I have promised to answer all comers; in accordance with the wishes of the company, [then, continue] and ask of me any question which you like.

Soc.   Let me tell you then, Gorgias, what surprises me in your words; though I dare say that you may be right, and I may have understood your meaning. You say that you can make any man, who will learn of you, a rhetorician?

Gor.   Yes.

Soc. Do you mean that you will teach him to gain the ears of the multitude on any subject, and this not by instruction but by persuasion?

Gor. Quite so.

Soc. You were saying, in fact, that the rhetorician will have, greater powers of persuasion than the physician even in a matter of health?

Gor. Yes, with the multitude—that is.

Soc. You mean to say, with the ignorant; for with those who know he cannot be supposed to have greater powers of persuasion.

Gor. Very true.

Soc. But if he is to have more power of persuasion than the physician, he will have greater power than he who knows?

Gor. Certainly.

Soc. Although he is not a physician:—is he?

Gor. No.

Soc. And he who is not a physician must, obviously, be ignorant of what the physician knows.

Gor. Clearly.

Soc. Then, when the rhetorician is more persuasive than the physician, the ignorant is more persuasive with the ignorant than he who has knowledge?—is not that the inference?

Gor. In the case supposed:—Yes.

Soc. And the same holds of the relation of rhetoric to all the other arts; the rhetorician need not know the truth about things; he has only to discover some way of persuading the ignorant that he has more knowledge than those who know?

Gor. Yes, Socrates, and is not this a great comfort?—not to have learned the other arts, but the art of rhetoric only, and yet to be in no way inferior to the professors of them?

Soc. Whether the rhetorician is or [is] not inferior on this account is a question which we will hereafter examine if the enquiry is likely to be of any service to us; but I would rather begin by asking, whether he is as ignorant of the just and unjust, base and honourable, good and evil, as he is of medicine and the other arts; I mean to say, does he really know anything of what is good and evil, base or honourable, just or unjust in them; or has he only a way with the ignorant of persuading them that he not knowing is to be esteemed to know more about these things than some one else who knows? Or must the pupil know these things and come to you knowing them before he can acquire the art of rhetoric? If he is ignorant, you who are the teacher of rhetoric will not teach him—it is not your business; but you will make him seem to the multitude to know them, when he does not know them; and seem to be a good man, when he is not. Or will you be unable to teach him rhetoric at all, unless he knows the truth of these things first? What is to be said about all this? By heavens, Gorgias, I wish that you would reveal to me the power of rhetoric, as you were saying that you would.

Gor. Well, Socrates, I suppose that if the pupil does chance not to know them, he will have to learn of me these things as well.

Soc. Say no more, for there you are right; and so he whom you make a rhetorician must either know the nature of the just and unjust already, or he must be taught by you.

Gor. Certainly.

Soc. Well, and is not he who has learned carpentering a carpenter?

Gor. Yes.

Soc. And he who has learned music a musician?

Gor. Yes.

Soc. And he who has learned medicine is a physician, in like manner? He who has learned anything whatever is that which his knowledge makes him.

Gor. Certainly.

Soc. And in the same way, he who has learned what is just is just?

Gor. To be sure.

Soc.   And he who is just may be supposed to do what is just?

Gor.   Yes.

Soc.   And must not the just man always desire to do what is just?

Gor.   That is clearly the inference.

Soc.   Surely, then, the just man will never consent to do injustice?

Gor.   Certainly not.

Soc.   And according to the argument the rhetorician must be a just man?

Gor.   Yes.

Soc.   And will therefore never be willing to do injustice?

Gor.   Clearly not.

Soc.   But do you remember saying just now that the trainer is not to be accused or banished if the pugilist makes a wrong use of his pugilistic art; and in like manner, if the rhetorician makes a bad and unjust use of rhetoric, that is not to be laid to the charge of his teacher, who is not to be banished, but the wrong-doer himself who made a bad use of his rhetoric—he is to be banished—was not that said?

Gor.   Yes, it was.

Soc.   But now we are affirming that the aforesaid rhetorician will never have done injustice at all?

Gor.   True.

Soc.   And at the very outset, Gorgias, it was said that rhetoric treated of discourse, not [like arithmetic] about odd and even, but about just and unjust? Was not this said?

Gor.   Yes.

Soc.   I was thinking at the time, when I heard you saying so, that rhetoric, which is always discoursing about justice, could not possibly be an unjust thing. But when you added, shortly afterwards, that the rhetorician might make a bad use of rhetoric I noted with surprise the inconsistency into which you had fallen; and I said, that if you thought, as I did, that there

was a gain in being refuted, there would be an advantage in going on with the question, but if not, I would leave off. And in the course of our investigations, as you will see yourself, the rhetorician has been acknowledged to be incapable of making an unjust use of rhetoric, or of willingness to do injustice. By the dog, Gorgias, there will be a great deal of discussion, before we get at the truth of all this.

Pol.   And do even you, Socrates, seriously believe what you are now saying about rhetoric? What! because Gorgias was ashamed to deny that the rhetorician knew the just and the honourable and the good, and admitted that to any one who came to him ignorant of them he could teach them, and then out of this admission there arose a contradiction—the thing which you dearly love, and to which not he, but you, brought the argument by your captious questions—[do you seriously believe that there is any truth in all this?] For will any one ever acknowledge that he does not know, or cannot teach, the nature of justice? The truth is, that there is great want of manners in bringing the argument to such a pass.

Soc.   Illustrious Polus, the reason why we provide ourselves with friends and children is, that when we get old and stumble, a younger generation may be at hand to set us on our legs again in our words and in our actions: and now, if I and Gorgias are stumbling, here are you who should raise us up; and I for my part engage to retract any error into which you may think that I have fallen—upon one condition:

Pol.   What condition?

Soc.   That you contract, Polus, the prolixity of speech in which you indulged at first.

Pol.   What! do you mean that I may not use as many words as I please?

Soc.   Only to think, my friend, that having come on a visit to Athens, which is the most free-spoken state in Hellas, you when you got there, and you alone, should be deprived of the power of speech—that would be hard indeed. But then consider my case:—shall not I be very hardly used, if, when you are making a long oration, and refusing to answer what you are asked, I am compelled to stay and listen to you, and may not go away? I say rather, if you have a real interest in the argument, or, to repeat my former expression, have any desire to set it on its legs, take back any statement which you please; and in your turn ask and answer, like myself and Gorgias—refute and be refuted: for I suppose that you would claim to know what Gorgias knows—would you not?

Pol. Yes.

Soc. And you, like him, invite any one to ask you about anything which he pleases, and you will know how to answer him?

Pol. To be sure.

Soc. And now, which will you do, ask or answer?

Pol. I will ask; and do you answer me, Socrates, the same question which Gorgias, as you suppose, is unable to answer: What is rhetoric?

Soc. Do you mean what sort of an art?

Pol. Yes.

Soc. To say the truth, Polus, it is not an art at all, in my opinion.

Pol. Then what, in your opinion, is rhetoric?

Soc. A thing which, as I was lately reading in a book of yours, you say that you have made an art.

Pol. What thing?

Soc. I should say a sort of experience.

Pol. Does rhetoric seem to you to be an experience?

Soc. That is my view, but you may be of another mind.

Pol. An experience in what?

Soc. An experience in producing a sort of delight and gratification.

Pol. And if able to gratify others, must not rhetoric be a fine thing?

Soc. What are you saying, Polus? Why do you ask me whether rhetoric is a fine thing or not, when I have not as yet told you what rhetoric is?

Pol. Did I not hear you say that rhetoric was a sort of experience?

Soc. Will you, who are so desirous to gratify others, afford a slight gratification to me?

Pol. I will.

Soc. Will you ask me, what sort of an art is cookery?

Pol. What sort of an art is cookery?

Soc. Not an art at all, Polus.

Pol. What then?

Soc. I should say an experience.

Pol. In what? I wish that you would explain to me.

Soc. An experience in producing a sort of delight and gratification, Polus.

Pol. Then are cookery and rhetoric the same?

Soc. No, they are only different parts of the same profession.

Pol. Of what profession?

Soc. I am afraid that the truth may seem discourteous; and I hesitate to answer, lest Gorgias should imagine that I am making fun of his own profession. For whether or no this is that art of rhetoric which Gorgias practises I really cannot tell:—from what he was just now saying, nothing appeared of what he thought of his art, but the rhetoric which I mean is a part of a not very creditable whole.

Gor. A part of what, Socrates? Say what you mean, and never mind me.

Soc. In my opinion then, Gorgias, the whole of which rhetoric is a part is not an art at all, but the habit of a bold and ready wit, which knows how to manage mankind: this habit I sum up under the word "flattery"; and it appears to me to have many other parts, one of which is cookery, which may seem to be an art, but, as I maintain, is only an experience or routine and not an art:—another part is rhetoric, and the art of attiring and sophistry are two others: thus there are four branches, and four different things answering to them. And Polus may ask, if he likes, for he has not as yet been informed, what part of flattery is rhetoric: he did not see that I had not yet answered him when he proceeded to ask a further question: Whether I do not think rhetoric a fine thing? But I shall not tell him whether rhetoric is a fine thing or not, until I have first answered, "What is rhetoric?" For that would not be right, Polus; but I shall be happy to answer, if you will ask me, What part of flattery is rhetoric?

Pol. I will ask and do you answer? What part of flattery is rhetoric?

Soc. Will you understand my answer? Rhetoric, according to my view, is the ghost or counterfeit of a part of politics.

Pol. And noble or ignoble?

Soc. Ignoble, I should say, if I am compelled to answer, for I call what is bad ignoble: though I doubt whether you understand what I was saying before.

Gor. Indeed, Socrates, I cannot say that I understand myself.

Soc. I do not wonder, Gorgias; for I have not as yet explained myself, and our friend Polus, colt by name and colt by nature, is apt to run away.

Gor. Never mind him, but explain to me what you mean by saying that rhetoric is the counterfeit of a part of politics.

Soc. I will try, then, to explain my notion of rhetoric, and if I am mistaken, my friend Polus shall refute me. We may assume the existence of bodies and of souls?

Gor. Of course.

Soc. You would further admit that there is a good condition of either of them?

Gor. Yes.

Soc. Which condition may not be really good, but good only in appearance? I mean to say, that there are many persons who appear to be in good health, and whom only a physician or trainer will discern at first sight not to be in good health.

Gor. True.

Soc. And this applies not only to the body, but also to the soul: in either there may be that which

gives the appearance of health and not the reality?

Gor. Yes, certainly.

Soc. And now I will endeavour to explain to you more clearly what I mean: The soul and body being two, have two arts corresponding to them: there is the art of politics attending on the soul; and another art attending on the body, of which I know no single name, but which may be described as having two divisions, one of them gymnastic, and the other medicine. And in politics there is a legislative part, which answers to gymnastic, as justice does to medicine; and the two parts run into one another, justice having to do with the same subject as legislation, and medicine with the same subject as gymnastic, but with a difference. Now, seeing that there are these four arts, two attending on the body and two on the soul for their highest good; flattery knowing, or rather guessing their natures, has distributed herself into four shams or simulations of them; she puts on the likeness of some one or other of them, and pretends to be that which she simulates, and having no regard for men's highest interests, is ever making pleasure the bait of the unwary, and deceiving them into the belief that she is of the highest value to them. Cookery simulates the disguise of medicine, and pretends to know what food is the best for the body; and if the physician and the cook had to enter into a competition in which children were the judges, or men who had no more sense than children, as to which of them best understands the goodness or badness of food, the physician would be starved to death. A flattery I deem this to be and of an ignoble sort, Polus, for to you I am now addressing myself, because it aims at pleasure without any thought of the best. An art I do not call it, but only an experience, because it is unable to explain or to give a reason of the nature of its own applications. And I do not call any irrational thing an art; but if you dispute my words, I am prepared to argue in defence of them.

Cookery, then, I maintain to be a flattery which takes the form of medicine; and tiring, in like manner, is a flattery which takes the form of gymnastic, and is knavish, false, ignoble, illiberal, working deceitfully by the help of lines, and colours, and enamels, and garments, and making men affect a spurious beauty to the neglect of the true beauty which is given by gymnastic.

I would rather not be tedious, and therefore I will only say, after the manner of the geometricians (for I think that by this time you will be able to follow)

as tiring : gymnastic :: cookery : medicine; or rather,

as tiring : gymnastic :: sophistry : legislation; and

as cookery : medicine :: rhetoric : justice.

And this, I say, is the natural difference between the rhetorician and the sophist, but by reason of their near connection, they are apt to be jumbled up together; neither do they know what to make of themselves, nor do other men know what to make of them. For if the body presided over itself, and were not under the guidance of the soul, and the soul did not discern and discriminate between cookery and medicine, but the body was made the judge of them, and the rule of judgment was the bodily delight which was given by them, then the word of Anaxagoras, that word with which you, friend Polus, are so well acquainted, would prevail far and wide: "Chaos" would come again, and cookery, health, and medicine would mingle in an indiscriminate mass. And now I have told you my notion of rhetoric, which is, in relation to the soul, what cookery is to the body. I may have been inconsistent in making a long speech, when I would not allow you to discourse at length. But I think that I may be excused, because you did not understand me, and could make no use of my answer when I spoke shortly, and therefore I had to enter into explanation. And if I show an equal inability to make use of yours, I hope that you will speak at equal length; but if I am able to understand you, let me have the benefit of your brevity, as is only fair: And now you may do what you please with my answer.

Pol. What do you mean? do you think that rhetoric is flattery?

Soc. Nay, I said a part of flattery—if at your age, Polus, you cannot remember, what will you do by-and-by, when you get older?

Pol. And are the good rhetoricians meanly regarded in states, under the idea that they are flatterers?

Soc. Is that a question or the beginning of a speech?

Pol. I am asking a question.

Soc. Then my answer is, that they are not regarded at all.

Pol. How not regarded? Have they not very great power in states?

Soc. Not if you mean to say that power is a good to the possessor.

[. . .]

7

RHETORIC

ARISTOTLE

BOOK I

1

RHETORIC [is] the counterpart of Dialectic. Both alike are concerned with such things as come, more or less, within the general ken of all men and belong to no definite science. Accordingly all men make use, more or less, of both; for to a certain extent all men attempt to discuss statements and to maintain them, to defend themselves and to attack others. Ordinary people do this either at random or through practice and from acquired habit. Both ways being possible, the subject can plainly be handled systematically, for it is possible to inquire the reason why some speakers succeed through practice and others spontaneously; and every one will at once agree that such an inquiry is the function of an art.

Now, the framers of the current treatises on rhetoric have constructed but a small portion of that art. The modes of persuasion are the only true constituents of the art: everything else is merely accessory. These writers, however, say nothing about enthymemes, which are the substance of rhetorical persuasion, but deal mainly with non-essentials. The arousing of prejudice, pity, anger, and similar emotions has nothing to do with the essential facts, but is merely a personal appeal to the man who is judging the case. Consequently if the rules for trials which are now laid down [in] some states—especially in well-governed states—were applied everywhere, such people would have nothing to say. All men, no doubt, think that the laws should prescribe such rules, but some, as in the court of Areopagus, give practical effect to their thoughts and forbid talk about non-essentials. This is sound law and custom. It is not right to pervert the judge by moving him to anger or envy or pity—one might as well warp a carpenter's rule before using it. Again, a litigant has clearly nothing to do but to show that the alleged fact is so or is not so, that it has or has

SOURCE: Aristotle. (c. 350 BC). *Rhetoric* (W. Rhys Roberts, Trans.; excerpts). Retrieved May 23, 2005, from http://infomotions .com/etexts/philosophy/400BC-301BC/aristotle-rhetoric-86.txt. (This document is in the public domain.)

not happened. As to whether a thing is important or unimportant, just or unjust, the judge must surely refuse to take his instructions from the litigants: he must decide for himself all such points as the law-giver has not already defined for him.

Now, it is of great moment that well-drawn laws should themselves define all the points they possibly can and leave as few as may be to the decision of the judges; and this for several reasons. First, to find one man, or a few men, who are sensible persons and capable of legislating and administering justice is easier than to find a large number. Next, laws are made after long consideration, whereas decisions in the courts are given at short notice, which makes it hard for those who try the case to satisfy the claims of justice and expediency. The weightiest reason of all is that the decision of the lawgiver is not particular but prospective and general, whereas members of the assembly and the jury find it their duty to decide on definite cases brought before them. They will often have allowed themselves to be so much influenced by feelings of friendship or hatred or self-interest that they lose any clear vision of the truth and have their judgement obscured by considerations of personal pleasure or pain. In general, then, the judge should, we say, be allowed to decide as few things as possible. But questions as to whether something has happened or has not happened, will be or will not be, is or is not, must of necessity be left to the judge, since the lawgiver cannot foresee them. If this is so, it is evident that any one who lays down rules about other matters, such as what must be the contents of the 'introduction' or the 'narration' or any of the other divisions of a speech, is theorizing about non-essentials as if they belonged to the art. The only question with which these writers here deal is how to put the judge into a given frame of mind. About the orator's proper modes of persuasion they have nothing to tell us; nothing, that is, about how to gain skill in enthymemes.

Hence it comes that, although the same systematic principles apply to political as to forensic oratory, and although the former is a nobler business, and fitter for a citizen, than that which concerns the relations of private individuals, these authors say nothing about political oratory, but try, one and all, to write treatises on the way to plead in court. The reason for this is that in political oratory there is less inducement to talk about nonessentials. Political oratory is less given to unscrupulous practices than forensic, because it treats of wider issues. In a political debate the man who is forming a judgement is making a decision about his own vital interests. There is no need, therefore, to prove anything except that the facts are what the supporter of a measure maintains they are. In forensic oratory this is not enough; to conciliate the listener is what pays here. It is other people's affairs that are to be decided, so that the judges, intent on their own satisfaction and listening with partiality, surrender themselves to the disputants instead of judging between them. Hence in many places, as we have said already, irrelevant speaking is forbidden in the law-courts: in the public assembly those who have to form a judgement are themselves well able to guard against that.

It is clear, then, that rhetorical study, in its strict sense, is concerned with the modes of persuasion. Persuasion is clearly a sort of demonstration, since we are most fully persuaded when we consider a thing to have been demonstrated. The orator's demonstration is an enthymeme, and this is, in general, the most effective of the modes of persuasion. The enthymeme is a sort of syllogism, and the consideration of syllogisms of all kinds, without distinction, is the business of dialectic, either of dialectic as a whole or of one of its branches. It follows plainly, therefore, that he who is best able to see how and from what elements a syllogism is produced will also be best skilled in the enthymeme, when he has further learnt what its subject-matter is and in what respects it differs from the syllogism of strict logic. The true and the approximately true are apprehended by the same faculty; it may also be noted that men have a sufficient natural instinct for what is true, and usually do arrive at the truth. Hence the man who makes a good guess at truth is likely to make a good guess at probabilities.

It has now been shown that the ordinary writers on rhetoric treat of non-essentials; it has also been shown why they have inclined more towards the forensic branch of oratory.

Rhetoric is useful (1) because things that are true and things that are just have a natural tendency to prevail over their opposites, so that if the decisions of judges are not what they ought to be, the defeat must be due to the speakers themselves, and they must be blamed accordingly. Moreover, (2) before some audiences not even the possession of the exactest knowledge will make it easy for what we say to produce conviction. For argument based on knowledge implies instruction, and there are people whom one cannot instruct. Here, then, we must use, as our modes of persuasion and argument, notions possessed by everybody, as we observed in the Topics when dealing with the way to handle a popular audience. Further, (3) we must be able to employ persuasion, just as strict reasoning can be employed, on opposite sides of a question, not in order that we may in practice employ it in both ways (for we must not make people believe what is wrong), but in order that we may see clearly what the facts are, and that, if another man argues unfairly, we on our part may be able to confute him. No other of the arts draws opposite conclusions: dialectic and rhetoric alone do this. Both these arts draw opposite conclusions impartially. Nevertheless, the underlying facts do not lend themselves equally well to the contrary views. No; things that are true and things that are better are, by their nature, practically always easier to prove and easier to believe in. Again, (4) it is absurd to hold that a man ought to be ashamed of being unable to defend himself with his limbs, but not of being unable to defend himself with speech and reason, when the use of rational speech is more distinctive of a human being than the use of his limbs. And if it be objected that one who uses such power of speech unjustly might do great harm, that is a charge which may be made in common against all good things except virtue, and above all against the things that are most useful, as strength, health, wealth, generalship. A man can confer the greatest of benefits by a right use of these, and inflict the greatest of injuries by using them wrongly.

It is clear, then, that rhetoric is not bound up with a single definite class of subjects, but is as universal as dialectic; it is clear, also, that it is useful. It is clear, further, that its function is not simply to succeed in persuading, but rather to discover the means of coming as near such success as the circumstances of each particular case allow. In this it resembles all other arts. For example, it is not the function of medicine simply to make a man quite healthy, but to put him as far as may be on the road to health; it is possible to give excellent treatment even to those who can never enjoy sound health. Furthermore, it is plain that it is the function of one and the same art to discern the real and the apparent means of persuasion, just as it is the function of dialectic to discern the real and the apparent syllogism. What makes a man a 'sophist' is not his faculty, but his moral purpose. In rhetoric, however, the term 'rhetorician' may describe either the speaker's knowledge of the art, or his moral purpose. In dialectic it is different: a man is a 'sophist' because he has a certain kind of moral purpose, a 'dialectician' in respect, not of his moral purpose, but of his faculty.

Let us now try to give some account of the systematic principles of Rhetoric itself—of the right method and means of succeeding in the object we set before us. We must make as it were a fresh start, and before going further define what rhetoric is.

2

Rhetoric may be defined as the faculty of observing in any given case the available means of persuasion. This is not a function of any other art. Every other art can instruct or persuade about its own particular subject-matter; for instance, medicine about what is healthy and unhealthy, geometry about the properties of magnitudes, arithmetic about numbers, and the same is true of the other arts and sciences. But rhetoric we look upon as the power of observing the means of persuasion on almost any subject presented to us;

and that is why we say that, in its technical character, it is not concerned with any special or definite class of subjects.

Of the modes of persuasion some belong strictly to the art of rhetoric and some do not. By the latter I mean such things as are not supplied by the speaker but are there at the outset—witnesses, evidence given under torture, written contracts, and so on. By the former I mean such as we can ourselves construct by means of the principles of rhetoric. The one kind has merely to be used, the other has to be invented.

Of the modes of persuasion furnished by the spoken word there are three kinds. The first kind depends on the personal character of the speaker; the second on putting the audience into a certain frame of mind; the third on the proof, or apparent proof, provided by the words of the speech itself. Persuasion is achieved by the speaker's personal character when the speech is so spoken as to make us think him credible. We believe good men more fully and more readily than others: this is true generally whatever the question is, and absolutely true where exact certainty is impossible and opinions are divided. This kind of persuasion, like the others, should be achieved by what the speaker says, not by what people think of his character before he begins to speak. It is not true, as some writers assume in their treatises on rhetoric, that the personal goodness revealed by the speaker contributes nothing to his power of persuasion; on the contrary, his character may almost be called the most effective means of persuasion he possesses. Secondly, persuasion may come through the hearers, when the speech stirs their emotions. Our judgements when we are pleased and friendly are not the same as when we are pained and hostile. It is towards producing these effects, as we maintain, that present-day writers on rhetoric direct the whole of their efforts. This subject shall be treated in detail when we come to speak of the emotions. Thirdly, persuasion is effected through the speech itself when we have proved a truth or an apparent truth by means of the persuasive arguments suitable to the case in question.

There are, then, these three means of effecting persuasion. The man who is to be in command of them must, it is clear, be able (1) to reason logically, (2) to understand human character and goodness in their various forms, and (3) to understand the emotions—that is, to name them and describe them, to know their causes and the way in which they are excited. It thus appears that rhetoric is an offshoot of dialectic and also of ethical studies. Ethical studies may fairly be called political; and for this reason rhetoric masquerades as political science, and the professors of it as political experts—sometimes from want of education, sometimes from ostentation, sometimes owing to other human failings. As a matter of fact, it is a branch of dialectic and similar to it, as we said at the outset. Neither rhetoric nor dialectic is the scientific study of any one separate subject: both are faculties for providing arguments. This is perhaps a sufficient account of their scope and of how they are related to each other.

With regard to the persuasion achieved by proof or apparent proof: just as in dialectic there is induction on the one hand and syllogism or apparent syllogism on the other, so it is in rhetoric. The example is an induction, the enthymeme is a syllogism, and the apparent enthymeme is an apparent syllogism. I call the enthymeme a rhetorical syllogism, and the example a rhetorical induction. Every one who effects persuasion through proof does in fact use either enthymemes or examples: there is no other way. And since every one who proves anything at all is bound to use either syllogisms or inductions (and this is clear to us from the Analytics), it must follow that enthymemes are syllogisms and examples are inductions. The difference between example and enthymeme is made plain by the passages in the Topics where induction and syllogism have already been discussed. When we base the proof of a proposition on a number of similar cases, this is induction in dialectic, example in rhetoric; when it is shown that, certain propositions being true, a further and quite distinct proposition must also be true in consequence, whether invariably or usually, this is called syllogism in dialectic, enthymeme in rhetoric. It is plain also that each of these types of oratory has its advantages. Types of oratory, I say: for what has been said in the Methodics applies equally well here; in some oratorical styles examples prevail, in others enthymemes; and in like manner, some orators are better at the former and some at the latter. Speeches that rely on examples are as persuasive as the other kind, but those which rely on enthymemes excite the louder applause. The sources of examples and enthymemes, and their proper uses, we will discuss later. Our next step is to define the processes themselves more clearly.

A statement is persuasive and credible either because it is directly self-evident or because it appears to be proved from other statements that are so. In either case it is persuasive because there is somebody whom it persuades. But none of the arts theorize about individual cases. Medicine, for instance, does not theorize about what will help to cure Socrates or Callias, but only about what will help to cure any or all of a given class of patients: this alone is business: individual cases are so infinitely various that no systematic knowledge of them is possible. In the same way the theory of rhetoric is concerned not with what seems probable to a given individual like Socrates or Hippias, but with what seems probable to men of a given type; and this is true of dialectic also. Dialectic does not construct its syllogisms out of any haphazard materials, such as the fancies of crazy people, but out of materials that call for discussion; and rhetoric, too, draws upon the regular subjects of debate. The duty of rhetoric is to deal with such matters as we deliberate upon without arts or systems to guide us, in the hearing of persons who cannot take in at a glance a complicated argument, or follow a long chain of reasoning. The subjects of our deliberation are such as seem to present us with alternative possibilities: about things that could not have been, and cannot now or in the future be, other than they are, nobody who takes them to be of this nature wastes his time in deliberation.

It is possible to form syllogisms and draw conclusions from the results of previous syllogisms; or, on the other hand, from premisses which have not been thus proved, and at the same time are so little accepted that they call for proof. Reasonings of the former kind will necessarily be hard to follow owing to their length, for we assume an audience of untrained thinkers; those of the latter kind will fail to win assent, because they are based on premisses that are not generally admitted or believed.

The enthymeme and the example must, then, deal with what is in the main contingent, the example being an induction, and the enthymeme a syllogism, about such matters. The enthymeme must consist of few propositions, fewer often than those which make up the normal syllogism. For if any of these propositions is a familiar fact, there is no need even to mention it; the hearer adds it himself. Thus, to show that Dorieus has been victor in a contest for which the prize is a crown, it is enough to say 'For he has been victor in the Olympic games', without adding 'And in the Olympic games the prize is a crown', a fact which everybody knows.

There are few facts of the 'necessary' type that can form the basis of rhetorical syllogisms. Most of the things about which we make decisions, and into which therefore we inquire, present us with alternative possibilities. For it is about our actions that we deliberate and inquire, and all our actions have a contingent character; hardly any of them are determined by necessity. Again, conclusions that state what is merely usual or possible must be drawn from premisses that do the same, just as 'necessary' conclusions must be drawn from 'necessary' premisses; this too is clear to us from the Analytics. It is evident, therefore, that the propositions forming the basis of enthymemes, though some of them may be 'necessary', will most of them be only usually true. Now the materials of enthymemes are Probabilities and Signs, which we can see must correspond respectively with the propositions that are generally and those that are necessarily true. A Probability is a thing that usually happens; not, however, as some definitions would suggest, anything whatever that usually happens, but only if it belongs to the class of the 'contingent' or 'variable'. It bears the same relation to that in respect of which it is probable as the universal bears to the particular. Of Signs, one kind bears the same relation to the statement it supports as the particular bears to the universal, the other the same as the universal bears to the particular. The infallible kind is a 'complete proof' (tekmerhiou); the fallible kind has no specific name. By infallible signs I mean those on which syllogisms proper may be based: and this shows us why this kind of Sign is called 'complete proof': when people think that what they have said cannot be refuted, they then think that they are bringing forward a 'complete proof', meaning that the matter has now been demonstrated and completed (peperhasmeuou); for the word 'perhas' has the same meaning (of 'end' or 'boundary') as the word 'tekmarh' in the ancient tongue. Now the one kind of Sign (that which bears to the proposition it supports the relation of particular to universal) may be illustrated thus. Suppose it were said, 'The fact that Socrates was wise and just is a sign that the wise are just'. Here we certainly have a Sign; but even though the proposition be true, the argument is refutable, since it does not form a syllogism. Suppose, on the other hand, it were said, 'The fact that he has a fever is a sign that he is ill', or, 'The fact that she is giving milk is a sign that she has lately borne a child'. Here we have the infallible kind of Sign, the only kind that constitutes a complete proof, since it is the only kind that, if the particular statement is true, is irrefutable. The other kind of Sign, that which bears to the proposition it supports the relation of universal to particular, might be illustrated by saying, 'The fact that he breathes fast is a sign that he has a fever'. This argument also is refutable, even if the statement about the fast breathing be true, since a man may breathe hard without having a fever.

It has, then, been stated above what is the nature of a Probability, of a Sign, and of a complete proof, and what are the differences between them. In the Analytics a more explicit description has been given of these points; it is there shown why some of these reasonings can be put into syllogisms and some cannot.

The 'example' has already been described as one kind of induction; and the special nature of the subject-matter that distinguishes it from the other kinds has also been stated above. Its relation to the proposition it supports is not that of part to whole, nor whole to part, nor whole to whole, but of part to part, or like to like. When two statements are of the same order, but one is more familiar than the other, the former is an 'example'. The argument may, for instance, be that Dionysius, in asking as he does for a body-guard, is scheming to make himself a despot. For in the past Peisistratus kept asking for a bodyguard in order to carry out such a scheme, and did make himself a despot as soon as he got it; and so did Theagenes at Megara; and in the same way all other instances known to the speaker are made into examples, in order to show what is not yet known, that Dionysius has the same purpose in making the same request: all these being instances of the one general principle, that a man who asks for a bodyguard is scheming to make himself a despot. We have now described the sources of those means of persuasion which are popularly supposed to be demonstrative.

There is an important distinction between two sorts of enthymemes that has been wholly overlooked by almost everybody—one that also subsists between the syllogisms treated of in dialectic. One sort of enthymeme really belongs to rhetoric, as one sort of syllogism really belongs to dialectic; but the other sort really belongs to other arts and faculties, whether to those we already exercise or to those we have not yet acquired. Missing this distinction, people fail to notice that the more correctly they handle their particular subject the further they are getting away from pure rhetoric or dialectic. This statement will be clearer if expressed more fully. I mean that the proper subjects of dialectical and rhetorical syllogisms are the things with which we say the regular or universal

Lines of Argument are concerned, that is to say those lines of argument that apply equally to questions of right conduct, natural science, politics, and many other things that have nothing to do with one another. Take, for instance, the line of argument concerned with 'the more or less'. On this line of argument it is equally easy to base a syllogism or enthymeme about any of what nevertheless are essentially disconnected subjects—right conduct, natural science, or anything else whatever. But there are also those special Lines of Argument which are based on such propositions as apply only to particular groups or classes of things. Thus there are propositions about natural science on which it is impossible to base any enthymeme or syllogism about ethics, and other propositions about ethics on which nothing can be based about natural science. The same principle applies throughout. The general Lines of Argument have no special subject-matter, and therefore will not increase our understanding of any particular class of things. On the other hand, the better the selection one makes of propositions suitable for special Lines of Argument, the nearer one comes, unconsciously, to setting up a science that is distinct from dialectic and rhetoric. One may succeed in stating the required principles, but one's science will be no longer dialectic or rhetoric, but the science to which the principles thus discovered belong. Most enthymemes are in fact based upon these particular or special Lines of Argument; comparatively few on the common or general kind. As in the [*topics*] therefore, so in this work, we must distinguish, in dealing with enthymemes, the special and the general Lines of Argument on which they are to be founded. By special Lines of Argument I mean the propositions peculiar to each several class of things, by general those common to all classes alike. We may begin with the special Lines of Argument. But, first of all, let us classify rhetoric into its varieties. Having distinguished these we may deal with them one by one, and try to discover the elements of which each is composed, and the propositions each must employ.

3

Rhetoric falls into three divisions, determined by the three classes of listeners to speeches. For of the three elements in speech-making—speaker, subject, and person addressed—it is the last one, the hearer, that determines the speech's end and object. The hearer must be either a judge, with a decision to make about things past or future, or an observer. A member of the assembly decides about future events, a juryman about past events: while those who merely decide on the orator's skill are observers. From this it follows that there are three divisions of oratory—(1) political, (2) forensic, and (3) the ceremonial oratory of display.

Political speaking urges us either to do or not to do something: one of these two courses is always taken by private counsellors, as well as by men who address public assemblies. Forensic speaking either attacks or defends somebody: one or other of these two things must always be done by the parties in a case. The ceremonial oratory of display either praises or censures somebody. These three kinds of rhetoric refer to three different kinds of time. The political orator is concerned with the future: it is about things to be done hereafter that he advises, for or against. The party in a case at law is concerned with the past; one man accuses the other, and the other defends himself, with reference to things already done. The ceremonial orator is, properly speaking, concerned with the present, since all men praise or blame in view of the state of things existing at the time, though they often find it useful also to recall the past and to make guesses at the future.

Rhetoric has three distinct ends in view, one for each of its three kinds. The political orator aims at establishing the expediency or the harmfulness of a proposed course of action; if he urges its acceptance, he does so on the ground that it will do good; if he urges its rejection, he does so on the ground that it will do harm; and all other points, such as whether the proposal is just or unjust, honourable or dishonourable, he brings in as subsidiary and relative to this main consideration. Parties in a law-case aim at establishing the justice or injustice of some action, and they too bring in all other points as subsidiary and relative to this one. Those who praise or attack a man aim at proving him worthy of honour or the reverse, and they too treat all other considerations with reference to this one.

That the three kinds of rhetoric do aim respectively at the three ends we have mentioned is shown by the fact that speakers will sometimes not try to establish anything else. Thus, the litigant will sometimes not deny that a thing has happened or that he has done harm. But that he is guilty of injustice he will never admit; otherwise there would be no need of a trial. So too, political orators often make any concession short of admitting that they are recommending their hearers to take an inexpedient course or not to take an expedient one. The question whether it is not unjust for a city to enslave its innocent neighbours often does not trouble them at all. In like manner those who praise or censure a man do not consider whether his acts have been expedient or not, but often make it a ground of actual praise that he has neglected his own interest to do what was honourable. Thus, they praise Achilles because he championed his fallen friend Patroclus, though he knew that this meant death, and that otherwise he need not die: yet while to die thus was the nobler thing for him to do, the expedient thing was to live on.

It is evident from what has been said that it is these three subjects, more than any others, about which the orator must be able to have propositions at his command. Now the propositions of Rhetoric are Complete Proofs, Probabilities, and Signs. Every kind of syllogism is composed of propositions, and the enthymeme is a particular kind of syllogism composed of the aforesaid propositions.

Since only possible actions, and not impossible ones, can ever have been done in the past or the present, and since things which have not occurred, or will not occur, also cannot have been done or be going to be done, it is necessary for the political, the forensic, and the ceremonial speaker alike to be able to have at their command propositions about the possible and the impossible, and about whether a thing has or has not occurred, will or will not occur. Further, all men, in giving praise or blame, in urging us to accept or reject proposals for action, in accusing others or defending themselves, attempt not only to prove the points mentioned but also to show that the good or the harm, the honour or disgrace, the justice or injustice, is great or small, either absolutely or relatively; and therefore it is plain that we must also have at our command propositions about greatness or smallness and the greater or the lesser—propositions both universal and particular. Thus, we must be able to say which is the greater or lesser good, the greater or lesser act of justice or injustice; and so on.

Such, then, are the subjects regarding which we are inevitably bound to master the propositions relevant to them. We must now discuss each particular class of these subjects in turn, namely those dealt with in political, in ceremonial, and lastly in legal, oratory.

4

First, then, we must ascertain what are the kinds of things, good or bad, about which the political orator offers counsel. For he does not deal with all things, but only with such as may or may not take place. Concerning things which exist or will exist inevitably, or which cannot possibly exist or take place, no counsel can be given. Nor, again, can counsel be given about the whole class of things which may or may not take place; for this class includes some good things that occur naturally, and some that occur by accident; and about these it is useless to offer counsel. Clearly counsel can only be given on matters about which people deliberate; matters, namely, that ultimately depend on ourselves, and which we have it in our power to set going. For we turn a thing over in our mind until we have reached the point of seeing whether we can do it or not.

Now to enumerate and classify accurately the usual subjects of public business, and further to frame, as far as possible, true definitions of them is a task which we must not attempt on the present occasion. For it does not belong to the art of rhetoric, but to a more instructive art and a more real branch of knowledge; and as it is, rhetoric has been given a far wider subject-matter than strictly belongs to it. The truth is, as indeed we have said already, that rhetoric is a combination of the science of logic and of the ethical branch of politics; and it is partly like dialectic, partly like sophistical reasoning. But the more we try to make either dialectic rhetoric not, what they really are, practical faculties, but sciences, the more we shall inadvertently be destroying their true nature; for we shall be re-fashioning them and shall be passing into the region of sciences dealing with definite subjects rather than simply with words and forms of reasoning. Even here, however, we will mention those points which it is of practical importance to distinguish, their fuller treatment falling naturally to political science.

The main matters on which all men deliberate and on which political speakers make speeches are some five in number: ways and means, war and peace, national defence, imports and exports, and legislation.

As to Ways and Means, then, the intending speaker will need to know the number and extent of the country's sources of revenue, so that, if any is being overlooked, it may be added, and, if any is defective, it may be increased. Further, he should know all the expenditure of the country, in order that, if any part of it is superfluous, it may be abolished, or, if any is too large, it may be reduced. For men become richer not only by increasing their existing wealth but also by reducing their expenditure. A comprehensive view of these questions cannot be gained solely from experience in home affairs; in order to advise on such matters a man must be keenly interested in the methods worked out in other lands.

As to Peace and War, he must know the extent of the military strength of his country, both actual and potential, and also the nature of that actual and potential strength; and further, what wars his country has waged, and how it has waged them. He must know these facts not only about his own country, but also about neighbouring countries; and also about countries with which war is likely, in order that peace may be maintained with those stronger than his own, and that his own may have power to make war or not against those that are weaker. He should know, too, whether the military power of another country is like or unlike that of his own; for this is a matter that may affect their relative strength. With the same end in view he must, besides, have studied the wars of other countries as well as those of his own, and the way they ended; similar causes are likely to have similar results.

With regard to National Defence: he ought to know all about the methods of defence in actual use, such as the strength and character of the defensive force and the positions of the forts—this last means that he must be well acquainted with the lie of the country—in order that a garrison may be increased if it is too small or removed if it is not wanted, and that the strategic points may be guarded with special care.

With regard to the Food Supply: he must know what outlay will meet the needs of his country; what kinds of food are produced at home and what imported; and what articles must be exported or imported. This last he must know in order that agreements and commercial treaties may be made with the countries concerned. There are, indeed, two sorts of state to which he must see that his countrymen give no cause for offence, states stronger than his own, and states with which it is advantageous to trade.

But while he must, for security's sake, be able to take all this into account, he must before all things understand the subject of legislation; for it is on a country's laws that its whole welfare depends. He must, therefore, know how many different forms of constitution there are; under what conditions each of these will prosper and by what internal developments or external attacks each of them tends to be destroyed. When I speak of destruction through internal developments I refer to the fact that all constitutions, except the best one of all, are destroyed both by not being pushed far enough and by being pushed too far. Thus, democracy loses its vigour, and finally passes into oligarchy, not only when it is not pushed far enough, but also when it is pushed a great deal too far; just as the aquiline and the snub nose not only turn into normal noses by not being aquiline or snub enough, but also by being too violently aquiline or snub arrive at a condition in which they no longer look like noses at all. It is useful, in framing laws, not only to study the past history of one's own country, in order to understand which constitution is desirable for it now, but also to have a knowledge of the constitutions of other nations, and so to learn for what kinds of nation the various kinds of constitution are suited. From this we can see that books of travel are useful aids to legislation, since from these we may learn the laws and customs of different races. The political speaker will also find the researches of historians useful. But all this is the business of political science and not of rhetoric.

These, then, are the most important kinds of information which the political speaker must possess. Let us now go back and state the premisses from which he will have to argue in favour of adopting or rejecting measures regarding these and other matters. . . .

8

A RHETORIC OF MOTIVES

KENNETH BURKE

INTRODUCTION

The only difficult portion of this book happens, unfortunately, to be at the start. There, selecting texts that are usually treated as pure poetry, we try to show why rhetorical and dialectical considerations are also called for. Since these texts involve an imagery of killing (as a typical text for today should) we note how, behind the surface, lies a quite different realm that has little to do with such motives. An imagery of killing is but one of many terminologies by which writers can represent the process of change. And while recognizing the sinister implications of a preference for homicidal and suicidal terms, we indicate that the principles of development or transformation ("rebirth") which they stand for are not strictly of such a nature at all.

We emerge from the analysis with the key term, "Identification." Hence, readers who would prefer to begin with it, rather than to worry a text

until it is gradually extricated, might go lightly through the opening pages, with the intention of not taking hold in earnest until they come to the general topic of *Identification,* on page 19.

Thereafter, with this term as instrument, we seek to mark off the areas of rhetoric, by showing how a rhetorical motive is often present where it is not usually recognized, or thought to belong. In part, we would but rediscover rhetorical elements that had become obscured when rhetoric as a term fell into disuse, and other specialized disciplines such as esthetics, anthropology, psychoanalysis, and sociology came to the fore (so that esthetics sought to outlaw rhetoric, while the other sciences we have mentioned took over, each in its own terms, the rich rhetorical elements that esthetics would ban).

But besides this job of reclamation, we also seek to develop our subject beyond the traditional bounds of rhetoric. There is an intermediate area of expression that is not wholly deliberate, yet not

SOURCE: Burke, K. (1969). *A rhetoric of motives.* Berkeley & Los Angeles: University of California Press. (pages xiii-xv, 20–26, 35–46). Reprinted by permission.

wholly unconscious. It lies midway between aimless utterance and speech directly purposive. For instance, a man who identifies his private ambitions with the good of the community may be partly justified, partly unjustified. He may be using a mere pretext to gain individual advantage at the public expense; yet he may be quite sincere, or even may willingly make sacrifices in behalf of such identification. Here is a rhetorical area not analyzable either as sheer design or as sheer simplicity. And we would treat of it here.

Traditionally, the key term for rhetoric is not "identification," but "persuasion." Hence, to make sure that we do not maneuver ourselves unnecessarily into a weak position, we review several classic texts which track down all the major implications of that term. Our treatment, in terms of identification, is decidedly not meant as a substitute for the sound traditional approach. Rather, as we try to show, it is but an accessory to the standard lore. And our book aims to make itself at home in both emphases.

Particularly when we come upon such aspects of persuasion as are found in "mystification," courtship, and the "magic" of class relationships, the reader will see why the classical notion of clear persuasive intent is not an accurate fit, for describing the ways in which the members of a group promote social cohesion by acting rhetorically upon themselves and one another. As W. C. Blum has stated the case deftly, "In identification lies the source of dedications and enslavements, in fact of cooperation."

All told, persuasion ranges from the bluntest quest of advantage, as in sales promotion or propaganda, through courtship, social etiquette, education, and the sermon, to a "pure" form that delights in the process of appeal for itself alone, without ulterior purpose. And identification ranges from the politician who, addressing an audience of farmers, says, "I was a farm boy myself," through the mysteries of social status, to the mystic's devout identification with the source of all being.

That the reader might find it gratifying to observe the many variations on our two interrelated themes, at every step we have sought to proceed by examples. Since we did not aim to write a compendium, we have not tried to cover the field in the way that a comprehensive historical survey might do—and another volume will be needed to deal adequately with the polemic kinds of rhetoric (such as the verbal tactics now called "cold war").

But we have tried to show what portions of other works should be selected as parts of a "course in rhetoric," and how they should be considered for our particular purposes. We have tried to show how rhetorical analysis throws light on literary texts and human relations generally. And while interested always in rhetorical devices, we have sought above all else to write a "philosophy of rhetoric."

We do not flatter ourselves that any one book can contribute much to counteract the torrents of ill will into which so many of our contemporaries have so avidly and sanctimoniously plunged. But the more strident our journalists, politicians, and alas! even many of our churchmen become, the more convinced we are that books should be written for tolerance and contemplation.

Part I: The Range of Rhetoric

[. . .]

Identification and "Consubstantiality"

A is not identical with his colleague, B. But insofar as their interests are joined, A is *identified* with B. Or he may *identify himself* with B even when their interests are not joined, if he assumes that they are, or is persuaded to believe so.

Here are ambiguities of substance. In being identified with B, A is "substantially one" with a person other than himself. Yet at the same time he remains unique, an individual locus of motives. Thus he is both joined and separate, at once a distinct substance and consubstantial with another.

While consubstantial with its parents, with the "firsts" from which it is derived, the off-spring is nonetheless apart from them. In this sense, there is nothing abstruse in the statement that the offspring both is and is not one with its parentage. Similarly, two persons may be identified in terms of some principle they share in common, an "identification" that does not deny their distinctness.

To identify A with B is to make A "consubstantial" with B. Accordingly, since our *Grammar of Motives* was constructed about "substance" as key term, the related rhetoric selects its nearest equivalent in the areas of persuasion and dissuasion, communication and polemic. And our third volume, *Symbolic of Motives,* should be built about *identity* as titular or ancestral term, the "first" to which all other terms could be reduced and from which they could then be derived or generated, as from a common spirit. The thing's *identity* would here be its uniqueness as an entity in itself and by itself, a demarcated unit having its own particular structure.

However, "substance" is an abstruse philosophic term, beset by a long history of quandaries and puzzlements. It names so paradoxical a function in men's systematic terminologies, that thinkers finally tried to abolish it altogether—and in recent years they have often persuaded themselves that they really did abolish it from their terminologies of motives. They abolished the *term,* but it is doubtful whether they can ever abolish the *function* of that term, or even whether they should *want* to. A doctrine of *consubstantiality,* either explicit or implicit, may be necessary to any way of life. For substance, in the old philosophies, was an *act;* and a way of life is an *acting-together;* and in acting together, men have common sensations, concepts, images, ideas, attitudes that make them *consubstantial.*

The *Grammar* dealt with the universal paradoxes of substance. It considered resources of placement and definition common to all thought. The *Symbolic* should deal with unique individuals, each its own peculiarly constructed act, or form. These unique "constitutions" being capable of treatment in isolation, the *Symbolic* should

consider them primarily in their capacity as singulars, each a separate universe of discourse (though there are also respects in which they are consubstantial with others of their kind, since they can be classed with other unique individuals as joint participants in common principles, possessors of the same or similar properties).

The *Rhetoric* deals with the possibilities of classification in its *partisan* aspects; it considers the ways in which individuals are at odds with one another, or become identified with groups more or less at odds with one another.

Why "at odds," you may ask, when the titular term is "identification"? Because, to begin with "identification" is, by the same token, though roundabout, to confront the implications of *division.* And so, in the end, men are brought to that most tragically ironic of all divisions, or conflicts, wherein millions of cooperative acts go into the preparation for one single destructive act. We refer to that ultimate *disease* of cooperation: *war.* (You will understand war much better if you think of it, not simply as strife come to a head, but rather as a disease, or perversion of communion. Modern war characteristically requires a myriad of constructive acts for each destructive one; before each culminating blast there must be a vast network of interlocking operations, directed communally.)

Identification is affirmed with earnestness precisely because there is division. Identification is compensatory to division. If men were not apart from one another, there would be no need for the rhetorician to proclaim their unity. If men were wholly and truly of one substance, absolute communication would be of man's very essence. It would not be an ideal, as it now is, partly embodied in material conditions and partly frustrated by these same conditions; rather, it would be as natural, spontaneous, and total as with those ideal prototypes of communication, the theologian's angels, or "messengers."

The *Grammar* was at peace insofar as it contemplated the paradoxes common to all men, the universal resources of verbal placement. The *Symbolic* should be at peace, in that the individual substances, or entities, or constituted acts are there considered in their uniqueness, hence outside the realm of conflict. For individual universes, as such, do not compete. Each merely *is,* being its own self-sufficient realm of discourse. And the *Symbolic* thus considers each thing as a set of interrelated terms all conspiring to round out their identity as participants in a common substance of meaning. An individual does in actuality compete with other individuals. But within the rules of *Symbolic,* the individual is treated merely as a self-subsistent unit proclaiming its peculiar nature. It is "at peace," in that its terms *cooperate* in modifying one another. But insofar as the individual is involved in conflict with other individuals or groups, the study of this same individual would fall under the head of *Rhetoric.* Or considered rhetorically, the victim of a neurotic conflict is torn by parliamentary wrangling; he is heckled like Hitler within. (Hitler is said to have confronted a constant wrangle in his private deliberations, after having imposed upon his people a flat choice between conformity and silence.) Rhetorically, the neurotic's every attempt to legislate for his own conduct is disorganized by rival factions within his own dissociated self. Yet, considered Symbolically, the same victim is technically "at peace," in the sense that his identity is like a unified, mutually adjusted set of terms. For even antagonistic terms, confronting each other as parry and thrust, can be said to "cooperate" in the building of an over-all form.

The *Rhetoric* must lead us through the Scramble, the Wrangle of the Market Place, the flurries and flare-ups of the Human Barnyard, the Give and Take, the wavering line of pressure and counterpressure, the Logomachy, the onus of ownership, the Wars of Nerves, the War. It too has its peaceful moments: at times its endless competition can add up to the transcending of itself. In ways of its own, it can move from the factional to the universal. But its ideal culminations are more often beset by strife as the condition of their organized expression, or material embodiment. Their very universality becomes transformed into a partisan weapon. For one need not scrutinize the concept of "identification" very sharply to see, implied in it at every turn, its ironic counterpart: division. Rhetoric is concerned with the state of Babel after the Fall. Its contribution to a "sociology of knowledge" must often carry us far into the lugubrious regions of malice and the lie.

The Identifying Nature of Property

Metaphysically, a thing is identified by its *properties.* In the realm of Rhetoric, such identification is frequently by property in the most materialistic sense of the term, economic property, such property as Coleridge, in his "Religious Musings," calls a

> twy-streaming fount,
>
> Whence Vice and Virtue flow, honey and gall

And later:

> From Avarice thus, from Luxury and War
>
> Sprang heavenly Science; and from Science, Freedom.

Coleridge, typically the literary idealist, goes one step further back, deriving "property" from the workings of "Imagination." But meditations upon the dual aspects of property as such are enough for our present purposes. In the surrounding of himself with properties that name his number or establish his identity, man is ethical. ("Avarice" is but the scenic word "property" translated into terms of an agent's attitude, or incipient act.) Man's moral growth is organized through properties, properties in goods, in services, in position or status, in citizenship, in reputation, in acquaintanceship and love. But however ethical such an array of identifications may be when considered in itself, its relation to other entities that are likewise forming their identity in terms of property can lead to turmoil and discord. Here is *par excellence* a topic to be considered in a rhetoric having "identification" as its key term. And we see why one should expect to get much insight from Marxism, as a study of capitalistic rhetoric. Veblen is also, from this point of view, to be considered a theorist of rhetoric. (And we know of no better way to quickly glimpse the range of rhetoric than to read, in succession, the articles on "Property" and "Propaganda" in *The Encyclopaedia of the Social Sciences.*)

Bentham's utilitarian analysis of language, treating of the ways in which men find "eulogistic coverings" for their "material interests," is thus seen to be essentially rhetorical, and to bear directly upon the motives of property as a rhetorical factor. Indeed, since it is so clearly a matter of rhetoric to persuade a man by identifying your cause with his interests, we note the ingredient of rhetoric in the animal experimenter's ways of conditioning, as animals that respond avidly at a food signal suggest, underlying even human motives, the inclination, like a house dog, to seek salvation in the Sign of the Scraped Plate. But the lessons of this "animal rhetoric" can mislead, as we learn from the United States' attempts to use food as an instrument of policy in Europe after the war. These efforts met with enough ill will to suggest that the careful "screening" of our representatives, to eliminate reformist tendencies as far as possible and to identify American aid only with conservative or even reactionary interests, practically *guaranteed* us a dismal rhetoric in our dealings with other nations. And when Henry Wallace, during a trip abroad, began earning for our country the genuine good will of Europe's common people and intellectual classes, the Genius of the Screening came into its own: our free press, as at one signal, began stoutly assuring the citizens of both the United States and Europe that Wallace did not truly represent us. What did represent us, presumably, was the policy of the Scraped Plate, which our officialdom now and then bestirred themselves to present publicly in terms of a dispirited "idealism," as heavy as a dead elephant. You see, we were not to be identified with very resonant things; our press assured our people that the outcome of the

last election had been a "popular mandate" to this effect. (We leave this statement unrevised. For the conditions of Truman's reelection, after a campaign in which he out-Wallaced Wallace, corroborated it "in principle.")

In pure identification there would be no strife. Likewise, there would be no strife in absolute separateness, since opponents can join battle only through a mediatory ground that makes their communication possible, thus providing the first condition necessary for their interchange of blows. But put identification and division ambiguously together, so that you cannot know for certain just where one ends and the other begins, and you have the characteristic invitation to rhetoric. Here is a major reason why rhetoric, according to Aristotle, "proves opposites." When two men collaborate in an enterprise to which they contribute different kinds of services and from which they derive different amounts and kinds of profit, who is to say, once and for all, just where "cooperation" ends and one partner's "exploitation" of the other begins? The wavering line between the two cannot be "scientifically" identified; rival rhetoricians can draw it at different places, and their persuasiveness varies with the resources each has at his command. (Where public issues are concerned, such resources are not confined to the intrinsic powers of the speaker and the speech, but depend also for their effectiveness upon the purely technical means of communication, which can either aid the utterance or hamper it. For a "good" rhetoric neglected by the press obviously cannot be so "communicative" as a poor rhetoric backed nation-wide by headlines. And often we must think of rhetoric not in terms of some one particular address, but as a general *body of identifications* that owe their convincingness much more to trivial repetition and dull daily reinforcement than to exceptional rhetorical skill.)

If you would praise God, and in terms that happen also to sanction one system of material property rather than another, you have forced Rhetorical considerations upon us. If you would praise science, however exaltedly, when that same science is at the service of imperialist-militarist expansion, here again you bring things within the orbit of Rhetoric. For just as God has been identified with a certain worldly structure of ownership, so science may be identified with the interests of certain groups or classes quite *unscientific* in their purposes. Hence, however "pure" one's motives may be actually, the impurities of identification lurking about the edges of such situations introduce a typical Rhetorical wrangle of the sort that can never be settled once and for all, but belongs in the field of moral controversy where men properly seek to "prove opposites."

Thus, when his friend, Preen, wrote of a meeting where like-minded colleagues would be present and would all be proclaiming their praise of science, Prone answered: "You fail to mention another colleague who is sure to be there too, unless you take care to rule him out. I mean John *Q.* Militarist-Imperialist." Whereat, Preen: "This John *Q.* Militarist-Imperialist must be quite venerable by now. I seem to have heard of him back in Biblical times, before Roger B. Science was born. Doesn't he get in everywhere, unless he is explicitly ruled out?" He does, thanks to the ways of identification, which are in accordance with the nature of property. And the rhetorician and the moralist become one at that point where the attempt is made to reveal the undetected presence of such an identification. Thus in the United States after the second World War, the temptations of such an identification became particularly strong because so much scientific research had fallen under the direction of the military. To speak merely in praise of science, without explicitly dissociating oneself from its reactionary implications, is to identify oneself with these reactionary implications by default. Many reputable educators could thus, in this roundabout way, *function* as "conspirators." In their zeal to get federal subsidies for the science department of their college or university, they could help to shape educational policies with the ideals of war as guiding principle.

[. . .]

Ingenuous and Cunning Identifications

The thought of self-deception brings up another range of possibilities here. For there is a wide range of ways whereby the rhetorical motive, through the resources of identification, can operate without conscious direction by any particular agent. Classical rhetoric stresses the element of explicit design in rhetorical enterprise. But one can systematically extend the range of rhetoric, if one studies the persuasiveness of false or inadequate terms which may not be directly imposed upon us from without by some skillful speaker, but which we impose upon ourselves, in varying degrees of deliberateness and unawareness, through motives indeterminately self-protective and/or suicidal. We shall consider these matters more fully later, when we study the rhetoric of *hierarchy* (or as it is less revealingly named, *bureaucracy*). And our later pages on Marx and Veblen would apply here. But for the present we might merely recall the psychologist's concept of "malingering," to designate the ways of neurotic persons who, though not actually ill, persuade themselves that they are, and so can claim the attentions and privileges of the ill (their feigned illness itself becoming, at one remove, genuine). Similarly, if a social or occupational class is not too exacting in the scrutiny of identifications that flatter its interests, its very philosophy of life is a profitable malingering (profitable at least until its inaccuracies catch up with it)—and as such, it is open to either attack or analysis, Rhetoric comprising both the *use* of persuasive resources (*rhetorica utens,* as with the philippics of Demosthenes) and the *study* of them (*rhetorica docens,* as with Aristotle's treatise on the "art" of Rhetoric).

This aspect of identification, whereby one can protect an interest merely by using terms not incisive enough to criticize it properly, often brings rhetoric to the edge of cunning. A misanthropic politician who dealt in mankind-loving imagery could still think of himself as rhetorically honest, if he meant to do well by his constituents yet thought that he could get their votes only by such display. Whatever the falsity in overplaying a role, there may be honesty in the assuming of that role itself; and the overplaying may be but a translation into a different medium of communication, a way of amplifying a statement so that it carries better to a large or distant audience. Hence, the persuasive identifications of Rhetoric, in being so directly designed for *use,* involve us in a special problem of *consciousness,* as exemplified in the Rhetorician's particular *purpose* for a given statement.

The thought gives a glimpse into rhetorical motives behind many characters in drama and fiction. Shakespeare's Iago and Molière's Tartuffe are demons of Rhetoric. Every word and act is addressed, being designed to build up false identifications in the minds of their victims. Similarly, there is a notable ingredient of Rhetoric in Stendhal's Julien Sorel, who combines "heightened consciousness" with "freedom" by a perversely frank decision to perfect his own kind of hypocrisy as a means of triumphing over the hypocrisy of others. All his actions thus become rhetorical, framed for their effect; his life is a spellbinding and spellbound address to an audience.

Did you ever do a friend an injury by accident, in all poetic simplicity? Then conceive of this same injury as done by sly design, and you are forthwith within the orbit of Rhetoric. If you, like the Stendhals and Gides, conceive a character by such sophistication, Rhetoric as the speaker's attempt to identify himself favorably with his audience then becomes so transformed that the work may seem to have been written under an esthetic of pure "expression," without regard for communicative appeal. Or it may appeal perversely, to warped motives within the audience. Or it may be but an internalizing of the rhetorical motive, as the very actions of such a representative figure take on a rhetorical cast. Hence, having woven a rhetorical motive so integrally into the very essence of his conception, the writer can seem to have ignored rhetorical considerations; yet, in the sheer effrontery of his protagonist there is embedded, however

disguised or transformed, an *anguish* of communication (communication being, as we have said, a generalized form of love).

As regards the rhetorical ways of Stendhal's hero, moving in the perverse freedom of duplicity: After the disclosure of his cunning, Julien abandons his complex rhetorical morality of hypocrisy-to-outhypocritize-the-hypocrites, and regains a new, suicidally poetic level of simplicity. *"Jamais cette tête n'avait été aussi poétique qu'au moment où elle allait tomber."* The whole structure of the book could be explained as the account of a hero who, by the disclosure of his Rhetoric, was jolted into a tragically direct poetic. Within the terms of the novel, "hypocrisy" was the word for "rhetoric," such being the quality of the rhetoric that marked the public life of France under the reign of *Napoléon le Petit.*

Rhetoric of "Address" (to the Individual Soul)

By our arrangement, the individual in his uniqueness falls under the head of Symbolic. But one should not thereby assume that what is known as "individual psychology" wholly meets the same test. Particularly in the Freudian concern with the neuroses of individual patients, there is a strongly rhetorical ingredient. Indeed, what could be more profoundly rhetorical than Freud's notion of a dream that attains expression by stylistic subterfuges designed to evade the inhibitions of a moralistic censor? What is this but the exact analogue of the rhetorical devices of literature under political or theocratic censorship? The *ego* with its *id* confronts the *super-ego* much as an orator would confront a somewhat alien audience, whose susceptibilities he must flatter as a necessary step towards persuasion. The Freudian psyche is quite a parliament, with conflicting interests expressed in ways variously designed to take the claims of rival factions into account.

The best evidence of a strongly rhetorical ingredient in Freud's view of the psyche is in his analysis of *Wit and Its Relation to the*

Unconscious. In particular, we think of Freud's concern with the role of an audience, or "third person," with whom the speaker establishes rapport, in their common enterprise directed against the butt of tendentious witticisms. Here is the purest rhetorical pattern: speaker and hearer as partners in partisan jokes made at the expense of another. If you "internalize" such a variety of motives, so that the same person can participate somewhat in all three positions, you get a complex individual of many voices. And though these may be treated, under the heading of Symbolic, as a concerto of principles mutually modifying one another, they may likewise be seen, from the standpoint of Rhetoric, as a parliamentary wrangle which the individual has put together somewhat as he puts together his fears and hopes, friendships and enmities, health and disease, or those tiny rebirths whereby, in being born to some new condition, he may be dying to a past condition, his development being dialectical, a series of terms in perpetual transformation.

Thus by a roundabout route we come upon another aspect of Rhetoric: its nature as *addressed,* since persuasion implies an audience. A man can be his own audience, insofar as he, even in his secret thoughts, cultivates certain ideas or images for the effect he hopes they may have upon him; he is here what Mead would call "an 'I' addressing its 'me' "; and in this respect he is being rhetorical quite as though he were using pleasant imagery to influence an outside audience rather than one within. In traditional Rhetoric, the relation to an external audience is stressed. Aristotle's Art of Rhetoric, for instance, deals with the appeal to audiences in this primary sense: It lists typical beliefs, so that the speaker may choose among them the ones with which he would favorably identify his cause or unfavorably identify the cause of an opponent; and it lists the traits of character with which the speaker should seek to identify himself, as a way of disposing an audience favorably towards him. But a modern "post-Christian" rhetoric must also concern itself with the thought that, under the heading of appeal to audiences, would also be included any ideas or images privately addressed to the individual self for moralistic or incantatory

purposes. For you become your own audience, in some respects a very lax one, in some respects very exacting, when you become involved in psychologically stylistic subterfuges for presenting your own case to yourself in sympathetic terms (and even terms that seem harsh can often be found on closer scrutiny to be flattering, as with neurotics who visit sufferings upon themselves in the name of very high-powered motives which, whatever their discomfiture, feed pride).

Such considerations make us alert to the ingredient of rhetoric in all *socialization,* considered as a *moralizing* process. The individual person, striving to form himself in accordance with the communicative norms that match the cooperative ways of his society, is by the same token concerned with the rhetoric of identification. To act upon himself persuasively, he must variously resort to images and ideas that are formative. Education ("indoctrination") exerts such pressure upon him from without; he completes the process from within. If he does not somehow act to tell himself (as his own audience) what the various brands of rhetorician have told him, his persuasion is not complete. Only those voices from without are effective which can speak in the language of a voice within.

Among the Tanala of Madagascar, it is said, most of those tribesmen susceptible to *tromba* ("neurotic seizure indicated by an extreme desire to dance") were found to be among the least favored members of the tribe. Such seizures are said to be a device that makes the possessed person "the center of all the attention." And afterwards, the richest and most powerful members of the sufferer's family foot the bill, so that "the individual's ego is well satisfied and he can get along quite well until the next tromba seizure occurs." In sum, "like most hysterical seizures, tromba requires an audience."

The citations are from A. Kardiner, *The Individual and His Society* (New York: Columbia University Press). They would suggest that, when asking what all would fall within the scope of our topic, we could also include a "rhetoric of hysteria." For here too are expressions which are *addressed*—and we confront an ultimate irony, in glimpsing how even a catatonic lapse into sheer automatism, beyond the reach of all normally linguistic communication, is in its origins communicative, addressed, though it be a paralogical appeal-that-ends-all-appeals.

Rhetoric and Primitive Magic

The Kardiner citations are taken from a paper by C. Kluckhohn on "Navaho Witchcraft," containing observations that would also bring witchcraft within the range of rhetoric. Indeed, where witchcraft is imputed as a motive behind the individual search for wealth, power, or vengeance, can we not view it as a primitive vocabulary of *individualism* emerging in a culture where *tribal* thinking had been uppermost, so that the individualist motive would be admitted and suspect? And any breach of identification with the tribal norms being sinister, do we not glimpse rhetorical motives behind the fact that Macbeth's private ambitions were figured in terms of witches?

At first glance we may seem to be straining the conception of rhetoric to the breaking point, when including even a treatise on primitive witchcraft within its range. But look again. Precisely at a time when the *term* "rhetoric" had fallen into greatest neglect and disrepute, writers in the "social sciences" were, under many guises, making good contributions to the New Rhetoric. As usual with modern thought, the insights gained from *comparative culture* could throw light upon the classic approach to this subject; and again, as usual with modern thought, this light was interpreted in terms that concealed its true relation to earlier work. And though the present writer was strongly influenced by anthropological inquiries into primitive magic, he did not clearly discern the exact relation between the anthropologist's concern with magic and the literary critic's concern with communication until he had systematically worked on this *Rhetoric* for some years. Prior to this discovery, though he persisted in anthropological hankerings, he did so with a bad conscience; and he was half willing to agree with literary opponents who considered such concerns alien to the study of literature proper.

Now, in noting methodically how the anthropologist's account of magic can belong in a rhetoric, we are better equipped to see exactly wherein the two fields of inquiry diverge. Anthropology is a gain to literary criticism only if one knows how to "discount" it from the standpoint of rhetoric. And, ironically, anthropology can be a source of disturbance, not only to literary criticism in particular, but to the study of human relations in general, if one does not so discount it, but allows *its* terms to creep into one's thinking at points where issues *should* be studied explicitly in terms of rhetoric.

We saw both the respects in which the anthropologists' study of magic overlaps upon rhetoric and the respects in which they are distinct when we were working on a review of Ernst Cassirer's *Myth of the State*. The general proposition that exercised us can be stated as follows:

We must begin by confronting the typically scientist view of the relation between science and magic. Since so many apologists of modern science, following a dialectic of simple antithesis, have looked upon magic merely as an early form of bad science, one seems to be left only with a distinction between bad science and good science. Scientific knowledge is thus presented as a terminology that gives an accurate and critically tested description of reality; and magic is presented as antithetical to such science. Hence magic is treated as an early uncritical attempt to do what science does, but under conditions where judgment and perception were impaired by the naïvely anthropomorphic belief that the impersonal forces of nature were motivated by personal designs. One thus confronts a flat choice between a civilized vocabulary of scientific description and a savage vocabulary of magical incantation.

In this scheme, "rhetoric" has no systematic location. We recall noting the word but once in Cassirer's *Myth of the State,* and then it is used only in a random way; yet the book is really about nothing more nor less than a most characteristic concern of rhetoric: the manipulation of men's beliefs for political ends.

Now, the basic function of rhetoric, the use of words by human agents to form attitudes or to induce actions in other human agents, is certainly not "magical." If you are in trouble, and call for help, you are no practitioner of primitive magic. You are using the primary resource of human speech in a thoroughly realistic way. Nor, on the other hand, is your utterance "science," in the strict meaning of science today, as a "semantic" or "descriptive" terminology for charting the conditions of nature from an "impersonal" point of view, regardless of one's wishes or preferences. A call for help is quite "prejudiced"; it is the most arrant kind of "wishful thinking"; it is not merely descriptive, it is *hortatory*. It is not just trying to tell how things are, in strictly "scenic" terms; it is trying to move people. A call for help might, of course, include purely scientific statements, or preparations for action, as a person in need might give information about particular dangers to guard against or advantages to exploit in bringing help. But the call, in itself, as such, is not scientific; it is *rhetorical*. Whereas poetic language is a kind of symbolic action, for itself and in itself, and whereas scientific action is a preparation for action, rhetorical language is inducement to action (or to attitude, attitude being an incipient act).

If you have only a choice between magic and science, you simply have no bin in which to accurately place such a form of expression. Hence, since "the future" is not the sort of thing one can put under a microscope, or even test by a knowledge of *exactly equivalent conditions* in the past, when you turn to political exhortation, you are involved in decisions that necessarily lie beyond the strictly scientific vocabularies of description. And since the effective politician is a "spellbinder," it seems to follow by elimination that the hortatory use of speech for political ends can be called "magic," in the discredited sense of that term.

As a result, much analysis of political exhortation comes to look simply like a survival of primitive magic, whereas it should be handled in its own terms, as an aspect of what it really is: rhetoric. The approach to rhetoric in terms of "word magic" gets the whole subject turned backwards. Originally, the magical use of symbolism to affect natural processes by rituals and incantations was a mistaken transference of a proper linguistic function to an area for which it was not fit. The realistic use of addressed language to *induce action in people* became the magical use of addressed language to *induce motion in things* (things by nature alien to purely linguistic orders of motivation). If we then begin by treating this *erroneous* and *derived* magical use as *primary,* we are invited to treat a *proper* use of language (for instance, political persuasion) simply as a vestige of benightedly prescientific magic.

To be sure, the rhetorician has the tricks of his trade. But they are not mere "bad science"; they are an "art." And any overly scientist approach to them (treating them in terms of flat dialectical opposition to modern technology) must make our world look much more "neo-primitive" than is really the case. At the very least, we should note that primitive magic prevailed most strongly under social conditions where the rationalization of social effort in terms of money was negligible; but the rhetoric of modern politics would establish social identifications atop a way of life highly diversified by money, with the extreme division of labor and status which money served to rationalize.

Realistic Function of Rhetoric

Gaining courage as we proceed, we might even contend that we are not so much proposing to import anthropology into rhetoric as proposing that anthropologists recognize the factor of rhetoric in their own field. That is, if you look at recent studies of primitive magic from the standpoint of this discussion, you might rather want to distinguish between magic as "bad science" and magic as "primitive rhetoric." You then discover that anthropology does clearly recognize the rhetorical *function* in magic; and far from dismissing the rhetorical aspect of magic merely as bad science, anthropology recognizes in it a pragmatic device that greatly assisted the survival of cultures by promoting social cohesion. (Malinowski did much work along these lines, and the Kluckhohn essay makes similar observations about witchcraft.) But now that we have confronted the term "magic" with the term "rhetoric," we'd say that one comes closer to the true state of affairs if one treats the socializing aspects of magic as a "primitive rhetoric" than if one sees modern rhetoric simply as a "survival of primitive magic."

For rhetoric as such is not rooted in any past condition of human society. It is rooted in an essential function of language itself, a function that is wholly realistic, and is continually born anew; the use of language as a symbolic means of inducing cooperation in beings that by nature respond to symbols. Though rhetorical considerations may carry us far afield, leading us to violate the principle of autonomy separating the various disciplines, there is an intrinsically rhetorical motive, situated in the persuasive use of language. And this persuasive use of language is not derived from "bad science," or "magic." On the contrary, "magic" was a faulty derivation from it, "word magic" being an attempt to produce linguistic responses in kinds of beings not accessible to the linguistic motive. However, once you introduce this emendation, you can see beyond the accidents of language. You can recognize how much of value has been contributed to the New Rhetoric by these investigators, though their observations are made in terms that never explicitly confront the rhetorical ingredient in their field of study. We can place in terms of rhetoric all those statements by anthropologists, ethnologists, individual and social psychologists, and the like, that bear upon the *persuasive* aspects of language, the function of language as *addressed,* as direct or roundabout appeal to real or ideal audiences, without or within.

Are we but haggling over a term? In one sense, yes. We are offering a rationale intended to show how far one might systematically extend the term "rhetoric." In this respect, we are haggling over a term; for we must persist in tracking down the *function* of that term. But to note the ingredient of rhetoric lurking in such anthropologist's terms as "magic" and "witchcraft" is not to ask that the anthropologist replace his words with ours. We are certainly not haggling over terms in that sense. The term "rhetoric" is no substitute for "magic," "witchcraft," "socialization," "communication," and so on. But the term rhetoric designates a *function* which is present in the areas variously covered by those other terms. And we are asking only that this *function* be recognized for what it is: a linguistic function by nature as *realistic* as a proverb, though it may be quite far from the kind of realism found in strictly "scientific realism." For it is essentially a realism of the *act:* moral, persuasive—and acts are not "true" and "false" in the sense that the propositions of "scientific realism" are. And however "false" the "propositions" of primitive magic may be, considered from the standpoint of scientific realism, it is different with the peculiarly *rhetorical* ingredient in magic, involving ways of identification that contribute variously to social cohesion (either for the advantage of the community as a whole, or for the advantage of special groups whose interests are a burden on the community, or for the advantage of special groups whose rights and duties are indeterminately both a benefit and a tax on the community, as with some business enterprise in our society).

The "pragmatic sanction" for this function of magic lies outside the realm of strictly true-or-false propositions; it falls in an area of deliberation that itself draws upon the resources of rhetoric; it is itself a subject matter belonging to an art that can "prove opposites."

To illustrate what we mean by "proving opposites" here: we read an article, let us say, obviously designed to dispose the reading public favorably towards the "aggressive and expanding" development of American commercial interests in Saudi Arabia. It speaks admiringly of the tremendous changes which our policies of commerce and investment will introduce into a vestigially feudal culture, and of the great speed at which the rationale of finance and technology will accomplish these changes. When considering the obvious rhetorical intent of these "facts," we suddenly in a perverse *non sequitur,* remember a passage in the Kluckhohn essay, involving what we would now venture to call "the rhetoric of witchcraft":

In a society like the Navaho which is competitive and capitalistic, on the one hand, and still familistic on the other, any ideology which has the effect of slowing down economic mobility is decidedly adaptive. One of the most basic strains in Navaho society arises out of the incompatibility between the demands of familism and the emulation of European patterns in the accumulating of capital.

And in conclusion we are told that the "survival of the society" is assisted by "any pattern, such as witchcraft, which tends to discourage the rapid accumulation of wealth" (witchcraft, as an "ideology," contributing to this end by identifying new wealth with malign witchery). Now, when you begin talking about the optimum rate of speed at which cultural changes should take place, or the optimum proportion between tribal and individualistic motives that should prevail under a particular set of economic conditions, you are talking about something very important indeed, but you will find yourself deep in matters of rhetoric: for nothing is more rhetorical in nature than a deliberation as to what is too much or too little, too early or too late; in such controversies, rhetoricians are forever "proving opposites."

Where are we now? We have considered two main aspects of rhetoric: its use of *identification* and its nature as *addressed*. Since identification implies division, we found rhetoric involving us in matters of socialization and faction. Here was a wavering line between peace and conflict, since identification is got by property, which is ambivalently a motive of both morality and strife. And inasmuch as the ultimate of conflict is war or murder, we considered how such imagery can figure as a terminology of reidentification ("transformation" or "rebirth"). For in considering the wavering line between identification and division, we shall always be coming upon manifestations of the logomachy, avowed as in invective, unavowed as in stylistic subterfuges for presenting real divisions in terms that deny division.

We found that this wavering line between identification and division was forever bringing rhetoric against the possibility of malice and the lie; for if an identification favorable to the speaker or his cause is made to seem favorable to the audience, there enters the possibility of such "heightened consciousness" as goes with deliberate cunning. Thus, roundabout, we confronted the nature of rhetoric as *addressed* to audiences of the first, second, or third person. Socialization itself was, in the widest sense, found to be addressed. And by reason of such simultaneous identification-with and division-from as mark the choice of a scapegoat, we found that rhetoric involves us in problems related to witchcraft, magic, spellbinding, ethical promptings, and the like. And in the course of discussing these subjects, we found ourselves running into another term: persuasion. Rhetoric is the art of persuasion, or a study of the means of persuasion available for any given situation. We have thus, deviously, come to the point at which Aristotle begins his treatise on rhetoric.

So we shall change our purpose somewhat. Up to now, we have been trying to indicate what kinds of subject matter not traditionally labeled "rhetoric" should, in our opinion, also fall under this head. We would now consider varying views of rhetoric that have already prevailed; and we would try to "generate" them from the same basic terms of our discussion.

As for the relation between "identification" and "persuasion": we might well keep it in mind that a speaker persuades an audience by the use of stylistic identifications; his act of persuasion may be for the purpose of causing the audience to identify itself with the speaker's interests; and the speaker draws on identification of interests to establish rapport between himself and his audience. So, there is no chance of our keeping apart the meanings of persuasion, identification ("consubstantiality") and communication (the nature of rhetoric as "addressed"). But, in given instances, one or another of these elements may serve best for extending a line of analysis in some particular direction.

And finally: The use of symbols, by one symbol-using entity to induce action in another (persuasion properly addressed) is in essence not magical but *realistic*. However, the resources of identification whereby a sense of consubstantiality is symbolically established between beings of unequal status may extend far into the realm of the *idealistic*. And as we shall see later, when on the subject of order, out of this idealistic element there may arise a kind of magic or mystery that sets its mark upon all human relations.

9

BEYOND PERSUASION

A Proposal for an Invitational Rhetoric

SONJA K. FOSS AND CINDY L. GRIFFIN

cknowledgment of the patriarchal bias that undergirds most theories of rhetoric is growing steadily in the communication discipline. As feminist scholars have begun to explicate the ways in which standard theories of rhetoric embody patriarchal perspectives, they have identified communicative modes that previously have not been recognized or theorized because they are grounded in alternative values (see, for example, Edson, 1985; Elshtain, 1982; Foss & Foss, 1991; Foss, Foss, & Trapp, 1991; Foss & Griffin, 1992; Gearhart, 1979; Griffin, 1993; Kramarae, 1989; Shepherd, 1992). Attention to non-patriarchal forms of communication, feminist scholars argue, expands the scope of rhetorical theory and enhances the discipline's ability to explain diverse communicative phenomena successfully.

One manifestation of the patriarchal bias that characterizes much of rhetorical theorizing is the definition of rhetoric as persuasion. As far back as the Western discipline of rhetoric has been explored, rhetoric has been defined as the conscious intent to change others. As Shepherd (1992) notes, in humanistic, social scientific, and critical perspectives on communication, "interaction processes have typically been characterized essentially and primarily in terms of persuasion, influence, and power" (p. 204). Every communicative encounter has been viewed "as primarily an attempt at persuasion or influence, or as a struggle over power" (p. 206). As natural as an equation of rhetoric with persuasion seems for scholars of rhetoric, this conception is only one perspective on rhetoric and one, we suggest, with a patriarchal bias.

SOURCE: Foss, S. K., & Griffin, C. L. (1995). Beyond persuasion: A proposal for an invitational rhetoric. *Communication Monographs, 62*, 2–18. Reproduced by permission of Taylor & Francis Ltd., http://www.tandf.co.uk/journals.

Implicit in a conception of rhetoric as persuasion is the assumption that humans are on earth to alter the "environment and to influence the social affairs" of others. Rhetorical scholars "have taken as given that it is a proper and even necessary human function to attempt to change others" (Gearhart, 1979, p. 195). The desire to effect change is so pervasive that the many ways in which humans engage in activities designed for this purpose often go unnoticed:

> We conquered trees and converted them into a house, taking pride in having accomplished a difficult task. We conquered rivers and streams and converted them into lakes, marvelling in ourselves at the improvement we made on nature. We tramped with our conquering spaceboots on the fine ancient dust of the Moon and we sent our well-rehearsed statements of triumph back for a waiting world to hear. (Gearhart, 1979, p. 196)

Embedded in efforts to change others is a desire for control and domination, for the act of changing another establishes the power of the change agent over that other. In some instances, the power of the rhetor over another is overt, as it is, for example, in laws that exert control over women's bodies, such as those concerned with abortion. In securing the adherence of women to these laws, lawmakers have power over women and their lives. But even in cases where the strategies used are less coercive, rhetors who convince others to adopt their viewpoints exert control over part of those others' lives. A student who tells another student that she ought to take a particular course, for example, controls or influences the nature of another's life, if only for a few minutes, if the other enrolls in the course or even considers enrolling in it. We suggest that a strikingly large part of many individuals' lives is spent in such efforts to change others, even when the desired changes have absolutely no impact on the lives of the change agents. Whether a friend enrolls in a particular course, for example, often is irrelevant to a student's own life.

The reward gained from successful efforts to make others change is a "rush of power" (Gearhart, 1979, p. 201)—a feeling of self-worth that comes from controlling people and situations. The value of the self for rhetors in this rhetorical system comes from the rhetor's ability to demonstrate superior knowledge, skills, and qualifications—in other words, authority—in order to dominate the perspectives and knowledge of those in their audiences. The value of the self derives not from a recognition of the uniqueness and inherent value of each living being but from gaining control over others.

The act of changing others not only establishes the power of the rhetor over others but also devalues the lives and perspectives of those others. The belief systems and behaviors others have created for living in the world are considered by rhetors to be inadequate or inappropriate and thus in need of change. The speaker's role very often "may be best described as paternalistic" (Scott, 1991, p. 205) in that the rhetor adopts a " 'let me help you, let me enlighten you, let me show you the way' approach" (Gearhart, 1979, p. 195). Audience members are assumed to be naive and less expert than the rhetor if their views differ from the rhetor's own.

Rhetorical scholars have prided themselves on the eschewal of physical force and coercion and the use, in their place, of "language and metalanguage, with refined functions of the mind" (Gearhart, 1979, p. 195) to influence others and produce change. Although these discursive strategies allow more choice to the audience than do the supposedly more heavy-handed strategies of physical coercion, they still infringe on others' rights to believe as they choose and to act in ways they believe are best for them. Even discursive strategies can constitute a kind of trespassing on the personal integrity of others when they convey the rhetor's belief that audience members have inadequacies that in some way can be corrected if they adhere to the viewpoint of the rhetor. Such strategies disallow, in other words, the possibility that audience members are content with the belief systems they have developed, function happily with them, and do not perceive a need to change.

The traditional conception of rhetoric, in summary, is characterized by efforts to change others and thus to gain control over them, self-worth derived from and measured by the power exerted over others, and a devaluation of the life worlds of others. This is a rhetoric of patriarchy, reflecting its values of change, competition, and domination. But these are not the only values on which a rhetorical system can be constructed, and we would like to propose as one alternative a feminist rhetoric.

Although definitions of *feminism* vary, feminists generally are united by a set of basic principles. We have chosen to focus on three of these principles—equality, immanent value, and self-determination—to serve as the starting place for a new rhetoric. These principles are ones that explicitly challenge the positive value the patriarchy accords to changing and thus dominating others.

Primary among the feminist principles on which our proposed rhetoric is based is a commitment to the creation of relationships of equality and to the elimination of the dominance and elitism that characterize most human relationships. As Wood (1994) aptly summarizes this principle, "I don't accept oppression and domination as worthy human values, and I don't believe differences must be ranked on a continuum of good and bad. I believe there are better, more humane and enriching ways to live" (p. 4). Efforts to dominate and gain power over others cannot be used to develop relationships of equality, so feminists seek to replace the "alienation, competition, and dehumanization" that characterize relationships of domination with "intimacy, mutuality, and camaraderie" (hooks, 1984, p. 34).

Yet another principle that undergirds most feminisms is a recognition of the immanent value of all living beings. The essence of this principle is that every being is a unique and necessary part of the pattern of the universe and thus has value. Immanent value derives from the simple principle that "your life is worth something. . . . You need only be what you are" (Starhawk, 1987, pp. 115–116). Worth cannot be determined by positioning individuals on a hierarchy so they can be ranked and compared or by attending to emblems of external achievement, for worth

cannot be "earned, acquired, or proven" (Starhawk, 1987, p. 21). Concomitant with a recognition of the immanent value of another individual is the eschewal of forms of communication that seek to change that individual's unique perspective to that held by the rhetor.

Self-determination is a third principle that typically comprises a feminist world view. Grounded in a respect for others, self-determination allows individuals to make their own decisions about how they wish to live their lives. Self-determination involves the recognition that audience members are the authorities on their own lives and accords respect to others' capacity and right to constitute their worlds as they choose. As Johnson (1991) explains, this principle involves a trust that others are doing the best they can at the moment and simply need "to be unconditionally accepted as the experts on their own lives" (p. 162). When others are seen as experts who are making competent decisions about their lives, efforts by a rhetor to change those decisions are seen as a violation of their life worlds and the expertise they have developed.

Our purpose in this essay is to propose a definition and explication of a rhetoric built on the principles of equality, immanent value, and self-determination rather than on the attempt to control others through persuasive strategies designed to effect change. Although we believe that persuasion is often necessary, we believe an alternative exists that may be used in instances when changing and controlling others is not the rhetor's goal; we call this rhetoric *invitational rhetoric*. In what follows, we offer a description of this rhetoric, beginning with a discussion of its definition and purpose and then describing the communicative options available to rhetors who wish to use it. We conclude our essay with two examples of invitational rhetoric and a discussion of some implications of invitational rhetoric for rhetorical theory.

Although invitational rhetoric is constructed largely from feminist theory, the literature in which its principles and various dimensions have been theorized most thoroughly, we are not suggesting that only feminists have dealt with and developed its various components or that only feminists adhere to the principles on which it is based. Some dimensions of this rhetoric have been explicated by traditional rhetorical theorists, and we have incorporated their ideas into our description of this rhetoric. We also do not want to suggest that the rhetoric we propose describes how all women communicate or that it is or can be used only by women. Feminism "implies an understanding of inclusion with interests beyond women" (Wood, 1993, p. 39), and its aim is not to "privilege women over men" or "to benefit solely any specific group of women" (hooks, 1984, p. 26). The rhetoric we describe is a rhetoric used at various times by some women and some men, some feminists and some non-feminists. What makes it feminist is not its use by a particular population of rhetors but rather the grounding of its assumptions in feminist principles and theories. Our goal in offering this theory is to expand the array of communicative options available to all rhetors and to provide an impetus for more focused and systematic efforts to describe and assess rhetoric in all of its manifestations.

DEFINITION

Invitational rhetoric is an invitation to understanding as a means to create a relationship rooted in equality, immanent value, and self-determination. Invitational rhetoric constitutes an invitation to the audience to enter the rhetor's world and to see it as the rhetor does. In presenting a particular perspective, the invitational rhetor does not judge or denigrate others' perspectives but is open to and tries to appreciate and validate those perspectives, even if they differ dramatically from the rhetor's own. Ideally, audience members accept the invitation offered by the rhetor by listening to and trying to understand the rhetor's perspective and then presenting their own. When this happens, rhetor and audience alike contribute to the thinking about an issue so that everyone involved gains a greater understanding of the issue in its subtlety,

richness, and complexity. Ultimately, though, the result of invitational rhetoric is not just an understanding of an issue. Because of the nonhierarchical, nonjudgmental, nonadversarial framework established for the interaction, an understanding of the participants themselves occurs, an understanding that engenders appreciation, value, and a sense of equality.

The stance taken by invitational rhetors toward their audiences obviously is different from that assumed by traditional rhetors. Invitational rhetors do not believe they have the right to claim that their experiences or perspectives are superior to those of their audience members and refuse to impose their perspectives on them. Rhetors view the choices selected by audience members as right for them at that particular time, based on their own abilities to make those decisions. Absent are efforts to dominate another because the goal is the understanding and appreciation of another's perspective rather than the denigration of it simply because it is different from the rhetor's own. The result of the invitational rhetor's stance toward the audience is a relationship of equality, respect, and appreciation.

Invitational rhetoric is characterized, then, by the openness with which rhetors are able to approach their audiences. Burke (1969) suggests that rhetors typically adjust their conduct to the external resistance they expect in the audience or situation: "We in effect modify our own assertion in reply to its assertion" (p. 237). In invitational rhetoric, in contrast, resistance is not anticipated, and rhetors do not adapt their communication to expected resistance in the audience. Instead, they identify possible impediments to the creation of understanding and seek to minimize or neutralize them so they do not remain impediments.

Change may be the result of invitational rhetoric, but change is not its purpose. When change does occur as a result of understanding, it is different from the kind of change that typifies the persuasive interactions of traditional rhetoric. In the traditional model, change is defined as a shift in the audience in the direction requested by the rhetor, who then has gained some measure of power and control over the audience. In invitational rhetoric, change occurs in the audience or rhetor or both as a result of new understanding and insights gained in the exchange of ideas. As rhetors and audience members offer their ideas on an issue, they allow diverse positions to be compared in a process of discovery and questioning that may lead to transformation for themselves and others. Participants even may choose to be transformed because they are persuaded by something someone in the interaction says, but the insight that is persuasive is offered by a rhetor not to support the superiority of a particular perspective but to contribute to the understanding by all participants of the issue and of one another.

The internal processes by which transformation occurs also are different in invitational rhetoric. In traditional rhetoric, the change process often is accompanied by feelings of inadequacy, insecurity, pain, humiliation, guilt, embarrassment, or angry submission on the part of the audience as rhetors communicate the superiority of their positions and the deficiencies of those of the audience. In invitational rhetoric, on the other hand, rhetors recognize the valuable contributions audience members can make to the rhetors' own thinking and understanding, and they do not engage in strategies that may damage or sever the connection between them and their audiences. This does not mean that invitational rhetoric always is free of pain. In invitational rhetoric, there may be a wrenching loose of ideas as assumptions and positions are questioned as a result of an interaction, a process that may be uncomfortable. But because rhetors affirm the beliefs of and communicate respect for others, the changes that are made are likely to be accompanied by an appreciation for new perspectives gained and gratitude for the assistance provided by others in thinking about an issue.

COMMUNICATIVE OPTIONS

The process of engaging in invitational rhetoric assumes two primary rhetorical forms. One is offering perspectives, a mode by which rhetors put forward for consideration their perspectives; the second is the creation of external conditions that allow others to present their perspectives in an atmosphere of respect and equality.

Offering Perspectives

When rhetors do not seek to impose their positions on audience members in invitational rhetoric, the presentation and function of individual perspectives differ significantly from their nature and function in traditional rhetorics. Individual perspectives are articulated in invitational rhetoric as carefully, completely, and passionately as possible to give them full expression and to invite their careful consideration by the participants in the interaction. This articulation occurs not through persuasive argument but through offering—the giving of expression to a perspective without advocating its support or seeking its acceptance. Offering involves not probing or invading but giving, a process "of wrapping around the givee, of being available to her/him without insisting; our giving is a *presence,* an *offering,* an *opening*" (Gearhart, 1982, p. 198). In offering, rhetors tell what they currently know or understand; they present their vision of the world and show how it looks and works for them.

As a rhetorical form, offering may appear to be similar to some traditional rhetorical strategies, such as the use of personal narrative as a form of support for a rhetor's position. But narrative as offering functions differently from narrative as a means of support. It is presented in offering for the purpose of articulating a viewpoint but not as a means to increase the likelihood of the audience's adherence to that viewpoint. The offering of a personal narrative is, itself, the goal; the means and the ends are the same in offering. Offering is not based on a dichotomy of cause and effect, an action done in the present to affect the future. Instead, as Johnson (1989) explains, the "'means are the ends; . . . *how* we do something is *what* we get'" (p. 35). In this mode, then, a story is not told as a means of supporting or achieving some other end but as an end in itself—simply offering the perspective the story represents.

A critical dimension of the offering of a perspective, in whatever form it takes, is a willingness to yield. Not unlike Buber's (1965) notion of the "I-Thou" relationship, the basic movement of a willingness to yield is a turning toward the other. It involves meeting another's position "in its uniqueness, letting it have its impact" (p. xiv). Tracy (1987) explains the connection between the meeting of another's uniqueness and a willingness to yield: "To attend to the other as other, the different as different, is also to understand the different *as* possible" (p. 20). When they assume such a stance, rhetors communicate a willingness to call into question the beliefs they consider most inviolate and to relax their grip on those beliefs. The process is not unlike the self-risk that Natanson (1965) describes as the risking

> of the self's world of feeling, attitude, and the total subtle range of its affective and conative sensibility. . . . [W]hen I truly risk myself in arguing I open myself to the viable possibility that the consequence of an argument may be to make me *see* something of the structure of my immediate world. (p. 15)

Scott (1976) calls this self-risk "a grave risk: the risk of the self that resides in a value structure" (p. 105). Thus, the perspective presented through offering represents an initial, tentative commitment to that perspective—one subject to revision as a result of the interaction.

A few specific examples of offering may clarify the nature of this rhetorical form. Although much rarer than we would like, offering sometimes occurs in academic settings when faculty members and/or students gather to discuss a topic of mutual interest. When they enter the interaction with a goal not of converting others to their positions but of sharing what they know, extending one another's ideas, thinking critically about all the ideas offered, and coming to an understanding of the subject and of one another, they are engaged in offering. Offering also is marked by discursive forms such as "I tried this

solution when that happened to me; I thought it worked well" or "What would happen if we introduced the idea of ___ into this problem?" rather than statements with forms such as "You really ought to do ___" or "Your idea is flawed because you failed to take into account ___."

Offering may occur not only in small-group settings but also in formal presentational contexts. A rhetor who presents her ideas at an academic colloquium, for example, engages in offering when she presents her ideas as valuable yet also as tentative. She acknowledges the fact that her work is in progress; thus, she is open to the ideas of others so she can continue to revise and improve it. She builds on and extends the work of others rather than tearing their ideas apart in an effort to establish the superiority of her own. In an offering mode, she provides explanations for the sources of her ideas rather than marshalling evidence to establish their superiority. Audience members, too, may engage in offering behavior. They do so when they ask questions and make comments designed not to show the stupidity or error of the perspective presented or to establish themselves as more powerful or expert than the presenter. Instead, their questions and suggestions are aimed at learning more about the presenter's ideas, understanding them more thoroughly, nurturing them, and offering additional ways of thinking about the subject for everyone involved in the interaction.

We have tried to write this essay using such features of the offering form. We present a *proposal* for an invitational rhetoric, for example, a word we chose deliberately to suggest that what we present here is only one of many equally legitimate perspectives possible. We suggest that invitational rhetoric is a viable form of interaction in many instances but do not assert that it is the only appropriate form of rhetoric and should be used in all situations or contexts. We acknowledge the importance and usefulness of traditional theories of rhetoric even as we propose an alternative to them, and we try to build on and extend the work of other theorists—both traditional and feminist—rather than characterizing their work as inaccurate or misguided. Although we are constrained somewhat by the format of a journal article, we see this essay as in progress and plan to continue to work on our ideas; the responses of some of our colleagues and the reviewers and editor of *Communication Monographs* already have helped us clarify and improve our description of this rhetoric. We have attempted, then, to model the offering of a perspective within the perimeters allowed by a framework of scholarly discourse.

Offering also may be seen in the nonverbal realm; a perspective may be offered in the clothing individuals wear, the places in which and how they live, and in all of the symbolic choices rhetors make that reveal their perspectives. This kind of offering is illustrated by Purple Saturday, sponsored by the Women's Caucus at Speech Communication Association (SCA) conventions. On Purple Saturday, the women attending the convention (and those men who wish to show their support for women) are asked to wear purple, a color of the early women's suffrage movement, to proclaim women's solidarity and presence in SCA. When women wear purple on Saturday at the convention, they are not trying to persuade others to become feminists, to accept feminist scholarship, or to value women. Instead, they are simply offering a perspective so that those who wish to learn more about feminist scholarship or to join in the celebration of feminism may do so. Although not designed to influence others to change in particular directions, such nonverbal offerings may have that effect; some who view the wearing of purple by others at a convention may choose, for example, to explore or engage in feminist research themselves.

Another form offering may take, particularly in a hostile situation or when a dominant perspective is very different from the one held by the rhetor, is re-sourcement (Gearhart, 1982). Re-sourcement is a response made by a rhetor according to a framework, assumptions, or principles other than those suggested in the precipitating message. In using re-sourcement, the rhetor deliberately draws energy from a new source—a source other than the individual or system that provided the initial frame for the issue. It is a means, then, of communicating a perspective that is different from that of the individual who produced the message to which the rhetor is responding. Re-sourcement is not unlike Burke's (1984) notion of perspective by incongruity, but in re-sourcement, the juxtaposition of two systems or frameworks is split between rhetor and audience, with one reflected in the original message, the other in the response.

Re-sourcement involves the two processes of disengagement from the framework, system, or principles embedded in the precipitating message and the creative development of a response so that the issue is framed differently. Rorty's (1986) description of the process of generating new vocabularies points to this two-part process: "The idea is to get a vocabulary which is (at the moment) incommensurable with the old in order to draw attention away from the issues stated in the old, and thereby help people to forget them" (p. 114). In Forget's (1989) words, this kind of communication is "a swerve, a leap to the other side, which lets us . . . deploy another logic or system" (p. 136).

Although a refusal to engage in conflict or interaction under the terms proposed by a rhetor sometimes is seen as a negative, ineffective form of communication because it is interpreted as disconfirmation (e.g., Veenendall & Feinstein, 1990) or as a kind of manipulation associated with passive-aggressive behavior, it can be a positive response to a situation. It allows rhetors to continue to value themselves as well as the audience because it communicates that they are not willing to allow the audience to violate their integrity. Re-sourcement also opens up possibilities for future rhetorical choices, providing more options for rhetors than were previously available. As later options, rhetors who use re-sourcement may articulate their positions through more traditional forms of offering or standard forms of persuasion.

An example of re-sourcement is provided by Starhawk (1987) in her description of an incident that followed the blockade of the Livermore Weapons Lab in California to protest its development of nuclear weapons. She and other women were arrested and held in a school gym, and during their confinement, a woman was chased into the gym by six guards. She dove into a cluster of women, and they held on to her as the guards pulled at her legs, trying to extract her from the group. The guards were on the verge of beating the women when one woman sat down and began to chant. As the other women followed suit, the guards' actions changed in response:

> They look bewildered. Something they are unprepared for, unprepared even to name, has arisen in our moment of common action. They do not know what to do. And so, after a moment, they withdraw. . . . In that moment in the jail, the power of domination and control met something outside its comprehension, a power rooted in another source. (p. 5)

The guards' message was framed in a context of opposition, violence, hostility, and fear; the women, in contrast, chose to respond with a message framed in terms of nonviolence and connection.

Re-sourcement in a discursive form is exemplified in a story told by Watzlawick, Weakland, and Fisch (1974) about a police officer who was

> issuing a citation for a minor traffic violation when a hostile crowd began to gather around him. By the time he had given the offender his ticket, the mood of the crowd was ugly and the sergeant was not certain he would be able to get back to the relative safety of his patrol car. It then occurred to him to announce in a loud voice: "You have just witnessed the issuance of a traffic ticket by a member of your Oakland Police Department." And while the bystanders were busy trying to fathom the deeper meaning of this all too obvious communique, he got into his cruiser and drove off. (pp. 108–109)

The initial message presented to the police officer was framed in the context of opposition and hostility; he chose, however, to respond with a message grounded in a framework of simple explanation, cooperation, and respect. Re-sourcement, as a means of offering, allowed him to diffuse the situation and to communicate his own perspective—that he was doing the job he was hired by the crowd members, as taxpayers, to do.

External Conditions

Offering can occur whether or not an audience chooses to join with a rhetor in a process of discovery and understanding. But if invitational rhetoric is to result in *mutual* understanding of perspectives, it involves not only the offering of the rhetor's perspective but the creation of an atmosphere in which audience members' perspectives also can be offered. We propose that to create such an environment, an invitational rhetoric must create three external conditions in the interaction between rhetors and audience members—safety, value, and freedom. These are states or prerequisites required if the possibility of mutual understanding is to exist.

The condition of *safety* involves the creation of a feeling of security and freedom from danger for the audience. Rhetoric contributes to a feeling of safety when it conveys to audience members that the ideas and feelings they share with the rhetor will be received with respect and care. When rhetoric establishes a safe context, the rhetor makes no attempt to hurt, degrade, or belittle audience members or their beliefs, and audience members do not fear rebuttal of or retribution for their most fundamental beliefs. Even in a volatile situation such as that described by Starhawk, when the guards were about to beat a woman seeking safe haven in a group of protesters, rhetoric that promotes a feeling of safety can be created. In this case, the women did nothing to endanger the guards or make them feel as though they would be hurt. They did not fight them physically or argue against the guards' use of force; neither did they engage in verbal abuse or ridicule the guards' training and beliefs about how to deal with prisoners.

Rhetoric that contributes to a feeling of safety also provides some means for audience members to order the world so it seems coherent and makes sense to them. When audience members feel their sense of order is threatened or challenged, they are more likely to cling to familiar ways of thinking and to be less open to understanding the perspectives of others. When a safe environment is created, then, audience members trust the rhetor and feel the rhetor is working with and not against them.

The condition of *value* is the acknowledgment that audience members have intrinsic or immanent worth. This value is what Benhabib (1992) calls "*the principle of universal moral respect*"— "the right of all beings capable of speech and action to be participants" in the conversation (p. 29). Barrett (1991) describes this condition as "respectfully, affirming others" while at the same time "one affirms oneself" (p. 148).

Value is created when rhetors approach audience members as "unrepeatable individuals" and eschew "distancing, depersonalizing, or paternalistic attitudes" (Walker, 1989, pp. 22, 23). As a result, audience members feel their identities are not forced upon or chosen for them by rhetors. Rhetors do not attempt to fit audience members into any particular roles but face "the 'otherness of the other,' one might say to face their 'alterity,' their irreducible distinctness and difference from the self" (Benhabib, 1992, p. 167). Rhetors celebrate the unique and individual identities of audience members—what Benhabib (1992) describes as

> the actuality of my choices, namely to how I, as a finite, concrete, embodied individual, shape and fashion the circumstances of my birth and family, linguistic, cultural and gender identity into a coherent narrative that stands as my life's story. (pp. 161–162)

One way in which rhetoric may contribute to the acknowledgment and celebration of freely chosen, unique identities by audience members is through a process Gendlin (1978) calls "*absolute listening*" (p. 116), Morton (1985) describes as "hearing to speech" (p. 202), and Johnson (1987) terms "hearing into being"

(p. 130). In such rhetoric, listeners do not interrupt, comfort, or insert anything of their own as others tell of their experiences. Such a stance contrasts with typical ways of listening, in which "we nearly always stop each other from getting very far inside. Our advice, reactions, encouragements, reassurances, and well-intentioned comments actually prevent people from feeling understood" (Gendlin, 1978, p. 116) and encourage them to direct their comments toward listeners' positions or orientations (Johnson, 1987). While speaking to listeners who do not insert themselves into the talk, individuals come to discover their own perspectives. Morton (1985) quotes a woman's description of her experience in the process of being heard to speech: " 'You didn't smother me. You gave it [my voice] space to shape itself. You gave it time to come full circle' " (p. 205).

Value is conveyed to audience members when rhetors not only listen carefully to the perspectives of others but try to think from those perspectives. Benhabib's (1992) notion of the "'reversibility of perspectives'" (p. 145) is relevant here; it is the capacity to reverse perspectives and to reason from the standpoint of others, "making present to oneself what the perspectives of others involved are or could be" (p. 137). When value is created in a communicative situation, audience members feel rhetors see them as significant individuals and appreciate and attend to their uniqueness. They feel rhetors care about them, understand their ideas, and allow them to contribute in significant ways to the interaction.

Freedom, the power to choose or decide, is a third condition whose presence in an environment is a prerequisite for the possibility of mutual understanding. In invitational rhetoric, rhetors do not place restrictions on an interaction. Participants can bring any and all matters to the interaction for consideration; no subject matter is off limits, and all presuppositions can be challenged. The rhetor's ideas also are not privileged over those of the audience in invitational rhetoric. All the participants in the interaction are able, in Barrett's (1991) words, to "speak up, to speak out" (p. 148). Benhabib (1992) calls this "*the principle of egalitarian reciprocity*" (p. 29); within conversations, it suggests, "each has the same symmetrical rights to various speech acts, to initiate new topics, to ask for reflection about the presuppositions of the conversation, etc." (p. 29).

Freedom also is developed when a rhetor provides opportunities for others to develop and choose options from alternatives they, themselves, have created. Rather than presenting a predetermined set of options from which individuals may choose, a rhetor who wishes to facilitate freedom allows audience members to develop the options that seem appropriate to them, allowing for the richness and complexity of their unique subjective experiences. Perspectives are articulated as a means to widen options—to generate more ideas than either rhetors or audiences had initially—in contrast to traditional rhetoric, where rhetors seek to limit the options of audiences and encourage them to select the one they advocate.

Freedom of choice is made available to audiences, as well, in that, in invitational rhetoric, the audience's lack of acceptance of or adherence to the perspective articulated by the rhetor truly makes no difference to the rhetor. Some audience members will choose to try to understand the perspective of the rhetor, but others will not. Of those who do, some will choose to accept the perspective offered by the rhetor, but others will not. Either outcome—acceptance or rejection—is seen as perfectly acceptable by the invitational rhetor, who is not offended, disappointed, or angry if audience members choose not to adopt a particular perspective. Should the audience choose not to accept the vision articulated by the rhetor, the connection between the rhetor and the audience remains intact, and the audience still is valued and appreciated by the rhetor. The maintenance of the connection between rhetors and audiences is not dependent on rhetors' approval of the choices made by audience members. Rogers' (1962) notion of unconditional positive regard suggests the nature of the autonomy the rhetor accords the audience; the audience has the freedom to make choices without the possibility of losing the respect of the rhetor.

ILLUSTRATIONS

Invitational rhetoric offers an invitation to understanding—to enter another's world to better understand an issue and the individual who holds a particular perspective on it. Ultimately, its purpose is to provide the basis for the creation and maintenance of relationships of equality. Its primary communicative options are offering perspectives and the creation of the external conditions of safety, value, and freedom that enable audience members to present their perspectives to the rhetor. In this section, we present two examples of invitational rhetoric to clarify its primary features.

The first example is the acceptance speech given by Adrienne Rich when she was awarded the National Book Awards' prize for poetry in 1974 (Rich, Lorde, & Walker, 1974/1994). When Rich accepted the award, she read a statement that she had prepared with Alice Walker and Audre Lorde—both of whom also had been nominated for the prize. In the statement, the three women announced that they were accepting the award together: "We, Audre Lorde, Adrienne Rich, and Alice Walker, together accept this award in the name of all the women whose voices have gone and still go unheard in a patriarchal world" (p. 148).

The statement clearly articulated the women's own position: "We believe that we can enrich ourselves more in supporting and giving to each other than by competing against each other; and that poetry—if it *is* poetry—exists in a realm beyond ranking and comparison" (p. 148). They presented no arguments in favor of their belief, however, nor did they argue against the position held by representatives of the National Book Awards. Thus, they did not seek the adherence of others to their perspective but simply offered their own vision.

The speech illustrates re-sourcing as a form of offering in that the women communicated their differences with the hierarchical, competitive framework established by the National Book Awards simply by not communicating within the terms of that framework: "None of us could accept this money for herself" (p. 148). They chose to respond within a different framework—one based on support and cooperation—by accepting the prize in the name of all women: "We will share this prize among us, to be used as best we can for women" (p. 148).

The three external conditions of safety, value, and freedom required for others to present their perspectives were created by the speech. The rhetors communicated safety when they suggested that they regarded the perspective of the judges as a legitimate one that they would treat with respect and care. "We appreciate the good faith of the judges for this award" (p. 148), they stated.

They accorded value in very specific ways to many individuals, both those in their immediate audience and others:

> We dedicate this occasion to the struggle for self-determination of all women, of every color, identification, or derived class: the poet, the housewife, the lesbian, the mathematician, the mother, the dishwasher, the pregnant teenager, the teacher, the grandmother, the prostitute, the philosopher, the waitress, the women who will understand what we are doing here and those who will not understand yet. (pp. 148–149)

They not only recognized these diverse and unique individuals but credited them as sources for their own work, calling them "the silent women whose voices have been denied us, the articulate women who have given us strength to do our work" (p. 149).

The brevity of the speech precluded the opportunity for the extensive development of freedom for the audience, but it is evident in that Rich, Walker, and Lorde do not specify particular options for action for women; they leave open to women whatever routes of "self-determination" (p. 148) they, themselves, choose. Nor do they suggest the kind of support women should give to each other or the particular contributions other women have made to them. Their ambiguity in these areas leaves open options for the audience and does not confine the terms of the interaction they initiated.

Feminist and animal-rights activist Sally Miller Gearhart (1993) provides a second example of invitational rhetoric in her narration of her interaction with an anti-abortion advocate. In the interaction, Gearhart used both traditional and invitational rhetoric, so her narrative provides a useful contrast between the two and the kinds of results each tends to produce. On a trip with a friend to upstate New York, Gearhart encountered a man in the Kennedy airport "railing about all these women and abortion rights." Because of her own pro-choice beliefs, Gearhart

> took him on. As a matter of fact, I took him on so loudly that we gathered a little crowd there in the Kennedy airport. I was screaming at him; I was trying to make him change. It was not successful, and it was pretty ugly, as a matter of fact. . . . They didn't have to actually physically separate us, but it was close to that.

An hour later, as she was boarding the shuttle bus to take her to Plattsburg, her destination, Gearhart encountered the man again: "There was only one seat on that bus, and guess who it was next to? . . . He looked at me and I looked at him as if to say, 'Oh, my God, what are we going to do?'" Rather than continue to engage the man as she had in the airport, Gearhart decided to try something different—to engage in what we suggest was invitational rhetoric: "I decided that what I would do was to try to approach this man with something different . . . and so I began asking him about his life and about the things that he did," seeking to understand his perspective and the reasons it made sense to him. "In fact," Gearhart explains, "it was even worse than I had originally thought. In fact, he was a chemist, and he had experimented on animals. He had grown up as a hunter and, of course, all that is absolutely counter to the things that I believe." But rather than attempting to convince him of the error of his ways, Gearhart continued to listen to the man, and he did the same as she shared her own perspectives and experiences with him.

The invitational rhetoric in which the two engaged brought Gearhart and the man together, although neither one "had changed our original position." As the two crossed paths for the third time in the parking lot, waiting for their respective rides, they started walking toward each other. Gearhart finishes the story:

> I don't know which one of us did it first, but I guess maybe I flung open my arms and he flung open his arms and we came together in this terrific hug, both of us in tears, sobbing, crying like babies. I said, "You know, I don't know what has happened here, but my life has been totally changed after today." And he said, "My life is totally changed, too, and I don't know what's happened."

We suggest that what happened was that the two individuals had offered their perspectives and listened to and acknowledged one another's perspectives in an environment of safety, value, and freedom. Their communication thus invited understanding and brought them to a new place of awareness of and appreciation for one another. Gearhart's (1993) summary of the experience is an excellent summary of invitational rhetoric: "It's a way to disagree and at the same time not to hurt each other and to respect each other and to have, actually, something very close and tender."

We see the statement of Rich, Lorde, and Walker and Gearhart's interaction as invitational, then, in that both were rooted in the principles of equality, immanent value, and respect for others and validation of their perspectives. Rich, Lorde, and Walker offered a perspective and communicated its difference with that of the judges, but they neither sought adherence for it nor denigrated the different viewpoint of the judges. Gearhart also offered a perspective very different from that of her acquaintance and listened to one very different from her own without seeking adherence or pronouncing judgment. Each rhetor created conditions of safety, value, and freedom,

contributing to an environment in which audience members were able to present their different perspectives. The result was an understanding on which relationships of equality and respect could be built.

IMPLICATIONS FOR RHETORICAL THEORY

The expansion of the notion of rhetoric to include invitational rhetoric has several implications for rhetorical theory. The introduction of invitational rhetoric into the scope of rhetorical theory challenges the presumption that has been granted to persuasion as the interactional goal in the rhetorical tradition. Identification and explication of a rhetoric not grounded in the intent to produce a desired change in others undermine the position of privilege accorded to efforts to influence in rhetoric. The existence of invitational rhetoric encourages the exploration of yet other rhetorics that do not involve this singular interactional goal.

A second implication is that invitational rhetoric may contribute to the efforts of communication scholars who are working to develop models for cooperative, nonadversarial, and ethical communication. Such a goal, for example, is espoused by Herrick (1992), in his discussion of the link between rhetoric and ethics, when he suggests "that a virtue approach to rhetorical ethics may provide the kind of flexible, yet directive, ethic needed" to maintain the democratic nature of a pluralistic social order (p. 147). Van Eemeren and Grootendorst (1992) also propose such a goal in their book on argumentation; their approach is designed to create an open and free exchange and responsible participation in cooperative, dialogic communication. The framework provided by invitational rhetoric may allow such theorists to achieve their laudatory missions more easily by contributing to a reconciliation of goals and means (Makau, in press). According to Herrick's and van Eemeren and Grootendorst's definitions of rhetoric as a process in which rhetors seek to secure the acceptance of their perspectives by others, rhetors tend to see their audiences as opponents and sometimes may be tempted to engage in questionable ethical practices to win their "battles" with them. Rules thus are required to contain the interaction that results from the use of such strategies. Invitational rhetoric may serve as a way to allow these scholars to develop models for interaction not characterized by the opposition and competition that make the achievement of their goal difficult.

The introduction of invitational rhetoric to the array of rhetorical forms available also serves a greater heuristic, inventive function than rhetoric previously has allowed. Traditional theories of rhetoric occur within preimposed or preconceived frameworks that are reflexive and reinforce the vocabularies and tenets of those frameworks. In rhetoric in which the rhetor seeks to impose change on others, an idea is adapted to the audience or is presented in ways that will be most persuasive to the audience; as a result, the idea stays lodged within the confines of the rhetorical system in which it was framed. Others may challenge the idea but only within the confines of the framework of the dispute already established. The inventive potential of rhetoric is restricted as the interaction converts the idea to the experience required by the framework.

Invitational rhetoric, on the other hand, aims at converting experience "to one of the many views which are indeterminately possible" (Holmberg, 1977, p. 237). As a result, much is open in invitational rhetoric that is not in traditional rhetorics—the potential of the audience to contribute to the generation of ideas is enhanced, the means used to present ideas are not those that limit the ideas to what is most persuasive for the audience, the view of the kind of environment that can be created in the interaction is expanded, and the ideas that can be considered multiply. The privileging of invention in invitational rhetoric allows for the development of interpretations, perspectives, courses of actions, and solutions to problems different from those allowed in traditional models of rhetoric. Rather than the discovery of how to make a case, invitational rhetoric employs invention to discover more cases, a process Daly (1984) describes as

one of creating "an atmosphere in which further creativity may flourish. . . . [w]e become breathers/creators of free space. We are windy, stirring the stagnant spaces with life" (p. 18).

The inclusion of an invitational rhetoric in the array of rhetorics available suggests the need to revise and expand rhetorical constructs of various kinds to take into account the nature and function of this form. Invitational rhetoric suggests, for example, that the traditional view of the audience as an opponent ought to be questioned. It challenges the traditional conception of the notion of rhetorical strategies as means to particular ends in that in invitational rhetoric, the means constitute the ends. It suggests the need for a new schema of ethics to fit interactional goals other than inducement of others to adherence to the rhetor's own beliefs.

Finally, invitational rhetoric provides a mode of communication for women and other marginalized groups to use in their efforts to transform systems of domination and oppression. At first glance, invitational rhetoric may seem to be incapable of resisting and transforming oppressive systems such as patriarchy because the most it seems able to do is to create a space in which representatives of an oppressive system understand a different—in this case, a feminist—perspective but do not adopt it. Although invitational rhetoric is not designed to create a specific change, such as the transformation of systems of oppression into ones that value and nurture individuals, it may produce such an outcome. Invitational rhetoric may resist an oppressive system simply because it models an alternative to the system by being "itself an Other way of thinking/speaking" (Daly, 1978, p. xiii)—it presents an alternative feminist vision rooted in affirmation and respect and thus shows how an alternative looks and works. Invitational rhetoric thus may transform an oppressive system precisely because it does not engage that system on its own terms, using arguments developed from the system's framework or orientation. Such arguments usually are co-opted by the dominant system (Ferguson, 1984) and provide the impetus "to strengthen, refine, and embellish the original edifice," entrenching the system further (Johnson, 1989, pp. 16–17). Invitational rhetoric, in contrast, enables rhetors to disengage from the dominance and mastery so common to a system of oppression and to create a reality of equality and mutuality in its place, allowing for options and possibilities not available within the familiar, dominant framework.

Our interest in inserting invitational rhetoric into the scope of rhetorical theory is not meant to suggest that it is an ideal for which rhetors should strive or that it should or can be used in all situations. Invitational rhetoric is one of many useful and legitimate rhetorics, including persuasion, in which rhetors will want to be skilled. With the identification of the rhetorical mode of invitational rhetoric, however, rhetors will be able to recognize situations in which they seek not to persuade others but simply to create an environment that facilitates understanding, accords value and respect to others' perspectives, and contributes to the development of relationships of equality.

REFERENCES

Barrett, H. (1991). *Rhetoric and civility: Human development, narcissism, and the good audience.* New York: State University of New York Press.

Benhabib, S. (1992). *Situating the self: Gender, community and postmodernism in contemporary ethics.* New York: Routledge.

Buber, M. (1965). *Between man and man* (R.G. Smith, Trans.). New York: Macmillan.

Burke, K. (1969). *A grammar of motives.* Berkeley: University of California Press.

Burke, K. (1984). *Attitudes toward history* (3rd ed.). Berkeley: University of California Press.

Daly, M. (1978). *Gyn! ecology: The metaethics of radical feminism.* Boston: Beacon.

Daly, M. (1984). *Pure lust: Elemental feminist philosophy.* Boston: Beacon.

Edson, B. A. (1985). Bias in social movement theory: A view from a female-systems perspective. *Women's Studies in Communication, 8,* 34–45.

Elshtain, J. B. (1982). Feminist discourse and its discontents: Language, power, and meaning. *Signs, 7,* 603–621.

Ferguson, K. E. (1984). *The feminist case against bureaucracy.* Philadelphia: Temple University Press.

Ferguson, M. (1980). *The aquarian conspiracy: Personal and social transformation in the 1980s.* Los Angeles: J.P. Tarcher.

Forget, P. (1989). Argument(s). In D. Michelfelder & R. Palmer (Eds.), *Dialogue and deconstruction: The Gadamer-Derrida encounter* (pp. 129–149). Albany, NY: SUNY Press.

Foss, K. A., & Foss, S. K. (1991). *Women speak: The eloquence of women's lives.* Prospect Heights, IL: Waveland.

Foss, S. K., Foss, K. A., & Trapp, R. (1991). *Contemporary perspectives on rhetoric* (rev. ed.). Prospect Heights, IL: Waveland.

Foss, S. K., & Griffin, C. L. (1992). A feminist perspective on rhetorical theory: Toward a clarification of boundaries. *Western Journal of Communication, 56,* 330–349.

Gearhart, S. M. (1979). The womanization of rhetoric. *Women's Studies International Quarterly, 2,* 195–201.

Gearhart, S. (1982). Womanpower: Energy resourcement. In C. Spretnak (Ed.), *The politics of women's spirituality: Essays on the rise of spiritual power within the feminist movement* (pp. 194–206). Garden City, NY: Anchor.

Gearhart, S. M. (1993, January). [Videotaped interview with Sonja K. Foss and members of the Feminist Rhetorical Theory class, Ohio State University].

Gendlin, E. T. (1978). *Focusing.* New York: Everest.

Griffin, C. L. (1993). Women as communicators: Mary Daly's hagography as rhetoric. *Communication Monographs, 60,* 158–177.

Herrick, J. A. (1992). Rhetoric, ethics, and virtue. *Communication Studies, 43,* 133–149.

Holmberg, C. (1977). Dialectical rhetoric and rhetorical rhetoric. *Philosophy and Rhetoric, 10,* 232–243.

hooks, b. (1984). *Feminist theory: From margin to center.* Boston: South End.

Johnson, S. (1987). *Going out of our minds: The metaphysics of liberation.* Freedom, CA: Crossing.

Johnson, S. (1989). *Wildfire: Igniting the she/volution.* Albuquerque, NM: Wildfire.

Johnson, S. (1991). *The ship that sailed into the living room: Sex and intimacy reconsidered.* Estancia, NM: Wildfire.

Kramarae, C. (1989). Feminist theories of communication. In E. Barnouw (Ed.), *International encyclopedia of communications* (Vol. 2, pp. 157–160). New York: Oxford University Press.

Makau, J. M. (in press). [Review of *Argumentation, communication and fallacies: A pragma-dialectical perspective*]. *Philosophy and Rhetoric*.

Morton, N. (1985). *The journey is home*. Boston: Beacon.

Natanson, M. (1965). The claims of immediacy. In M. Natanson & H. W. Johnstone, Jr. (Eds.), *Philosophy, rhetoric and argumentation* (pp. 10–19). University Park: Pennsylvania State University Press.

Rich, A., Lorde, A., & Walker, A. (1994). A statement for voices unheard: A challenge to the National Book Awards. In S.K. Foss & K.A. Foss, *Inviting transformation: Presentational speaking for a changing world* (pp. 148–149). Prospect Heights, IL: Waveland. (Speech presented 1974)

Rogers, C. R. (1962). The interpersonal relationship: The core of guidance. *Harvard Educational Review, 32*, 416–429.

Rorty, R. (1986). Beyond realism and anti-realism. In L. Nagl & R. Heinrich (Eds.), *Wo steht die Analytische Philosophie heute?* (pp. 103–115). Vienna, Austria: Oldenbourg.

Scott, R. L. (1976). Dialogue and rhetoric. In J. Blankenship & H. Stelzner (Eds.), *Rhetoric and communication: Studies in the University of Illinois tradition* (pp. 99–109). Urbana: University of Illinois Press.

Scott, R. L. (1991). The necessary pluralism of any future history of rhetoric. *Pre/Text, 12*, 195–209.

Shepherd, G.J. (1992). Communication as influence: Definitional exclusion. *Communication Studies, 43*, 203–219.

Starhawk. (1987). *Truth or dare: Encounters with power, authority, and mystery*. San Francisco: Harper and Row.

Starhawk. (1988). *Dreaming the dark: Magic, sex and politics* (rev. ed.). Boston: Beacon.

Tracy, D. (1987). *Plurality and ambiguity: Hermeneutics, religion, hope*. San Francisco: Harper and Row.

van Eemeren, F. H., & Grootendorst, R. (1992). *Argumentation, communication and fallacies: A pragma-dialectical perspective*. Hillsdale, NJ: Lawrence Erlbaum.

Veenendall, T. L., & Feinstein, M. C. (1990). *Let's talk about relationships*. Prospect Heights, IL: Waveland.

Walker, M. U. (1989). Moral understandings: Alternative "epistemology" for a feminist ethics. *Hypatia, 4*, 15–28.

Watzlawick, P., Weakland, J. H., & Fisch, R. (1974). *Change: Principles of problem formation and problem resolution*. New York: W.W. Norton.

Wood, J. T. (1993). Enlarging conceptual boundaries: A critique of research in interpersonal communication. In S.P. Bowen & N. Wyatt (Eds.), *Transforming visions: Feminist critiques in communication studies* (pp. 19–49). Cresskill, NJ: Hampton.

Wood, J. T. (1994). *Gendered lives: Communication, gender, and culture*. Belmont, CA: Wadsworth.

Projects for Rhetorical Theorizing

Additional Readings on Rhetorical Theory

A. Plato's critique was directed against Sophistic rhetoric. To learn more about the theoretical concepts in sophistic rhetoric: Duncan (1938); Rosenmeyer (1955); Enos (1993); Poulakos (1995).

B. To learn more about rhetorical theory in general: Sloane (2001); Hauser (2002).

C. To learn more about Burke: Burke (1966); Burke (1969a, 1969b); Rueckert (1982).

D. To learn more about feminist rhetoric and other contemporary perspectives on rhetoric: Foss, Foss, and Trapp (1985); Foss and Griffin (1992); Foss, Foss, and Griffin (1999).

Application Exercise

Collect example(s) of contemporary rhetoric in any of the following ways. Take what you think was a poor speech given by a public official and rewrite it based on your theoretical understandings of rhetoric. Collect a set of texts and identify what, if any, shared rhetorical strategies are being used in today's public-mass discourse. Locate within your community a community of practitioners who you think are being productive with their rhetoric. Identify the rhetorical strategies being used in this community of practice. For the set of strategies in your collected texts, what would thinkers in this unit have to say about these strategies? What do these strategies have to say to the thinkers in this unit?

Projects

1. Building on the proposal of Foss and Griffin (reading 9), one may be drawn toward asking, what is the place of debate and persuasion in modern society? While Foss and Griffin provide one point of view on this topic, not all scholars agree. Tannen (1998) and Cameron (2000) provide two different contrasting views. Examine these different perspectives and develop a theoretically informed answer to the question.

2. Building on the ideas of Burke (reading 8), one may be drawn to look around at texts and ask the question, What is the rhetoric in texts such as photographs, works of fiction, films, music lyrics, the music charts, popular magazines, product labels, blueprints, campaign slogans, institutional insignia, billboards, cookbooks, driver education manuals, baseball cards, storefronts, mall layouts, and Internet search engine results? Burke himself has examined the rhetoric of religion (Burke, 1970); others have examined the rhetoric of science (e.g., Nelson, Megill, & McCloskey, 1987), while many other texts have been examined under the heading visual rhetoric (Hill & Helmers, 2004; Rice, 2004; Gallagher & Zagacki, 2005). Focusing on a specific kind of

text, examine a set of such texts and propose a theory of the rhetoric in these texts.

3. If the language in all of the texts listed in the previous project is rhetorical, one might begin to ask, is all language rhetorical? And what would it mean to take a rhetorical perspective on human interaction in general? Some scholars within the rhetorical tradition (Scott, 1967; Scott, 1976; Gill, 1994), as well as scholars from disciplines such as psychology that have adopted a rhetorical perspective (Edwards & Potter, 1992; Potter, 1996), have proposed that how we think and talk in our everyday discourse is rhetorical in nature. How we conceptualize and make sense of things, what we remember, and how we describe things are just some of the aspects that scholars have discussed as rhetorical. Focusing on a sample of everyday talk, provide a rhetorical interpretation of this talk by identifying rhetorical strategies used as well as addressing the idea of how to talk about everyday talk as rhetoric.

4. Building on Plato's critique of the public discourse of his day, one might be drawn to look closely at the public speakers of today. As such, one could examine the problem of elected public officials who many claim are poor public speakers. Theorizing about this problem might entail asking some of the following questions: Could it be that these speakers are using strategies other than traditional public speaking strategies to communicate their messages? Do they perhaps use personal persuasion strategies in public forums? One could also theorize about the principles, ideals, and even theories that these speakers rely on when choosing these particular communication techniques. What are the conceptions in the current sociohistorical surround that indicate the potential usefulness of such strategies?

5. Another potential problem arises when thinking about Burke as well as Aristotle and Plato and looking at public discourse today. As some, such as Hauser (1999), point out, the modern public is not the same as the Greek *polis* where all citizens attempted to persuade each other through debate. Relatedly, as Van Eemeren, Grootendorst, Jackson, and Jacobs (1993) noticed in their examination of witnessing and heckling, often public speakers are not speaking to each other but rather are performing for their own crowds. This notion of performance is paramount in Burke (reading 8) as he talks about the human drama and how people act as performers. As Senate debates become a few senators talking to C-SPAN cameras with a nearly empty chamber behind them, one could examine the problem of rhetorical performance. In many ways this project can be seen as a modern-day version of Aristotle's project. What are the ways of thinking and talking that are needed to have productive public interchange of ideas today? Theorizing this problem could entail developing conceptions for and ways of talking about nonperformative public rhetoric, examining nonperformative rhetorical practices, and thinking about training for nonperformative rhetors.

REFERENCES

Burke, K. (1966). *Language as symbolic action: Essays on life, literature, and method.* Berkeley: University of California Press.

Burke, K. (1969a). *A grammar of motives.* Berkeley: University of California Press.

Burke, K. (1969b). *A rhetoric of motives.* Berkeley: University of California Press.

Burke, K. (1970). *The rhetoric of religion: Studies in logology.* Berkeley: University of California Press.

Cameron, D. (2000). *Good to talk? Living and working in a communication culture.* London: Sage.

Duncan, T. S. (1938). Gorgias' theories of art. *Classical Journal, 33,* 402–413.

Edwards, D., & Potter, J. (1992). *Discursive psychology.* London: Sage.

Enos, R. L. (1993). *Greek rhetoric before Aristotle.* Prospect Heights, IL: Waveland Press.

Foss, K. A., Foss, S. K., & Griffin, C. L. (1999). *Feminist rhetorical theories.* Thousand Oaks, CA: Sage.

Foss, K. A., Foss, S. K., & Griffin, C. L. (Eds.). (2003). *Readings in feminist rhetorical theory.* Thousand Oaks, CA: Sage.

Foss, S. K., Foss, K. A., & Trapp, R. (1985). *Contemporary perspectives on rhetoric.* Prospect Heights, IL: Waveland Press.

Foss, S. K., Foss, K. A., & Trapp, R. (2002). *Readings in contemporary rhetoric.* Prospect Heights, IL: Waveland Press.

Foss, S. K., & Griffin, C. L. (1992). A feminist perspective on rhetorical theory: Toward a classification of boundaries. *Western Journal of Communication, 56,* 330–349.

Gallagher, V., & Zagacki, K. (2005). Visibility and rhetoric: The power of visual images in Norman Rockwell's depictions of civil rights. *Quarterly Journal of Speech, 91*(2), 175–200.

Gill, A. (1994). *Rhetoric and human understanding.* Prospect Heights, IL: Waveland Press.

Hauser, G. A. (1999). *Vernacular voices: The rhetorics of publics and public spheres.* Columbia: University of South Carolina Press.

Hauser, G. A. (2002). *An introduction to rhetorical theory* (2nd ed.). Prospect Heights, IL: Waveland Press.

Hill, C. A., & Helmers, M. (Eds.). (2004). *Defining visual rhetorics.* Mahwah, NJ: Lawrence Erlbaum.

Nelson, J. S., Megill, A., & McCloskey, D. N. (1987). *The rhetoric of the human sciences: Language and argument in scholarship and public affairs.* Madison: University of Wisconsin Press.

Potter, J. (1996). *Representing reality: Discourse, rhetoric, and social construction.* Thousand Oaks, CA: Sage.

Poulakos, J. (1995). *Sophistical rhetoric in classical Greece.* Columbia: University of South Carolina Press.

Rice, J. (2004). A critical review of visual rhetoric in a postmodern age: Complementing, extending, and presenting new ideas. *Review of Communication, 4*(1–2), 63–74.

Rosenmeyer, T. G. (1955). Gorgias, Aeschyles, and Apate. *American Journal of Philology, 76,* 225–260.

Rueckert, W. H. (1982). *Kenneth Burke and the drama of human relations* (2nd ed.). Berkeley: University of California Press.

Scott, R. L. (1967). On viewing rhetoric as epistemic. *Central States Speech Journal, 18,* 9–17.

Scott, R. L. (1976). On viewing rhetoric as epistemic: Ten years later. *Central States Speech Journal, 27,* 258–266.

Sloane, T. O. (Ed.). (2001). *Encyclopedia of rhetoric.* New York: Oxford University Press.

Tannen, D. (1998). *The argument culture: Moving from debate to dialogue.* New York: Random House.

Van Eemeren, F. H., Grootendorst, R., Jackson, S., & Jacobs, S. (1993). *Reconstructing argumentative discourse.* Tuscaloosa: University of Alabama Press.

UNIT IV   INTRODUCTION

THE SEMIOTIC TRADITION

Moving from the rhetorical tradition to the semiotic tradition is kind of like moving from examining how to make the best bread for the occasion to understanding the molecular structure and chemical processes of the yeast. From a semiotic perspective, sign systems and the use of signs are the productive agents of thought and society. While discursive psychology and theories of rhetoric as epistemic blur the line between rhetoric and discourse in general (see Projects for Rhetorical Theorizing, project 3), the rhetorical tradition theorizes communication primarily as an art of discourse of speakers (rhetors) addressing audiences. Semioticians, however, theorize communication as intersubjective mediation by signs— that is, as a process in which language and other sign systems come to have shared meanings and thereby serve as a medium for common understanding between individuals (subjects).

Semiotics foregrounds understanding rather than persuasion as the essential problem of communication, thinking and talking about communication with metadiscursive concepts such as sign, meaning, cognition, code, medium, and discourse. Metadiscourse itself, a concept central to the metatheoretical perspective of this book, is a semiotic idea. Semioticians address communication by examining phenomena such as the structure of language and other systems of signs, the relationship between language and thought, and the communicative uses of signs. Extensions of semiotic thinking about language include structuralist explorations of society and social institutions (Sturrock, 2003). The five readings in this unit provide insight into some of the foundational concepts in semiotics as well as a range of thinking about communication in the semiotic tradition.

John Locke (1632–1704) was the first modern philosopher to pose the problem of communication in semiotic terms, as the problem of sharing ideas through signs. Indeed, he has been called the inventor of the modern concept of communication as transmission (Peters, 1989). Peters shows how Locke's formulation of the problem of communication reflected his individualistic political philosophy in the sociohistorical context of early capitalist societies.

Locke's individualistic, empiricist analysis of language, although quite outdated with respect to current semiotic theory, still forms the implicit background for a great deal of popular advice on how to communicate clearly and avoid misunderstanding. A prominent example is the 20th-century language reform movement known as General Semantics (Hayakawa & Hayakawa, 1949/1990; Korzybski, 1933/1958). General semanticists' criticisms of the abuse of language clearly echo those of Locke, whose *Essay Concerning Human Understanding* (from which our first reading in this unit is excerpted) was first published in 1690.

Responding in part to what he saw as the obfuscating use of language by academic philosophers and religious thinkers, Locke's analysis of the inherent imperfection of words as well as the additional imperfection brought about by the intentional misuse of language can be seen as theorizing the *problem of communication via words*. According to Locke, taking the three reasons for communication to be to share one's thoughts with another, to do so quickly, and to show one's knowledge of things, words serve none of these ends very well. Unless the word used excites the same meaning in the mind of the hearer as it does in the speaker, none of the ends of communication can be achieved. This, for Locke, is the problem of words.

Yet in some ways it is not the imperfection of words that is the most problematic aspect of communicating via words. This imperfection of words allows speakers to abuse words by doing things such as not having an idea in mind when using a word, using a word in a way that does not match the idea commonly associated with that word, or using words inconsistently. Interestingly Locke also cites as an abuse the use, by those engaged in the practice of disputing, of the same word to mean different things, and notes that highly valuing skill in disputing increases this type of abuse. Indeed, in a passage infamous among rhetoricians, he condemns the whole art of rhetoric as a "powerful instrument of error and deceit" (reading 10). What is interesting about Locke's views on the misuse of language is that he sees it as problematic not only because it can lead to bad public decisions or untruthful ideas in the hearer, as Plato might critique, but more fundamentally because it leads to misunderstanding. This emphasis on understanding is one distinction that separates the semiotic tradition from the rhetorical tradition, in which persuasive use of language is more central. In keeping with the goal of understanding, Locke proposes a set of practical guidelines for avoiding the abuse of words.

Jumping forward to the late 19th century, the semiotic tack of looking at signs and the individual is seen in the work of Charles Sanders Peirce (1839–1914). Peirce was a logician and experimental scientist whom the philosopher William James regarded as the founder of American Pragmatism. Exploring scientific and logical truth through applying scientific methods to philosophical issues in order to clarify the meaning of ideas, Peirce pursued the possibility of abductive reasoning. Abductive reasoning is distinct from deductive and inductive reasoning and seeks to generate explanations for surprising ideas. One way to state the problem that Peirce theorized is *the problem of reasoning through signs*.

In contrast to Saussure's two-sided model of the sign (to be discussed later in this unit introduction), at the center of Peirce's theorizing about signs is a triadic process involving a sign, an object, and an idea (which itself is a sign in someone's mind) that forms the connection between the sign and the object. In other writings, Peirce called this process of signification *semiosis*, called the three elements the *representamen* (sign), the object, and the *interpretant* (the idea that connects the sign and the object), and defined a sign as "something which stands for something to somebody in some respect or capacity" (Peirce, 1955, p. 99).

This triadic sign provides an explanation for how ideas chain together in the mind of an individual. The chain ensues because an interpretant can also be a representamen that elicits the production of another interpretant, and so on. One thought leads to another. A dyadic sign does not explain this chaining of ideas, but this triadic sign provides the foundation for thinking and talking about thought as consisting only of signs. Not all experience is semiotic.

As in Peirce's opening example, experience can consist of pure unreflective feelings, or of reactions brought about by interruptions of feeling states. But to the extent that experience involves thought and reasoning, it is constituted through signs. This is the process of semiosis. Further exploring the nature of semiosis, Peirce identifies three types of signs, icons, indices, and symbols, and explains that language is of the symbolic type.

Moving ahead slightly to the early 20th century, theorizing the *problem of language as an autonomous system*, Ferdinand de Saussure advances the proposal that language should be studied as a socially instituted system of signs that exists "outside the individual who can never create nor modify it by himself" (reading 12). Previously language had always been studied in conjunction with something else, such as speech or sound, and some theorists such as Locke had focused on the meanings of individual words without understanding how the words of a language form a structured, interdependent system. However, when language is understood as a structured object clearly distinct from its use in articulate speech, it becomes possible to elucidate what is fundamental and what is accidental to signs. We can also see that language is not the only socially instituted system of signs that express ideas, although it is the most important such system. Other systems of signs include military signs, rituals, and social customs, among others. Saussure concludes that a science of semiology is needed in order to fully understand the life of signs in society.

Saussure's articulation of the structure of language as an autonomous object provided key concepts within the semiotic tradition. Elsewhere in his *Course in General Linguistics* (1916/1959), Saussure defined a sign as a two-sided psychological entity consisting of the signifier (sound-image) and the signified (the concept that the sound-image signifies). This two-sided conceptualization of the sign,

the arbitrary relationship between signifier and signified (there is no natural connection between words and what they mean), the linear nature of the signifier, and the dual nature of language as both mutable and immutable are key concepts in Saussure's theory. These concepts elucidate both the nature of linguistic signs and the relationship between language as a system of signs and history.

The complexity of language is a key to understanding the stability of language. The sheer number of signs and the web of connections between them is simply too large to change quickly or radically. Additionally, even though the relationship between concept and sign-image is arbitrary, it is fixed by the conventions of the linguistic community. Although there are important differences, this Saussurean idea harkens back to Locke's discussion of the common meaning of a word. This relation between language and the larger society is a key notion within some strands of the semiotic tradition. Just as interaction between individuals is mediated by signs, so is the interaction between individuals and society. Despite the stability of language and the impossibility of changing it by conscious choice, the arbitrariness of the signifier-signified relationship does allow for shifts in meaning to occur through time. So while things mostly stay the same, change is unavoidable. Language is both immutable and mutable.

Saussure laid the foundation for French structuralism, a movement of thought that became highly influential in the second half of the 20th century (Sturrock, 2003). Just as the various phonemes (the meaningful sounds) of a language do not exist independently as individuals but form a tightly structured system generated by an underlying set of contrasts (like the single sound feature that differentiates both *pat* from *bat* and *pill* from *bill*), structuralists argued that the diversity within every type of cultural phenomenon, ranging from myths to fashions to ideologies, is produced by some underlying structure of conceptual distinctions. Individual entities—including conscious human individuals, or *subjects*—have no definite meaning in themselves but only by virtue of their positions within larger systems of signification. Poststructuralist thought, while questioning the stability of underlying structures, has retained structuralism's anti-individualism and its view that meaning is generated within systems of signs.

The next piece, by Roland Barthes, extends Saussure's structuralist approach to examine nonlinguistic but language-like signs. A photograph is not linguistic, yet it is a sign; it represents something and has a meaning. In his study of the photographic image in newspapers, Barthes theorizes *the problem of connotative meanings in seemingly objective signs.* This communication problem is closely related to the problem of propaganda that Burke theorized in the rhetorical tradition (see the introduction to unit III): the problem that even apparently neutral and objective uses of symbols actually function persuasively.

A photograph is an especially interesting sign because it is seemingly completely denotative: an exact representation of the scene photographed, having essentially a literal or objective meaning. Denotative meaning is the specific object that a sign signifies. In this sense, a photo simply denotes whatever was photographed. Connotations are meanings associated with a sign by the code (language or other semiotic system) of which the sign is a part. For example, the word *justice* has no denotation (no specific object that it refers to) in the abstract yet is highly meaningful (has rich connotations) to any speaker of English.

Barthes claims that no code is used to construct a photographic image per se; therefore, it apparently has no connotation. However, he goes on to discuss the connotative procedures, techniques ranging from trick effects to the simple placement of objects in a photo, that are used to attach connotative meanings to these nonlinguistic signs. Captions and headlines also change the connotative meanings of news

photos. A picture of a man simply denotes the man who was photographed, but it can have very different connotations if captioned *John Doe, Tour de France winner* or *John Doe, charged with embezzlement.* Connotations are supplied by the readers of the newspaper from their stock of current knowledge and cultural mythology (sports hero mythology or business corruption mythology, depending on the caption). The presence of a photo gives these ethical and ideological connotations an aura of objectivity that they would not have if expressed in words alone.

Barthes's approach to semiotic theorizing shows some blending of traditions. He incorporates elements of literary criticism (an approach usually associated with rhetoric), and his critique of culture is seen by some as a precursor to critical cultural studies, which in this volume is considered within the critical tradition. This blending of traditions can also be seen in the last reading in this unit. Through introducing hermeneutical ideas, John Durham Peters blends semiotics and phenomenology (see unit V). Theorizing the *problem of disconnection,* Peters models communication not as seeking to achieve shared meanings but as the dissemination of signs. The 20th-century fixation with trying to communicate with aliens, like the 19th-century fascination with psychic communication and spiritualism, evidences that communication can only be undertaken to achieve a very different kind of understanding than has often been assumed in the semiotic tradition. Communication is not about finding the right words to achieve shared meaning, but is rather about finding ways to achieve fellowship with otherness. Harkening back to Saussure, Peters addresses the limits of democracy due to the linearity of language and the consequent limitation of being able to hear only one speaker at a time. Drawing on Peirce, he addresses the idea that all communication—including our inner thought processes—is conducted in signs. Signs and only signs connect us to others—even very different others like animals, ecosystems, aliens, and our own interiority. His poetic example of communication among dolphins provides a model of how communication takes place between individuals who work under the assumption of connection. When he writes of dolphins, "Theirs is a life of sporting firstness," he refers to Peirce's category of *firstness,* or immediate, unreflective feeling (reading 14). So, it seems, a final proposal in this piece is that there are conceptions and practices of communication where dissemination—the pure flow of signs—and direct contact with others, perhaps the experience of dialogue, are indistinguishable.

As you read these pieces, you may find yourself asking some of the general questions associated with the project of theorizing, such as, What communication problems does the lens of semiotic theory illuminate? How much do you align with semiotic thought? How does it inform your own theories of communication? What techniques does semiotics provide to manage the communication difficulties you experience? What new ideas and vocabulary do you now have to talk about communication? Where do you now see signs and signification that you didn't previously? Additionally, questions about the tradition may seem relevant: How tightly does the tradition hold together? Are the conceptions of signs and codes similar enough in all these pieces that they all belong in the same tradition? What is it about semiotics that leads to so much blending with other traditions?

Other questions may emerge as you compare these theorists to each other: What exactly is a sign? Is there an idea that *sign* should be reserved for while using other terms for related yet different ideas about signs? Why is it that Locke's ideas have remained in the general talk about communication across time, even though later semiotic theorists have largely rejected them? How do the ideas of each of these theorists compare and contrast with Locke? Does exploring the difference between Peirce's and Saussure's notions of signs provide any insight into the nature of theorizing within a sociohistorical context? Should Barthes's notion of connotation creation be applied to all signs, linguistic and nonlinguistic? What about Peters's notions; how would the other theorists respond to his proposal? What about the fixation with communicating via codes and the quest for connection? Is there something about the nature of signs that fosters this condition? These are some questions that may lead to further development of ways of talking and thinking within the semiotic tradition.

References

Hayakawa, S. I., & Hayakawa, A. R. (1990). *Language in thought and action* (5th rev. ed.). San Diego, CA: Harcourt Brace Jovanovich. (Original work published 1949)

Korzybski, A. (1958). *Science and sanity: An introduction to non-Aristotelian systems and general semantics* (4th ed.). Lakeville, CT: The International Non-Aristotelian Library. (Original work published 1933).

Locke, J. (1979). *An essay concerning human understanding* (P. H. Nidditch, Ed.). New York: Oxford University Press. (Original work published 1690)

Peirce, C. S. (1955). *Philosophical writings of Peirce* (J. Buchler, Ed.). New York: Dover.

Peters, J. D. (1989). John Locke, the individual, and the origin of communication. *Quarterly Journal of Speech, 75,* 387–399.

Saussure, F. de. (1959). *Course in general linguistics* (W. Baskin, Trans.; C. Bally & A. Sechehaye [with A. Reidlinger], Eds.). New York: Philosophical Library. (Original work published 1916)

Sturrock, J. (2003). *Structuralism* (2nd ed.). Malden, MA: Blackwell.

10

THE ABUSE OF WORDS

JOHN LOCKE

Words are used for recording and communicating our thoughts. From what has been said in the foregoing chapters, it is easy to perceive what imperfection there is in language, and how the very nature of words makes it almost unavoidable for many of them to be doubtful and uncertain in their significations. To examine the perfection or imperfection of words, it is necessary first to consider their use and end: for as they are more or less fitted to attain that, so they are more or less perfect. We have, in the former part of this discourse often, upon occasion, mentioned a double use of words.

First, One for the recording of our own thoughts.

Secondly, The other for the communicating of our thoughts to others.

As to the first of these, for the recording our own thoughts for the help of our own memories, whereby, as it were, we talk to ourselves, any words will serve the turn. For since sounds are voluntary and indifferent signs of any ideas, a man may use what words he pleases to signify his own ideas to himself: and there will be no imperfection in them, if he constantly use the same sign for the same idea: for then he cannot fail of having his meaning understood, wherein consists the right use and perfection of language.

Secondly, As to communication by words, that too has a double use.

I. Civil.

II. Philosophical.

First, by their civil use, I mean such a communication of thoughts and ideas by words, as may serve for the upholding common conversation and commerce, about the ordinary affairs and conveniences of civil life, in the societies of men, one amongst another.

Secondly, by the philosophical use of words, I mean such a use of them as may serve to convey the precise notions of things, and to express in general propositions certain and undoubted truths, which the mind may rest upon and be satisfied with in its search after true knowledge. These two uses are very distinct; and a great deal less exactness will serve in the one than in the other, as we shall see in what follows.

SOURCE: Locke, J. (1690). *An essay concerning human understanding* (excerpts). Retrieved from http://www.infomotions .com/etexts/philosophy/1600-1699/locke-essay-113.txt. (This document is in the public domain.)

The chief end of language in communication being to be understood, words serve not well for that end, neither in civil nor philosophical discourse, when any word does not excite in the hearer the same idea which it stands for in the mind of the speaker. Now, since sounds have no natural connexion with our ideas, but have all their signification from the arbitrary imposition of men, the doubtfulness and uncertainty of their signification, which is the imperfection we here are speaking of, has its cause more in the ideas they stand for than in any incapacity there is in one sound more than in another to signify any idea: for in that regard they are all equally perfect. That then which makes doubtfulness and uncertainty in the signification of some more than other words, is the difference of ideas they stand for.

[. . .]

Besides the imperfection that is naturally in language, and the obscurity and confusion that is so hard to be avoided in the use of words, there are several wilful faults and neglects which men are guilty of in this way of communication, whereby they render these signs less clear and distinct in their signification than naturally they need to be.

First, In this kind the first and most palpable abuse is, the using of words without clear and distinct ideas; or, which is worse, signs without anything signified. Of these there are two sorts:

I. One may observe, in all languages, certain words that, if they be examined, will be found in their first original, and their appropriated use, not to stand for any clear and distinct ideas. These, for the most part, the several sects of philosophy and religion have introduced. For their authors or promoters, either affecting something singular, and out of the way of common apprehensions, or to support some strange opinions, or cover some weakness of their hypothesis, seldom fail to coin new words, and such as, when they come to be examined, may justly be called insignificant terms. For, having either had no determinate collection of ideas annexed to them when they were first invented; or at least such as, if well examined, will be found inconsistent, it is no wonder,

if, afterwards, in the vulgar use of the same party, they remain empty sounds, with little or no signification, amongst those who think it enough to have them often in their mouths, as the distinguishing characters of their Church or School, without much troubling their heads to examine what are the precise ideas they stand for. I shall not need here to heap up instances; every man's reading and conversation will sufficiently furnish him. Or if he wants to be better stored, the great mintmasters of this kind of terms, I mean the Schoolmen and Metaphysicians (under which I think the disputing natural and moral philosophers of these latter ages may be comprehended) have wherewithal abundantly to content him.

II. Others there be who extend this abuse yet further, who take so little care to lay by words, which, in their primary notation have scarce any clear and distinct ideas which they are annexed to, that, by an unpardonable negligence, they familiarly use words which the propriety of language has affixed to very important ideas, without any distinct meaning at all. Wisdom, glory, grace, &c., are words frequent enough in every man's mouth; but if a great many of those who use them should be asked what they mean by them, they would be at a stand, and not know what to answer: a plain proof, that, though they have learned those sounds, and have them ready at their tongues ends, yet there are no determined ideas laid up in their minds, which are to be expressed to others by them.

[. . .]

Secondly, Another great abuse of words is inconstancy in the use of them. It is hard to find a discourse written on any subject, especially of controversy, wherein one shall not observe, if he read with attention, the same words (and those commonly the most material in the discourse, and upon which the argument turns) used sometimes for one collection of simple ideas, and sometimes for another; which is a perfect abuse of language. Words being intended for signs of my ideas, to make them known to others, not by any natural signification, but by a voluntary imposition, it is plain cheat and abuse, when I make them stand sometimes for one thing and sometimes for another; the wilful doing whereof can be imputed to nothing but great folly, or greater dishonesty. And a man, in his accounts with another may, with as much fairness make the characters of numbers stand sometimes for one and sometimes for another collection of units: v.g. this character 3, stand sometimes for three, sometimes for four, and sometimes for eight, as in his discourse or reasoning make the same words stand for different collections of simple ideas. If men should do so in their reckonings, I wonder who would have to do with them? One who would speak thus in the affairs and business of the world, and call 8 sometimes seven, and sometimes nine, as best served his advantage, would presently have clapped upon him, one of the two names men are commonly disgusted with. And yet in arguings and learned contests, the same sort of proceedings passes commonly for wit and learning; but to me it appears a greater dishonesty than the misplacing of counters in the casting up a debt; and the cheat the greater, by how much truth is of greater concernment and value than money.

Thirdly, Another abuse of language is an affected obscurity; by either applying old words to new and unusual significations; or introducing new and ambiguous terms, without defining either; or else putting them so together, as may confound their ordinary meaning. Though the Peripatetick philosophy has been most eminent in this way, yet other sects have not been wholly clear of it. There are scarce any of them that are not cumbered with some difficulties (such is the imperfection of human knowledge) which they have been fain to cover with obscurity of terms, and to confound the signification of words, which, like a mist before people's eyes, might hinder their weak parts from being discovered. That body and extension in common use, stand for two distinct ideas, is plain to any one that will but reflect a little. For were their signification precisely the same, it would be as proper, and as intelligible to say, "the body of an extension," as the "extension of a body"; and yet there are those who find it necessary to confound their signification. To this abuse, and the mischiefs of confounding the signification of words, logic, and the liberal sciences as they have been handled in the schools, have given reputation; and the admired Art of Disputing hath added much to the natural imperfection of languages, whilst it has been made use of and fitted to perplex the signification of words, more than to discover the knowledge and truth of things: and he that will look into that sort of learned writings, will find the words there much more obscure, uncertain, and undetermined in their meaning, than they are in ordinary conversation.

This is unavoidably to be so, where men's parts and learning are estimated by their skill in disputing. And if reputation and reward shall attend these conquests, which depend mostly on the fineness and niceties of words, it is no wonder if the wit of man so employed, should perplex, involve, and subtilize the signification of sounds, so as never to want something to say in opposing or defending any question; the victory being adjudged not to him who had truth on his side, but the last word in the dispute.

[. . .]

Whether any by-interests of these professions have occasioned this, I will not here examine; but I leave it to be considered, whether it would not be well for mankind, whose concernment it is to know things as they are, and to do what they ought, and not to spend their lives in talking about them, or tossing words to and fro— whether it would not be well, I say, that the use of words were made plain and direct; and that language, which was given us for the improvement of knowledge and bond of society, should not be employed to darken truth and unsettle people's rights; to raise mists, and render unintelligible both morality and religion? Or that at least, if this will happen, it should not be thought learning or knowledge to do so?

Fourthly, Another great abuse of words, is the taking them for things. This, though it in some degree concerns all names in general, yet more particularly affects those of substances. To this abuse those men are most subject who most confine their thoughts to any one system, and give themselves up into a firm belief of the perfection of any received hypothesis: whereby they come to be persuaded that the terms of that sect are so suited to the nature of things, that they perfectly correspond with their real existence. Who is there that has been bred up in the Peripatetick philosophy, who does not think the Ten Names, under which are ranked the Ten Predicaments, to be exactly conformable to the nature of things? Who is there of that school that is not persuaded that substantial forms, vegetative souls, abhorrence of a vacuum, intentional species, &c., are something real? These words men have learned from their very entrance upon knowledge, and have found their masters and systems lay great stress upon them: and therefore they cannot quit the opinion, that they are conformable to nature, and are the representations of something that really exists. The Platonists have their soul of the world, and the Epicureans their endeavour towards motion in their atoms when at rest. There is scarce any sect in philosophy has not a distinct set of terms that others understand not. But yet this gibberish, which, in the weakness of human understanding, serves so well to palliate men's ignorance, and cover their errors, comes, by familiar use amongst those of the same tribe, to seem the most important part of language, and of all other the terms the most significant: and should aerial and aetherial vehicles come once, by the prevalency of that doctrine, to be generally received anywhere, no doubt those terms would make impressions on men's minds, so as to establish them in the persuasion of the reality of such things, as much as Peripatetick forms and intentional species have heretofore done.

[. . .]

Fifthly, Another abuse of words is the setting them in the place of things which they do or can by no means signify. We may observe that in the general names of substances whereof the nominal essences are only known to us when we put them into propositions, and affirm or deny anything about them, we do most commonly tacitly suppose or intend, they should stand for the real essence of a certain sort of substances. For, when a man says gold is malleable, he means and would insinuate something more than this. That

what I call gold is malleable (though truly it amounts to no more) but would have this understood, viz. That gold, i.e. what has the real essence of gold, is malleable; which amounts to thus much, that malleableness depends on, and is inseparable from the real essence of gold. But a man, not knowing wherein that real essence consists, the connexion in his mind of malleableness is not truly with an essence he knows not, but only with the sound gold he puts for it.

[. . .]

But however preposterous and absurd it be to make our names stand for ideas we have not, or (which is all one) essences that we know not, it being in effect to make our words the signs of nothing; yet it is evident to any one who ever so little reflects on the use men make of their words, that there is nothing more familiar. When a man asks whether this or that thing he sees, let it be a drill, or a monstrous foetus, be a man or no; it is evident the question is not, Whether that particular thing agree to his complex idea expressed by the name man: but whether it has in it the real essence of a species of things which he supposes his name man to stand for. In which way of using the names of substances, there are these false suppositions contained:

First, that there are certain precise essences according to which nature makes all particular things, and by which they are distinguished into species. That everything has a real constitution, whereby it is what it is, and on which its sensible qualities depend, is past doubt: but I think it has been proved that this makes not the distinction of species as we rank them, nor the boundaries of their names.

Secondly, this tacitly also insinuates, as if we had ideas of these proposed essences. For to what purpose else is it, to inquire whether this or that thing have the real essence of the species man, if we did not suppose that there were such a specific essence known? Which yet is utterly false. And therefore such application of names as would make them stand for ideas which we have not, must needs cause great disorder in discourses and reasonings about them, and be a great inconvenience in our communication by words.

Sixthly, there remains yet another more general, though perhaps less observed, abuse of words; and that is, that men having by a long and familiar use annexed to them certain ideas, they are apt to imagine so near and necessary a connexion between the names and the signification they use them in, that they forwardly suppose one cannot but understand what their meaning is; and therefore one ought to acquiesce in the words delivered, as if it were past doubt that, in the use of those common received sounds, the speaker and hearer had necessarily the same precise ideas. Whence presuming, that when they have in discourse used any term, they have thereby, as it were, set before others the very thing they talked of. And so likewise taking the words of others as naturally standing for just what they themselves have been accustomed to apply them to, they never trouble themselves to explain their own, or understand clearly others' meaning. From whence commonly proceeds noise, and wrangling, without improvement or information; whilst men take words to be the constant regular marks of agreed notions, which in truth are no more but the voluntary and unsteady signs of their own ideas. And yet men think it strange, if in discourse, or (where it is often absolutely necessary) in dispute, one sometimes asks the meaning of their terms: though the arguings one may every day observe in conversation make it evident, that there are few names of complex ideas which any two men use for the same just precise collection. It is hard to name a word which will not be a clear instance of this. Life is a term, none more familiar. Any one almost would take it for an affront to be asked what he meant by it. And yet if it comes in question, whether a plant that lies ready formed in the seed have life; whether the embryo in an egg before incubation, or a man in a swoon without sense or motion, be alive or no; it is easy to perceive that a clear, distinct, settled idea does not always accompany the use of so known a word as that of life is. Some gross and confused conceptions men indeed ordinarily have, to which they apply the common words of their language; and such a loose use of their words serves them well enough in their ordinary discourses or affairs. But this is not sufficient for philosophical inquiries. Knowledge and reasoning require precise determinate ideas. And though men will not be so importunately dull as not to understand what others say, without demanding an explication of their terms; nor so troublesomely critical as to correct others in the use of the words they receive from them: yet, where truth and knowledge are concerned in the case, I know not what fault it can be, to desire the explication of words whose sense seems dubious; or why a man should be ashamed to own his ignorance in what sense another man uses his words; since he has no other way of certainly knowing it but by being informed. This abuse of taking words upon trust has nowhere spread so far, nor with so ill effects, as amongst men of letters. The multiplication and obstinacy of disputes, which have so laid waste the intellectual world, is owing to nothing more than to this ill use of words. For though it be generally believed that there is great diversity of opinions in the volumes and variety of controversies the world is distracted with; yet the most I can find that the contending learned men of different parties do, in their arguings one with another, is, that they speak different languages. For I am apt to imagine, that when any of them, quitting terms, think upon things, and know what they think, they think all the same: though perhaps what they would have be different.

To conclude this consideration of the imperfection and abuse of language. The ends of language in our discourse with others being chiefly these three: First, to make known one man's thoughts or ideas to another; Secondly, to do it with as much ease and quickness as possible; and, Thirdly, thereby to convey the knowledge of things: language is either abused or deficient, when it fails of any of these three.

First, Words fail in the first of these ends, and lay not open one man's ideas to another's view: 1. When men have names in their mouths without any determinate ideas in their minds, whereof they are the signs: or, 2. When they apply the common received names of any language to ideas, to which the common use of that language does not apply them: or, 3. When they apply them very unsteadily, making them stand, now for one, and by and by for another idea.

Secondly, Men fail of conveying their thoughts with all the quickness and ease that may be, when they have complex ideas without having any distinct names for them. This is sometimes the fault of the language itself, which has not in it a sound yet applied to such a signification; and sometimes the fault of the man, who has not yet learned the name for that idea he would show another.

Thirdly, There is no knowledge of things conveyed by men's words, when their ideas agree not to the reality of things. Though it be a defect that has its original in our ideas, which are not so conformable to the nature of things as attention, study, and application might make them, yet it fails not to extend itself to our words too, when we use them as signs of real beings, which yet never had any reality or existence.

How men's words fail in all these: First, He that hath words of any language, without distinct ideas in his mind to which he applies them, does, so far as he uses them in discourse, only make a noise without any sense or signification; and how learned soever he may seem, by the use of hard words or learned terms, is not much more advanced thereby in knowledge, than he would be in learning, who had nothing in his study but the bare titles of books, without possessing the contents of them. For all such words, however put into discourse, according to the right construction of grammatical rules, or the harmony of well-turned periods, do yet amount to nothing but bare sounds, and nothing else.

Secondly, He that has complex ideas, without particular names for them, would be in no better case than a bookseller, who had in his warehouse volumes that lay there unbound, and without titles, which he could therefore make known to others only by showing the loose sheets, and communicate them only by tale. This man is hindered in his discourse, for want of words to communicate his complex ideas, which he is therefore forced to make known by an enumeration of the simple ones that compose them; and so is fain often to use twenty words, to express what another man signifies in one.

Thirdly, He that puts not constantly the same sign for the same idea, but uses the same words sometimes in one and sometimes in another signification, ought to pass in the schools and conversation for as fair a man, as he does in the market and exchange, who sells several things under the same name.

Fourthly, He that applies the words of any language to ideas different from those to which the common use of that country applies them, however his own understanding may be filled with truth and light, will not by such words be able to convey much of it to others, without defining his terms. For however the sounds are such as are familiarly known, and easily enter the ears of those who are accustomed to them; yet standing for other ideas than those they usually are annexed to, and are wont to excite in the mind of the hearers, they cannot make known the thoughts of him who thus uses them.

Fifthly, He that imagined to himself substances such as never have been, and filled his head with ideas which have not any correspondence with the real nature of things, to which yet he gives settled and defined names, may fill his discourse, and perhaps another man's head with the fantastical imaginations of his own brain, but will be very far from advancing thereby one jot in real and true knowledge.

He that hath names without ideas, wants meaning in his words, and speaks only empty sounds. He that hath complex ideas without names for them, wants liberty and dispatch in his expressions, and is necessitated to use periphrases. He that uses his words loosely and unsteadily will either be not minded or not understood. He that applies his names to ideas different from their common use, wants propriety in his language, and speaks gibberish. And he that hath the ideas of substances disagreeing with the real existence of things, so far wants the materials of true knowledge in his understanding, and hath instead thereof chimeras.

[. . .]

Since wit and fancy find easier entertainment in the world than dry truth and real knowledge, figurative speeches and allusion in language will hardly be admitted as an imperfection or abuse of it. I confess, in discourses where we seek rather pleasure and delight than information and improvement, such ornaments as are borrowed from them can scarce pass for faults. But yet if we would speak of things as they are, we must allow that all the art of rhetoric, besides order and clearness; all the artificial and figurative application of words eloquence hath invented, are for nothing else but to insinuate wrong ideas, move the passions, and thereby mislead the judgment; and so indeed are perfect cheats: and therefore, however laudable or allowable oratory may render them in harangues and popular addresses, they are certainly, in all discourses that pretend to inform or instruct, wholly to be avoided; and where truth and knowledge are concerned, cannot but be thought a great fault, either of the language or person that makes use of them. What and how various they are, will be superfluous here to take notice; the books of rhetoric which abound in the world, will instruct those who want to be informed: only I cannot but observe how little the preservation and improvement of truth and knowledge is the care and concern of mankind; since the arts of fallacy are endowed and preferred. It is evident how much men love to deceive and be deceived, since rhetoric, that powerful instrument of error and deceit, has its established professors, is publicly taught, and has always been had in great reputation: and I doubt not but it will be thought great boldness, if not brutality, in me to have said thus much against it. Eloquence, like the fair sex, has too prevailing beauties in it to suffer itself ever to be spoken against. And it is in vain to find fault with those arts of deceiving, wherein men find pleasure to be deceived.

11

What Is a Sign?

Charles Sanders Peirce

§1. This is a most necessary question, since all reasoning is an interpretation of signs of some kind. But it is also a very difficult question, calling for deep reflection.[1]

It is necessary to recognize three different states of mind. First, imagine a person in a dreamy state. Let us suppose he is thinking of nothing but a red color. Not thinking about it, either, that is, not asking nor answering any questions about it, not even saying to himself that it pleases him, but just contemplating it, as his fancy brings it up. Perhaps, when he gets tired of the red, he will change it to some other color,—say a turquoise blue,—or a rose-color;—but if he does so, it will be in the play of fancy without any reason and without any compulsion. This is about as near as may be to a state of mind in which something is present, without compulsion and without reason; it is called Feeling. Except in a half-waking hour, nobody really is in a state of feeling, pure and simple. But whenever we are awake, something is present to the mind, and what is present, without reference to any compulsion or reason, is feeling.

Second, imagine our dreamer suddenly to hear a loud and prolonged steam whistle. At the instant it begins, he is startled. He instinctively tries to get away; his hands go to his ears. It is not so much that it is unpleasing, but it forces itself so upon him. The instinctive resistance is a necessary part of it: the man would not be sensible his will was borne down, if he had no self-assertion to be borne down. It is the same when we exert ourselves against outer resistance; except for that resistance we should not have anything upon which to exercise strength. This sense of acting and of being acted upon, which is our sense of the reality of things,—both of outward things and of ourselves,—may be called the sense of Reaction. It does not reside in any

SOURCE: Peirce, C. S. (1998). What is a sign? In Peirce Edition Project (Eds.), *The Essential Peirce: Selected Philosophical Writings, Volume 2 (1893–1913)* (pp. 4–10). Bloomington, IN: Indiana University Press. ISBN 0-253-21190-5

one Feeling; it comes upon the breaking of one feeling by another feeling. It essentially involves two things acting upon one another.

Third, let us imagine that our now-awakened dreamer, unable to shut out the piercing sound, jumps up and seeks to make his escape by the door, which we will suppose had been blown to with a bang just as the whistle commenced. But the instant our man opens the door let us say the whistle ceases. Much relieved, he thinks he will return to his seat, and so shuts the door, again. No sooner, however, has he done so than the whistle recommences. He asks himself whether the shutting of the door had anything to do with it; and once more opens the mysterious portal. As he opens it, the sound ceases. He is now in a third state of mind: he is *Thinking.* That is, he is aware of learning, or of going through a process by which a phenomenon is found to be governed by a rule, or has a general knowable way of behaving. He finds that one action is the means, or middle, for bringing about another result. This third state of mind is entirely different from the other two. In the second there was only a sense of brute force; now there is a sense of government by a general rule. In Reaction only two things are involved; but in government there is a third thing which is a means to an end. The very word *means* signifies something which is in the middle between two others. Moreover, this third state of mind, or Thought, is a sense of learning, and learning is the means by which we pass from ignorance to knowledge. As the most rudimentary sense of Reaction involves two states of Feeling, so it will be found that the most rudimentary Thought involves three states of Feeling.

As we advance into the subject, these ideas, which seem hazy at our first glimpse of them, will come to stand out more and more distinctly; and their great importance will also force itself upon our minds.

§2. There are three kinds of interest we may take in a thing. First, we may have a primary interest in it for itself. Second, we may have a secondary interest in it, on account of its reactions with other things. Third, we may have a mediatory interest in it, in so far as it conveys to a mind an idea about a thing. In so far as it does this, it is a *sign,* or representation.

§3. There are three kinds of signs. Firstly, there are *likenesses,* or icons; which serve to convey ideas of the things they represent simply by imitating them. Secondly, there are *indications,* or indices; which show something about things, on account of their being physically connected with them. Such is a guidepost, which points down the road to be taken, or a relative pronoun, which is placed just after the name of the thing intended to be denoted, or a vocative exclamation, as "Hi! there," which acts upon the nerves of the person addressed and forces his attention. Thirdly, there are *symbols,* or general signs, which have become associated with their meanings by usage. Such are most words, and phrases, and speeches, and books, and libraries.

Let us consider the various uses of these three kinds of signs more closely.

§4. *Likenesses.* Photographs, especially instantaneous photographs, are very instructive, because we know that they are in certain respects exactly like the objects they represent. But this resemblance is due to the photographs having been produced under such circumstances that they were physically forced to correspond point by point to nature. In that aspect, then, they belong to the second class of signs, those by physical connection. The case is different, if I surmise that zebras are likely to be obstinate, or otherwise disagreeable animals, because they seem to have a general resemblance to donkeys, and donkeys are self-willed. Here the donkey serves precisely as a probable likeness of the zebra. It is true we suppose that resemblance has a physical cause in heredity; but then, this hereditary affinity is itself only an inference from the likeness between the two animals, and we have not (as in the case of the photograph) any independent knowledge of the circumstances of the production of the two species. Another example of the use of a likeness is the design an artist draws of a statue, pictorial composition, architectural elevation, or piece of decoration, by the contemplation of which he can ascertain whether what he proposes will be beautiful and

Figures 11.1 & 11.2

satisfactory. The question asked is thus answered almost with certainty because it relates to how the artist will himself be affected. The reasoning of mathematicians will be found to turn chiefly upon the use of likenesses, which are the very hinges of the gates of their science. The utility of likenesses to mathematicians consists in their suggesting, in a very precise way, new aspects of supposed states of things. For example, suppose we have a winding curve, with continual points where the curvature changes from clockwise to counter-clockwise and conversely as in Figure 11.1. Let us further suppose that this curve is continued so that it crosses itself at every such point of reversed bending in another such point. The result appears in Figure 11.2. It may be described as a number of ovals flattened together, as if by pressure. One would not perceive that the first description and the second were equivalent, without the figures. We shall find, when we get further into the subject, that all these different uses of likeness may be brought under one general formula.

In intercommunication, too, likenesses are quite indispensable. Imagine two men who know no common speech, thrown together remote from the rest of the race. They must communicate; but how are they to do so? By imitative sounds, by imitative gestures, and by pictures. These are three kinds of likenesses. It is true that they will also use other signs, finger-pointings, and the

like. But, after all, the likenesses will be the only means of describing the qualities of the things and actions which they have in mind. Rudimentary language, when men first began to talk together, must have largely consisted either in directly imitative words, or in conventional names which they attached to pictures. The Egyptian language is an excessively rude one. It was, as far as we know, the earliest to be written; and the writing is all in pictures. Some of these pictures came to stand for sounds,—letters and syllables. But others stand directly for ideas. They are not nouns; they are not verbs; they are just pictorial ideas.

§5. *Indications.* But pictures alone,—pure likenesses,—can never convey the slightest information. Thus, Figure 11.3 suggests a wheel. But it leaves the spectator uncertain whether it is a copy of something actually existing or a mere play of fancy. The same thing is true of general language and of all *symbols.* No combination of words (excluding proper nouns, and in the absence of gestures or other indicative concomitants of speech) can ever convey the slightest information. This may sound paradoxical; but the following imaginary little dialogue will show how true it is:

Two men, A and B, meet on a country road, when the following conversation ensues.

    B. The owner of that house is the richest man in these parts.

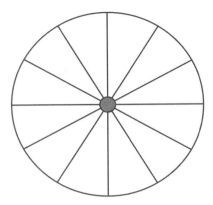

Figure 11.3

A. What house?

B. Why do you not see a house to your right about seven kilometres distant, on a hill?

A. Yes, I think I can descry it.

B. Very well; that is the house.

Thus, A has acquired information. But if he walks to a distant village and says "the owner of a house is the richest man in those parts," the remark will refer to nothing, unless he explains to his interlocutor how to proceed from where he is in order to find that district and that house. Without that, he does not indicate what he is talking about. To identify an object, we generally state its place at a stated time; and in every case must show how an experience of it can be connected with the previous experience of the hearer. To state a time, we must reckon from a known epoch,—either the present moment, or the assumed birth of Christ, or something of the sort. When we say the epoch must be known, we mean it must be connected with the hearer's experience. We also have to reckon in units of time; and there is no way of making known what unit we propose to use except by appealing to the hearer's experience. So no place can be described, except relatively to some known place; and the unit of distance used must be defined by reference to some bar or other object which people can actually use directly or indirectly in measurement. It is true that a map is very useful in designating a place; and a map is a sort of picture. But unless the map carries a mark of a known locality, and the scale of miles, and the points of the compass, it no more shows where a place is than the map in *Gulliver's Travels* shows the location of Brobdingnag.[2] It is true that if a new island were found, say, in the Arctic Seas, its location could be approximately shown on a map which should have no lettering, meridians, nor parallels; for the familiar outlines of Iceland, Nova Zemla, Greenland, etc., serve to indicate the position. In such a case, we should avail ourselves of our knowledge that there is no second place that any being on this earth is likely to make a map of which has outlines like those of the Arctic shores. This experience of the world we live in renders the map something more than a mere icon and confers upon it the added characters of an *index*. Thus, it is true that one and the same sign may be at once a likeness and an indication. Still, the offices of these orders of signs are totally different. It may be objected that likenesses as much as indices[3] are founded on experience, that an image of red is meaningless to the color blind, as is that of erotic passion to the child. But these are truly objections which help the distinction; for it is *not* experience, but the *capacity* for experience, which they show is requisite for a likeness; and this is requisite, not in order that the likeness should be interpreted, but in order that it should at all be presented to the sense. Very different is the case of the inexperienced and the experienced person meeting the same man and noticing the same peculiarities, which to the experienced man indicate a whole history, but to the inexperienced reveal nothing.

Let us examine some examples of indications. I see a man with a rolling gait. This is a probable indication that he is a sailor. I see a bowlegged man in corduroys, gaiters, and a jacket. These are probable indications that he is a jockey or something of the sort. A weathercock *indicates* the direction of the wind. A sun-dial or a clock *indicates* the time of day. Geometricians mark letters against the different parts of their diagrams and then use those letters to indicate those parts. Letters are similarly used by lawyers and others. Thus, we may say: If *A* and *B* are married to one another and *C* is their child while *D* is brother of *A,* then *D* is uncle of *C.* Here *A, B, C,* and *D* fulfill the office of relative pronouns, but are more convenient since they require no special collocation of words. A rap on the door is an indication. Anything which focuses the attention is an indication. Anything which startles us is an indication, in so far as it marks the junction between two portions of experience. Thus a tremendous thunderbolt indicates that something considerable happened, though we may not know precisely what the event was. But it may be expected to connect itself with some other experience.

§6. *Symbols.* The word *symbol* has so many meanings that it would be an injury to the language to add a new one. I do not think that the signification I attach to it, that of a conventional sign, or one depending upon habit (acquired or inborn), is so much a new meaning as a return to the original meaning. Etymologically, it should mean a thing thrown together, just as *embolon* (embolum) is a thing thrown into something, a bolt, and *parabolon* (parabolum) is a thing thrown besides, collateral security, and *upobolon* (hypobolum) is a thing thrown underneath, an antenuptial gift. It is usually said that in

the word *symbol,* the throwing together is to be understood in the sense of to conjecture; but were that the case, we ought to find that *sometimes,* at least, it meant a conjecture, a meaning for which literature may be searched in vain. But the Greeks used "throw together" (*sumballein*) very frequently to signify the making of a contract or convention. Now, we do find symbol (*sumbolon*) early and often used to mean a convention or contract. Aristotle calls a noun a "symbol," that is, a conventional sign.[4] In Greek,[5] a watch-fire is a "symbol," that is, a signal agreed upon; a standard or ensign is a "symbol," a watch-word is a "symbol," a badge is a "symbol"; a church creed is called a symbol, because it serves as a badge or shibboleth; a theatre-ticket is called a "symbol"; any ticket or check entitling one to receive anything is a "symbol." Moreover, any expression of sentiment was called a "symbol." Such were the principal meanings of the word in the original language. The reader will judge whether they suffice to establish my claim that I am not seriously wrenching the word in employing it as I propose to do.

Any ordinary word, as "give," "bird," "marriage," is an example of a symbol. It is *applicable to whatever may be found to realize the idea connected with the word;* it does not, in itself, identify those things. It does not show us a bird, nor enact before our eyes a giving or a marriage, but supposes that we are able to imagine those things, and have associated the word with them.

§7. A regular progression of one, two, three may be remarked in the three orders of signs, Likeness, Index, Symbol. The likeness has no dynamical connection with the object it represents; it simply happens that its qualities resemble those of that object, and excite analogous sensations in the mind for which it is a likeness. But it really stands unconnected with them. The index is physically connected with its object; they make an organic pair. But the interpreting mind has nothing to do with this connection, except remarking it, after it is established. The symbol is connected with its object by virtue of the idea of the symbol-using mind, without which no such connection would exist.

Every physical force reacts between a pair of particles, either of which may serve as an index of the other. On the other hand, we shall find that every intellectual operation involves a triad of symbols.

§8. A symbol, as we have seen, cannot indicate any particular thing; it denotes a kind of thing. Not only that, but it is itself a kind and not a single thing. You can write down the word "star"; but that does not make you the creator of the word, nor if you erase it have you destroyed the word. The word lives in the minds of those who use it. Even if they are all asleep, it exists in their memory. So we may admit, if there be reason to do so, that generals are mere words without at all saying, as Ockham supposed,[6] that they are really individuals.

Symbols grow. They come into being by development out of other signs, particularly from likenesses or from mixed signs partaking of the nature of likenesses and symbols. We think only in signs. These mental signs are of mixed nature; the symbol-parts of them are called concepts. If a man makes a new symbol, it is by thoughts involving concepts. So it is only out of symbols that a new symbol can grow. *Omne symbolum de symbolo.*[7] A symbol, once in being, spreads among the peoples. In use and in experience, its meaning grows. Such words as *force, law, wealth, marriage,* bear for us very different meanings from those they bore to our barbarous ancestors. The symbol may, with Emerson's sphynx,[8] say to man,

Of thine eye I am eyebeam.

§9. In all reasoning, we have to use a mixture of *likenesses, indices,* and *symbols.* We cannot dispense with any of them. The complex whole may be called a *symbol;* for its symbolic, living character is the prevailing one. A metaphor is not always to be despised: though a man may be said to be composed of living tissues, yet portions of his nails, teeth, hair, and bones, which are most necessary to him, have ceased to undergo the metabolic processes which constitute life, and there are liquids in his body which are not alive. Now, we may liken the indices we use in reasoning to the hard parts of the body, and the likenesses we use to the blood: the one holds us stiffly up to the realities, the other with its swift changes supplies the nutriment for the main body of thought.

Suppose a man to reason as follows: The Bible says that Enoch and Elijah were caught up into heaven; then, either the Bible errs, or else it is not strictly true that all men are mortal. What the Bible is, and what the historic world of men is, to which this reasoning relates, must be shown by indices. The reasoner makes some sort of mental diagram by which he sees that his alternative conclusion must be true, if the premise is so; and this diagram is an *icon* or likeness. The rest is symbols; and the whole may be considered as a modified symbol. It is not a dead thing, but carries the mind from one point to another. The art of reasoning is the art of marshalling such signs, and of finding out the truth.

NOTES

1. Section numbers, which in the manuscript begin with §31, here begin with §1, since the first chapter of Peirce's projected book is not included.

2. Book II of Jonathan Swift's *Gulliver's Travels* opens on a fanciful map of Brobdingnag merged into a map of the North American Pacific coast.

3. Peirce wrote "signs" instead of "indices," a mistake given the preceding context. Some early writings, however, do refer to indices as "signs" (see EP1:7).

4. De interpretatione, II.16a.12.

5. Peirce wrote "in Greek" rather than "in Greece" because he is working through the list of alternative translations provided by Liddell and Scott's *Greek-English Lexicon* under the entry σύμβολου.

6. Cf. William of Ockham's *Summa totius logicae,* part i, ch. 14.

7. "Every symbol follows from a symbol."

8. Peirce often quotes this verse from the fourteenth stanza of Emerson's poem "The Sphinx" (*Dial,* Jan. 1841).

12

THE OBJECT OF LINGUISTICS

FERDINAND DE SAUSSURE

1. DEFINITION OF LANGUAGE

What is both the integral and concrete object of linguistics? The question is especially difficult; later we shall see why; here I wish merely to point up the difficulty.

Other sciences work with objects that are given in advance and that can then be considered from different viewpoints; but not linguistics. Someone pronounces the French word *nu* 'bare': a superficial observer would be tempted to call the word a concrete linguistic object; but a more careful examination would reveal successively three or four quite different things, depending on whether the word is considered as a sound, as the expression of an idea, as the equivalent of Latin *nudum,* etc. Far from it being the object that antedates the viewpoint, it would seem that it is the viewpoint that creates the object; besides, nothing tells us in advance that one way of considering the fact in question takes precedence over the others or is in any way superior to them.

Moreover, regardless of the viewpoint that we adopt, the linguistic phenomenon always has two related sides, each deriving its values from the other. For example:

1) Articulated syllables are acoustical impressions perceived by the ear, but the sounds would not exist without the vocal organs; an *n,* for example, exists only by virtue of the relation between the two sides. We simply cannot reduce language to sound or detach sound from oral articulation; reciprocally, we cannot define the movements of the vocal organs without taking into account the acoustical impression.

2) But suppose that sound were a simple thing: would it constitute speech? No, it is only the instrument of thought; by itself, it has no existence. At this point a new and redoubtable relationship arises: a sound, a complex acoustical-vocal unit, combines in turn with an idea to form a complex physiological-psychological unit. But that is still not the complete picture.

SOURCE: de Saussure, F. (1959). *Course in general linguistics* (W. Baskin, Trans.; C. Bally & A. Sechehaye with A. Reidlinger, Eds.). New York: Philosophical Library. (pp. 7–17)

3) Speech has both an individual and a social side, and we cannot conceive of one without the other. Besides:

4) Speech always implies both an established system and an evolution; at every moment it is an existing institution and a product of the past. To distinguish between the system and its history, between what it is and what it was, seems very simple at first glance; actually the two things are so closely related that we can scarcely keep them apart. Would we simplify the question by studying the linguistic phenomenon in its earliest stages—if we began, for example, by studying the speech of children? No, for in dealing with speech, it is completely misleading to assume that the problem of early characteristics differs from the problem of permanent characteristics. We are left inside the vicious circle.

From whatever direction we approach the question, nowhere do we find the integral object of linguistics. Everywhere we are confronted with a dilemma: if we fix our attention on only one side of each problem, we run the risk of failing to perceive the dualities pointed out above; on the other hand, if we study speech from several viewpoints simultaneously, the object of linguistics appears to us as a confused mass of heterogeneous and unrelated things. Either procedure opens the door to several sciences—psychology, anthropology, normative grammar, philology, etc.—which are distinct from linguistics, but which might claim speech, in view of the faulty method of linguistics, as one of their objects.

As I see it there is only one solution to all the foregoing difficulties: from the very outset we must put both feet on the ground of language and use language as the norm of all other manifestations of speech. Actually, among so many dualities, language alone seems to lend itself to independent definition and provide a fulcrum that satisfies the mind.

But what is language [*langue*]? It is not to be confused with human speech [*langage*], of which it is only a definite part, though certainly an essential one. It is both a social product of the faculty of speech and a collection of necessary conventions that have been adopted by a social body to permit individuals to exercise that faculty. Taken as a whole, speech is many-sided and heterogeneous; straddling several areas simultaneously—physical, physiological, and psychological—it belongs both to the individual and to society; we cannot put it into any category of human facts, for we cannot discover its unity.

Language, on the contrary, is a self-contained whole and a principle of classification. As soon as we give language first place among the facts of speech, we introduce a natural order into a mass that lends itself to no other classification.

One might object to that principle of classification on the ground that since the use of speech is based on a natural faculty whereas language is something acquired and conventional, language should not take first place but should be subordinated to the natural instinct.

That objection is easily refuted.

First, no one has proved that speech, as it manifests itself when we speak, is entirely natural, i.e. that our vocal apparatus was designed for speaking just as our legs were designed for walking. Linguists are far from agreement on this point. For instance Whitney, to whom language is one of several social institutions, thinks that we use the vocal apparatus as the instrument of language purely through luck, for the sake of convenience: men might just as well have chosen gestures and used visual symbols instead of acoustical symbols. Doubtless his thesis is too dogmatic; language is not similar in all respects to other social institutions; moreover, Whitney goes too far in saying that our choice happened to fall on the vocal organs; the choice was more or less imposed by nature. But on the essential point the American linguist is right: language is a convention, and the nature of the sign that is agreed upon does not matter. The question of the vocal apparatus obviously takes a secondary place in the problem of speech.

One definition of *articulated speech* might confirm that conclusion. In Latin, *articulus* means a member, part, or subdivision of a sequence; applied to speech, articulation designates either the subdivision of a spoken chain into syllables or the subdivision of the chain of meanings into significant units; *gegliederte Sprache* is used in the second sense in German. Using the second definition, we can say that what is natural to mankind is not oral speech but the faculty of constructing a language, i.e. a system of distinct signs corresponding to distinct ideas.

Broca discovered that the faculty of speech is localized in the third left frontal convolution; his discovery has been used to substantiate the attribution of a natural quality to speech. But we know that the same part of the brain is the center of *everything* that has to do with speech, including writing. The preceding statements, together with observations that have been made in different cases of aphasia resulting from lesion of the centers of localization, seem to indicate: (1) that the various disorders of oral speech are bound up in a hundred ways with those of written speech; and (2) that what is lost in all cases of aphasia or agraphia is less the faculty of producing a given sound or writing a given sign than the ability to evoke by means of an instrument, regardless of what it is, the signs of a regular system of speech. The obvious implication is that beyond the functioning of the various organs there exists a more general faculty which governs signs and which would be the linguistic faculty proper. And this brings us to the same conclusion as above.

To give language first place in the study of speech, we can advance a final argument: the faculty of articulating words—whether it is natural or not—is exercised only with the help of the instrument created by a collectivity and provided for its use; therefore, to say that language gives unity to speech is not fanciful.

2. Place of Language in the Facts of Speech

In order to separate from the whole of speech the part that belongs to language, we must examine the individual act from which the speaking-circuit can be reconstructed. The act requires the presence of at least two persons; that is the minimum number necessary to complete the circuit. Suppose that two people, A and B, are conversing with each other, as in Figure 12.1.

Suppose that the opening of the circuit is in A's brain, where mental facts (concepts) are associated with representations of the linguistic sounds (sound-images) that are used for their expression. A given concept unlocks a corresponding sound-image in the brain; this purely *psychological* phenomenon is followed in turn by a *physiological* process: the brain transmits an impulse corresponding to the image to the organs used in producing sounds. Then the

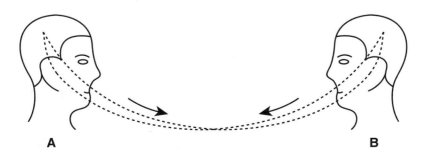

A   B

Figure 12.1

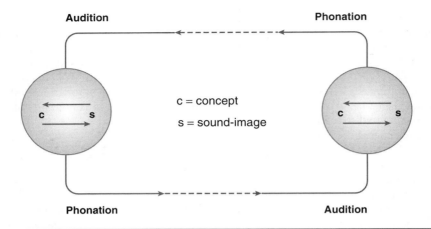

Figure 12.2

sound waves travel from the mouth of A to the ear of B: a purely *physical* process. Next, the circuit continues in B, but the order is reversed: from the ear to the brain, the physiological transmission of the sound-image; in the brain, the psychological association of the image with the corresponding concept. If B then speaks, the new act will follow—from his brain to A's—exactly the same course as the first act and pass through the same successive phases, which I shall diagram [as in Figure 12.2].

The preceding analysis does not purport to be complete. We might also single out the pure acoustical sensation, the identification of that sensation with the latent sound-image, the muscular image of phonation, etc. I have included only the elements thought to be essential, but the drawing brings out at a glance the distinction between the physical (sound waves), physiological (phonation and audition), and psychological parts (word-images and concepts). Indeed, we should not fail to note that the word-image stands apart from the sound itself and that it is just as psychological as the concept which is associated with it.

The circuit that I have outlined can be further divided into:

(a)   an outer part that includes the vibrations of the sounds which travel from the mouth to the ear, and an inner part that includes everything else;

(b)   a psychological and a nonpsychological part, the second including the physiological productions of the vocal organs as well as the physical facts that are outside the individual;

(c)   an active and a passive part: everything that goes from the associative center of the speaker to the ear of the listener is active, and everything that goes from the ear of the listener to his associative center is passive;

(d)   finally, everything that is active in the psychological part of the circuit is executive $(c \to s)$, and everything that is passive is receptive $(s \to c)$.

We should also add the associative and co-ordinating faculty that we find as soon as we leave isolated signs; this faculty plays the dominant role in the organization of language as a system.

But to understand clearly the role of the associative and co-ordinating faculty, we must leave the individual act, which is only the embryo of speech, and approach the social fact.

Among all the individuals that are linked together by speech, some sort of average will be set up: all will reproduce—not exactly of course, but approximately—the same signs united with the same concepts.

How does the social crystallization of language come about? Which parts of the circuit are involved? For all parts probably do not participate equally in it.

The nonpsychological part can be rejected from the outset. When we hear people speaking a language that we do not know, we perceive the sounds but remain outside the social fact because we do not understand them.

Neither is the psychological part of the circuit wholly responsible: the executive side is missing, for execution is never carried out by the collectivity. Execution is always individual, and the individual is always its master: I shall call the executive side *speaking [parole]*.

Through the functioning of the receptive and co-ordinating faculties, impressions that are perceptibly the same for all are made on the minds of speakers. How can that social product be pictured in such a way that language will stand apart from everything else? If we could embrace the sum of word-images stored in the minds of all individuals, we could identify the social bond that constitutes language. It is a storehouse filled by the members of a given community through their active use of speaking, a grammatical system that has a potential existence in each brain, or, specifically, in the brains of a group of individuals. For language is not complete in any speaker; it exists perfectly only within collectivity.

In separating language from speaking we are at the same time separating: (1) what is social from what is individual; and (2) what is essential from what is accessory and more or less accidental.

Language is not a function of the speaker; it is a product passively assimilated by the individual. It never requires premeditation, and reflection enters in only for the purpose of classification, which we shall take up later.

Speaking, on the contrary, is an individual act. It is wilful and intellectual. Within the act, we should distinguish between: (1) the combinations by which the speaker uses the language code expressing his own thought; and (2) the psychophysical mechanism that allows him to exteriorize those combinations.

Note that I have defined things rather than words; these definitions are not endangered by certain ambiguous words that do not have identical meanings in different languages. For in German *Sprache* means both "language" and "speech"; *Rede* almost corresponds to "speaking" but adds the special connotation of "discourse." Latin *sermo* designates both "speech" and "speaking," while *lingua* means "language," etc. No word corresponds exactly to any of the notions specified above; that is why all definitions of words are made in vain; starting from words in defining things is a bad procedure.

To summarize, these are the characteristics of language:

1) Language is a well-defined object in the heterogeneous mass of speech facts. It can be localized in the limited segment speaking-circuit where an auditory image becomes associated with a concept. It is the social side of speech, outside the individual who can never create nor modify it by himself; it exists only by means of a sort of contract signed by the members of a community. Moreover, the individual must always serve an apprenticeship in order to learn the functioning of language; a child assimilates it only gradually. It is such a distinct thing that a man deprived of the use of speaking retains it provided that he understands the vocal signs that he hears.

2) Language, unlike speaking, is something that we can study separately. Although dead languages are no longer spoken, we can easily assimilate their linguistic organisms. We can dispense with the other elements of speech; indeed, the science of language is possible only if the other elements are excluded.

3) Whereas speech is heterogeneous, language, as defined, is homogeneous. It is a system of signs in which the only essential thing is the union of meanings and sound-images, and in which both parts of the sign are psychological.

4) Language is concrete, no less so than speaking; and this is a help in our study of it. Linguistic signs, though basically psychological, are not abstractions; associations which bear the stamp of collective approval—and which added together constitute language—are realities that have their seat in the brain. Besides, linguistic signs are tangible; it is possible to reduce them to conventional written symbols, whereas it would be impossible to provide detailed photographs of acts of speaking [*actes de parole*]; the pronunciation of even the smallest word represents an infinite number of muscular movements that could be identified and put into graphic form only with great difficulty. In language, on the contrary, there is only the sound-image, and the latter can be translated into a fixed visual image. For if we disregard the vast number of movements necessary for the realization of sound-images in speaking, we see that each sound-image is nothing more than the sum of a limited number of elements or phonemes that can in turn be called up by a corresponding number of written symbols. The very possibility of putting the things that relate to language into graphic form allows dictionaries and grammars to represent it accurately, for language is a storehouse of sound-images, and writing is the tangible form of those images.

3. PLACE OF LANGUAGE IN HUMAN FACTS: SEMIOLOGY

The foregoing characteristics of language reveal an even more important characteristic. Language, once its boundaries have been marked off within the speech data, can be classified among human phenomena, whereas speech cannot.

We have just seen that language is a social institution; but several features set it apart from other political, legal, etc. institutions. We must call in a new type of facts in order to illuminate the special nature of language.

Language is a system of signs that express ideas, and is therefore comparable to a system of writing, the alphabet of deaf-mutes, symbolic rites, polite formulas, military signals, etc. But it is the most important of all these systems.

A science that studies the life of signs within society is conceivable; it would be a part of social psychology and consequently of general psychology; I shall call it *semiology*[1] (from Greek *smeîon* 'sign'). Semiology would show what constitutes signs, what laws govern them. Since the science does not yet exist, no one can say what it would be; but it has a right to existence, a place staked out in advance. Linguistics is only a part of the general science of semiology; the laws discovered by semiology will be applicable to linguistics, and the latter will circumscribe a well-defined area within the mass of anthropological facts.

To determine the exact place of semiology is the task of the psychologist.[2] The task of the linguist is to find out what makes language a special system within the mass of semiological data. This issue will be taken up again later; here I wish merely to call attention to one thing: if I have succeeded in assigning linguistics a place among the sciences, it is because I have related it to semiology.

Why has semiology not yet been recognized as an independent science with its own object like all the other sciences? Linguists have been going around in circles: language, better than anything else, offers a basis for understanding the semiological problem; but language must, to put it correctly, be studied in itself; heretofore language has almost always been studied in connection with something else, from other viewpoints.

There is first of all the superficial notion of the general public: people see nothing more than a name-giving system in language, thereby prohibiting any research into its true nature.

Then there is the viewpoint of the psychologist, who studies the sign mechanism in the individual; this is the easiest method, but it does not lead beyond individual execution and does not reach the sign, which is social.

Or even when signs are studied from a social viewpoint, only the traits that attach language to the other social institutions—those that are more or less voluntary—are emphasized; as a result, the goal is by-passed and the specific characteristics of semiological systems in general and of language in particular are completely ignored. For the distinguishing characteristic of the sign—but the one that is least apparent at first sight—is that in some way it always eludes the individual or social will.

In short, the characteristic that distinguishes semiological systems from all other institutions shows up clearly only in language where it manifests itself in the things which are studied least, and the necessity or specific value of a semiological science is therefore not clearly recognized. But to me the language problem is mainly semiological, and all developments derive their significance from that important fact. If we are to discover the true nature of language we must learn what it has in common with all other semiological systems; linguistic forces that seem very important at first glance (e.g., the role of the vocal apparatus) will receive only secondary consideration if they serve only to set language apart from the other systems. This procedure will do more than to clarify the linguistic problem. By studying rites, customs, etc. as signs, I believe that we shall throw new light on the facts and point up the need for including them in a science of semiology and explaining them by its laws.

NOTES

1. *Semiology* should not be confused with *semantics,* which studies changes in meaning, and which Saussure did not treat methodically [. . .] [Ed.]

2. Cf. A. Naville, *Classification des Sciences,* (2nd. ed.), p. 104. [Ed.] The scope of semiology (or semiotics) is treated at length in Charles Morris' *Signs, Language and Behavior* (New York: Prentice-Hall, 1946). [Tr.]

13

THE PHOTOGRAPHIC MESSAGE

ROLAND BARTHES

The press photograph is a message. Considered overall this message is formed by a source of emission, a channel of transmission and a point of reception. The source of emission is the staff of the newspaper, the group of technicians certain of whom take the photo, some of whom choose, compose and treat it, while others, finally, give it a title, a caption and a commentary. The point of reception is the public which reads the paper. As for the channel of transmission, this is the newspaper itself, or, more precisely, a complex of concurrent messages with the photograph as centre and surrounds constituted by the text, the title, the caption, the lay-out and, in a more abstract but no less 'informative' way, by the very name of the paper (this name represents a knowledge that can heavily orientate the reading of the message strictly speaking: a photograph can change its meaning as it passes from the very conservative *L'Aurore* to the communist *L'Humanité*). These observations are not without their importance for it can readily be seen that in the case of the press photograph the three traditional parts of the message do not call for the same method of investigation. The emission and the reception of the message both lie within the field of a sociology: it is a matter of studying human groups, of defining motives and attitudes, and of trying to link the behaviour of these groups to the social totality of which they are a part. For the message itself, however, the method is inevitably different: whatever the origin and the destination of the message, the photograph is not simply a product or a channel but also an object endowed with a structural autonomy. Without in any way intending to divorce this object from its use, it is necessary to provide for a specific method prior to sociological analysis and which can only be the immanent analysis of the unique structure that a photograph constitutes.

SOURCE: Barthes, R. (1977). *Image, music, text* (S. Heath, Trans.; pp. 15–31). New York: Hill and Wang. "The Photographic Message" from IMAGE/MUSIC/TEXT by Roland Barthes, translated by Stephen Heath. English translation copyright © 1977 by Stephen Heath. Reprinted by permission of Hill and Wang, a division of Farrar, Straus and Giroux, LLC.

Naturally, even from the perspective of a purely immanent analysis, the structure of the photograph is not an isolated structure; it is in communication with at least one other structure, namely the text—title, caption or article—accompanying every press photograph. The totality of the information is thus carried by two different structures (one of which is linguistic). These two structures are co-operative but, since their units are heterogeneous, necessarily remain separate from one another: here (in the text) the substance of the message is made up of words; there (in the photograph) of lines, surfaces, shades. Moreover, the two structures of the message each occupy their own defined spaces, these being contiguous but not 'homogenized', as they are for example in the rebus which fuses words and images in a single line of reading. Hence, although a press photograph is never without a written commentary, the analysis must first of all bear on each separate structure; it is only when the study of each structure has been exhausted that it will be possible to understand the manner in which they complement one another. Of the two structures, one is already familiar, that of language (but not, it is true, that of the 'literature' formed by the language-use of the newspaper; an enormous amount of work is still to be done in this connection), while almost nothing is known about the other, that of the photograph. What follows will be limited to the definition of the initial difficulties in providing a structural analysis of the photographic message.

The Photographic Paradox

What is the content of the photographic message? What does the photograph transmit? By definition, the scene itself, the literal reality. From the object to its image there is of course a reduction—in proportion, perspective, colour—but at no time is this reduction a *transformation* (in the mathematical sense of the term). In order to move from the reality to its photograph it is in no way necessary to divide up this reality into units and to constitute these units as signs, substantially different from the object they communicate; there is no necessity to set up a relay, that is to say a code, between the object and its image. Certainly the image is not the reality but at least it is its perfect *analogon* and it is exactly this analogical perfection which, to common sense, defines the photograph. Thus can be seen the special status of the photographic image: *it is a message without a code;* from which proposition an important corollary must immediately be drawn: the photographic message is a continuous message.

Are there other messages without a code? At first sight, yes: precisely the whole range of analogical reproductions of reality—drawings, paintings, cinema, theatre. In fact, however, each of those messages develops in an immediate and obvious way a supplementary message, in addition to the analogical content itself (scene, object, landscape), which is what is commonly called the *style* of the reproduction; second meaning, whose signifier is a certain 'treatment' of the image (result of the action of the creator) and whose signified, whether aesthetic or ideological, refers to a certain 'culture' of the society receiving the message. In short, all these 'imitative' arts comprise two messages: a *denoted* message, which is the *analogon* itself, and a *connoted* message, which is the manner in which the society to a certain extent communicates what it thinks of it. This duality of messages is evident in all reproductions other than photographic ones: there is no drawing, no matter how exact, whose very exactitude is not turned into a style (the style of 'verism'); no filmed scene whose objectivity is not finally read as the very sign of objectivity. Here again, the study of these connoted messages has still to be carried out (in particular it has to be decided whether what is called a work of art can be reduced to a system of significations); one can only anticipate that for all these imitative arts—when common—the code of the connoted system is very likely constituted either by a universal symbolic order or by a period rhetoric, in short by a stock of stereotypes (schemes, colours, graphisms, gestures, expressions, arrangements of elements).

When we come to the photograph, however we find in principle nothing of the kind, at any rate as regards the press photograph (which is never an 'artistic' photograph). The photograph professing to be a mechanical analogue of reality, its first-order message in some sort completely fills its substance and leaves no place for the development of a second-order message. Of all the structures of information,[1] the photograph appears as the only one that is exclusively constituted and occupied by a 'denoted' message, a message which totally exhausts its mode of existence. In front of a photograph, the feeling of 'denotation' or if one prefers, of analogical plenitude, is so great that the description of a photograph is literally impossible; *to describe* consists precisely in joining to the denoted message a relay or second-order message derived from a code which is that of language and constituting in relation to the photographic analogue, however much care one takes to be exact, a connotation: to describe is thus not simply to be imprecise or incomplete, it is to change structures, to signify something different to what is shown.[2]

This purely 'denotative' status of the photograph, the perfection and plenitude of its analogy, in short its 'objectivity', has every chance of being mythical (these are the characteristics that common sense attributes to the photograph). In actual fact, there is a strong probability (and this will be a working hypothesis) that the photographic message too—at least in the press—is connoted. Connotation is not necessarily immediately graspable at the level of the message itself (it is, one could say, at once invisible and active, clear and implicit) but it can already be inferred from certain phenomena which occur at the levels of the production and reception of the message: on the one hand, the press photograph is an object that has been worked on, chosen, composed, constructed, treated according to professional, aesthetic or ideological norms which are so many factors of connotation; while on the other, this same photograph is not only perceived, received, it is *read,* connected more or less consciously by the public that consumes it to a traditional stock of signs. Since every sign supposes a code, it is this code (of connotation) that one should try to establish. The photographic paradox can then be seen as the co-existence of two messages, the one without a code (the photographic analogue), the other with a code (the 'art', or the treatment, or the 'writing', or the rhetoric, of the photograph); structurally, the paradox is clearly not the collusion of a denoted message and a connoted message (which is the—probably inevitable—status of all the forms of mass communication), it is that here the connoted (or coded) message develops on the basis of a message *without a code*. This structural paradox coincides with an ethical paradox: when one wants to be 'neutral', 'objective', one strives to copy reality meticulously, as though the analogical were a factor of resistance against the investment of values (such at least is the definition of aesthetic 'realism'); how then can the photograph be at once 'objective' and 'invested', natural and cultural? It is through an understanding of the mode of imbrication of denoted and connoted messages that it may one day be possible to reply to that question. In order to undertake this work, however, it must be remembered that since the denoted message in the photograph is absolutely analogical, which is to say *continuous,* outside of any recourse to a code, there is no need to look for the signifying units of the first-order message; the connoted message on the contrary does comprise a plane of expression and a plane of content, thus necessitating a veritable decipherment. Such a decipherment would as yet be premature, for in order to isolate the signifying units and the signified themes (or values) one would have to carry out (perhaps using tests) directed readings, artificially varying certain elements of a photograph to see if the variations of forms led to variations in meaning. What can at least be done now is to forecast the main planes of analysis of photographic connotation.

CONNOTATION PROCEDURES

Connotation, the imposition of second meaning on the photographic message proper, is realized at the different levels of the production of the photograph (choice, technical treatment, framing, lay-out) and represents, finally, a coding of the photographic analogue. It is thus possible to separate out various connotation procedures, bearing in mind however that these procedures are in no way units of signification such as a subsequent analysis of a semantic kind may one day manage to define; they are not strictly speaking part of the photographic structure. The procedures in question are familiar and no more will be attempted here than to translate them into structural terms. To be fully exact, the first three (trick effects, pose, objects) should be distinguished from the last three (photogenia, aestheticism, syntax), since in the former the connotation is produced by a modification of the reality itself, of, that is, the denoted message (such preparation is obviously not peculiar to the photograph). If they are nevertheless included amongst the connotation procedures, it is because they too benefit from the prestige of the denotation: the photograph allows the photographer to *conceal elusively* the preparation to which he subjects the scene to be recorded. Yet the fact still remains that there is no certainty from the point of view of a subsequent structural analysis that it will be possible to take into account the material they provide.

1. *Trick effects.* A photograph given wide circulation in the American press in 1951 is reputed to have cost Senator Millard Tydings his seat; it showed the Senator in conversation with the Communist leader Earl Browder. In fact, the photograph had been faked, created by the artificial bringing together of the two faces. The methodological interest of trick effects is that they intervene without warning in the plane of denotation; they utilize the special credibility of the photograph—this, as was seen, being simply its exceptional power of denotation—in order to pass off as merely denoted a message which is in reality heavily connoted; in no other treatment does connotation assume so completely the 'objective' mask of denotation. Naturally, signification is only possible to the extent that there is

a stock of signs, the beginnings of a code. The signifier here is the conversational attitude of the two figures and it will be noted that this attitude becomes a sign only for a certain society, only given certain values. What makes the speakers' attitude the sign of a reprehensible familiarity is the tetchy anti-Communism of the American electorate; which is to say that the code of connotation is neither artificial (as in a true language) nor natural, but historical.

2. *Pose.* Consider a press photograph of President Kennedy widely distributed at the time of the 1960 election: a half-length profile shot, eyes looking upwards, hands joined together. Here it is the very pose of the subject which prepares the reading of the signifieds of connotation: youthfulness, spirituality, purity. The photograph clearly only signifies because of the existence of a store of stereotyped attitudes which form ready-made elements of signification (eyes raised heavenwards, hands clasped). A 'historical grammar' of iconographic connotation ought thus to look for its material in painting, theatre, associations of ideas, stock metaphors, etc., that is to say, precisely in 'culture'. As has been said, pose is not a specifically photographic procedure but it is difficult not to mention it insofar as it derives its effect from the analogical principle at the basis of the photograph. The message in the present instance is not 'the pose' but 'Kennedy praying': the reader receives as a simple denotation what is in actual fact a double structure—denoted-connoted.

3. *Objects.* Special importance must be accorded to what could be called the posing of objects, where the meaning comes from the objects photographed (either because these objects have, if the photographer had the time, been artificially arranged in front of the camera or because the person responsible for lay-out chooses a photograph of this or that object). The interest lies in the fact that the objects are accepted inducers of associations of ideas (bookcase = intellectual) or, in a more obscure way, are veritable symbols (the door of the gas-chamber for Chessman's execution with its reference to

the funeral gates of ancient mythologies). Such objects constitute excellent elements of signification: on the one hand they are discontinuous and complete in themselves, a physical qualification for a sign, while on the other they refer to clear, familiar signifieds. They are thus the elements of a veritable lexicon, stable to a degree which allows them to be readily constituted into syntax. Here, for example, is a 'composition' of objects: a window opening on to vineyards and tiled roofs; in front of the window a photograph album, a magnifying glass, a vase of flowers. Consequently, we are in the country, south of the Loire (vines and tiles), in a bourgeois house (flowers on the table) whose owner, advanced in years (the magnifying glass), is reliving his memories (the photograph album)—François Mauriac in Malagar (photo in *Paris-Match*). The connotation somehow 'emerges' from all these signifying units which are nevertheless 'captured' as though the scene were immediate and spontaneous, that is to say, without signification. The text renders the connotation explicit, developing the theme of Mauriac's ties with the land. Objects no longer perhaps possess a *power,* but they certainly possess meanings.

4. *Photogenia.* The theory of photogenia has already been developed (by Edgar Morin in *Le Cinéma ou l'homme imaginaire*[3]) and this is not the place to take up again the subject of the general signification of that procedure; it will suffice to define photogenia in terms of informational structure. In photogenia the connoted message is the image itself, 'embellished' (which is to say in general sublimated) by techniques of lighting, exposure and printing. An inventory needs to be made of these techniques, but only insofar as each of them has a corresponding signified of connotation sufficiently constant to allow its incorporation in a cultural lexicon of technical 'effects' (as for instance the 'blurring of movement' or 'flowingness' launched by Dr. Steinert and his team to signify space-time). Such an inventory would be an excellent opportunity for distinguishing aesthetic effects from signifying effects—unless perhaps it be recognized that in

photography, contrary to the intentions of exhibition photographers, there is never *art* but always *meaning;* which precisely would at last provide an exact criterion for the opposition between good painting, even if strongly representational, and photography.

5. *Aestheticism.* For if one can talk of aestheticism in photography, it is seemingly in an ambiguous fashion: when photography turns painting, composition or visual substance treated with deliberation in its very material 'texture', it is either so as to signify itself as 'art' (which was the case with the 'pictorialism' of the beginning of the century) or to impose a generally more subtle and complex signified than would be possible with other connotation procedures. Thus Cartier-Bresson constructed Cardinal Pacelli's reception by the faithful of Lisieux like a painting by an early master. The resulting photograph, however, is in no way a painting: on the one hand, its display of aestheticism refers (damagingly) to the very idea of a painting (which is contrary to any true painting); while on the other, the composition signifies in a declared manner a certain ecstatic spirituality translated precisely in terms of an objective spectacle. One can see here the difference between photograph and painting: in a picture by a Primitive, 'spirituality' is not a signified but, as it were, the very being of the image. Certainly there may be coded elements in some paintings, rhetorical figures, period symbols, but no signifying unit refers to spirituality, which is a mode of being and not the object of a structured message.

6. *Syntax.* We have already considered a discursive reading of object-signs within a single photograph. Naturally, several photographs can come together to form a sequence (this is commonly the case in illustrated magazines); the signifier of connotation is then no longer to be found at the level of any one of the fragments of the sequence but at that—what the linguists would call the suprasegmental level—of the concatenation. Consider for example four snaps of a presidential shoot at Rambouillet: in each, the illustrious sportsman (Vincent Auriol)

is pointing his rifle in some unlikely direction, to the great peril of the keepers who run away or fling themselves to the ground. The sequence (and the sequence alone) offers an effect of comedy which emerges, according to a familiar procedure, from the repetition and variation of the attitudes. It can be noted in this connection that the single photograph, contrary to the drawing, is very rarely (that is, only with much difficulty) comic; the comic requires movement, which is to say repetition (easy in film) or typification (possible in drawing), both these 'connotations' being prohibited to the photograph.

Text and Image

Such are the main connotation procedures of the photographic image (once again, it is a question of techniques, not of units). To these may invariably be added the text which accompanies the press photograph. Three remarks should be made in this context.

Firstly, the text constitutes a parasitic message designed to connote the image, to 'quicken' it with one or more second-order signifieds. In other words, and this is an important historical reversal, the image no longer *illustrates* the words; it is now the words which, structurally, are parasitic on the image. The reversal is at a cost: in the traditional modes of illustration the image functioned as an episodic return to denotation from a principal message (the text) which was experienced as connoted since, precisely, it needed an illustration; in the relationship that now holds, it is not the image which comes to elucidate or 'realize' the text, but the latter which comes to sublimate, patheticize or rationalize the image. As however this operation is carried out accessorily, the new informational totality appears to be chiefly founded on an objective (denoted) message in relation to which the text is only a kind of secondary vibration, almost without consequence. Formerly, the image illustrated the text (made it clearer); today, the text loads the image, burdening it with a culture, a moral, an imagination.

Formerly, there was reduction from text to image; today, there is amplification from the one to the other. The connotation is now experienced only as the natural resonance of the fundamental denotation constituted by the photographic analogy and we are thus confronted with a typical process of naturalization of the cultural.

Secondly, the effect of connotation probably differs according to the way in which the text is presented. The closer the text to the image, the less it seems to connote it; caught as it were in the iconographic message, the verbal message seems to share in its objectivity, the connotation of language is 'innocented' through the photograph's denotation. It is true that there is never a real incorporation since the substances of the two structures (graphic and iconic) are irreducible, but there are most likely degrees of amalgamation. The caption probably has a less obvious effect of connotation than the headline or accompanying article: headline and article are palpably separate from the image, the former by its emphasis, the latter by its distance; the first because it breaks, the other because it distances the content of the image. The caption, on the contrary, by its very disposition, by its average measure of reading, appears to duplicate the image, that is, to be included in its denotation.

It is impossible however (and this will be the final remark here concerning the text) that the words 'duplicate' the image; in the movement from one structure to the other second signifieds are inevitably developed. What is the relationship of these signifieds of connotation to the image? To all appearances, it is one of making explicit, of providing a stress; the text most often simply amplifying a set of connotations already given in the photograph. Sometimes, however, the text produces (invents) an entirely new signified which is retroactively projected into the image, so much so as to appear denoted there. '*They were near to death, their faces prove it*', reads the headline to a photograph showing Elizabeth and Philip leaving a plane—but at the moment of the photograph the two still knew nothing of the accident they had just escaped.

Sometimes too, the text can even contradict the image so as to produce a compensatory connotation. An analysis by Gerbner (*The Social Anatomy of the Romance Confession Cover-girl*) demonstrated that in certain romance magazines the verbal message of the headlines, gloomy and anguished, on the cover always accompanied the image of a radiant cover-girl; here the two messages enter into a compromise, the connotation having a regulating function, preserving the irrational movement of projection-identification.

PHOTOGRAPHIC INSIGNIFICANCE

We saw that the code of connotation was in all likelihood neither 'natural' nor 'artificial' but historical, or, if it be preferred, 'cultural'. Its signs are gestures, attitudes, expressions, colours or effects, endowed with certain meanings by virtue of the practice of a certain society: the link between signifier and signified remains if not unmotivated, at least entirely historical. Hence it is wrong to say that modern man projects into reading photographs feelings and values which are characteral or 'eternal' (infra- or transhistorical), unless it be firmly specified that *signification* is always developed by a given society and history. Signification, in short, is the dialectical movement which resolves the contradiction between cultural and natural man.

Thanks to its code of connotation the reading of the photograph is thus always historical; it depends on the reader's 'knowledge' just as though it were a matter of a real language [*langue*], intelligible only if one has learned the signs. All things considered, the photographic 'language' ['*langage*'] is not unlike certain ideographic languages which mix analogical and specifying units, the difference being that the ideogram is experienced as a sign whereas the photographic 'copy' is taken as the pure and simple denotation of reality. To find this code of connotation would thus be to isolate, inventoriate and structure all the 'historical' elements of the photograph, all the parts of the photographic surface which derive their very discontinuity from a certain knowledge on the reader's part, or, if one prefers, from the reader's cultural situation.

This task will perhaps take us a very long way indeed. Nothing tells us that the photograph contains 'neutral' parts, or at least it may be that complete insignificance in the photograph is quite exceptional. To resolve the problem, we would first of all need to elucidate fully the mechanisms of reading (in the physical, and no longer the semantic, sense of the term), of the perception of the photograph. But on this point we know very little. How do we read a photograph? What do we perceive? In what order, according to what progression? If, as is suggested by certain hypotheses of Bruner and Piaget, there is no perception without immediate categorization, then the photograph is verbalized in the very moment it is perceived; better, it is only perceived verbalized (if there is a delay in verbalization there is disorder in perception, questioning, anguish for the subject, traumatism, following G. Cohen-Séat's hypothesis with regard to filmic perception). From this point of view, the Image—grasped immediately by an inner metalanguage, language itself—in actual fact has no denoted state, is immersed for its very social existence in at least an initial layer of connotation, that of the categories of language. We know that every language takes up a position with regard to things, that it connotes reality, if only in dividing it up; the connotations of the photograph would thus coincide, *grosso modo*, with the overall connotative planes of language.

In addition to 'perceptive' connotation, hypothetical but possible, one then encounters other, more particular, modes of connotation, and firstly a 'cognitive' connotation whose signifiers are picked out, localized, in certain parts of the analogon. Faced with such and such a townscape, I *know* that this is a North African country because on the left I can see a sign in Arabic script, in the centre a man wearing a gandoura, and so on. Here the reading closely depends on my culture, on my knowledge of the world, and it is probable that a good press photograph (and they are all good, being selected) makes ready play with the supposed knowledge of its readers, those prints being chosen which comprise the greatest possible quantity of information of this kind in such a way as to render the reading fully satisfying. If one photographs Agadir in ruins, it is better to have a few signs of 'Arabness' at one's disposal, even though 'Arabness' has nothing to do with the disaster itself; connotation drawn from knowledge is always a reassuring force—man likes signs and likes them clear.

Perceptive connotation, cognitive connotation; there remains the problem of ideological (in the very wide sense of the term) or ethical connotation, that which introduces reasons or values into the reading of the image. This is a strong connotation requiring a highly elaborated signifier of a readily syntactical order: conjunction of people (as was seen in the discussion of trick effects), development of attitudes, constellation of objects. A son has just been born to the Shah of Iran and in a photograph we have: royalty (cot worshipped by a crowd of servants gathering round), wealth (several nursemaids), hygiene (white coats, cot covered in Plexiglass), the nevertheless human condition of kings (the baby is crying)—all the elements, that is, of the myth of princely birth as it is consumed today. In this instance the values are apolitical and their lexicon is abundant and clear. It is possible (but this is only a hypothesis) that political connotation is generally entrusted to the text insofar as political choices are always, as it were, in bad faith: for a particular photograph I can give a right-wing reading or a left-wing reading (see in this connection an IFOP survey published by *Les Temps modernes* in 1955). Denotation, or the appearance of denotation, is powerless to alter political opinions: no photograph has ever convinced or refuted anyone (but the photograph can 'confirm') insofar as political consciousness is perhaps non-existent outside the *logos:* politics is what allows *all* languages.

These few remarks sketch a kind of differential table of photographic connotations, showing, if nothing else, that connotation extends a long way. Is this to say that a pure denotation, a *this-side of language,* is impossible? If such a denotation exists, it is perhaps not at the level of what ordinary language calls the insignificant, the neutral, the objective, but, on the contrary, at the level of absolutely traumatic images. The trauma is a suspension of language, a blocking of meaning. Certainly situations which are normally traumatic can be seized in a process of photographic signification but then precisely they are indicated via a rhetorical code which distances, sublimates and pacifies them. Truly traumatic photographs are rare, for in photography the trauma is wholly dependent on the certainty that the scene 'really' happened: *the photographer had to be there* (the mythical definition of denotation). Assuming this (which, in fact, is already a connotation), the traumatic photograph (fires, shipwrecks, catastrophes, violent deaths, all captured 'from life as lived') is the photograph about which there is nothing to say; the shock-photo is by structure insignificant: no value, no knowledge, at the limit no verbal categorization can have a hold on the process instituting the signification. One could imagine a kind of law: the more direct the trauma, the more difficult is connotation; or again, the 'mythological' effect of a photograph is inversely proportional to its traumatic effect.

Why? Doubtless because photographic connotation, like every well-structured signification, is an institutional activity; in relation to society overall, its function is to integrate man, to reassure him. Every code is at once arbitrary and rational; recourse to a code is thus always an opportunity for man to prove himself, to test himself through a reason and a liberty. In this sense, the analysis of codes perhaps allows an easier and surer historical definition of a society than the analysis of its signifieds, for the latter can often appear as trans-historical, belonging more to an anthropological base than to a proper history. Hegel gave a better definition of the ancient Greeks by outlining the manner in which they made nature signify than by describing the totality of their 'feelings and beliefs' on the subject. Similarly, we can perhaps do better than to take stock directly of the ideological contents of our age; by trying to reconstitute in its specific structure the code of connotation of a mode of communication as important as the press photograph we may hope to find, in their very subtlety, the forms our society uses to ensure its peace of mind and to grasp thereby the magnitude, the detours and the underlying function of that activity. The prospect is the more appealing in that, as was said at the beginning, it develops with regard to the photograph in the form of a paradox—that which makes of an inert object a language and which transforms the unculture of a 'mechanical' art into the most social of institutions.

NOTES

1. It is a question, of course, of 'cultural' or culturalized structures, not of operational structures. Mathematics, for example, constitutes a denoted structure without any connotation at all; should mass society seize on it, however, setting out for instance an algebraic formula in an article on Einstein, this originally purely mathematical message now takes on a very heavy connotation, since it *signifies* science.

2. The description of a drawing is easier, involving, finally, the description of a structure that is already connoted, fashioned with a *coded* signification in view. It is for this reason perhaps that psychological texts use a great many drawings and very few photographs.

3. [Edgar Morin, *Le Cinéma ou l'homme imaginaire,* Paris 1956.]

14

COMMUNICATION WITH ALIENS

JOHN DURHAM PETERS

I firmly disbelieve, myself, that our human experience is the highest form of experience in the universe.

—William James,
Pragmatism, Lecture 8

Humans have long imagined themselves in contact with super- and subhuman intelligences; it is a specieswide longing. Before the twentieth century many philosophers had great interest in the inhabitants of other worlds, but as with animal communication, only since the late nineteenth century has the dream of empirical contact with beings not of this planet been pursued as a scientific enterprise.[1] With the modern attack, led by Marx, Feuerbach, Nietzsche, and Freud, on the human imagination as an unwitting maker of all kinds of fantastical others (gods, demons, angels, munchkins, trolls, water sprites, and spirits of

all sorts), science has compensated by seeking contact with objective others—animals, aliens, "primitives," the unconscious. In research on extraterrestrial intelligence, as on animal communication, all kinds of strategies have been sought to transcend the inevitability of one-way communication. Any message we receive must decisively prove to be immune to our own fabrications. As in Dorothy Parker's anxious monologue, we wait for a telephone call. The quest for contact with aliens is a leading example of the dialectic of enlightenment, the persistence of myth at the heart of the most secular enterprises. Even more, it is an allegory of faith in a disenchanted universe.

The search for extraterrestrial intelligence (SETI), an international scientific effort of varying fortunes since its start in the late 1950s, is perhaps the most sustained examination of communication—and communication breakdown—in late twentieth-century culture.[2] SETI is a child of the twentieth century. The project presupposes knowledge of the speed of light, the measurement

SOURCE: Peters, J. D. (1999). *Speaking into the air: A history of the idea of communication.* Chicago, IL: University of Chicago Press. Pages 246–261.

of vast distance, the discovery of radio waves, means of sorting signal from noise (such as cryptography and information theory), high-speed computers, and the longing to break through the circle of our own cognitions to touch otherness. The titles of recent articles on SETI tell a tale of communicative pathos: Is anyone out there? Are we alone? An invitation to strangers. Who's there? Still listening. Tuning in to out there. The next voice you hear. Earthlings are figured as Miss Lonelyhearts waiting by the telephone. The literature on SETI, both scientific and popular, is rife with explicit discussion of communication. SETI not only is the project of understanding radio emissions from deep space but is also implicitly a sustained inquiry into our earthly dilemmas about communication. It is a fertile field for exploring the philosophical consequences of storage and transmission capacities across vast expanses of time and space. Perhaps we are interested in communication with aliens because we live among alien communications. Every owner of a radio or television set possesses both a time machine and a teleportation device for alien personages.

Interstellar communication is riddled with astronomical gaps: mind numbing distances, ranging from four light-years to billions; delays between call and response that could outlast a thousand earth generations; the problem of signal persistence through Doppler shifts, space-time distortion, and signal scatter caused by cosmic dust and gases; and the prospect of such a radical otherness in our interlocutors that their math, their being in time, or their bodies might be like nothing in our ken. Their strangeness could put all other strangeness to shame. They might count with irrational numbers or communicate by modes of being instead of perceptible signals. Any message they send to us might never be recognized as a message. Codes for them might look like nature to us. The whir of the cicadas might be a message they are sending. Their sensitivity to quantities too vast or infinitesimal, or to matter too gross or subtle for the frame of our senses and minds, or even their time scale, might be so queer that no junction could

ever be made. If we couldn't understand a lion who spoke, why would we understand an alien? Across such desperate distance, any evidence of the will to communicate may always be underdetermined, subject to all kinds of alternative explanations.[3]

Extraterrestrial communication, more than any other situation, clearly shows that communication at a distance always comes out of the past. Any "message" received from a distant planet comes from a point already lost to time. If we were to receive a broadcast from a world near Arcturus, say, thirty-eight light-years away, we would hear only what the intelligences there had to say to us thirty-eight years ago. The "now" of reception would be the "then" of transmission. Communication with galactically distant worlds is an archaeological dig. Our dialogic couplings will be wildly asynchronous. SETI, by extremity of exaggeration, reveals what late nineteenth-century spiritualists knew: the unity of communication at a distance and communication with the dead.

Indeed, what psychical research was to the late nineteenth century, SETI is to the late twentieth. In both, highly respected scientists investigate topics that popular culture both abounds in and disdains as frivolous: spirits and aliens. Both draw on extant communications technology and practices. Psychical research owes an immense amount to the telegraph, telephone, and wireless for its imagery, as we have seen, and SETI is the latest step in the wireless imagination. Frank Drake, the founder in 1959 of Project Ozma, the first attempt to eavesdrop or tune in on the broadcasts of distant civilizations, and one of the senior players in SETI, compares any message we might send to faraway worlds to "an interstellar fax."[4] Both psychical research and SETI confront massive but mockingly inconclusive quantities of data with the hope that a junction can be made. Both deal with the most poignant human concerns: mourning, cosmic loneliness, contact with the dead and distant (psychical research) or alien and distant (SETI). Both are moved by faith in the other's existence without the ability to take hold of a sure connection. Both imagine a universe humming with conversations we are unable, for whatever reasons, to tap. As James C. Fletcher, twice the head of NASA and an active supporter of SETI, wrote, "We should begin to listen to other civilizations in the galaxy. It must be full of voices, calling from star to star in a myriad of tongues."[5] Both psychical research and SETI develop innovative methodologies for sorting messages from static, signal from noise. Psychical investigation into telepathy was the origin of randomized design; the experimenter could thus be completely blind to any order created (e.g., in the arrangement of playing cards) so as to bar any unwitting collaboration from his or her own unconscious.[6] Information theory and cryptography, likewise, make SETI conceivable; it is fitting that Stanislaw Lem makes a mathematician with special expertise in statistics the hero of his SETI novel *His Master's Voice* (1968), a brilliantly dizzying meditation on the hermeneutic undecidabilities of a letter from the stars, a text outside any known relationship.[7] Both inquiries have produced methods to restrain the human rage for order, the will to impose meaning on randomness or otherness, and our overzealousness in credulity.

In fact there is a historical link between psychical research and SETI. Oliver Lodge, who in the 1890s wrote of the powers of radio to create direct communication between distant brains and was later an active psychical researcher, was also apparently the first to have the idea of using radio as an instrument of exploration in astronomy. He sought to identify solar radio emissions, but there was too much electrical interference in Liverpool—perhaps owing in part to the sparking of the electrical trams on the streets.[8] His plea for psychical research applies equally well to SETI: "Clearly the conclusion [that the chasm between the living and the dead can be bridged] is either folly and self-deception, or it is a truth of the utmost importance to humanity."[9] Cambridge University, and more specifically the Cavendish Laboratory, was the headquarters not only for many of the late nineteenth-century physicists who both hypothesized the ether and engaged in psychical research, but also of many of the key

innovations after World War II in radio astronomy, which completely transformed our understanding of the universe. Since Newton a place of grace and order, the universe of radio astronomy is a Shiva's dance of creation and destruction, spectacular explosions of supernovas, and such unexpected weirdnesses as twin stars, quasars, dark matter, and black holes. The notion to use radio as an instrument of communication rather than of inquiry, however, appeared only in the late 1950s, with Project Ozma.

Reading some of the founding SETI articles from the late 1950s, like messages sent from distant planets forty light-years away, one is struck by how much they assume science is the universal language. In the founding article of SETI, Giuseppe Cocconi and Philip Morrison thought it "highly probable that for a long time [extraterrestrial societies] will have been expecting the development of science near the Sun." Once we receive and answer their signal, we would enter into "the community of intelligence," a sort of intergalactic invisible college.[10] The SETI scientists have a touching confidence that messages from other worlds would be sent by scientists eager to engage in scholarly exchange rather than by mindless bureaucrats, conquistadores, or con artists. Further, underlying early SETI documents is a rather apocalyptically tinged story of technological progress, with the hopes that more "advanced" civilizations could help us skip over intermediate stages without destroying ourselves in the meantime. One scientist even proposed that the apparent silence of the cosmos "may simply be that the mortality rate for advanced civilizations is too high for them to become abundant in the Galaxy."[11]

Radio begins as a séance, fragmentary messages flying through space, trying to make links with some listener, as in Rudyard Kipling's story "Wireless"; in SETI it ends where it began, in the quest for junction, beaming messages into space, scanning the heavens for proof of intelligible fabrication. The link between DX-ing, spiritualism, and SETI is explicit in the 1997 film *Contact*, based on the Carl Sagan novel by the same name. As a child the heroine, played by

Jodie Foster, is an amateur radio operator, who calls "CQ, CQ" into the great beyond. When she is orphaned, her DX-ing becomes a kind of quest for her dead parents. In adulthood she is a beleaguered SETI researcher who finally hits the jackpot—a message that beats out, rap by rap, the sequence of prime numbers from 1 to 100. In the climax, she travels to a distant world where she has a reunion with her father, or rather with an alien presence using her father as a reassuring simulation through which to speak to her. SETI is here figured as a quest for contact with the dead and others across distance. Of course the "contact" she has made leaves no decisive objective evidence except eighteen hours of static-filled tapes, such that the question of the reality of the junction (versus a huge hallucination? on her part) is, as always, left naggingly open. The possibility of communication is the twentieth century's version of the mystery of faith.

SETI seeks a true signal amid an infinity of noise; thus by far the most effort has been put into listening rather than sending. Like William James looking for evidence of immortality in the "bosh" of mediumistic performance, K looking for recognition from the Castle, or a lover listening to ten million radio voices for a telephonic message from his or her beloved, SETI faces the vertigo of infinitesimally small odds. The SETI scientist is in a position analogous to that of the radio listener trying to find out whether the voice of Kate Smith or Rudy Vallee is sincere, since he or she must sort out all the potential false sources of noise from the universe. The universe itself emits all manner of radio signals; the first pulsar, for example, was discovered in 1967 and was first thought to be an amazingly insistent radio signal from a remote intelligent civilization. The Cambridge astronomer and Nobel laureate Antony Hewish even hushed up the discovery for six months for fear of causing a public uproar if it really was some kind of distant signal. (It turned out to be a neutron star rotating on its axis at astounding speed.)[12] Indeed, the receipt of an alien signal, especially if it was a declaration of war or the design for a super weapon, could pose a profound question of public relations, not to

mention defense; there is even a worldwide pact among researchers not to respond at once if some message does come, lest we inadvertently step into some intergalactic conflict.[13] Radio astronomers are supposed to act initially as what Internet culture calls "lurkers"—those who read messages but do not make themselves known by actually posting one.

SETI recognizes the gaps of which communication is made. Galactic conversation can be nothing but alternating broadcasts. As Stanislaw Lem notes, "When 'questions' were separated from the 'answers' they received by a time that was on the order of centuries, it was hard to call such an exchange 'dialogue.' "[14] Much of SETI's strategy is explicitly the one-way work of eavesdropping. Astronomer Freeman Dyson, a long-time leader in SETI, proposed surveillance as the best course for discerning intelligent life in the universe: rather than DX-ing with the universe (searching for the most distant signal possible), we should inspect the vast archives of photographic data of deep space for evidence of cosmic engineering (specifically so-called Dyson spheres, huge solar power stations that would serve as proof of distant alien intelligence).[15] SETI offers a nice catalog of the pieces that result once dialogue is, in Paul Ricoeur's word, "exploded." There is spying (I receive a signal not meant for me without your knowing it), hailing (I recognize you as a potential interlocutor), recognition (you "copy" my recognition with a counterhailing), and interaction. The enormous elongation of the communication circuit in deep space, like the equally radical extensions of the telegraph or photograph, reveal that the fundamental problem of communication is not adjusting semantics so we mean the same things with words, but figuring out ways to come into fellowship with otherness.

SETI faces a task suited for Kabbalists: scanning an infinite text for the name of names. It must employ search strategies in impossibly vast aggregates. Prophets heard voices from the heavens, but SETI researchers have to contend with the gigabytes of radio emissions naturally produced by the universe, to say nothing of the interference they produce for themselves (the electrical trams of Liverpool, or Clever Hans problems). SETI might rightly take its place among the theological and interpersonal abysses of the twentieth century. Kafka and Borges understand best the stakes of the quest for intelligible order in a pulsating cosmos. Borges's story "The Library of Babel" is a delirium of tedious infinities. This library contains every possible combination of all the letters of the Roman alphabet bound in volumes of 410 pages each. The number of volumes is very large, but not infinite. We know beyond the shadow of a doubt that there is somewhere in the library of Babel the greatest literary work possible with these letters, the Miltonic epic Keats would have written had he lived or sublimities Proust only dreamed of: yet there are billions of variants of this grand work, slightly diminished, and an even greater all but infinity of utter nonsense. We are unable to know if we have found it, since there are a hundred thousand versions perfect in everything but a single typo and a billion slightly blemished versions, and all but an aleph-null of deformed pieces. The absolute confidence that the masterpiece exists— along with every possible masterpiece—goes together with the sure knowledge that it cannot be found. The masterpiece cannot announce itself as such. Somewhere in the library there is even a volume that explicates the order of the library—a catalog—but it too exists in a billion spurious versions.

Borges gives us an allegory of inability to connect: theologically, statistically, communicatively. His library is dissemination taken to an infinite extreme. One-to-one contact becomes impossible. Just so, we may know for sure that the animal hurts, but access to that pain is forever barred; we may believe the chances tiny that we are alone in the universe, but the others are so far away. The Library of Babel is an allegory of the minimal odds of our own existence, and still we exist. We seem an exception in the universe, and yet mundanity cloaks us on every side. SETI is an emblem of the hermeneutic giddiness that faces anyone staring into the abyss; our attempts to "communicate" have only made it worse.

One thing that distinguishes SETI from previous attempts to communicate with the heavens is the acute sense of the possibility of error. A 1959 article important in launching the movement nicely stated the grand prize: "indisputable identification as an artificial signal."[16] The issue was how to know a bona fide signal from other worlds—what others since have called "an intelligible beacon"[17] or "a nonrandom possibly intelligent transmission."[18] To be taken as a message, a signal must have an extremely low probability of being either a random or a natural product. Russian exoscientists made "artificiality criteria" a topic of very sophisticated study, including analysis of the statistical properties of signals.[19] Sought is an unmistakable signature of artifice, of a will to communicate—a concerto, pi to one hundred places, or some other feat of a playful (nonutilitarian) intelligence. Increased capacities of data processing have only escalated the pathos of infinity. Like a Penelope waiting for a rendezvous with an Odysseus she doesn't know if she will recognize, SETI scientists look for incontrovertible tokens. They seek a sign.

The image of the earth alone in the universe is analogous to the idealist's "man" cooped up in his room: both long not to be alone, to find a sign of something that is not a projection of the self. Though we live amid alien human intelligences— music, mathematics, art, and argument—a simple SOS from Tau Ceti would electrify the whole world. It is not only, contra Turing, intelligence or, contra Shannon, information that concerns us in communication, but the body it comes from. What SETI hopes for is the self-consciousness that the other is communicating, a sign rather than a signal: nothing would quite thrill like call letters, a break in the flow of programming to "identify oneself" (phrase of Hegelian wonder). Call letters would meet the precise definition of a social sign for George Herbert Mead: a sign used by the self to connect it to others. As one astrophysicist said, "We're looking for the one combination that says, 'Hi there.' "[20] The grand prize of communication at a distance recurs: Come here, I want you.

Otherness turns out, alas, always to be internally defined. In 1959 Cocconi and Morrison offered an elegant and influential argument for using the natural wavelength of the hydrogen atom as the logical frequency to send an interstellar message, assuming that to be a universal constant. But it is a postulate, like the Kantian or Jamesian varieties, that the aliens would also think to broadcast on that wavelength. SETI is a fine example of the post-Kantian problematic of how to recognize authentic empirical inputs within the all-coloring powers of human cognition. Today some scientists fear that the "pollution" of the electromagnetic spectrum by earth's own broadcasting may be so severe that the search may have to shift from radio to the optical band. As interference makes earth-bound scanning impossible, astronomers may either shift to infrared and visible wavelengths or use space stations to scan for signals from deep space.[21] The Drake equation, which gives grounds for calculating the likelihood of intelligent life elsewhere in the universe, estimates the longevity of a communicating civilization at one million years. Perhaps Drake should have calculated instead the span between the discovery of radio and the filling of the spectrum—more like one hundred years in the case of earth history. The shift in strategy from radio to optics is motivated, of course, not by any sense that extraterrestrials might have shifted their signals to a higher frequency but by the capacities of *our* instruments, which always constitute the ceiling on communication. When the aliens in *Contact* communicate with Jodie Foster via her father's persona, they say they are trying to soften the shock of the experience for her, but they end up depriving her of proof of having burst the bubble of solipsism.

The basic assumption of SETI—that a signal must stand in stark contrast to the rest of nature— is based on a shrinkage of the realm of the semiotic. In romanticism, with such thinkers as Ritter, Schelling, or even Kant's notion of a *Chiffenschrift der Natur* (hieroglyphics of nature), nature was once assumed to be a text written in cipher; more anciently it was assumed to be full of cryptic messages intelligible to the sage or soothsayer. We have seen, since, a recession in the general supply of meaning. In nature we have come to assume that all those obvious but unintelligible and apparently unauthored patterns— sunsets, cries of birds, the guts of a lamb, or the fabric of clouds—are not the work of a conscious intelligence that we can interpret. The pathetic fallacy, animism, and anthropocentrism have all been scared out of us. And so solipsism is inescapable, since the only source of intelligible order is within us. Our lack of confidence in the objectivity of meanings is one key source of the pervasive sense of communication breakdown.

Some exoscientists have not stopped short at receiving messages but have sent messages to space—potentially the ultimate dead letter. Carl Sagan and others designed a message to be sent to outer space with *Voyager* in the 1970s that was supposed to be stripped of any extraneous cultural coding. Twenty-five years later this image already seems an emanation from an alien civilization, with its 1970s hairdos, vision of gender (the man takes the lead in greeting while the woman stands in a pose half demure, half sexy), and race (the couple are clearly white, though whites are not the majority race of the planet). Even in its attempts to transcend itself, a historical moment only reveals its blindness to its own face. By transposing the passage of time to flight across space, SETI offers lessons in the philosophy of history: what is hardest to recapture of the past is not its treasure-house of information about itself but its ignorance of what is most obvious to later observers. The attempt to send a message on a spacecraft is almost amusing, considering just how "hot" our planet has been over the past century in its emissions on the electromagnetic spectrum. Why the aliens should prefer the message on *Voyager* to all the episodes of *I Love Lucy, The Twilight Zone, Gilligan's Island*, or any other signal we earthlings have sent zooming through interstellar space is anyone's guess. SETI scientists at times evince a touching faith that the extraterrestrials would share their preference for Bach or mathematics over rock and roll or Scrabble.[22]

The aliens populate cinema, television, and the tabloids, all of which assume that contact has been made and take it from there with bathos or horror. SETI in contrast scrupulously scrutinizes the alternative hypotheses and wants pure, intelligible other mind, not just patters created by the reader, pulsars, background radiation, or a passing airliner or satellite. Nature and self are systematically excluded as authors: intentional otherness must break through. But Plato and Hegel would remind us that if the other has no body whose presence we could desire, then what makes us think minds can make contact? We might even, like Maxwell's glass lenses that never touch, be surrounded by extraterrestrial intelligence, only to never come in contact.

This is indeed the oddest thing about SETI—that we are so plainly surrounded with alien intelligences—bees, whales, porpoises, chimpanzees, DNA molecules, computers, dung beetles, slime mold, even the planet as an ecosystem—but still feel lonely and unable to communicate.[23] How much intelligence and wisdom are found in Chinese civilization, for instance, and how ignorant the West continues to be of it![24] Why do we seek distant alien intelligence when we hardly know what to do with our own? The huge barrier here is the strangeness that we never see: our own faces. We haunt ourselves like aliens. The main ghost that stalks me is my self, the only person whom everyone else knows but I never can. As Peirce wrote, "Facts that stand before our face and eyes and stare us in the face are far from being, in all cases, the ones most easily discerned."[25] Our failure to recognize ourselves fuels our thirst for confirmation from alien intelligences. "It is only when we think of ourselves on the receiving end that imagination seems to fail us."[26] The issue is our failure to enter into a common realm with the other: we are back with all the misfires and distortions that Socrates sketches.

The problem may be less our loneliness than our too stringent sense of communication. If we thought of communication as the occasional touch of otherness rather than a conjunction of consciousness, we might be less restrictive in our quest for nonearthly intelligence. What is the human truth of SETI? That the mundane is only a small pocket of the extraordinary. Of the billions of solar systems, we know of only one so able to support life. An orbit slightly closer to the sun, a tilt of the earth's axis by a few more degrees, or an errant comet all could have made life on earth impossible. Of the five billion years of earth's existence, humanoids have existed for one thousandth of that time. Civilization as we know it (with its writing, war, patriarchy) has existed for one thousandth of that. We are, as the romantics all insisted, the great exception to the universe, the rare case, the completion of nature, the way that the universe comes to self-consciousness.

The question should be, then, not how we break through the sludge of habit to rediscover the hidden strangeness of things, but how we ever managed to convince ourselves that anything was not a dissemination of intelligence. Boredom is the amazing achievement, not wonder. Our senses can catch only a narrow portion of the spectrum: the cosmic rays, rainbows above or below the range of visible light, or tectonic groans of the earth all elude us. What the moralists have said about the universe, science since Faraday has proved to be empirically true: We are immersed in a sea of intelligence that we cannot fully understand or even sense. Emerson's point about spiritualism applies equally to SETI: Why search so wistfully in a corner when the whole universe is a message? SETI research reminds one of Thoreau's quip about those who tried to measure the depths of Walden Pond: "They were paying out the rope in the vain attempt to fathom their truly immeasurable capacity for marvellousness."[27] In the 1890s William Crookes, Charles Sanders Peirce, Henry Adams, and many lesser spirits were delirious about the chances for human connection via waves naturally emitted from our persons. The hope for brain waves, however, remains constrained by the dullness of our instrumentation; perhaps it is simply our narrow bandwidth that makes telepathy a dream, the privacy of pain a given, and democracy always bounded by the dynamics of a conversation in which only one person can speak at a time.

Instead of being terrorized by the quest for communication with aliens, we should recognize its ordinariness. There is no other kind of communication. All our converse with others is via signs, those creatures from outer and inner space. This was a central tenet of Peirce, who led the pragmatist revolt against Cartesian hierarchies. His essay "Some Consequences of Four Incapacities" (1868) directly attacks introspection and Descartes, offers a behavioral understanding of communication, is open to the animal or the inhuman as a potential partner, and relinquishes any claim of special privilege for the human mind—which Peirce, borrowing a line from Shakespeare's *Measure for Measure*, called "man's glassy essence." Not afraid of the charge of animism, Peirce takes human beings and words as continuous. "It may be said that man is conscious, while a word is not. But consciousness is a very vague term . . . consciousness, being a mere sensation, is only a part of the *material quality* of the man-sign." If words do not have consciousness, in what sense do people have it? Significance, in other words, does not need a live body; a word in itself can radiate meaning, in the same way that a phonograph or photograph can hold thought in objective form. Peirce argued "that a person is nothing but a symbol involving a general idea," and he later drew the even more radical conclusion that "every general idea has the unified living feeling of a person."[28] The criterion of life, then, does not suffice to distinguish humans from signs. "The man-sign acquires information, and comes to mean more than he did before. But so do words." Words mean what people have made them mean, but people mean nothing that words have not taught them to say. Words have their associations and communities, just as people or animals do. "In fact, therefore, men and words reciprocally educate each other; each increase in a man's information involves, and is involved by, a corresponding increase of a word's information."[29]

Peirce's argument is not only a critique of Cartesian high-handedness, or a semiotic animism that ascribes objective reality to meanings, as semantic theorists would fear, but an effort to invite us into a beloved community, one that includes all forms of intelligence as our partners in some way, at least in some future horizon. Though his thinking about evolutionary love and corporate personality ranks among the most wonderful and strange to come from the pragmatist tradition, and though he clearly does believe (in contrast to James) in the ultimate possibility of something like shared brain space, the ascription of independent intelligence to signs might be seen as Peirce's response to a communicative universe in which persons obeyed new laws of motion, scattering themselves into all fields in which signs may play.[30] We play host to signs like alien spores that have taken us over. Instead of taking signs as meaningful because they have an animating mind behind them, it is sounder to think of minds as themselves signs mixed with mortal life. The signs are as conscious as we are; they too have inner lives. Peirce's theory of signs is historically indebted to an age when intelligence can be stored in media.

Clearly, then, neither Peirce nor James is a defender of some sort of humanism, of "man" as the measure of all things. They recognize, in contrast, our fundamental inhumanity in the sense that we are always more or less than human. They do so with a quality of mercy that other antihumanisms such as behaviorism and poststructuralism often lack. They say not that inner life is a mentalist figment but that interiority appears as an other; that its form is polymorphous; that we find our inner life dispersed pluralistically across the fields of our experience. Inner life is best thought of not as a control panel presided over by a homunculus, but as behavior continuous with all else that we do. The inner and the outer are two sides of the same Möbius strip. We honor, not demean, the riches of inner life by seeing it as one kind of complex behavior not appreciably different from any other we engage in.

The pragmatists teach us that we should care for children, animals, the mad, the deformed, spirits and the dead, aliens and nature not because they potentially have a inner life of reason that can lay claim to our recognition (as Descartes might have it) but because they share our world and our shape. We should relate to animals not because they have minds, but because they have vertebrae, need oxygen, or feel pain. Our obligation to other creatures comes not from our ability to tap into their inner life but from a primordial kinship deriving from a common biological history, as variant forms of intelligent life that God or nature has seen fit to produce. The kinship we share with all creation is written into our bodies before we ever make mental contact (a lesson the pragmatists learned from Emerson and Darwin alike). This is a commonsense fact of compassion rather than an epistemological conundrum of other minds. Against the impasses of solipsism James wrote: "Men who see each other's bodies sharing the same space, treading the same earth, splashing the same water, making the same air resonant, and pursuing the same game and eating out of the same dish, will practically never believe in a pluralism of solipsistic worlds." A behaviorist query—Do we in fact cooperate?—is the question pragmatism poses to the worries about the impossibility of communication. Lovable form trumps abstract impossibilities. "The practical point of view brushes such metaphysical cobwebs away."[31]

This recognition involves a softening of the heart, an admission of the inefficacy of our glassy essence against the awe of strangeness. Interior consciousness ceases to be the criterion of humanness. The refusal to probe inner life can lead in the more militant direction of depriving all beings of an inner life (some forms of behaviorism) or in the wilder and superior direction of granting an admirable but inaccessible innerness to all creatures, of giving, like Emerson or Whitman, a welcome to the universe—democracy in the best, full sense. A true democracy would have to include a much wider range of creatures than humans, for humans themselves are many creatures. Full democracy would be transspecies, transgender, transrace, transregion, transclass, transage, transhuman: what Emerson called "the democracy of chemistry." Even the dead would be invited.

The problem of communication in the twentieth century arises with much less exotic partners than aliens, animals, and machines, although again it is already a failure of recognition that we think of these creatures rather than ourselves as exotic. All the gaps and breakdowns we find with them we find among ourselves. But they also give us a way to imagine different worlds in which we might dwell. Consider the dolphins. Dolphins have no hands, so they have no works—no weapons, no records, no history, no government, no property, no law, no crime, no punishment.[32] No dolphin is married to any other dolphin, but all dolphins are kin. They are the true idyll of communism as Marx dreamed it. There is no forbidden fruit to expel them from Eden. They are naked and not ashamed. They are some of the aliens among us; women are some other aliens, as are men. So is the self: I am the thing from outer space (the ancients knew this). I am the UFO haunting everything (Novalis, Coleridge, and Emerson all knew this). So the dolphins sing and mate and play and eat and swim. They roll, exempt from the regime of secondness. What collective poetry, oral histories, symphonies of discussions over hundreds of leagues, fondness, relationships they must have. Voices that travel for hundreds of miles, allowing completely asynchronous dialogues. What friendships. What grief at the loss of a fellow to the nets or the killer whales. What philosophical dialogues, with no record but the consciousness of the community that listens. All conversation would be a reading of the archive of the community, as conversational turns traveling across great stretches of water would come to each participant in a unique order. Each response would appear in its true light as a new beginning. Dialogue and dissemination would be indistinguishable. The sea must be the original agora, the place of speech. But the dolphins have no agonistics because there is no drive to besting or individuation; their works of verbal invention are collective compositions. Theirs is a life of sporting firstness. If the hearing capacities of the dolphins are as advanced as our vision, dolphins may be exempt from the hardest argument against democracy: the ability of only one person to speak and be heard at a time. Dolphins can perhaps hear many of their fellows speaking at once; they would not be torn by the unfortunate mismatch between hearing and speaking, which makes democracy ever subject to constraints of scale. The party would be a party always, a polylogue in which everyone spoke and everyone heard. Such is perhaps the vision we should take away from a century's attempt to make contact with alien creatures.

NOTES

1. On the philosophical history of such interest, see Lewis White Beck, "Extraterrestrial Intelligent Life," in *Extraterrestrials: Science and Alien Intelligence,* ed. Edward Regis Jr. (Cambridge: Cambridge University Press, 1935), 3–18.

2. It is also sometimes known as CETI, communication (or contact) with extraterrestrial intelligence.

3. Dennis Overbye, "The Big Ear," *Omni* 13 (December 1990): 44. Frank Drake has suggested that our most likely interlocutors in SETI are immortal beings who have infinite patience to await our response.

4. David Graham, "Intergalactic Conversations," *Technology Review* 96 (February–March 1993): 20–21.

5. James C. Fletcher quoted in Roger D. Launius, "A Western Mormon in Washington, D.C.: James C. Fletcher, NASA, and the Final Frontier," *Pacific Historical Review* 64 (May 1995): 233.

6. Ian Hacking, "Telepathy: Origins of Randomization in Experimental Design," *Isis* 79 (1988): 427–51.

7. Stanislaw Lem, *His Master's Voice,* trans. Michael Kandel (New York: Harvest/HBJ, 1968).

8. Nigel Calder, *Radio Astronomy* (New York: Roy, 1958), 11.

9. Oliver Lodge, *Raymond, or Life and Death, with Examples of the Evidence of Survival of Memory and Affection after Death* (New York: Doran, 1916), 389.

10. Giuseppe Cocconi and Philip Morrison, "Searching for Interstellar Communications," *Nature* 184 (19 September 1959): 844.

11. R. N. Bracewell, "Communications from Superior Galactic Communities," *Nature* 185 (28 May 1960): 671.

12. S. A. Kaplan, "Exosociology: The Search for Signals from Extraterrestrial Civilizations," in *Extraterrestrial Civilizations: Problems of Interstellar Communication,* ed. S. A. Kaplan, trans. from Russian (Jerusalem: Keter Press, 1971), 7.

13. Graham, "Intergalactic Conversations," 20.

14. Lem, *His Master's Voice,* 103.

15. Freeman Dyson, "Search for Artificial Stellar Sources of Infrared Radiation," *Science* 131 (1959): 1667–68. Dyson also has a Cambridge connection: B.A. in mathematics, 1945.

16. Cocconi and Morrison, "Searching for Interstellar Communications," 846.

17. Alan Lightman, "E. T. Call Harvard," *Science* 85 (September 1985): 20–22.

18. Gregg Easterbrook, "Are We Alone?" *Atlantic Monthly,* August 1988, 27.

19. L. M. Gindilis, "The Possibility of Radio Communication with Extraterrestrial Civilizations," in *Extraterrestrial Civilizations: Problems of Interstellar Communication,* ed. S. A. Kaplan, trans. from Russian (Jerusalem: Keter Press, 1971), 103–8. The Eastern Europeans have led the way in these inquiries, in science on the one hand and in literature and cinema on the other.

20. Kent Cullers, quoted in Overbye, "Big Ear," 48.

21. Robert Naeye, "SETI at the Crossroads," *Sky and Telescope,* November 1992, 514.

22. *Mother Earth News* 122 (March–April 1990), in its twentieth anniversary issue, sent an open letter to the great blue yonder, apologizing in effect for the bad condition of the planet!

23. This and many other excellent points are made in Anthony Weston, "Radio Astronomy as Epistemology: Some Philosophical Reflections on the Contemporary Search for Extraterrestrial Intelligence" in *Monist* 71, 1 (1988): 88–100.

24. Naeye, "SETI at the Crossroads," 515.

25. Charles Sanders Peirce, "The Law of Mind," *Monist* 2, 4 (1892): 559.

26. Weston, "Radio Astronomy as Epistemology," 91.

27. Henry David Thoreau, *Walden* (1854; New York: Norton, 1975), 189.

28. Charles Sanders Peirce, "Man's Glassy Essence," *Monist* 3, 1 (1892): 21.

29. Charles Sanders Peirce, "Some Consequences of Four Incapacities" (1868), in *Philosophical Writings of Peirce*, ed. Justus Buchler (New York: Dover, 1955), 249.

30. A helpful explication and critique is Jürgen Habermas, "Peirce and Communication," in *Peirce and Contemporary Thought*, ed. Kenneth Laine Ketner (New York: Fordham University Press, 1995), 243–66.

31. William James, "The Function of Cognition," in *The Writings of William James: A Comprehensive Edition*, ed. John J. McDermott (Chicago: University of Chicago Press, 1977), 146.

32. Loren Eiseley, "The Long Loneliness: Man and the Porpoise," in *A Writer's Reader,* ed. Donald Hall and D. L. Emblen (Boston: Little, Brown, 1979), 140–47.

PROJECTS FOR SEMIOTIC THEORIZING

ADDITIONAL READINGS ON SEMIOTICS

A. To learn more about semiotics in general: Bouissac (1998); Chandler (2002); Leeds-Hurwitz (1993); Morris (1930); Ogden and Richards (1959); Peirce (1992).

B. Saussure laid the foundation for structuralism. To learn more about structuralism: Saussure (1916/1959); Levi-Strauss (1963, 1966); Sturrock (2003).

C. To learn more about language-like semiotic codes: Barthes (1983).

D. To learn more about cognitive psychology and links to Peircean ideas: Miller and Johnson-Laird (1976); Schank and Abelson (1977); Gardner (1985, 2004); Johnson-Laird (1988).

APPLICATION EXERCISE

Explore the nature of signs by doing one of the following. Make up a word and start using it in your daily speech. Who asks about the word—people you know well, people you don't? Who begins to use the word? Does the word start to appear in print anywhere? Trace the history of a specific word as it has changed meaning over time. How have talking, thinking, and/or institutional decision making changed as the meaning of this word has changed? Have three or four people look at the same photograph and each write out what the picture shows. Do the same with a photo accompanying a news article. Compare and contrast the descriptions. Are the news photo descriptions more similar or more different than those of the stand-alone picture? Why is this the case?

PROJECTS

1. Just as the Peters reading may lead one to think about phenomenology, reading Chang in the next unit on the phenomenological tradition may lead one to think about semiotics. Chang's idea of the paradox of unstable meaning is in keeping with post-structuralist theorists such as Derrida (1978). Although many post-structuralists who have incorporated some of Peirce's thinking take this approach to meaning, some semiotic theorists, such as Ellis (1991, 1995), argue for the possibility of stable meaning. Compare these ideas on meaning and theorize about the stability of meaning and what that means for practicing communication.

2. Thinking about Barthes, one may be drawn to asking about the possibility of nonlinguistic codes. Some thinkers who have studied the origin of human language, such as Langer (1953; 1972, see pp. 265–316; 1979), have differentiated between discursive (such as language) and presentational (such as art) symbolic forms, whereas Burke (1953) has discussed qualitative form. Compare discursive symbols with other symbolic forms such as articulated

presentational symbols and theorize about the potential of nonlinguistic ways of communicating meaning.

3. Peters looks at Carl Sagan's book *Contact* as seen in the Jodie Foster version of the movie by the same name and addresses the fascination with SETI (the search for extraterrestrial intelligence) and communicating as integral to this search. To see if the problem of connection is prevalent in fictionalized accounts of contacting or encountering aliens, examine other science fiction movies and books such as Madeleine L'Engle's *Wrinkle in Time* or the movie *Starman,* (Carpenter, 1984) staring Jeff Bridges and Karen Allen, to see if similar or different conceptions of communication are in these works.

4. As mentioned in the introduction to this volume, many of Locke's ideas about communication are still influential today, especially in nonacademic arenas. Examine popular conceptions of communication such as seen in self-help books and TV talk shows to see if Locke's principles for avoiding the abuse of language are evident in this popular talk about communication. Theorize about the popular conception of communication and how this came to be the popular conception. Is it the case that Lockean ideas are the basis for popular ideas about communication? Or is popular theorizing changing? Is there evidence that Peters's theorizing on communication and connection is becoming part of the popular conception and practice of communication? Compare your conclusions to studies of popular ideas about communication by Cameron (2000) and Carbaugh (1988).

5. Looking across thinkers, one may be drawn to think about the nature of understanding as seen in different conceptions of the relationship between language, thought, speech, and meaning. Locke talks about words matching ideas. Peirce links thought processes and signs. Saussure advocates studying language as an autonomous system separate from speech. Peters addresses the contiguity of human beings and words as they reciprocally educate each other. Outside the semiotic tradition, theorists such as Vygotsky (1978, 1986) examine the connection between external speech and internal speech, proposing that higher psychological processes develop through an internalization process where external speech (talk with others) precedes internal speech and thought. Barthes's proposal of connotative techniques adds another angle on the idea of creating meaning. Comparing and contrasting some of these views, work to answer these questions: What is understanding and how is it achieved? Do this through theorizing the relationship between language, words, thought, speech, and meaning. In this theorizing you may want to address questions such as these: Are there a variety of speech-meaning processes? Is there a distinct line of progression in understanding meaning across these thinkers? Does the difference between a dyadic sign-referent relationship and a triadic relationship lead to different ways of conceptualizing understanding? Does language impact thought differently than speech? Do nonlinguistic signs impact thought differently than linguistic signs? Does connection precede or result from communication? Does connection equal understanding?

REFERENCES

Barthes, R. (1983). *The fashion system* (M. Ward & R. Howard, Trans.). New York: Hill and Wang.

Bouissac, P. R. (Ed.). (1998). *Encyclopedia of semiotics.* New York: Oxford University Press.

Burke, K. (1953). *Counterstatement.* Los Altos, CA: Hermes.

Cameron, D. (2000). *Good to talk? Living and working in a communication culture.* London: Sage.

Carbaugh, D. (1988). *Talking American: Cultural discourse on Donohue.* Norwood, NJ: Ablex.

Carpenter, J. (Director). (1984). *Starman* [Motion picture]. United States: Sony Picture Home Entertainment.

Chandler, D. (2002). *Semiotics: The basics.* New York: Routledge.

Chang, B. G. (1996). *Deconstructing communication: Representation, subject, and economies of exchange.* Minneapolis: University of Minnesota Press.

Derrida, J. (1978). *Writing and difference* (A. Bass, Trans.). Chicago: University of Chicago Press.

Ellis, D. G. (1991). Post-structuralism and language: Non-sense. *Communication Monographs, 58*(2), 213–224.

Ellis, D. G. (1995). Fixing communicative meaning: A coherentist theory. *Communication Research, 22*(5), 515–544.

Gardner, H. (1985). *The mind's new science: A history of the cognitive revolution.* New York: Basic Books.

Gardner, H. (2004). *Changing minds: The art and science of changing our own and other people's minds.* Boston: Harvard Business School Press.

Johnson-Laird, P. N. (1988). *The computer and the mind: An introduction to cognitive science.* Cambridge, MA: Harvard University Press.

Langer, S. K. (1953). *Feeling and form: A philosophy of art developed from philosophy in a new key.* New York: Charles Scribner's Sons.

Langer, S. K. (1972). *Mind: An essay on human feeling* (Vol. 2). Baltimore: Johns Hopkins University Press.

Langer, S. K. (1979). *Philosophy in a new key: A study in the symbolism of reason, rite, and art* (3rd ed.). Cambridge, MA: Harvard University Press.

Leeds-Hurwitz, W. (1993). *Semiotics and communication: Signs, codes, cultures.* Hillsdale, NJ: Lawrence Erlbaum.

L'Engle, M. (1962). *A wrinkle in time.* New York: Farrar, Straus, and Giroux.

Levi-Strauss, C. (1963). *Structural anthropology* (C. Jacobson & B. C. Schoepf, Trans.). New York: Basic Books.

Levi-Strauss, C. (1966). *The savage mind.* Chicago: University of Chicago Press.

Miller, G. A., & Johnson-Laird, P. N. (1976). *Language and perception.* Cambridge, MA: Belknap Press.

Morris, C. (1930). *Foundations of the theory of signs.* Chicago: University of Chicago Press.

Ogden, C. K., & Richards, I. A. (1959). *The meaning of meaning: A study of the influence of language upon thought and of the science of symbolism.* New York: Harcourt Brace.

Peirce, C. S. (1992). *The essential Peirce: Selected philosophical writings* (Vol. 2; N. Houser & C. Kloesel, Eds.). Bloomington: Indiana University Press.

Saussure, F. de. (1959). *Course in general linguistics* (W. Baskin, Trans.; C. Bally & A. Sechehaye [with A. Reidlinger], Eds.). New York: Philosophical Library. (Original work published 1916)

Schank, R. C., & Abelson, R. P. (1977). *Scripts, plans, goals, and understanding: An inquiry into human knowledge structures.* Hillsdale, NJ: Lawrence Erlbaum.

Sturrock, J. (2003). *Structuralism* (2nd ed.). Malden, MA: Blackwell.

Vygotsky, L. S. (1978). *Mind in society: The development of higher psychological processes.* Cambridge, MA: Harvard University Press.

Vygotsky, L. S. (1986). *Thought and language.* Cambridge, MA: MIT Press.

UNIT V   INTRODUCTION

THE PHENOMENOLOGICAL TRADITION

The phenomenological tradition conceptualizes communication as dialogue or the experience of otherness. Although a progression of ideas certainly can be seen across the four readings in this unit, all are concerned with questions such as these: What do we do with experience? What is the experience of being a person in communication? What are the limits and possibilities of understanding others? Responding to those questions, the phenomenological tradition theorizes communication by using concepts such as experience, dialogue, authenticity, interpretation, and otherness.

The philosopher Edmund Husserl (1859–1938) conceived phenomenology as a rigorous scientific method for analyzing conscious experience. In contrast to the natural attitude of everyday life, in which we seldom question the basis of our perceptions, Husserl's method of phenomenology involves bracketing or disregarding the particular contents of an experience in order to reveal essential structures and transcendental (beyond experience) conditions that make the experience possible. To take a relatively simple example, our visual experience of solid physical objects takes for granted certain essential properties, such as the fact that objects have more than one side and appear differently when seen from different perspectives. These taken-for-granted properties are the basis for our confidence that we are seeing the same objects from different points of view even though their appearance constantly changes as we move around them. Without this transcendental experiential structure for perceiving objects, the changing appearance of a single object while we move around it might lead us to think we were seeing multiple objects instead of the same object from different views.

Phenomenology rejects any absolute distinction between objectivity and subjectivity because every conscious experience involves both. Experience is a relation between a conscious subject who is having the experience and objects in the world that are intended (constituted in consciousness) by the subject. Consciousness is always consciousness *of* something, yet it is only our consciousness that picks objects out from the continuous flow of the world around us and constitutes them as distinct, identifiable things. The objective world can be carved up and experienced in many different ways depending on how we happened to interact with it; however, subjective experience is not something made up entirely inside our heads. It is our consciousness of things we encounter in the world.

Among the many kinds of things we experience, one especially important kind consists of others—conscious beings like ourselves with whom we can communicate. A phenomenological theory of communication attempts to explain this kind of experience, but in doing so it confronts an essential paradox. Genuine communication (often called dialogue in this tradition) requires that we experience others *as others,* that is, as conscious beings in their own right, in and for themselves, but we can never actually experience another person's unique consciousness. Therefore, we can never quite experience others as others. What then is the basis for any genuine relationship to other people? How is authentic communication possible? The readings in this section illustrate several different approaches to this *problem of knowing the other.*

The first reading is a short excerpt from Husserl's *Cartesian Meditations: An Introduction to Phenomenology* (1929–1931/1960), in which he confronts the classic phenomenological problem of the other: If phenomenological epoché (i.e., bracketing) finally reduces everything to the purified experience of a solitary *transcendental ego* or abstracted individual, then doesn't phenomenology degenerate into a kind of solipsism—a radical subjectivism that cannot acknowledge the reality of any other's experience? Husserl's strategy for solving this problem is sketched in the final paragraph of the reading and elaborated in subsequent sections of his book. Since we do apparently experience others as actual others with their own experiences, what we must now do, he suggests, is to undertake a careful phenomenological analysis of the structure of experiences in which we recognize and verify the experiences of others by analogy with our own experiences. In other words, you cannot directly experience another person's experiences, but you can understand those experiences by assuming that they resemble your own.

Critics of Husserl's transcendental phenomenology have considered this to be an inadequate solution to the problem because it continues to reduce the other to an element constituted in one's own experience, hence not a genuine other. As Chang writes, "Inasmuch as the other ego is derivative from my ego, what Husserl calls the " 'illusion' of solipsism cannot be said to be dissolved" (1996, p. 28).

But does this dry conclusion capture what happens when we actually experience dialogue with another person? As interpreted by Pilotta and Mickunas (1990), dialogue is an experience of communicating with another person about something. In genuine dialogue, the attention of both partners is focused on their mutual involvement in whatever they are doing or talking about together: "In the dialogical context the other is experienced not as an object given to the subject to be deciphered but as a dialogical partner" (Pilotta & Mickunas, 1990, p. 62). Phenomenological thinkers have attempted to describe this subtle experience of dialogue with the other, to distinguish genuine dialogue from inauthentic forms of communication that may have the appearance of dialogue, and to understand the conditions that promote or inhibit dialogue.

Martin Buber's theologically influenced concept of dialogue as turning toward the other (reading 16) and Hans-Georg Gadamer's ideal of conversation as a form of "hermeneutical experience" (reading 17) illustrate how different threads of the phenomenological tradition replaced Husserl's idea of the transcendental ego with dialogue defined as a special kind of experience that happens between self and other.

In the excerpts we have assembled from his classic essay on "Dialogue," Buber (1947/2002) describes the authentic experience of movement toward the other that is dialogue, distinguishes it from various forms of monologue or false dialogue, and applies it to problems of community in modern group and organizational life. The early 20th-century social environment in which Buber wrote was increasingly dominated by impersonal bureaucracy, large-scale industrialization, and mass communication. Genuine human relationships seemed increasingly rare and threatened by inauthentic simulations of dialogue that are really forms of monologue in disguise. Is this problem any less real today than it was then? Buber's theory of communication addresses this *problem of monologue*. His essay opens with examples illustrating ineffable experiences of momentary communion with others, showing that dialogue can be entirely wordless and yet deeply meaningful. These are not mystical experiences, according to Buber, although their meaning cannot be explained in words and one example (perhaps representing an experience of God) occurred to him only in dreams. Another example, described later in the essay, occurred between the young Buber and a horse. Are these poetically rendered examples realistic instances of communication?

In attempting to characterize these experiences, Buber notes the difference between merely observing and truly becoming aware of another being. When two beings turn toward each other and experience their awareness of each other as mutual, then there is dialogue. A person whose basic attitude toward life is to be open and receptive to this kind of experience can be said to be living the life of dialogue. Buber distinguishes the genuine experience of dialogue from mere information exchange (technical dialogue) and several forms of false dialogue such as debate and friendly chitchat. The basic movement of dialogue, he says, is to focus on the other, whereas the basic movement of monologue is reflexion, or focus on the self.

Although dialogue requires focus on the other, Buber emphasizes that dialogue does not involve a merger of two beings into one or any loss of individuality. Dialogue is an "I-Thou" relationship between beings that maintain their distinctness from each other. This idea allows Buber to distinguish a genuine

community in which members retain their individuality while striving to realize a common goal from a collectivity that requires members to subordinate themselves to group conformity.

In the concluding section on confirmation, Buber argues for the realistic possibility of dialogue. Dialogue is possible between opponents if they are truly open to each other and each seriously engages with what the other has to say. And dialogue is possible in the practical world of business and industry, despite all the pressures of modern life that militate against it. This is possible, he writes, if we choose to experience the organization not as "a structure of mechanical centres of force and their organic servants" but rather "as an association of persons with faces and names and biographies" (reading 16).

Gadamer's theory of communication resembles Buber's but makes an important shift in emphasis. Buber's concept of dialogue emphasizes direct mutual awareness and openness to one another as unique beings. Gadamer's parallel concept of conversation emphasizes the object or subject matter of conversation that brings people together in dialogue. An I-Thou relationship arises from our mutual engagement with something we are talking about and both trying to understand from our different views. Gadamer compares the process of conversation to that of interpreting a literary text or translating from one language to another. Although these subtle comparisons may challenge the reader's comprehension, they repay the effort of reading with glimpses of a different vision of communication.

Gadamer's *Truth and Method* (1960/1989), from which our reading is excerpted, is not primarily about dialogue or interpersonal communication. It is a treatise on philosophical hermeneutics, which addresses *the problem of understanding*. Hermeneutics is the art of interpretation. Originally a method for interpreting ancient texts, it was later applied to other areas of historical and cultural understanding. Gadamer's philosophical hermeneutics, building on Heidegger's (1927/1996) hermeneutic phenomenology, relates hermeneutics to our essential way of being in the world—the experience of expanding our horizons of understanding as we encounter new situations.

Tradition plays a necessary role in Gadamer's theory. We are only able to make sense of ourselves and the world around us because our consciousness has been shaped by history and traditions in ways we are largely unaware of. As we encounter new situations that may violate some of our traditional assumptions, if we are open to what is going on, our awareness expands and our understanding of the tradition evolves. This is what Gadamer called hermeneutical experience. Gadamer was especially interested in art and culture as sources of hermeneutical experience. Great works of literature and art, like laws and sacred texts, deepen the meaning of life and provide wisdom but need to be constantly reinterpreted as we encounter them from new situations. A similar kind of creative encounter with tradition also happens when we engage in conversations with others who have different views. We are able to communicate with others insofar as we share a common language and tradition, but each of us has experienced a different range of situations, so our understandings of the world have evolved in different ways. Hermeneutical experience is about coming to understand those differences and in the process, coming to understanding the world and ourselves differently.

Gadamer's effort to understand hermeneutical experience at the deepest level itself challenges many traditional understandings of tradition, experience, and language. The passages we have excerpted from *Truth and Method* focus on Gadamer's view of interpretation as an I-Thou relationship, the question-answer logic that underlies hermeneutic experience, and the central role of language in constituting our world of meaning.

Gadamer begins by noting that we encounter tradition primarily in the form of language. Because we experience language as a *Thou* (like someone speaking to us), that is also how we experience tradition. Although a traditional hermeneutical activity like reading a text is clearly different from interpersonal dialogue, in both cases we experience a Thou who speaks to us in language from a common tradition. Exploring subtle parallels between these two experiences, Gadamer distinguishes what he calls the "historically effected consciousness" that enables genuine hermeneutic or dialogical experience from two lesser forms of consciousness that he identifies as knowledge of human nature and historical consciousness. Gadamer does not explicitly mention Buber in this passage, but his discussion of three ways of experiencing the I-Thou relationship shows Buber's influence as well as their shared tradition of German philosophy going back to Hegel in the early 19th century. For Gadamer, a necessary element of genuine hermeneutical experience, whether in interpersonal dialogue or when interpreting a work of art, is openness to learning from the other, which "involves recognizing that I myself must accept some things that are against me, even though no one else forces me to do so" (reading 17).

Gadamer goes on to explain that the ability to have experiences requires asking questions. A questioning attitude implies openness and acknowledges "a radical negativity: the knowledge of not knowing" (reading 17). Despite the ordinary connotations of the word *negative*, in Gadamer's hermeneutical perspective the negative aspect of experience is basically a good thing. Genuine experience always involves some negative challenge to our traditional assumptions. The challenge is logically equivalent to asking a question that leads to a dialectical process of interpretation and growth of understanding, much like the question-answer procedure of Plato's dialogues. A genuine question expresses openness but also a particular focus of curiosity that limits the type of answer that is sought. There is no fixed method for asking questions, but questions will naturally occur to someone who really wants to know and who acknowledges not knowing. Every real conversation follows a similar question-answer logic, although not usually in the literal form of a series of questions and answers. The conversation flows freely because the participants do not guide it according to any preconceived plan. They follow the subject matter wherever it goes in a common search for truth, with each comment raising some challenge to understanding that leads on to the next. How does this hermeneutical question-answer logic differ from the methods of questioning that, are often recommended for active listening?

After an interesting digression on the declining art of letter writing (which might stimulate a project of theorizing the question-answer logics of newer media such as e-mail and text messaging), Gadamer further examines the analogy between conversation and textual interpretation as forms of hermeneutic experience. He notes in both cases that the primary focus is on understanding the object or subject matter and that the understanding is expressed in language. Coming to an understanding means creating a common language that expresses that understanding. Expanding this point, Gadamer discusses translation between languages as an extreme case of what always happens in conversation or textual interpretation, which is to find language for expressing the same object in different worlds of meaning. The key point, is that this process must all occur in language because, as Gadamer goes on to explain, our "world of meaning" is coextensive with our language and the two evolve together in hermeneutical experience. In stark contrast to Locke and much of traditional

semiotics and philosophy of language, Gadamer says that words are not just "handy tools" for expressing already-existing thoughts; "concepts are constantly in the process of being formed" as we apply our language to new situations (reading 17). How do Locke's and Gadamer's different views of language explain their different views of communication?

The Chang reading is taken from the conclusion of his book, *Deconstructing Communication* (1996). Chang's theory, which uses techniques of deconstruction developed by the poststructuralist philosopher Jacques Derrida and others, rather than seeking a solution to the problem of knowing the other, recovers the paradoxical undecidability of communication that Husserl, Buber, and Gadamer (like most theorists of communication) attempted to avoid. Personal authenticity and genuine openness to the other, Chang suggests, can only be achieved by recognizing that communication, in the sense of truly understanding another person's experience, is impossible. Routine interaction and meaningless chitchat can give the illusion that we are communicating, as Buber pointed out, but any attempt to overcome radical otherness—to share a message that goes beyond what is already familiar—is likely to leave the recipient merely speechless and feeling stupid. The paradox is that communication, for all its impossibility, at the same time is unavoidable. We cannot not communicate (see reading 20 in the next unit for a different treatment of this theme), because when face-to-face with another person, we cannot avoid the implicit obligation to try to understand each other. So we are always communicating despite the impossibility of doing so: at least the fact that we are communicating, if not the particular experience we are trying to communicate, is successfully communicated. "Communication," Chang concludes, "is possible and is impossible. If communication is anything at all, it is an *undecidable*" (reading 18).

Other questions, in addition to ones we have already mentioned along the way, may arise as you read this unit. What problems of communication do these phenomenological theories most clearly illuminate? Do they speak to problems frequently encountered in your own experience? Do they suggest useful ways of approaching those problems? What distinctive ways of talking about communication does phenomenology provide, and how do they differ from ways of talking found in other units of this book? For what purposes does this tradition seem more or less useful than others? What does it mean to be authentic in our relationships? What is required to really understand another person's experiences? Is this possible at all? Is it necessary at all? What kind of understanding does an authentic relationship require? Is Husserl's solution to the problem of knowing others sufficient? Buber's? Gadamer's? How would these other theorists respond to Chang's claim that communication is undecidable? Does Chang's theory of communication possibly owe more to Husserl—or even to John Locke—that he might like to admit? Is the emphasis on authenticity that runs through the phenomenological tradition always an appropriate or very helpful criterion for evaluating communication?

REFERENCES

Buber, M. (2002). Dialogue (R. G. Smith, Trans.). In *Between man and man* (pp. 1–45). London: Routledge. (Original work published 1947)

Chang, B. G. (1996). *Deconstructing communication: Representation, subject, and economies of exchange.* Minneapolis: University of Minnesota Press.

Gadamer, H.-G. (1989). *Truth and method* (J. Weinsheimer & D. Marshall, Trans.; 2nd ed.). New York: Crossroad. (Original work published 1960)

Heidegger, M. (1996). *Being and time: A translation of Sein und Zeit* (J. Stambaugh, Trans.). Albany: State University of New York Press. (Original work published 1927)

Husserl, E. (1960). *Cartesian meditations: An introduction to phenomenology* (D. Cairns, Trans.). The Hague, The Netherlands: M. Nijhoff. (Original work published 1929–1931)

Pilotta, J. J., & Mickunas, A. (1990). *Science of communication: Its phenomenological foundation.* Hillsdale, NJ: Lawrence Erlbaum.

15

The Problem of Experiencing Someone Else

Edmund Husserl

§ *42. Exposition of the problem of experiencing someone else, in rejoinder to the objection that phenomenology entails solipsism.*

As the point of departure for our new meditations, let us take what may seem to be a grave objection. The objection concerns nothing less than the claim of transcendental phenomenology to be itself transcendental *philosophy* and therefore its claim that, in the form of a constitutional problematic and theory moving within the limits of the transcendentally reduced ego, it can solve the transcendental problems pertaining to the *Objective world.* When I, the meditating I, reduce myself to my absolute transcendental ego by phenomenological epoché do I not become *solus ipse;* and do I not remain that, as long as I carry on a consistent self-explication under the name phenomenology? Should not a phenomenology that proposed to solve the problems of Objective being, and to present itself actually as

philosophy, be branded therefore as transcendental solipsism?

Let us consider the matter more closely. Transcendental reduction restricts me to the stream of my pure conscious processes and the unities constituted by their actualities and potentialities. And indeed it seems[1] obvious that such unities are inseparable from my ego and therefore belong to his concreteness itself.

But what about other egos, who surely are not a mere intending and intended *in me,* merely synthetic unities of possible verification *in me,* but, according to their sense, precisely *others*? Have we not therefore done transcendental realism an injustice? The doctrine may lack a phenomenological foundation; but essentially it is right in the end, since it looks for a path from the immanency of the ego to the transcendency of the Other. Can we, as phenomenologists, do anything but agree with this and say: "The Nature

SOURCE: Husserl, E. (1960). *Cartesian meditations: An introduction to phenomenology* (D. Cairns, Trans.). The Hague: M. Nijhoff. (Pages 89–90). Used with kind permission from Springer Science and Business Media.

and the whole world that are constituted 'immanently' in the ego are only my 'ideas' and have behind them the world that exists in itself. The way to this world must still be sought."? Accordingly can we avoid saying likewise: "The very question of the possibility of actually transcendent knowledge—above all, that of the possibility of my going outside my ego and reaching other egos (who, after all, as others, are not actually in me but only consciously intended in me)—this question cannot be asked purely phenomenologically"? Is it not *self-understood* from the very beginning that my field of transcendental knowledge does not reach beyond my sphere of transcendental experience and what is synthetically comprised therein? Is it not self-understood that all of that is included without residue in my own transcendental ego?

But perhaps there is some mistake in thoughts like these. Before one decides in favor of them and the "self-understood" propositions they exploit, and then perchance embarks on dialectical argumentations and self-styled "metaphysical" hypotheses (whose supposed possibility may turn out to be complete absurdity), it might indeed be more fitting to undertake the *task of phenomenological explication* indicated in this connexion by the "alter ego" and carry it through in concrete work. We must, after all, obtain for ourselves insight into the explicit and implicit intentionality wherein the alter ego becomes evinced and verified in the realm of our transcendental ego; we must discover in what intentionalities, syntheses, motivations, the sense "other ego" becomes fashioned in me[2] and, under the title, harmonious experience of someone else, becomes verified as existing and even as itself there in its own manner. These experiences and their works are facts belonging to my[3] phenomenological sphere. How else than by examining them can I explicate the sense, existing others, in all its aspects?

NOTES

1. Marginal note: Seems? Is.
2. The phrase rendered by "in me" crossed out.
3. The word [rendered] as "belonging to my" crossed out. Marginal comment: "The dangerous first person singular! This should be expanded terminologically."

16

DIALOGUE

MARTIN BUBER

SECTION ONE: DESCRIPTION

Original Remembrance

Through all sorts of changes the same dream, sometimes after an interval of several years, recurs to me. I name it the dream of the double cry. Its context is always much the same, a "primitive" world meagrely equipped. I find myself in a vast cave, like the Latomias of Syracuse, or in a mud building that reminds me when I awake of the villages of the fellahin, or on the fringe of a gigantic forest whose like I cannot remember having seen.

The dream begins in very different ways, but always with something extraordinary happening to me, for instance, with a small animal resembling a lion-cub (whose name I know in the dream but not when I awake) tearing the flesh from my arm and being forced only with an effort to loose its hold. The strange thing is that this first part of the dream story, which in the

duration as well as the outer meaning of the incidents is easily the most important, always unrolls at a furious pace as though it did not matter. Then suddenly the pace abates: I stand there and cry out. In the view of the events which my waking consciousness has I should have to suppose that the cry I utter varies in accordance with what preceded it, and is sometimes joyous, sometimes fearful, sometimes even filled both with pain and with triumph. But in my morning recollection it is neither so expressive nor so various. Each time it is the same cry, inarticulate but in strict rhythm, rising and falling, swelling to a fulness which my throat could not endure were I awake, long and slow, quiet, quite slow and very long, a cry that is a song. When it ends my heart stops beating. But then, somewhere, far away, another cry moves towards me, another which is the same, the same cry uttered or sung by another voice. Yet it is not the same cry, certainly no "echo" of my cry but rather its true rejoinder, tone for tone not repeating mine, not even in a

---

SOURCE: Buber, M. (2002). Dialogue (R. G. Smith, Trans.). In *Between man and man* (pp. 1–45; excerpts from pp. 1–7, 9–12, 22–29, 35–37, 39–45). London: Routledge.

weakened form, but corresponding to mine, answering its tones—so much so, that mine, which at first had to my own ear no sound of questioning at all, now appear as questions, as a long series of questions, which now all receive a response. The response is no more capable of interpretation than the question. And yet the cries that meet the one cry that is the same do not seem to be the same as one another. Each time the voice is new. But now, as the reply ends, in the first moment after its dying fall, a certitude, true dream certitude comes to me that *now it has happened.* Nothing more. Just this, and in this way— *now it has happened.* If I should try to explain it, it means that that happening which gave rise to my cry has only now, with the rejoinder, really and undoubtedly happened.

After this manner the dream has recurred each time—till once, the last time, now two years ago. At first it was as usual (it was the dream with the animal), my cry died away, again my heart stood still. But then there was quiet. There came no answering call. I listened, I heard no sound. For I *awaited* the response for the first time; hitherto it had always surprised me, as though I had never heard it before. Awaited, it failed to come. But now something happened with me. As though I had till now had no other access from the world to sensation save that of the ear and now discovered myself as a being simply equipped with senses, both those clothed in the bodily organs and the naked senses, so I exposed myself to the distance, open to all sensation and perception. And then, not from a distance but from the air round about me, noiselessly, came the answer. Really it did not come; it was there. It had been there—so I may explain it—even before my cry: there it was, and now, when I laid myself open to it, it let itself be received by me. I received it as completely into my perception as ever I received the rejoinder in one of the earlier dreams. If I were to report with what I heard it I should have to say "with every pore of my body." As ever the rejoinder came in one of the earlier dreams this corresponded to and answered my cry. It exceeded the earlier rejoinder in an unknown perfection which is hard to define, for it resides in the fact that it was already there.

When I had reached an end of receiving it, I felt again that certainty, pealing out more than ever, that *now it has happened.*

Silence Which Is Communication

Just as the most eager speaking at one another does not make a conversation (this is most clearly shown in that curious sport, aptly termed discussion, that is, "breaking apart," which is indulged in by men who are to some extent gifted with the ability to think), so for a conversation no sound is necessary, not even a gesture. Speech can renounce all the media of sense, and it is still speech.

Of course I am not thinking of lovers' tender silence, resting in one another, the expression and discernment of which can be satisfied by a glance, indeed by the mere sharing of a gaze which is rich in inward relations. Nor am I thinking of the mystical shared silence, such as is reported of the Franciscan Aegidius and Louis of France (or, almost identically, of two rabbis of the Hasidim) who, meeting once, did not utter a word, but "taking their stand in the reflection of the divine Face" experienced one another. For here too there is still the expression of a gesture, of the physical attitude of the one to the other.

What I am thinking of I will make clear by an example.

Imagine two men sitting beside one another in any kind of solitude of the world. They do not speak with one another, they do not look at one another, not once have they turned to one another. They are not in one another's confidence, the one knows nothing of the other's career, early that morning they got to know one another in the course of their travels. In this moment neither is thinking of the other; we do not need to know what their thoughts are. The one is sitting on the common seat obviously after his usual manner, calm, hospitably disposed to everything that may come. His being seems to say it is too little to be ready, one must also be really *there*. The other, whose attitude does not betray him, is a man who holds himself in reserve, withholds himself. But if we know about him we know that a childhood's spell is laid on him, that his withholding of himself is something other than an attitude, behind all attitude is entrenched the impenetrable inability to communicate himself. And now—let us imagine that this is one of the hours which succeed in bursting asunder the seven iron bands about our heart— imperceptibly the spell is lifted. But even now the man does not speak a word, does not stir a finger. Yet he does something. The lifting of the spell has happened to him—no matter from where—without his doing. But this is what he does now: he releases in himself a reserve over which only he himself has power. Unreservedly communication streams from him, and the silence bears it to his neighbour. Indeed it was intended for him, and he receives it unreservedly as he receives all genuine destiny that meets him. He will be able to tell no one, not even himself, what he has experienced. What does he now "know" of the other? No more knowing is needed. For where unreserve has ruled, even wordlessly, between men, the word of dialogue has happened sacramentally.

Opinions and the Factual

Human dialogue, therefore, although it has its distinctive life in the sign, that is in sound and gesture (the letters of language have their place in this only in special instances, as when, between friends in a meeting, notes describing the atmosphere skim back and forth across the table), can exist without the sign, but admittedly not in an objectively comprehensible form. On the other hand an element of communication, however inward, seems to belong to its essence. But in its highest moments dialogue reaches out even beyond these boundaries. It is completed outside contents, even the most personal, which are or can be communicated. Moreover it is completed not in some "mystical" event, but in one that is in the precise sense factual, thoroughly

dovetailed into the common human world and the concrete time-sequence.

One might indeed be inclined to concede this as valid for the special realm of the erotic. But I do not intend to bring even this in here as an explanation. For Eros is in reality much more strangely composed than in Plato's genealogical myth, and the erotic is in no way, as might be supposed, purely a compressing and unfolding of dialogue. Rather do I know no other realm where, as in this one (to be spoken of later), dialogue and monologue are so mingled and opposed. Many celebrated ecstasies of love are nothing but the lover's delight in the possibilities of his own person which are actualized in unexpected fulness.

I would rather think of something unpretentious yet significant—of the glances which strangers exchange in a busy street as they pass one another with unchanging pace. Some of these glances, though not charged with destiny, nevertheless reveal to one another two dialogical natures.

But I can really show what I have in mind only by events which open into a genuine change from communication to communion, that is, in an embodiment of the word of dialogue.

What I am here concerned with cannot be conveyed in ideas to a reader. But we may represent it by examples—provided that, where the matter is important, we do not eschew taking examples from the inmost recesses of the personal life. For where else should the like be found?

My friendship with one now dead arose in an incident that may be described, if you will, as a broken-off conversation. The date is Easter 1914. Some men from different European peoples had met in an undefined presentiment of the catastrophe, in order to make preparations for an attempt to establish a supra-national authority. The conversations were marked by that unreserve, whose substance and fruitfulness I have scarcely ever experienced so strongly. It had such an effect on all who took part that the fictitious fell away and every word was an actuality. Then as we discussed the composition of the larger circle from which public initiative should proceed (it was decided that it should meet in August of the same year) one of us, a man of passionate concentration and judicial power of love, raised the consideration that too many Jews had been nominated, so that several countries would be represented in unseemly proportion by their Jews. Though similar reflections were not foreign to my own mind, since I hold that Jewry can gain an effective and more than merely stimulating share in the building of a steadfast world of peace only in its own community and not in scattered members, they seemed to me, expressed in this way, to be tainted in their justice. Obstinate Jew that I am, I protested against the protest. I no longer know how from that I came to speak of Jesus and to say that we Jews knew him from within, in the impulses and stirrings of his Jewish being, in a way that remains inaccessible to the peoples submissive to him. "In a way that remains inaccessible to you"—so I directly addressed the former clergyman. He stood up, I too stood, we looked into the heart of one another's eyes. "It is gone," he said, and before everyone we gave one another the kiss of brotherhood.

The discussion of the situation between Jews and Christians had been transformed into a bond between the Christian and the Jew. In this transformation dialogue was fulfilled. Opinions were gone, in a bodily way the factual took place.

[. . .]

Setting of the Question

The life of dialogue is not limited to men's traffic with one another; it is, it has shown itself to be, a relation of men to one another that is only represented in their traffic.

Accordingly, even if speech and communication may be dispensed with, the life of dialogue seems, from what we may perceive, to have inextricably joined to it as its minimum constitution one thing, the mutuality of the inner action. Two men bound together in dialogue must obviously be turned to one another, they must therefore—no matter with what measure of activity or indeed of consciousness of activity—have turned to one another.

It is good to put this forward so crudely and formally. For behind the formulating question about the limits of a category under discussion is hidden a question which bursts all formulas asunder.

Observing, Looking On, Becoming Aware

We may distinguish three ways in which we are able to perceive a man who is living before our eyes. (I am not thinking of an object of scientific knowledge, of which I do not speak here.) The object of our perception does not need to know of us, of our being there. It does not matter at this point whether he stands in a relation or has a standpoint towards the perceiver.

The *observer* is wholly intent on fixing the observed man in his mind, on "noting" him. He probes him and writes him up. That is, he is diligent to write up as many "traits" as possible. He lies in wait for them, that none may escape him. The object consists of traits, and it is known what lies behind each of them. Knowledge of the human system of expression constantly incorporates in the instant the newly appearing individual variations, and remains applicable. A face is nothing but physiognomy, movements nothing but gestures of expression.

The *onlooker* is not at all intent. He takes up the position which lets him see the object freely, and undisturbed awaits what will be presented to him. Only at the beginning may he be ruled by purpose, everything beyond that is involuntary. He does not go around taking notes indiscriminately, he lets himself go, he is not in the least afraid of forgetting something ("Forgetting is good," he says). He gives his memory no tasks, he trusts its organic work which preserves what is worth preserving. He does not lead in the grass as green fodder, as the observer does; he turns it and lets the sun shine on it. He pays no attention to traits ("Traits lead astray," he says). What stands out for him from the object is not "character" and not "expression" ("The interesting is not important," he says). All great artists have been onlookers.

But there is a perception of a decisively different kind.

The onlooker and the observer are similarly orientated, in that they have a position, namely, the very desire to perceive the man who is living before our eyes. Moreover, this man is for them an object separated from themselves and their personal life, who can in fact for this sole reason be "properly" perceived. Consequently what they experience in this way, whether it is, as with the observer, a sum of traits, or, as with the onlooker, an existence, neither demands action from them nor inflicts destiny on them. But rather the whole is given over to the aloof fields of aesthesis.

It is a different matter when in a receptive hour of my personal life a man meets me about whom there is something, which I cannot grasp in any objective way at all, that "says something" to me. That does not mean, says to me what manner of man this is, what is going on in him, and the like. But it means, says something *to me,* addresses something to me, speaks something that enters my own life. It can be something about this man, for instance that he needs me. But it can also be something about myself. The man himself in his relation to me has nothing to do with what is said. He has no relation to me, he has indeed not noticed me at all. It is not he who says it to me, as that solitary man silently confessed his secret to his neighbour on the seat; but *it* says it.

To understand "say" as a metaphor is not to understand. The phrase "that doesn't say a thing to me" is an outworn metaphor; but the saying I am referring to is real speech. In the house of speech are many mansions, and this is one of the inner.

The effect of having this said to me is completely different from that of looking on and observing. I cannot depict or denote or describe the man in whom, through whom, something has been said to me. Were I to attempt it, that would be the end of saying. This man is not my object; I have got to do with him. Perhaps I have to accomplish something about him; but perhaps I have only to learn something, and it is only a matter of my "accepting." It may be that I have to answer at once, to this very man before me; it may be that the saying has a long and manifold transmission before it, and that I am to answer some other person at some other time and place, in who knows what kind of speech, and that it is now only a matter of taking the answering on myself. But in each instance a word demanding an answer has happened to me.

We may term this way of perception *becoming aware.* It by no means needs to be a man of whom I become aware. It can be an animal, a plant, a stone. No kind of appearance or event is fundamentally excluded from the series of the things through which from time to time something is said to me. Nothing can refuse to be the vessel for the Word. The limits of the possibility of dialogue are the limits of awareness.

[. . .]

SECTION TWO: LIMITATION

The Realms

The realms of the life of dialogue and the life of monologue do not coincide with the realms of dialogue and monologue even when forms without sound and even without gesture are included. There are not merely great spheres of the life of dialogue which in appearance are not dialogue, there is also dialogue which is not the dialogue of life, that is, it has the appearance but not the essence of dialogue. At times, indeed, it seems as though there were only this kind of dialogue.

I know three kinds. There is genuine dialogue—no matter whether spoken or silent—where each of the participants really has in mind the other or others in their present and particular being and turns to them with the intention of establishing a living mutual relation between himself and them. There is technical dialogue, which is prompted solely by the need of objective understanding. And there is monologue disguised as dialogue, in which two or more men, meeting in space, speak each with himself in strangely tortuous and circuitous ways and yet imagine they have escaped the torment of being thrown back on their own resources. The first kind, as I have said, has become rare; where it arises, in no matter how "unspiritual" a form, witness is borne on behalf of the continuance of the organic substance of the human spirit. The second belongs to the inalienable sterling quality of "modern existence." But real dialogue is here continually hidden in all kinds of odd corners and, occasionally in an unseemly way, breaks surface surprisingly and inopportunely—certainly still oftener it is arrogantly tolerated than downright scandalizing—as in the tone of a railway guard's voice, in the glance of an old newspaper vendor, in the smile of the chimney-sweeper. And the third. . . .

A *debate* in which the thoughts are not expressed in the way in which they existed in the mind but in the speaking are so pointed that they may strike home in the sharpest way, and moreover without the men that are spoken to being regarded in any way present as persons; a *conversation* characterized by the need neither to communicate something nor to learn something nor to influence someone nor to come into connexion with someone, but solely by the desire to have one's own self-reliance confirmed by marking the impression that is made, or if it has become unsteady to have it strengthened; a *friendly chat* in which each regards himself as absolute and legitimate and the other as relativized and questionable; a *lovers' talk* in which both partners alike enjoy their own glorious soul and their precious experience—what an underworld of faceless spectres of dialogue!

The life of dialogue is not one in which you have much to do with men, but one in which you really have to do with those with whom you have to do. It is not the solitary man who lives the life of monologue, but he who is incapable of making real in the context of being the community in which, in the context of his destiny, he moves. It is, in fact, solitude which is able to show the innermost nature of the contrast. He who is living the life of dialogue receives in the ordinary course of the hours something that is said and feels himself approached for an answer. But also in the vast blankness of, say, a companionless mountain wandering that which confronts him, rich in change, does not leave him. He who is

living the life of monologue is never aware of the other as something that is absolutely not himself and at the same time something with which he nevertheless communicates. Solitude for him can mean mounting richness of visions and thoughts but never the deep intercourse, captured in a new depth, with the incomprehensibly real. Nature for him is either an *état d'âme,* hence a "living through" in himself or it is a passive object of knowledge, either idealistically brought within the soul or realistically alienated. It does not become for him a word apprehended with senses of beholding and feeling.

Being, lived in dialogue, receives even in extreme dereliction a harsh and strengthening sense of reciprocity; being, lived in monologue, will not, even in the tenderest intimacy, grope out over the outlines of the self.

This must not be confused with the contrast between "egoism" and "altruism" conceived by some moralists. I know people who are absorbed in "social activity" and have never spoken from being to being with a fellow-man. I know others who have no personal relation except to their enemies, but stand in such a relation to them that it is the enemies' fault if the relation does not flourish into one of dialogue.

Nor is dialogic to be identified with love. I know no one in any time who has succeeded in loving every man he met. Even Jesus obviously loved of "sinners" only the loose, lovable sinners, sinners against the Law; not those who were settled and loyal to their inheritance and sinned against him and his message. Yet to the latter as to the former he stood in a direct relation. Dialogic is not to be identified with love. But love without dialogic, without real outgoing to the other, reaching to the other, and companying with the other, the love remaining with itself—this is called Lucifer.

Certainly in order to be able to go out to the other you must have the starting place, you must have been, you must be, with yourself. Dialogue between mere individuals is only a sketch, only in dialogue between persons is the sketch filled in. But by what could a man from being an individual so really become a person as by the strict and sweet experiences of dialogue which teach him the boundless contents of the boundary?

What is said here is the real contrary of the cry, heard at times in twilight ages, for universal unreserve. He who can be unreserved with each passer-by has no substance to lose; but he who cannot stand in a direct relation to each one who meets him has a fulness which is futile. Luther is wrong to change the Hebrew "companion" (out of which the Seventy had already made one who is near, a neighbour) into "nearest." . . . If everything concrete is equally near, equally nearest, life with the world ceases to have articulation and structure, it ceases to have human meaning. But nothing needs to mediate between me and one of my companions in the companionship of creation, whenever we come near one another, because we are bound up in relation to the same centre.

The Basic Movements

I term basic movement an essential action of man (it may be understood as an "inner" action, but it is not there unless it is there to the very tension of the eyes' muscles and the very action of the foot as it walks), round which an essential attitude is built up. I do not think of this happening in time, as though the single action preceded the lasting attitude; the latter rather has its truth in the accomplishing, over and over again, of the basic movement, without forethought but also without habit. Otherwise the attitude would have only aesthetic or perhaps also political significance, as a beautiful and as an effective lie. The familiar maxim, "An attitude must first be adopted, the rest follows of itself" ceases to be true in the circle of essential action and essential attitude—that is, where we are concerned with the wholeness of the person.

The basic movement of the life of dialogue is the turning towards the other. That, indeed, seems to happen every hour and quite trivially. If you look at someone and address him you turn to him, of course with the body, but also in the requisite measure with the soul, in that you direct your attention to him. But what of all this is an essential action done with the essential being? In this way, that out of the incomprehensibility of what lies to hand this one person steps forth and becomes a presence. Now to our perception the world ceases to be an insignificant multiplicity of points to one of which we pay momentary attention. Rather it is a limitless tumult round a narrow breakwater, brightly outlined and able to bear heavy loads—limitless, but limited by the breakwater, so that, though not engirdled, it has become finite in itself, been given form, released from its own indifference. And yet none of the contacts of each hour is unworthy to take up from our essential being as much as it may. For no man is without strength for expression, and our turning towards him brings about a reply, however imperceptible, however quickly smothered, in a looking and sounding forth of the soul that are perhaps dissipating in mere inwardness and yet do exist. The notion of modern man that this turning to the other is sentimental and does not correspond to the compression of life today is a grotesque error, just as his affirmation that turning to the other is impractical in the bustle of this life today is only the masked confession of his weakness of initiative when confronted with the state of the time. He lets it dictate to him what is possible or permissible, instead of stipulating, as an unruffled partner, what is to be stipulated to the state of *every* time, namely, what space and what form it is bound to concede to creaturely existence.

The basic movement of the life of monologue is not turning away as opposed to turning towards; it is "reflexion."

When I was eleven years of age, spending the summer on my grandparents' estate, I used, as often as I could do it unobserved, to steal into the stable and gently stroke the neck of my darling, a broad dapple-grey horse. It was not a casual delight but a great, certainly friendly, but also deeply stirring happening. If I am to explain it now, beginning from the still very fresh memory of my hand, I must say that what I experienced in touch with the animal was the Other, the immense otherness of the Other, which, however, did not remain strange like the otherness of the ox and the ram, but rather let me draw near and touch it. When I stroked the mighty mane, sometimes marvellously smooth-combed, at other times just as astonishingly wild, and felt the life beneath my hand, it was as though the element of vitality itself bordered on my skin, something that was not I, was certainly not akin to me, palpably the other, not just another, really the Other itself; and yet it let me approach, confided itself to me, placed itself elementally in the relation of *Thou* and *Thou* with me. The horse, even when I had not begun by pouring oats for him into the manger, very gently raised his massive head, ears flicking, then snorted quietly, as a conspirator gives a signal meant to be recognizable only by his fellow-conspirator; and I was approved. But once—I do not know what came over the child, at any rate it was childlike enough—it struck me about the stroking, what fun it gave me, and suddenly I became conscious of my hand. The game went on as before, but something had changed, it was no longer the same thing. And the next day, after giving him a rich feed, when I stroked my friend's head he did not raise his head. A few years later, when I thought back to the incident, I no longer supposed that the animal had noticed my defection. But at the time I considered myself judged.

Reflexion is something different from egoism and even from "egotism." It is not that a man is concerned with himself, considers himself, fingers himself, enjoys, idolizes and bemoans himself; all that can be added, but it is not integral to reflexion. (Similarly, to the turning towards the other, completing it, there can be added the realizing of the other in his particular existence, even the encompassing of him, so that the situations common to him and oneself are experienced also from his, the other's, end.) I term it reflexion when a man withdraws from accepting with his essential being another person in his particularity—a particularity which is by no means to be circumscribed by the circle of his own self, and though it substantially touches and moves his soul is in no way immanent in it—and lets the other exist only as his own experience, only as a "part of myself." For then dialogue becomes a fiction, the mysterious intercourse between two human worlds only a game, and in the rejection of the real life confronting him the essence of all reality begins to disintegrate.

The Wordless Depths

Sometimes I hear it said that every *I and Thou* is only superficial, deep down word and response cease to exist, there is only the one primal being unconfronted by another. We should plunge into the silent unity, but for the rest leave its relativity to the life to be lived, instead of imposing on it this absolutized *I* and absolutized *Thou* with their dialogue.

Now from my own unforgettable experience I know well that there is a state in which the bonds of the personal nature of life seem to have fallen away from us and we experience an undivided unity. But I do not know—what the soul willingly imagines and indeed is bound to imagine (mine too once did it)—that in this I had attained to a union with the primal being or the godhead. That is an exaggeration no longer permitted to the responsible understanding. Responsibly—that is, as a man holding his ground before reality—I can elicit from those experiences only that in them I reached an undifferentiable unity of myself without form or content. I may call this an original pre-biographical unity and suppose that it is hidden unchanged beneath all biographical change, all development and complication of the soul. Nevertheless, in the honest and sober account of the responsible understanding this unity is nothing but the unity of this soul of mine, whose "ground" I have reached, so much so, beneath all formations and contents, that my spirit has no choice but to understand it as the groundless. . . . But the basic unity of my own soul is certainly beyond the reach of all the multiplicity it has hitherto received from life, though not in the least beyond individuation, or the multiplicity of all the souls in the world of which it is one—existing but once, single, unique, irreducible, this creaturely one: one of the human souls and not the "soul of the All"; a defined and particular being and not

"Being"; the creaturely basic unity of a creature, bound to God as in the instant before release the creature is to the *creator spiritus,* not bound to God as the creature to the *creator spiritus* in the moment of release.

The unity of his own self is not distinguishable in the man's feeling from unity in general. For he who in the act or event of absorption is sunk beneath the realm of all multiplicity that holds sway in the soul cannot experience the cessation of multiplicity except as unity itself. That is, he experiences the cessation of his own multiplicity as the cessation of mutuality, as revealed or fulfilled absence of otherness. The being which has become one can no longer understand itself on this side of individuation nor indeed on this side of *I and Thou.* For to the border experience of the soul "one" must apparently mean the same as "the One."

But in the actuality of lived life the man in such a moment is not above but beneath the creaturely situation, which is mightier and truer than all ecstasies. He is not above but beneath dialogue. He is not nearer the God who is hidden above *I and Thou,* and he is farther from the God who is turned to men and who gives himself as the *I* to a *Thou* and the *Thou* to an *I,* than that other who in prayer and service and life does not step out of the position of confrontation and awaits no wordless unity, except that which perhaps bodily death discloses.

Nevertheless, even he who lives the life of dialogue knows a lived unity: the unity of *life,* as that which once truly won is no more torn by any changes, not ripped asunder into the everyday creaturely life and the "deified" exalted hours; the unity of unbroken, raptureless perseverance in concreteness, in which the word is heard and a stammering answer dared.

[. . .]

Community

In the view customary to-day, which is defined by politics, the only important thing in groups, in the present as in history, is what they aim at and what they accomplish. Significance is ascribed to what goes on within them only in so far as it influences the group's action with regard to its aim. Thus it is conceded to a band conspiring to conquer the state power that the comradeship which fills it is of value, just because it strengthens the band's reliable assault power. Precise obedience will do as well, if enthusiastic drill makes up for the associates remaining strangers to one another; there are indeed good grounds for preferring the rigid system. If the group is striving even to reach a higher form of society then it can seem dangerous if in the life of the group itself something of this higher form begins to be realized in embryo. For from such a premature seriousness a suppression of the "effective" impetus is feared. The opinion apparently is that the man who whiles away his time as a guest on an oasis may be accounted lost for the project of irrigating the Sahara.

[. . .]

The feeling of community does not reign where the desired change of institutions is wrested in common, but without community, from a resisting world. It reigns where the fight that is fought takes place from the position of a community struggling for its own reality as a community. But the future too is decided here at the same time; all political "achievements" are at best auxiliary troops to the effect which changes the very core, and which is wrought on the unsurveyable ways of secret history by the moment of realization. No way leads to any other goal but to that which is like it.

But who in all these massed, mingled, marching collectivities still perceives what that is for which he supposes he is striving—what community is? They have all surrendered to its counterpart. Collectivity is not a binding but a bundling together: individuals packed together, armed and equipped in common, with only as much life from man to man as will inflame the marching step. But community, growing community (which is all we have known so far) is the being no longer side by side but *with* one another of a multitude of persons. And this multitude, though it also moves towards one goal, yet experiences everywhere a turning to, a dynamic facing of, the other, a flowing from *I* to *Thou.* Community is where community happens. Collectivity is based on an organized atrophy of personal existence, community on its increase and conformation in life lived towards one another. The modern zeal for collectivity is a flight from community's testing and consecration of the person, a flight from the vital dialogic, demanding the staking of the self, which is in the heart of the world.

[. . .]

SECTION THREE: CONFIRMATION

Conversation With the Opponent

I hope for two kinds of readers for these thoughts: for the *amicus* who knows about the reality to which I am pointing with a finger I should like to be able to stretch out like Grünewald's Baptist; and for the *hostis* or *adversarius* who denies this reality and therefore contends with me, because I point to it (in his view misleadingly) as to a reality. Thus he takes what is said here just as seriously as I myself do, after long waiting writing what is to be written—just as seriously, only with the negative sign. The mere *inimicus,* as which I regard everyone who wishes to relegate me to the realm of ideology and there let my thoughts count, I would gladly dispense with.

I need say nothing at this point to the *amicus.* The hour of common mortality and the common way strikes in his and in my ears as though we stood even in the same place with one another and knew one another.

But it is not enough to tell the *adversarius* here what I am pointing at—the hiddenness of his personal life, his secret, and that, stepping over a carefully avoided threshold, he will discover what he denies. It is not enough. I dare not turn aside his gravest objection. I must accept it, as and where it is raised, and must answer.

So now the *adversarius* sits, facing me in his actual form as he appears in accordance with the spirit of the time, and speaks, more above and beyond me than towards and to me, in accents and attitude customary in the universal duel, free of personal relation.

"In all this the actuality of our present life, the conditioned nature of life as a whole, is not taken into account. All that you speak of takes place in the never-never-land, not in the social context of the world in which we spend our days, and by which if by anything our reality is defined. Your 'two men' sit on a solitary seat, obviously during a holiday journey. In a big city office you would not be able to let them sit, they would not reach the 'sacramental' there. Your 'interrupted conversation' takes place between intellectuals who have leisure a couple of months before the huge mass event to spin fantasies of its prevention through a spiritual influence. That may be quite interesting for people who are not taken up with any duty. But is the business employee to 'communicate himself without reserve' to his colleagues? Is the worker at the conveyor belt to 'feel himself addressed in what he experiences'? Is the leader of a gigantic technical undertaking to 'practise the responsibility of dialogue'? You demand that we enter into the situation which approaches us, and you neglect the enduring situation in which everyone of us, so far as we share in the life of community, is elementally placed. In spite of all references to concreteness, all that is pre-war individualism in a revised edition."

And I, out of a deep consciousness of how almost impossible it is to think in common, if only in opposition, where there is no common experience, reply.

Before all, dear opponent, if we are to converse with one another and not at and past one another, I beg you to notice that I do not demand. I have no call to that and no authority for it. I try only to say that there is something, and to indicate how it is made: I simply record. And how could the life of dialogue be demanded? There is no ordering of dialogue. It is not that you *are* to answer but that you *are able.*

You are really able. The life of dialogue is no privilege of intellectual activity like dialectic. It does not begin in the upper story of humanity. It begins no higher than where humanity begins. There are no gifted and ungifted here, only those who give themselves and those who withhold themselves. And he who gives himself tomorrow is not noted to-day, even he himself does not know that he has it in himself, that we have it in ourselves, he will just find it, "and finding be amazed."

You put before me the man taken up with duty and business. Yes, precisely him I mean, him in the factory, in the shop, in the office, in the mine, on the tractor, at the printing-press: man. I do not seek for men. I do not seek men out for myself, I accept those who are there, I have them, I have him, in mind, the yoked, the wheel-treading, the conditioned. Dialogue is not an affair of spiritual luxury and spiritual luxuriousness, it is a matter of creation, of the creature, and he is that, the man of whom I speak, he is a creature, trivial and irreplaceable.

In my thoughts about the life of dialogue I have had to choose the examples as "purely" and as much in the form of paradigm as memory presented them to me in order to make myself intelligible about what has become so unfamiliar, in fact so sunk in oblivion. For this reason I appear to draw my tales from the province which you term the "intellectual," in reality only from the province where things succeed, are rounded off, in fact are exemplary. But I am not concerned with the pure; I am concerned with the turbid, the repressed, the pedestrian, with toil and dull contraryness—and with the break-through. With the break-through and not with a perfection, and moreover with the break-through not out of despair with its murderous and renewing powers; no, not with the great catastrophic break-through which happens once for all (it is fitting to be silent for a while about that, even in one's own heart), but with the breaking through from the status of the dully-tempered disagreeableness, obstinacy, and contraryness in which the man, whom I pluck at random out of the tumult, is living and out of which he can and at times does break through.

Whither? Into nothing exalted, heroic or holy, into no Either and no Or, only into this tiny strictness and grace of every day, where I have to do with just the very same "reality" with whose duty and business I am taken up in such a way, glance to glance, look to look, word to word, that I experience it as reached to me and myself to it,

it as spoken to me and myself to it. And now, in all the clanking of routine that I called my reality, there appears to me, homely and glorious, the effective reality, creaturely and given to me in trust and responsibility. We do not find meaning lying in things nor do we put it into things, but between us and things it can happen.

It is not sufficient, dear opponent, first of all to ascribe to me the pathos of "all or nothing" and then to prove the impossibility of my alleged demand. I know neither what all nor what nothing is, the one appears to me to be as inhuman and contrived as the other. What I am meaning is the simple *quantum satis* of that which this man in this hour of his life is able to fulfil and to receive—if he gives himself. That is, if he does not let himself be deceived by the compact plausibility that there are places excluded from creation, that he works in such a place and is able to return to creation when his shift is over; or that creation is outstripped, that it once was but is irrevocably over, now there is business and now it is a case of stripping off all romanticism, gritting the teeth and getting through with what is recognized as necessary. I say—if he does not let himself be deceived.

No factory and no office is so abandoned by creation that a creative glance could not fly up from one working-place to another, from desk to desk, a sober and brotherly glance which guarantees the reality of creation which is happening—*quantum satis*. And nothing is so valuable a service of dialogue between God and man as such an unsentimental and unreserved exchange of glances between two men in an alien place.

But is it irrevocably an alien place? Must henceforth, through all the world's ages, the life of the being which is yoked to business be divided in two, into alien "work" and home "recovery"? More, since evenings and Sundays cannot be freed of the workday character but are unavoidably stamped with it, must such a life be divided out between the business of work and the business of recovery without a remainder of directness, of unregulated surplus—of freedom? (And the freedom I mean is established by no new order of society.)

Or does there already stir, beneath all dissatisfactions that can be satisfied, an unknown and primal and deep dissatisfaction for which there is as yet no recipe of satisfaction anywhere, but which will grow to such mightiness that it dictates to the technical leaders, the promoters, the inventors, and says, "Go on with your rationalizing, but humanize the rationalizing *ratio* in yourselves. Let it introduce the living man into its purposes and its calculations, him who longs to stand in a mutual relation with the world." Dear opponent, does the longing already stir in the depths—an impulse to great construction or a tiny spark of the last revolution—to fill business with the life of dialogue? That is, in the formulation of the *quantum satis,* the longing for an order of work in which business is so continually soaked in vital dialogic as the tasks to be fulfilled by it allow? And of the extent to which they can allow it there is scarcely an inkling to-day, in an hour when the question which I put is at the mercy of the fanatics, blind to reality, who conform to the time, and of the heralds, blind to possibility, of the impervious tragedy of the world.

Be clear what it means when a worker can experience even his relation to the machine as one of dialogue, when, for instance, a compositor tells that he has understood the machine's humming as "a merry and grateful smile at me for helping it to set aside the difficulties and obstructions which disturbed and bruised and pained it, so that now it could run free." Must even you not think then of the story of Androclus and the Lion?

But when a man draws a lifeless thing into his passionate longing for dialogue, lending it independence and as it were a soul, then there may dawn in him the presentiment of a world-wide dialogue, a dialogue with the world-happening that steps up to him even in his environment, which consists partly of things. Or do you seriously think that the giving and taking of signs halts on the threshold of that business where an honest and open spirit is found?

You ask with a laugh, can the leader of a great technical undertaking practise the responsibility of dialogue? He can. For he practises it when he makes present to himself in its concreteness, so far as he can, *quantum satis,* the business which he leads. He practises it when he experiences it, instead of as a structure of mechanical centres of force and their organic servants (among which latter there is for him no differentiation but the functional one), as an association of persons with faces and names and biographies, bound together by a work that is represented by, but does not consist of, the achievements of a complicated mechanism. He practises it when he is inwardly aware, with a latent and disciplined fantasy, of the multitude of these persons, whom naturally he cannot separately know and remember as such; so that now, when one of them for some reason or other steps really as an individual into the circle of his vision and the realm of his decision, he is aware of him without strain not as a number with a human mask but as a person. He practises it when he comprehends and handles these persons as persons—for the greatest part necessarily indirectly, by means of a system of mediation which varies according to the extent, nature and structure of the undertaking, but also directly, in the parts which concern him by way of organization. Naturally at first both camps, that of capital and that of the proletariat, will decry his masterly attitude of fantasy as fantastic nonsense and his practical attitude to persons as dilettantist. But just as naturally only until his increased figures of production accredit him in their eyes. (By this of course is not to be implied that those increases necessarily come to pass: between truth and success there is no prestabilized harmony.) Then, to be sure, something worse will follow. He will be pragmatically imitated, that is, people will try to use his "procedure" without his way of thinking and imagining. But this demoniac element inherent in spiritual history (think only of all the magicizing of religion) will, I think, shipwreck here on the power of discrimination in men's souls. And meanwhile it is to be hoped that a new generation will arise, learning from what is alive, and will take all this in real seriousness as he does.

Unmistakably men are more and more determined by "circumstances." Not only the absolute mass but also the relative might of social objectives is growing. As one determined partially by them the individual stands in each moment before concrete reality which wishes to reach out to him and receive an answer from him; laden with the situation he meets new situations. And yet in all the multiplicity and complexity he has remained Adam. Even now a real decision is made in him, whether he faces the speech of God articulated to him in things and events—or escapes. And a creative glance towards his fellow-creature can at times suffice for response.

Man is in a growing measure sociologically determined. But this growing is the maturing of a task not in the "ought" but in the "may" and in "need," in longing and in grace. It is a matter of renouncing the pantechnical mania or habit with its easy "mastery" of every situation; of taking everything up into the might of dialogue of the genuine life, from the trivial mysteries of everyday to the majesty of destructive destiny.

The task becomes more and more difficult, and more and more essential, the fulfilment more and more impeded and more and more rich in decision. All the regulated chaos of the age waits for the break-through, and wherever a man perceives and responds, he is working to that end.

17

THE HERMENEUTICAL EXPERIENCE

HANS-GEORG GADAMER

Hermeneutical experience is concerned with *tradition*. This is what is to be experienced. But tradition is not simply a process that experience teaches us to know and govern; it is *language*—i.e., it expresses like a Thou. A Thou is not an object; it relates itself to us. It would be wrong to think that this means that what is experienced in tradition is to be taken as the opinion of another person, a Thou. Rather, I maintain that the understanding of tradition does not take the traditionary text as an expression of another person's life, but as a meaning that is detached from the person who means it, from an I or a Thou. Still, the relationship to the Thou and the meaning of experience implicit in that relation must be capable of teaching us something about hermeneutical experience. For tradition is a genuine partner in dialogue, and we belong to it as does the I with a Thou.

It is clear that the *experience of the Thou* must be special because the Thou is not an object but is in relationship with us. For this reason the elements we have emphasized in the structure of experience will undergo a change. Since here the object of experience is a person, this kind of experience is a moral phenomenon—as is the knowledge acquired through experience, the understanding of the other person. Let us therefore consider the change that occurs in the structure of experience when it is experience of the Thou and when it is hermeneutical experience.

There is a kind of experience of the Thou that tries to discover typical behavior in one's fellowmen and can make predictions about others on the basis of experience. We call this knowledge of human nature. We can understand the other person in the same way that we understand any other typical event in our experiential field—i.e., he is predictable. His behavior is as much a means to our end as any other means. From the moral point of view this orientation toward the Thou is purely self-regarding and contradicts the moral definition of man. As we know, in interpreting the categorical imperative Kant said,

SOURCE: Gadamer, H.-G. (1989). *Truth and method* (2nd ed.; J. Weinsheimer & D. Marshall, Trans.; excerpts from pp. 358–369, 378–379, 383–385, 387–388, 401–404). New York: Crossroad. Excerpts from *Truth and Method,* Second, Revised edition by Hans-Georg Gadamer. Translation rev. by J. Weinsheimer & D. G. Marshall. English translation, second revised edition, © 1989 by The Crossroad Publishing Company. Reprinted with the permission of the publisher, The Continuum International Publishing Group.

239

inter alia, that the other should never be used as a means but always as an end in himself.

If we relate this form of the I-Thou relation—the kind of understanding of the Thou that constitutes knowledge of human nature to the hermeneutical problem, the equivalent is naive faith in method and in the objectivity that can be attained through it. Someone who understands tradition in this way makes it an object—i.e., he confronts it in a free and uninvolved way—and by methodically excluding everything subjective, he discovers what it contains. We saw that he thereby detaches himself from the continuing effect of the tradition in which he himself has historical reality. It is the method of the social sciences, following the methodological ideas of the eighteenth century and their programmatic formulation by Hume, ideas that are a clichéd version of scientific method.[1] But this covers only part of the actual procedure of the human sciences, and even that is schematically reduced, since it recognizes only what is typical and regular in behavior. It flattens out the nature of hermeneutical experience in precisely the same way as we have seen in the teleological interpretation of the concept of induction since Aristotle.

A second way in which the Thou is experienced and understood is that the Thou is acknowledged as a person, but despite this acknowledgment the understanding of the Thou is still a form of self-relatedness. Such self-regard derives from the dialectical appearance that the dialectic of the I-Thou relation brings with it. This relation is not immediate but reflective. To every claim there is a counterclaim. That is why it is possible for each of the partners in the relationship reflectively to outdo the other. One claims to know the other's claim from his point of view and even to understand the other better than the other understands himself. In this way the Thou loses the immediacy with which it makes its claim. It is understood, but this means it is co-opted and preempted reflectively from the standpoint of the other person. Because it is a mutual relationship, it helps to constitute the reality of the I-Thou relationship itself. The inner historicity of all the relations in the lives of men consists in the fact that there is a constant struggle for mutual recognition. This can have very varied degrees of tension, to the point of the complete domination of one person by the other. But even the most extreme forms of mastery and slavery are a genuine dialectical relationship of the kind that Hegel has elaborated.[2]

The experience of the Thou attained here is more adequate than what we have called the knowledge of human nature, which merely seeks to calculate how the other person will behave. It is an illusion to see another person as a tool that can be absolutely known and used. Even a slave still has a will to power that turns against his master, as Nietzsche rightly said.[3] But the dialectic of reciprocity that governs all I-Thou relationships is inevitably hidden from the consciousness of the individual. The servant who tyrannizes his master by serving him does not believe that he is serving his own aims by doing so. In fact, his own self-consciousness consists precisely in withdrawing from the dialectic of this reciprocity, in reflecting himself out of his relation to the other and so becoming unreachable by him. By understanding the other, by claiming to know him, one robs his claims of their legitimacy. In particular, the dialectic of charitable or welfare work operates in this way, penetrating all relationships between men as a reflective form of the effort to dominate. The claim to understand the other person in advance functions to keep the other person's claim at a distance. We are familiar with this from the teacher-pupil relationship, an authoritative form of welfare work. In these reflective forms the dialectic of the I-Thou relation becomes more clearly defined.

In the hermeneutical sphere the parallel to this experience of the Thou is what we generally call *historical consciousness*. Historical consciousness knows about the otherness of the other, about the past in its otherness, just as the understanding of the Thou knows the Thou as a person. In the otherness of the past it seeks not the instantiation of a general law but something historically unique. By claiming to transcend its own conditionedness completely in knowing the other, it is involved in a false dialectical appearance, since it is actually seeking to master the past, as it were. This need not be accompanied by the speculative claim of a philosophy of world history; as an ideal of perfect enlightenment, it sheds light on the process of experience in the historical sciences, as we find, for example, in Dilthey. In my analysis of hermeneutical consciousness I have shown that the dialectical illusion which historical consciousness creates, and which corresponds to the dialectical illusion of experience perfected and replaced by knowledge, is the unattainable ideal of the Enlightenment. A person who believes he is free of prejudices, relying on the objectivity of his procedures and denying that he is himself conditioned by historical circumstances, experiences the power of the prejudices that unconsciously dominate him as a vis a tergo. A person who does not admit that he is dominated by prejudices will fail to see what manifests itself by their light. It is like the relation between I and Thou. A person who reflects himself out of the mutuality of such a relation changes this relation and destroys its moral bond. *A person who reflects himself out of a living relationship to tradition destroys the true meaning of this tradition in exactly the same way.* In seeking to understand tradition historical consciousness must not rely on the critical method with which it approaches its sources, as if this preserved it from mixing in its own judgments and prejudices. It must, in fact, think within its own historicity. To be situated within a tradition does not limit the freedom of knowledge but makes it possible.

Knowing and recognizing this constitutes the third, and highest, type of hermeneutical experience: the openness to tradition characteristic of historically effected consciousness. It too has a real analogue in the experience of the Thou. In human relations the important thing is, as we have seen, to experience the Thou truly as a Thou—i.e., not to overlook his claim but to let him really say something to us. Here is where openness belongs. But ultimately this openness does not exist for the person who speaks; rather anyone who listens is fundamentally open. Without such openness to one another there is no genuine human bond. Belonging together always

also means being able to listen to one another. When two people understand each other, this does not mean that one person "understands" the other. Similarly, "to hear and obey someone" (auf jemanden hören) does not mean simply that we do blindly what the other desires. We call such a person slavish (hörig). Openness to the other, then, involves recognizing that I myself must accept some things that are against me, even though no one else forces me to do so.

[. . .]

This indicates the direction our inquiry must take. We will now examine the *logical structure of openness* that characterizes hermeneutical consciousness, recalling the importance of the concept of the question to our analysis of the hermeneutical situation. It is clear that the structure of the question is implicit in all experience. We cannot have experiences without asking questions. Recognizing that an object is different, and not as we first thought, obviously presupposes the question whether it was this or that. From a logical point of view, the openness essential to experience is precisely the openness of being either this or that. It has the structure of a question. And just as the dialectical negativity of experience culminates in the idea of being perfectly experienced i.e., being aware of our finitude and limitedness so also the logical form of the question and the negativity that is part of it culminate in a radical negativity: the knowledge of not knowing. This is the famous Socratic docta ignorantia which, amid the most extreme negativity of doubt, opens up the way to the true superiority of questioning. We will have to consider *the essence of the question* in greater depth if we are to clarify the particular nature of hermeneutical experience.

The essence of the question is to have sense. Now sense involves a sense of direction. Hence the sense of the question is the only direction from which the answer can be given if it is to make sense. A question places what is questioned in a particular perspective. When a question arises, it breaks open the being of the object, as it were. Hence the logos that explicates this opened up being is an answer. Its sense lies in the sense of the question.

Among the greatest insights that Plato's account of Socrates affords us is that, contrary to the general opinion, it is more difficult to ask questions than to answer them. When the partners in the Socratic dialogue are unable to answer Socrates' awkward questions and try to turn the tables by assuming what they suppose is the preferable role of the questioner, they come to grief.[4] Behind this comic motif in the Platonic dialogues there is the critical distinction between authentic and inauthentic dialogue. To someone who engages in dialogue only to prove himself right and not to gain insight, asking questions will indeed seem easier than answering them. There is no risk that he will be unable to answer a question. In fact, however, the continual failure of the interlocutor shows that people who think they know better cannot even ask the right questions. In order to be able to ask, one must want to know, and that means knowing that one does not know. In the comic confusion between question and answer, knowledge and ignorance that Plato describes, there is a profound recognition of the *priority of the question* in all knowledge and discourse that really reveals something of an object. Discourse that is intended to reveal something requires that that thing be broken open by the question.

For this reason, dialectic proceeds by way of question and answer or, rather, the path of all knowledge leads through the question. To ask a question means to bring into the open. The openness of what is in question consists in the fact that the answer is not settled. It must still be undetermined, awaiting a decisive answer. The significance of questioning consists in revealing the questionability of what is questioned. It has to be brought into this state of indeterminacy, so that there is an equilibrium between pro and contra. The sense of every question is realized in passing through this state of indeterminacy, in which it becomes an open question. Every true question requires this openness. Without it, it is basically no more than an apparent question. We are familiar with this from the example of the pedagogical question, whose paradoxical difficulty consists in the fact that it is a question without a questioner.

Or from the rhetorical question, which not only has no questioner but has no object.

The openness of a question is not boundless. It is limited by the horizon of the question. A question that lacks this horizon is, so to speak, floating. It becomes a question only when its fluid indeterminacy is concretized in a specific "this or that." In other words, the question has to be posed. Posing a question implies openness but also limitation. It implies the explicit establishing of presuppositions, in terms of which can be seen what still remains open. Hence a question can be asked rightly or wrongly, according as it reaches into the sphere of the truly open or fails to do so. We say that a question has been put wrongly when it does not reach the state of openness but precludes reaching it by retaining false presuppositions. It pretends to an openness and susceptibility to decision that it does not have. But if what is in question is not foregrounded, or not correctly foregrounded, from those presuppositions that are really held, then it is not brought into the open and nothing can be decided.

This is shown clearly in the case of the slanted question that we are so familiar with in everyday life. There can be no answer to a slanted question because it leads us only apparently, and not really, through the open state of indeterminacy in which a decision is made. We call it slanted rather than wrongly put because there is a question behind it—i.e., there is an openness intended, but it does not lie in the direction in which the slanted question is pointing. The word "slanted" refers to something that has deviated from the right direction. The slant of a question consists in the fact that it does not give any real direction, and hence no answer to it is possible. Similarly, we say that statements which are not exactly wrong but also not right are "slanted." This too is determined by their sense—i.e., by their relation to the question. We cannot call them wrong, since we detect something true about them, but neither can we properly call them right because they do not correspond to any meaningful question and hence have no correct meaning unless they are themselves corrected. Sense is always sense of direction for a possible question. Correct sense must accord with the direction in which a question points.

Insofar as a question remains open, it always includes both negative and positive judgments. This is the basis of the essential relation between question and knowledge. For it is the essence of knowledge not only to judge something correctly but, at the same time and for the same reason, to exclude what is wrong. Deciding the question is the path to knowledge. What decides a question is the preponderance of reasons for the one and against the other possibility. But this is still not full knowledge. The thing itself is known only when the counterinstances are dissolved, only when the counterarguments are seen to be incorrect.

[. . .]

There is no such thing as a method of learning to ask questions, of learning to see what is questionable. On the contrary, the example of Socrates teaches that the important thing is the knowledge that one does not know. Hence the Socratic dialectic—which leads, through its art of confusing the interlocutor, to this knowledge— creates the conditions for the question. All questioning and desire to know presupposes a knowledge that one does not know; so much so, indeed, that a particular lack of knowledge leads to a particular question.

Plato shows in an unforgettable way where the difficulty lies in knowing what one does not know. It is the power of opinion against which it is so hard to obtain an admission of ignorance. It is opinion that suppresses questions. Opinion has a curious tendency to propagate itself. It would always like to be the general opinion, just as the word that the Greeks have for opinion, doxa, also means decision made by the majority in the council assembly. How, then, can ignorance be admitted and questions arise?

Let us say first of all that it can occur only in the way any idea occurs to us. It is true that we do speak of ideas occurring to us less in regard to questions than to answers—e.g., the solution of problems; and by this we mean to say that there is no methodical way to arrive at the solution. But we also know that such ideas do not occur to us entirely unexpectedly. They always presuppose an orientation toward an area of openness from which the idea can occur—i.e., they presuppose questions. The real nature of the sudden idea is perhaps less that a solution occurs to us like an answer to a riddle than that a question occurs to us that breaks through into the open and thereby makes an answer possible. Every sudden idea has the structure of a question. But the sudden occurrence of the question is already a breach in the smooth front of popular opinion. Hence we say that a question too "occurs" to us, that it "arises" or "presents itself" more than that we raise it or present it.

We have already seen that, logically considered, the negativity of experience implies a question. In fact we have experiences when we are shocked by things that do not accord with our expectations. Thus questioning too is more a passion than an action. A question presses itself on us; we can no longer avoid it and persist in our accustomed opinion.

It seems to conflict with these conclusions, however, that the Socratic-Platonic dialectic raises the art of questioning to a conscious art; but there is something peculiar about this art. We have seen that it is reserved to the person who wants to know—i.e., who already has questions. The art of questioning is not the art of resisting the pressure of opinion; it already presupposes this freedom. It is not an art in the sense that the Greeks speak of techne, nor a craft that can be taught or by means of which we could master the discovery of truth. The so called epistemological digression of the *Seventh Letter* is directed, rather, to distinguishing the unique art of dialectic from everything that can be taught and learned. The art of dialectic is not the art of being able to win every argument. On the contrary, it is possible that someone practicing the art of dialectic—i.e., the art of questioning and of seeking truth—comes off worse in the argument in the eyes of those listening to it. As the art of asking questions, dialectic proves its value because only the person who knows how to ask questions is able to persist in his questioning, which involves being able to preserve his orientation toward openness. The art of questioning is the art of questioning ever further—i.e., the art of thinking. It is called dialectic because it is the art of conducting a real dialogue.

To conduct a dialogue requires first of all that the partners do not talk at cross purposes. Hence it necessarily has the structure of question and answer. The first condition of the art of conversation is ensuring that the other person is with us. We know this only too well from the reiterated yesses of the interlocutors in the Platonic dialogues. The positive side of this monotony is the inner logic with which the subject matter is developed in the conversation. To conduct a conversation means to allow oneself to be conducted by the subject matter to which the partners in the dialogue are oriented. It requires that one does not try to argue the other person down but that one really considers the weight of the other's opinion. Hence it is the art of testing.[5] But the art of testing is the art of questioning. For we have seen that to question means to lay open, to place in the open. As against the fixity of opinions, questioning makes the object and all its possibilities fluid. A person skilled in the "art" of questioning is a person who can prevent questions from being suppressed by the dominant opinion. A person who possesses this art will himself search for everything in favor of an opinion. Dialectic consists not in trying to discover the weakness of what is said, but in bringing out its real strength. It is not the art of arguing (which can make a strong case out of a weak one) but the art of thinking (which can strengthen objections by referring to the subject matter).

The unique and continuing relevance of the Platonic dialogues is due to this art of strengthening, for in this process what is said is continually transformed into the uttermost possibilities of its rightness and truth, and overcomes all opposition that tries to limit its validity. Here again it is not simply a matter of leaving the subject undecided. Someone who wants to know something cannot just leave it a matter of mere opinion, which is to say that he cannot hold himself aloof from the opinions that are in question.[6] The speaker (der Redende) is put to the question (zur Rede gestellt) until the truth of what is under discussion

(wovon der Rede ist) finally emerges. The maieutic productivity of the Socratic dialogue, the art of using words as a midwife, is certainly directed toward the people who are the partners in the dialogue, but it is concerned merely with the opinions they express, the immanent logic of the subject matter that is unfolded in the dialogue. What emerges in its truth is the logos, which is neither mine nor yours and hence so far transcends the interlocutors' subjective opinions that even the person leading the conversation knows that he does not know. As the art of conducting a conversation, dialectic is also the art of seeing things in the unity of an aspect (sunoran eis heneidos)—i.e., it is the art of forming concepts through working out the common meaning. What characterizes a dialogue, in contrast with the rigid form of statements that demand to be set down in writing, is precisely this: that in dialogue spoken language—in the process of question and answer, giving and taking, talking at cross purposes and seeing each other's point—performs the communication of meaning that, with respect to the written tradition, is the task of hermeneutics. Hence it is more than a metaphor; it is a memory of what originally was the case, to describe the task of hermeneutics as entering into dialogue with the text. That this interpretation is performed by spoken language does not mean that it is transposed into a foreign medium; rather, being transformed into spoken language represents the restoration of the original communication of meaning. When it is interpreted, written tradition is brought back out of the alienation in which it finds itself and into the living present of conversation, which is always fundamentally realized in question and answer.

[. . .]

The primacy of conversation can also be seen in derivative forms in which the relation between question and answer is obscured. Letters, for example, are an interesting intermediate phenomenon: a kind of written conversation that, as it were, stretches out the movement of talking at cross purposes and seeing each other's point. The art of writing letters consists in not letting what one says become a treatise on the subject but in making it acceptable to the correspondent. But on the other hand it also consists in preserving and fulfilling the standard of finality that everything stated in writing has. The time lapse between sending a letter and receiving an answer is not just an external factor, but gives this form of communication its special nature as a particular form of writing. So we note that speeding up the post has not improved this form of communication but, on the contrary, has led to a decline in the art of letter writing.

[. . .]

When we try to examine the hermeneutical phenomenon through the model of conversation between two persons, the chief thing that these apparently so different situations—understanding a text and reaching an understanding in a conversation—have in common is that both are concerned with a subject matter that is placed before them. Just as each interlocutor is trying to reach agreement on some subject with his partner, so also the interpreter is trying to understand what the text is saying. This understanding of the subject matter must take the form of language. It is not that the understanding is subsequently put into words; rather, the way understanding occurs—whether in the case of a text or a dialogue with another person who raises an issue with us—is the coming-into-language of the thing itself. Thus we will first consider the structure of dialogue proper, in order to specify the character of that other form of dialogue that is the understanding of texts. Whereas up to now we have framed the constitutive significance of the *question* for the hermeneutical phenomenon in terms of conversation, we must now demonstrate the linguisticality of dialogue, which is the basis of the question, as an element of hermeneutics.

Our first point is that the language in which something comes to speak is not a possession at the disposal of one or the other of the interlocutors. Every conversation presupposes a common language, or better, creates a common language. Something is placed in the center, as the Greeks say, which the partners in dialogue both share, and concerning which they can exchange ideas with one another. Hence reaching an understanding on the subject matter of a conversation necessarily means that a common language must be first worked out in the conversation. This is not an external matter of simply adjusting our tools; nor is it even right to say that the partners adapt themselves to one another but, rather, in a successful conversation they both come under the influence of the truth of the object and are thus bound to one another in a new community. To reach an understanding in a dialogue is not merely a matter of putting oneself forward and successfully asserting one's own point of view, but being transformed into a communion in which we do not remain what we were.[7]

[. . .]

We say that we "conduct" a conversation, but the more genuine a conversation is, the less its conduct lies within the will of either partner. Thus a genuine conversation is never the one that we wanted to conduct. Rather, it is generally more correct to say that we fall into conversation, or even that we become involved in it. The way one word follows another, with the conversation taking its own twists and reaching its own conclusion, may well be conducted in some way, but the partners conversing are far less the leaders than the led. No one knows in advance what will "come out" of a conversation. Understanding or its failure is like an event that happens to us. Thus we can say that something was a good conversation or that it was ill fated. All this shows that a conversation has a spirit of its own, and that the language in which it is conducted bears its own truth within it—i.e., that it allows something to "emerge" which henceforth exists.

In our analysis of romantic hermeneutics we have already seen that understanding is not based on transposing oneself into another person, on one person's immediate participation with another. To understand what a person says is, as we saw, to come to an understanding about the subject matter, not to get inside another person and relive his experiences (Erlebnisse). We emphasized that the experience (Erfahrung) of meaning that takes place in understanding always includes application. Now we are to note *that this whole process is verbal*. It is not for nothing that the special problematic of understanding and the attempt to master it as an art—the concern of hermeneutics—belongs traditionally to the sphere of grammar and rhetoric. Language is the medium in which substantive understanding and agreement take place between two people.

In situations where coming to an understanding is disrupted or impeded, we first become conscious of the conditions of all understanding. Thus the verbal process whereby a conversation in two different languages is made possible through translation is especially informative. Here the translator must translate the meaning to be understood into the context in which the other speaker lives. This does not, of course, mean that he is at liberty to falsify the meaning of what the other person says. Rather, the meaning must be preserved, but since it must be understood within a new language world, it must establish its validity within it in a new way. Thus every translation is at the same time an interpretation. We can even say that the translation is the culmination of the interpretation that the translator has made of the words given him.

The example of translation, then, makes us aware that language as the medium of understanding must be consciously created by an explicit mediation. This kind of explicit process is undoubtedly not the norm in a conversation. Nor is translation the norm in the way we approach a foreign language. Rather, having to rely on translation is tantamount to two people giving up their independent authority. Where a translation is necessary, the gap between the spirit of the original words and that of their reproduction must be taken into account. It is a gap that can never be completely closed. But in these cases understanding does not really take place between the partners of the conversation, but between the interpreters, who can really have an encounter in a common world of understanding. (It is well known that nothing is more difficult than a dialogue in two different languages in which one person speaks one and the other person the other, each understanding the other's language but not speaking it. As if impelled by a higher force, one of the languages always tries to establish itself over the other as the medium of understanding.)

Where there is understanding, there is not translation but speech. To understand a foreign language means that we do not need to translate it into our own. When we really master a language, then no translation is necessary—in fact, any translation seems impossible. Understanding how to speak is not yet of itself real understanding and does not involve an interpretive process; it is an accomplishment of life. For you understand a language by living in it—a statement that is true, as we know, not only of living but dead languages as well. Thus the hermeneutical problem concerns not the correct mastery of language but coming to a proper understanding about the subject matter, which takes place in the medium of language. Every language can be learned so perfectly that using it no longer means translating from or into one's native tongue, but thinking in the foreign language. Mastering the language is a necessary precondition for coming to an understanding in a conversation. Every conversation obviously presupposes that the two speakers speak the same language. Only when two people can make themselves understood through language by talking together can the problem of understanding and agreement even be raised. Having to depend on an interpreter's translation is an extreme case that doubles the hermeneutical process, namely the conversation: there is one conversation between the interpreter and the other, and a second between the interpreter and oneself.

Conversation is a process of coming to an understanding. Thus it belongs to every true conversation that each person opens himself to the other, truly accepts his point of view as valid and transposes himself into the other to such an extent that he understands not the particular individual but what he says. What is to be grasped is the substantive rightness of his opinion, so that we can be at one with each other on the subject. Thus we do not relate the other's opinion to him but to our own opinions and views. Where a person is concerned with the other as individuality—e.g., in a therapeutic conversation or the interrogation of a man accused of a crime—this is not really a situation in which two people are trying to come to an understanding.[8]

Everything we have said characterizing the situation of two people coming to an understanding in conversation has a genuine application to hermeneutics, which is concerned with *understanding texts.*

[. . .]

Reaching an understanding in conversation presupposes that both partners are ready for it and are trying to realize the full value of what is alien and opposed to them. If this happens mutually, and each of the partners, while simultaneously holding on to his own arguments, weighs the counter-arguments, it is finally possible to achieve—in an imperceptible but not arbitrary reciprocal translation of the other's position (we call this an exchange of views)—a common diction and a common dictum.

[. . .]

In bridging the gulf between languages, the translator clearly exemplifies the reciprocal relationship that exists between interpreter and text, and that corresponds to the reciprocity involved in reaching an understanding in conversation. For every translator is an interpreter. The fact that a foreign language is being translated means that this is simply an extreme case of hermeneutical difficulty—i.e., of alienness and its conquest. In fact all the "objects" with which traditional hermeneutics is concerned are alien in the same unequivocally defined sense. The translator's task of re-creation differs only in degree, not in kind, from the general hermeneutical task that any text presents.

This is not to say, of course, that the hermeneutic situation in regards to texts is exactly the same as that between two people in conversation. Texts are "enduringly fixed expressions of life"[9] that are to be understood; and that means that one partner in the hermeneutical conversation, the text, speaks only through the other partner, the interpreter. Only through him are the written marks changed back into meaning. Nevertheless, in being changed back by understanding, the subject matter of which the text speaks itself finds expression. It is like a

real conversation in that the common subject matter is what binds the two partners, the text and the interpreter, to each other. When a translator interprets a conversation, he can make mutual understanding possible only if he participates in the subject matter under discussion; so also in relation to a text it is indispensable that the interpreter participate in its meaning.

Thus it is perfectly legitimate to speak of a *hermeneutical conversation.* But from this it follows that hermeneutical conversation, like real conversation, finds a common language, and that finding a common language is not, any more than in real conversation, preparing a tool for the purpose of reaching understanding but, rather, coincides with the very act of understanding and reaching agreement. Even between the partners of this "conversation" a communication like that between two people takes place that is more than mere accommodation. The text brings a subject matter into language, but that it does so is ultimately the achievement of the interpreter. Both have a share in it.

[. . .]

We must rightly understand the fundamental priority of language asserted here. Indeed, language often seems ill suited to express what we feel. In the face of the overwhelming presence of works of art, the task of expressing in words what they say to us seems like an infinite and hopeless undertaking. The fact that our desire and capacity to understand always go beyond any statement that we can make seems like a critique of language. But this does not alter the fundamental priority of language. The possibilities of our knowledge seem to be far more individual than the possibilities of expression offered by language. Faced with the socially motivated tendency toward uniformity with which language forces understanding into particular schematic forms which hem us in, our desire for knowledge tries to escape from these schematizations and predecisions. However, the critical superiority which we claim over language pertains not to the conventions of verbal expression but to the conventions of meaning that have become sedimented in language. Thus that superiority says nothing against the essential connection between understanding and language. In fact it confirms this connection. For all critique that rises above the schematism of our statements in order to understand finds its expression in the form of language. Hence language always forestalls any objection to its jurisdiction. Its universality keeps pace with the universality of reason. Hermeneutical consciousness only participates in what constitutes the general relation of equivalence to its possible interpretation, and if there are basically no bounds set to understanding, then the verbal form in which this understanding is interpreted must contain within it an infinite dimension that transcends all bounds. Language is the language of reason itself.

One says this, and then one hesitates. For this makes language so close to reason—which means, to the things it names—that one may ask why there should be different languages at all, since all seem to have the same proximity to reason and to objects. When a person lives in a language, he is filled with the sense of the unsurpassable appropriateness of the words he uses for the subject matter he is talking about. It seems impossible that other worlds in other languages could name the things equally well. The suitable word always seems to be one's own and unique, just as the thing referred to is always unique. The agony of translation consists ultimately in the fact that the original words seem to be inseparable from the things they refer to, so that to make a text intelligible one often has to give an interpretive paraphrase of it rather than translate it. The more sensitively our historical consciousness reacts, the more it seems to be aware of the untranslatability of the unfamiliar. But this makes the intimate unity of word and thing a hermeneutical scandal. How can we possibly understand anything written in a foreign language if we are thus imprisoned in our own?

It is necessary to see the speciousness of this argument. In actual fact the sensitivity of our historical consciousness tells us the opposite. The work of understanding and interpretation always remains meaningful. This shows the superior universality with which reason rises above the limitations of any given language. The hermeneutical experience is the corrective by means of which the thinking reason escapes the prison of language, and it is itself verbally constituted.

From this point of view the problem of language does not present itself in the same way as *philosophy of language* raises it. Certainly the variety of languages in which linguistics is interested presents us with a question. But this question is simply how every language, despite its difference from other languages, can say everything it wants. Linguistics teaches us that every language does this in its own way. But we then ask how, amid the variety of these forms of utterance, there is still the same unity of thought and speech, so that everything that has been transmitted in writing can be understood. Thus we are interested in the opposite of what linguistics tries to investigate.

The intimate unity of language and thought is the premise from which linguistics too starts. It is this alone that has made it a science. For only because this unity exists is it worthwhile for the investigator to make the abstraction which causes language to be the object of his research. Only by breaking with the conventionalist prejudices of theology and rationalism could Herder and Humboldt learn to see languages as views of the world. By acknowledging the unity of thought and language they could envision the task of comparing the various forms of this unity. We are starting from the same insight but going, as it were, in the opposite direction. Despite the multiplicity of ways of speech, we are trying to keep in mind the indissoluble unity of thought and language as we encounter it in the hermeneutical phenomenon, namely as the unity of understanding and interpretation.

Thus the question that concerns us is *the conceptual character* of all understanding. This only appears to be a secondary question. We have seen that conceptual interpretation is the realization of the hermeneutical experience itself. That is why our problem is so difficult. The interpreter does not know that he is bringing himself and his own concepts into the interpretation. The verbal formulation is so much part of the interpreter's mind that he never becomes aware of it as an object. Thus it is understandable that this side of the hermeneutic process has been wholly ignored. But there is the further point that the situation has been confused by incorrect *theories of language.* It is obvious that an instrumentalist theory of signs which sees words and concepts as handy tools has missed the point of the hermeneutical phenomenon. If we stick to what takes place in speech and, above all, in every dialogue with tradition carried on by the human sciences, we cannot fail to see that here concepts are constantly in the process of being formed. This does not mean that the interpreter is using new or unusual words. But the capacity to use familiar words is not based on an act of logical subsumption, through which a particular is placed under a universal concept. Let us remember, rather, that understanding always includes an element of application and thus produces an ongoing process of concept formation. We must consider this now if we want to liberate the verbal nature of understanding from the presuppositions of philosophy of language. The interpreter does not use words and concepts like a craftsman who picks up his tools and then puts them away. Rather, we must recognize that all understanding is interwoven with concepts and reject any theory that does not accept the intimate unity of word and subject matter.

Indeed, the situation is even more difficult. It is doubtful that the *concept of language* that modern linguistics and philosophy of language take as their starting point is adequate to the situation. It has recently been stated by some linguists—and rightly so—that the modern concept of language presumes a verbal consciousness that is itself a product of history and does not apply to the beginning of the historical process, especially to what language was for the Greeks.[10] From the complete unconsciousness of language that we find in classical Greece, the path leads to the instrumentalist devaluation of language that we find in modern times. This process of increasing consciousness, which also involves a change in the attitude to language, makes it possible for "language" as such—i.e., its form, separated from all content—to become an independent object of attention.

We can doubt whether this view's characterization of the relation between language behavior and language theory is correct, but there is no doubt that the science and philosophy of language operate on the premise that their only concern is the *form* of language. Is the idea of form still appropriate here? Is language a symbolic form, as Cassirer calls it? Does this take account of the fact that language is unique in embracing everything—myth, art, law, and so on—that Cassirer also calls symbolic form?[11]

In analyzing the hermeneutical phenomenon we have stumbled upon the universal function of language. In revealing the verbal nature of the hermeneutical phenomenon, we see that it has a universal significance. Understanding and interpretation are related to verbal tradition in a specific way. But at the same time they transcend this relationship not only because all the creations of human culture, including the nonverbal ones, can be understood in this way, but more fundamentally because everything that is intelligible must be accessible to understanding and to interpretation. What is true of understanding is just as true of language. Neither is to be grasped simply as a fact that can be empirically investigated. Neither is ever simply an object but instead comprehends everything that can ever be an object.[12]

NOTES

1. Cf. our remarks on this in the "Introduction" *[in Truth and Method].*

2. Cf. the outstanding analysis of this reflective dialectic of I and Thou in Karl Löwith, *Das Individuum in der Rolle des Mitmenschen* (1928) and my review of it in *Logos,* 18 (1929) [*GW,* IV].

3. *Thus Spake Zarathustra,* II, "Of self-overcoming."

4. Cf. the argument concerning the form of discourse in the *Protagoras,* 355ff.

5. Aristotle, *Metaphysics,* 1004 b 25: *esti de he dialektike peirastike.* Here we can already discern the idiom of being led, which is the real sense of dialectic, in that the testing of an opinion gives it the chance to conquer and hence puts one's own previous opinion at risk.

6. See above pp. 292f., 336f.

7. Cf. my "Was ist Wahrheit?," *Kleine Schriften,* I, 46–58 (*GW,* II, 44–56).

8. If one transposes oneself into the position of another with the intent of understanding not the truth of what he is saying, but him, the questions asked in such a conversation are marked by the inauthenticity described above (pp. 362f.).

9. Droysen, *Historik,* ed. Hübner (1937), p. 63.

10. Johannes Lohmann in *Lexis* III and elsewhere.

11. Cf. Ernst Cassirer, *Wesen und Wirkung des Symbolbegriffs* (1956), which chiefly contains the essays published in the Wartburg Library Series. R. Hönigswald, *Philosophie und Sprache* (1937), starts his critique here.

12. Hönigswald puts it this way: "Language is not only a fact, but a principle" (op. cit., p. 448).

18

DECONSTRUCTING COMMUNICATION

BRIANKLE G. CHANG

Till human voices wake us, and we drown.

—T. S. Eliot

Don't start from the good old things, but the bad new ones.

—Bertolt Brecht

Imagine three situations:

1. Someone came and said something to me. I understood her, I knew what she wanted, and I responded. We talked for a while until we both had to leave. A few days later, I had forgotten about the incident. I did not remember who she was, and I did not remember what we talked about. I know incidents like this have happened before, and I know similar events will happen again. Looking back at it now, I cannot say that I know anything about it—I have forgotten about *that* incident.

2. Someone dropped by my office to say hello. Glad to see him, I invited him in. We chatted about the weather and the news, all the while sipping tea. Hours later, he left, and I went back to my work. This has happened before, though not as frequently as I would like. But right now, that is not something I worry about; in fact, after he left, I did not think much about our visit—except that I vaguely remember that we both enjoyed it.

3. Someone came and said something to me. This time, something strange happened. I did not understand what she was saying, and I did not know how to respond. I was puzzled, and I am still puzzled. An incident like this, as far as I can recollect, has never happened to me before, and I would hate to experience it again. But right now, I cannot help thinking about it; I cannot

SOURCE: Chang, B. G. (1996). *Deconstructing communication: Representation, subject, and economies of exchange.* Minneapolis, MN: University of Minnesota Press. ("Conclusion," pages 221–228.)

help wondering what has happened or why it happened, although I still do not have the vaguest idea what she said, and I do not think I would know how to respond if it were to happen again. I felt stupid then, and I feel stupid now. Perhaps it was my fault; perhaps . . .

In each of these situations, something happened: Someone came to me and said something. Silence was broken; utterances were made; as a result, life's flow was interrupted, momentarily. In the first and second situations, not only did the visitor say something to me, but I also responded in kind. What ensued could only be described as a conversation, a free exchange in which meaningful sounds replaced the silence that characterized our individual existence before the encounter. In that exchange, information—significant or trivial—was shared; questions—intelligent or foolish—were asked and answered; issues—pressing or irrelevant—were discussed; mutual concerns—sincere or pretended—were expressed. Because of this exchange, we understood one another a little better; because of this exchange, we, as Schutz might say, grew a little older together—aging through time spent talking to one another. Despite the semantic mobility of the word *communication,* we can justifiably conclude that there was a situation of communication: There took place (an event of) communication, an event that occurred as the happening of mutual understanding.

Not all conversations are equally memorable; every conversation does not impact on our lives equally. In fact, most of the conversations we have, save perhaps a few precious ones, are forgotten shortly after the event. Life goes on, as the cliché goes, irrespective of the little interruptions that talk might create. As in the first situation, the conversation that occupied me for a while soon evaporated after the fact, receding into nothingness, becoming irretrievable. Looking back now, I do not remember a thing. It is as if nothing happened.

That most conversations soon recede into nothingness after the fact can occur for a reason other than either our forgetfulness or the lack of clarity of what was talked about. A different

kind of "nothingness" can take over our communication, weakening its force, depleting its significance, until the event leaves no vestige of itself and becomes indistinguishable from the first kind of nothingness. This is what happened in the second situation: Someone visited me, and we had a pleasant conversation. But it was a conversation about nothing, about nothing in particular, for no sooner did the conversation begin than it slipped into utter triviality, into the vapidity of a quotidian act whose purpose, despite the momentary pleasure it afforded, was, as we say, to kill time. Although the utterances exchanged between my visitor and me were neither garbled nor indecipherable nor meaningless, the conversation as a whole did not *mean* anything; it was limited, as it were, to the *there* and *then* and was quickly swamped by the mindless routine of life, becoming shapeless, faded, and finally, gone. What we said to one another has become, for all its clarity at the moment, an idle vehicle, a vehicle without content, a vehicle in which "nothing" was said. What happened in this case can only be called "chatter" or "idle talk"—a kind of communication in which nothing of consequence is communicated except the act of communicating itself, its ritualistic insignificant repetitions. In this situation, "the vehicles of communication," as Peter Fenves puts it, "carry nothing of *weight.*Communication continues to take place, and its pace may very well accelerate, but everything is still somehow idle. In such non-movement—or incessant movement at a standstill—empty and idle talk finds its point of departure: the vehicle of communication, language as structure and act, remains in operation, but it no longer *works,* for whatever it carries is somehow 'nothing.' "[1] In a way similar to what happened in the first situation, a comparable nothingness also took over the communication between me and my second visitor.

That even the most enjoyable of all our conversations can deflate into "idle chatter," spiraling down to "nothingness," reflects the fact that, as existentialists are never tired of saying, we live for the most part *inauthentically.* To the extent that *inauthenticity,* which, one should note, does not connote any moral or ethical deficiency, characterizes our ordinary mode of being, idle chatter, its about-nothingness, will never cease to haunt the episodes of our conversing acts without which what is called the social would not even be able to ascend above its epiphenomenal threshold. In view of the two kinds of nothingness that routinely annihilate our communication, the third situation becomes singularly interesting—not merely because it poses an intellectual problem or practical exigency, but because it creates an uncanny dislocation in me, an existential crisis that no experience and no wisdom can alleviate.

In contrast to what took place in the first two situations, something profoundly strange happened in the third one. Someone came and said something to me, but instead of responding, I became speechless. In fact, I was at a complete loss, unable to make any sense of what was happening. Silence was broken, but it soon resumed. I heard something, but frustration or a sense of my own stupidity was my only response, a silent response that only widened the gap of nonrecognition between her and me. I had every reason to believe that she must have said and meant something, but her message, as it were, remained null, incapable of reaching me. Her message, if it carried what she intended it to mean, appeared too "proper to" her to be communicative, too pure to mean anything to me, that is, too idio(t)lectic not to lapse into sheer noise, into a string of disturbing sounds that remind me of, among other things, my stupidity or ineptitude. This idiolectic message formed a rift between us by forming a void in me. Consequently, there was no exchange, no understanding, and we can only conclude, no communication.

Yes, there was an event; yes, an event began, barely, when she began to say something. But this event did not come to fruition, for nothing, nothing really, happened—except a sudden defamiliarization of my world, an unforeseen estrangement brought about by the least violent of all acts—the mere emitting of sounds—that toppled the sense-structure of my life world.

After she breached my silent existence, silence returned, devouring both of us again by expropriating my ability to respond. So nothing, nothing really, happened. But this nothing, compared to "idle chatter" and the "forgetfulness" of an ordinary conversation, was much more dramatic. It produced in me an effect like no other. Considering what happened, or rather, what failed to take place, I must confess that I was profoundly affected by it. In fact, I am still living that event through the unique nothingness brought home to me by the incident, suffering from it, agonizing over it as an event that keeps returning as a nonevent. In any case, the undeniable fact is that there *was* an event, there *took place* a situation that, although nothing, nothing really, happened in it, is still happening now. It was like a traumatic "primal scene," forever gone but constantly coming back.

It is not difficult to see that, contrary to the current widespread ideology, the only communication worth its name takes place in situations like the third one. These situations, despite their variable forms and contents, display the possibility, in a much more powerful fashion than do the first two, of demonstrating the criteria by which we determine whether an event is truly communicative or not. "Something is communicated to me in a strong sense, or *there is* an event of communication," as Geoffrey Bennington remarks, "only when I do not have available to me the means to decode a transparent message. This implies that there is communication only when there is a moment, however minimal, of nonunderstanding, of *stupidity* with respect to what is said."[2] *Communication thus implies noncomprehension,* for I am most firmly placed in a situation of communication with the other only when I recognize that someone has come to me but do not understand why and do not quite understand what he, she, or it says. Was there even an utterance? Was that utterance, if there was one, directed toward me? If so, why? It is this sense of apprehension or uncertainty about what is to unfold and the subsequent noncomprehension of what is unfolding that open the space of communication from which it is always too late for one to retreat.

As Bennington concludes: "Communication takes place, if at all, in a fundamental and irreducible uncertainty as to the very fact and possibility of communication."[3]

The truth of communication thus shows itself to be duplicitous: Communication can actually take place when it *appears not to* take place, and it can appear to take place when actually it fails to even begin. This possible failure of communication, the "irreducible uncertainty" implied in the very fact of communication, as reflected in my stupid noncomprehension vis-à-vis my visitor, is constitutive of communication in the same way that silence is constitutive of sounds, or that noise is constitutive of transmittable signals. As can now be inferred from my last hypothetical scenario, the constitutive stupidity on my part, taken to the limit, means that the space of communication is most radically itself, most radically open to the coming of the other, when I am not even sure whether someone has come and said something. At the same time, and from a slightly different point of view, it also means that communication becomes virtual only when its space is heterogeneous, when it is invaded by an alien, an inscrutable other that embodies a void, a nothing as the I-know-not-what, which I, having been invited into that space, cannot ignore. It is this alien invasion that creates a crisis in me, and it is this crisis that causes the event of communication to occupy me, to take its place in me—in spite of its nothingness, in spite of the void it induces in me.

Here we arrive at the most radical of the conclusions about communication that I have tried to convey: The impossibility of communication is the birth *to* its possibility. Recall my visitor in the third situation. By uttering to me meaningless sounds, she might be trying to avoid being communicative. But her very attempt to avoid communication testifies to the force of its necessity and thus confirms the singular law of communication—communication cannot *not* take place—one of whose effects, as I became painfully aware, is my uncanny experience of feeling stupid. The communication of a void therefore does not and cannot avoid communication, for "a void of communication," as Fenves critically observes, "is communicated whenever communication is avoided."[4] Whether my visitor intended it or not, her avoiding communication nevertheless communicates a void to me. As long as she came to me, the "not" of her communication cannot not be, which is to say, her noncommunication is an impossibility.

That the impossibility of communication constitutes its possibility means that communication knows no negativity, that "a 'not' of communication is under every condition impossible."[5] This is not simply because there is a theoretical difficulty in literally and genuinely communicating about nothing, or that incommunicability, to the extent that it can be formulated into a concept, can always be communicated; rather, it is because even noncommunication, or successful refusal to communicate, such as deliberate silence, voluntary mutism, counterfactual fabrications, or a masterful feigning of stupidity, carries with it at every turn the promise, which is to say the threat, of its own negation.

This impossibility of annulling communication, taken to the limit, reveals that communication is governed—even before it begins—by (the force of) an imperative that binds the one to the other in an authorless contract. "When someone (?) comes (?) and says (?) something (?)," I immediately enter into the space of an imperative, just as he/she/it does.[6] Immediately and imperceptibly, there emerges an unsigned but effective contract between us, indispensable to what is taking place, namely, that you, the addresser, are addressing me, the addressee. This contract communicates to us, before our communication, its force—forcing us to obey, forcing upon us the demand to respond. Communicated to us as an imperative, this demand cannot be excommunicated. It is a universal demand of exchange that interpellates the self and the other as communicating subjects by interpolating both into a measureless cycle of credit and debit, giving and returning, taking and keeping. As such, it demands our responsibility to respond to one another, despite the fact that I do not understand what you say, and that you are uncertain whether I will be saying anything back at all. By laying down the law for respons(e)ibility irrespective of the possibility that that response may not be forthcoming, this demand legislates promise, establishing a contract capable of having itself enforced in the future. This contract of anticipatory response, based on the decree of reciprocity, thus nullifies the possibility of any negativity of communication by bringing about a *contra*communication: a communication against (non)communication, a communication that crosses itself out by communicating.[7]

Seen in this light, we, as communicating subjects, can no longer be regarded as free agents who choose (or choose not) to communicate. For the exoteric autonomy of the subjects in communication, of my visitors and me, and of everyone else, too, is in effect a conditioned freedom bestowed on us by a prior contract. Agency, as the freedom *to* exchange, therefore means the universal responsibility to honor a contract delivered to us by we-know-not-what and from we-know-not-where. It is by obeying this imperative that we, as communicators, can be free *to* communicate as well as *not to* communicate.

Communication cannot not take place. This is the paradoxical freedom of communication, the unbearable freedom that one cannot not communicate, even if one chooses not to do so. One cannot not communicate; "communication cannot be avoided even when the void of communication, its negativity, is communicated."[8] This is the agony of communication, the ordeal of the *autonomos* of the communicating subjects, caused by what I called earlier the "postal paradox of communication." This agony, this ordeal, accompanies communication at every turn. As a result, we, the communicating subjects, are both autonomous and other-dependent—free to receive as well as to reject the other and yet bound to play this double role by the contractual force of an *an-archic* imperative. By the same token, communication theorists, to the extent that their metareflective statements say something—intelligible or not—about communication, are destined to reenact the same double play, exhibiting, in their very enunciations, the kind of duplicity that cannot not take place whenever one meets and says something to the other. That being the case, theorizing, particularly theorizing about communication, will never be more than an exploration. I choose the word *exploration* purposefully. Exploration does not entail end; it does not guarantee any final discovery any more than it predicts the attainability of some ultimate truth. Always *liminal,* that is, always *transitional,* communication theories, like any conversation worth its name, will never be able to have the last word on the subject matter they choose to address; their ostensive ending— whether it is caused by the addresser's avoidance of being communicative, by the addressee's stupid noncomprehension, or by the message's own vacuousness—is but a promise that another ending will come.

Ending, like beginning, cannot but take place. One way to end—arbitrarily and temporarily, of course—my argument in this book is to say that communication, like such philosophemes as presence, identity, origin, structure, and the like, is an *undecidable.* By focusing on the universal media of communication, sign and meaning, the purpose of my analysis has been to show that all communicative events, to the extent that they manage to transmit certain messages, are internally split and therefore thwarted by the very acts that materialize them. This, as Derrida reminds us, and as any deconstructive analysis worth the name demonstrates, "is something that happens—it just happens."[9] It happens in the ancient "quarrel" between philosophy and poetry (Plato's *diaphora*); it happens when philosophical heroism (Hegel) meets homoerotic fantasies (Genet); it happens when speech-act theory (John Searle) begins to speak to grammatology (Derrida); and I know it happens between conversing friends, as evidenced by my hypothetical scenario. Although its happening is never *thetic* (which in Greek means "to place," which is *ponere/positum* in Latin), it will certainly take place whenever someone comes and says something. So the best way for me to end this written communication is to repeat what I have been trying to say all along: Communication is possible and is impossible. If communication is anything at all, it is an *undecidable.* As you, my reader, can see now, I can only return in the end to where I began: "Il faut Parler. Parler sans pouvoir." One must communicate, communicate without the ability to do so.

NOTES

---

1. Peter Fenves, *"Chatter": Language and History in Kierkegaard* (Stanford, Calif.: Stanford University Press, 1993), p. 2.

2. Geoffrey Bennington, *Legislations: The Politics of Deconstruction* (London: Verso, 1994), p. 2.

3. Ibid.

4. Peter Fenves, *"Chatter,"* p. 145.

5. Ibid., pp. 143–44.

6. Geoffrey Bennington, *Legislations,* p. 2.

7. Peter Fenves, *"Chatter,"* pp. 149–50. My use of the term "*contra*communication" differs slightly from Fenves's use.

8. Ibid., p. 146.

9. Gary A. Olson, "Jacques Derrida on Rhetoric and Composition: A Conversation," *Journal of Advanced Composition* 10, no. 1 (1990): 12.

PROJECTS FOR PHENOMENOLOGICAL THEORIZING

ADDITIONAL READINGS ON PHENOMENOLOGY

A. To learn more about the phenomenological tradition in communication theory: Anton (2001); Chang (1996); Langsdorf (1994); Lanigan (1992); Pilotta and Mickunas (1990).

B. To learn more about theories of dialogue: Anderson, Baxter, and Cissna (2004).

C. To learn more about hermeneutics: Heidegger (1927/1996), Gadamer (1960/1989), and Ricoeur (1990/1992) for key philosophical works; Palmer (1969) for a concise history; Deetz (1990) for applications to interpersonal communication.

APPLICATION EXERCISE

To explore phenomenological dialogue, try the following three exercises. First, talk to someone you know until you find something that you disagree on. Continue to talk to each other until both of you can articulate the other person's opinion. Second, talk to someone who looks different than you do. Talk to them until you find something about which you have a different perspective. Continue to talk until both of you can articulate both the perspective of the other and the experiences of the other that led to the other having that perspective. Third, talk to someone who you think holds different beliefs-values than you do. Talk to that person until you are both able to articulate three things: the other person's contrasting belief, what led the other person to have that belief, and something on which the two of you agree. How were experiences of these three exercises similar and different from each other?

PROJECTS

1. An important moment in the history of dialogue occurred in 1957 in a public interview between Buber and Rogers, a psychotherapist famous for his influential work in client-centered therapy. Communication scholars Rob Anderson and Kenneth Cissna have published an edited transcript (Anderson & Cissna, 1997) and extensive commentary (Cissna & Anderson, 2002) on the Buber-Rogers dialogue. Arnett (1986) also compared Buber's and Rogers's theories. Key writings include Buber (1923/1987, 1947/2002) and Rogers (1961, 1970). Compare these two views of dialogue with regard to their assumptions about concepts such as human nature, the self, and relationships. How are they similar and different in their approach to practical problems?

2. Bohm (1996), a prominent British physicist, developed a popular approach to dialogue that has received relatively little comment from communication scholars. Compare Bohm's ideas about dialogue to Buber on the I-Thou relationship, Rogers on encounters and client-centered therapy, and Gadamer on genuine conversation.

What is distinctive about Bohm's approach? Critique the underlying assumptions of Bohm's theory from a phenomenological viewpoint.

3. Phenomenological theorists are often critical of rhetoric for ethical reasons, regarding it as a form of monologue or inauthentic (strategic) communication. What would each of the theorists in this unit probably have to say about rhetoric? Would some be more accepting of rhetoric than others? How do these views of rhetoric compare with Plato's and Foss and Griffin's critiques (unit III)? Also see Cissna and Anderson's chapter, "A Rhetorical Approach to Dialogue" (2002, pp. 15–34). Is dialogue a practical alternative to the art of rhetoric for conducting public discourse?

4. The role of semiotic signs and symbols in communication is disputed by phenomenologists. Stewart (1995, 1996) is a communication theorist who has been particularly critical of what he calls "the symbol model," defining communication instead as unmediated "articulate contact" between people. In this unit's readings, Buber writes about wordless dialogue and Gadamer criticizes the semiotic philosophy of language. Also compare Anton's (1999) view on this issue. Which phenomenological thinkers have most influenced Stewart's critique of semiotics? How might the various semiotic thinkers in unit IV respond to his critique? Are semiotics and phenomenology incompatible? Are both traditions useful for addressing different kinds of communication problems? Have semiotic phenomenologists such as Lanigan (1992) succeeded in combining the two traditions?

5. Phenomenological ideas about dialogue and openness to others seem particularly relevant to social problems related to diversity, identity, and difference (of social class, gender, sexuality, race-ethnicity, religion, etc.). Anderson et al. (2004) subtitled their book on dialogue *Theorizing Difference in Communication Studies*. Take for example the personal experiences in higher education reported by Allen, Orbe, and Olivas (1999). Do the readings in this unit provide

helpful ways of talking about those experiences? What are the prospects for productive dialogue between members of different racial and ethnic groups in our society? For somewhat contrasting views in the academic context, see the chapters by Deetz and Simpson and by McPhail in Anderson et al. (2004).

REFERENCES

Allen, B. J., Orbe, M. P., & Olivas, M. R. (1999). The complexity of our tears: Dis/enchantment and (in)difference in the academy. *Communication Theory, 9*, 402–429.

Anderson, R., Baxter, L. A., & Cissna, K. N. (Eds.). (2004). *Dialogue: Theorizing difference in communication studies*. Thousand Oaks, CA: Sage.

Anderson, R., & Cissna, K. N. (1997). *The Martin Buber-Carl Rogers dialogue: A new transcript with commentary*. Albany: State University of New York Press.

Anton, C. (1999). Beyond the constitutive-representational dichotomy: The phenomenological notion of intentionality. *Communication Theory, 9*, 26–57.

Anton, C. (2001). *Selfhood and authenticity*. Albany: State University of New York Press.

Arnett, R. C. (1986). *Communication and community: Implications of Martin Buber's dialogue*. Carbondale: Southern Illinois University Press.

Bohm, D. (1996). *On dialogue* (L. Nichol, Ed.). London: Routledge.

Buber, M. (1987). *I and thou* (R. G. Smith, Trans.; 2nd ed.). New York: Scribners. (Original work published 1923)

Buber, M. (2002). *Between man and man*. New York: Routledge. (Original work published 1947)

Chang, B. G. (1996). *Deconstructing communication: Representation, subject, and economies of exchange*. Minneapolis: University of Minnesota Press.

Cissna, K. N., & Anderson, R. (2002). *Moments of meeting: Buber, Rogers, and the potential for public dialogue*. Albany: State University of New York Press.

Deetz, S. (1990). Reclaiming the subject matter as a guide to mutual understanding: Effectiveness and ethics in interpersonal interaction. *Communication Quarterly, 38*, 226–243.

Gadamer, H.-G. (1989). *Truth and method* (J. Weinsheimer & D. Marshall, Trans.; 2nd ed.). New York: Crossroad. (Original work published 1960)

Heidegger, M. (1996). *Being and time: A translation of Sein und Zeit* (J. Stambaugh, Trans.). Albany: State University of New York Press. (Original work published 1927)

Langsdorf, L. (Ed.). (1994). Phenomenology in communication research [Special issue]. *Human Studies, 17*(1), 1–162.

Lanigan, R. L. (1992). *The human science of communicology: A phenomenology of discourse in Foucault and Merleau-Ponty.* Pittsburgh, PA: Duquesne University Press.

Palmer, R. E. (1969). *Hermeneutics.* Evanston, IL: Northwestern University Press.

Pilotta, J. J., & Mickunas, A. (1990). *Science of communication: Its phenomenological foundation.* Hillsdale, NJ: Lawrence Erlbaum.

Ricoeur, P. (1992). *Oneself as another* (K. Blamey, Trans.). Chicago: University of Chicago Press. (Original work published 1990)

Rogers, C. R. (1961). *On becoming a person.* Boston: Houghton Mifflin.

Rogers, C. R. (1970). *Carl Rogers on encounter groups.* New York: HarperCollins.

Stewart, J. (1995). *Language as articulate contact: Toward a post-semiotic philosophy of communication.* Albany: State University of New York Press.

Stewart, J. (Ed.). (1996). *Beyond the symbol model: Reflections on the representational nature of language.* Albany: State University of New York Press.

UNIT VI   INTRODUCTION

THE CYBERNETIC TRADITION

Playing off the title of the last reading in this section, one can ask, What is information? The cybernetic tradition conceptualizes communication as information processing, and yet what exactly is information? Is it the *ones* and *zeros* of machine language? Is it the messages sent by dogs to inform each other that what they are doing is playing and not fighting? Is it the messages of the man staring off into space on the bench at the bus stop? In the cybernetic tradition, scholars talk and think about concepts such as systems, processing, information, messages, senders, receivers, probability, entropy, self-organization, autopoiesis, and feedback. Often, theorizing in this tradition is discussed in terms of modeling. The language of mathematics and computation is common in this tradition, and yet some scholars in this tradition build their work around families, patients with mental disorders, or animal communication. One challenge in investigating this tradition is to nail down the idea of information, and yet the difficulty of isolating this central concept is as much in keeping with the tradition as the concept of information itself. The cybernetic tradition often leads to a holistic approach to understanding communication, and variations of a holistic approach can be seen in each of the readings in this unit.

The mathematical theory of information, developed by Claude Shannon and presented to a wider audience in collaboration with Warren Weaver (Shannon & Weaver, 1949; Weaver, 1949) was a landmark work that gave impetus to the cybernetic tradition. Although these readings are not included in this unit for reasons of space, the cybernetic tradition cannot be understood without some understanding of information theory. Shannon and Weaver can be seen as theorizing the *problem of achieving smooth information flow*. In his work to provide electrical engineers with a theory that could help them build better telecommunications systems, Shannon applied statistical principles to the transfer of information. The system needed to transmit information smoothly, so the information would not stack up and bog down the system—think of a continual busy signal because there is no room for more impulses to travel in the channel. To avoid such pileup, the designers of systems needed to know how much information would need to flow through the cables. The calculation of channel capacity also needed to take account of noise or random blips in a signal that interfere with the process of transmission. Using an idea of entropy that can be illustrated by the number of yes-no questions one would need to have answered to determine the answer to some given question (somewhat like the game of 20 questions), Shannon worked probabilistically to calculate the amount of information that would flow through the phone lines. The theory showed that effective transmission of information requires efficient coding of messages (logically equivalent to winning at 20 questions by asking the smallest number of questions possible). Yet effective transmission also requires a certain amount of redundancy to compensate for the presence of noise in the communication channel. Without any redundancy at all, a single blip of noise would destroy the signal. Using the mathematical formulas of information theory, engineers could build systems in which the necessary amount of information could flow smoothly.

Shannon and Weaver (1949) illustrated their theory with a linear model of communication that ever since has been commonly taught with variations as *the model of communication*. The model pictures communication by a series of boxes and arrows showing how a message flows from a communication source to a destination with noise interfering. This diagram was presented as a general model that applies to any form of communication, not just signals traveling through telephone wires. Although they acknowledged that the transmission of meaning in communication involves more than just the physical transmission of a signal, Shannon and Weaver speculated that the theory could eventually be extended to provide precise mathematical explanations of meaning and communication effects (see pp. 24–28). To make a long story short, this extension of the theory was never successfully accomplished. Therefore, although Shannon's mathematical approach continues to be useful for telecommunications engineering, its application to other aspects of human communication has been very limited and imprecise. For example, there is some value in the insight that redundancy plays a

necessary role in communication, even if the redundancy of meaning is impossible to measure precisely in any real situation. However, the one-way linear model is commonly criticized for failing to include a practically essential element of communication: feedback, the receiver's response to the message.

Feedback is the central concept of another landmark theory represented by the first reading in this unit. Writing at about the same time as Shannon and Weaver, Norbert Wiener (1948) coined the term *cybernetics*, although in our reading he tells of earlier uses of the term. The reading is taken from *The Human Use of Human Beings: Cybernetics and Society* (Wiener, 1954), a nonmathematical presentation of Wiener's theory of cybernetics for general readers. His work can be seen as theorizing the *problem of human-machine communication*. Stated generally, Wiener explains how human communication is parallel to machine communication. It is not that humans communicate one way to each other and in a different way with machines. Rather, the principles of machine communication can be used to explain human communication. In this case, information is that which is exchanged as communicators adapt to the outer world to have some control over the outer world. Communication is a response to an environment, and a message is a form of pattern and organization. Modern machines respond via their sensors, and their feedback mechanisms respond to actual performance. For example, an elevator opens when it actually reaches a floor, not when it formulaically should reach a floor. It is the feedback mechanisms that allow the system to have control rather than being taken over by nature's tendency toward disorganization.

Similarly, just like machines, human communicators receive feedback based on their actual performance, not their intentions, and these regulatory processes control the communicator's responses to the environment. In other words, we communicate in response to something (similar to the elevator call button being pushed); the feedback we receive from others is feedback to our actual communication, not what we merely intended to communicate (that is, what others actually heard and did, not what was in our minds to say); and the adjustments we make (whatever next actions we take) are based on the feedback we receive (what people actually said and did, not what happened in their minds). Thus, communication consists of feedback and response patterns. Examining society from this perspective, one can see how adjustments are made to fend off nature's tendency toward disorganization and how movement's tendency toward purposive ends becomes possible.

Gregory Bateson (1972; Ruesch & Bateson, 1968) is another important figure in the cybernetic tradition not directly represented in this volume for reasons of space (although many of his ideas are referenced by Watzlawick, Beavin, and Jackson in reading 20). His work, which used concepts from semiotics and mathematical logic to extend cybernetic theory to address distinctive aspects of interaction through signs and symbols in humans and higher animals, could be seen as theorizing *the problem of metacommunication*. Bateson examined a wide variety of interactions ranging from animal communication to therapy with mental patients. In examining animal communication, Bateson saw that dogs can tell when they are fighting and when they are playing, even though their actions when fighting or playing look very similar. Play, to Bateson, was a key evolutionary step, and animals' ability to communicate to each other that "this is play" shows their metacommunicative ability. Human interaction also is infused with these unstated metamessages. Interaction has both a *report*, or informational, aspect and a *command,* or framing, aspect, which establishes the relationship between the communicators. That we

engage in multiple layers of communication (simultaneously communicating about the frame and the message within the frame) produces a paradox of abstraction, and it is this paradox that keeps language changing and developing rather than becoming a rigid game with fixed rules. These layers of messages, if used skillfully by a therapist, can also lead to a schizophrenic changing her frame of interpretation.

The second piece in this unit builds on Bateson's ideas and theorizes a similar problem. The authors were associated with the Mental Research Institute in Palo Alto, California, members of which had worked with Bateson in earlier studies of the double bind in mental patients. The double bind is a repetitive pattern of interaction in which a victim is both confronted with contradictory messages at different levels of abstraction and prevented from leaving the situation or metacommunicating about the contradiction. For example, there could be a pattern of interaction between a mother and child in which the mother verbally says something such as *come here, I love you* while nonverbally signaling the child to stay away. The child is powerless to leave the relationship or to question the contradiction, which the mother will consistently deny. The child is likely to generalize this interactional pattern to other relationships and as a result becomes emotionally disturbed and uncommunicative. In this regard, the double bind resembles forms of "discursive closure" theorized by the critical theorist Stanley Deetz (reading 34).

The piece included here presents five axioms that Watzlawick, Beavin, and Jackson (1967) proposed as part of their calculus of human communication. These are notions that are commonly taught in interpersonal communication courses, and as one reads this piece, one can gain a deeper sense of the context of these axioms and how they are relevant for understanding interpersonal communication. For instance, the well-known axiom *one cannot not communicate* involves the accompanying notion that one cannot not respond. The man sitting on the park bench staring into space is communicating, and anyone who encounters that communication responds to it in some way, even if only by trying to appear to ignore it. The communicator and the responder are connected. They are parts of a communication system. (How does this differ from Chang's [reading 18] phenomenological argument that communication is unavoidable?)

In emphasizing and examining communication as a system, these theorists also theorize the problem of the whole. The five axioms (the impossibility of not communicating, the content and relationship levels of communication, punctuation of the sequence of events, digital and analogic communication, and symmetrical and complementary interaction) provide a set of fundamentals that draw focus to the system of communication rather than the individuals involved in the communication. This idea of looking at how the system works, rather than at the parts of the system individually, itself is a hallmark of the cybernetic tradition.

The third reading in this unit is an interesting conjunction of cybernetic (information processing) and social psychological theory applied to mass communication. Lang theorizes *the problem of information processing by television viewers*. To understand how a TV message affects viewers, intentionally and unintentionally, Lang provides a theory of cognitive processing of messages. There are three components to this processing: encoding, storage, and retrieval. However, the processing system is limited in that there are only so many processing resources available to the system. If too many resources are allocated to encoding, for example, there may not be enough resources to allow thorough storage of the message. Additionally, there are characteristics of messages, such as being unexpected,

that seem to automatically elicit encoding, and so if the message continually breaks expectations, the allocation of resources will be greatly skewed toward encoding so the receiver may encode a lot but not do much other processing. As Lang points out, although this theory can potentially lead to new models of how to construct and present TV messages, this idea of limited capacity is not limited to understanding mass media messages but can be applied to processing messages in other communication contexts as well.

The final piece in this unit is by the German social theorist Niklas Luhmann and examines the difference between the psychic system (individual consciousness) and the communication system (social). In theorizing *the problem of the systemic autonomy of communication*, using the ideas of autopoiesis and self-organizing systems, Luhmann makes the paradoxical-sounding claim that only communication communicates. Just as does consciousness, communication operates as a closed, autonomous system. What is communicated depends on the system, not on what the individual participants in the communication would like to be communicated. Although conscious entities are needed for communication to happen, they are not part of the communication per se. Communication either happens or it does not. Either a communication system organizes itself and communication happens or it does not. However, although communication and consciousness are distinct, they can disturb each other. When communication occurs, a consciousness is forced to accept or reject the communication. Because of the social-psychic divide, one can avoid the risk of communication when rejection is likely, and in fact institutions are constructed that facilitate this avoidance. Due to this divide, there are things that can be handled communicatively, but this is not the same as handling things in the individual consciousness.

After reading the pieces in this unit, the question asked at the outset may still be relevant: What is information? The question of how well this tradition holds together may also arise. How related are the notions of information and of system in these readings? Are there enough shared strands of thought that cybernetics is a distinct way of conceptualizing communication? What is it that sets this tradition apart from the others? How is the conception of information processing different from those of the art of discourse (rhetoric), shared meaning (semiotics), and experience of the other (phenomenology)? Do the thinkers in this unit seem to build on each other, or has this tradition been built by thinkers coming from different directions yet ending up proposing related ideas? How does the Luhmann piece relate to the others? What are the implications of his argument?

Scholars such as Lang may lead one to think and talk about everyday technical problems of message construction and technical system construction. How do communication systems need to be engineered? What message constructions will lead a TV viewer to attend, process, and be able to recall a televised message? Other readings may lead to thinking about the similarity and differences of machine, human, and animal communication. Do humans communicate with each other just as computers communicate with each other? Can studying animal communication provide a valuable and informative model for analyzing the process of human communication? One may want to extend from the machine-human-animal comparisons to ask more generalized questions, such as questions concerning the similarities and differences between systems of different types.

Additionally, the Lang and the Luhmann readings bring up the notion of mind. Is the mind an information processing machine? What is gained by taking this information systems approach to understanding mind? Is there a divide between the individual mind and communication? What is the relationship between communication and the individual? Is the Lang piece about mind? Is her model only applicable to the mental processing of mediated messages, or can it be used to model the processing of messages in face-to-face interaction? What is the difference between processing messages in face-to-face interaction and processing audience-directed messages such as television, movies, or even public speeches?

What about the idea of studying the whole rather than the parts? What is gained by taking this perspective? What practices can be viewed as systems? How large can a communication system be? Is a whole society, even the entire world, a communication system? Wiener seems to indicate that cybernetics can provide a grand theory that explains all communication, that understanding the technical level of communication can provide valuable insight into all other levels of communication. How plausible are those claims? Is the idea of information processing too general to be relevant to any specific communication practice?

Finally, some of the ideas in this tradition have had quite a bit of staying power. Why is this so? Why is the Shannon and Weaver model (1949) still so commonly referred to? Is it especially relevant for some reason? Why are the Watzlawick et al. (1967) axioms of communication so popularly taught in communication courses? Are these ideas taught in ways that seem in keeping with their presentation in these original texts? All of these questions are worthy of reflection, as well as some of the basic theorizing questions: What new vocabulary do you have? What do you see as a communication system that you did not previously? How do these readings support and call into question your own thoughts about communication? There are many questions that can be thought about as one reads the selections in this unit.

REFERENCES

Bateson, G. (1972). *Steps to an ecology of mind.* New York: Ballantine Books.

Ruesch, J., & Bateson, G. (1968). *Communication: The social matrix of psychiatry.* New York: W. W. Norton.

Shannon, C. E., & Weaver, W. (1949). *The mathematical theory of communication.* Urbana: University of Illinois Press.

Watzlawick, P., Beavin, J. H., & Jackson, D. D. (1967). *Pragmatics of human communication: A study of interactional patterns, pathologies, and paradoxes.* New York: W. W. Norton.

Weaver, W. (1949). The mathematics of communication. *Scientific American, 181,* 11–15.

Wiener, N. (1948). *Cybernetics.* New York: John Wiley & Sons.

Wiener, N. (1954). *The human use of human beings: Cybernetics and society.* Boston: Houghton Mifflin.

19

Cybernetics in History

Norbert Wiener

Since the end of World War II, I have been working on the many ramifications of the theory of messages. Besides the electrical engineering theory of the transmission of messages, there is a larger field which includes not only the study of language but the study of messages as a means of controlling machinery and society, the development of computing machines and other such automata, certain reflections upon psychology and the nervous system, and a tentative new theory of scientific method. This larger theory of messages is a probabilistic theory, an intrinsic part of the movement that owes its origin to Willard Gibbs and which I have described in the introduction.

Until recently, there was no existing word for this complex of ideas, and in order to embrace the whole field by a single term, I felt constrained to invent one. Hence "Cybernetics," which I derived from the Greek word kubernētēs, or "steersman," the same Greek word from which we eventually derive our word "governor." Incidentally, I found later that the word had already been used by Ampère with reference to political science, and had been introduced in another context by a Polish scientist, both uses dating from the earlier part of the nineteenth century.

I wrote a more or less technical book entitled *Cybernetics* which was published in 1948. In response to a certain demand for me to make its ideas acceptable to the lay public, I published the first edition of *The Human Use of Human Beings* in 1950. Since then the subject has grown from a few ideas shared by Drs. Claude Shannon, Warren Weaver, and myself, into an established region of research. Therefore, I take this opportunity occasioned by the reprinting of my book to bring it up to date, and to remove certain defects and inconsequentialities in its original structure.

In giving the definition of Cybernetics in the original book, I classed communication and control together. Why did I do this? When I

SOURCE: Wiener, N. (1954). *The human use of human beings: Cybernetics and society* (pp. 15–27). Boston: Houghton Mifflin.

communicate with another person, I impart a message to him, and when he communicates back with me he returns a related message which contains information primarily accessible to him and not to me. When I control the actions of another person, I communicate a message to him, and although this message is in the imperative mood, the technique of communication does not differ from that of a message of fact. Furthermore, if my control is to be effective I must take cognizance of any messages from him which may indicate that the order is understood and has been obeyed.

It is the thesis of this book that society can only be understood through a study of the messages and the communication facilities which belong to it; and that in the future development of these messages and communication facilities, messages between man and machines, between machines and man, and between machine and machine, are destined to play an ever increasing part.

When I give an order to a machine, the situation is not essentially different from that which arises when I give an order to a person. In other words, as far as my consciousness goes I am aware of the order that has gone out and of the signal of compliance that has come back. To me, personally, the fact that the signal in its intermediate stages has gone through a machine rather than through a person is irrelevant and does not in any case greatly change my relation to the signal. Thus the theory of control in engineering, whether human or animal or mechanical, is a chapter in the theory of messages.

Naturally there are detailed differences in messages and in problems of control, not only between a living organism and a machine, but within each narrower class of beings. It is the purpose of Cybernetics to develop a language and techniques that will enable us indeed to attack the problem of control and communication in general, but also to find the proper repertory of ideas and techniques to classify their particular manifestations under certain concepts.

The commands through which we exercise our control over our environment are a kind of information which we impart to it. Like any form of information, these commands are subject to disorganization in transit. They generally come through in less coherent fashion and certainly not more coherently than they were sent. In control and communication we are always fighting nature's tendency to degrade the organized and to destroy the meaningful; the tendency, as Gibbs has shown us, for entropy to increase.

Much of this book concerns the limits of communication within and among individuals. Man is immersed in a world which he perceives through his sense organs. Information that he receives is co-ordinated through his brain and nervous system until, after the proper process of storage, collation, and selection, it emerges through effector organs, generally his muscles. These in turn act on the external world, and also react on the central nervous system through receptor organs such as the end organs of kinaesthesia; and the information received by the kinaesthetic organs is combined with his already accumulated store of information to influence future action.

Information is a name for the content of what is exchanged with the outer world as we adjust to it, and make our adjustment felt upon it. The process of receiving and of using information is the process of our adjusting to the contingencies of the outer environment, and of our living effectively within that environment. The needs and the complexity of modern life make greater demands on this process of information than ever before, and our press, our museums, our scientific laboratories, our universities, our libraries and textbooks, are obliged to meet the needs of this process or fail in their purpose. To live effectively is to live with adequate information. Thus, communication and control belong to the essence of man's inner life, even as they belong to his life in society.

The place of the study of communication in the history of science is neither trivial, fortuitous, nor new. Even before Newton such problems were current in physics, especially in the work of Fermat, Huygens, and Leibnitz, each of whom shared an interest in physics whose focus was not mechanics but optics, the communication of visual images.

Fermat furthered the study of optics with his principle of minimization which says that over any sufficiently short part of its course, light follows the path which it takes the least time to traverse. Huygens developed the primitive form of what is now known as "Huygens' Principle" by saying that light spreads from a source by forming around that source something like a small sphere consisting of secondary sources which in turn propagate light just as the primary sources do. Leibnitz, in the meantime, saw the whole world as a collection of beings called "monads" whose activity consisted in the perception of one another on the basis of a pre-established harmony laid down by God, and it is fairly clear that he thought of this interaction largely in optical terms. Apart from this perception, the monads had no "windows," so that in his view all mechanical interaction really becomes nothing more than a subtle consequence of optical interaction.

A preoccupation with optics and with message, which is apparent in this part of Leibnitz's philosophy, runs through its whole texture. It plays a large part in two of his most original ideas: that of the *Characteristica Universalis,* or universal scientific language, and that of the *Calculus Ratiocinator,* or calculus of logic. This Calculus Ratiocinator, imperfect as it was, was the direct ancestor of modern mathematical logic.

Leibnitz, dominated by ideas of communication, is, in more than one way, the intellectual ancestor of the ideas of this book, for he was also interested in machine computation and in automata. My views in this book are very far from being Leibnitzian, but the problems with which I am concerned are most certainly Leibnitzian. Leibnitz's computing machines were only an offshoot of his interest in a computing language, a reasoning calculus which again was in his mind, merely an extention of his idea of a complete artificial language. Thus, even in his computing machine, Leibnitz's preoccupations were mostly linguistic and communicational.

Toward the middle of the last century, the work of Clerk Maxwell and of his precursor,

Faraday, had attracted the attention of physicists once more to optics, the science of light, which was now regarded as a form of electricity that could be reduced to the mechanics of a curious, rigid, but invisible medium known as the ether, which, at the time, was supposed to permeate the atmosphere, interstellar space and all transparent materials. Clerk Maxwell's work on optics consisted in the mathematical development of ideas which had been previously expressed in a cogent but non-mathematical form by Faraday. The study of ether raised certain questions whose answers were obscure, as, for example, that of the motion of matter through the ether. The famous experiment of Michelson and Morley, in the nineties, was undertaken to resolve this problem, and it gave the entirely unexpected answer that there simply was no way to determine the motion of matter through the ether.

The first satisfactory solution to the problems aroused by this experiment was that of Lorentz, who pointed out that if the forces holding matter together were conceived as being themselves electrical or optical in nature, we should expect a negative result from the Michelson-Morley experiment. However, Einstein in 1905 translated these ideas of Lorentz into a form in which the unobservability of absolute motion was rather a postulate of physics than the result of any particular structure of matter. For our purposes, the important thing is that in Einstein's work, light and matter are on an equal basis, as they had been in the writings before Newton; without the Newtonian subordination of everything else to matter and mechanics.

In explaining his views, Einstein makes abundant use of the observer who may be at rest or may be moving. In his theory of relativity it is impossible to introduce the observer without also introducing the idea of message, and without, in fact, returning the emphasis of physics to a quasi-Leibnitzian state whose tendency is once again optical. Einstein's theory of relativity and Gibbs' statistical mechanics are in sharp contrast, in that Einstein, like Newton, is still talking primarily in terms of an absolutely rigid dynamics not introducing the idea of probability. Gibbs' work, on the other hand, is probabilistic from the very start, yet both directions of work represent a shift in the point of view of physics in which the world as it actually exists is replaced in some sense or other by the world as it happens to be observed, and the old naïve realism of physics gives way to something on which Bishop Berkeley might have smiled with pleasure.

At this point it is appropriate for us to review certain notions pertaining to entropy which have already been presented in the introduction. As we have said the idea of entropy represents several of the most important departures of Gibbsian mechanics from Newtonian mechanics. In Gibbs' view we have a physical quantity which belongs not to the outside world as such, but to certain sets of possible outside worlds, and therefore to the answer to certain specific questions which we can ask concerning the outside world. Physics now becomes not the discussion of an outside universe which may be regarded as the total answer to all the questions concerning it, but an account of the answers to much more limited questions. In fact, we are now no longer concerned with the study of all possible outgoing and incoming messages which we may send and receive, but with the theory of much more specific outgoing and incoming messages; and it involves a measurement of the no-longer infinite amount of information that they yield us.

Messages are themselves a form of pattern and organization. Indeed, it is possible to treat sets of messages as having an entropy like sets of states of the external world. Just as entropy is a measure of disorganization, the information carried by a set of messages is a measure of organization. In fact, it is possible to interpret the information carried by a message as essentially the negative of its entropy, and the negative logarithm of its probability. That is, the more probable the message, the less information it gives. Clichés, for example, are less illuminating than great poems.

I have already referred to Leibnitz's interest in automata, an interest incidentally shared by his contemporary, Pascal, who made real contributions to the development of what we now know as the desk adding-machine. Leibnitz saw in the concordance of the time given by clocks set at the same time, the model for the pre-established harmony of his monads. For the technique embodied in the automata of his time was that of the clockmaker. Let us consider the activity of the little figures which dance on the top of a music box. They move in accordance with a pattern, but it is a pattern which is set in advance, and in which the past activity of the figures has practically nothing to do with the pattern of their future activity. The probability that they will diverge from this pattern is nil. There is a message indeed; but it goes from the machinery of the music box to the figures, and stops there. The figures themselves have no trace of communication with the outer world, except this one-way stage of communication with the pre-established mechanism of the music box. They are blind, deaf, and dumb, and cannot vary their activity in the least from the conventionalized pattern.

Contrast with them the behavior of man or indeed of any moderately intelligent animal such as a kitten. I call to the kitten and it looks up. I have sent it a message which it has received by its sensory organs, and which it registers in action. The kitten is hungry and lets out a pitiful wail. This time it is the sender of a message. The kitten bats at a swinging spool. The spool swings to its left, and the kitten catches it with its left paw. This time messages of a very complicated nature are both sent and received within the kitten's own nervous system through certain nerve end-bodies in its joints, muscles, and tendons; and by means of nervous messages sent by these organs, the animal is aware of the actual position and tensions of its tissues. It is only through these organs that anything like a manual skill is possible.

I have contrasted the prearranged behavior of the little figures on the music box on the one hand, and the contingent behavior of human beings and animals on the other. But we must not suppose that the music box is typical of all machine behavior.

The older machines, and in particular the older attempts to produce automata, did in fact function on a closed clockwork basis. But modern automatic machines such as the controlled missile, the proximity fuse, the automatic door opener, the control apparatus for a chemical factory, and the rest of the modern armory of automatic machines which perform military or industrial functions, possess sense organs; that is, receptors for messages coming from the outside. These may be as simple as photoelectric cells which change electrically when a light falls on them, and which can tell light from dark, or as complicated as a television set. They may measure a tension by the change it produces in the conductivity of a wire exposed to it, or they may measure temperature by means of a thermocouple, which is an instrument consisting of two distinct metals in contact with one another through which a current flows when one of the points of contact is heated. Every instrument in the repertory of the scientific-instrument maker is a possible sense organ, and may be made to record its reading remotely through the intervention of appropriate electrical apparatus. Thus the machine which is conditioned by its relation to the external world, and by the things happening in the external world, is with us and has been with us for some time.

The machine which acts on the external world by means of messages is also familiar. The automatic photoelectric door opener is known to every person who has passed through the Pennsylvania Station in New York, and is used in many other buildings as well. When a message consisting of the interception of a beam of light is sent to the apparatus, this message actuates the door, and opens it so that the passenger may go through.

The steps between the actuation of a machine of this type by sense organs and its performance of a task may be as simple as in the case of the electric door; or it may be in fact of any desired degree of complexity within the limits of our engineering techniques. A complex action is one in which the data introduced, which we call the *input,* to obtain an effect on the outer world, which we call the *output,* may involve a large number of combinations. These are combinations, both of the data put in at the moment and of the records taken from the past stored data which we call the *memory.* These are recorded in the machine. The most complicated machines yet made which transform input data into output data are the high-speed electrical computing machines, of which I shall speak later in more detail. The determination of the mode of conduct of these machines is given through a special sort of input, which frequently consists of punched cards or tapes or of magnetized wires, and which determines the way in which the machine is going to act in one operation, as distinct from the way in which it might have acted in another. Because of the frequent use of punched or magnetic tape in the control, the data which are fed in, and which indicate the mode of operation of one of these machines for combining information, are called the *taping.*

I have said that man and the animal have a kinaesthetic sense, by which they keep a record of the position and tensions of their muscles. For any machine subject to a varied external environment to act effectively it is necessary that information concerning the results of its own action be furnished to it as part of the information on which it must continue to act. For example, if we are running an elevator, it is not enough to open the outside door because the orders we have given should make the elevator be at that door at the time we open it. It is important that the release for opening the door be dependent on the fact that the elevator is actually at the door; otherwise something might have detained it, and the passenger might step into the empty shaft. This control of a machine on the basis of its *actual* performance rather than its *expected* performance is known as *feedback,* and involves sensory members which are actuated by motor members and perform the function of *tell-tales* or *monitors*—that is, of elements which indicate a performance. It is the function of these mechanisms to control the mechanical tendency toward disorganization; in other words, to produce a temporary and local reversal of the normal direction of entropy.

I have just mentioned the elevator as an example of feedback. There are other cases where the importance of feedback is even more apparent. For example, a gun-pointer takes information from his instruments of observation, and conveys it to the gun, so that the latter will point in such a direction that the missile will pass through the moving target at a certain time. Now, the gun itself must be used under all conditions of weather. In some of these the grease is warm, and the gun swings easily and rapidly. Under other conditions the grease is frozen or mixed with sand, and the gun is slow to answer the orders given to it. If these orders are reinforced by an extra push given when the gun fails to respond easily to the orders and lags behind them, then the error of the gun-pointer will be decreased. To obtain a performance as uniform as possible, it is customary to put into the gun a control feedback element which reads the lag of the gun behind the position it should have according to the orders given it, and which uses this difference to give the gun an extra push.

It is true that precautions must be taken so that the push is not too hard, for if it is, the gun will swing past its proper position, and will have to be pulled back in a series of oscillations, which may well become wider and wider, and lead to a disastrous instability. If the feedback system is itself controlled—if, in other words, its own entropic tendencies are checked by still other controlling mechanisms—and kept within limits sufficiently stringent, this will not occur, and the existence of the feedback will increase the stability of performance of the gun. In other words, the performance will become less dependent on the frictional load; or what is the same thing, on the drag created by the stiffness of the grease.

Something very similar to this occurs in human action. If I pick up my cigar, I do not will to move any specific muscles. Indeed in many cases, I do not know what those muscles are. What I do is to turn into action a certain feedback mechanism; namely, a reflex in which the amount by which I have yet failed to pick up the cigar is turned into a new and increased order to the lagging muscles, whichever they may be. In this way, a fairly uniform voluntary command will enable the same task to be performed from widely varying initial positions, and irrespective of the decrease of contraction due to fatigue of the muscles. Similarly, when I drive a car, I do not follow out a series of commands dependent simply on a mental image of the road and the task I am doing. If I find the car swerving too much to the right, that causes me to pull it to the left. This depends on the actual performance of the car, and not simply on the road; and it allows me to drive with nearly equal efficiency a light Austin or a heavy truck, without having formed separate habits for the driving of the two. I shall have more to say about this in the chapter in this book on special machines, where we shall discuss the service that can be done to neuropathology by the study of machines with defects in performance similar to those occurring in the human mechanism.

It is my thesis that the physical functioning of the living individual and the operation of some of the newer communication machines are precisely parallel in their analogous attempts to control entropy through feedback. Both of them have sensory receptors as one stage in their cycle of operation: that is in both of them there exists a special apparatus for collecting information from the outer world at low energy levels, and for making it available in the operation of the individual or of the machine. In both cases these external messages are not taken *neat*, but through the internal transforming powers of the apparatus, whether it be alive or dead. The information is then turned into a new form available for the further stages of performance. In both the animal and the machine this performance is made to be effective on the outer world. In both of them, their *performed* action on the outer world, and not merely their *intended* action, is reported back to the central regulatory apparatus. This complex of behavior is ignored by the average man, and in particular does not play the role that it should in our habitual analysis of society; for just as individual physical responses may be seen from this point of view, so may the organic responses of society itself. I do not mean that the sociologist is unaware of the existence and complex nature of communications in society, but until recently he has tended to overlook the extent to which they are the cement which binds its fabric together.

We have seen in this chapter the fundamental unity of a complex of ideas which until recently had not been sufficiently associated with one another, namely, the contingent view of physics that Gibbs introduced as a modification of the traditional, Newtonian conventions, the Augustinian attitude toward order and conduct which is demanded by this view, and the theory of the message among men, machines, and in society as a sequence of events in time which, though it itself has a certain contingency, strives to hold back nature's tendency toward disorder by adjusting its parts to various purposive ends.

20

Some Tentative Axioms of Communication

Paul Watzlawick, Janet Helmick Beavin, and Don D. Jackson

2.1 Introduction

The conclusions reached in the first chapter generally emphasized the inapplicability of many traditional psychiatric notions to our proposed framework and so may seem to leave very little on which the study of the pragmatics of human communication could be based. We want to show next that this is not so. However, to do this, we have to start with some simple properties of communication that have fundamental interpersonal implications. It will be seen that these properties are in the nature of axioms within our hypothetical calculus of human communication. When these have been defined we will be in a position to consider some of their possible pathologies in Chapter 3.

2.2 The Impossibility of Not Communicating

2.21

First of all, there is a property of behavior that could hardly be more basic and is, therefore, often overlooked: behavior has no opposite. In other words, there is no such thing as nonbehavior or, to put it even more simply: one cannot *not* behave. Now, if it is accepted that all behavior in an interactional situation[1] has message value, i.e., is communication, it follows that no matter how one may try, one cannot *not* communicate. Activity or inactivity, words or silence all have message value: they influence others and these others, in turn, cannot *not* respond to these

SOURCE: Watzlawick, P., Beavin, J. H., & Jackson, D. D. (1967). *Pragmatics of human communication: A study of interactional patterns, pathologies, and paradoxes* (pp. 48–71). New York, NY: W. W. Norton & Company. Copyright © 1967 by W. W. Norton & Company, Inc. Used by permission of W. W. Norton & Company, Inc.

communications and are thus themselves communicating. It should be clearly understood that the mere absence of talking or of taking notice of each other is no exception to what has just been asserted. The man at a crowded lunch counter who looks straight ahead, or the airplane passenger who sits with his eyes closed, are both communicating that they do not want to speak to anybody or be spoken to, and their neighbors usually "get the message" and respond appropriately by leaving them alone. This, obviously, is just as much an interchange of communication as an animated discussion.[2]

Neither can we say that "communication" only takes place when it is intentional, conscious, or successful, that is, when mutual understanding occurs. Whether message sent equals message received is an important but different order of analysis, as it must rest ultimately on evaluations of specific, introspective, subject-reported data, which we choose to neglect for the exposition of a behavioral-theory of communication. On the question of misunderstanding, our concern, given certain formal properties of communication, is with the development of related pathologies, aside from, indeed in spite of, the motivations or intentions of the communicants.

2.22

In the foregoing, the term "communication" has been used in two ways: as the generic title of our study, and as a loosely defined unit of behavior. Let us now be more precise. We will, of course, continue to refer to the pragmatic aspect of the theory of human communication simply as "communication." For the various units of communication (behavior), we have sought to select terms which are already generally understood. A single communicational unit will be called a *message* or, where there is no possibility of confusion, *a* communication. A series of messages exchanged between persons will be called *interaction*. (For those who crave more precise quantification, we can only say that the sequence we refer to by the term "interaction" is greater than

one message but not infinite.) Finally, in Chapters 4–7, we will add *patterns of interaction,* which is a still higher-level unit of human communication.

Further, in regard to even the simplest possible unit, it will be obvious that once we accept all behavior as communication, we will not be dealing with a monophonic message unit, but rather with a fluid and multifaceted compound of many behavioral modes—verbal, tonal, postural, contextual, etc.—all of which qualify the meaning of all the others. The various elements of this compound (considered as a whole) are capable of highly varied and complex permutations, ranging from the congruent to the incongruent and paradoxical. The pragmatic effect of these combinations in interpersonal situations will be our interest herein.

2.23

The impossibility of not communicating is a phenomenon of more than theoretical interest. It is, for instance, part and parcel of the schizophrenic "dilemma." If schizophrenic behavior is observed with etiological considerations in abeyance, it appears that the schizophrenic tries *not to communicate*. But since even nonsense, silence, withdrawal, immobility (postural silence), or any other form of denial is itself a communication, the schizophrenic is faced with the impossible task of denying that he is communicating and at the same time denying that his denial is a communication. The realization of this basic dilemma in schizophrenia is a key to a good many aspects of schizophrenic communication that would otherwise remain obscure. Since any communication, as we shall see, implies commitment and thereby defines the sender's view of his relationship with the receiver, it can be hypothesized that the schizophrenic behaves as if he would avoid commitment by not communicating. Whether this is his purpose, in the causal sense, is of course impossible of proof; that this is the effect of schizophrenic behavior will be taken up in greater detail in [a later section].

2.24

To summarize, a metacommunicational axiom of the pragmatics of communication can be postulated: *one cannot not communicate.*

2.3 THE CONTENT AND RELATIONSHIP LEVELS OF COMMUNICATION

2.31

Another axiom was hinted at in the foregoing when it was suggested that any communication implies a commitment and thereby defines the relationship. This is another way of saying that a communication not only conveys information, but that at the same time it imposes behavior. Following Bateson (Ruesch & Bateson, 1951, pp. 179–81), these two operations have come to be known as the "report" and the "command" aspects, respectively, of any communication. Bateson exemplifies these two aspects by means of a physiological analogy: let *A, B,* and *C* be a linear chain of neurons. Then the firing of neuron *B* is both a "report" that neuron *A* has fired and a "command" for neuron *C* to fire.

The report aspect of a message conveys information and is, therefore, synonymous in human communication with the *content* of the message. It may be about anything that is communicable regardless of whether the particular information is true or false, valid, invalid, or undecidable. The command aspect, on the other hand, refers to what sort of a message it is to be taken as, and, therefore, ultimately to the relationship between the communicants. All such *relationship* statements are about one or several of the following assertions: "This is how I see myself . . . this is how I see you . . . this is how I see you seeing me . . ." and so forth in theoretically infinite regress. Thus, for instance, the messages "It is important to release the clutch gradually and smoothly" and "Just let the clutch go, it'll ruin the transmission in no time" have approximately the same information content (report aspect), but they

obviously define very different relationships. To avoid any misunderstanding about the foregoing, we want to make it clear that relationships are only rarely defined deliberately or with full awareness. In fact, it seems that the more spontaneous and "healthy" a relationship, the more the relationship aspect of communication recedes into the background. Conversely, "sick" relationships are characterized by a constant struggle about the nature of the relationship, with the content aspect of communication becoming less and less important.

2.32

It is quite interesting that before behavioral scientists began to wonder about these aspects of human communication, computer engineers had come across the same problem in their work. It became clear to them that when communicating with an artificial organism, their communications had to have both report and command aspects. For instance, if a computer is to multiply two figures, it must be fed this information (the two figures) *and* information about this information: the command "multiply them."

Now, what is important for our consideration is the relation existing between the content (report) and the relationship (command) aspects of communication. In essence it has already been defined in the preceding paragraph when it was mentioned that a computer needs *information* (data) and *information about this information* (instructions). Clearly, then, the instructions are of a higher logical type than the data; they are *metainformation* since they are information *about* information, and any confusion between the two would lead to a meaningless result.

2.33

If we now return to human communication, we see that the same relation exists between the report and the command aspects: the former conveys the "data" of the communication, the latter how this communication is to be taken. "This is an order" or "I am only joking" are verbal examples of such communications about communication. The relationship can also be expressed nonverbally by shouting or smiling or in a number of other ways. And the relationship may be clearly understood from the context in which the communication takes place, e.g., between uniformed soldiers, or in a circus ring.

The reader will have noticed that the relationship aspect of a communication, being a communication about a communication, is, of course, identical with the concept of metacommunication elaborated in the first chapter, where it was limited to the conceptual framework and to the language the communication analyst must employ when communicating about communication. Now it can be seen that not only he but everyone is faced with this problem. The ability to metacommunicate appropriately is not only the *conditio sine qua non* of successful communication, but is intimately linked with the enormous problem of awareness of self and others. This point will be explained in greater detail in s. 3.3. For the moment, and by way of illustration, we merely want to show that messages can be constructed, especially in written communication, which offer highly ambiguous metacommunicational clues. As Cherry (1961, p. 120) points out, the sentence "Do you think that one will do?" can have a variety of meanings, according to which word is to be stressed—an indication that written language usually does not supply. Another example would be a sign in a restaurant reading "Customers who think our waiters are rude should see the manager," which, at least in theory, can be understood in two entirely different ways. Ambiguities of this kind are not the only possible complications arising out of the level structure of all communication; consider, for instance, a notice that reads "Disregard This Sign." As we shall see in the chapter on paradoxical communication, confusions or contaminations between these levels—communication and metacommunication—may lead to impasses identical in structure to those of the famous paradoxes in logic.

2.34

For the time being let us merely summarize the foregoing into another axiom of our tentative calculus: *Every communication has a content and a relationship aspect such that the latter classifies the former and is therefore a metacommunication.*[3]

2.4 THE PUNCTUATION OF THE SEQUENCE OF EVENTS

2.41

The next basic characteristic of communication we wish to explore regards interaction—exchanges of messages—between communicants. To an outside observer, *a series of communications can be viewed as an uninterrupted sequence of interchanges.* However, the participants in the interaction always introduce what, following Whorf (1956), Bateson and Jackson have termed the "punctuation of the sequence of events." They state:

> The stimulus-response psychologist typically confines his attention to sequences of interchange so short that it is possible to label one item of input as "stimulus" and another item as "reinforcement" while labelling what the subject does between these two events as "response." Within the short sequence so excised, it is possible to talk about the "psychology" of the subject. In contrast, the sequences of interchange which we are here discussing are very much longer and therefore have the characteristic that every item in the sequence is simultaneously stimulus, response, and reinforcement. A given item of A's behavior is a stimulus insofar as it is followed by an item contributed by B and that by another item contributed by A. But insofar as A's item is sandwiched between two items contributed by B, it is a response. Similarly A's item is a reinforcement insofar as it follows an item contributed by B. The ongoing interchanges, then, which we are here discussing, constitute a chain of overlapping triadic links, each of which is comparable to a stimulus-response-reinforcement sequence. We can take any triad of our interchange and see it as a single trial in a stimulus-response learning experiment.

If we look at the conventional learning experiments from this point of view, we observe at once that repeated trials amount to a differentiation of relationship between the two organisms concerned—the experimenter and his subject. The sequence of trials is so punctuated that it is always the experimenter who seems to provide the "stimuli" and the "reinforcements," while the subject provides the "responses." These words are here deliberately put in quotation marks because the role definitions are in fact only created by the willingness of the organisms to accept the system of punctuation. The "reality" of the role definitions is only of the same order as the reality of a bat on a Rorschach card—a more or less over-determined creation of the perceptive process. The rat who said "I have got my experimenter trained. Each time I press the lever he gives me food" was declining to accept the punctuation of the sequence which the experimenter was seeking to impose.

> It is still true, however, that in a long sequence of interchange, the organisms concerned—especially if these be people—will in fact punctuate the sequence so that it will appear that one or the other has initiative, dominance, dependency or the like. That is, they will set up between them patterns of interchange (about which they may or may not be in agreement) and these patterns will in fact be rules of contingency regarding the exchange of reinforcement. While rats are too nice to re-label, some psychiatric patients are not, and provide psychological trauma for the therapist! (Bateson & Jackson, 1964, pp. 273–74)

It is not the issue here whether punctuation of communicational sequence is, in general, good or bad, as it should be immediately obvious that punctuation *organizes* behavioral events and is therefore vital to ongoing interactions. Culturally, we share many conventions of punctuation which, while no more or less accurate than other views of the same events, serve to organize common and important interactional sequences. For example, we call a person in a group behaving in one way the "leader" and another the "follower," although on reflection it

is difficult to say which comes first or where one would be without the other.

2.42

Disagreement about how to punctuate the sequence of events is at the root of countless relationship struggles. Suppose a couple have a marital problem to which he contributes passive withdrawal, while her 50 per cent is nagging criticism. In explaining their frustrations, the husband will state that withdrawal is his only *defense against* her nagging, while she will label this explanation a gross and willful distortion of what "really" happens in their marriage: namely, that she is critical of him *because of* his passivity. Stripped of all ephemeral and fortuitous elements, their fights consist in a monotonous exchange of the messages "I withdraw because you nag" and "I nag because you withdraw." This type of interaction has already been mentioned briefly in s. 1.65. Represented graphically, with an arbitrary beginning point, their interaction looks somewhat like [the diagram in Figure 20.1].

It can be seen that the husband only perceives triads 2–3–4, 4–5–6, 6–7–8, etc., where his behavior (solid arrows) is "merely" a response to her behavior (the broken arrows). With her it is exactly the other way around; she punctuates the sequence of events into the triads 1–2–3, 3–4–5, 5–6–7, etc., and sees herself as only reacting to, but not determining, her husband's behavior. In conjoint psychotherapy with couples one is frequently struck by the intensity of what in traditional psychotherapy would be referred to as "reality distortion" on the part of both parties. It is often hard to believe that two individuals could have such divergent views on many elements of joint experience. And yet the problem lies primarily in an area already frequently mentioned: their inability to metacommunicate about their respective patterning of their interaction. This interaction is of an oscillatory yes-no-yes-no-yes nature which theoretically can go on ad infinitum and almost invariably is accompanied, as we shall see later, by the typical charges of badness or madness.

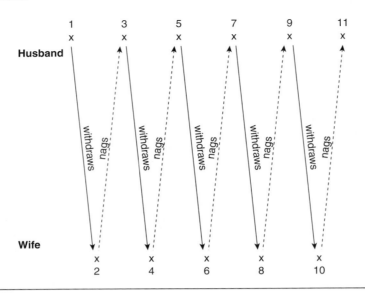

Figure 20.1

International relations, too, are rife with analogous patterns of interaction; take for instance C. E. M. Joad's analysis of arms races:

> ... if, as they maintain, the best way to preserve peace is to prepare war, it is not altogether clear why all nations should regard the armaments of other nations as a menace to peace. However, they do so regard them, and are accordingly stimulated to increase their armaments to overtop the armaments by which they conceive themselves to be threatened. ... These increased arms being in their turn regarded as a menace by nation A whose allegedly defensive armaments have provoked them, are used by nation A as a pretext for accumulating yet greater armaments where-with to defend itself against the menace. Yet these greater armaments are in turn interpreted by neighbouring nations as constituting a menace to themselves and so on ... (Joad, 1939, p. 69)

2.43

Again, mathematics supplies a descriptive analogy: the concept of "infinite, oscillating series." While the term itself was introduced much later, series of this kind were studied in a logical, consistent manner for the first time by the Austrian priest Bernard Bolzano shortly before his death in 1848, when, it would appear, he was deeply involved with the meaning of infinity. His thoughts appeared posthumously in the form of a small book entitled *The Paradoxes of the Infinite* (Bolzano, 1889), which became a classic of mathematical literature. In it Bolzano studied various kinds of series (S), of which perhaps the simplest is the following:

$$S = a - a + a - a + a - a + a - a + a - a + a - a + a - \ldots$$

For our purposes this series may be taken to stand for a communicational sequence of assertions and denials of message *a*. Now, as Bolzano showed, this sequence can be grouped—or, as we would say, punctuated—in several different, but arithmetically correct, ways.[4] The result is a different limit for the series depending on how one chooses to punctuate the sequence of its elements, a result which consternated many mathematicians, including Leibnitz. Unfortunately, as far as we can see, the solution of the paradox offered eventually by Bolzano is of no help in the analogous communicational dilemma. There, as

Bateson [personal communication] suggests, the dilemma arises out of the spurious punctuation of the series, namely, the pretense that it has a beginning, and this is precisely the error of the partners in such a situation.

2.44

Thus we add a third metacommunicational axiom: *The nature of a relationship is contingent upon the punctuation of the communicational sequences between the communicants.*

2.5 DIGITAL AND ANALOGIC COMMUNICATION

2.51

In the central nervous system the functional units (neurons) receive so-called quantal packages of information through connecting elements (synapses). Upon arrival at the synapses these "packages" produce excitatory or inhibitory postsynaptic potentials that are summed up by the neuron and either cause or inhibit its firing. This specific part of neural activity, consisting in the occurrence or nonoccurrence of its firing, therefore conveys binary digital information. The humoral system, on the other hand, is not based on digitalization of information. This system communicates by releasing discrete quantities of specific substances into the bloodstream. It is further known that the neural and the humoral modes of intraorganismic communication exist not only side by side, but that they complement and are contingent upon each other, often in highly complex ways.

The same two basic modes of communication can be found at work in the field of man-made organisms:[5] there are computers which utilize the all-or-none principle of vacuum tubes or transistors and are called *digital,* because they are basically calculators working with digits; and there is another class of machines that manipulate discrete, positive magnitudes—the analogues of the data—and hence are called *analogic.* In digital computers both data and instructions are processed in the form of numbers so that often, especially in the case of the instructions, there is only an arbitrary correspondence between the particular piece of information and its digital expression. In other words, these numbers are arbitrarily assigned code names which have as little resemblance to actual magnitudes as do the telephone numbers assigned to the subscribers. On the other hand, as we have already seen, the analogy principle is the essence of all analogic computation. Just as in the humoral system of natural organisms the carriers of information are certain substances and their concentration in the bloodstream, in analogue computers data take the form of discrete and, therefore, always positive quantities, e.g., the intensity of electrical currents, the number of revolutions of a wheel, the degree of displacement of components, and the like. A so-called tide machine (an instrument composed of scales, cogs, and levers formerly used to compute the tides for any given time) can be considered a simple analogue computer, and, of course, Ashby's homeostat, mentioned in Chapter 1, is a paradigm of an analogue machine, even though it does not compute anything.

2.52

In human communication, objects—in the widest sense—can be referred to in two entirely different ways. They can either be represented by a likeness, such as a drawing, or they can be referred to by a name. Thus, in the written sentence "The cat has caught a mouse" the nouns could be replaced by pictures; if the sentence were spoken, the actual cat and the mouse could be pointed to. Needless to say, this would be an unusual way of communicating, and normally the written or spoken "name," that is, the word, is used. These two types of communication—the one by a self-explanatory likeness, the other by a word—are, of course, also equivalent to the concepts of the analogic and the digital respectively. Whenever a word is used to *name* something it is obvious that the relation between the name and the thing named is an arbitrarily established one.

Words are arbitrary signs that are manipulated according to the logical syntax of language. There is no particular reason why the three letters "c-a-t" should denote a particular animal. In ultimate analysis it is only a semantic convention of the English language, and outside this convention there exists no other correlation between any word and the thing it stands for, with the possible but insignificant exception of onomatopoeic words. As Bateson and Jackson point out: "There is nothing particularly five-like in the number five; there is nothing particularly table-like in the word 'table'" (Bateson & Jackson, 1964, p. 271).

In analogic communication, on the other hand, there *is* something particularly "thing-like" in what is used to express the thing. Analogic communication can be more readily referred to the thing it stands for. The difference between these two modes of communication may become somewhat clearer if it is realized that no amount of listening to a foreign language on the radio, for example, will yield an understanding of the language, whereas some basic information can fairly easily be derived from watching sign language and from so-called intention movements, even when used by a person of a totally different culture. Analogic communication, we suggest, has its roots in far more archaic periods of evolution and is, therefore, of much more general validity than the relatively recent, and far more abstract, digital mode of verbal communication.

What then is analogic communication? The answer is relatively simple: it is virtually a nonverbal communication. This term, however, is deceptive, because it is often restricted to body movement only, to the behavior known as kinesics. We hold that the term must comprise posture, gesture, facial expression, voice inflection, the sequence, rhythm, and cadence of the words themselves, and any other nonverbal manifestation of which the organism is capable, as well as the communicational clues unfailingly present in any *context* in which an interaction takes place.[6]

2.53

Man is the only organism known to use both the analogic and the digital modes of communication.[7] The significance of this is still very inadequately understood, but can hardly be overrated. On the one hand there can be no doubt that man communicates digitally. In fact, most, if not all, of his civilized achievement would be unthinkable without his having evolved digital language. This is particularly important for the sharing of information about *objects* and for the time-binding function of the transmission of knowledge. And yet there exists a vast area where we rely almost exclusively on analogic communication, often with very little change from the analogic inheritance handed down to us from our mammalian ancestors. This is the area of *relationship*. Based on Tinbergen (1953) and Lorenz (1952), as well as his own research, Bateson (1955) has shown that vocalizations, intention movements, and mood signs of animals are analogic communications by which they define the nature of their relationships, rather than making denotative statements about objects. Thus, to take one of his examples, when I open the refrigerator and the cat comes, rubs against my legs, and mews, this does not mean "I want milk"—as a human being would express it—but invokes a specific relationship, "Be mother to me," because such behavior is only observed in kittens in relation to adult cats, and never between two grown-up animals. Conversely, pet lovers often are convinced that their animals "understand" their speech. What the animal does understand, needless to say, is certainly not the meaning of the words, but the wealth of analogic communication that goes with speech. Indeed, wherever relationship is the central issue of communication, we find that digital language is almost meaningless. This is not only the case between animals and between man and animal, but in many other contingencies in human life, e.g., courtship, love, succor, combat, and, of course, in all dealings with very young children or severely disturbed mental patients. Children, fools, and animals have always been credited with particular intuition regarding the sincerity or insincerity of human attitudes, for it is easy to profess something verbally, but difficult to carry a lie into the realm of the analogic.

In short, if we remember that every communication has a content and a relationship aspect, we can expect to find that the two modes of communication not only exist side by side but complement each other in every message. We can further expect to find that the content aspect is likely to be conveyed digitally whereas the relationship aspect will be predominantly analogic in nature.

2.54

In this correspondence lies the pragmatic importance of certain differences between the digital and analogic modes of communication which will now be considered. In order to make these differences clear, we can return to the digital and analogic modes as represented in artificial communication systems.

The performance, accuracy, and versatility of the two types of computers—digital and analogue—are vastly different. The analogues used in analogue computers in lieu of actual magnitudes can never be more than approximations of the real values, and this ever-present source of inaccuracy is further increased during the process of the computer operations themselves. Cogs, gears, and transmissions can never be built to perfection, and even when analogue machines rely entirely on discrete intensities of electrical currents, electrical resistances, rheostats, and the like, these analogues are still subject to virtually uncontrollable fluctuations. A digital machine, on the other hand, could be said to work with perfect precision if space for storing digits were not restricted, thus making it necessary to round off any results having more digits than the machine could hold. Anyone who has used a slide rule (an excellent example of an analogue computer) knows that he can only get an approximate result, while any desk calculator will supply an exact result, as long as the digits required do not exceed the maximum the calculator can handle.

Apart from its perfect precision, the digital computer has the enormous advantage of being not only an arithmetic, but also a *logical,* machine. McCulloch and Pitts (1943) have shown that the sixteen truth functions of the logical calculus can be represented by combinations of all-or-none organs, so that, for instance,

the summation of two pulses will represent the logical "and," the mutual exclusiveness of two pulses represents the logical "or," a pulse which inhibits the firing of an element represents negation, etc. Nothing even remotely comparable is possible in analogue computers. Since they operate only with discrete, positive quantities they are unable to represent any negative value, including negation itself, or any of the other truth functions.

Some of the characteristics of computers also apply to human communication: digital message material is of a much higher degree of complexity, versatility, and abstraction than analogic material. Specifically, we find that analogue communication has nothing comparable to the logical syntax of digital language. This means that in analogic language there are no equivalents for such vitally important elements of discourse as "if—then," "either—or," and many others, and that the expression of abstract concepts is as difficult, if not impossible, as in primitive picture writing, where every concept can only be represented by its physical likeness. Furthermore, analogic language shares with analogic computing the lack of the simple negative, i.e., an expression for "not."

To illustrate: there are tears of sorrow and tears of joy, the clenched fist may signal aggression or constraint, a smile may convey sympathy or contempt, reticence can be interpreted as tactfulness or indifference, and we wonder if perhaps all analogic messages have this curiously ambiguous quality, reminiscent of Freud's *Gegensinn der Urworte* (antithetical sense of primal words). Analogic communication has no qualifiers to indicate which of two discrepant meanings is implied, nor any indicators that would permit a distinction between past, present, or future.[8] These qualifiers and indicators do, of course, exist in digital communication. But what is lacking in digital communication is an adequate vocabulary for the contingencies of relationship.

Man, in his necessity to combine these two languages, either as sender or receiver, must constantly *translate* from the one into the other, and in doing so encounters very curious dilemmas, which will be taken up in greater detail in the chapter on pathological communication (s. 3.5).

For in human communication, the difficulty of translation exists both ways. Not only can there be no translation from the digital into the analogic mode without great loss of information (see 3.55. on hysterical symptom formation), but the opposite is also extraordinarily difficult: to *talk about* relationship requires adequate translation from the analogic into the digital mode of communication. Finally we can imagine similar problems when the two modes must coexist, as Haley has noted in his excellent chapter, "Marriage Therapy":

> When a man and a woman decide their association should be legalized with a marriage ceremony, they pose themselves a problem which will continue through the marriage: now that they are married are they staying together because they wish to or because they must? (Haley, 1963, p. 119)

In the light of the foregoing, we would say that when to the mostly analogic part of their relationship (courtship behavior) is added a digitalization (the marriage contract) an unambiguous definition of their relationship becomes very problematic.[9]

2.55

To summarize: *Human beings communicate both digitally and analogically. Digital language has a highly complex and powerful logical syntax but lacks adequate semantics in the field of relationship, while analogic language possesses the semantics but has no adequate syntax for the unambiguous definition of the nature of relationships.*

2.6 SYMMETRICAL AND COMPLEMENTARY INTERACTION

2.61

In 1935 Bateson reported on an interactional phenomenon which he observed in the Iatmul tribe in New Guinea and which, in his book *Naven* (1958), published a year later, he dealt with in greater detail. He called this phenomenon *schismogenesis* and defined it as *a process of differentiation in the norms of individual behavior resulting from cumulative interaction between individuals.* In 1939 Richardson (1956) applied this concept to his analyses of war and foreign politics; since 1952 Bateson and others have demonstrated its usefulness in the field of psychiatric research (Cf. Watzlawick, 1964, pp. 7–17; also Sluzki & Beavin, 1965). This concept, which, as we can see, has a heuristic value beyond the confines of any one discipline, was elaborated by Bateson in *Naven* as follows:

> When our discipline is defined in terms of the reactions of an individual to the reactions of other individuals, it is at once apparent that we must regard the relationship between two individuals as liable to alter from time to time, even without disturbance from outside. We have to consider, not only A's reactions to B's behaviour, but we must go on to consider how these affect B's later behaviour and the effect of this on A.
>
> It is at once apparent that many systems of relationship, either between individuals or groups of individuals, contain a tendency towards progressive change. If, for example, one of the patterns of cultural behaviour, considered appropriate in individual A, is culturally labelled as an assertive pattern, while B is expected to reply to this with what is culturally regarded as submission, it is likely that this submission will encourage a further assertion, and that this assertion will demand still further submission. We have thus a potentially progressive state of affairs, and unless other factors are present to restrain the excesses of assertive and submissive behavior, A must necessarily become more and more assertive, while B will become more and more submissive; and this progressive change will occur whether A and B are separate individuals or members of complementary groups.
>
> Progressive changes of this sort we may describe as *complementary* schismogenesis. But there is another pattern of relationships between individuals or groups of individuals which equally contains the germs of progressive change. If, for example, we find boasting as the cultural pattern of behaviour in one group, and that the other group replies to this with boasting, a competitive

situation may develop in which boasting leads to more boasting, and so on. This type of progressive change we may call *symmetrical* schismogenesis. (Bateson, 1958, pp. 176–77)

2.62

The two patterns just described have come to be used without reference to the schismogenetic process and are now usually referred to simply as symmetrical and complementary interaction. They can be described as relationships based on either equality or difference. In the first case the partners tend to mirror each other's behavior, and thus their interaction can be termed *symmetrical*. Weakness or strength, goodness or badness, are not relevant here, for equality can be maintained in any of these areas. In the second case one partner's behavior complements that of the other, forming a different sort of behavioral Gestalt, and is called *complementary*. Symmetrical interaction, then, is characterized by equality and the minimization of difference, while complementary interaction is based on the maximization of difference.

There are two different positions in a complementary relationship. One partner occupies what has been variously described as the superior, primary, or "one-up" position, and the other the corresponding inferior, secondary, or "one-down" position. These terms are quite useful as long as they are not equated with "good" or "bad," "strong" or "weak." A complementary relationship may be set by the social or cultural context (as in the cases of mother and infant, doctor and patient, or teacher and student), or it may be the idiosyncratic relationship style of a particular dyad. In either case, it is important to emphasize the interlocking nature of the relationship, in which dissimilar but fitted behaviors evoke each other. One partner does not impose a complementary relationship on the other, but rather each behaves in a manner which presupposes, while at the same time providing reasons for, the behavior of the other: their definitions of the relationship (s. 2.3) fit.

2.63

A third type of relationship has been suggested—"metacomplementary," in which *A* lets or forces *B* to be in charge of him; by the same reasoning, we could also add "pseudosymmetry," in which *A* lets or forces *B* to be symmetrical. This potentially infinite regress can, however, be avoided by recalling the distinction made earlier (s. 1.4) between the observation of behavioral redundancies and their inferred explanations, in the form of mythologies; that is, we are interested in *how* the pair behave without being distracted by why (they believe) they so conduct themselves. If, though, the individuals involved avail themselves of the multiple levels of communication (s. 2.22) in order to express different patterns on different levels, paradoxical results of significant pragmatic importance may arise (s. 5.41; 6.42, ex. 3; 7.5, ex. 2d).

2.64

The potential pathologies (escalation in symmetry and rigidity in complementarity) of these modes of communication will be dealt with in the next chapter. For the present, we can state simply our last tentative axiom: *All communicational interchanges are either symmetrical or complementary, depending on whether they are based on equality or difference.*

2.7 SUMMARY

Regarding the above axioms in general, some qualifications should be re-emphasized. First, it should be clear that they are put forth tentatively, rather informally defined and certainly more preliminary than exhaustive. Second, they are, among themselves, quite heterogeneous in that they draw from widely ranging observations on communication phenomena. They are unified not by their origins but by their *pragmatic* importance, which in turn rests not so much on their particulars as on their *interpersonal* (rather than monadic) reference. Birdwhistell has even gone so far as to suggest that

> an individual does not communicate; he engages in or becomes part of communication. He may move, or make noises . . . but he does not communicate. In a parallel fashion, he may see, he may hear, smell, taste, or feel—but he does not communicate. In other words, he does not originate communication; he participates in it. Communication as a system, then, is not to be understood on a simple model of action and reaction, however complexly stated. As a system, it is to be comprehended on the transactional level. (Birdwhistell, 1959, p. 104)

Thus, the impossibility of not communicating makes all two-or-more-person situations *interpersonal,* communicative ones; the relationship aspect of such communication further specifies this same point. The pragmatic, interpersonal importance of the digital and analogic modes lies not only in its hypothesized isomorphism with content and relationship, but in the inevitable and significant ambiguity which both sender and receiver face in problems of translation from the one mode to the other. The description of problems of punctuation rests precisely on the underlying metamorphosis of the classic action-reaction model. Finally, the symmetry-complementarity paradigm comes perhaps closest to the mathematical concept of *function,* the individuals' positions merely being variables with an infinity of possible values whose meaning is not absolute but rather only emerges in relation to the other.

Notes

1. It might be added that, even alone, it is possible to have dialogues in fantasy, with one's hallucinations (Bateson, 1961), or with life (s. 8.3). Perhaps such internal "communication" follows some of the same rules which govern interpersonal communication; such unobservable phenomena, however, are outside the scope of our meaning of the term.
2. Very interesting research in this field has been carried out by Luft (1962), who studied what he calls "social stimulus deprivation." He brought two strangers together in a room, made them sit across from each other and instructed them "not to talk or communicate in any way." Subsequent interviews revealed the highly stressful nature of this situation. To quote the author:

. . . he has before him the other unique individual with his ongoing, though muted, behavior. At this point, it is postulated, that true interpersonal testing takes place, and only part of this testing may be done consciously. For example, how does the other subject respond to him and to the small non-verbal cues which he sends out? Is there an attempt at understanding his enquiring glance, or is it coldly ignored? Does the other subject display postural cues of tension, indicating some distress at confronting him? Does he grow increasingly comfortable, indicating some kind of acceptance, or will the other treat him as if he were a thing, which did not exist? These and many other kinds of readily discernible behavior appear to take place. . . .

3. We have chosen, somewhat arbitrarily, to say that the relationship classifies, or subsumes, the content aspect, although it is equally accurate in logical analysis to say that the class is defined by its members and therefore the content aspect can be said to define the relationship aspect. Since our primary interest is not information exchange but the pragmatics of communication, we will use the former approach.

4. The three possible groupings ("punctuations") are:

$$S = (a - a) + (a - a) + (a - a) + (a - a) + . . .$$
$$= 0 + 0 + 0 + . . .$$
$$= 0$$

Another way of grouping the elements of the sequence would be:

$$S = a - (a - a) - (a - a) - (a - a) - (a - a) - . . .$$
$$= a - 0 - 0 - 0$$
$$= a$$

Still another way would be:

$$S = a - (a - a + a - a + a - a + a - . . .)$$

and since the elements contained in the brackets are nothing but the series itself, it follows that:

$$S = a - S$$

Therefore $2S = a$, and $S = \frac{a}{2}$ (Bolzano, 1889, pp. 49–50).

5. Interestingly enough, there is reason to believe that computer engineers arrived at this result quite independently from what the physiologists already knew at the time, a fact which in itself provides a beautiful illustration of von Bertalanffy's (1950) postulate that complex systems have their own inherent lawfulness that can be followed throughout the various systemic levels, i.e., the atomic, molecular, cellular, organismic, individual, societal, etc. The story goes that during an interdisciplinary gathering of scientists interested in feedback phenomena (probably one of the Josiah Mary Foundation meetings), the great histologist von Bonin was shown the wiring diagram of a selective reading device and immediately said: "But this is just a diagram of the third layer of the visual cortex . . ." We cannot vouch for the authenticity of this story, but would hold it with the Italian proverb "se non è vero, è ben trovato" (even if it is not true, it still makes a good story).

6. The paramount communicational significance of context is all too easily overlooked in the analysis of human communication, and yet anyone who brushed his teeth in a busy street rather than in his bathroom might be quickly carted off to a police station or to a lunatic asylum—to give just one example of the pragmatic effects of nonverbal communication.

7. There is reason to believe that whales and dolphins may also use digital communication, but the research in this area is not yet conclusive.

8. By now the reader will have discovered for himself how suggestive a similarity there exists between the analogic and the digital modes of communication and the psychoanalytic concepts of *primary* and *secondary* processes respectively. If transposed from the intrapsychic to the interpersonal frame of reference, Freud's description of the id becomes virtually a definition of analogic communication:

> The laws of logic—above all, *the law of contradiction* —do not hold for processes in the id. Contradictory impulses exist side by side without neutralizing each other or drawing apart . . . There is nothing in the id which can be compared to negation, and we are astonished to find in it an exception to the philosophers' assertion that space and time are necessary forms of our mental acts (Freud, 1933, p. 104; italics ours).

9. For the same reasons, it is possible to suggest that divorce would be experienced as something much more definite if the usually dry and uninspiring legal act of obtaining the final decree were implemented by some form of analogic ritual of final separation.

REFERENCES

Bateson, Gregory, "Culture Contact and Schismogenesis." *Man,* 35:178–83, 1935.

Bateson, Gregory, "A Theory of Play and Fantasy." *Psychiatric Research Reports,* 2:39–51, 1955.

Bateson, Gregory, *Naven,* 2nd ed. Stanford: Stanford University Press, 1958.

Bateson, Gregory, ed., *Perceval's Narrative, A Patient's Account of His Psychosis, 1830–1832.* Stanford: Stanford University Press, 1961.

Bateson, Gregory, personal communication.

Bateson, Gregory, and Jackson, Don D., "Some Varieties of Pathogenic Organization." In David McK. Rioch, ed., *Disorders of Communication,* Volume 42, Research Publications. Association for Research in Nervous and Mental Disease, 1964, pp. 270–83.

Bertalanffy, Ludwig von, "An Outline of General System Theory." *British Journal of the Philosophy of Science,* 1:134–165, 1950.

Birdwhistell, Ray L., "Contribution of Linguistic-Kinesic Studies to the Understanding of Schizophrenia." In Alfred Auerback, ed., *Schizophrenia. An Integrated Approach.* New York: The Ronald Press Company, 1959, pp. 99–123.

Bolzano, Bernard, *Paradoxien des Unendlichen* [Paradoxes of the Infinite], 2nd ed., Fr. Přihonsky, ed., Berlin: Mayer und Müller, 1889.

Cherry, Colin, *On Human Communication.* New York: Science Editions, 1961.

Freud, Sigmund, *New Introductory Lectures on Psychoanalysis.* New York: W. W. Norton & Company, Inc., 1933.

Haley, Jay, *Strategies of Psychotherapy.* New York: Grune & Stratton, Inc., 1963.

Joad, C. E. M., *Why War?* Harmondsworth: Penguin Special, 1939.

Lorenz, Konrad Z., *King Solomon's Ring.* London: Methuen, 1952.

Luft, Joseph, "On Non-verbal Interaction." Paper presented at the Western Psychological Association Convention, San Francisco, April 1962.

McCulloch, Warren S., and Pitts, Walter, "A Logical Calculus of the Ideas Immanent in Nervous Activity." *Bulletin of Mathematical Biophysics,* 5:115–33, 1943.

Richardson, Lewis Fry, "Mathematics of War and Foreign Politics." In James R. Newman, ed., *The World of Mathematics,* Volume 2. New York: Simon and Schuster, Inc., 1956, pp. 1240–53.

Ruesch, Jurgen, and Bateson, Gregory, *Communication: The Social Matrix of Psychiatry.* New York: Humanities Press, 1951.

Sluzki, Carlos E., and Beavin, Janet, "Simetría y complementaridad: una definición operacional y una tipología de parejas" [Symmetry and Complementarity: An Operational Definition and a Typology of Dyads]. *Acta psiquiátrica y psicológica de América latina,* 11:321–30, 1965.

Tinbergen, Nicolass, *Social Behavior in Animals with Special Reference to Vertebrates.* London: Methuen, 1953.

Watzlawick, Paul, *An Anthology of Human Communication; Text and Tape.* Palo Alto: Science and Behavior Books, 1964.

Whorf, Benjamin Lee, "Science and Linguistics." In John B. Carroll, ed., *Language, Thought, and Reality: Selected Writings of Benjamin Lee Whorf.* New York: John Wiley & Sons, Inc., 1956, pp. 207–19.

21

THE LIMITED CAPACITY MODEL OF MEDIATED MESSAGE PROCESSING

ANNIE LANG

The goal of this paper is to present a limited capacity information-processing model of mediated message processing and to offer at least one measure of each part of this information-processing model. Using this approach and these measures, researchers should be able to track the content of mediated messages into, through, and back out of the message recipient's information-processing system (the "black box"). The ability to do this will allow us to craft messages that convey their information better and to understand better how our messages may cause very real effects, both intended and unintended.

The model presented here is a data-driven model. Its roots lie in the information-processing tradition of cognitive psychology (Lachman, Lachman, & Butterfield, 1979) and in the social scientific effects research in mass communication

(Berger & Chaffee, 1989). The model, as it stands now, is the product of a series of empirical studies that arose from the application of the information-processing model to questions of interest to effects researchers. It provides both a conceptual-theoretical framework for asking questions about the cognitive processing underlying media effects and an operational conceptualization that provides a methodological tool to measure each theorized process and mechanism.

[. . .]

LIMITED CAPACITY INFORMATION-PROCESSING APPROACH TO MEDIATED COMMUNICATION

The particular information-processing model presented here (Lang, 1992; 1995; Lang & Basil,

SOURCE: Lang, A. (2000). The limited capacity model of mediated message processing. *Journal of Communication, 50*, 46–70 (46–55 and 66–70). Used by permission of the International Communication Association.

1998) was specifically developed to investigate how people process television messages. It is an amalgam of many information-processing models developed over the past 30 years (Eysenck, 1993; Lachman, Lachman, & Butterfield, 1979). The model has two major assumptions. First, people are information processors. A major task that people engage in is the processing of information. The basic parts of information processing are to perceive stimuli, turn them into mental representations, do mental work on those representations, and reproduce them in the same or in an altered form. Second, a person's ability to process information is limited. Processing messages requires mental resources, and people have only a limited (and perhaps fixed) pool of mental resources. You can think about one thing, or two, or maybe seven, at the same time, but eventually all your resources are being used, and the system cannot think yet another thing without letting a previous thought go.

Information processing, in this model, is conceived of as a group of simultaneously occurring component processes (or subprocesses) that people perform on stimuli and on the mental representation of stimuli that they construct. Some of these subprocesses are automatic and some are controlled (Shiffrin & Schneider, 1977). Automatic processes happen without conscious volition on the part of the message recipient. Controlled processes are those that people intend. This model proposes three major subprocesses of information processing: (a) encoding; (b) storage; and (c) retrieval. Though the discussion of this model will proceed in a linear fashion, the processes discussed are continuous and iterative. It is assumed that the human brain can, and usually does, engage in all of these processes simultaneously.

Encoding

The subprocess of encoding involves getting the message out of the environment (i.e., off the page or off the screen) and into a person's brain. Historically, in the mass communication field, we have operationally equated this step with measures of exposure, such as the number of hours spent with the medium, or through measures of attention. Many communication models and theories treat this step in the information-processing sequence as simple and dichotomous—as a necessary, but not sufficient, condition on the road to communication effects. Not so, in the model presented here. Rather, this initial passage from environmental stimulus to mental representation is conceived of as being complex, idiosyncratic, and inexact.

This model theorizes that there are three processes involved in converting a message into a mental representation in the brain. First, the message must engage the sensory receptors, that is, eyes, ears, nose, mouth, skin (Eysenck, 1993). This can be thought of as exposure or perception. Information gathered by the sensory receptors enters some kind of sensory store (Zechmeister & Nyberg, 1982). Research on these sensory stores suggests that there is a specific sensory store for each sense, and that these stores may be virtually unlimited. However, the storage here is very short-lived. Information resides in these stores for periods ranging from about 300 msec for the visual (called iconic) store (Coltheart, 1975; Holding, 1975) to 4 or 5 seconds for the auditory (called echoic) store (Crowder, 1976). If a bit of information is not selected for further processing, it is written over by new information and lost.

If a person is exposed to a mediated message, the message should automatically make it into the sensory store. The sensory stores, however, hold more information than a person can be aware of or attend to. Only a fraction of the information held in the sensory stores moves on into active (or short-term or working) memory. The encoding subprocess is a two-step process through which specific bits of information[1] contained in the original message are selected from the myriad information bits available in the sensory store and transformed into activated mental representations in working or short-term memory. The mental representation of the message that is activated in working memory is not a veridical or precise representation of the message, but rather a representation that reflects both which specific bits of information any given person has selected for representation and the act of constructing a mental representation, which is affected in turn by the goals, knowledge, and environment of the person receiving the message.

The initial step in the encoding process is the determination of which bits of information will be transformed into mental representations. This selection process is driven by both automatic (unintentional) and controlled (intentional) processes.

Controlled selection processes reflect the viewer's goals. You might, for example, decide to notice what color shirts people were wearing in a movie; as a result, shirt color would always be selected into short-term memory while you were watching.

Automatic selection processes are unintentional and unconscious and are activated by the stimulus. Two major types of stimuli activate automatic selection processes: (a) information that is relevant to the goals and needs of the individual, and (b) information that represents change or an unexpected occurrence in the environment (Graham, 1997; Ohman, 1997). Automatic selection processes that are related to individual goals and relevance will vary across situations, cultures, and individuals. On the other hand, automatic selection processes related to stimulus characteristics, such as novelty, change, and intensity, are likely to be the same across individuals within a culture, though the standards of what is novel may vary from culture to culture.

The process of encoding a message, thus, does not produce a precise one-to-one correspondence between the message and the mental representation of the message. The encoded message is neither an exact nor a complete replica of the original message. Rather it is an idiosyncratic representation of the message that is constructed by the viewer. It contains only a small fraction of the total information contained in the original message.

In this model there is nothing simple about exposure and attention. Rather, all the bits of information in a mediated message must engage the sensory receptors and enter the sensory store,

where a fraction of them are selected (as a result of automatic and controlled selection processes) and transformed into mental representations in a person's working memory. This is the process of encoding. What a person does with this mental representation of the message is the basis upon which many theories of communication are built. One of the obvious things that people must do is to transfer some of that information from short-term memory to some longer term store.

Storage

Memory theory is a complex and fast-changing area of research. How many types of stores there are, whether they are limited or not, the mechanisms through which memories are stored, are all disputed questions. Recent methodological innovations (e.g., PET, FMRI, single-cell recording techniques, and neurochemical investigations) are rapidly altering our knowledge about where and how memory works. This model uses a general associative network model of memory, but does not take a stance on the specifics of memory architecture and operation.

Associative network models conceptualize individual memories as being connected to other related memories by associations (or links). When a memory is in use, it is activated. Activation can travel through associations, a process that renders related memories more active, or available, than unrelated memories (Eysenck, 1993; Eysenck & Keane, 1990; Klimesch, 1994). This model does not draw a sharp distinction between short- and long-term memory. Short-term or working memory is conceptualized as activated memories within the larger inactive (or long-term) memory. It is conceivable that working memory is just the subset of all memories that are active at any given time. The state of being concurrently activated may be the process that builds associations among new and old mental representations.

During the encoding subprocess, a mental representation of the message is constructed in working or activated memory. Initially, this newly encoded "message information" is activated but has associations only with the other information concurrently active in short-term memory. As a person thinks about the message, more and more associations between the "new" information and old information are formed.

The more a person links a new bit of information into this associative memory network, the better that information is stored. This process of linking newly encoded information to previously encoded information (or memories) is called storage. The more associations are formed between new and old information, the more completely the new information is stored. The result of the storage process is a continuum from poorly stored (few associations and links) to thoroughly stored (many associations and links). Some bits of information in the encoded mental representations of messages may be more thoroughly stored than others. In other words, all of the bits of information encoded from a message do not receive equivalent amounts of processing during storage. Some parts will be more thoroughly stored while other parts receive only cursory storage.

Retrieval

The final subprocess in this model is retrieval. This is the process of reactivating a stored mental representation of some aspect of the message. Put another way, retrieval is the process of searching the associative memory network for a specific piece of information and reactivating it in working memory. By and large, the more associative links there are to a piece of information, that is, the more thoroughly it has been stored, the more readily retrievable it is.

In addition to conceptualizing retrieval as an outcome associated with learning the content of a message, this model also conceptualizes retrieval as an ongoing process during message reception. We activate or retrieve relevant previously stored knowledge from long-term memory as we receive messages in order to comprehend and store them. A message about an election, for example, will result in concurrent retrieval of what you know about elections in general, and about this election in particular, in order for you to understand the message and store this new election information into your associative network. This concurrent retrieval process also plays a role in the storage process because concurrent retrieval causes the simultaneous activation of old and new information.

Any one of these subprocesses—encoding, storage, or retrieval—can be performed in a cursory or a thorough manner. How thoroughly a subprocess is performed and how many resources are allocated to the subprocess affect the likelihood that subsequent or concurrent subprocesses will be performed thoroughly. Memory for a message is, therefore, a composite of the outcome of all three subprocesses.

Information Processing and Limited Capacity

Many things affect how thoroughly a message is processed, that is, how much of the information in the message is encoded, stored, and ultimately retrievable. A major contributing factor is whether or not the recipient of the message has sufficient processing resources available to process the message. There are two main reasons why messages may not be thoroughly processed. First, the message recipient may choose to allocate fewer resources to the task than it requires. Second, the message may require more resources than the message recipient has available to allocate to the task. In either case, fewer resources are allocated to the task of processing a message than it requires, and the message, therefore, will not be thoroughly processed.

This model suggests that processing resources are independently allocated to the three major subprocesses of encoding, storage, and retrieval.[2] As a result, one subprocess (encoding, for example) may be allocated sufficient resources for thorough processing while the other, simultaneously occurring subprocesses (i.e., storage and retrieval) may receive insufficient resources to be performed optimally.

A LIMITED CAPACITY INFORMATION-PROCESSING APPROACH TO TELEVISION VIEWING

What follows is a more concrete application of the model to a specific mediated-message context, that of watching television. What happens when limited capacity information processors (i.e., people) allocate their limited resources to television viewing?

Television as a Psychological Stimulus

First things first. We begin with the question, what is television? From an information-processing perspective, a television message is made up of two streams of variably redundant information, one audio and one video. These streams of information are continuous, and their pace is not generally under the control of the viewer. Much communication research has focused on the content of television (sports, violence, sex, news). Both the audio and the video channels carry story or content information. They also, however, contain a great deal of video and audio structural information (e.g., luminance levels, cuts, slow motion, animation, zooms, pans, video graphics, frequency levels, sound effects, music, rate of presentation, narrative structure). The television message is made up of both content and structural information.

To understand how television messages are processed, we must examine how both the structure and the content of the medium interact with each of the models' subprocesses. The following three sections of this paper consider the effects of both content and structure on encoding, storage, and retrieval.

Television Messages and Encoding

The first subprocess in the information-processing model described here is the encoding of the message into working memory. Encoding is an ongoing process. People are continuously selecting (unconsciously and consciously) information from their environment and encoding it into short-term memory. The discussion here attempts to determine which bits of information in a mediated message are most likely to be encoded into working memory. As discussed above, two types of information are most likely to be selected for encoding into working memory: (a) information relevant to the goals of the individual, and (b) information that is novel, unexpected, or representative of change in the environment. How do these types of information get selected?

This model suggests that one of the automatic selection mechanisms steering the selection of information to be encoded is the orienting response, or OR (Ohman, 1979; 1997). The orienting response, first proposed by Pavlov (1927), is an automatic (some say reflexive) physiological and behavioral response that occurs in response to novel or signal stimuli. A signal stimulus has some meaning for a person—the person's name, for instance. Signal stimuli change from person to person, culture to culture, and even from one situation to another. Once a stimulus has acquired signal status, however, the orienting response will be elicited by it. A novel stimulus is one that represents a change in the environment or an unexpected occurrence. In the context of viewing a television message, novelty or change is interpreted within the context of that television message. When an orienting response occurs, the viewer orients his or her sensory receptors toward the stimulus that caused the response, and an organized set of physiological responses accompanies this behavioral response (Lynn, 1966). The response set includes vasodilation of the blood vessels to the head, decrease in the alpha frequency of the EEG, slowing of the heart, increases in skin conductance and skin temperature, and general vasoconstriction of the blood vessels to the major muscle groups. Research suggests that this physiological response set is associated with attention (quieting of the body and increase in blood flow to the brain) and stimulus intake (Campbell, Wood, &

McBride, 1997; Graham, 1997; Hoffman, 1997; Kimmel, Van Olst, & Orlebeke, 1979).

It has been suggested that the orienting response is one of the selection mechanisms that determines what information in the sensory store gets selected to be encoded into working memory (Ohman, 1979, 1997). The model being presented here suggests that many aspects of the structure and content of television messages elicit orienting responses in television viewers. The orienting response causes an automatic allocation of processing resources to the task of encoding the stimulus that elicited the orienting response. This increase in resources allocated to encoding increases the amount of information that can be selected from sensory store and encoded into working memory at that point in time, so long as the television viewer has sufficient available resources to respond to the call for additional resources made by the orienting response.

Consider the case mentioned earlier in which a person has made a controlled decision to notice the color of the actors' shirts. In that case, shirt color becomes a signal stimulus. As a result, whenever a shirt appears, the viewer will orient to the color of the shirt, additional resources will be allocated to encoding the shirt color, and this viewer will encode more information about shirt colors than a viewer who has not made this strategic choice. Thus, the orienting response, as a selection mechanism, can account for both individual choices, about what in the message is relevant and also for universal responses to novelty, structure, and unexpected content.[3]

Television Messages and Storage

What determines how much and which parts of a message are stored? As discussed above, both automatic and controlled processes are likely to be operating here, so storage is affected by both individual differences and by the resource limitations of the human information-processing system. In addition, in the television-viewing situation (because the message is continuous), encoding and storage likely limit

one another. To the extent that a message elicits frequent orienting responses, there will be frequent calls for processing resources to encode the message, which may cause a disproportionate amount of processing resources to be automatically allocated to the encoding subprocess. This will decrease the amount of resources that are unallocated and therefore available to be allocated to storage. How many of the remaining resources are allocated to storage will be primarily dependent on the goals and needs of the individual. A person who is watching primarily for entertainment, for example, may not be purposely allocating his or her limited processing resources to storage. This person is "running on automatic." As a result, only sufficient information to follow the story may be stored. The stored information may form associative links primarily with other information from the story, and not be much integrated into already existing memory structures. Because long-term memory is not a goal of this individual, only a small portion of previously stored knowledge may be activated during viewing.

On the other hand, a person watching a television message on which he or she expects to be tested (e.g., watching a science video in school) may make a serious attempt to allocate resources to storage so as to be able to pass the test. In this case, the calls for attention made by structural features may actually interfere with the process of storage because they may "steal" resources from storage in order to allocate them to encoding. In addition, this viewer is likely to allocate a fair number of resources to retrieving what he or she already knows about this topic from long-term memory in order to integrate new knowledge with old knowledge. This viewer is much more likely to run into a resource-limited situation than the person watching to be entertained, since this viewer is purposely allocating resources to storage and retrieval in order to learn and retain the content of the message. On the other hand, because this person is allocating resources to storage and concurrent retrieval, he or she is likely to process the message more fully than someone who is allocating fewer resources, despite the fact that overload will limit the availability of required resources and, therefore, how thoroughly he or she is able to process the message.

In the same way that the orienting response allocates resources to encoding, there appear to be other automatic processes that operate to automatically allocate resources to storage. A specific mechanism, akin to the orienting response, has not yet been proposed for this task. Research suggests, however, that certain types of stimuli are stored much better than other types of stimuli, a phenomenon that may indicate some sort of automatic allocation process. In particular, stimuli that elicit emotion appear to be stored much better than stimuli that do not elicit emotion (Bradley, Greenwald, Petry, & P. J. Lang, 1992; Christianson, 1992; Lang, Dhillon, & Dong, 1995; Reeves, Newhagen, Maibach, Basil, & Kurz, 1991; Thorson & Friestad, 1989). This model suggests that emotion-eliciting stimuli may cause the automatic allocation of additional processing resources to storage.

Television Messages and Retrieval

Two aspects of the retrieval process need to be considered: later retrieval of message content and concurrent retrieval of already known information during viewing. First, consider later retrieval, or memory, for the message content. If the content of a television message has been selected from sensory store, encoded into working memory, and thoroughly stored, then it should be retrievable for use at a later date (that test on the science program). Later retrieval of the information contained in a message differs significantly from the storage and encoding subprocesses in that it is not performed during viewing. In the television-viewing situation, the viewer must keep up with the message. If you don't encode some aspect of a scene and the scene changes, that's it, you didn't encode it. Similarly, if you don't store something that you encoded, that information will remain unlinked or poorly linked. On the other hand, later

retrieval of a message's content is not necessarily constrained by time and resources.

Concurrent retrieval, on the other hand, the process of continuously retrieving previously known information during viewing to aid understanding and storage, is constrained by time and resource availability. The demand placed on resources by the need to retrieve information from long-term memory will increase the resources required to process a message and thereby decrease the resources available to be allocated to encoding and storage.

A message that requires viewers to recall facts they already know in order to follow the message will require more resources than one that does not require much background. Further, how available this past knowledge is, that is, how hard it is to retrieve the previously known facts, will also affect how many resources the subprocess requires. If the viewer is an expert in the message area, then retrieval of background information will require few resources, as the associative memory network will be complex and available. If the person knows little about the topic, the retrieval of what information the viewer does know may require many resources, and this will greatly limit his or her ability to learn the new information. In this regard, the model is quite consistent with research in communication, starting with the "knowledge gap," that suggests that the more you know about something the easier it is to learn more about it.

Summary

Briefly, then, this model describes television watching as a combination of controlled and automatic resource allocation mechanisms that combine to allocate processing resources to the encoding, storage, and retrieval of the bits of information that make up a television message. When a viewer has insufficient resources available to perform all of these subprocesses thoroughly, some aspects of processing will suffer. Both the structure and the content of television elicit orienting responses. These orienting responses call processing resources to the encoding process. Certain message characteristics, such as emotion, as well as the goals of the viewer, may increase the resources allocated to storage, which in turn may increase how much and how well content information is stored. Finally, the need to retrieve previous knowledge in order to understand the message also demands resources during viewing and influences how easily information can be stored.

[. . .]

The model as it stands now is a work in progress. Other researchers, working within its framework, may apply the model to other areas of interest to communication scholars and extend the model both theoretically and methodologically. Future research using the model might, for example, explore the use of implicit memory measures as an indicator of concurrent retrieval or investigate how individual and message factors influence the accuracy of the construction of the mental representation during encoding.

This model should prove useful both to researchers and, eventually, to producers by increasing our understanding of how the content and structure of a medium interact with a user's information-processing system and to determine which parts and how much of communication messages are remembered. This model should allow us to better understand how micro- and macroelements of individuals, societies, and cultures shape the communication process.

Notes

1. "Information" or "bit of information" is used here to indicate all the individual units of structure and content that make up a message. These bits of information range from purely structural information like luminance levels, color spectrum, audio frequency, and size and location in the visual field, to larger, more content-related units like words, pictures, and actions, and to even larger metaconstructions, such as expressions, tone, intentions, etc. Any given message contains countless bits of information that may or may not be selected and encoded into working memory.

2. This model is a single-pool model. It assumes that all resources can be allocated to any of these three processes. The possibility exists, of course, that each of these processes might have its own pool of resources. The debate among theorists about multiple-pool vs. single-pool models is hotly contested and continuous. A good review of this literature can be found in Basil (1994a). To date, the data generated by the model presented here have supported the continued use of a single-pool model.

3. Of course, encoding does not occur only in response to orienting. People encode information continuously as they make sense of their environment. However, the orienting response does account for variation in the amount of processing resources allocated to encoding. To some extent this moment-to-moment variation in processing resource allocation can be predicted across subject as a function of the novelty and signal status of the elements of the stimulus message.

References

Alwitt, L. F., Anderson, D. R., Lorch, E. P., & Levin, S. R. (1980). Preschool children's visual attention to attributes of television. *Human Communication Research, 7,* 52–67.

Anderson, D. R., & Levin, S. R. (1976). Young children's attention to *Sesame Street. Child Development, 47,* 806–811.

Basil, M. (1994a). Multiple resource theory I: Application to television viewing. *Communication Research, 21,* 177–207.

Basil, M. (1994b). Secondary reaction-time measures. In A. Lang (Ed.), *Measuring psychological responses to media messages* (pp. 85–98). Hillsdale, NJ: Erlbaum.

Berger, C. R., & Chaffee, S. H. (1989). *Handbook of communication science.* Newbury Park, CA: Sage.

Bolls, P., Hibbs, H., & Lang, A. (1995, February). *A message is a message is a message . . . Structure predicts memory for random television messages.* Presented to the Mass Communication Interest Group of the Western Speech Communication Association, Portland, OR.

Bolls, P., Potter, R., & Lang, A. (1996, April). Television arousal and memory: The effects of production pacing and arousing content on encoding, storage, and retrieval of television messages. In M. Gasser (Ed.), *Online proceedings of the 1996 Midwest Artificial Intelligence and Cognitive Science Conference.* URL http://www.cs.indiana.edu/event/maics96/Proceedings/Bolls/bolls.html

Borse, J., David, P., Dent, D., Lang, A., Potter, R., Bolls, P., Zhou, S., Schwartz, N., & Trout, G. (1997, August). *Extra/Extra./Read all about it: Attention and memory for deviant and imagistic headlines.* Paper presented to the Theory and Methodology Division of the Association for Education in Journalism and Mass Communication, Chicago.

Bradley, M. M., Greenwald, M. K., Petry, M. C., & Lang, P. J. (1992). Remembering pictures: Pleasure and arousal in memory. *Journal of Experimental Psychology, 18,* 379–390.

Campbell, B. A., Wood, G., & McBride, T. (1997). Origins of orienting and defensive responses: An evolutionary perspective. In P. J. Lang, R. F. Simons, & M. Balaban (Eds.), *Attention and orienting: Sensory and motivational processes* (pp. 41–58). Hillsdale, NJ: Erlbaum.

Chew, F. (1994). Interest, the knowledge gap, and television programming. *Journal of Broadcasting and Electronic Media, 38,* 271–288.

Christianson, S. (1992). *The handbook of emotion and memory: Research and theory.* Hillsdale, NJ: Erlbaum.

Christianson, S., Goodman, J., & Loftus, E. F. (1992). Eyewitness memory for stressful events: Methodological quandaries and ethical dilemmas. In S. Christianson (Ed.), *The handbook of emotion and memory: Research and theory* (pp. 217–244). Hillsdale, NJ: Erlbaum.

Columbo, M., & D'Amato, M. R. (1986). A comparison of visual and auditory short-term memory in monkeys (Cebus apella). *Quarterly Journal of Experimental Psychology, 38,* 425–428.

Coltheart, M. (1975). Iconic memory and visible persistence. *Perception & Psychophysics, 27,* 183–228.

Craik, F. I., & Lockhart, R. S. (1972). Levels of processing: A framework for memory research. *Journal of Verbal Learning and Verbal Behavior, 11,* 671–684.

Crowder, R. G. (1976). *Principles of learning and memory.* Hillsdale, NJ: Erlbaum.

Davidson, R., Schwartz, G., Saron, C., Bennet, J., & Goleman, D. (1979). Frontal versus parietal EEG asymmetry during positive and negative affect. *Psychophysiology, 2,* 202–203.

Dimmond, S. J., Farrington, L., & Johnson, P. (1976). Differing emotional responses from right and left hemispheres. *Nature, 261,* 690–692.

Eysenck, M. W. (1993). *Principles of cognitive psychology.* Hillsdale, NJ: Erlbaum.

Eysenck, M. W., & Keane, M. T. (1990). *Cognitive psychology: A student's handbook.* Hove, UK: Erlbaum.

Gantz, W. (1978). How uses and gratifications affect recall of television news. *Journalism Quarterly, 55,* 664–672.

Geiger, S., & Reeves, B. (1993). The effects of scene changes and semantic relatedness on attention to television. *Communication Research, 20,* 155–175.

Grabe, M., Lang, A., Zhou, S., & Bolls, P. (1999, May). *The impact of education on information processing: An experimental investigation of the knowledge gap.* Paper presented to the Information Systems Division of the International Communication Association, San Francisco, CA.

Graham, F. K. (1997). Afterward: Pre-attentive processing and passive and active attention. In P. J. Lang, R. F. Simons, & M. Balaban (Eds.), *Attention and orienting: Sensory and motivational processes* (pp. 417–452). Hillsdale, NJ: Erlbaum.

Graham, F. K., & Clifton, R. K. (1966). Heart-rate change as a component of the orienting response. *Psychological Bulletin, 65,* 305–320.

Grimes, T. (1991). Mild auditory-visual dissonance in television news may exceed viewer attentional capacity. *Human Communication Research, 18,* 268–298.

Gunter, B. (1987). *Poor reception: Misunderstanding and forgetting broadcast news.* Hillsdale, NJ: Erlbaum.

Hasher, L., & Zacks, R. T. (1979). Automatic and effortful processes in memory. *Journal of Experimental Psychology: General, 108,* 356–388.

Heurer, F., & Reisberg, D. (1992). Emotion, arousal, and memory for detail. In S. Christianson (Ed.), *The handbook of emotion and memory: Research and theory* (pp. 151–180). Hillsdale, NJ: Erlbaum.

Hibbs, H., Bolls, P., & Lang, A. (1995, May). *The medium is the memory: Using structural features to predict memory for random television messages.* Presented to the Information Systems Division of the International Communication Association, Albuquerque, NM.

Hoffman, H. S. (1997). Attention factors in the elicitation and modification of the startle reaction. In E. J. Lang, R. F. Simons, & M. Balaban (Eds.),

Attention and orienting: Sensory and motivational processes (pp. 185–204). Hillsdale, NJ: Erlbaum.

Holding, D. H. (1975). Sensory storage reconsidered. *Memory & Cognition, 3,* 31–41.

Katz, E., Adoni, H., & Parness, P. (1977). Remembering the news: What the picture adds to recall. *Journalism Quarterly, 54,* 231–239.

Kawahara, K., Bolls, P., Hansell, R., Lang, A., Potter, R., & Dent, D. (1996, May). *The effects of production pacing and content arousal on viewers allocation of capacity to encoding and storage of television messages.* Paper presented to the International Communication Association, Information Systems Division, Chicago, IL.

Kimmel, H. D., Van Olst, E. H., & Orlebeke, J. F. (1979). *The orienting reflex in humans.* Hillsdale, NJ: Erlbaum.

Klimesch, W. (1994). *The structure of long-term memory: A connectivity model of semantic processing.* Hillsdale, NJ: Erlbaum.

Lachman, R., Lachman, J. L., & Butterfield, E. C. (1979). *Cognitive psychology and information processing: An introduction.* Hillsdale, NJ: Erlbaum.

Lang, A. (1989). The effects of chronological presentation of information on processing and memory for broadcast news. *Journal of Broadcasting and Electronic Media, 33,* 441–452.

Lang, A. (1990). Involuntary attention and physiological arousal evoked by structural features and mild emotion in TV commercials. *Communication Research, 17,* 275–299.

Lang, A. (1991). Emotion, formal features, and memory for televised political advertisements. In F. Biocca (Ed.), *Television and political advertising, Vol. 1: Psychological processes* (pp. 221–244). Hillsdale, NJ: Erlbaum.

Lang, A. (1992, May). *A limited capacity theory of television viewing.* Paper presented to the Information Systems Division of the International Communication Association, Miami, FL.

Lang, A. (1995). Defining audio/video redundancy from a limited capacity information processing perspective. *Communication Research, 22,* 86–115.

Lang, A., & Basil, M. D. (1998). Attention, resource allocation, and communication research: What do secondary task reaction times measure anyway? In M. Roloff (Ed.), *Communication Yearbook 21.* Thousand Oaks, CA: Sage.

Lang, A., Bolls, P., & Kawahara, K. (1996, April). The effects of arousing message content and structural complexity on television viewers' level of arousal and allocation of processing resources. The proceedings of the Midwest Artificial Intelligence and Cognitive Science Conference, http://www.cs.indiana.edu/event/maics96/procedings.html.

Lang, A., Bolls, P., Potter, R., & Kawahara, K. (1999). The effects of production pacing and arousing content on the information processing of television messages. *Journal of Broadcasting and Electronic Media, 43*(4), 451–475.

Lang, A., Dhillon, P., & Dong, Q. (1995). Arousal, emotion, and memory for television messages. *Journal of Broadcasting and Electronic Media, 38,* 1–15.

Lang, A., & Friestad, M. (1993). Emotion, hemispheric specialization, and visual and verbal memory for television messages. *Communication Research, 20,* 647–670.

Lang, A., Geiger, S., Strickwerda, M., & Sumner, J. (1993). The effects of related and unrelated cuts on viewers memory for television: A limited capacity theory of television viewing. *Communication Research, 20,* 4–29.

Lang, A., Newhagen, J., & Reeves, B. (1996). Negative video as structure: Emotion, attention, capacity, and memory. *Journal of Broadcasting and Electronic Media, 40,* 460–477.

Lang, A., & Potter, R. (1996, August). *Arousing messages: Reaction time, capacity, encoding.* Paper presented to the annual convention of the Association for Education in Journalism and Mass Communication, Anaheim, CA.

Lang, A., Sias, P., Chantrill, P., & Burek, J. A. (1995). Tell me a story: Narrative structure and memory for television messages. *Communication Reports, 8*(2), 1–9.

Lang, P. J., Bradley, M. M., & Cuthbert, B. N. (1997). Motivated attention: Affect, activation, and action. In P. J. Lang, R. F. Simons, & M. Balaban (Eds.), *Attention and orienting: Sensory and motivational processes* (pp. 97–136). Hillsdale, NJ: Erlbaum.

Lynn, R. (1966). *Attention, arousal, and the orientation reaction.* Oxford, UK: Pergamon Press.

McGaugh, J. L. (1992). Affect, neuromodulatory systems, and memory storage. In S. Christianson (Ed.), *The handbook of emotion and memory: Research and theory* (pp. 245–268). Hillsdale, NJ: Erlbaum.

Metcalfe, J. (1991). Recognition failure and the composite memory trace in CHARM. *Psychological Review, 98,* 529–553.

Newhagen, J., & Reeves, B. (1992). This evening's bad news: Effects of compelling negative television news images on memory. *Journal of Communication, 42,* 25–41.

Ohman, A. (1979). The orientations response, attention, and learning: An information-processing perspective. In H. D. Kimmel, E. H. Van Olst, & J. F. Orlebeke (Eds.), *The orienting reflex in humans* (pp. 443–472). Hillsdale, NJ: Erlbaum.

Ohman, A. (1997). As fast as the blink of an eye: Evolutionary preparedness for preattentive processing of threat. In P. J. Lang, R. F. Simons, & M. Balaban (Eds.), *Attention and orienting: Sensory and motivational processes* (pp. 165–184). Hillsdale, NJ: Erlbaum.

Olien, C. N., Donohue, G. A., & Tichenor, P. J. (1982). *Massacommunicatie, 10*(3), 81–87.

Pavlov, I. P. (1927). *Conditional reflexes: An investigation of the physiological activity of the cerebral cortex.* London: Wexford University Press.

Potter, R. F., Bolls, P., Lang, A., Zhou, S., Schwartz, N., Borse, J., Trout, G., & Dent, D. (1997, August). *What is it? Orienting to structural features of radio messages.* Paper presented to the Theory and Methodology Division of the Association for Education in Journalism and Mass Communication, Chicago.

Potter, R., Lang, A., & Bolls, P. (1997, August). Orienting responses to structural features of media. *Psychophysiology, 34,* Supplement 1, p. S72.

Potter, R., Lang, A., & Bolls, P. (1998, August). *Identifying structural features of radio: Orienting and memory for radio messages.* Paper submitted to the Association for Education in Journalism and Mass Communication, Theory and Methodology Division, Baltimore, MD.

Reeves, B., Lang, A., Thorson, E., & Rothschild, M. (1988). Hemispheric lateralization and the processing of emotional television scenes. *Human Communication Research, 15,* 493–508.

Reeves, B., & Nass, C. (1996). *The media equation: How people treat computers, television, and new media like real people and places.* Cambridge, UK: Cambridge University Press.

Reeves, B., Newhagen, J., Maibach, E., Basil, M., & Kurz, K. (1991). Negative and positive television messages: Effects of message type and message context on attention and memory. *American Behavioral Scientist, 34,* 679–694.

Reeves, B., Thorson, E., Rothschild, M., McDonald, D., Hirsch, J., & Goldstein, R. (1985). Attention to television: Intra stimulus effects of movement and scene changes on alpha variation over time. *International Journal of Neuroscience, 25,* 241–255.

Reeves, B., Thorson, E., & Schleuder, J. (1986). Attention to television: Psychological theories and chronometric measures. In J. Bryant & D. Zillmann (Eds.), *Perspectives on media effects* (pp. 251–279). Hillsdale, NJ: Erlbaum.

Revelle, W., & Loftus, D. A. (1992). The implications of arousal effects for the study of affect and memory. In S. Christianson (Ed.), *The handbook of emotion and memory: Research and theory* (pp. 113–150). Hillsdale, NJ: Erlbaum.

Rubin, A. (1994). Media uses and effects: A uses and gratifications perspective. In J. Bryant & D. Zillmann (Eds.), *Media effects: Advances in theory and research* (pp. 417–427). Hillsdale, NJ: Erlbaum.

Shiffrin, R. M., & Schneider, W. (1977). Controlled and automatic human information processing: Perceptual learning, automatic attending, and a general theory. *Psychological Review, 84,* 127–190.

Singer, J. (1980). The power and limitations of television: A cognitive-affective analysis. In P. Tannenbaum (Ed.), *The entertainment functions of television* (pp. 36–42). Hillsdale, NJ: Erlbaum.

Spear, N. E., & Riccio, D. C. (1994). *Memory: Phenomena and principles.* Boston, MA: Allyn & Bacon.

Thorson, E. (1990). Processing television commercials. In B. Dervin, L. Grossberg, & E. Wartella (Eds.), *Paradigm dialogues in communication, Vol. II: Exemplars.* Newbury Park, CA: Sage.

Thorson, E., & Friestad, M. (1989). The effects of emotion on episodic memory for television commercials. In P. Cafferata & A. Tybout (Eds.), *Cognitive and affective responses to advertising* (pp. 305–325). Lexington, MA: D. C. Heath.

Thorson, E., & Lang, A. (1992). Effects of television video graphics and lecture familiarity on adult cardiac orienting responses and memory. *Communication Research, 19,* 346–369.

Thorson, E., Reeves, B., & Schleuder, J. (1985). Message complexity and attention to television. *Communication Research, 12,* 427–454.

Thorson, E., Reeves, B., & Schleuder, J. (1986). Attention to local and global complexity in television messages. In M. L. McLaughlin (Ed.), *Communication Yearbook 10.* Beverly Hills, CA: Sage.

Tulving, E. (1972). Relation between encoding specificity and levels of processing. In L. S. Cermak & F. I. M. Craik (Eds.), *Levels of processing in human memory.* Hillsdale, NJ: Erlbaum.

Tulving, E., & Osier, S. (1968). Effectiveness of retrieval cues in memory for words. *Journal of Experimental Psychology, 77,* 593–601.

Tulving, E., & Thompson, D. M. (1973). Encoding specificity and retrieval processes in episodic memory. *Psychological Review, 80,* 352–373.

Yoon, K., Bolls, B., & Lang, A. (1998). The effects of arousal on liking and believability of commercials. *Journal of Marketing Communications, 4,* 101–114.

Yuille, J. C., & Tollestrup, P. A. (1992). A model of diverse effects of emotion on eyewitness memory. In S. Christianson (Ed.), *The handbook of emotion and memory: Research and theory* (pp. 201–216). Hillsdale, NJ: Erlbaum.

Zechmeister, E. B., & Nyberg, S. E. (1982). *Human memory: An introduction to research and theory.* Monterey, CA: Brooks/Cole.

Zhou, S., Schwartz, N., Bolls, P., Potter, R. P., Lang, A., Trout, G., Funabiki, R., Borse, J., & Dent, D. (1997, August). *When an edit is an edit can an edit be too much? The effects of edits on arousal, attention, and memory for television messages.* Paper presented to the Theory and Methodology Division of the Association for Education in Journalism and Mass Communication, Chicago, IL.

22

WHAT IS COMMUNICATION?

NIKLAS LUHMANN

I.

My purpose is to criticize the common understanding of communication and to replace it with a different version. But before I begin I would like to make some remarks about the scientific context in which this change is to be accomplished.

I can begin from an uncontested fact. The well-known distinction between psychology and sociology, and over a hundred years of specialized research, have led to the understanding that psychical and social systems can no longer be integrated. No researcher can survey the entire body of knowledge in either of these disciplines. However, this much is clear—in both cases we are concerned with systems that possess highly complex structures and whose dynamics, for any observer, are opaque and incapable of being regulated. Nevertheless, there are always concepts and theories that ignore this or try to screen it out systematically. In sociology the concepts of action and communication belong to the residue of such an attempt. Normally they are employed in reference to a subject. This means that they

assume an author, characterized as an individual or subject to whom the action or communication can be attributed. Therefore the concepts of "subject" and "individual" function as empty formulas for an, in itself, highly complex state of affairs falling within the domain of psychology and no longer concerning sociology. If one challenges this interpretation—and that is what I intend to do—then one usually encounters the objection that ultimately it is persons, individuals, or subjects who act or communicate. On the contrary, I would like to maintain that *only communication can communicate* and that only within such a network of communication is what we understand as action created.

My second preliminary remark concerns the interesting recent developments in general systems theory or the cybernetics of self-referential systems that earlier were found under the title of self-organization but are currently under the title of autopoiesis. The present state of research itself is incomplete and controversial. But an epistemologically satisfactory reformulation of the theoretical means of investigation—encompassing

SOURCE: Luhmann, N. (1992). What is communication? *Communication Theory, 2*(3), 251–259. Used by permission of the International Communication Association.

biology, psychology, and sociology—is clearly visible. Those who prefer a multileveled architecture can, in this case, observe a reformulation of theory that occurs on several different levels at the same time and that also calls into question the distinction of levels that logic suggests. Contrary to the basic assumptions of the philosophical tradition, self-reference (or reflexiveness) is not a property peculiar to thought or consciousness but instead a general principle of system formation with special consequences for the structure of complexity and evolution. An unavoidable consequence of this is that there are many different possibilities for observing the world, depending on the reference system that is taken as basic. Or in other words, evolution has led to a world that has many different possibilities for observing itself without characterizing any one of these possibilities as the best one. Every theory that addresses this issue must find itself at the level of observing observations—at the level of second-order cybernetics in Heinz von Foerster's (1981) sense.

My question is now, how does a sociological theory of social systems appear if it seriously tries to address these theoretical developments? My suspicion is that one must not begin with the concept of action but with the concept of communication. For it is not action but rather communication that is an unavoidably social operation and at the same time an operation that necessarily comes into play whenever social situations arise.

In the main part of my presentation I would like to try to present a corresponding concept of communication, one that avoids all reference to consciousness or life because it is situated on a different level of the realization of autopoietic systems. But I must at the same time caution that this is not to be taken to mean that communication is possible without life and consciousness. It is also impossible without carbon, without moderate temperatures, without the earth's magnetic field or the atomic cohesiveness of matter. In view of the complexity of the world, not all the conditions of the possibility of any state of affairs can be included in this concept because

then it would lose all contour and applicability for use in the construction of theories.

II.

Just like life and consciousness, communication is an emergent reality, a state of affairs *sui generis*. It arises through a synthesis of three different selections, namely, selection of *information,* selection of the *utterance* of this information, and a selective *understanding or misunderstanding* of this utterance and its information.

None of these components can be present by itself. Only together can they create communication. Only together—and that means only when their selectivity can be made congruent. Therefore communication occurs only when a difference of utterance and information is understood. That distinguishes it from the mere perception of the behavior of others. In understanding, communication grasps a distinction between the information value of its content and the reasons for which the content was uttered. It can thereby emphasize one or the other side. It can concern itself more with the information itself or more with the expressive behavior. But it always depends on the fact that *both* are experienced as *selection* and *thereby* distinguished. In other words, one must be able to assume that the information is not self-understood but requires a separate decision. This is also true when the utterer utters something about himself or herself. As long as these distinctions are not made we are dealing with a mere perception.

It is of considerable importance to retain this distinction between communication and perception, although, and even precisely because, communication provides many possibilities for an accompanying perception. Nevertheless, a perception remains above all a psychical event without communicative existence. Within the communicative process it is incapable of immediate connection. What another has perceived can neither be confirmed nor repudiated, neither questioned nor answered. It remains enclosed within consciousness and opaque for the communication system as well as for another consciousness. Of course, it can become an external occasion for successive communication. Participants can mention their own perceptions and the accompanying interpretations of the situation in the communication, but only according to the laws proper to the communication system, for example, only in the form of language, only through taking into consideration the amount of time involved, only through appearing, making one's presence felt and explaining oneself—thus only under discouragingly difficult circumstances.

In addition to information and utterance, understanding is a selection, too. Understanding is never the mere duplication of the utterance in another consciousness but a condition of connection with further communication in the communication system, that is, a condition of the autopoiesis of social systems. Whatever the participants may understand in their own self-referentially closed consciousnesses, the communication system works out its own understanding or misunderstanding. And to this purpose it creates its own processes of self-observation and self-control.

One can communicate about understanding, misunderstanding, and non-understanding—of course, only under the highly specific conditions of the autopoiesis of the communication system and not simply as the participants would like. Thus the utterance "You don't understand me" remains ambivalent and communicates this ambivalence at the same time. On one hand, it says, "you are not ready to accept what I want to tell you" and attempts to provoke the admission of this fact. On the other, it is the utterance of the information that the communication cannot be continued under this condition of nonunderstanding. And third, it is the continuation of communication. It is thus paradoxical communication. The normal technique for dealing with difficulties of communication is simply further inquiry and clarification in the normal, routine communication about communication without any particular emotional burden. And this normal routine is broken by those who try to assign the failure or the danger of failure of communication within the

communication itself. "You don't understand me" only camouflages the difficulty of the problem of acceptance or rejection with a semantics that suggests that the problem is, nevertheless, to be solved through communication about communication.

III.

What is new about this concept of communication? And what are the consequences of the innovation? The distinction of the three components of information, utterance, and understanding is not new. A similar distinction is to be found in the work of Karl Bühler (1934) with respect to the different functions of linguistic communication. Thinkers like Austin (1962) and Searle (1969) have developed this distinction into a theory of act types and speech acts. And Jürgen Habermas (1979) has added to this a typology of validity claims that are implicit in the communication. All this begins, however, from an understanding of communication in terms of action and thus views the process of communication as a successful or unsuccessful *transmission* of messages, information, or understanding expectations. However, in a systems-theoretic approach it is the very *emergence of communication* that is emphasized. Nothing is transmitted. Redundancy is created in the sense that the communication creates a memory that can be called on by many persons in quite different ways. When A announces something to B, further communication can be directed to either A or B. The system pulsates as it were with a constant creation of overflow and selection. When writing and printing were invented this process of systems formation was enormously increased with consequences for social structure, semantics, indeed for language itself, that only gradually entered the purview of research.

Thus the three components of information, utterance, and understanding must not be interpreted as functions, acts, or horizons of validity claims, although one may admit that these are possible ways of applying them. There are no building blocks of communication that exist independently and only need to be assembled by someone (a subject, perhaps?). Instead it is a matter of different selections whose selectivity and selective domain are constituted by the communication itself. There is no information outside of communication, no utterance outside of communication, no understanding outside of communication—and not simply in the causal sense for which information is the cause of the utterance and the utterance the cause of the understanding, but rather in the circular sense of reciprocal presupposition.

A communication system is therefore a completely closed system that creates the components out of which it arises through communication itself. In this sense a communication system is an autopoietic system that (re)produces everything that functions as a unity for the system through the system itself. Of course, this can occur only in an environment and depending on environmental restrictions.

Formulated more concretely, this means that the communication system itself specifies not only its elements—whatever the ultimate units of communication are—but also its structures. What is not communicated cannot contribute anything to it. Only communication can influence communication. Only communication can break down the units of communication (e.g., analyze the selective horizon of information or seek the reasons for an utterance). And only communication can control and repair communication. As can readily be seen, the practice of carrying out such reflexive operations is extraordinarily demanding and is restricted by the characteristics of the autopoiesis of communication. There is a limit to the exactness that can be attained. Sooner or later, and usually sooner, the bounds of communication are reached, or patience—that is, the burden that the psychical environment can accept—is exhausted. Or finally an interest in other themes or partners supervenes.

IV.

The argument of the circular, autopoietic closure of the system is not easy to accept. Some conceptual experimentation is required before its advantages can be seen. The same is true of a second argument closely related to it. Communication has no goal or end, no immanent entelechy. It occurs or it does not—that is all that can be said about it. In this way the theory of autopoiesis is not in the spirit of Aristotle but rather of Spinoza.

Of course, goal-directed episodes can be formed within the communication system insofar as autopoiesis functions, just as consciousness can establish episodic goals without making goal positing the goal of the system. Any other interpretation would have to justify why the system continues after it has attained its goal. Or one would have to say, and not for the first time, that death is the goal or end of life.

In many cases it is implicitly assumed that communication aims at consensus, seeks agreement. The theory of the rationality of communicative action developed by Habermas (1979) is built on this premise. But in fact it is empirically false. Communication can be used to indicate dissent. Strife can be sought. And there is no reason to suppose that the seeking of consensus is any more rational than the seeking of dissent. This depends entirely on the themes of communication and the partners. Of course, communication is impossible without some consensus. But it is equally impossible devoid of all dissent. What it necessarily presupposes is that the question of consensus or dissent can be left aside concerning those themes that are momentarily not topical. And even in the case of actual themes—even when one finally finds a parking spot and after a long walk arrives at the cafe where reputedly the best coffee in Rome can be found and enjoys one's drink—where is the consensus or dissent, as long as the enjoyment is not spoiled by communication?

Systems theory replaces the consensus-directed entelechy with another argument: Communication leads to a decision whether the uttered and understood information is to be accepted or rejected. A message is believed or not. This is the first alternative created by communication and with it the risk of rejection. It forces a decision to be made that would not have occurred without the communication. In this respect all communication involves risk. This risk is a very important morphogenetic factor because it leads to the establishment of institutions that guarantee acceptability even in the case of improbable communications. But, on the other hand, it can also—and this seems to me to be the case for Far Eastern cultures—increase sensibility. Communication with a likelihood of rejection is avoided or one tries to fulfill wishes before they are uttered. And it is precisely in this way that one can indicate restrictions. Communication continues as long as it does not encounter contradiction or is not disturbed by an indication of acceptance or rejection.

In other words—to repeat an oft made important point—communication bifurcates reality. It creates two versions—a yes version and a no version—and thereby forces selection. And it is precisely in the fact that something must happen (even if this is an explicitly communicated break-off of communication) that the autopoiesis of the system resides, guaranteeing for itself its own continuability.

Focusing on the alternative of acceptance or rejection is therefore nothing more than the autopoiesis of communication itself. It identifies the position of connection for the next communication that can now either build on an already attained consensus or seek dissent. Or it can attempt to conceal the problem and avoid it in the future. Nothing that can be communicated escapes this hard and fixed bifurcation—with one exception: the world (understood in the phenomenological sense) as the ultimate horizon in which everything occurs but cannot itself be qualified positively or negatively, accepted or rejected, and is co-produced in all meaningful communication as the condition of accessibility of further communication.

V.

Now let me test this general theoretical approach on a particular question. Through the efforts of Neo-Kantianism and Jürgen Habermas we have become accustomed to suspect the presence of validity claims at this point and are encouraged to test them. The truth of the matter is both simpler and at the same time more complicated.

What is empirically observable is, first of all, that values are involved in communication by implication. They are assumed, hinted at. For example, no one directly says, "I am for peace. I value my health." This is avoided for well-known reasons: It would bifurcate into the possibilities of acceptance and rejection, which is exactly what is unnecessary in the case of values—or so one thinks, in any event.

Values hold through the assumption of their validity. Anyone who communicates in this way enjoys a kind of value bonus. For then it is the burden of the other to say if he or she is not in agreement. One operates, as it were, under the aegis of the beauty and goodness of values, and profits from the fact that anyone who wants to protest must assume the burden of complexity. He/she assumes the onus of argumentation. He/she runs the risk of having to think innovatively and of being isolated. And since it is always the case that more values are implied than can be thematized in the next move, selection, rejection, and modification are an almost hopeless undertaking. Therefore—instead of values—preferences, interests, prescriptions, and programs are discussed. None of this means that there exists a system of values or that value orders are structured transitively or hierarchically. Nor does it mean, and this is important, that values are a matter of psychologically stable structures. On the contrary, values seem to lead an extraordinarily labile psychological existence. They are used on one occasion and not on another without being supported by a psychological deep structure. Their stability is, as I would like to formulate it provocatively, an exclusively communicative artifact. And the autopoietic system of consciousness deals with them as it pleases. It is precisely because structures of the autopoiesis of the social system operate in this case that the semantics of values is appropriate to use in the presentation of the foundations of a social system. Their stability rests on a recursive assumption and testing of the semantics with which this functions at any time. The *basis of validity* is recursiveness, reinforced by the communicative disadvantage of contradiction.

Whatever else consciousness thinks is an entirely different mater. In due time it will come to recognize that value consensus is as unavoidable as it is innocuous. For there is no self-execution of values. And everything that they seem to require can be allowed to slip by in the execution, of course in the name of values.

VI.

Such a profound revision of the conceptual framework of communication systems will surely have consequences for the diagnosis and therapy of the states of systems that are viewed as pathological. The author does not claim any kind of competence in this area, above all that kind of automatic self-correction that arises from a familiarity with the milieu. Nevertheless, in a kind of summary fashion, I would like to illuminate several points that might serve as an occasion for reconstructing well-known phenomena.

First of all, this account emphasizes the difference between psychical and social systems. The former operate on the basis of consciousness, the latter on the basis of communication. Both are self-referentially closed systems that are limited to their own mode of autopoietic reproduction. A social system cannot think and a psychical system cannot communicate. There are, however, immense and highly complex causal interdependencies. Closure does not mean that no reciprocity exists or that such interconnections cannot be observed and described by an observer. It does require, however, that the initial situation of autopoietic closure enters into the description. This means that one must take into account the fact that effects can arise only through the co-operation of the system experiencing them. And one must also remember that the systems are opaque to each another and therefore cannot reciprocally steer each other.

A consequence of this account is that consciousness contributes only noise, disturbance, or perturbation to communication and vice versa.

In fact, if you observe a communication process you have to be familiar with the preceding communication, ultimately with its themes and what can be said meaningfully about them. As such, you do not have to have a knowledge of the conscious structures of the individuals.

But, of course, this point of departure needs refinement since communication systems very often thematize persons and since consciousness has become accustomed to prefer certain words, to tell certain stories and to identify itself, in part, with communication. Thus an observer can recognize highly structured interdependencies between psychical and social systems. Nevertheless, the psychical selectivity of communicative events in the experience of the participants is something completely different from the social selectivity. A mere consideration of what we ourselves say suffices to make us aware of how carefully we must select in order to be able to say what can be said, how much an emitted word is no longer what was thought and intended, how much one's own consciousness dances about the words like a will-o'-the-wisp, using and mocking them, meaning and not meaning them at the same time, letting them rise and fall, how it has them on the tip of its tongue and desperately wants to say them and then without any good reason does not do so. Were we to try to observe our own consciousness moving from thought to thought we would indeed be fascinated by language. But we would also experience the non-communicative, purely internal use of linguistic symbols and a genuine depth of conscious actuality in the background, one on which the words sail like little ships connected one to another but without itself being consciousness.

This superiority of consciousness to communication (to which, of course, a superiority of communication to consciousness corresponds in the converse system reference) becomes completely clear when one realizes that consciousness is not only concerned with words and vague word and propositional ideas but also and preeminently with perception and with the imaginative depiction and effacement of images. Even during speaking, consciousness is incessantly concerned with perceptions. In my own case it often happens that in the act of formulating I see the pictures of the written words (a state of affairs that has never, as far as I can see, been noted by research into culture's transposition into the written form [*Verschriftlichung*]). And the extent to which one can be diverted from the observation of others by one's own talking, or still be able to process sense impressions while attending to the train of conversation, varies from person to person.

All this makes it necessary to adapt communication to this will-o'-the-wisp of consciousness when we change the system reference again to that of the social system of communication. Of course, this does not mean that communication carries consciousness along piece by piece. Instead, consciousness—whatever else it may be thinking—is maneuvered by communication into a situation of forced choice. Or at least that is how it appears from the point of view of communication. Communication can be accepted or rejected in a way that is communicatively understandable. And naturally the range of themes can be factored so that a decision is broken down into several decisions. The autopoietic autonomy of consciousness, so to say, is represented and compensated in communication by binarization. A decision that can be handled in communication takes the place of a meaninglessly noisy environment of a decision, for example, yes or no, further inquiry, perhaps hesitation, delay, doubt. In other words, communication can be disturbed by consciousness and even foresees this; but this always happens in ways that can be connected with further communication and thus can be handled communicatively. In this way a confusion of the autopoiesis of the systems is avoided despite a high degree of coevolution and reciprocal interaction.

I am well aware that this analysis still does not suffice to describe what we experience as a pathological state of the system. In terms of this theory, reciprocal noise, disturbance, perturbation, and so on, are the normal case for which a normal interception and absorption capacity exists, psychically as well as socially. Supposedly a sense of the pathological occurs only when certain thresholds of tolerance are transcended. Or one could possibly say, when the memory of the system is brought into play and experiences of disturbances are stored, combined, represented again, and amplified by the reinforcement of deviation and hypercorrection, and when an increased capacity for the same is called on. Be that as it may, from the theoretical position that I have attempted to outline, one would have to distinguish clearly between psychical and social pathologies and be especially careful if one wants to view either as the indicator or even the cause of the other.

References

Austin, J. L. (1962). *How to do things with words.* Cambridge, MA: Harvard University Press.

Bühler, K. (1934). *Sprachtheorie.* Jena: Fischer.

Habermas, J. (1979). *Communication and the evolution of society.* (T. McCarthy, Trans.). Boston: Beacon Press.

Searle, J. (1969). *Speech acts: An essay in the philosophy of language.* Cambridge: Cambridge University Press.

von Foerster, H. (1981). *Observing systems.* Seaside, CA: InterSystems.

Projects for Cybernetic Theorizing

Additional Readings on Cybernetics

A. To learn more about the cybernetic tradition in general: Ashby (1956); Broadhurst and Darnell (1965); Heims (1980, 1991); Krippendorff (1989); Shannon and Weaver (1949); Weaver (1949); Wiener (1948, 1954). *The Principia Cybernetica Web* (http://pespmc1.vub.ac.be) is an excellent online resource.

B. To learn more about Bateson, the Interactional View, and applications of Bateson's cybernetic theory to psychology and interpersonal and organizational communication: Bateson (1972); Cronen, Pearce, and Snavely (1979); Rogers and Escudero (2004); Ruesch and Bateson (1968); Watzlawick, Beavin, and Jackson (1967); Watzlawick and Weakland (1977); Weick (1979); Wilder and Weakland (1981).

C. To learn more about autopoiesis, self-organizing systems, and second order cybernetics with applications to sociology and organizational communication: Maturana and Varela (1980); Luhmann (1989, 1990); Steier (1991); Contractor (1999); Taylor (2001).

D. To learn more about cognitive communication theory and especially about action assembly theory: Greene (1984, 1995, 1997).

Application Exercise

Working off the idea that communication is a system, examine who is part of the communication system when gathering information on the Internet. Determine a fact you want to ascertain, or better yet a question you want to answer. Search on the Internet until you have found your answer. Now work to trace all the participants in the communication system you have just been a part of in answering your question. Also answer the following questions. What are the controls (feedback mechanisms) in this system? Do some of these mechanisms work in conjunction with a person's limited processing capacity? Develop an argument to support your answer to the following question: Is the answer you obtained from the Internet a result of information flow that can be explained in some respects by Shannon and Weaver's theory?

Projects

1. As noted in the introduction to this unit, Shannon and Weaver speculated that Shannon's mathematical theory of information might become the basis for a general theory of communication, but that development has never successfully occurred and the applications to human communication have turned out to be very limited. For various views on this issue, read Broadhurst and Darnell (1965), Finn and Roberts (1984), MacKay (1969), and Ritchie (1986, 1991a, 1991b). Imagine a society in which Shannon and Weaver's theory did provide an accurate description of human communication. What would it be like to live in that world?

2. Theorists such as those cited in paragraph B under additional readings theorize relationships as cybernetic systems. Relationships are the patterns of interaction between people. As such, a family is a system of interaction. The attention is removed from the individuals and the focus is on the sequences and organization of the messages—that is, on the system. For this project, speculate about how such a focus might work on analyzing a large-scale system (e.g., escalation of a conflict or the removal or addition of a particular participant in the interaction). Some potential large-scale systems might be long-term group conflicts (Palestinian-Israeli in the Middle East, Catholic-Protestant in Northern Ireland), removal of totalitarian rule (the dynamics in the Balkan states or the former USSR), external intervention (Afghanistan, Iraq), national policy debates (in the United States, the War on Drugs, or the culture wars), the potential for stability in countries with competing factions and/or warlords (Somalia), outbursts of ethnic violence such as those in France and Australia in 2005, or terrorism as a means of political communication. How can a cybernetic approach aid in our understanding of these situations? What can a cybernetic approach tell us about what has happened and what will happen? Identify the communication sequences in the situation, and hypothesize about communication moves that might continue or could potentially alter the current system. Could a cybernetic approach be useful in the construction of public policy and decisions about intervention by external participants in the system?

3. Some communication theorists have proposed formal mathematical models as a precise way of describing and explaining communication processes. For examples of this approach, read Fink (1993) and Woelfel and Fink (1980). How successful have these models been in achieving their scientific goals? What seem to be the advantages and disadvantages of mathematical modeling as an approach to communication theory? Is there a difference between modeling technical communications systems and modeling human communication? Does a mathematical modeling approach dehumanize communication or does it provide tools to practically improve our communication?

4. Identify problems in communication in an organization or group and theorize these using the ideas of self-organizing systems (paragraph C under additional readings). What new picture of communication in an organization emerges through such a theorizing? Are new remedies generated? Do these seem like remedies that participants would have the skills to implement, or does it seem the tendency is to have and build skills more in accord with a mechanical (or some other) model?

5. With the unlocking of the genetic code, one way of looking at DNA is as information. The possibility now exists of biological computers going beyond pacemakers and hearing aids to more sophisticated interweaving of technology and organisms. What implications does thinking of biology as an information system have for communication (see Braman, 2004)? Luhmann might lean toward a nonnormative (descriptive rather than value-based) exploration of the biological information system. Work to build a nonnormative (or normative) model based on these ideas of biological information and theorize what communication practices might be informed and might be able to inform such a model.

REFERENCES

Ashby, W. R. (1956). *An introduction to cybernetics.* London: Chapman & Hall.

Bateson, G. (1972). *Steps to an ecology of mind.* New York: Ballantine Books.

Braman, S. (Ed.). (2004). *Biotechnology and communication: The meta-technologies of information.* Mahwah, NJ: Lawrence Erlbaum.

Broadhurst, A. R., & Darnell, D. K. (1965). Introduction to cybernetics and information theory. *Quarterly Journal of Speech, 51*(4), 442–453.

Contractor, N. S. (1999). Self-organizing systems research in the social sciences: Reconciling the metaphors and the models. *Management Communication Quarterly, 13*(1), 154–166.

Cronen, V. E., Pearce, W. B., & Snavely, L. M. (1979). A theory of rule-structure and types of episodes and a study of perceived enmeshment in undesired repetitive patterns ("URPs"). In D. Nimmo (Ed.), *Communication Yearbook 3* (pp. 225–240). New Brunswick, NJ: Transaction.

Fink, E. L. (Ed.). (1993). Symposium: Communication theory, mathematical models, and social policy. *Journal of Communication, 43*(1), 4–100.

Finn, S., & Roberts, D. (1984). Source, destination, and entropy: Reassessing the role of information theory in communication research. *Communication Research, 11*, 453–476.

Greene, J. O. (1984). A cognitive approach to human communication: An action assembly theory. *Communication Monographs, 51*(4), 289–306.

Greene, J. O. (1995). Production of messages in pursuit of multiple social goals: Action assembly theory contributions to the study of cognitive encoding processes. In B. Burleson (Ed.), *Communication Yearbook 18* (pp. 26–53). Thousand Oaks, CA: Sage.

Greene, J. O. (Ed.). (1997). *Message production: Advances in communication theory*. Mahwah, NJ: Lawrence Erlbaum.

Heims, S. J. (1980). *John Von Neumann and Norbert Weiner: From mathematics to the technologies of life and death*. Cambridge, MA: MIT Press.

Heims, S. J. (1991). *The cybernetics group*. Cambridge, MA: MIT Press.

Krippendorff, K. (1989). Cybernetics. In E. Barnouw, G. Gerbner, W. Schramm, T. L. Worth, & L. Gross (Eds.), *International encyclopedia of communications* (Vol. 1, pp. 443–446). New York: Oxford University Press.

Luhmann, N. (1989). *Ecological communication* (J. Bednarz Jr., Trans.). Chicago: University of Chicago Press.

Luhmann, N. (1990). *Essays on self-reference*. New York: Columbia University Press.

MacKay, D. M. (1969). *Information, mechanism and meaning*. Cambridge, MA: MIT Press.

Maturana, H. R., & Varela, F. J. (1980). *Autopoiesis and cognition: The realization of the living* (Vol. 42). Dordecht, Holland: D. Reidel.

Ritchie, L. D. (1986). Shannon and Weaver: Unraveling the paradox of information. *Communication Research, 13*, 278–298.

Ritchie, L. D. (1991a). Another turn of the information revolution: Relevance, technology, and the information society. *Communication Research, 18*, 412–427.

Ritchie, L. D. (1991b). *Information*. Newbury Park, CA: Sage.

Rogers, L. E., & Escudero, V. (2004). *Relational communication: An interactional perspective to the study of process and form*. Mahwah, NJ: Lawrence Erlbaum.

Ruesch, J., & Bateson, G. (1968). *Communication: The social matrix of psychiatry*. New York: W. W. Norton.

Shannon, C. E., & Weaver, W. (1949). *The mathematical theory of communication*. Urbana: University of Illinois Press.

Steier, F. (Ed.). (1991). *Research and reflexivity*. Newbury Park, CA: Sage.

Taylor, J. R. (2001). The 'rational' organization reconsidered: An exploration of some of the organizational implications of self-organizing. *Communication Theory, 11*, 137–177.

Watzlawick, P., Beavin, J. H., & Jackson, D. D. (1967). *Pragmatics of human communication: A study of interactional patterns, pathologies, and paradoxes*. New York: W. W. Norton.

Watzlawick, P., & Weakland, J. H. (Eds.). (1977). *The interactional view: Studies at the Mental Research Institute Palo Alto, 1965–1974*. New York: W. W. Norton.

Weaver, W. (1949). The mathematics of communication. *Scientific American, 181*, 11–15.

Weick, K. E. (1979). *The social psychology of organizing* (2nd ed.). Reading, MA: Addison-Wesley.

Wiener, N. (1948). *Cybernetics*. New York: John Wiley & Sons.

Wiener, N. (1954). *The human use of human beings: Cybernetics and society*. Boston: Houghton Mifflin.

Wilder, C., & Weakland, J. H. (Eds.). (1981). *Rigor and imagination: Essays from the legacy of Gregory Bateson*. New York: Praeger.

Woelfel, J., & Fink, E. L. (1980). *The measurement of communication processes: Galileo theory and method*. New York: Academic Press.

UNIT VII   INTRODUCTION

THE SOCIOPSYCHOLOGICAL TRADITION

I f the parts of this book were constructed in proportion to the prominence of each tradition in most communication theory textbooks, the unit on sociopsychological theory would be significantly larger than it is. This is one of the newest traditions of communication theory, its history much shorter than rhetoric or semiotics, but during its time it has been the dominant source of theory for social scientific communication studies. It is the tradition that has provided theoretically informed corrections of many naive assumptions about the psychological processes involved in communication, generated a wealth of experimentally tested hypotheses, and provided rigorous criteria for researching and theorizing.

As mentioned in the introduction to the rhetoric unit, the social scientific approach often is seen in opposition to humanistic approaches such as rhetoric. Within the sociopsychological tradition, communication is conceptualized as a process of social interaction. That communication is infused with causal forces of social influence and that these forces can be understood scientifically are hallmark emphases within this tradition. Thus empiricism, the careful experimental testing of claims about the communication process, is also a hallmark of the sociopsychological tradition. Much of the work in this tradition is focused on particular contexts of communication, meaning that there are interpersonal theories, organizational theories, mass communication theories, and so on. Within these contexts are subcontexts such as media and children, problem-solving groups, and cross-sex friendships. Other theories examine specific processes such as persuasion, conflict, and relational communication.

Tracing the history of the sociopsychological tradition of communication theory is interwoven with tracing the emergence of communication as a unique modern academic discipline of study. This history begins within the academic field of experimental social psychology in the early decades of the 20th century, a time at which the modern disciplines of psychology and sociology were being actively defined and institutionalized. Social psychology—the study of behavior in social contexts—emerged as an interdisciplinary field that overlapped the two disciplines. However, instead of breaking off from both and forming a separate, unified discipline, social psychology split into two camps that are associated with two different traditions of communication theory. The impulse to bring those two traditions of thought (and others) together in an interdisciplinary alliance for the study of communication was an important factor leading to the eventual emergence of a communication discipline (for various perspectives on this see Delia, 1987; Dennis & Wartella, 1996; Rogers, 1994).

The sociological branch of social psychology looks at human interaction primarily from the standpoint of society. It tends to use field research methods such as surveys and participant observation. It sees communication as a process of symbolic interaction that both produces and depends on the larger social order, thus contributing to what we call the sociocultural tradition of communication theory (see unit VIII, especially the Mead reading).

The psychological branch of social psychology looks at human interaction primarily from the standpoint of the individual. It tends to use laboratory-based, experimental methods. It sees communication as a process in which individuals interact, thereby influencing each other's cognitions, emotions, and behaviors. Interaction may occur face-to-face or through media, including mass mediated messages addressed to many individuals at once. It was in this psychological branch of social psychology that the sociopsychological tradition of communication theory originated.

Interestingly, psychologists did not initially use the word *communication* to describe this sociopsychological process. It was only in the 1940s, when communication research came to prominence as an interdisciplinary academic field, that experimental social psychologists began writing about communication explicitly. A paper by Hovland (1948), the first reading in this unit, is one of the earliest writings we have found in which an experimental social psychologist commented extensively on communication. However, the underlying sociopsychological approach to the study of interaction had been clearly articulated by 1919 and entered the mainstream of experimental social psychology in the 1920s. Floyd H. Allport (1919, 1924) drew a bright line of separation between the psychological approach, which he advocated, and group-based, sociological approaches, which he

rejected as unscientific. Social psychology, he wrote, "must be studied . . . in the specific reactions and interactions of persons. . . . True causes must be sought by the scientific method, that is by the scrutiny of individual cases in which direct or indirect social stimulation has produced definite responses" (1919, p. 298). In his 1924 textbook, Allport "presented a program for the development of social psychology that would very much come to define psychological social psychology thereafter" (Parkovnick, 2000, p. 429).

This concern with the scientific method in the field of communication theory is seen quite vividly in Festinger (1950), who addressed the need for strict theory and the issues of precision as well as of exploring "real" phenomena. In this early example of explicit communication theorizing by a social psychologist, Festinger argued that a theory must be empirically influenceable. In other words, a theory must generate hypotheses, those hypotheses must be testable, and the theory must be responsive to the results of those tests. To be useful from a sociopsychological point of view, a theory needs to be empirically testable and the hypotheses need to be grounded in a coherent model of communicative functioning. Sociopsychological theories of communication are often as much addressed to problems of scientific method as they are to practical communication problems. For that reason, we mention both kinds of problems when introducing each theory.

The first reading (Hovland, 1948) is interesting in many ways. While it lays out a framework for the study of communication—communicator, stimulus, communicatee, and response of communicatee—it also addresses the idea that communication needs to be studied by psychologists, sociologists, anthropologists, and political scientists as well as by communication practitioners. Of note here is the lack of mention of study by communication theorists, but at this time communication was not yet recognized as an academic discipline.

As can be seen in the constructs of stimulus and response, the language of the experimental psychology of Hovland's day is central in this proposed framework. This framework for study could be seen as a response to *the problem of numbers and distance.* As labor and management get further apart, public officials no longer hold town meetings, and Americans need to communicate with Russians, the principles and laws of communication need to be understood. As Hovland surveys what is known so far and points out potential sources for hypotheses, he links the success of the science of communication to the development of more and more sophisticated experimental techniques undertaken as a combined effort by social scientists.

Moving forward a few decades, Berger and Calabrese (1975) presented one of the first original sociopsychological theories developed within the communication discipline. This second reading can be seen as a response to both a communication problem and a problem in scientific empiricism. *The problem of forming interpersonal relationships*, as Berger and Calabrese point out in the conclusion of their article, is especially salient in a fast-changing, mobile society in which we are constantly meeting new people. Berger and Calabrese address this communication problem with a formal set of axioms and theorems designed to explain the initial phases— entry phase, personal phase, and exit phase—of interpersonal interaction between strangers. Berger and Calabrese also developed their theory to address what might be called *the problem of communication theory.* Near the beginning of the article, they point out that communication research had depended heavily on theories borrowed from social psychology and express what has become a common complaint among communication scholars: that theories in social psychology seldom focus directly on the communication process itself. Although constructs borrowed from other disciplines have been beneficial, there is a need for the generation and testing of communication-specific constructs. We need scientifically rigorous theories that explain actual processes of interpersonal interaction. Berger and Calabrese addressed that need with an empirically testable theory that explains interaction. One interesting feature marking this as a native communication theory is that the key concept of *uncertainty* is a nonmathematical application of the (cybernetic tradition) concept of *entropy* from Shannon and Weaver's (1948) theory of information. As is integral in theorizing within the sociopsychological tradition, Berger and Calabrese stress that their theory is open to revision through empirical research, and the hope of these theorists is that the program of research generated from these initial axioms will go on to examine later phases of interpersonal relationships.

The Bandura (2001) chapter is included in this book because it is currently one of the most important sociopsychological theories in the field of mass communication. Interestingly, it does not meet Berger and Calabrese's call for a communication-centric theory. It arose out of studying the psychology of observational learning. However, it is clearly an example of a formal sociopsychological theory derived from a program of empirical research. Begun not long after Festinger (1950) wrote, the theory of social cognition has been continuously studied and adapted in an empirical fashion. The detail in the theory has evolved over the years. This theory and program of research can be seen as a response to a problem in empiricism we might call *the problem of the social-psychological divide.* As discussed in the article's conclusion, Bandura's aim for this theory is to provide a framework in which the sociological and psychological determinants of behavior can be treated in a complementary fashion. Rather than looking at either sociological impacts or psychological impacts on behavior, using this theory one can examine both in combination.

The practical communication problem that this theory is designed to address is *the problem of media effects,* which it does by identifying "the psychosocial mechanisms through which symbolic communication influences human thought, affect and action" (reading 25).

The final reading in this unit (Poole, 1998) circles back to a key theoretical issue from the very dawn of the sociopsychological tradition. Floyd Allport (not to be confused with his brother, Gordon Allport, who is mentioned by Poole) argued forcefully that the essential unit of study in social psychology should not be the group but rather the individual in a group context. He wrote,

> We may conclude then that the greatest incubus in social psychology is the unwarranted emphasis placed upon the group. We have been so busy talking about group types, group interests, group consciousness, and the degree of group solidarity, that we have forgotten that the locus of all psychology, individual or social, is in the neuromotor system of the individual. (Allport, 1919, p. 298)

Poole argues just as forcefully from an exactly opposite view, claiming that the group should be the fundamental unit of study in communication research. For Poole, the focus on either the micro (individual) or the macro (organizational or societal) has ignored many important aspects of communication. Like other sociopsychological theorists, Poole's project of theorizing responds to methodological problems in empiricism as well as practical problems in communication. He mentions two empirical problems (the problem of intersubjectivity and the problem of boundaries) that might be summarized as *the problem of emergence*—the problem of explaining phenomena that are "not located in any individual, but are intersubjective in that they are maintained by the interaction system of the group (or society)" (reading 26). Poole

proposes switching from an individual focus (as he argues, social and organization phenomena, due to their complexity, end up being studied at the individual level as well) to a dyadic, or better yet a group focus in research. The boundary problem and intersubjectivity can best be studied in groups because the group is large enough to see these emergent phenomena but also small enough to see the individuals.

An interesting note in this piece that harks back to Hovland (1948) is the idea that this charge to focus on the group level may not be taken up by many researchers due to the complexity of constructing experimental designs to study phenomena at the group level. Once again, the success or even probability of programmatic research depends on the ability to create ways to control and measure communication phenomena empirically. However, in light of "the current emphasis on teamwork, quality, social responsibility, and empowerment in societal discourse" (reading 26), Poole argues that communication theorists should be paying more attention to group communication phenomena. Although there are many, many pieces that could be included in this section, these four provide insight into the social-psychological tradition. Theory construction through focusing on a specifiable communication phenomenon, empirically testable theory, propositions that are tested, programmatic research, debate about the kind of phenomena that should be studied due to their likelihood to produce useful theory, and the need to continually create new ways to design experiments and measure communication are all key elements within this tradition. One question that certainly might be addressed as one reads these articles is, Why has this tradition been so dominant within the communication discipline. Additionally, what is the relationship between the kind of empirical theory construction within this tradition and the kind of theorizing proposed throughout this volume? Is there a divide between these kinds of theorizing, or can they inform each other? A final question about theory that may be addressed though consideration of these readings is the one raised early in the tradition by scholars such as Festinger (1950): What makes a theory useful?

Other questions might revolve around Poole's proposition concerning the issue of units of study as well as questions about the potential to have general communication theory versus context-specific theories. Are there constructs that could be examined to understand communication in general? Or does the phenomenon need to be more specified than that in order to have useful theories? What about focusing on context theories as opposed to process theories? What are the advantages and disadvantages of each approach? Although the Berger and Calabrese (1975) piece was discussed here as a context-specific theory, could this also be seen as a process theory? What about Bandura (2001)?

Questions might also revolve around the selections included in this unit. Are there arguments to make for including pieces other than these? Is there a core to this tradition? Is there a set of pieces that one needs to read to be fluent in this tradition? Or does one need to be area specific and focus on theories in a certain context or a certain process to be fluent in this tradition? What about the link between theory and research method? Is there a rigid link between theory and experimental design in this tradition, or can other methods lead to an empirically built theory? What kinds of experimental design would be necessary to undertake Poole's (1998) direction?

As mentioned at the beginning of this unit introduction, these four readings provide a very small sample of work in this tradition and are not intended to represent the range of the tradition. Part of the project of theorizing is to continue to examine each of the traditions as well as the idea of traditions in general as a way to think about the field of communication theory. Should some traditions be more central than others within the discipline? Should sociopsychological theory be the most central because it is most strongly dedicated to the goals of empirical science? Are other traditions now becoming more central, and if so, is that desirable or not? Are things changing in the discipline? And if things are changing, what is the place of not only the sociopsychological tradition but also the idea of traditions? If they are not changing, how might this idea of seven different traditions represented in this volume be a construct that can be used to keep things the same or be used to bring about change?

REFERENCES

Allport, F. H. (1919). Behavior and experiment in social psychology. *Journal of Abnormal Psychology, 14,* 297–306.

Allport, F. H. (1924). *Social psychology.* Boston: Houghton Mifflin.

Bandura, A. (2001). Social cognitive theory of mass communications. In J. Bryant & D. Zillman (Eds.), *Media effects: Advances in theory and research* (2nd ed., pp. 121–153). Hillsdale, NJ: Lawrence Erlbaum.

Berger, C. R., & Calabrese, R. J. (1975). Some explorations in initial interaction and beyond: Toward a developmental theory of interpersonal communication. *Human Communication Research, 1*(2), 99–112.

Delia, J. G. (1987). Communication research: A history. In C. R. Berger & S. H. Chaffee (Eds.), *Handbook of communication science* (pp. 20–98). Newbury Park, CA: Sage.

Dennis, E. E., & Wartella, E. (Eds.). (1996). *American communication research: The remembered history.* Mahwah, NJ: Lawrence Erlbaum.

Festinger, L. (1950). Informal social communication. *Psychological Review, 57,* 271–282.

Hovland, C. (1948). Social communication. *Proceedings of the American Philosophical Society, 92*, 371–375.

Parkovnick, S. (2000). Contextualizing Floyd Allport's *Social Psychology. Journal of the History of the Behavioral Sciences, 36*(4), 429–441.

Poole, M. S. (1998). The small group should be *the* fundamental unit of communication research. In J. S. Trent (Ed.), *Communication: Views from the helm for the 21st century* (pp. 94–97). Boston: Allyn & Bacon.

Rogers, E. M. (1994). *A history of communication study: A biographical approach.* New York: Free Press.

Shannon, C. E., & Weaver, W. (1948). *The mathematical theory of communication.* Urbana: University of Illinois Press.

23

SOCIAL COMMUNICATION

CARL HOVLAND

Communication as an *art* has had a very long history. The writer, the orator, the public relations counsellor, and the advertiser have been leading practitioners of this art. Communication as a field of scientific inquiry, on the other hand, has been of fairly recent origin. Within the last decade or so, however, there has developed the promise of a genuine science of communication—a systematic attempt to formulate in rigorous fashion the principles by which information is transmitted and opinions and attitudes formed.

The development of this new field has been at least in part a response to the growing urgency of the problem. In industry the increasing concentration of control has widened the gap between workers and management and the feeling has arisen on both sides of the need for more effective intercommunications. The different frames of reference of management and of the worker have intensified this problem. The next speaker on the program will discuss this topic in connection with labor-management studies.

In our national life the same gap between lawmaker and citizen exists. Formal means of intercommunication have helped somewhat. The radio has brought the political leader closer to the voter and the public opinion poll has brought the views of the citizens more closely to the attention of the lawmaker. But there is still felt by many the lack of more effective intercommunication to replace the lost intimacy of the town meeting in the early days of our democracy.

On the international scene the same lack of communication appears. I recently heard one of our important United Nations officials say "If only we could communicate with the Russians." There is here not the problem of physical communication, but of psychological communication, not a language barrier alone but ideological barriers to communication.

The problem of communications is made more challenging by the fact that it is not an area for an isolated specialist. Adequate understanding of the problems of this field depends on a wider variety of talent and range of specialization than

SOURCE: Hovland, C. (1948). Social communication. *Proceedings of the American Philosophical Society, 92*, 371–375.

almost any other problem in the social sciences. A real science of communication will require the cooperation of both the practitioner and the scientist. Thus the newspaper editor, the radio broadcaster, the movie producer, as well as the psychologist, the sociologist, the anthropologist, and the political scientist have important roles to perform.[1]

Numerous definitions of the term "communication" have been given but for purposes of the present discussion I should like to define communication as the process by which an individual (the communicator) transmits stimuli (usually verbal symbols) to modify the behavior of other individuals (communicatees).

This definition thus defines the research task as being the analysis of four factors: (1) the *communicator* who transmits the communication; (2) the *stimuli* transmitted by the communicator; (3) the *individuals* who respond to the communication; (4) the *responses* made to the communication by the communicatee. In addition, we must analyze the *laws* and *principles* relating the above elements.

Numerous studies have been made of the communicator and how his characteristics affect the response of those receiving the communication.[2] In this category belong such important problems as the effect of communications in which the true communicator is not revealed, and the effectiveness of appeals made by the communicator in person compared with those in which the message is transmitted through radio, motion pictures or other media.

Analysis of the second factor, the stimuli, has been the most thoroughly studied. In fact when mention is made of communication analysis, or of institutes of communication, which are springing up on all sides, this is the aspect usually meant. With the growing complexity of our civilization just knowing what material is being transmitted is a gigantic and important task. Analysis of the material transmitted through the various channels of communication has required the development of precise quantitative techniques. The study of the stimuli transmitted by the communicator employs the familiar technique of *content*

analysis. Just before the war and during the war work on this problem made rapid strides. The studies of Lasswell, Kris, and Speier on analysis of enemy propaganda through newspapers, radio, and movies constitute good examples of the developments of the last few years in this area. These methods provide analysis in terms of the subject matter of a communication, its thematic content, type of symbolization, kinds of rhetorical devices used, syntactical characteristics, etc.[3] Without the thorough description made possible by these new and more precise methods of describing the content aspect of the stimuli the task of formulating principles and generalizations would be most difficult.

Because the stimuli used in communication are primarily verbal symbols it is important to understand the role of language in communication. Recent developments in the analysis of language and the field of semantics promise important application to the science of communication.[4] The analysis of this problem requires taking into account not only the differences between the languages of different nations but the equally critical problem of the differences in language between groups within our own society—e. g., between the scientist and the layman or between labor and management.

Scientific studies of the material transmitted try to be objective and uninterested in the *values* of the material transmitted. So it is at this point that research must be supplemented by studies of other groups—of the regulation of communication, the maintenance of a free press, and the variety of topics surveyed by the Commission on Freedom of the Press.[5] Here the philosopher, the student of government, and the lawyer, all have a significant place. Research can provide them with objective data basic to their analysis particularly in connection with evaluating the effect of various communication policies.

We now turn to the third of our problems—the analysis of the individual who receives the communication. Here we have the core of the problem of individual psychology. What are the motives of the individuals, what are their capacities, how do their predispositions influence the way in which they react to various stimuli presented? While psychology is most concerned with these problems, other adjacent disciplines have made significant contributions to our understanding. Psychiatry and psychoanalysis have contributed to the analysis of the complex motives of the individual. Anthropological research in our own culture has shown us how the dominant motives and patterns of an individual can be predicted from factors such as his occupation and social class. Thus important information about the individual to be affected by the communication is furnished by census-type data. Just knowing that an individual is twenty-one years of age, wealthy, and has a high intelligence test score permits us to make highly significant predictions of the individual's motives, habits, and capacity to learn, which are extremely relevant to the type of communication used. Procedures derived from clinical psychology and first-hand knowledge of the individual permit still better prediction. This field appears very promising for future developments in our understanding of communication. Studies of other cultures and other national patterns is an integral part of this problem. Better understanding of the countries of Eastern Europe, for example, and consequent better communication with them requires extensive research on the predispositions of individual in various cultures of the world. Work on this problem is now being begun at a number of centers.

The fourth facet of analysis is that of responses to communication. Some aspects of this problem are much more developed than others. One of the simplest responses is that of attention to the communication. Studies of what readers have noticed in communication and what they have read, for example, in the daily newspapers, are relatively numerous. Within the last few years there have been increasingly frequent attempts to relate simple responses, like reading behavior, to the characteristics of the individual responding. Such studies relate readership to sex, educational level, age group, etc.

Similarly a great deal of research on the response side has been done in the field of radio. But here the primary emphasis has been on the responses of listening and enjoyment. Devices for recording of responses of like or dislike have been of some assistance in this phase of the problem.[6] Only recently have there been corresponding studies of the effectiveness of radio in influencing opinion and in transmitting information.[7] Much the same has been true of the large amount of research that has gone into the analysis of response to the movies. The emphasis has been on what do people like. This has been the aspect that has had the great commercial backing. The beginnings of interest in other directions were shown in the Payne Fund studies on the effects of the movies on a wide variety of phases of social behavior.[8] The work which we did during the war on the analysis of the effectiveness of the films prepared by the Army to give soldiers the background of the war and our participation in it may also be mentioned.[9] Here the responses studied were in terms of the amount of information received, the opinions which were changed, and the effect of changes in information and opinion on motivation.

The analysis of response to communication has been enormously facilitated by recent improvements in technique. Public opinion methods have made rapid strides as will be seen from the papers presented this afternoon. But these methods do not suffice for the many aspects to be covered. Intensive interview methods are needed on many phases of the problem. For some phases of the problem adaptations of clinical procedures will probably prove essential to understand fully the total impact of communication. Another aspect of the problem requiring much further work is that of relating the different types of responses made to communication. This includes study of how changes in opinion and verbal statement are related to other phases of behavior like social action. This brings in the fascinating problem of how to change the way an individual perceives a problem and how changes in his perception affect his other actions.

Our research task also includes the formulation of principles and laws relating the stimuli, the individual, and the response. Here we are immediately stuck by the wide generality of the problem. We find that the principles needed for an understanding of communication are the very ones needed for an understanding of other aspects of behavior all the way from psychological warfare to individual psychotherapy in a face-to-face situation. We are thus at once benefited by the years of basic work that have gone into analysis of psychological behavior and its change, and at the same time confronted anew in changed form with the many large unsolved problems of human relations.

We are, of course, benefited in the search for principles by the years of experience of practitioners of the communication art. Let us survey briefly these contributions.

The field of education has made significant contributions. On the problems of how to transmit factual information, for example, the work of the last twenty years has been very enlightening. But even more significant problems exist in the field of communication of values and attitudes. Here we are largely in unknown territory, with a strong realization on the part of educators of the magnitude of the problem and its importance but with little dependable information at hand.

Another important source of hypotheses is the work which has been done on discussion groups. From wide practical experience a number of excellent books have been written on how to conduct discussion groups, strategic and tactical procedures, and the like.[10] Few of these recommendations have been put to experimental test but there are contained in these books numerous important ideas which should be evaluated.

Some systematic work directed toward study of discussion groups was done by our research group during the war to determine the type of leadership which is most effective and the effectiveness of various types of presentation. Extensive studies of the effectiveness of group discussion were carried out during the war by the late Kurt Lewin and his associates.[11] Their studies indicated that group discussion followed by a group decision to carry out some particular social action, like eating less white bread, or trying out meat substitutes, was more effective than

lectures and individual decision. This research raises a large number of important questions for research as to the factors responsible for the alleged effectiveness of group decision, such as the interelationships between the members of the group, the personality characteristics of those who are and are not influenced by the group pressures, and the like. Such research should greatly clarify our understanding of the interrelationships of the individual and the group in communication. Other significant work is being planned in the analysis of conference discussions and their effectiveness in various situations.

Work on psychotherapy has been of value as a source of hypotheses. This represents an important form of communication—of the face-to-face variety. From the extensive work on this problem many hypotheses have developed which if confirmed should be applicable to mass communication as well. Let me quote a single example. It has long been a belief on the part of many psychotherapists that decisions reached independently by the client or patient are apt to be more influential and lasting than those suggested by the therapist. Some work has been done along this line for individual psychotherapy. How about this generalization at the mass communication level? Is it more effective to present evidence for the point being communicated without drawing the implied conclusion and letting the communicatee draw the conclusion? Or is it better to present the evidence and also draw the conclusion for the reader or hearer? Preliminary work we have underway seems to indicate that an important variable is the intelligence of the individual or group addressed. With the more intelligent members of the audience the effects may be more lasting when they participated in the decision process but with less intelligent members the correct conclusion may not always be seen and grasped without being made explicitly by the communication.

Advertising wisdom yields a number of important hypotheses. Where systematic results are available they have considerable significance because of the fact that the objective of the communication is usually clearly defined. This is in contrast to certain other areas where people are eager to communicate but it is extremely difficult to define what they are trying to communicate so that one can make any adequate evaluation of the success of the effort.

There are a number of important limitations, however, to work in advertising as a source of principles of communication.

The first is the fact that many of the results are kept confidential because of their commercial value. A second difficulty is the complexity of the situation in which research is carried on. Organizations frequently have simultaneous radio, newspaper, magazine, and poster advertising with complex temporal relations which make it difficult to attribute results to specifiable causes. Thirdly, the research has been done primarily without reference to theoretical systematization so that it is difficult to generalize the results to new situations. Results are most frequently of the type that ad *A* produces more sales than ad *B*, but without any systematic account of the respects in which the two ads were the same and in which they were different.

Lastly, important ideas have come from analysis of problems of communication in industry. The importance of this problem was clearly shown by the early studies of Mayo[12] and others. A book like that of Chester Barnard[13] on leadership has a large number of significant hypotheses as to the role of communications, the formal and informal channels which exist within an organization and the barriers to more effective communication up and down the lines of organization and across them. Systematic work is being begun on the problem of communication within management, between management and the worker, and between management and the public.

The problem confronting us currently is not then lack of ideas and hypotheses. These as we have seen are available on every side. What are primarily lacking are two things: (1) lack of a comprehensive theoretical structure to embrace the diverse ideas and hunches from the various fields and (2) systematic experimental work to check and verify or refute the hypotheses obtaining.

In systematizing the field the work which has been done on the psychology of learning has proved of enormous help. This is not unexpected when we stop to consider that communication is essentially that phase of learning in which the conditions for learning are set up by another individual, the communicator. Thus all teaching is communicating.

As a result of the intimate relationship of communication to learning we have a quite sizeable body of principles already available to guide us in the development of a science of communication. We know the elements which are most relevant to analysis of this process—stimuli, responses, motives, and rewards. We know something about the conditions under which new habits are acquired. We know what happens when the four elements are appropriately timed and what happens when they are not.

These principles tie together a lot of the hunches derived from some of the practical groups mentioned earlier. But they also tend to make us skeptical of some of the theories advanced by some communicators. Let me cite one example.

Many advertisers assert that any communication will be effective if it is repeated frequently enough. Psychological theory, on the other hand, stresses the fact that repetition will only be effective when the proper combinations of the other elements of motive, reward, and response are observed. Without a response leading to satisfaction not learning, but "unlearning" should occur. At the superficial level we could say that many repetitions will strengthen the desired behavior but the strengthening is not the result of repetition alone.

This approach of the advertiser to the problem of communication is illustrated in the story in today's *New York Times* concerning a planned campaign to eliminate race prejudice.

> An aggressive national advertising campaign utilizing virtually every type of medium reaching the public, with the objective of "making racial prejudice as unpopular as B.O." will be carried on by the Advertising Council, Inc., it was announced yesterday.
>
> During a press conference prior to the announcement of the campaign, Lee Bristol, vice

president of Bristol-Myers and campaign coordinator, said: "Every means of advertising which could probably be useful will be mobilized in this fight against prejudice. Some of the best brains in the advertising profession have donated their time and talent to the design of striking posters and eloquent statements of the American creed. Through business facilities we will use advertising in newspapers, magazines, over the air, in outdoor display panels, and subway car cards."

Discussing the program, Edward Royal, council campaign manager, said it would be pushed strongly in the South. "We know that there is some support in the South already," Mr. Royal asserted. "We intend to hit the South as hard and as often as we can and feel reasonably certain that much of our material will be run in Southern newspapers and other media consistently."[14]

The objective is a worthy one and communication media may have an important role in attacking this problem, but I am sure you will feel from Mr. Wirth's paper later in the program that some important elements of the problem have not been sufficiently taken into account. However, if the copy for the campaign is adequately keyed to important personal motives, repetition will increase the chances of an individual's being exposed to the communication.

I have stressed the role of psychological theory. Equally important is the development of sociological and anthropological theories concerning communications. The way in which communication is transmitted in various types of social structure is an obvious example where the individual and the group are interdependent. Even more significant is the fact that understanding of the reward system for individuals is only possible in the light of the structure of the individual's society, and that sociological and anthropological analyses of what gets rewarded and what gets punished in the society as a whole, and more particularly in the subgroups of the society, has a most important function.

This brief survey has, I hope, shown that within the last decade there have been developed the basic materials needed to support an all-out offensive in developing a science of communication. The improved techniques for the analysis of the content of communication, the recent improvement in methods of studying the behavior elicited by communication, and the availability of both accumulated experience and some systematic theory make it possible to set up more critical observation and experiments. It appears quite likely that we shall witness substantial progress within the next years on this important new frontier.

NOTES

1. This is well illustrated in the diversity of contributors to the recent symposium: Communication and social action, Yeager, W. H., and W. E. Utterback, ed., *Annals Amer. Acad. Pol. and Soc. Sci.* 250, 1947.

2. *Cf.* e. g., Smith, B. L., The political communication specialist of our times, pp. 31–73, in Smith, B. L., H. D. Lasswell, and R. D. Casey, *Propaganda, communication, and public opinion,* Princeton Univ. Press, 1946.

3. Lasswell, H. D., Describing the contents of communications, pp. 74–94, in Smith, B. L., H. D. Lasswell, and R. D. Casey, *op. cit.*

4. *Cf.* e. g., Johnson, W., *People in quandaries; the semantics of personal adjustment,* N.Y., Harper, 1946.

5. Chafee, Z., *Government and mass communication,* 2 v., Univ. of Chicago Press, 1947.

6. Hallonquist, T., and E. A. Suchman, Listening to the listener, pp. 265–334, in *Radio research, 1943–1945,* Lazarsfeld, P. F., and F. N. Stanton, ed., N.Y., Duell, Sloan, and Pearce, 1944.

7. *Cf.,* e. g., Wilson, E. C., The effectiveness of documentary broadcasts, *Public Opin. Quart.* 12: 19–29, 1948.

8. Charters, W. W., *Motion pictures and youth: a summary,* N.Y., Macmillan, 1933.

9. *Experiments on mass communication* (to be published).

10. *Cf.,* e. g., Elliott, H. S., *The process of group thinking,* N.Y., Association Press, 1928.

11. Lewin, K., Forces behind food habits and methods of change, pp. 35–65, in The problem of changing food habits, *Bull. Nat. Res. Council,* No. 108, Oct. 1943.

12. Mayo, E., *The human problems of an industrial civilization,* N.Y., Macmillan, 1933.

13. Barnard, C. I., *The functions of the executive,* Harvard Univ. Press, 1938.

14. *New York Times* for Feb. 6, 1948.

24

SOME EXPLORATIONS IN INITIAL INTERACTION AND BEYOND

Toward a Developmental Theory of Interpersonal Communication

CHARLES R. BERGER AND RICHARD J. CALABRESE

When communication researchers have conducted empirical research on the interpersonal communication process, they have tended to employ social psychological theories as starting points. Theories relevant to such areas as person perception, social exchange, and interpersonal balance have frequently been employed as frameworks from which to derive testable hypotheses about the interpersonal communication process. While it is true that Newcomb's (1953) balance formulation and subsequent research on the acquaintance process (Newcomb, 1961) do include communication-relevant constructs, his theory does not focus on several important aspects of interpersonal communication. Obviously, Asch's (1946) work in the area of person perception and subsequent developments in that area (Kaplan & Anderson, 1973) are also relevant to the study of interpersonal communication. However, here too we find that these formulations do not directly focus upon the interpersonal communication process.

The present model seeks to remedy this situation by employing communication-relevant constructs which, in turn, lead to the formation of hypotheses which directly involve communication behavior. In constructing the theory, we have elected to focus our attention on the initial phases of interaction between strangers. Our

SOURCE: Berger, C., & Calabrese, R. (1975). Some explorations in initial interaction and beyond: Toward a developmental theory of interpersonal communication. *Human Communication Research, Vol. 1*, 99–112. Used by permission of the International Communication Association.

hope is that through subsequent research and theoretical extension, the model can be used to make predictions about and explain interpersonal communication phenomena which occur later in relationships. In our explication of the model, we have attempted to include previous research findings which lend support to our axioms and theorems.

DEVELOPMENTAL STAGES

Before we consider specific constructs and their relationships with each other, we feel it useful to provide some idea of the *possible stages* by which the communication transaction might be viewed. For purposes of the discussion, it is assumed that the persons involved in the communication transaction are strangers. We have labeled the first stage of the transaction the *entry phase*. One reason for the use of the term "entry" is that when strangers are faced with each other in a particular situation, their communication behaviors are, in part, determined by a set of communication rules or norms. Some rules are implicit; persons may not be able to verbalize them or indicate where they acquired them. Other rules are quite explicit and the individual might be able to indicate verbally what the rule is and where he acquired his knowledge of the rule. For example, two persons might both say "please" when asking someone to pass them something. One person might indicate that he said "please" because it "is the polite thing to do," while the other person might indicate that he said "please" because it is "natural" and not necessarily "polite." From this example it would seem that the first person is more *aware* of the "rule" which guided his behavior. Of course, it would also be possible for a person to be more or less certain about the appropriateness of a particular behavior. Some persons consistently have to concern themselves about the "appropriateness" of their behavior in particular situations, while others do not. These individual differences would suggest that the learning of rules and norms appropriate to situations, whether through

direct instruction or social modeling, is not uniform for all individuals.

Findings to be discussed later indicate that during the entry phase, communication content is somewhat structured. For example, message content tends to be focused on demographic kinds of information. The amount of information asked for and given by the interactants tends to be symmetric. During the latter phases of the entry stage, persons begin to explore each other's attitudes and opinions. The kinds of attitude issues explored are of rather low consequence or low involvement. By the end of the entry phase, the interactants have a fairly confident estimate of whether or not they will develop their relationship toward a more intimate level.

The second phase of the communication transaction we have labeled the *personal phase.* This phase begins when the interactants engage in communication about central attitudinal issues, personal problems, and basic values. This phase could begin after a few minutes of interaction; however, in most informal communication situations, the personal phase does not appear until the individuals involved have interacted on repeated occasions. While there are almost always rules and norms which regulate communication behavior in most situations, when interactants have moved to the personal phase, communication is more spontaneous and less constrained by social desirability norms. During this phase, persons may talk about socially undesirable aspects of their personalities and social relations. In the entry phase, such information is not usually sought or given.

The final phase of the transaction we have called the *exit phase.* During this phase decisions are made concerning the desirability of future interaction. Frequently, these decisions are discussed and plans for future interaction made. At a more macroscopic level of analysis, the exit phase of a relationship may occur over several interactions. Divorce is probably a good example. In most instances, it is probably the case that the final physical act of parting is preceded in time by a series of interactions and decisions which produce the final behavior. Knapp, Hart, Friedrich, and Shulman (1973) have begun to study the kinds of non-verbal behaviors which occur during the exit phase of a particular communication transaction. Their data suggest several behaviors which signal the end of a particular encounter.

By employing these descriptive categories we do not mean to imply that the phases are exhaustive or necessarily exclusive. Moreover, there are probably conditions under which the entry phase will be of relatively short duration and the interactants will move rapidly to the personal phase. Of course, it is also possible that because of certain information gained during the entry phase, the interaction will be terminated and the personal phase skipped entirely. All of these possibilities will be discussed in greater detail. By employing certain constructs, we feel that we can provide adequate explanations for these kinds of phenomena.

Axioms

Verbal Communication and Uncertainty

Central to the present theory is the assumption that when strangers meet, their primary concern is one of uncertainty reduction or increasing predictability about the behavior of both themselves and others in the interaction. This assumption is consistent with Heider's (1958) notion that man seeks to "make sense" out of events he perceives in his environment. By uncertainty we mean at least two things. First, at the very beginning of a particular encounter, there are a number of alternative ways in which each interactant *might behave*. Thus, one task for each interactant is to attempt to *predict* the most likely alternative actions the other person might take. Moreover, the individual interactant must then select from his own available response alternatives those which might be most appropriate to the predicted action of the other. However, before such response selection can occur, the individual must reduce his uncertainty about the other; that is, narrow the range of alternatives about the other's

probable future behavior. He must attempt to develop predictions about the other *before* the other acts. In the first sense of uncertainty reduction, the individual is engaged in a *proactive* process of creating predictions.

The second sense of uncertainty concerns the problem of *retroactively* explaining the other's behavior. For example, a target person might say something or act in a particular way which induces the other interactant to ask himself or others, "I wonder what he meant by that?" In almost any situation, there are a number of plausible alternative attributions one might make for a particular communicative act. The problem here is for the individual to reduce the number of plausible alternative explanations for the other person's behavior. Thus, in our view, uncertainty involves both prediction and explanation components.

The view of uncertainty explicated above follows from Heider's (1958) seminal attribution work and is consistent with later attribution formulations. Jones, Kanouse, Kelley, Nisbett, Valins, and Weiner (1972), Kelley (1967), and Kelley (1973) generally take the view that we strive to make our own behavior and the behavior of others *predictable,* and we try to develop causal structures which provide *explanations* for our own behavior as well as the behavior of others. Within this framework, interpersonal communication behavior plays at least two different roles. First, we must attempt to develop predictions about and explanations for our own and others' communication behavior; that is, communication behavior itself is something which we endeavor to predict and explain. Second, communication behavior is one vehicle through which such predictions and explanations are themselves formulated. Attribution theorists have been quick to point out that such predictions and explanations generally yield *imperfect knowledge* of ourselves and others. However, it is significant that such imperfect knowledge does *guide our total behavior toward others.* Thus, crucial to an understanding of a given individual's communication behavior is a knowledge of the kinds of predictions and explanations the individual has for the behavior of the person with whom he is interacting.

Such theorists as Adams (1965), Altman and Taylor (1973), Homans (1961), and Thibaut and Kelley (1959) have argued that reward/cost ratios determine whether or not an interaction will continue. Following from their position, one might argue that since uncertainty reduction is rewarding, the notion of rewards/costs is coterminous with the uncertainty construct. This analysis is somewhat faulty for the following reasons. While uncertainty may be rewarding up to a point, the ability to completely predict another's behavior might lead to boredom. Boredom in an interpersonal relationship might well be a cost rather than a reward. Moreover, since it is difficult to stipulate on an *a priori* basis just what is likely to be rewarding in a particular relationship, we feel that the reward/cost notion is of limited value in the construction of theory designed to predict rather than to retrodict interaction outcomes. Thus, we feel that uncertainty reduction is a more fruitful organizing construct than is reward/cost.

There are data which support the assertion that at the beginning of the entry phase uncertainty is relatively high and is subsequently reduced as a function of time. For example, Lalljee and Cook (1973) found that as interactions between strangers progressed, filled pause rate decreased while speech rate increased. Pause rate and speech rate were employed as two empirical indicators of uncertainty. In addition, it was found that a measure of anxiety, the non-ah speech disturbance ratio, did not decrease as the interaction progressed. This latter finding was interpreted as lowering the plausibility of the rival hypothesis that the decrease in pause rate was directly related to anxiety reduction.

The preceding discussion of the uncertainty construct and the empirical evidence provided by Lalljee and Cook (1973) suggest the following axiom:[1]

> AXIOM 1: *Given the high level of uncertainty present at the onset of the entry phase, as the amount of verbal communication between strangers increases, the level of uncertainty for each interactant in the relationship will decrease. As uncertainty is further reduced, the amount of verbal communication will increase.*

This axiom posits a reciprocal causal relationship between the amount of verbal communication and the level of uncertainty reduction; i.e., reduction in uncertainty level feeds back to determine the amount of verbal communication. The previously cited Lalljee and Cook study *which allowed for two-way exchange* found that the number of words per minute uttered by interactants *increased* significantly over a nine minute period. However, a study by Berger and Larimer (1974) revealed that when *feedback was not allowed* between strangers, the number of words per minute uttered *decreased* significantly over a four minute period. In this study, subjects were led to believe that they were talking to a person in another room whose picture they possessed. Actually, the pictures had been previously scaled for physical attractiveness (high, moderate, or low). While no differential effects were found for the physical attractiveness variable, across all conditions there were significant decreases in verbal output over time. The present formulation would suggest that since the subjects did not receive any feedback from the targets, the subjects' levels of uncertainty about the targets remained at a high level. The persistent high level of uncertainty about the target persons reduced the amount of communication directed toward them.

The Communication Environment and Uncertainty

The basal level of uncertainty a person has about a stranger can be modulated by the communication situation itself. For example, the street of a large city provides an observer with relatively little information about the persons walking along it. By contrast, an observer at a political rally for a particular candidate may be able to infer, with a high probability of being correct, the political attitudes of those present at the rally. In situations where uncertainty levels are reduced by the situation itself, conversations are likely to begin by focusing on content areas related to the situation. Two persons meeting for the first time at a political rally might well open a conversation by discussing the particular candidate and expressing their views about him. In other circumstances, the same two persons might begin a conversation by focusing upon each other's backgrounds. Thus, we recognize that uncertainty level may be influenced by the communication situation itself.

Nonverbal Affiliative Expressiveness and Uncertainty

For the same reason that high uncertainty levels at the beginning of the encounter lower the amount of verbal communication during that period, uncertainty also acts to lower nonverbal expressions of affiliation. There are a number of empirical indicators of nonverbal affiliative behavior which have been shown to be positively correlated with each other. For example, in a factor analytic study of various verbal and non-verbal dimensions in an initial interaction situation, Mehrabian (1971a) found significant positive correlations between such variables as total statements per minute, percent duration of eye contact, head nods per minute, positive verbal content, head and arm gestures per minute, and pleasantness of vocal expressions. These and other variables loaded on a factor labeled *affiliative behavior*. A second study by Mehrabian and Ksionzky (1971) found much the same pattern of factor loadings for the same variables as those used in the Mehrabian study. It is interesting to note that in both of these factor analyses, distance between the interactants was not associated with the affiliative behavior factor.

In comparing the results of these two studies with the results of other prior research on the distance-liking relationship, Mehrabian (1971b) points out that several experimental studies have supported an inverse relationship between liking and physical distance; persons who like each other tend to stand closer to each other. Mehrabian explains this apparent inconsistency by arguing that in both the factor analytic studies cited above, the distance between the interactants was averaged over the duration of the interaction. Studies which show liking to be associated with smaller interaction distances

usually use *initial* distance between interactants as the primary dependent variable.

The above discussion of the nature of the nonverbal affiliative expressiveness dimension and its relationship to level of uncertainty suggests the following axiom:

> AXIOM 2: *As nonverbal affiliative expressiveness increases, uncertainty levels will decrease in an initial interaction situation. In addition, decreases in uncertainty level will cause increases in nonverbal affiliative expressiveness.*

Uncertainty and Information Seeking

Given the relatively high level of uncertainty existing at the onset of the entry phase, one would expect persons in the situation to interrogate each other in order to gain information which might be instrumental in uncertainty reduction. Thus, one might expect interactants to engage in more question asking in the initial phases of the interaction. Moreover, the kinds of questions asked during the beginning of the entry phase might be ones which demand relatively short answers. For example, requests for such information as one's occupation, hometown, places of prior residence, and so on, generally call for relatively short responses. It seems that if an individual gives a relatively long response to such questions, he is generally judged somewhat negatively, especially when a detailed answer to the question was not explicitly called for. The predominance of short-answer questions during the early stages of the entry phase allows interactants to sample a number of different attributes in a relatively short time.

The preceding line of argument leads to the following axiom:

> AXIOM 3: *High levels of uncertainty cause increases in information seeking behavior. As uncertainty levels decline, information seeking behavior decreases.*

Data reported by Frankfurt (1965) support the relationship posited in Axiom 3. In this study, the number of questions asked to another in a simulated communication situation declined through time.

Uncertainty and Intimacy Level of Communication Content

We assume, as does Goffman (1959), that persons generally prefer to have smoothly running interpersonal relationships. Goffman argues that persons frequently assist each other in their performances so that each performer will maintain "face." Given this assumption and the relatively high level of uncertainty existing at the beginning of the entry phase, we might ask what is the least disruptive way of reducing uncertainty about the other? One strategy might be to ask the other how he feels about a variety of political and social issues. The problem with this strategy is that persons may disagree on such issues which, in turn, may lead to disruptions of their relationship. A better strategy would be to ask for and give biographical and demographic information during the entry phase. Dissimilarities along these dimensions probably have a relatively trivial negative impact on the interaction system. However, *similarities and dissimilarities in background characteristics might lead to the development of predictions of similarity or dissimilarity on more crucial attitudinal issues.* Thus, not only might uncertainty be reduced, predicted similarities or differences might also determine: (1) whether or not the interaction system will continue to exist and/or (2) whether or not the interactants will engage in a discussion of more intimate issues. For if two persons predict that they have widely differing beliefs on intimate and consequential issues and if they wish to have a smoothly running interaction, they will probably choose to avoid discussions of the issues of potential conflict.

The preceding discussion suggests the following axiom concerning the relationship between uncertainty and intimacy level.

AXIOM 4: *High levels of uncertainty in a relationship cause decreases in the intimacy level of communication content. Low levels of uncertainty produce high levels of intimacy.*

In their discussion of social penetration theory, Altman and Taylor (1973) argue that intimacy level of communication content tends to increase through time. However, their explanation of this phenomenon rests on the notion that as a relationship becomes more rewarding and less costly, persons will become more intimate. Our explanation of the same phenomenon is that as persons continue to communicate with each other, their uncertainty about each other decreases. Decreases in uncertainty lead to increases in intimacy level of communication.

Taylor and Altman (1966) had both college students and navy recruits sort 671 conversational topics along an intimacy continuum. Generally it was found that topics falling into such categories as biographical, hobbies and interests, and current events received low intimacy ratings, while topics falling into the categories of religion, sex, and personal attitudes received higher intimacy ratings. Taylor and Altman suggest that the statements scaled in their study can be used as guidelines for developing rating systems to score the intimacy level of communication content. Sermat and Smyth (1973) followed Taylor and Altman's recommendation and were able to obtain acceptable interjudge reliabilities of content intimacy in their study. However, Cozby (1973) has pointed out that the kinds of topics which Taylor and Altman scaled for intimacy value may be quite different from the kinds of communication content actually passed during an interaction. For example, according to the Taylor and Altman scaling study, talking about movies is a relatively low intimacy communication topic. However, there is probably a great deal of difference in perceived intimacy between a conversation in which the interactants talk about the movie "Mary Poppins" and one in which they exchange their views on "Deep Throat." Thus, although the Taylor and Altman study may provide us with rather general guidelines about the intimacy level of communication content, more specific kinds of content within general topic areas must be assessed for intimacy value.

A study by Berger (1973) revealed that during the course of interaction between strangers, the amount of demographic (low intimacy) information asked for and given was highest during the first minute of interaction. After the first minute, statistically significant decreases in the amount of demographic information exchanged were observed; while the amounts of information asked for and given in such more intimate categories as "attitudes and opinions" and "other persons" increased. Studies by Cozby (1972), Ehrlich and Graeven (1971), Sermat and Smyth (1973), Taylor, Altman, and Sorrentino (1969), and Taylor, Altman, and Wheeler (1973) also support the development of intimacy through time.

These outcomes are in agreement with the observations of Altman and Taylor (1973) who suggest that the early stages of the development of a relationship are characterized by exchanges of "superficial" information. While we agree that most observers would tend to judge a conversation consisting of exchanges of biographical information "superficial," we feel that the kinds of information asked for and given during the initial phases of the entry stage are crucial for the development of inferences about the persons rendering the information.

As Jones and Goethals (1972) have pointed out, primacy effects are more the rule than the exception in person perception research. There are conditions under which recency effects will obtain, but because of the prevalence of primacy effects, we are forced to conclude that information exchanged early in the interaction has functional significance for the actors involved. Knowing that a given individual is a college professor may well help to reduce uncertainty about his political and social attitudes. Obviously, many of the inferences drawn may be inaccurate. Nevertheless, persons do encode messages on the basis of such "imperfect knowledge."

Uncertainty and Reciprocity Rate

The notion that a reciprocity norm acts to control information exchange in an interaction has been advanced by Gouldner (1960). Research in the area of interviewer-interviewee speech behavior suggests that interviewees tend to match variations in the rate of interviewer

speech behavior (Matarazzo, Wiens & Saslow, 1965). Furthermore, evidence supporting the proposition that the amount of information exchanged in an interaction tends to be reciprocal has been reported by Worthy, Gary, and Kahn (1969). While these studies support the existence of a reciprocity norm in interaction, the underlying explanation for the phenomenon is not clear.

In view of the present formulation and the previous argument that persons prefer smoothly running interactions to ones in which there is great stress (Goffman, 1959), it seems reasonable to assume that the easiest way in which to reduce mutual uncertainty would be to ask for and give the same kinds of information at the same rate of exchange. In this way, no one interactant in the system would be able to gain *information power* over the other. Moreover, it also seems reasonable to assume that as uncertainty is reduced, there is less need for symmetric exchanges of information at a rapid rate. That is, it becomes more possible for greater time lags to occur between speaking and listening. Once uncertainty is at relatively low levels, one person might be able to talk to another for long periods of time without fear of being accused of "dominating the conversation." However, if a given individual plays the speaker for long periods of time during the entry phase, he would most probably be accused of dominating the conversation and the probability that the interaction would continue would be reduced. Thus, when uncertainty is high, reciprocity rate will also be high. As uncertainty is reduced, reciprocity rate decreases. Formally stated:

AXIOM 5: *High levels of uncertainty produce high rates of reciprocity. Low levels of uncertainty produce low reciprocity rates.*

Altman and Taylor (1973) have argued that the reciprocity construct is of limited value in the development of a theory of interaction development since there has been little in the way of *explanation* provided for the reciprocity phenomenon; i.e., merely asserting that a particular norm exists does not ipso facto explain its existence. However, we feel that the requirement for even uncertainty reduction in order to avoid asymmetries in information power distribution provides an explanation for the reciprocity norm's appearance during initial interaction.

Jourard (1960) found evidence suggestive of a "dyadic effect" concerning the intimacy level of self-disclosure. In this study he found that persons who disclosed more to others reported that they also received high amounts of disclosure from others. Subsequent experimental evidence (Worthy, Gary & Kahn, 1969; Ehrlich & Graeven, 1971; Cozby, 1972; Sermat & Smyth, 1973) suggests that when an individual discloses intimate information to another, the other tends to reciprocate at that level of intimacy. Moreover, Sermat and Smyth (1973) found that when a confederate continued to demand higher levels of disclosure through the questions he asked the subject, while at the same time refusing to disclose intimate information about himself, the subject tended to lower his level of liking for the confederate. However, when the confederate matched the subject's level of disclosure and then demanded disclosure at a higher intimacy level, the subject was more willing to meet the confederate's disclosure request. These studies together with Axiom 5 suggest that early in a relationship it is crucial for the interactants to convey information evenly and at a fairly rapid rate and to disclose information which is at about the same intimacy level. Violations of one or more of these rules raise the probability of dissolution of the relationship.

Similarity and Uncertainty

Most social psychological theories concerned with friendship formation have employed the notion of *similarity* of some sort as an antecedent of liking. Byrne (1971), Duck (1973), Homans (1961), Newcomb (1953), and Newcomb (1961) have argued that similarities along such dimensions as attitudes and conceptual structure produce interpersonal attraction, while dissimilarity produces negative interpersonal affect. Byrne employs a reinforcement framework to explain the similarity-attraction relationship. He argues that attitude agreements are rewarding and that such rewards lead to liking. By contrast, balance theorists (Heider, 1958) explain the similarity-liking relationship by arguing that shared affect toward an object will result in pressures toward liking. Recently, Duck (1973) has developed a "filter hypothesis" which asserts that different kinds of similarity are important for liking at different phases of the relationship. He suggests that at the early stages of a relationship, similarity of attitudes tends to be a strong determinant of liking; however, as the relationship progresses, *conceptual similarity* along both content and structural dimensions becomes the significant determinant of attraction. Duck employs Kelly's (1955) theory of personal constructs as a conceptual basis for his predictions. He reports several studies, employing a modified version of the Role Rep Test, which show that friends do have significantly higher levels of conceptual similarity than randomly formed dyads.

There is an impressive amount of evidence (Berscheid & Walster, 1969; Byrne, 1971) to demonstrate a positive relationship between attitude similarity and interpersonal attraction. Moreover, Duck's (1973) research supports a positive relationship between similarity of conceptual structure and friendship formation. In our view, both types of similarity act to reduce the level of uncertainty in a relationship; i.e., similarity of attitudes and conceptual structure produces decreases in uncertainty, while dissimilarities along attitude and conceptual dimensions raise uncertainty levels. Why do disagreements along attitude dimensions tend to raise uncertainty? After all, if a person holds an opinion opposed to mine, does that not reduce my uncertainty about him?

In order to answer the above question, we must consider the influence of affect direction on the number of alternative attributions generated about a person. Koenig (1971) has argued that when we dislike another person, social norms demand that we provide explanations for our dislike. When we like someone, however, we do not have to provide explanations for our liking. This phenomenon Koenig has labeled "justification"; i.e., we must justify our negative affect toward others. Koenig presents data which lend support to his justification hypothesis. Moreover, in research currently being conducted by Berger, a tendency has been found for persons to make more causal attributions for a disagreement between two persons than when the two persons show agreement. In these studies, subjects are presented with alleged conversations in which persons show either attitude agreement or attitude disagreement. Some studies have involved tape recorded conversations while others have used transcriptions of conversations. After the subjects read through or listen to the conversations, they are asked to list as many reasons (attributions) as they can for the agreement or disagreement shown by the persons in the conversation. Data from one of the studies indicate that subjects who were presented with a conversation in which disagreement occurred make more attributions than do subjects who are presented with agreeable conversations. These data suggest that as dissimilarity between persons increases, uncertainty in terms of number of alternative explanations for behavior also increases. Similarity reduces the necessity for the generation of a large number of alternatives for explaining behavior. The preceding line of argument suggests the following axiom:

AXIOM 6: *Similarities between persons reduce uncertainty, while dissimilarities produce increases in uncertainty.*

Uncertainty and Liking

As we noted in the previous section, a number of social psychologists have adduced evidence supportive of a positive relationship between similarity and liking. Furthermore, two main theoretical positions have been employed to explain this relationship: (1) reinforcement theory and (2) cognitive consistency theories. Earlier in this paper we suggested some inadequacies of the reinforcement approach to the study of interaction development. We have also argued that

similarity-dissimilarity is connected to uncertainty level. By making such a connection, we are subsuming the notion of similarity-dissimilarity and the related notions of balance under the broader conceptual umbrella of uncertainty. This formulation is consistent with the suggestion made by Berkowitz (1969) that "the striving for cognitive balance may actually only be a special case of a desire for certainty" (p. 96).

When persons are unable to make sense out of their environment, they usually become anxious. Moreover, Festinger (1954) has suggested that persons seek out similar others who are proximate when they experience a high level of uncertainty regarding the appropriateness of their behavior and/or opinions in a particular situation. Schachter's (1959) research on anxiety and affiliation tends to confirm this social comparison theory prediction for first born children. In view of the tendency to seek out similar others in order to reduce uncertainty, reduction of uncertainty by such means should tend to produce liking. This line of reasoning leads to the following axiom regarding the relationship between uncertainty and liking:

AXIOM 7: *Increases in uncertainty level produce decreases in liking; decreases in uncertainty level produce increases in liking.*

Taken together, Axioms 6 and 7 suggest that uncertainty level mediates between similarity and liking. It should be clear, however, that variables other than similarity-dissimilarity influence uncertainty level. Thus, an observed relationship between uncertainty level and liking may be due to similarity and/or the amount of communication that two persons have had with each other.

THEOREMS

From the preceding seven axioms, it is possible to deduce the following 21 theorems. Existing evidence relevant to the relationship posited by the theorem will be cited.

THEOREM 1: *Amount of verbal communication and nonverbal affiliative expressiveness are positively related.*

The relationship suggested by Theorem 1 has been verified in at least two factor analytic studies (Mehrabian, 1971a; Mehrabian & Ksionzky, 1971). In both studies such variables as total number of statements per minute and number of declarative statements per minute were found to correlate positively and significantly with such indices of nonverbal behavior as percent duration of eye contact, head nods per minute, hand and arm gestures per minute, and pleasantness of vocal expressions. The observed correlations among these empirical indicators of the amount of verbal communication and the amount of nonverbal affiliative expressiveness lend support to Theorem 1.

THEOREM 2: *Amount of communication and intimacy level of communication are positively related.*

While no study has directly related these two variables, the Lalljee and Cook (1973) finding that as an interaction progresses the number of words uttered per unit of time increases and the finding that intimacy levels of communication content increase with passage of time would suggest the relationship posited by Theorem 2.

THEOREM 3: *Amount of communication and information seeking behavior are inversely related.*

Indirect support for Theorem 3 can be derived from the Lalljee and Cook (1973) and the Frankfurt (1965) studies. As was noted above, Lalljee and Cook found significant increases in speech rate over a nine minute initial interaction period. Frankfurt reported data which supported the proposition that as an interaction progresses, the number of questions asked decreases. Taken together, these findings would suggest an inverse relationship between the amount of communication and the amount of information seeking behavior.

THEOREM 4: *Amount of communication and reciprocity rate are inversely related.*

While there are no data bearing directly upon the veracity of Theorem 4, the suggestions that as the relationship continues the amount of communication will increase and that greater time lags in reciprocity will be tolerated as the relationship continues both lend support to Theorem 4. However, the notion that reciprocity rate will decrease through time is one which needs to be verified empirically.

THEOREM 5: *Amount of communication and liking are positively related.*

Empirical support for the above proposition has been obtained by Lott and Lott (1961) and Moran (1966). In both of these studies it was found that persons who expressed liking for each other communicated more than persons who were strangers or persons who did not work together well. In his discussion of group cohesiveness and quantity of interaction, Shaw (1971) concludes that cohesiveness and amount of verbal interaction are positively related.

THEOREM 6: *Amount of communication and similarity are positively related.*

Data supportive of Theorem 6 have been presented by Schachter (1959). Following from Festinger's (1954) social comparison theory, Schachter found that persons preferred to affiliate with similar others. While Theorem 6 would seem to hold for initial interaction situations, there is some evidence that under certain conditions, dissimilarities between persons will produce increases in the amount of communication. Schachter (1951) found that the amount of communication directed toward a deviant in a group tended to increase through time. In highly cohesive groups to which the group task was highly relevant, the amount of communication directed toward the deviant tended to increase at first, then to decrease. The discrepancy between these findings and the social comparison theory findings seems to involve the nature of the interaction situation. Schachter's (1951) deviation-rejection study involved a *group* of persons interacting for the purpose of producing solutions to a problem; i.e., the group was explicitly *task oriented*. By contrast, the findings related to social comparison theory seem to be more relevant to situations in which the "task" confronting the *individual* is one of establishing the appropriateness of his opinions and behavior. For purposes of the formulation, the relationship between amount of communication and similarity suggested by the data relevant to social comparison theory would seem to be most appropriate, since the present theory deals with initial interaction situations between strangers.

THEOREM 7: *Nonverbal affiliative expressiveness and intimacy level of communication content are positively related.*

THEOREM 8: *Nonverbal affiliative expressiveness and information seeking are inversely related.*

THEOREM 9: *Nonverbal affiliative expressiveness and reciprocity rate are inversely related.*

There is little, if any, direct or indirect empirical evidence bearing upon the above three theorems. Studies involving intimacy level of communication content, information seeking, and reciprocity rate have not related these variables to nonverbal indices of affiliative behavior. Thus, research is needed to determine whether empirical hypotheses derived from the above three theorems hold.

THEOREM 10: *Nonverbal affiliative expressiveness and liking are positively related.*

The previously cited Mehrabian factor analytic studies as well as the research in the area of visual interaction summarized by Exline (1971) tend to support the above theorem. Persons who are attracted to each other have higher levels of eye contact, greater numbers of head nods and hand gestures per unit of time, and more frequent displays of pleasant facial expressions than persons who dislike each other.

THEOREM 11: *Nonverbal affiliative expressiveness and similarity are positively related.*

We know of no studies which provide direct support for Theorem 11, although it seems reasonable to assume that since liking and nonverbal affiliative expressiveness have been found to be positively related, similarity and nonverbal affiliative expressiveness should also be found to be positively related.

THEOREM 12: *Intimacy level of communication content and information seeking are inversely related.*

THEOREM 13: *Intimacy level of communication content and reciprocity rate are inversely related.*

There are no data which provide direct support for these two theorems. Altman and Taylor's (1973) social penetration theory and research suggest, however, that intimacy levels of communication increase through time, while information seeking attempts decrease. These tendencies lend some support to Theorem 12.

THEOREM 14: *Intimacy level of communication content and liking are positively related.*

One implication of Theorem 14 is that persons tend to disclose intimate information to persons they like and withhold intimate information from persons whom they do not like. In a review of self-disclosure literature relevant to this issue, Pearce and Sharp (1973) concluded that self-disclosure generally occurs within the context of positive relationships. However, these authors caution that there is some contradictory evidence which suggests that the relationship between disclosure and liking is probably a complex one.

THEOREM 15: *Intimacy level of communication content and similarity are positively related.*

THEOREM 16: *Information seeking and reciprocity rate are positively related.*

THEOREM 17: *Information seeking and liking are negatively related.*

THEOREM 18: *Information seeking and similarity are negatively related.*

There is no evidence that bears directly upon the above four theorems. However, since Theorems 17 and 18 appear to be non-commonsensical predictions, further comment is in order. First, Theorem 17 suggests that as liking increases in a relationship, the amount of information seeking behavior will decrease. One operational indicator of information seeking suggested earlier was the number of questions asked per unit of time. It would seem reasonable to suggest that as a relationship develops through time, there is less need for questions to be asked. Frankfurt's (1965) findings support this suggestion. As the relationship develops, persons are more willing to proffer information about themselves without specifically being asked for it. Thus, if positive affect does develop in a relationship through the reduction of uncertainty then the necessity for extensive interrogation would also tend to decrease, thus producing a negative relationship between information seeking and liking. In the case of Theorem 18, we have suggested that similarity tends to reduce uncertainty and that reductions of uncertainty obviate the necessity for extensive verbal interrogation. Thus, we would expect to find that similarity and information seeking are negatively related.

THEOREM 19: *Reciprocity rate and liking are negatively related.*

THEOREM 20: *Reciprocity rate and similarity are negatively related.*

THEOREM 21: *Similarity and liking are positively related.*

While there appears to be little evidence bearing on Theorems 19 and 20, there is an incredible amount of support for the similarity-attraction relationship. Byrne's (1971) research relevant to the attraction paradigm not only demonstrates that attitude similarity produces attraction, Byrne, Clore, and Worchel (1966) found that persons are more attracted to others who are perceived to be from economic backgrounds similar to their own. In addition, Duck (1973) has found that

conceptual similarity is positively related to friendship formation. It should be kept in mind, however, that the present theory explains the above empirical findings by employing the uncertainty construct as a mediating variable. This implies that if the effects of uncertainty were statistically removed from the similarity-attraction relationship, the similarity-attraction relationship would weaken significantly.

BEYOND INITIAL INTERACTION

For the present time, we have elected to confine our theory to the initial stages of interaction between strangers. Obviously, a full blown theory of interaction development would have to stipulate broader boundary conditions than the present one. We feel that one critical construct which might be part of such an extension is *frequency of contact.* The reason for our view is simply that in all probability, persons who do not have frequent contact with each other become uncertain about each other; i.e., as the time between contacts increases, persons' opinions, beliefs, and behaviors can change due to the influence of other persons and events. When two persons face each other after a long period of separation, they may have to go through a certain amount of biographic-demographic scanning behavior in order to "update" their "knowledge" of each other. Thus, because of the possible strong link between contact frequency and uncertainty level, an extension of the present formulation would have to take into account this relationship.

In a broader social perspective, Toffler (1970) has suggested that the rate of social change in the United States is increasing. One ingredient in the accelerated rate of change is the high level of mobility experienced by both individuals and families. If the rate of social change is indeed increasing and persons are becoming more mobile, then the necessity for going through the process explicated by the present model increases. Persons who experience frequent moves and the necessity of making new friends must go through the uncertainty reduction process more frequently than less mobile persons. The crucial social question is whether there is an upper limit of uncertainty that the individual can tolerate. If there is, then it would seem imperative that techniques be developed to help highly mobile persons form stable relationships with others as quickly as possible. For example, perhaps information about new neighbors could be provided to a family about to move into a new neighborhood. Advanced information about neighbors might aid the new family in their adaptation to the new environment. While this process may seem "artificial" and not very "spontaneous," it could help the highly mobile family anchor themselves more quickly in their new environment.

We believe that the present formulation serves to bring together a diverse body of findings as well as to generate predictions for future research. Some of the theorems generated by the model have already received strong empirical support while others have not been subjected to direct test. Obviously, there are other relevant constructs which might be explicitly incorporated into the model. Some of these constructs will no doubt be derived from the failure of the present model to predict particular relationships. Thus, our view is that the present formulation is a first effort. Hopefully, subsequent research and reformulation will result in a more general theory of the developmental aspects of interpersonal communication.

NOTE

1. The procedure for explicating the axioms and theorems of the present theory is taken from Blalock (1969). Blalock suggests that assumed causal relationships be stated as axioms and statements of covariation stated as theorems.

REFERENCES

Adams, J. S. Inequity in social exchange. In L. Berkowitz (Ed.), *Advances in experimental social psychology,* Vol. 2. New York: Academic Press, 1965, 267–299.

Altman, I., & Taylor, D. A. *Social penetration: The development of interpersonal relationships.* New York: Holt, Rinehart and Winston, 1973.

Asch, S. E. Forming impressions of personality. *Journal of Abnormal and Social Psychology,* 1946, 41, 258–290.

Berger, C. R. The acquaintance process revisited: Explorations in initial interaction. Paper presented at the annual convention of the Speech Communication Association, New York, November, 1973.

Berger, C. R., & Larimer, M. W. When beauty is only skin deep: The effects of physical attractiveness, sex and time on initial interaction. Paper presented at the annual convention of the International Communication Association, New Orleans, April, 1974.

Berkowitz, L. Social motivation. In G. Lindzey and E. Aronson (Eds.), *The handbook of social psychology,* Vol. 3. Reading, Mass: Addison Wesley, 1969, 50–135.

Berscheid, E., & Walster, E. H. *Interpersonal attraction.* Reading, Mass: Addison Wesley, 1969.

Blalock, H. M. *Theory construction: From verbal to mathematical formulations.* Englewood Cliffs, N.J.: Prentice-Hall, 1969.

Byrne, D. *The attraction paradigm.* New York: Academic Press, 1971.

Byrne, D., Clore, G. L., & Worchel, P. The effect of economic similarity-dissimilarity on interpersonal attraction. *Journal of Personality and Social Psychology,* 1966, 4, 220–224.

Cozby, P. C. Self-disclosure, reciprocity and liking. *Sociometry,* 1972, 35, 151–160.

Cozby, P. C. Self-disclosure: A literature review. *Psychological Bulletin,* 1973, 79, 73–89.

Duck, S. W. *Personal relationships and personal constructs: A study of friendship formation.* New York: Wiley, 1973.

Ehrlich, H. J., & Graeven, D. B. Reciprocal self-disclosure in a dyad. *Journal of Experimental Social Psychology,* 1971, 7, 389–400.

Exline, R. V. Visual interaction: The glances of power and preference. In J. K. Cole (Ed.), *Nebraska symposium on motivation.* Lincoln: University of Nebraska Press, 1971, 163–206.

Festinger, L. A theory of social comparison processes. *Human Relations,* 1954, 7, 117–140.

Frankfurt, L. P. The role of some individual and interpersonal factors on the acquaintance process. Unpublished doctoral dissertation, The American University, 1965.

Goffman, E. *The presentation of self in everyday life.* New York: Doubleday Press, 1959.

Gouldner, A. W. The norm of reciprocity: A preliminary statement. *American Sociological Review,* 1960, 25, 161–178.

Heider, F. *The psychology of interpersonal relations.* New York: Wiley, 1958.

Homans, G. C. *Social behavior: Its elementary forms.* New York: Harcourt, Brace and World, Inc., 1961.

Jones, E. E., & Goethals, G. R. Order effects in impression formation: Attribution context and the nature of the entity. In E. E. Jones, D. E. Kanouse, H. H. Kelley, R. E. Nesbitt, S. Valins, and B. Weiner, *Attribution: Perceiving the causes of behavior.* Morristown: General Learning Press, 1972.

Jones, E. E., Kanouse, D. E., Kelley, H. H., Nisbett, R. E., Valins, S., & Weiner, B. *Attribution: Perceiving the causes of behavior.* Morristown: General Learning Press, 1972.

Jourard, S. Knowing, liking, and the "dyadic effect" in men's self-disclosure. *Merrill Palmer Quarterly of Behavior and Development,* 1960, 6, 178–186.

Kaplan, M. F., & Anderson, N. H. Information integration theory and reinforcement theory as approaches to interpersonal attraction. *Journal of Personality and Social Psychology,* 1973, 28, 301–312.

Kelley, H. H. Attribution theory in social psychology. In D. Levine (Ed.), *Nebraska symposium on motivation.* Lincoln: University of Nebraska Press, 1967, 192–240.

Kelley, H. H. The processes of causal attribution. *American Psychologist,* 1973, 28, 107–128.

Kelly, G. A. *The psychology of personal constructs.* New York: Norton, 1955.

Knapp, M. L., Hart, R. P., Friedrich, G. W., & Shulman, G. M. The rhetoric of goodbye: Verbal and nonverbal correlates of human leave taking. *Speech Monographs,* 1973, 40, 182–198.

Koenig, F. Positive affective stimulus value and accuracy of role perception. *British Journal of Social and Clinical Psychology,* 1971, 10, 385–386.

Lalljee, M., & Cook, M. Uncertainty in first encounters. *Journal of Personality and Social Psychology,* 1973, 26, 137–141.

Lott, A. J., & Lott, B. E. Group cohesiveness, communication level, and conformity. *Journal of Abnormal and Social Psychology,* 1961, 62, 408–412.

Matarazzo, J. D., Wiens, A. N., & Saslow, G. Studies of interview speech behavior. In L. Krasner and L. P. Ullman (Eds.), *Research in behavior modification: New developments and implications.* New York: Holt, Rinehart and Winston, 1965, 179–210.

Mehrabian, A. Verbal and nonverbal interaction of strangers in a waiting situation. *Journal of Experimental Research in Personality,* 1971, 5, 127–138. (a)

Mehrabian, A. Nonverbal communication. In J. K. Cole (Ed.), *Nebraska symposium on motivation.* Lincoln: University of Nebraska Press, 1971. (b)

Mehrabian, A., & Ksionzky, S. Factors of interpersonal behavior and judgment in social groups. *Psychological Reports,* 1971, 28, 483–492.

Moran, G. Dyadic interaction and orientational consensus. *Journal of Personality and Social Psychology,* 1966, 4, 94–99.

Newcomb, T. An approach to the study of communicative acts. *Psychological Review,* 1953, 60, 393–404.

Newcomb, T. *The acquaintance process.* New York: Holt, Rinehart and Winston, 1961.

Pearce, W. B., & Sharp, S. M. Self-disclosing communication. *Journal of Communication,* 1973, 23, 409–425.

Schachter, S. Deviation, rejection, and communication. *Journal of Abnormal and Social Psychology,* 1951, 46, 190–207.

Schachter, S. *The psychology of affiliation: Experimental studies of the sources of gregariousness.* Stanford: Stanford University Press, 1959.

Sermat, V., & Smyth, M. Content analysis of verbal communication in the development of a relationship: Conditions influencing self-disclosure. *Journal of Personality and Social Psychology,* 1973, 26, 332–346.

Shaw, M. E. *Group dynamics: The psychology of small group behavior.* New York: McGraw-Hill, 1971.

Taylor, D. A., & Altman, I. Intimacy-scaled stimuli for use in studies of interpersonal relationships. Bethesda: Naval Medical Research Institute, 1966, Tech. Report No. 9, MF022.01.03-1002.

Taylor, D. A., Altman, I., & Sorrentino, R. Interpersonal exchange as a function of rewards and costs and situational factors: Expectancy confirmation-disconfirmation. *Journal of Experimental Social Psychology,* 1969, 5, 324–339.

Taylor, D. A., Altman, I., & Wheeler, L. Self-disclosure in isolated groups. *Journal of Personality and Social Psychology,* 1973, 26, 39–47.

Thibaut, J. W., & Kelley, H. H. *The social psychology of groups.* New York: Wiley, 1959.

Toffler, A. *Future shock.* New York: Random House, 1970.

Worthy, M., Gary, A. L., & Kahn, G. M. Self-disclosure as an exchange process. *Journal of Personality and Social Psychology,* 1969, 13, 59–64.

25

SOCIAL COGNITIVE THEORY OF MASS COMMUNICATION

ALBERT BANDURA

Because of the influential role the mass media play in society, understanding the psychosocial mechanisms through which symbolic communication influences human thought, affect and action is of considerable import. Social cognitive theory provides an agentic conceptual framework within which to examine the determinants and mechanisms of such effects. Human behavior has often been explained in terms of unidirectional causation, in which behavior is shaped and controlled either by environmental influences or by internal dispositions. Social cognitive theory explains psychosocial functioning in terms of triadic reciprocal causation (Bandura, 1986). In this transactional view of self and society, personal factors in the form of cognitive, affective, and biological events; behavioral patterns; and environmental events all operate as interacting determinants that influence each other bidirectionally (Figure 25.1).

Social cognitive theory is founded in an agentic perspective (Bandura, 1986, 2000a). People are self-organizing, proactive, self-reflecting, and self-regulating, not just reactive organisms shaped and shepherded by environmental events or inner forces. Human self-development, adaptation, and change are embedded in social systems. Therefore, personal agency operates within a broad network of sociostructural influences. In these agentic transactions, people are producers as well as products of social systems. Personal agency and social structure operate as codeterminants in an integrated causal structure rather than as a disembodied duality.

Seen from the sociocognitive perspective, human nature is a vast potentiality that can be fashioned by direct and observational experience into a variety of forms within biological limits. To say that a major distinguishing mark

SOURCE: Bandura, A. (2001). Social cognitive theory of mass communication. In J. Bryant & D. Zillman (Eds.), *Media effects: Advances in theory and research* (2nd ed., 121–153). Hillsdale, NJ: Lawrence Erlbaum.

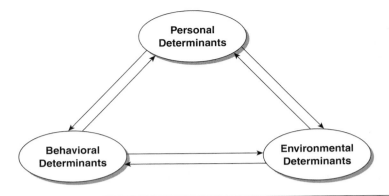

Figure 25.1   Schematization of Triadic Reciprocal Causation in the Causal Model of Social
Cognitive Theory

of humans is their endowed plasticity is not to
say that they have no nature or that they come
structureless (Midgley, 1978). The plasticity,
which is intrinsic to the nature of humans,
depends upon neurophysiological mechanisms
and structures that have evolved over time.
These advanced neural systems specialized for
processing, retaining, and using coded information provide the capacity for the very capabilities that are distinctly human–generative
symbolization, forethought, evaluative self-
regulation, reflective self-consciousness, and
symbolic communication. These capabilities are
addressed in the sections that follow.

SYMBOLIZING CAPABILITY

Social cognitive theory accords a central role
to cognitive, vicarious, self-regulatory, and self-
reflective processes. An extraordinary capacity
for symbolization provides humans with a powerful tool for comprehending their environment
and creating and regulating environmental events
that touch virtually every aspect of their lives.
Most external influences affect behavior through
cognitive processes rather than directly. Cognitive
factors partly determine which environmental

events will be observed, what meaning will be
conferred on them, whether they leave any lasting
effects, what emotional impact and motivating
power they will have, and how the information
they convey will be organized for future use. It is
with symbols that people process and transform
transient experiences into cognitive models that
serve as guides for judgment and action. Through
symbols, people give meaning, form, and continuity to their experiences.

People gain understanding of causal relationships and expand their knowledge by operating
symbolically on the wealth of information
derived from personal and vicarious experiences.
They generate solutions to problems, evaluate
their likely outcomes, and pick suitable options
without having to go through a laborious behavioral search. Through the medium of symbols
people can communicate with others at any distance in time and space. However, in keeping
with the interactional perspective, social cognitive theory devotes much attention to the social
origins of thought and the mechanisms through
which social factors exert their influence on cognitive functioning. The other distinctive human
capabilities are founded on this advanced capacity for symbolization.

[. . .]

VICARIOUS CAPABILITY

Psychological theories have traditionally emphasized learning by the effects of one's actions. If knowledge and skills could be acquired only by response consequences, human development would be greatly retarded, not to mention exceedingly tedious and hazardous. A culture could never transmit its language, mores, social practices, and requisite competencies if they had to be shaped tediously in each new member by response consequences without the benefit of models to exemplify the cultural patterns. Shortening the acquisition process is vital for survival as well as for self-development because natural endowment provides few inborn skills, hazards are ever present, and errors can be perilous. Moreover, the constraints of time, resources, and mobility impose severe limits on the places and activities that can be directly explored for the acquisition of new knowledge and competencies.

Humans have evolved an advanced capacity for observational learning that enables them to expand their knowledge and skills rapidly through information conveyed by the rich variety of models. Indeed, virtually all behavioral, cognitive, and affective learning from direct experience can be achieved vicariously by observing people's actions and its consequences for them (Bandura, 1986; Rosenthal & Zimmerman, 1978). Much social learning occurs either designedly or unintentionally from models in one's immediate environment. However, a vast amount of information about human values, styles of thinking, and behavior patterns is gained from the extensive modeling in the symbolic environment of the mass media.

A major significance of symbolic modeling lies in its tremendous reach and psychosocial impact. Unlike learning by doing, which requires altering the actions of each individual through repeated trial-and-error experiences, in observational learning a single model can transmit new ways of thinking and behaving simultaneously to countless people in widely dispersed locales. There is another aspect of symbolic modeling that magnifies its psychological and social impact. During the course of their daily lives, people have direct contact with only a small sector of the physical and social environment. They work in the same setting, travel the same routes, visit the same places, and see the same set of friends and associates. Consequently, their conceptions of social reality are greatly influenced by vicarious experiences—by what they see, hear, and read—without direct experiential correctives. To a large extent, people act on their images of reality. The more people's images of reality depend upon the media's symbolic environment, the greater is its social impact (Ball-Rokeach & DeFleur, 1976).

Most psychological theories were cast long before the advent of extraordinary advances in the technology of communication. As a result, they give insufficient attention to the increasingly powerful role that the symbolic environment plays in present-day human lives. Whereas previously, modeling influences were largely confined to the behavior patterns exhibited in one's immediate environment, the accelerated growth of video delivery technologies has vastly expanded the range of models to which members of society are exposed day in and day out. By drawing on these modeled patterns of thought and behavior, observers can transcend the bounds of their immediate environment. New ideas, values, behavior patterns and social practices are now being rapidly diffused by symbolic modeling worldwide in ways that foster a globally distributed consciousness (Bandura, 1986, 2000d). Because the symbolic environment occupies a major part of people's everyday lives, much of the social construction of reality and shaping of public consciousness occurs through electronic acculturation. At the societal level, the electronic modes of influence are transforming how social systems operate and serving as a major vehicle for sociopolitical change. The study of acculturation in the present electronic age must be broadened to include electronic acculturation.

Mechanisms Governing Observational Learning

Because symbolic modeling is central to full understanding of the effects of mass communication, the modeling aspect of social cognitive theory is discussed in somewhat greater detail. Observational learning is governed by four subfunctions which are summarized in Figure 25.2.

Attentional processes determine what is selectively observed in the profusion of modeling influences and what information is extracted from ongoing modeled events. A number of factors influence the exploration and construal of what is modeled. Some of these determinants concern the cognitive skills, preconceptions and value preferences of the observers. Others are related to the salience, attractiveness, and functional value of the modeled activities themselves. Still other factors are the structural arrangements of human interactions and associational networks, which largely determine the types of models to which people have ready access.

People cannot be much influenced by observed events if they do not remember them.

A second major subfunction governing observational learning concerns the construction of cognitive representations. In social cognitive theory, observers construct generative conceptions of styles of behavior from modeled exemplars rather than merely scripts from habitual routines. Retention involves an active process of transforming and restructuring information conveyed by modeled events into rules and conceptions for memory representation. Retention is greatly aided by symbolic transformations of modeled information into memory codes and cognitive rehearsal of the coded information. Preconceptions and affective states exert biasing influences on these representational activities. Similarly, recall involves a process of reconstruction rather than simply retrieval of registered events.

In the third subfunction in modeling—the behavioral production process—symbolic conceptions are translated into appropriate courses of action. This is achieved through a conception-matching process in which conceptions guide the construction and execution of behavior patterns which are then compared against the conceptual model for adequateness. The

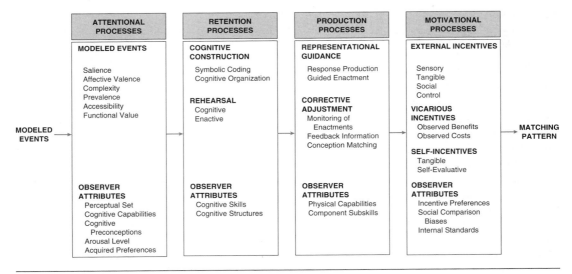

Figure 25.2   The Four Major Subfunctions Governing Observational Learning and the Influential Factors Operating Within Each Subfunction

behavior is modified on the basis of the comparative information to achieve close correspondence between conception and action. The mechanism for translating cognition into action involves both transformational and generative operations. Execution of a skill must be constantly varied to suit changing circumstances. Adaptive performance, therefore, requires a generative conception rather than a one-to-one mapping between cognitive representation and action. By applying an abstract specification of the activity, people can produce many variations on the skill. Conceptions are rarely transformed into masterful performance on the first attempt. Monitored enactments serve as the vehicle for transforming knowledge into skilled action. Performances are perfected by corrective adjustments during behavior production. The more extensive the subskills that people possess, the easier it is to integrate them to produce new behavior patterns. When deficits exist, the subskills required for complex performances must first be developed by modeling and guided enactment.

The fourth subfunction in modeling concerns motivational processes. Social cognitive theory distinguishes between acquisition and performance because people do not perform everything they learn. Performance of observationally learned behavior is influenced by three major types of incentive motivators—direct, vicarious, and self-produced. People are more likely to exhibit modeled behavior if it results in valued outcomes than if it has unrewarding or punishing effects. The observed detriments and benefits experienced by others influence the performance of modeled patterns in much the same way as do directly experienced consequences. People are motivated by the successes of others who are similar to themselves, but are discouraged from pursuing courses of behavior that they have seen often result in adverse consequences. Personal standards of conduct provide a further source of incentive motivation. The self-approving and self-censuring reactions people generate to their own behavior regulate which observationally learned activities they are

most likely to pursue. They pursue activities they find self-satisfying and give them a sense of worth but reject those they personally disapprove.

The different sources of consequences may operate as complimentary or opposing influences on behavior (Bandura, 1986). Behavior patterns are most firmly established when social and self-sanctions are compatible. Under such conditions, socially approvable behavior is a source of self-pride and socially disapprovable behavior is self-censured. Behavior is especially susceptible to external influences in the absence of countervailing self-sanctions. People who are not much committed to personal standards adopt a pragmatic orientation, tailoring their behavior to fit whatever the situation seems to call for (Snyder & Campbell, 1982). They become adept at reading social situations and guiding their actions by expediency.

One type of conflict between social and self-produced sanctions arises when individuals are socially punished for behavior they highly value. Principled dissenters and nonconformists often find themselves in this predicament. Here, the relative strength of self-approval and social censure determine whether the behavior will be restrained or expressed. Should the threatened social consequences be severe, people hold in check self-praiseworthy acts in risky situations but perform them readily in relatively safe settings. These are individuals, however, whose sense of self-worth is so strongly invested in certain convictions that they will submit to prolonged maltreatment rather than accede to what they regard as unjust or immoral.

People commonly experience conflicts in which they are socially pressured to engage in behavior that violates their moral standards. When self-devaluative consequences outweigh the benefits for socially accommodating behavior, the social influences do not have much sway. However, the self-regulation of conduct operates through conditional application of moral standards. We shall see shortly that self-sanctions can be weakened or nullified by selective disengagement of internal control.

Abstract Modeling

Modeling is not merely a process of behavioral mimicry, as commonly misconstrued. The proven skills and established customs of a culture may be adopted in essentially the same form as they are exemplified because of their high functional value. However, in most activities, subskills must be improvised to suit varying circumstances. Modeling influences convey rules for generative and innovative behavior as well. This higher-level learning is achieved through abstract modeling. Rule-governed judgments and actions differ in specific content and other details while embodying the same underlying rule. For example, a model may confront moral conflicts that differ widely in content but apply the same moral standard to them. In this higher form of abstract modeling, observers extract the rule governing the specific judgments or actions exhibited by others. Once they learn the rule, they can use it to judge or generate new instances of behavior that go beyond what they have seen or heard.

[. . .]

Modeling also plays a prominent role in creativity. Creativeness rarely springs entirely from individual inventiveness. By refining preexisting innovations, synthesizing them into new procedures and adding novel elements, something new is created (Bandura, 1986; Bolton, 1993; Fimrite, 1977). When exposed to models of differing styles of thinking and behaving, observers vary in what they adopt and thereby create new blends of personal characteristics that differ from the individual models. Modeling new perspectives and innovative styles of thinking also fosters creativity by weakening conventional mind sets (Harris & Evans, 1973).

Motivational Effects

The discussion thus far has centered on the acquisition of knowledge, cognitive skills and new styles of behavior through observational learning. Social cognitive theory distinguishes among several modeling functions, each governed by different determinants and underlying mechanisms. In addition to cultivating new competencies, modeling influences have strong motivational effects. Vicarious motivators are rooted in outcome expectations formed from information conveyed by the rewarding and punishing outcomes of modeled courses of action. Seeing others gain desired outcomes by their actions can create outcome expectancies that function as positive incentives; observed punishing outcomes can create negative outcome expectancies that function as disincentives. These motivational effects are governed by observers' judgments of their ability to accomplish the modeled behavior, their perception of the modeled actions as producing favorable or adverse consequences, and their inferences that similar or unlike consequences would result if they, themselves, were to engage in similar activities.

[. . .]

Vicariously created motivators have been studied most extensively in terms of the inhibitory and disinhibitory effects of modeled transgressive, aggressive and sexual behavior with accompanying outcomes (Bandura, 1973; Berkowitz, 1984; Malamuth & Donnerstein, 1984; Paik & Comstock, 1994; Zillmann & Bryant, 1984).

Transgressive behavior is regulated by two major sources of sanctions—social sanctions and internalized self-sanctions. Both control mechanisms operate anticipatorily. In motivators arising from social sanctions, people refrain from transgressing because they anticipate that such conduct will bring them social censure and other adverse consequences. In motivators rooted in self-reactive control, people refrain from transgressing because such conduct will give rise to self-reproach. Media portrayals can alter perceived social sanctions by the way in which the consequences of different styles of conduct are portrayed. For example, televised aggression is often exemplified in ways that tend to weaken restraints over aggressive conduct (Goranson, 1970; Halloran & Croll, 1972; Larsen, 1968). In televised representations of human discord, physical aggression is a preferred solution to interpersonal conflicts; it is acceptable and

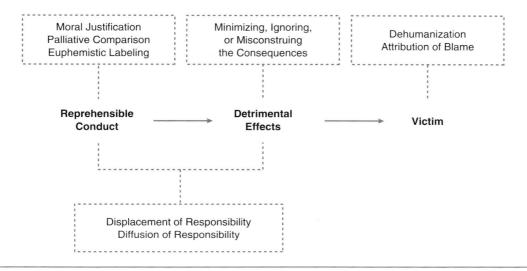

Figure 25.3   Mechanisms Through Which Self-Sanctions Are Selectively Activated and Disengaged From
Detrimental Conduct at Critical Points in the Self-Regulatory Process

relatively successful; and it is socially sanctioned
by superheroes triumphing over evil by violent
means. Such portrayals legitimize, glamorize
and trivialize human violence.

Inhibitory and disinhibitory effects stemming
from self-sanctions are mediated largely through
self-regulatory mechanisms. After standards
have been internalized, they serve as guides and
deterrents to conduct by the self-approving and
self-reprimanding consequences people produce
for themselves. However, moral standards do not
function as fixed internal regulators of conduct.
Self-regulatory mechanisms do not operate
unless they are activated, and there are many
processes by which moral reactions can be disengaged from inhumane conduct (Bandura,
1991b, 1999b). Selective activation and disengagement of internal control permits different
types of conduct with the same moral standards.
Figure 25.3 shows the points in the self-regulatory
process at which moral control can be disengaged from censurable conduct.

One set of disengagement practices operates
on the construal of the behavior itself by *moral
justification.* People do not ordinarily engage
in reprehensible conduct until they have justified to themselves the morality of their actions.
What is culpable is made personally and socially
acceptable by portraying it in the service of
moral purposes. Moral justification is widely
used to support self-serving and otherwise culpable conduct. Moral judgments of conduct are
also partly influenced by what it is compared
against. Self-deplored acts can be made benign
or honorable by contrasting them with more
flagrant transgressions. Because examples of
human culpability abound, they lend themselves
readily to cognitive restructuring of transgressive conduct by such *advantageous comparison.*
Activities can take on a very different appearance depending on what they are called.
Sanitizing *euphemistic labeling* provides
another convenient device for masking reprehensible activities or even conferring a
respectable status upon them. Through convo-
luted verbiage, reprehensible conduct is made
benign and those who engage in it are relieved
of a sense of personal agency.

Cognitive restructuring of behavior through moral justifications and palliative characterizations is the most effective psychological mechanism for promoting transgressive conduct. This is because moral restructuring not only eliminates self-deterrents but engages self-approval in the service of transgressive exploits. What was once morally condemnable becomes a source of self-valuation.

Ball-Rokeach (1972) attaches special significance to evaluative reactions and social justifications presented in the media, particularly in conflicts of power. This is because relatively few viewers experience sufficient inducement to use the aggressive strategies they have seen, but the transmitted justifications and evaluations can help to mobilize public support for policy actions favoring either social control or social change. The justificatory changes can have widespread social and political ramifications.

The mass media, especially television, provide the best access to the public through its strong drawing power. For this reason, television is increasingly used as the principle vehicle of justification. Struggles to legitimize and gain support for one's values and causes and to discredit those of one's opponents are now waged more and more through the electronic media (Ball-Rokeach, 1972; Bandura, 1990; Bassiouni, 1981). Because of its potential influence, the communication system itself is subject to constant pressures from different factions within society seeking to sway it to their ideology. Research on the role of the mass media in the social construction of reality carries important social implications.

Self-sanctions are activated most strongly when personal causation of detrimental effects is apparent. Another set of disengagement practices operates by obscuring or distorting the relationship between actions and the effects they cause. People will behave in ways they normally repudiate if a legitimate authority sanctions their conduct and accepts responsibility for its consequences (Milgram, 1974). Under conditions of *displacement of responsibility,* people view their actions as springing from the dictates of others rather than their being personally responsible for them. Since they are not the actual agent of their actions, they are spared self-prohibiting reactions. The deterrent power of self-sanctions is also weakened when the link between conduct and its consequences is obscured by *diffusion of responsibility* for culpable behavior. Through division of labor, diffusion of decision making, and group action, people can behave detrimentally without any one person feeling personally responsible (Kelman & Hamilton, 1989). People behave more injuriously under diffused responsibility than when they hold themselves personally accountable for what they do (Bandura, Underwood, & Fromson, 1975; Diener, 1977).

Additional ways of weakening self-deterring reactions operate through *disregard or distortion of the consequences of action.* When people pursue detrimental activities for personal gain or because of social inducements, they avoid facing the harm they cause or they minimize it. They readily recall the possible benefits of the behavior but are less able to remember its harmful effects (Brock & Buss, 1962, 1964). In addition to selective inattention and cognitive distortion of effects, the misrepresentation may involve active efforts to discredit evidence of the harm they cause. As long as the detrimental results of one's conduct are ignored, minimized, distorted, or disbelieved there is little reason for self-censure to be activated.

The final set of disengagement practices operates at the point of recipients of detrimental acts. The strength of self-evaluative reactions to detrimental conduct partly depends on how the perpetrators view the people toward whom the behavior is directed. To perceive another as human enhances empathetic or vicarious reactions through perceived similarity (Bandura, 1992). As a result, it is difficult to mistreat humanized persons without risking self-condemnation. Self-sanctions against cruel conduct can be disengaged or blunted by *dehumanization,* which divests people of human qualities or invests them with bestial qualities. While dehumanization weakens self-restraints against cruel conduct

(Diener, 1977; Zimbardo, 1969), humanization fosters considerate, compassionate behavior (Bandura et al., 1975).

Attribution of blame to one's antagonists is still another expedient that can serve self-exonerative purposes. Deleterious interactions usually involve a series of reciprocally escalative actions, in which the antagonists are rarely fault-less. One can always select from the chain of events an instance of the adversary's defensive behavior and view it as the original instigation. Injurious conduct thus becomes a justifiable defensive reaction to belligerent provocations. Others can, therefore, be blamed for bringing suffering on themselves. Self-exoneration is sim-ilarly achievable by viewing one's detrimental conduct as forced by circumstances rather than as a personal decision. By blaming others or cir-cumstances, not only are one's own actions excusable but one can even feel self-righteous in the process.

Because internalized controls can be selec-tively activated and disengaged, marked changes in moral conduct can be achieved without changing people's personality structures, moral principles, or self-evaluative systems. It is self-exonerative processes rather than character flaws that account for most inhumanities. The massive threats to human welfare stem mainly from deliberate acts of principle rather than from unrestrained acts of impulse.

The mechanisms of moral disengagement largely govern what is commonly labeled [the] "disinhibitory effect" of televised influences. Research in which the different disengagement factors are systematically varied in media por-trayals of inhumanities attests to the disin-hibitory power of mass media influences (Berkowitz & Green, 1967; Donnerstein, 1984; Meyer, 1972). Viewers' punitiveness is enhanced by exposure to media productions that morally justify injurious conduct, blame and dehumanize victims, displace or diffuse personal responsibil-ity, and sanitize destructive consequences. Research assessing self-reactive control provides evidence that sanctioning social conditions are linked to self-regulatory influences which, in

turn, are linked to injurious conduct (Bandura et al., 1975). The same disengagement mecha-nisms are enlisted heavily by members of the television industry in the production of programs that exploit human brutality for commercial pur-poses (Baldwin & Lewis, 1972; Bandura, 1973).

[. . .]

SOCIAL CONSTRUCTION OF REALITY

Televised representations of social realities reflect ideological bents in their portrayal of human nature, social relations, and the norms and structure of society (Adoni & Mane, 1984; Gerbner, 1972). Heavy exposure to this symbolic world may eventually make the televised images appear to be the authentic state of human affairs. Some disputes about the vicarious cultivation of beliefs [have] arisen over findings from corre-lational studies using global indices based on amount of television viewing (Gerbner, Gross, Morgan, & Signorielli, 1981; Hirsch, 1980). Televised influence is best defined in terms of the contents people watch rather than the sheer amount of television viewing. More particular-ized measures of exposure to the televised fare show that heavy television viewing shapes view-ers' beliefs and conceptions of reality (Hawkins & Pingree, 1982). The relationship remains when other possible contributing factors are simultaneously controlled.

Vicarious cultivation of social conceptions is most clearly revealed in studies verifying the direction of causality by varying experimentally the nature and amount of exposure to media influences. Controlled laboratory studies provide converging evidence that television portrayals shape viewers' beliefs (Flerx, Fidler, & Rogers, 1976; O'Bryant & Corder-Bolz, 1978). Portrayals in the print media similarly shape con-ceptions of social reality (Heath, 1984; Siegel, 1958). To see the world as the televised messages portray it is to harbor some misconceptions. Indeed, many of the shared misconceptions about occupational pursuits, ethnic groups, minorities, the elderly, social and sex roles, and other aspects of life are at least partly cultivated through symbolic modeling of stereotypes (Bussey & Bandura, 1999; Buerkel-Rothfuss & Mayes, 1981; McGhee & Frueh, 1980). Verification of personal conceptions against televised versions of social reality can thus foster some collective illusions.

SOCIAL PROMPTING OF HUMAN BEHAVIOR

The actions of others can also serve as social prompts for previously learned behavior that observers can perform but have not done so because of insufficient inducements, rather than because of restraints. Social prompting effects are distinguished from observational learning and disinhibition because no new behavior has been acquired, and disinhibitory processes are not involved because the elicited behavior is socially acceptable and not encumbered by restraints.

The influence of models in activating, channeling, and supporting the behavior of others is abundantly documented in both laboratory and field studies (Bandura, 1986). By exemplification one can get people to behave altruistically, to volunteer their services, to delay or seek gratification, to show affection, to select certain foods and drinks, to choose certain kinds of apparel, to converse on particular topics, to be inquisitive or passive, to think creatively or conventionally, or to engage in other permissible courses of action. Thus, the types of models who predominate within a social milieu partly determine which human qualities, from among many alternatives, are selectively activated. The actions of models acquire the power to activate and channel behavior when they are good predictors for observers that positive results can be gained by similar conduct.

The fashion and taste industries rely heavily on the social prompting power of modeling. Because the potency of vicarious influences can be enhanced by showing modeled acts bringing rewards, vicarious outcomes figure prominently in advertising campaigns. Thus, drinking a certain brand of wine or using a particular shampoo wins the loving admiration of beautiful people, enhances job performance, masculinizes self-conception, actualizes individualism and authenticity, tranquilizes irritable nerves, invites social recognition and amicable reactions from total strangers, and arouses affectionate overtures from spouses.

The types of vicarious outcomes, model characteristics, and modeling formats that are selected vary depending on what happens to be in vogue at the time. Model characteristics are varied to boost the persuasiveness of commercial messages. Prestigeful models are often enlisted to capitalize on the high regard in which they are held. The best social sellers depend on what happens to be popular at the moment. Drawing on evidence that similarity to the model enhances modeling, some advertisements portray common folk achieving wonders with the wares advertised. Because vicarious influence increases with multiplicity of modeling (Perry & Bussey, 1979), the beers, soft drinks, and snacks are being consumed with gusto in the advertised world by groups of wholesome, handsome, fun-loving models. Eroticism is another stimulant that never goes out of style. Therefore, erotic modeling does heavy duty in efforts to command attention and to make advertised products more attractive to potential buyers (Kanungo & Pang, 1973; Peterson & Kerin, 1979).

In sum, modeling influences serve diverse functions—as tutors, motivators, inhibitors, disinhibitors, social prompters, emotion arousers, and shapers of values and conceptions of reality. Although the different modeling functions can operate separately, in nature they often work in concert. Thus, for example, in the spread of new styles of aggression, models serve as both teachers and disinhibitors. When novel conduct is punished, observers learn the conduct that was punished as well as the restraints. A novel example can both teach and prompt similar acts.

DUAL-LINK VERSUS MULTI-PATTERN FLOW OF INFLUENCE

It has been commonly assumed in theories of mass communication that modeling influences operate through a two-step diffusion process. Influential persons pick up new ideas from the media and pass them on to their followers through personal influence. Some communication researchers have claimed that the media can only reinforce preexisting styles of behavior but cannot create new ones (Klapper, 1960). Such a view is at variance with a vast body of evidence. Media influences create personal attributes as well as alter preexisting ones (Bandura, 1986; Williams, 1986).

The different modes of human influence are too diverse in nature to have a fixed path of influence or strengths. Most behavior is the product of multiple determinants operating in concert. Hence, the relative contribution of any given factor in a pattern of influences can change depending on the nature and strength of coexisting determinants. Even the same determinant operating within the same causal structure of factors can change in its causal contribution with further experience (Wood & Bandura, 1989). In the case of atypical behavior, it is usually produced by a unique constellation of the determinants, such that if any one of them were absent the behavior would not have occurred. Depending on their quality and coexistence of other determinants, media influences may be subordinate to, equal to, or outweigh nonmedia influences. Given the dynamic nature of multifaceted causal structures, efforts to affix an average strength to a given mode of influence calls to mind the nonswimming analyst who drowned while trying to cross a river that averaged three feet in depth.

[. . .]

Chaffee (1982) reviews substantial evidence that calls into question the prevailing view that interpersonal sources of information are necessarily more persuasive than media sources.

People seek information that may be potentially useful to them from different sources. Neither informativeness, credibility, nor persuasiveness are uniquely tied to interpersonal sources or to media sources. How extensively different sources are used depends, in large part, on their accessibility and the likelihood that they will provide the kinds of information sought.

Modeling affects the adoption of new social practices and behavior patterns in several ways. It instructs people about new ways of thinking and behaving by informative demonstration or description. Learning about new things does not rely on a fixed hierarchy of sources. Efficacious modeling not only cultivates competencies but also enhances the sense of personal efficacy needed to transform knowledge and skills into successful courses of action (Bandura, 1997). The relative importance of interpersonal and media sources of information in initiating the adoption process varies for different activities and for the same activity at different stages in the adoption process (Pelz, 1983). Models motivate as well as inform and enable. People are initially reluctant to adopt new practices that involve costs and risks until they see the advantages that have been gained by early adopters. Modeled benefits accelerate social diffusion by weakening the restraints of the more cautious potential adopters. As acceptance spreads, the new ways gain further social support. Models also display preferences and evaluative reactions, which can alter observers' values and standards. Changes in evaluative standards affect receptivity to the activities being modeled. Models not only exemplify and legitimate new practices, they also serve as advocates for them by directly encouraging others to adopt them.

In effecting large-scale changes, communications systems operate through two pathways. . . . In the direct pathway, communications media promote changes by informing, modeling, motivating, and guiding participants. In the socially mediated pathway, media influences are used to link participants to social networks and community settings. These places provide continued

350 • READING 25

personalized guidance, as well as natural incentives and social supports for desired changes (Bandura, 1997, 2000d). The major share of behavior changes is promoted within these social milieus. People are socially situated in interpersonal networks. When media influences lead viewers to discuss and negotiate matters of import with others in their lives, the media set in motion transactional experiences that further shape the course of change. This is another socially mediated process through which symbolic communications exert their effect.

The absence of individualized guidance limits the power of one-way mass communications. The revolutionary advances in interactive technologies provide the means to expand the reach and impact of communications media. On the input side, communications can now be personally tailored to factors that are causally related to the behavior of interest. Tailored communications are viewed as more relevant and credible, are better remembered and are more effective in influencing behavior than general messages (Kreuter, Strecher, & Glassman, 1999). On the behavioral guidance side, interactive technologies provide a convenient means of individualizing the type and level of behavioral guidance needed to bring desired changes to fruition (Bandura, 2000c). In the population-based approaches the communications are designed to inform, enable, motivate, and guide people to effect personal and social changes. In implementing the social linking function, communications media can connect people to interactive online self-management programs that provide intensive individualized guidance in their homes when they want it (Bandura, 2000d; Taylor, Winzelberg, & Celio, 2001).

In short, there is no single pattern of social influence. The media can implant ideas either directly or through adopters. Analyses of the role of mass media in social diffusion must distinguish between their effect on learning modeled activities and on their adoptive use, and examine how media and interpersonal influences affect these separable processes. In some instances the media both teach new forms of behavior and create motivators for action by altering people's value preferences, efficacy beliefs, outcome expectations, and perception of opportunity structures. In other instances, the media teach but other adopters provide the incentive motivation to perform what has been learned observationally. In still other instances, the effect of the media may be entirely socially mediated. That is, people who have had no exposure to the media are influenced by adopters who have had the exposure and then, themselves, become the transmitters of the new ways. Within these different patterns of social influence, the media can serve as originating, as well as reinforcing, influences.

The hierarchical pattern is more likely to obtain for the print media, which has a more limited audience, than for the ubiquitous video media. Communication technologies and global interconnectedness provide people with ready direct access to information worldwide independently of time and place and unfettered by institutional and moneyed gatekeepers. The public is less dependent on a mediated filter-down system of persuasion and enlightenment. These vastly expanded opportunities for self-directedness underscore the growing primacy of agentic initiative in human adaptation and change in the electronic era (Bandura, 1997, 2000d). Ready access to communication technologies will not necessarily enlist active participation unless people believe that they can achieve desired results by this means. Perceived personal and collective efficacy partly determines the extent to which people use this resource and the purposes to which they put it.

SOCIAL DIFFUSION THROUGH SYMBOLIC MODELING

Much of the preceding discussion has been concerned mainly with modeling at the individual level. As previously noted, a unique property of modeling is that it can transmit information of virtually limitless variety to vast numbers of people simultaneously through the medium of symbolic modeling. Extraordinary advances in technology of communication are transforming the nature, reach, speed and loci of human influence (Bandura, 2000d). These technological developments have radically altered the social diffusion process. The video system feeding off telecommunications satellites has become the dominant vehicle for disseminating symbolic environments. Social practices are not only being widely diffused within societies, but ideas, values, and styles of conduct are being modeled worldwide.

The electronic media are coming to play an increasingly influential role in transcultural change. Televised modeling is now being used to effect social change at community and society-wide levels (Bandura, 1997; Sabido, 1981; Singhal & Rogers, 1999; Winett, Leckliter, Chinn, Stahl, & Love, 1985).

There are three major components of a sociocognitive communications model for social change. The first component is a *theoretical model* that specifies the determinants of psychosocial change and the mechanisms through which they produce their effects. This knowledge provides the guiding principles. The second component is a *translational and implementational model* that converts theoretical principles into an innovative operational model by specifying the content, strategies of change, and their mode of implementation. The third component is a social *diffusion model* on how to promote the adoption of psychosocial programs in diverse cultural milieus. It does so by making functional adaptations of the programs to different socio-structural circumstances, providing incentives and enabling guidance, and enlisting the necessary resources to achieve success.

In applications to the most urgent global problems, this communication model uses long-running dramatic serials on television or radio as the vehicle of change. The story lines model family planning, women's equality, environmental conservation, AIDS prevention, and a variety of beneficial life skills. The dramatizations inform, enable, guide, and motivate people to effect personal lifestyle changes and to alter detrimental societal norms and practices. The dramatizations further assist people in their efforts at personal and social change by linking them to enabling and supportive subcommunities and beneficial human services. Over 80 worldwide applications of this creative format in Africa, Asia and Latin America are enhancing people's efficacy to exercise control over their family lives, raising the status of women to have a say in their reproductive and social lives, promoting contraceptive methods, lowering the rates of childbearing, and fostering the adoption of AIDS prevention practices (Bandura, in press; Rogers et al, 1999; Vaughan et al., 2000). The higher the exposure to the modeled values and lifestyles, the stronger the impact (Rogers et al., 1999; Westoff & Rodriguez, 1995).

Social cognitive theory analyzes social diffusion of new behavior patterns in terms of three constituent processes and the psychosocial factors that govern them. These include the acquisition of knowledge about innovative behaviors; the adoption of these behaviors in practice; and the social networks through which they spread and are supported. Diffusion of innovation follows a common pattern (Robertson, 1971; Rogers, 1995). New ideas and social practices are introduced by notable example. Initially, the rate of adoption is slow because new ways are unfamiliar, customs resist change and results are uncertain. As early adopters convey more information about how to apply the new practices and their potential benefits, the innovation is adopted at an accelerating rate. After a period in which the new practices spread rapidly, the rate of diffusion slows down. The use of the innovation then either stabilizes or declines, depending upon its relative functional value.

[. . .]

Social Networks and Flow of Diffusion

The third major factor that affects the diffusion process concerns social network structures. People are enmeshed in networks of relationships that include occupational colleagues, organizational members, kinships, and friendships, just to mention a few. They are linked not only directly by personal relationships. Because acquaintanceships overlap different network clusters, many people become linked to each other indirectly by interconnected ties. Social structures comprise clustered networks of people with various ties among them, as well as persons who provide connections to other clusters through joint membership or a liaison role. Clusters vary in their internal structure, ranging from loosely knit ones to those that are densely interconnected. Networks also differ in the number and pattern of structural linkages between clusters. They may have many common ties or function with a high degree of separateness. In addition to their degree of interconnectedness, people vary in the positions and status they occupy in particular social networks which can affect their impact on what spreads through their network. One is more apt to learn about new ideas and practices from brief contacts with casual acquaintances than from intensive contact in the same circle of close associates. This path of influence creates the seemingly paradoxical effect that innovations are extensively diffused to cohesive groups through weak social ties (Granovetter, 1983).

Information regarding new ideas and practices is often conveyed through multilinked relationships (Rogers & Kincaid, 1981). Traditionally, the communication process has been conceptualized as one of unidirectional persuasion flowing from a source to a recipient. Rogers emphasizes the mutuality of influence in interpersonal communication. People share information, give meaning by mutual feedback to the information they exchange, gain understanding of each other's views, and influence each other. Specifying the channels of influence through which innovations are dispersed provides greater understanding of the diffusion process than simply plotting the rate of adoptions over time.

There is no single social network in a community that serves all purposes. Different innovations engage different networks. For example, birth control practices and agricultural innovations diffuse through quite different networks within the same community (Marshall, 1971). To complicate matters further, the social networks that come into play in initial phases of diffusion may differ from those that spread the innovation in subsequent phases (Coleman, Katz, & Menzel, 1966). Adoption rates are better predicted from the network that subserves a particular innovation than from a more general communication network. This is not to say that there is no generality to the diffusion function of network structures. If a particular social structure subserves varied activities, it can help to spread the adoption of innovations in each of those activities.

People with many social ties are more apt to adopt innovations than those who have few ties to others (Rogers & Kincaid, 1981). Adoption rates increase as more and more people in one's personal network adopt an innovation. The effects of social connectedness on adoptive behavior may be mediated through several processes. Multilinked relations can foster adoption of innovations because they convey more factual information, they mobilize stronger social influences, or it may be that people with close ties are more receptive to new ideas than those who are socially estranged. Moreover, in social transactions, people see their associates adopt innovations as well as talk about them. Multiple modeling alone can increase adoptive behavior (Bandura, 1986; Perry & Bussey, 1979).

If innovations are highly conspicuous, they can be adopted directly without requiring interaction among adopters. Television is being increasingly used to forge large single-link structures, in which many people are linked directly to the media source, but they may have little or no direct relations with each other. For example, television evangelists attract loyal followers who adopt the transmitted precepts as guides for how to behave in situations involving moral, social and political issues. Although they share a common bond to the media source, most members of an electronic community may never see each other. Political power structures are similarly being transformed by the creation of new constituencies tied to a single media source, but with little interconnectedness. Mass marketing techniques, using computer identification and mass mailings, create special-interest constituencies that by-pass traditional political organizations in the exercise of political influence.

The evolving information technologies will increasingly serve as a vehicle for building social networks. Online transactions transcend the barriers of time and space (Hiltz & Turoff, 1978; Wellman, 1997). Through interactive electronic networking people link together in widely dispersed locales, exchange information, share new ideas, and transact any number of pursuits. Virtual networking provides a flexible means for creating diffusion structures to serve given purposes, expanding their membership, extending them geographically, and disbanding them when they have outlived their usefulness.

Although structural interconnectedness provides potential diffusion paths, psychosocial factors largely determine the fate of what diffuses through those paths. In other words, it is the transactions that occur within social relationships rather than the ties, themselves, that explain adoptive behavior. The course of diffusion is best understood by considering the interactions among psychosocial determinants of adoptive behavior, the properties of innovations that facilitate or impede adoption, and the network structures that provide the social pathways of influence. Sociostructural and psychological determinants of adoptive behavior should, therefore, be treated as complementary factors in an integrated comprehensive theory of social diffusion, rather than be cast as rival theories of diffusion.

References

Adoni, H., & Mane, S. (1984). Media and the social construction of reality: Toward an integration of theory and research. *Communication Research, 11,* 323–340.

Baldwin, T. F., & Lewis, C. (1972). Violence in television: The industry looks at itself. In G. A. Comstock & E. A. Rubinstein (Eds.), *Television and social behavior: Vol. 1. Media content and control* (pp. 290–373). Washington, DC: U.S. Government Printing Office.

Ball-Rokeach, S. J. (1972). The legitimation of violence. In J. F. Short, Jr. & M. E. Wolfgang (Eds.), *Collective violence* (pp. 100–111). Chicago: Aldine-Atherton.

Ball-Rokeach, S., & DeFleur, M. (1976). A dependency model of mass media effects. *Communication Research, 3,* 3–21.

Bandura, A. (1973). *Aggression: A social learning analysis.* Upper Saddle River, NJ: Prentice Hall.

Bandura, A. (1982). The psychology of chance encounters and life paths. *American Psychologist, 37,* 747–755.

Bandura, A. (1986). *Social foundations of thought and action: A social cognitive theory.* Upper Saddle River, NJ: Prentice Hall.

Bandura, A. (1990). Mechanisms of moral disengagement. In W. Reich (Ed.), *Origins of terrorism: Psychologies, ideologies, theologies, states of mind* (pp. 162–191). Cambridge: Cambridge University Press.

Bandura, A. (1991a). Self-regulation of motivation through anticipatory and self-regulatory mechanisms. In R. A. Dienstbier (Ed.), *Perspectives on motivation: Nebraska symposium on motivation* (Vol. 38, pp. 69–164). Lincoln: University of Nebraska Press.

Bandura, A. (1991b). Social cognitive theory of moral thought and action. In W. M. Kurtines & J. L. Gewirtz (Eds.), *Handbook of moral behavior and development* (Vol. A, pp. 45–103). Hillsdale, NJ: Lawrence Erlbaum Associates.

Bandura, A. (1992). Social cognitive theory and social referencing. In S. Feinman (Ed.), *Social referencing and the social construction of reality in infancy* (pp. 175–208). New York: Plenum Press.

Bandura, A. (1997). *Self-efficacy: The exercise of control.* New York: Freeman.

Bandura, A. (1999a). A social cognitive theory of personality. In L. Pervin & O. John (Eds.), *Handbook of personality* (2nd ed., pp. 154–196). New York: Guilford Publications.

Bandura, A. (1999b). Moral disengagement in the perpetration of inhumanities. *Personality and Social Psychology Review* [Special Issue on Evil and Violence], *3,* 193–209.

Bandura, A. (2000a). Self-regulation of motivation and action through perceived self-efficacy. In E. A. Locke (Ed.), *Handbook of principles of organization behavior* (pp. 120–136). Oxford, England: Blackwell.

Bandura, A. (2000b). Exercise of human agency through collective efficacy. *Current Directions in Psychological Science, 9,* 75–78.

Bandura, A. (2000c). Health promotion from the perspective of social cognitive theory. In P. Norman, C. Abraham, & M. Conner (Eds.), *Understanding and changing health behaviour* (pp. 299–339). Reading, England: Harwood.

Bandura, A. (2000d). Growing primacy of human agency in adaptation and change in the electronic era. Keynote address delivered at "New Media in the Development of Mind," Naples, Italy, October 6, 2000.

Bandura, A. (2001). Social cognitive theory: An agentic perspective. In S. T. Fiske (Ed.), *Annual review of psychology* (Vol. 52, pp. 1–26). Palo Alto: Annual Reviews, Inc.

Bandura, A. (in press). Environmental sustainability through sociocognitive approaches to deceleration of population growth. In P. Schmuch & W. Schultz (Eds.), *The psychology of sustainable development.* Dordrecht, The Netherlands: Kluwer.

Bandura, A., Underwood, B., & Fromson, M. E. (1975). Disinhibition of aggression through diffusion of responsibility and dehumanization of victims. *Journal of Research in Personality, 9,* 253–269.

Bassiouni, M. C. (1981). Terrorism, law enforcement, and the mass media: Perspectives, problems, proposals. *The Journal of Criminal Law & Criminology, 72,* 1–51.

Beck, K. H., & Lund, A. K. (1981). The effects of health threat seriousness and personal efficacy upon intentions and behavior. *Journal of Applied Social Psychology, 11,* 401–405.

Berkowitz, L. (1984). Some effects of thoughts on anti- and prosocial influences of media events: A cognitive-neoassociation analysis. *Psychological Bulletin, 95,* 410–427.

Berkowitz, L., & Green, R. G. (1967). Stimulus qualities of the target of aggression: A further study. *Journal of Personality and Social Psychology, 5,* 364–368.

Bolton, M. K. (1993). Imitation versus innovation: Lessons to be learned from the Japanese. *Organizational Dynamics,* 30–45.

Brock, T. C., & Buss, A. H. (1962). Dissonance, aggression, and evaluation of pain. *Journal of Abnormal and Social Psychology, 65,* 197–202.

Brock, T. C., & Buss, A. H. (1964). Effects of justification for aggression and communication with the victim on postaggression dissonance. *Journal of Abnormal and Social Psychology, 68,* 403–412.

Buerkel-Rothfuss, N. L., & Mayes, S. (1981). Soap opera viewing: The cultivation effect. *Journal of Communication, 31,* 108–115.

Bussey, K., & Bandura, A. (1999). Social cognitive theory of gender development and differentiation. *Psychological Review, 106,* 676–713.

Cantor, J., & Wilson, B. J. (1988). Helping children cope with frightening media presentations. *Current Psychological Research and Reviews, 7,* 58–75.

Chaffee, S. H. (1982). Mass media and interpersonal channels: Competitive, convergent, or complementary? In G. Gumpert & R. Cathart (Eds.), *Inter/ Media: Interpersonal communication in a media world* (pp. 57–77). New York: Oxford University Press.

Coleman, J. S., Katz, E., & Menzel, H. (1966). *Medical innovation: A diffusion study.* New York: Bobbs-Merrill.

Diener, E. (1977). Deindividuation: Causes and consequences. *Social Behavior and Personality, 5,* 143–156.

Donnerstein, E. (1984). Pornography: Its effect on violence against women. In N. M. Malamuth & E. Donnerstein (Eds.), *Pornography and sexual aggression* (pp. 53–81). New York: Academic Press.

Duncker, K. (1938). Experimental modification of children's food preferences through social suggestion. *Journal of Abnormal Social Psychology, 33,* 489–507.

Dysinger, W. S., & Ruckmick, C. A. (1993). *The emotional responses of children to the motion-picture situation.* New York: Macmillan.

Falmagne, R. J. (1975). *Reasoning: Representation and process in children and adults.* Hillsdale, NJ: Lawrence Erlbaum Associates.

Fimrite, R. (1977, September). A melding of men all suited to a T. *Sports Illustrated,* 91–100.

Flerx, V. C., Fidler, D. S., & Rogers, R. W. (1976). Sex role stereotypes: Developmental aspects and early intervention. *Child Development, 47,* 998–1007.

Gerbner, G. (1972). Communication and social environment. *Scientific American, 227,* 153–160.

Gerbner, G., Gross, L., Morgan, M., & Signorielli, N. (1981). A curious journey into the scary world of Paul Hirsch. *Communication Research, 8,* 39–72.

Goranson, R. E. (1970). Media violence and aggressive behavior: A review of experimental research. In L. Berkowitz (Ed.), *Advances in experimental social psychology* (Vol. 5, p. 231). New York: Academic Press.

Granovetter, M. (1983). The strength of weak ties: A network theory revisited. In R. Collins (Ed.), *Sociological theory 1983* (pp. 201–233). San Francisco: Jossey-Bass.

Hall, J. R. (1987). *Gone from the promised land: Jonestown in American cultural history.* New Brunswick, NJ: Transaction Books.

Halloran, J. D., & Croll, P. (1972). Television programs in Great Britain: Content and control. In G. A. Comstock & E. A. Rubinstein (Eds.), *Television and social behavior: Vol. 1. Media content and control* (pp. 415–492). Washington, DC: U.S. Government Printing Office.

Harris, M. B., & Evans, R. C. (1973). Models and creativity. *Psychological Reports, 33,* 763–769.

Hawkins, R. P., & Pingree, S. (1982). Television's influence on social reality. In D. Pearl, L. Bouthilet, & J. Lazar (Eds.), *Television and behavior: Ten years of scientific progress and implications for the eighties* (Vol. II, pp. 224–247). Rockville, MD: National Institute of Mental Health.

Heath, L. (1984). Impact of newspaper crime reports on fear of crime: Multimethodological investigation. *Journal of Personality and Social Psychology, 47,* 263–276.

Hiltz, S. R., & Turoff, M. (1978). *The network nation: Human communication via computer.* Reading, MA: Addison-Wesley.

Hirsch, P. M. (1980). The "scary world of the nonviewer" and other anomalies: A reanalysis of Gerbner et al.'s findings on cultivation analysis. Part 1. *Communication Research, 7,* 403–456.

Kanungo, R. N., & Pang, S. (1973). Effects of human models on perceived product quality. *Journal of Applied Psychology, 57,* 172–178.

Kelman, H. C., & Hamilton, V. L. (1989). *Crimes of obedience: Toward a social psychology of authority and responsibility.* New Haven, CT: Yale University Press.

Klapper, J. T. (1960). *The effects of mass communication.* New York: Free Press.

Kreuter, M. W., Strecher, V. J., & Glassman, B. (1999). One size does not fit all: The case for tailoring print materials. *Annals of Behavioral Medicine, 21*(4), 276–283.

Larsen, O. N. (Ed.). (1968). *Violence and the mass media.* New York: Harper & Row.

Maibach, E. W., Flora, J., & Nass, C. (1991). Changes in self-efficacy and health behavior in response to a minimal contact community health campaign. *Health Communication, 3,* 1–15.

Malamuth, N. M., & Donnerstein, E. (Eds.). (1984). *Pornography and sexual aggression.* New York: Academic Press.

Marshall, J. F. (1971). Topics and networks in intra-village communication. In S. Polgar (Ed.), *Culture and population: A collection of current studies* (pp. 160–166). Cambridge, MA: Schenkman Publishing Company.

McGhee, P. E., & Frueh, T. (1980). Television viewing and the learning of sex-role stereotypes. *Sex Roles, 6,* 179–188.

Meichenbaum, D. (1984). Teaching thinking: A cognitive-behavioral perspective. In R. Glaser, S. Chipman, & J. Segal (Eds.), *Thinking and learning skills (Vol. 2): Research and open questions* (pp. 407–426). Hillsdale, NJ: Lawrence Erlbaum Associates.

Meyer, T. P. (1972). Effects of viewing justified and unjustified real film violence on aggressive behavior. *Journal of Personality and Social Psychology, 23,* 21–29.

Meyerowitz, B. E., & Chaiken, S. (1987). The effect of message framing on breast self-examination attitudes, intentions, and behavior. *Journal of Personality and Social Psychology, 52,* 500–510.

Midgley, D. F. (1976). A simple mathematical theory of innovative behavior. *Journal of Consumer Research, 3,* 31–41.

Midgley, M. (1978). *Beast and man: The roots of human nature.* Ithaca, NY: Cornell University Press.

Milgram, S. (1974). *Obedience to authority: An experimental view.* New York: Harper & Row.

O'Bryant, S. L., & Corder-Bolz, C. R. (1978). The effects of television on children's stereotyping of women's work roles. *Journal of Vocational Behavior, 12,* 233–244.

Ostlund, L. E. (1974). Perceived innovation attributes as predictors of innovativeness. *Journal of Consumer Research, 1,* 23–29.

Paik, H., & Comstock, G. (1994). The effects of television violence on antisocial behavior: A meta-analysis. *Communication Research, 21,* 516–546.

Pelz, D. C. (1983). Use of information channels in urban innovations. *Knowledge, 5,* 3–25.

Perry, D. G., & Bussey, K. (1979). The social learning theory of sex differences: Imitation is alive and well. *Journal of Personality and Social Psychology, 37,* 1699–1712.

Peterson, R. A., & Kerin, R. A. (1979). The female role in advertisements: Some experimental evidence. *Journal of Marketing, 41,* 59–63.

Rimal, R. N. (2000). Closing the knowledge-behavior gap in health promotion: The mediating role of self-efficacy. *Health Communication, 12,* 219–237.

Robertson, T. S. (1971). *Innovative behavior and communication.* New York: Holt, Rinehart & Winston.

Rogers, E. M. (1987). Progress, problems and prospects for network research: Investigating relationships in the age of electronic communication technologies. *Social Networks, 9,* 285–310.

Rogers, E. M. (1995). *Diffusion of innovations* (4th ed.). New York: Free Press.

Rogers, E. M., & Kincaid, D. L. (1981). *Communication networks: Toward a new paradigm for research.* New York: Free Press.

Rogers, E. M., & Shoemaker, F. (1971). *Communication of innovations: A cross-cultural approach* (2nd ed.). New York: Free Press.

Rogers, E. M., Vaughan, P. W., Swalehe, R. M. A., Roa, N., Svenkerud, P., & Sood, S. (1999). Effects of an entertainment-education radio soap opera on Family Planning behavior in Tansania. *Studies in Family Planning, 30,* 192–211.

Rosenthal, T. L., & Zimmerman, B. J. (1978). *Social learning and cognition.* New York: Academic Press.

Sabido, M. (1981). *Towards the social use of soap operas.* Mexico City, Mexico: Institute for Communication Research.

Siegel, A. E. (1958). The influence of violence in the mass media upon children's role expectation. *Child Development, 29,* 35–56.

Singhal, A., & Rogers, E. M. (1999). *Entertainment-education: A communication strategy for social change.* Mahwah, NJ: Lawrence Erlbaum Associates.

Slater, M. D. (1989). Social influences and cognitive control as predictors of self-efficacy and eating behavior. *Cognitive Therapy and Research, 13,* 231–245.

Snyder, M. (1980). Seek, and ye shall find: Testing hypotheses about other people. In E. T. Higgins, C. P. Herman, & M. P. Zanna (Eds.), *Social cognition: The Ontario Symposium on Personality and Social Psychology* (Vol. 1, pp. 105–130). Hillsdale, NJ: Lawrence Erlbaum Associates.

Snyder, M., & Campbell, B. H. (1982). Self-monitoring: The self in action. In J. Suls (Ed.), *Psychological perspectives on the self* (pp. 185–207). Hillsdale, NJ: Lawrence Erlbaum Associates.

Taylor, C. B., Winzelberg, A., & Celio, A. (2001). Use of interactive media to prevent eating disorders. In R. Striegel-Moor & L. Smolak (Eds.), *Eating disorders: Innovative directions for research and practice* (pp. 255–270). Washington, DC: American Psychological Association.

Tornatzky, L. G., & Klein, K. J. (1982). Innovation characteristics and innovation adoption implementation: A meta-analysis of findings. *IEEE Transactions of Engineering and Management, EM-29,* 28–45.

Vaughan, P. W., Rogers, E. M., Singhal, A., & Swalehe, R. M. (2000). Entertainment-education and HIV/AIDS prevention: A field experiment in Tanzania. *Journal of Health Communication, 5,* 81–100.

Watt, J. G., Jr., & van den Berg, S. A. (1978). Time series analysis of alternative media effects theories. In R. D. Ruben (Ed.), *Communication yearbook 2* (pp. 215–224). New Brunswick, NJ: Transaction Books.

Wellman, B. (1997). An electronic group is virtually a social network. In S. Kielser (Ed.), *Culture of the Internet* (pp. 179–205). Mahwah, NJ: Lawrence Erlbaum Associates.

Westoff, C. F., & Rodriguez, G. (1995). The mass media and family planning in Kenya. *International Family Planning Perspectives, 21,* 26–31.

Williams, T. M. (Ed.). (1986). *The impact of television: A natural experiment in three communities.* New York: Academic Press.

Wilson, B. J., & Cantor, J. (1985). Developmental differences in empathy with a television protagonist's fear. *Journal of Experimental Child Psychology, 39,* 284–299.

Winett, R. A., Leckliter, I. N., Chinn, D. E., Stahl, B. N., & Love, S. Q. (1985). The effects of television modeling on residential energy conservation. *Journal of Applied Behavior Analysis, 18,* 33–44.

Wood, R. E., & Bandura, A. (1989). Social cognitive theory of organizational management. *Academy of Management Review, 14,* 361–384.

Zaltman, G., & Wallendorf, M. (1979). *Consumer behavior: Basic findings and management implications.* New York: Wiley.

Zillmann, D., & Bryant, J. (1984). Effects of massive exposure to pornography. In N. M. Malamuth & E. Donnerstein (Eds.), *Pornography and sexual aggression* (pp. 115–138). New York: Academic Press.

Zimbardo, P. G. (1969). The human choice: Individuation, reason, and order versus deindividuation, impulse, and chaos. In W. J. Arnold & D. Levine (Eds.), *Nebraska Symposium on Motivation, 1969* (pp. 237–309). Lincoln: University of Nebraska Press.

26

THE SMALL GROUP SHOULD BE *the* FUNDAMENTAL UNIT OF COMMUNICATION RESEARCH

MARSHALL SCOTT POOLE

The study of group communication has always attracted the interest of a relatively small set of communication scholars. The number who focus on this topic has fluctuated over the years, with the peaks coming in the late 40s, the late 60s and early 70s, and now again in the early 90s. The fluctuation seems to be highly correlated with the concern for groups in society as a whole, as Steiner (1974) noted. In periods that emphasize individualism and social stability, such as the early 80s, the area does not fare well, while in times that emphasize collectivism and social change, such as the 60s, the area tends to enjoy relative prosperity. With the current emphasis on teamwork, quality, social responsibility, and empowerment in societal discourse, the area is currently experiencing an upswing.

"Experiencing an upswing" is, of course, a relative statement. Generally the number of active group communication researchers (those who produce at least 1 relevant article or convention paper per year) seems to peak at about 30, with maybe 100 others producing the occasional piece.

I have argued elsewhere (Poole, 1996) that the field of group studies is actually rather large, if we consider the entire group of interested scholars scattered across fields like communication, psychology, political science, management, and social work. If these scholars could form a more closely knit research community, the area

SOURCE: Poole, M. S. (1998). The small group should be *the* fundamental unit of communication research. In J. S. Trent (Ed.), *Communication: Views from the helm for the 21st century* (pp. 94–97). Boston, MA: Allyn & Bacon.

would no longer be peripheral. This possibility notwithstanding, in this essay I would like to focus on the issue of why group communication is not more central in our field.

Here I want to argue that the group should be THE basic unit of analysis in communication research. Despite the fact that most influential theories of communication focus on the individual or on larger social units, I believe there is a more appropriate nexus of analytic interests. The small group, composed of 3 to 10 members, is the minimal unit of analysis in which the social context of communication comes into play, yet the individuality of the actors can be discerned. Hence, it seems natural to take the small group as the basic experimental and analytical unit for communication research.

This idea seemed obvious to social scientists working before 1950. Mead, Cooley, Newcomb, Lewin, Gordon Allport, and Hadley Cantril took as given the notion that the individual can be understood only as part of a larger system. They analyzed subjects such as attitude formation and change, cognition, and action—subjects which most in our field treat as individual-level phenomena—in the context of social groups such as the family, a circle of friends, a neighborhood, or a community. For these seminal thinkers, individual behavior could not be divorced from its surround, and the small group was a critical part of this surround. The small group was the locus for the construction of social reality, with its associated ways of thinking, evaluating, and acting. Socialization occurred through small groups, especially the family, but also through church groups and classrooms. While some of these same scholars, especially Lewin, laid the groundwork for the individually oriented psychological research which predominated in the 1950s and after, always in the background of their work was the small group as the locus of individual and interpersonal processes. Unfortunately, as studies emphasizing the individual moved to the forefront, their group foundations were forgotten. As this work influenced communication inquiry, it transmitted a presumption toward the individual.

This was reinforced by early models of communication that drew on Shannon's formulation of mediated communication, which linked a single source and a single receiver. Originally directed to the problem of designing electronic communication systems, the Shannon model focused on a single source sending to a single receiver. Because human communication processes were not the impetus for Shannon's model, there was no need to factor in the social situation that surrounded human communication. Other influences on communication, such as the social influence of the group context or other group members, were lumped together and defined as noise, which interfered with the fidelity of transmission. This approach implicitly deemphasized other communicators or complex nets of communicators in communication theory. This valorization of the individual and the dyadic linkage was further reinforced by the transformation of Shannon into the SMCR model. With its affinities to the rhetorical tradition (S = rhetor, R = audience, etc.) this model further solidified attention on individual senders and receivers. Even later complexifications of this model, which tried to take into account other people and contextual factors that influenced communication, left primary emphasis on two folks, the individual sender and receiver.

This perspective was further reinforced by the dominant cultural assumptions of U.S. society. The assumption that the group is the basic building block of society runs counter to one of the cherished values of U.S. culture, individualism. As a result of the widespread emphasis on individualism, most people value the individual over the group and attribute more "reality" and impact to individuals than to groups. They may even regard groups as a hindrance to decisive action, which is seen as depending on individual initiative or on supra-individual entities, such as organizations.

It is, of course, impossible to deny that groups matter if we consider the family, the peer group, the classroom, the work group. However, I believe that the general tendency to ignore and devalorize groups per se is reflected in the diaspora of research on specific types of groups across numerous sectors of our field. Families are studied in interpersonal or relational communication, work groups in organizational communication, and interest and legislative groups in political communication. Propp and Kreps (1996) review many of these lines of research and call for more interchange among them. However, it seems unlikely to me that such interchange will elevate the group from its secondary status.

Entertain for a moment the possibility that the individual is not the basic building block of communication theory. To do so is to take seriously the arguments of various postmodernists, who argued for a "decentering" and denial of the unitary subject; of R. D. Laing, who analyzed the fragmented self; of George Herbert Mead, who saw the self as changing from situation to situation; and of Erving Goffman, who theorized the construction of selves. If not the individual, what should be the basic building block of communication theory?

A number of alternatives have been presented. Many media researchers would argue for whole societies; organizational researchers would advance entire organizations; and theorists of many types would advocate "discursive formations" of various types. While all of these are worthwhile candidates, I believe that most studies of these entities have in common the following flaw: Each of these large units is so complex in itself that a theoretical analysis is driven to treat them as though they were individuals. So societies are most often treated as individual entities; if their subdivisions or classes are recognized these are most often treated as entities in their own right, and studied in isolation, rather than as a group of components that influence each other in any meaningful sense. In the same vein, organizations tend to be treated either as unities or decomposed into components which are approached as isolated unities. While much is made of tracing "fractures" in discursive formations, by far the largest part of scholarship on such formations treats them as individual unities. In short, most scholarly analyses of organizations, societies, or discursive formations in communication treat them as giant individuals, much as more micro theories focus on individual human organisms. The problem here is that, again, the influence of other giant individuals on the central subject is omitted from most of these theories. These macro

level theories are like the micro level theories which valorize the individual writ large.

Theories which take organizations, societies, or discursive formations as their basic unit have another problem. They omit (or at least relegate to the background) the role of the organic human being in communication. Focusing on larger units downplays the role of the human as efficient and final cause of communication. While theories at the macro level will always be important to communication, they must ultimately be grounded in human action.

There are only two units of analysis which facilitate the detailed study of human communicative exchanges in context, the dyad and the small group. Both units promise insights into the nature of interaction because they enable researchers to witness message production and reception processes. Both are simple enough to enable study of individual cognitive and affective processes which influence and are influenced by communication. And both mediate the influence of context and the larger organization and society on individuals and the communicative process.

However, I believe the group is superior to the dyad in one important respect: the group includes multiple others. The dyad provides a useful and realistic model for communication because it includes *an* other. Including only one other, however, does not adequately capture the complex nature of social situations. Multiple others, up to the number that a communicator can take into account as individuals, should be included in the basic unit. The German sociologist Georg Simmel understood this at the turn of the century. His incisive analysis of the role of numbers in social interaction indicated that the dyad was a very unusual unit, lacking the characteristics of more numerous groups. Unlike dyads, groups of three or more have a future even if one member departs (the more members they have the more secure their future); because of their future, they have a degree of social reality for the subject that the dyad does not. Because the group captures the full "bite" of the social situation and confronts the communicator with several others, it offers the richest base for developing communication theory and research.

Cognitive studies indicate that humans can attend to more than 1 person at a time, but there are limits to human processing capacity which suggest that 5 to 10 others should be the maximum who can be considered as individuals at any one time. This suggests that relatively small groups are the maximum size necessary to invoke the social situation as transmitted by individuals.

Focusing on the group requires us to address several problems which have not received much attention by those plying individual-centered or society-centered models. First, there is the *problem of intersubjectivity*: fully realized groups are emergents, with properties which are more than a combination of the beliefs and attitudes of the individuals who make them up. Certain properties of groups (and societies for that matter) are not located in any individual, but are intersubjective in that they are maintained by the interaction system of the group (or society). How do emergents arise and how are intersubjective constructs created and maintained? These are very slippery issues, issues not often dealt with in individual- or dyad-based theory and research; unfortunately societal- or organizational-based theories have largely ignored this question. Turning our attention to the group forces us to confront this central problem which is directly connected to issues such as the creation of social reality, the nature of meaning, and the relation of action and structure.

Second, there is the *boundary problem*. As Linda Putnam and Cynthia Stohl have argued, groups are constantly having to reestablish and renegotiate their boundaries. Group boundaries are permeable, due to communication between groups, overlapping membership with other groups, relationships among group members in other contexts, and fluctations in membership. Being able to maintain boundaries that preserve their identities as groups while at the same time managing and profiting from their permeability is a key issue not only for groups but also for all communication relationships. The nature of boundaries determines the character of the context for communication, and hence the influences that come to bear on the communicator.

These are thorny problems, but ones that an adequate theory of communication should grapple with. They supplement traditional issues that have arisen in communication studies which take the dyad as the central unit. These issues are just as relevant for larger units such as organizations and societies as they are for groups, but they are posed in manageable terms when groups are studied.

Despite the potential benefits of moving to the group as the unit of analysis, there is a price to be paid. Studying multiple interactors requires more time and effort (for the data yielded) than studying individuals or dyads or survey research in large social formations. The time-consuming and difficult task of coding, and then making sense of complex group data in quantitative group studies, is only one of the difficulties that would confront researchers. The problem inherent in trying to ensure large samples of even three-person groups is another. The complicated theories and methods required to represent and explain interaction among multiple actors is yet another.

These difficulties, combined with the general predilection toward the individual, suggest that adherents will not flock to my position. However, theoretical gains almost always come at the price of complexity. I suggest it is a price worth paying.

REFERENCES

Poole, M. S. (1996). Breaking the isolation of small group communication studies. *Communication Studies, 45*, 20–28.
Propp, K. M., & Kreps, G. L. (1996). A rose by any other name: The vitality of small group communication research. *Communication Studies, 45*, 7–19.
Putnam, L. L., & Stohl, C. (1996). Bona fide groups: An alternative perspective for communication and small group decision making. In R. Y. Hirokawa & M. S. Poole (Eds.), *Communication and group decision making* (pp. 147–178). Newbury Park, CA: Sage.
Steiner, I. D. (1974). Whatever happened to the group in social psychology? *Journal of Experimental Social Psychology, 10*, 94–108.

PROJECTS FOR SOCIOPSYCHOLOGICAL THEORIZING

ADDITIONAL READINGS ON THE SOCIOPSYCHOLOGICAL TRADITION

A. To learn more about social psychology: Hogg and Cooper (2003); Greenwood (2004).

B. To learn more about communication skills and trait theories: Greene and Burleson (2003); McCroskey, Daly, Martin, and Beatty (1998).

C. To learn more about persuasion theory: Dilliard and Pfau (2002); O'Keefe (2002).

D. To learn more about interpersonal and family communication theory: Braithwaite and Baxter (2006); Knapp and Daly (2002).

E. To learn more about group and organizational communication theory: Frey, Gouran, and Poole (1999); Jablin and Putnam (2000); Poole and Hollingshead (2004).

F. To learn more about intercultural communication theory: Gudykunst (2004); Y. Y. Kim (2001); Ting-Toomey (2000).

G. To learn more about mass communication theory: Bryant and Miron (2004); Giles (2003).

APPLICATION EXERCISE

Sociopsychological communication theories offer possible explanations for the causes and effects of communicative behavior. For example, Berger and Calabrese attempted to explain the causes and effects of interpersonal uncertainty reduction, while Bandura attempted to explain the causes and effects of social-cognitive learning from the media. To apply a theory in this tradition, it is necessary to find practical situations in which the causal processes specified by a particular theory seem to be operating. Or, conversely, one can begin with a particular practical situation and look for theories that explain what is causing something to happen. Try this application exercise with one or more theories or situations. Select a sociopsychological communication theory that seems interesting and identify a practical situation to which the theory seems to apply. Or select an interesting practical situation and identify a sociopsychological communication theory that seems to explain what is going on. How easy was it to match theories and situations? How confident are you that the causal relations specified by a particular theory actually occur in a particular situation? Why or why not? Could the same effects be explained by more than one different theory? Did the application seem potentially useful? For example, does the theory suggest ways the situation could be managed or influenced more effectively?

PROJECTS

1. Using citation indexes, review articles, and other reference works, examine the status of one or two specific programs of research in the sociopsychological tradition. Search for empirical research based on a particular theory such as

Berger and Calabrese, Bandura, or any socio-psychological theory mentioned in the additional readings (not all theories cited in general reference works are in this tradition). Has the theory been definitively supported or falsified by empirical research? Are scholars still actively developing the theory? Has it been superseded by other theories? What do your answers suggest about the way theories develop in the sociopsychological tradition? An extension of this project would be to look at the impact the theory has had on popular understanding of communication. Has this theory influenced the way people communicate and/or talk about communication?

2. As formulated in the preceding unit on cybernetics and in this unit, Lang and Bandura both theorize the problem of mass-mediated message effects. Compare and contrast these two theoretical formulations. Do they have different things to say about the communication of mass media messages? Are the practical implications of these theorizations different? How can or should mass media messages be constructed to achieve particular effects? How can or should viewers interact with these messages? Do neither, either, or both of these theories apply to messages other than mass media ones? Do these two theories lead to distinct conversations about messages, or can they inform each other and be part of the same larger theoretical conversation? Using these two theories as a case study, one can begin to address the larger questions of how the cybernetic and sociopsychological traditions intersect or diverge from each other and how they might be able to inform each other.

3. Further pursuing the relation between cybernetic and sociopsychological theories, how is the concept of uncertainty reduction in Berger and Calabrese related to the concept of entropy in Shannon and Weaver's information theory? Does this comparison suggest how cybernetic ideas are changed when brought into the sociopsychological tradition? What is gained or lost in translating a concept from cybernetics to

social psychology? There are at least two larger questions here. First, what is gained or lost when importing an idea from any other tradition into the sociopsychological tradition, for example, when an idea from another tradition is operationalized for purposes of empirical testing? Second, in general, can ideas from one tradition be transported to another tradition without changing them in some important ways? Do some traditions seem more or less closely aligned with each other so that movement of ideas from one to the other is easier or harder? Similarly, just as the idea of entropy-uncertainty reduction has appeared in two traditions, are there other ideas that appear in multiple traditions? How does the commonality or lack of commonality of ideas in different traditions bode for cross-tradition conversation and theorizing?

4. How would one go about undertaking Poole's charge to make the group the fundamental unit of analysis? What was Allport's (1919) argument about making the individual the fundamental unit of analysis? Is the individual level of analysis foundational for sociopsychological theorizing? Berger's (1997) theorizing of cognitive processes of planning strategic communication is another example of the individual-level approach. Try to imagine how the process of planning strategic communication could be examined while taking the group as the unit of analysis. Could experiments be designed to study planning at a group level of analysis? What would be gained or lost by doing so, as compared with studies of individual cognition? Poole talks about the difficulty of experimental design at the group level. He has done some research investigating real-world groups (Kuhn & Poole, 2000), and some group theorists such as Frey (1994, 2003) advance that group researchers should focus on real groups and their actual interaction. Are the methods used by researchers in Frey's edited volumes experimental methods? Are they empirical methods? How is the theorizing and researching in these volumes different from that in Berger and Calabrese, Berger (1997), or

Bandura? The larger question here may be, Would taking the group as a unit of analysis alter the way that theorizing and research is conducted in the sociopsychological tradition?

5. An important strand of theorizing in the sociopsychological tradition is the trait approach, which focuses on individual personality characteristics, such as communication apprehension or shyness, that influence communication behavior (McCroskey et al., 1998). Beatty, McCroskey, and Valencic (2001) have argued that at least some of these traits have a genetic basis (are at least partly determined by biology rather than culture). An interesting critique of the trait approach comes from within the tradition. M.-S. Kim (2002) argues that theories premised on Western individualism do not explain the interaction of Asian peoples, and proposes to retheorize constructs like communication apprehension based on a non-Western conception of identity. Looking at some of the theory and research on communicator traits, what is the merit of Kim's critique? Does it seem that certain specific trait theories contain a Western bias, or is it that taking a trait approach at all is based on Western assumptions? Yamagata et al. (2006) provide evidence that the same basic personality traits occur in different cultures, perhaps even universally. To what extent do or do not their findings undermine Kim's critique of Western trait theories? Is there other research, such as some nonverbal studies (Segerstrale & Molnar, 1997), that may call into question (or support) the idea of cross-cultural generalizability of sociopsychological theories?

REFERENCES

Allport, F. H. (1919). Behavior and experiment in social psychology. *Journal of Abnormal Psychology, 14*, 297–306.

Beatty, M. J., McCroskey, J. C., & Valencic, K. M. (2001). *The biology of communication: A communibiological perspective.* Cresskill, NJ: Hampton Press.

Berger, C. R. (1997). *Planning strategic interaction: Attaining goals through communicative action.* Mahwah, NJ: Lawrence Erlbaum.

Braithwaite, D. O., & Baxter, L. A. (Eds.). (2006). *Engaging theories in family communication: Multiple perspectives.* Thousand Oaks, CA: Sage.

Bryant, J., & Miron, D. (2004). Theory and research in mass communication. *Journal of Communication, 54*(4), 662–704.

Dilliard, J. P., & Pfau, M. (2002). *The persuasion handbook: Developments in theory and practice.* Thousand Oaks, CA: Sage.

Fink, E. L., & McPhee, R. D. (Eds.). (1999). Special issue: Analyses of HCR and the communication discipline. *Human Communication Research, 25*(4), 453–631.

Frey, L. (Ed.). (1994). *Group communication in context: Studies of natural groups.* Hillsdale, NJ: Lawrence Erlbaum.

Frey, L. (Ed.). (2003). *Group communication in context: Studies in bona fide groups* (2nd ed.). Mahwah, NJ: Lawrence Erlbaum.

Frey, L. R., Gouran, D. S., & Poole, M. S. (Eds.). (1999). *The handbook of group communication theory and research.* Thousand Oaks, CA: Sage.

Giles, D. C. (2003). *Media psychology.* Mahwah, NJ: Lawrence Erlbaum.

Greene, J. O., & Burleson, B. R. (Eds.). (2003). *Handbook of communication and social interaction skills.* Mahwah, NJ: Lawrence Erlbaum.

Greenwood, J. D. (2004). *The disappearance of the social in American social psychology.* Cambridge: Cambridge University Press.

Gudykunst, W. B. (Ed.). (2004). *Theorizing about intercultural communication.* Thousand Oaks, CA: Sage.

Hogg, M. A., & Cooper, J. (Eds.). (2003). *The Sage handbook of social psychology.* Thousand Oaks, CA: Sage.

Jablin, F. M., & Putnam, L. (Eds.). (2000). *The new handbook of organizational communication: Advances in theory, research, and methods.* Thousand Oaks, CA: Sage.

Kim, M.-S. (2002). *Non-Western perspectives on human communication.* Thousand Oaks, CA: Sage.

Kim, Y. Y. (2001). *Becoming intercultural: An integrative theory of communication and cross-cultural adaptation.* Thousand Oaks, CA: Sage.

Knapp, M. L., & Daly, J. A. (Eds.). (2002). *Handbook of interpersonal communication.* Thousand Oaks, CA: Sage.

Kuhn, T., & Poole, M. S. (2000). Do conflict management styles affect group decision making: Evidence from a longitudinal field study. *Human Communication Research, 26*(4), 558–590.

McCroskey, J. C., Daly, J. A., Martin, M. M., & Beatty, M. J. (Eds.). (1998). *Communication and personality: Trait perspectives.* Cresskill, NJ: Hampton Press.

O'Keefe, D. J. (2002). *Persuasion: Theory and research* (2nd ed.). Thousand Oaks, CA: Sage.

Poole, M. S., & Hollingshead, A. B. (Eds.). (2004). *Theories of small groups: Interdisciplinary perspectives.* Thousand Oaks, CA: Sage.

Segerstrale, U., & Molnar, P. (1997). *Nonverbal communication: Where nature meets culture.* Mahwah, NJ: Lawrence Erlbaum.

Ting-Toomey, S. (2000). *Negotiating identity: Communicating across cultures.* New York: Guilford.

Yamagata, S., Suzuki, A., Ando, J., Ono, Y., Kijima, N., Yoshimura, K., et al. (2006). Is the genetic structure of human personality universal? A cross-cultural twin study from North America, Europe, and Asia. *Journal of Personality and Social Psychology, 90*(6), 987–998.

UNIT VIII   INTRODUCTION

THE SOCIOCULTURAL TRADITION

For theories in the sociocultural tradition, communication is a process essentially involved with concepts such as social structures, identities, norms, rituals, and collective belief systems. How does communication function to produce, maintain, and change social formations ranging from small groups to the global system? How do variations in culture and society affect communication? How are interactions among individual members of society conducted? How do individuals relate to larger-scale collectivities and social processes? These questions are at the heart of the sociocultural tradition, which may be the broadest, most complex, and least unified of the seven theoretical traditions surveyed in this book.

Society would be impossible without communication. By the same token, communication would be impossible or severely limited in the absence of shared patterns of action and meaning that enable mutual understanding—that is, in the absence of society and a common culture. Although few if any theorists would disagree with either of these propositions, they have approached this essential communication-society relationship in highly diverse ways. Unlike sociopsychological theories of communication, which are numerous but fairly uniform in their underlying metatheoretical assumptions, sociocultural approaches range across fundamentally different theoretical styles.

A key distinction that helps explain some of the diversity in this tradition is the distinction between macro and micro approaches. Macrosocial theories such as functionalism (Merton, 1957) and structuralism (Lévi-Strauss, 1963) view communication from a big picture standpoint of society as a whole, while microsocial theories like symbolic interactionism (Blumer, 1968) and ethnomethodology (Garfinkel, 1967/1987) zoom in to examine the details of individual and group participation in social life. The macro-micro distinction in social theory extends the arguments about group versus individual approaches to sociopsychological theory discussed by Poole in the previous unit. From a macro view, an entire society can be seen as a functioning system with collectively produced, emergent properties such as culture and social class structure that cannot be fully explained in terms of individual or small group behavior. Large-scale social forces such as urbanization, economic competition, and the spread of new technologies determine the aggregate behavior of individuals and groups. Microsocial theories grew out of the sociological branch of social psychology as discussed in the introduction to unit VII. From a micro view, individual action and creativity become more apparent. Individuals make strategic choices in response to their particular social circumstances. The macro and micro views both clearly have some validity, but how best to integrate them is a matter of dispute. Some theories are exclusively macro or micro while some, for example structuration theory (Giddens, 1984), attempt to combine both approaches.

The readings in this unit have been selected to represent some (only some) of the tradition's theoretical diversity while also giving a rough sense of historical development. The sequence of readings alternates between primarily micro (Mead; Taylor, Groleau, Heaton, & Van Every) and macro (Poster; Cameron) approaches and illustrates different ways of relating the two views. The readings in unit I on the historical and cultural roots of communication theory provide useful background, especially Mattelart's account of the origins of functionalist ideas about circulation through networks and Carey's transmission and ritual models (which draw from theories of functionalism and symbolic anthropology, respectively). One question that may seem to be continually present when investigating this tradition (a question also raised by the overall approach taken in this book and especially in unit I) is this: As the sociohistorical context changes, does not only the focus and terminology used but also the nature of communication itself change?

George Herbert Mead's *Mind, Self, and Society* (1934), the book from which our first reading is excerpted, theorizes the process in which mind, self, and society develop together through symbolic interaction. How communication shapes individual identities, making both individuality and social community possible, is the question at the heart of this investigation. Mead compares and contrasts animal and human interaction. Animal communication is a process of action and reaction, for example when a sentinel in a group of animals reacts to the presence of danger, thus alerting other animals in the group to respond. (Mead refers to individual animals as "forms" and

uses the term "gesture" to mean any interactive behavior.) Although human interaction can be similar to animal communication (Mead mentions behavior in crowds as an example), the evolution of language and other symbolic forms introduced an additional, distinctively human type of communication that makes possible the distinct kind of social order characteristic of human groups. Stated in terms of Peirce's semiotic theory (unit IV, reading 11), which was an important influence on Mead, animal communication relies exclusively on indexes whereas human communication also uses symbols. Symbolic communication involves what Mead called taking the role or attitude of the other. In learning to speak a human language as children, we learn to shift among different points of view, hearing our own words as if we were someone else, imagining their responses. The child's own sense of self gradually develops in this process of experiencing the self through the anticipated reactions of others. It is this taking the attitude of others and anticipating their responses that makes cooperative social activity possible. It is this cooperative activity that is the basis of community. Importantly for Mead, engaging in community is not something that leads to one losing one's individuality. One can only become an individual (in the sense of having a unique self-concept) as a member of a community, by engaging with others in cooperative activity, thereby learning to evaluate and control one's own conduct from the collective standpoint of the group (a standpoint Mead called the "generalized other"). Mead's theory moves from a micro toward a macro view of society by showing how symbolic interaction among individuals produces social order.

An important practical theme addressed in this reading is *the problem of cross-community communication*. That community arises from members taking the attitudes of one another leads to the fact that communities will be different based on the differences in cooperative activity that form them. Leaders who are able to cooperate in communities outside of their own can play an important linking role, making communication across different communities possible, as can journalists and novelists who familiarize audiences with attitudes in different communities. However, for Mead, an American pragmatist thinker, cross-community communication only becomes possible when there is something practical about which to communicate. Communication does not go on by itself in the abstract. If there is no cooperative activity across communities, there can be no cross-community communication. Fortunately, all human communities have in common religion (or neighborliness as he sometimes refers to it), seeking to help the less fortunate, and economics, seeking to trade extra goods to get extra from others. These shared attitudes of assistance and exchange can allow for cross-community communication. An ideal, democratic society for Mead would be one in which each member developed his or her own individuality to the fullest, performing his or her particular social functions while taking the attitudes of everyone else in society who might be affected. A perfect society would be characterized by perfect communication.

In the next piece, Mark Poster applies post-structuralist theory to examine the instability of identities and meanings in the new electronic media environment, which he terms "the mode of information," and calls for new theories that address *the problem of communication in the postmodern world*. Post-structuralism is a theoretical approach influenced by semiotics and phenomenology that generally emphasizes the instability and contestability of meanings in societal discourses. According to Poster's version of post-structuralism, the now fading modern society with its emphasis on rationality and stable personal identities was the product of

a print-based literate culture in which words were fixed on the page and readers were positioned vis-à-vis authors in certain ways. In the emerging new culture of digital electronic communication, meanings and personal identities (*subject positions*) become progressively more fragmented and fluid. (The term subject position emphasizes that personal identities are produced as one is positioned within particular societal discourses, for example discourses about gender or age.)

Poster highlights some interesting aspects of new media. He writes about the special powers of the TV ad where the voice-over allows the viewer to connect images that normally would not co-occur and the ad "invites the viewer to identify with the commodity" (reading 28). A second phenomenon is the identity that we have in the cyber world, where our *favorites* or recommendations specifically for each of us show up when we log into a Web site. We exist in databases. Linking to theories of Baudrillard and Foucault, Poster talks about society as a collage of theme parks and the impact the unseen guards have on us as the electronic world creates categories and those categories start to have an impact on us and the decisions we make. With the introduction of computer-based writing—Poster's third example—the mutability of the electronic word has replaced the stability and authorship of the written word. Linking to ideas of Derrida, Poster argues that communication functions differently now and is impacting both communal and individual identities.

He then proposes something that extends a key theme from the readings in unit I and is also developed by Cameron in this unit: the historical and cultural relativity of the very idea of communication. Rather than theorize on the basis of pure mathematical ideas, as Wiener did (referring to cybernetic theory, see unit VI), theory should respond to the actual conditions of communication and culture as influenced by changing media technologies. Some protest movements and feminist ethics have challenged the rational paradigm in communication theory, and this is the kind of direction that is needed, according to Poster. Hegemony (implicit domination) only works when it is unrecognized, he claims (a claim that is debatable). To understand and live in a postmodern world, the idea of the fixed stable nature of things needs to be challenged and new theories need to address the fluid actualities of that world. Concerned with exposing unrecognized structures of power, Poster's theory participates somewhat in the critical tradition (unit IX), although his primary purpose in this essay is to present a macro-sociocultural theory explaining the characteristics of communication in postmodern society.

The next reading is one of many responses to *the problem of coordinating communication to bring about organized collective action.* Taylor et al. theorize how communication aligns different perspectives (co-orientation) and how imbrication (overlapping) of levels of communication constitutes an organization. For Taylor et al., communication occurs at the intersection of what they call conversation (interaction process) and text (meaningful content), each of which has two aspects. Conversation consists of the circumstances or situatedness and the back and forth sequencing of interaction. Texts consist of the repertoire of things we know in common and the formal sequence of the communication (such as the rules of grammar). Communication is fundamentally pragmatic: It is about coordinated action, getting something done together. And just as can be seen in the example that opens this piece where the pilot and the jetway mover need to work together to get the passengers off the plane, co-orientation (coordinated orientation toward an object of action) is needed to get anything done. At the heart of this theory is a unique concept of collective agency based on co-orientation.

In Taylor et al.'s modified A-B-X model of co-orientation, X is the object: the thing talked about, something that needs to be acted upon. B is an agent who acts on behalf of A, another agent. A and B can be individuals (for example, a supervisor and an employee) but might also be categories of agents (the flight crew and the passengers on an airliner) or even entire organizations (an accounting firm and its corporate clients). This formula is the building block of an organization. As it builds and multiplies, a fractal pattern (a repetition of structure at different degrees of scale) can be seen as one sees more and more levels of agents who are involved in accomplishing a complex activity. The levels of activity are imbricated, meaning that the levels overlap like tiles on a roof to create a durable organizational infrastructure. But this is not the literal bricks-and-mortar structure of a building, and although Taylor et al. do not explicitly make this point, neither is it constructed essentially of signs and symbols as a semiotic theorist might claim; rather, the organization exists only in the ongoing, multilayered texts and conversations of communication as agents coordinate their practical activities.

In a large organization there are metalevels of conversation. Often the conversation one is engaged in is in fact a conversation about other conversations that are happening elsewhere in the organization. In these metaconversations, some speakers speak for other conversations (their departments), and the textual repertoires of interactants may be different (marketing draws on a different range of texts than finance or engineering). However, although there are multiple metalevels, the challenge of any organization is the same as any small group, which is to make itself into a collective agent: to get things done.

This piece is interesting for how it relates to a range of earlier readings. In some ways it is a microcosm of the sociocultural tradition in its attempts to show how the microstructure of interaction builds toward the larger social structure of organization, while at the same time representing or acting on behalf of that larger structure. The idea of co-orientation is reminiscent of Mead's concept of cooperation through taking the role of the other. Although Taylor et al. focus on micro and meso (intermediate) levels of structure rather than the macrolevel of society as a whole, in the end they refer to society and culture as the ultimate historical context in which organizations are constituted. Their analysis of the interplay between levels of organization has something in common with Poster's assumptions about the central role of discourse in positioning subjects (agents, for Taylor et al.) in larger structures. Even the cultural analysis of communication exemplified by Cameron (reading 30) has a role in this theory in explaining the repertoires of shared cultural knowledge (texts) that enable co-orientation. Taylor et al. integrate current ideas from several traditions of communication theory, including the semiotic (text, discourse, narrative), the phenomenological (objects, agents), the sociopsychological (co-orientation, interaction, influence), and the cybernetic (circular causation, embedded levels), although their primary focus on collective action in social systems puts them squarely in the sociocultural tradition. From that tradition they integrate concepts of structuration theory (Giddens, 1984), actor network theory (Latour, 1993), distributed cognition (Hutchins, 1995), interactionism (Goffman, 1963), and ethnomethodology (Boden, 1994), among other theories and approaches. Although no single reading could possibly represent the diversity of current sociocultural thinking, Taylor et al. have built an original communication theory on a broad base of the tradition.

The final reading in this unit, excerpted from the introductory chapter of Deborah Cameron's book *Good to Talk? Living and Working in a Communication Culture* (2000), examines popular ways of thinking and talking about communication in our own late modern society, with particular reference to the United Kingdom. She finds that the idea of communication in this culture "has been transformed into a technical skill, with its own professional experts and its own technical jargon" (reading 30). Communication is much talked about in the media, in business, in education, and in private life. Effective communication is considered the key to success and personal happiness, and many people would like to improve their communication skills.

Seeking a theoretical explanation for this recent cultural trend, Cameron looks to "economic and social developments of the historical period that is sometimes termed 'high' or 'late' modernity" (reading 30). Economic globalization seems to be an important influence. Two key concepts in Cameron's theoretical analysis are *reflexive modernity* and *enterprise culture.* Drawn from the social theory of Anthony Giddens (1991), reflexive modernity refers to a process in which expert technical knowledge is increasingly used to guide social practices of all kinds, including traditional practices like marriage and child rearing—and now, communication—that formerly were not regarded as technical topics. Even the self becomes a reflexive project as we seek expert advice from therapists and self-help books to become better, more effective people. Enterprise culture refers to a related process in which business values and "enterprising" personal traits like "resourcefulness, self-discipline, and openness to risk and change" are increasingly emphasized both in business and in non-business organizations such as universities and government agencies (reading 30). Responding to competitive pressures of the global economy demanding efficiency and innovation, the enterprise culture puts a premium on communication skills required by so-called "empowered" employees to perform effectively in teamwork and customer care. Communication becomes a standardized set of technical skills taught by experts even though, paradoxically, good communication also is still thought to require spontaneous, authentic self-expression.

Focusing again on everyday ideas about communication, Cameron notes an apparent contradiction between two commonplace ideas: That communication should be spontaneous and authentic (be yourself) and that communication is a set of technical skills that can be improved by training based on expert knowledge. Are these ideas contradictory? Can tensions between them be observed in situations that Cameron describes such as customer service, education, and therapy? Is there a similar paradox in the modern celebrity culture where the images of media stars and politicians tell us who they really are? If we think and talk about communication in this paradoxical fashion, do we actually communicate in a paradoxical manner as well? What in fact is *real* communication? As we have been seeing throughout this book, there are many possible answers to that last question!

A question posed earlier should now be raised again: As the sociohistorical context changes, does the nature of communication change, or does the nature of theorizing change? Do these readings show a change over time in the phenomenon of communication or simply different perspectives on something that has stayed essentially the same? Does this tradition develop as a new problem or set of related problems are identified and theorizing coalesces around those problems? What are the most important communication problems to be addressed by sociocultural theorizing today? Are globalization, multicultural diversity, and changing gender roles good examples? Are Poster's diagnosis of postmodern society and Cameron's analysis of "'high' or 'late' modernity" consistent with each other, or do they disagree in some ways? Can the communication problems of today be informed by the theories of yesterday? Is Mead's ideal human society, in which each person is able to take the role of everyone else whom he or she affects, making possible universal cooperation, an appropriate ideal for today's world? What are the barriers to achieving it? Are there ways to pull together strands from different traditions to build theories that let us identify and name current problems and

find productive ways to talk and think about them? Do Taylor et al. exemplify a good way of doing so? These are intriguing questions to address in light of the readings in this unit.

As well, the question of the changing nature of communication relates to this volume as a whole because one of our premises is that theorists theorize in response to problems experienced in their sociohistorical contexts. Poster calls for a new kind of theorizing grounded in actualities of culture and media. Is the project of theorizing in this volume a process of constructing such theories?

REFERENCES

Blumer, H. (1968). *Symbolic interactionism: Perspective and method.* Englewood Cliffs, NJ: Prentice-Hall.

Boden, D. (1994). *The business of talk: Organizations in action.* Cambridge, UK: Polity Press.

Cameron, D. (2000). *Good to talk? Living and working in a communication culture.* London: Sage.

Garfinkel, H. (1987). *Studies in ethnomethodology.* Cambridge, UK: Polity Press. (Original work published 1967)

Giddens, A. (1984). *The constitution of society: Outline of the theory of structuration.* Berkeley: University of California Press.

Giddens, A. (1991). *Modernity and self-identity: Self and society in the late modern age.* Stanford, CA: Stanford University Press.

Goffman, E. (1963). *Behavior in public places.* New York: Free Press.

Hutchins, E. (1995). *Cognition in the wild.* Cambridge, MA: MIT Press.

Latour, B. (1993). *We have never been modern.* Cambridge, MA: Harvard University Press.

Lévi-Strauss, C. (1963). *Structural anthropology* (C. Jacobson & B. C. Schoepf, Trans.). New York: Basic Books.

Mead, G. H. (1934). *Mind, self, and society from the standpoint of a social behaviorist* (C. W. Morris, Ed.). Chicago: University of Chicago Press.

Merton, R. K. (1957). *Social theory and social structure.* Glencoe, IL: The Free Press.

27

The Social Foundations and Functions of Thought and Communication

George Herbert Mead

In the same socio-physiological way that the human individual becomes conscious of himself he also becomes conscious of other individuals; and his consciousness both of himself and of other individuals is equally important for his own self-development and for the development of the organized society or social group to which he belongs.

The principle which I have suggested as basic to human social organization is that of communication involving participation in the other. This requires the appearance of the other in the self, the identification of the other with the self, the reaching of self-consciousness through the other. This participation is made possible through the type of communication which the human animal is able to carry out—a type of communication distinguished from that which takes place among other forms which have not this principle in their societies. I discussed the sentinel, so-called, that may be said to communicate his discovery of the danger to the other members, as the clucking of the hen may be said to communicate to the chick. There are conditions under which the gesture of one form serves to place the other forms in the proper attitude toward external conditions. In one sense we may say the one form communicates with the other, but the difference between that and self-conscious communication is evident. One form does not know that communication is taking place with the other. We get illustrations of that in what we term mob-consciousness, the attitude which an audience will take when under the influence of a great speaker. One is influenced by the attitudes of those about him, which are reflected back into

SOURCE: Mead, G. H. (1934). *Mind, self, and society from the standpoint of a social behaviorist* (C. W. Morris, ed.). Chicago, IL: University of Chicago Press. (Pages 253–260 and 325–328).

the different members of the audience so that they come to respond as a whole. One feels the general attitude of the whole audience. There is then communication in a real sense, that is, one form communicates to the other an attitude which the other assumes toward a certain part of the environment that is of importance to them both. That level of communication is found in forms of society which are of lower type than the social organization of the human group.

In the human group, on the other hand, there is not only this kind of communication but also that in which the person who uses this gesture and so communicates assumes the attitude of the other individual as well as calling it out in the other. He himself is in the role of the other person whom he is so exciting and influencing. It is through taking this role of the other that he is able to come back on himself and so direct his own process of communication. This taking the role of the other, an expression I have so often used, is not simply of passing importance. It is not something that just happens as an incidental result of the gesture, but it is of importance in the development of co-operative activity. The immediate effect of such role-taking lies in the control which the individual is able to exercise over his own response.[1] The control of the action of the individual in a co-operative process can take place in the conduct of the individual himself if he can take the role of the other. It is this control of the response of the individual himself through taking the role of the other that leads to the value of this type of communication from the point of view of the organization of the conduct in the group. It carries the process of co-operative activity farther than it can be carried in the herd as such, or in the insect society.

And thus it is that social control, as operating in terms of self-criticism, exerts itself so intimately and extensively over individual behavior or conduct, serving to integrate the individual and his actions with reference to the organized social process of experience and behavior in which he is implicated. The physiological mechanism of the human individual's central nervous system makes it possible for him to take the attitudes of other individuals, and the attitudes of the organized social group of which he and they are members, toward himself, in terms of his integrated social relations to them and to the group as a whole; so that the general social process of experience and behavior which the group is carrying on is directly presented to him in his own experience, and so that he is thereby able to govern and direct his conduct consciously and critically, with reference to his relations both to the social group as a whole and to its other individual members, in terms of this social process. Thus he becomes not only self-conscious but also self-critical; and thus, through self-criticism, social control over individual behavior or conduct operates by virtue of the social origin and basis of such criticism. That is to say, self-criticism is essentially social criticism, and behavior controlled by self-criticism is essentially behavior controlled socially.[2] Hence social control, so far from tending to crush out the human individual or to obliterate his self-conscious individuality, is, on the contrary, actually constitutive of and inextricably associated with that individuality; for the individual is what he is, as a conscious and individual personality, just in as far as he is a member of society, involved in the social process of experience and activity, and thereby socially controlled in his conduct.

The very organization of the self-conscious community is dependent upon individuals taking the attitude of the other individuals. The development of this process, as I have indicated, is dependent upon getting the attitude of the group as distinct from that of a separate individual— getting what I have termed a "generalized other." I have illustrated this by the ball game, in which the attitudes of a set of individuals are involved in a co-operative response in which the different roles involve each other. In so far as a man takes the attitude of one individual in the group, he must take it in its relationship to the action of the other members of the group; and if he is fully to adjust himself, he would have to take the attitudes of all involved in the process. The degree, of course, to which he can do that is restrained by his capacity, but still in all intelligent processes we are able sufficiently to take the roles of those involved in the activity to make our own action intelligent. The degree to which the life of the whole community can get into the self-conscious life of the separate individuals varies enormously. History is largely occupied in tracing out the development which could not have been present in the actual experience of the members of the community at the time the historian is writing about. Such an account explains the importance of history. One can look back over that which took place, and bring out changes, forces, and interests which nobody at the time was conscious of. We have to wait for the historian to give the picture because the actual process was one which transcended the experience of the separate individuals.

Occasionally a person arises who is able to take in more than others of an act in process, who can put himself into relation with whole groups in the community whose attitudes have not entered into the lives of the others in the community. He becomes a leader. Classes under a feudal order may be so separate from each other that, while they can act in certain traditional circumstances, they cannot understand each other; and then there may arise an individual who is capable of entering into the attitudes of the other members of the group. Figures of that sort become of enormous importance because they make possible communication between groups otherwise completely separated from each other. The sort of capacity we speak of is in politics the attitude of the statesman who is able to enter into the attitudes of the group and to mediate between them by making his own experience universal, so that others can enter into this form of communication through him.

The vast importance of media of communication such as those involved in journalism is seen at once, since they report situations through which one can enter into the attitude and experience of other persons. The drama has served this function in presenting what have been felt to be important situations. It has picked out characters which lie in men's minds from tradition, as the Greeks did in their tragedies, and then expressed

through these characters situations which belong to their own time but which carry the individuals beyond the actual fixed walls which have arisen between them, as members of different classes in the community. The development of this type of communication from the drama into the novel has historically something of the same importance as journalism has for our own time. The novel presents a situation which lies outside of the immediate purview of the reader in such form that he enters into the attitude of the group in the situation. There is a far higher degree of participation, and consequently of possible communication, under those conditions than otherwise. There is involved, of course, in such a development the existence of common interests. You cannot build up a society out of elements that lie outside of the individual's life-processes. You have to presuppose some sort of co-operation within which the individuals are themselves actively involved as the only possible basis for this participation in communication. You cannot start to communicate with people in Mars and set up a society where you have no antecedent relationship. Of course, if there is an already existing community in Mars of the same character as your own, then you can possibly carry on communication with it; but a community that lies entirely outside of your own community, that has no common interest, no co-operative activity, is one with which you could not communicate.

In human society there have arisen certain universal forms which found their expression in universal religions and also in universal economic processes. These go back, in the case of religion, to such fundamental attitudes of human beings toward each other as kindliness, helpfulness, and assistance. Such attitudes are involved in the life of individuals in the group, and a generalization of them is found back of all universal religions. These processes are such that they carry with them neighborliness and, in so far as we have co-operative activity, assistance to those in trouble and in suffering. The fundamental attitude of helping the other person who is down, who finds himself in sickness or other misfortune, belongs to the very structure of the individuals in a human community. It can be found even under conditions where there is the opposing attitude of complete hostility, as in giving assistance to the wounded enemy in the midst of a battle. The attitude of chivalry, or the mere breaking of bread with another, identifies the individual with the other even if he is an enemy. Those are situations in which the individual finds himself in an attitude of co-operation; and it is out of situations like that, out of universal co-operative activity, that the universal religions have arisen. The development of this fundamental neighborliness is expressed in the parable of the good Samaritan.

On the other hand, we have a fundamental process of exchange on the part of individuals arising from the goods for which they have no immediate need themselves but which can be utilized for obtaining that which they do need. Such exchange can take place wherever individuals who have such surpluses are able to communicate with each other. There is a participation in the attitude of need, each putting himself in the attitude of the other in the recognition of the mutual value which the exchange has for both. It is a highly abstract relationship, for something which one cannot himself use brings him into relationship with anybody else in exchange. It is a situation which is as universal as that to which we have referred in the case of neighborliness. These two attitudes represent the most highly universal, and, for the time being, most highly abstract society. They are attitudes which can transcend the limits of the different social groups organized about their own life-processes, and may appear even in actual hostility between groups. In the process of exchange or assistance persons who would be otherwise hostile can come into an attitude of co-operative activity.

Back of these two attitudes lies that which is involved in any genuine communication. It is more universal in one respect than religious and economic attitudes, and less in another. One has to have something to communicate before communicating. One may seemingly have the symbol of another language, but if he has not any common ideas (and these involve common responses) with those who speak that language,

he cannot communicate with them; so that back even of the process of discourse must lie co-operative activity. The process of communication is one which is more universal than that of the universal religion or universal economic process in that it is one that serves them both. Those two activities have been the most universal co-operative activities. The scientific community is one which has come to be perhaps as universal in one sense, but even it cannot be found among people who have no conscious signs or literature. The process of communication is, then, in one sense more universal than these different co-operative processes. It is the medium through which these co-operative activities can be carried on in the self-conscious society. But one must recognize that it is a medium for co-operative activities; there is not any field of thought as such which can simply go on by itself. Thinking is not a field or realm which can be taken outside of possible social uses. There has to be some such field as religion or economics in which there is something to communicate, in which there is a co-operative process, in which what is communicated can be socially utilized. One must assume that sort of a co-operative situation in order to reach what is called the "universe of discourse." Such a universe of discourse is the medium for all these different social processes, and in that sense it is more universal than they; but it is not a process that, so to speak, runs by itself.

It is necessary to emphasize this because philosophy and the dogmas that have gone with it have set up a process of thought and a thinking substance that is the antecedent of these very processes within which thinking goes on. Thinking, however, is nothing but the response of the individual to the attitude of the other in the wide social process in which both are involved, and the directing of one's anticipatory action by these attitudes of the others that one does assume. Since that is what the process of thinking consists in, it cannot simply run by itself.

I have been looking at language as a principle of social organization which has made the distinctively human society possible. Of course, if there are inhabitants in Mars, it is possible for us to enter into communication with them in as far as we can enter into social relations with them. If we can isolate the logical constants which are essential for any process of thinking, presumably those logical constants would put us into a position to carry on communication with the other community. They would constitute a common social process so that one could possibly enter into a social process with any other being in any historical period or spatial position. By means of thought one can project a society into the future or past, but we are always presupposing a social relationship within which this process of communication takes place. The process of communication cannot be set up as something that exists by itself, or as a presupposition of the social process. On the contrary, the social process is presupposed in order to render thought and communication possible.

THE IDEAL OF A HUMAN SOCIETY

There is, of course, a certain common set of reactions which belong to all, which are not differentiated on the social side but which get their expression in rights, uniformities, the common methods of action which characterize members of different communities, manners of speech, and so on. Distinguishable from those is the identity which is compatible with the difference of social functions of the individuals, illustrated by the capacity of the individual to take the part of the others whom he is affecting, the warrior putting himself in the place of those whom he is proceeding against, the teacher putting himself in the position of the child whom he is undertaking to instruct. That capacity allows for exhibiting one's own peculiarities, and at the same time taking the attitude of the others whom he is himself affecting. It is possible for the individual to develop his own peculiarities, that which individualizes him, and still be a member of a community, provided that he is able to take the attitude of those whom he affects. Of course, the degree to which that takes place varies

tremendously, but a certain amount of it is essential to citizenship in the community.

One may say that the attainment of that functional differentiation and social participation in the full degree is a sort of ideal which lies before the human community. The present stage of it is presented in the ideal of democracy. It is often assumed that democracy is an order of society in which those personalities which are sharply differentiated will be eliminated, that everything will be ironed down to a situation where everyone will be, as far as possible, like everyone else. But of course that is not the implication of democracy: the implication of democracy is rather that the individual can be as highly developed as lies within the possibilities of his own inheritance, and still can enter into the attitudes of the others whom he affects. There can still be leaders, and the community can rejoice in their attitudes just in so far as these superior individuals can themselves enter into the attitudes of the community which they undertake to lead.

How far individuals can take the roles of other individuals in the community is dependent upon a number of factors. The community may in its size transcend the social organization, may go beyond the social organization which makes such identification possible. The most striking illustration of that is the economic community. This includes everybody with whom one can trade in any circumstances, but it represents a whole in which it would be next to impossible for all to enter into the attitudes of the others. The ideal communities of the universal religions are communities which to some extent may be said to exist, but they imply a degree of identification which the actual organization of the community cannot realize. We often find the existence of castes in a community which make it impossible for persons to enter into the attitude of other people although they are actually affecting and are affected by these other people. The ideal of human society is one which does bring people so closely together in their interrelationships, so fully develops the necessary system of communication, that the individuals who exercise their own peculiar functions can take the attitude of those whom they affect. The development of communication is not simply a matter of abstract ideas, but is a process of putting one's self in the place of the other person's attitude, communicating through significant symbols. Remember that what is essential to a significant symbol is that the gesture which affects others should affect the individual himself in the same way. It is only when the stimulus which one gives another arouses in himself the same or like response that the symbol is a significant symbol. Human communication takes place through such significant symbols, and the problem is one of organizing a community which makes this possible. If that system of communication could be made theoretically perfect, the individual would affect himself as he affects others in every way. That would be the ideal of communication, an ideal attained in logical discourse wherever it is understood. The meaning of that which is said is here the same to one as it is to everybody else. Universal discourse is then the formal ideal of communication. If communication can be carried through and made perfect, then there would exist the kind of democracy to which we have referred, in which each individual would carry just the response in himself that he knows he calls out in the community. That is what makes communication in the significant sense the organizing process in the community. It is not simply a process of transferring abstract symbols; it is always a gesture in a social act which calls out in the individual himself the tendency to the same act that is called out in others.

What we call the ideal of a human society is approached in some sense by the economic society on the one side and by the universal religions on the other side, but is not by any means fully realized. Those abstractions can be put together in a single community of the democratic type. As democracy now exists there is not this development of communication so that individuals can put themselves into the attitudes of those whom they affect. There is a consequent leveling-down, and an undue recognition of that

which is not only common but identical. The ideal of human society cannot exist as long as it is impossible for individuals to enter into the attitudes of those whom they are affecting in the performance of their own peculiar functions.

Notes

1. From the standpoint of social evolution, it is this bringing of any given social act, or of the total social process in which that act is a constituent, directly and as an organized whole into the experience of each of the individual organisms implicated in that act, with reference to which he may consequently regulate and govern his individual conduct, that constitutes the peculiar value and significance of self-consciousness in these individual organisms.

We have seen that the process or activity of thinking is a conversation carried on by the individual between himself and the generalized other; and that the general form and subject matter of this conversation is given and determined by the appearance in experience of some sort of problem to be solved. Human intelligence, which expresses itself in thought, is recognized to have this character of facing and dealing with any problem of environmental adjustment which confronts an organism possessing it. And thus, as we have also seen, the essential characteristic of intelligent behavior is delayed responses—a halt in behavior while thinking is going on; this delayed response and the thinking for the purposes of which it is delayed (including the final selection, as the result of the thinking, of the best or most expedient among the several responses possible in the given environmental situation) being made possible physiologically through the mechanism of the central nervous system, and socially through the mechanism of language.

2. Freud's conception of the psychological "censor" represents a partial recognition of this operation of social control in terms of self-criticism, a recognition, namely, of its operation with reference to sexual experience and conduct. But this same sort of censorship or criticism of himself by the individual is reflected also in all other aspects of his social experience, behavior, and relations—a fact which follows naturally and inevitably from our social theory of the self.

28

THE MODE OF INFORMATION
AND POSTMODERNITY

MARK POSTER

A post-structuralist approach to communication theory analyses the way electronically mediated communication (what I
call 'the mode of information') both challenges
and reinforces systems of domination that are
emerging in a postmodern society and culture.[1]
My general thesis is that the mode of information
enacts a radical reconfiguration of language, one
which constitutes subjects outside the pattern of
the rational, autonomous individual. This familiar
modern subject is displaced by the mode of
information in favour of one that is multiplied,
disseminated, and decentred, continuously interpellated as an unstable identity. At the level of
culture, this instability poses both dangers and
challenges which, if they become part of a political movement, or are connected with the politics
of feminism, ethnic/racial minorities, gay and lesbian positions, may lead to a fundamental challenge to modern social institutions and structures.

Communication theory needs to account for
electronically mediated communication and by
doing so take its proper place of importance in
general social theory. This importance has not
generally been recognized by the great theorists
of modern society who emphasized action
(labour) and institutions (bureaucracy) over language and communication. Marx and Weber, for
example, fall clearly within this tendency. Yet
their theories reflect the dominant communicational mode of their time, even though they failed
fully to take it into account. They were heirs
of the eighteenth century Enlightenment, an intellectual tradition that was profoundly rooted in
print culture. The Enlightenment theory of the
autonomous rational individual derived much
sustenance and reinforcement from the practice
of reading the printed page.[2] Hegel struck such a
chord when he referred to newspaper reading as
'the morning prayer of modern man'. The spatial

materiality of print—the linear display of sentences, the stability of the word on the page, the orderly, systematic spacing of black letters on a white background—enable readers to distance themselves from authors. These features of print promote an ideology of the critical individual, reading and thinking in isolation, outside the network of political and religious dependencies. In an opposite, but yet complementary way, print culture, by the materiality of the word on the page as compared with the evanescence of the word in oral culture, promotes the authority of the author, the intellectual and the theorist. This double movement engenders the reader as critic and the author as authority, an apparent opposition or contradiction but actually an oscillation of dominance characteristic of communication in modern society.

In the case of both the reader and the author print culture constitutes the individual as a subject, as transcendent to objects, as stable and fixed in identity, in short, as a grounded essence. And this feature of print culture is homologous with the figure of the subject in modern institutions—the capitalist market with its possessive individuals, the legal system with its 'reasonable man,' representative democracy with its secret ballots and presumption of individual self-interest, bureaucracy with its instrumental rationality, the factory with its Taylorite system, the educational system with its individualized examinations and records. In response to these developments, Marx theorized the emancipation of rational individuality through the class struggle and Weber regretted the fixing of instrumental rationality in unchangeable social organizations. Both presumed a configuration of the subject which was a product of print culture and both viewed modernity as the final instantiation of that social individual. However, both missed the role of communications in the process of constituting such subjects and both understood the process of subject constitution only in part. Marx realized that individuals change in different modes of production, but posited man as a 'species being' that communism would fully actualize, one that looks very much like the

Enlightenment's autonomous rational agent. Weber allowed four types of subjects (value rational, instrumental rational, emotional and traditional), understood them as in some sense historically produced, but saw modernity as inscribing only one, the instrumental rational. For both, history ended with the appearance of the autonomous rational agent as subject, as fixed essence.

The emergence of the mode of information, with its electronically mediated systems of communication, changes the way we think about the subject and promises to alter as well the shape of society. Electronic culture promotes the individual as an unstable identity, as a continuous process of multiple identity formation, and raises the question of a social form beyond the modern, the possibility of a postmodern society.[3] Electronic culture promotes theories (such as post-structuralism) that focus on the role of language in the process of the constitution of subjects. These theories undermine views of the reader and author as stable points of criticism and authority respectively. When print mediates the theorist's understanding of the subject, language is understood as representational, as an arbitrary system of signs, invoked by a thinker in order to point to objects. As long as this regime is in place, the subject remains a stable point, fixed in space and time. Figures that upset such an understanding of the subject—women, children, non-Europeans—are placed in the position of being Other, of not being taken seriously into account. When electronic communication is a factor in the theorist's understanding of the subject, language is understood as performative, rhetorical, as an active figuring and positioning of the subject. With the spread of this regime of communication, the subject can only be understood as partially stable, as repeatedly reconfigured at different points of time and space, as non-self-identical and therefore as always partly Other.

Electronic communications, like print, place a distance between the addressor and the addressee; they accentuate the feature of language that permits a gap between the speaker and the listener. This gap is often understood by proponents of modern print-oriented theory as efficiency. From smoke signals to communication satellites, the principle is the same: extend the human voice. Just as tools may heighten the powers of the muscles in the production of goods, they may amplify the larynx, allowing speech at a distance. Theories that view communication technology purely as a question of efficiency unduly discourage new questions that arise from electronic communication, placing them within the older paradigms generated to theorize oral and print culture. When electronic communication is seen as simply allowing greater spatial and temporal extension, the analyst reconfirms the figure of the autonomous rational individual and reinstates the stability of the subject.

In terms of politics oral communication, from the point of view of print culture, binds the individual in relations of political domination. When communication is restricted to speech (and manuscript as its simple extension), individuals are easily restrained in ties of dependence. By enlarging the gap mentioned above as inherent in language, print allows a distance to intervene between speaker and listener and this gap permits the individual to think, coolly to judge the words of the other without his or her overbearing presence—or so advocates of print culture contend.

Theorists of print culture interpret the gap as enhancing the powers of reason and permitting individual autonomy. In other words, they link the gap in language to the subject as centred in reason. The ideological force of modern Enlightenment communication theory derives in good part from this move, a move that incorporates print technology within modern social theory. But the stability of this move is always partial, always threatened. For the gap instantiated by print could be turned against modern theory: it could be appropriated by excluded groups such as workers, women and non-Europeans to promote their ends; it could be turned into cultural resistance as in avant-garde art movements since the Romantic period.[4] Nineteenth-century jeremiads against the dangers of reading novels are indications that the inducement to fantasy was one appropriation of the gap that resisted

its Enlightenment containment. As early as Rousseau's *Emile,* Sophie falls in love with Emile because he resembles a character in a novel she had read. Love was mediated by the gap inscribed in print.

Electronic culture permits a different interpretation of the gap. The tremendous extension of the space between speaker and listener in the mode of information upsets the confinement of the gap to the self-identical subject. The combination of enormous distances with temporal immediacy produced by electronic communications both removes the speaker from the listener and brings them together. These opposing tendencies—opposite from the point of view of print culture—reconfigure the position of the individual so drastically that the figure of the self, fixed in time and space, capable of exercising cognitive control over surrounding objects, may no longer be sustained. Language no longer represents a reality, no longer is a neutral tool to enhance the subject's instrumental rationality: language becomes or better reconfigures reality. And by doing so the subject is interpellated through language and cannot easily escape recognition of that interpellation. Electronic communication systematically removes the fixed points, the grounds, the foundations that were essential to modern theory. I shall illustrate these transformations of cultural and social life by diverse examples of electronically mediated communication: the TV ad, the database and computer writing. And I shall explore these examples from the post-structuralist perspectives of Jean Baudrillard, Michel Foucault and Jacques Derrida.

In the register of humanist morality, TV ads are manipulative, deceptive and repugnant; they solicit consumer decisions on 'irrational' grounds and encourage a 'quick-fix' drug mentality as a false solution to life's problems. In the register of marketing, TV ads are evaluated in relation to their ability 'to create effective demand' for the product. In the register of democratic politics, TV ads undermine the independent thinking of the electorate, diminishing its ability to distinguish truth from falsity, the real and the imaginary, and passifying it into a state of indifference. In the register of Marxist social criticism, TV ads stimulate false needs that detract from the revolutionary purpose of the working class and serve only to pump up an economy that is beyond the control of the producers. Each of these perspectives contains a degree of validity but none approaches the crucial issue of the role of TV ads in contemporary culture, none reveals the altered language structure of the ads, and, most importantly, none draws attention to the relation of language to culture in the constitution of new subject positions, that is, new places in the network of social communication. I contend that TV ads exploit electronic mediation so as to inscribe a new technology of power, one whose political effects need to be assessed in relation to the possible emergence of a postmodern society.

Like monologues, print and radio, TV ads are nominally unidirectional communications: the sender addresses the receiver. Yet all communications enable responses, feedbacks, replies, however delayed. Monologues are subject to interventions, print to reports or to conversations, radio to telephone call-ins. But each of these communication technologies is enunciated as unidirectional. The TV ad, unlike the other examples, easily combines images, sounds and writing. It displays moving, aural narratives of everyday reality, at times with great verisimilitude. Because they control the context, the background, as well as the text of the narrative, TV ads contain special powers. The 'reality' they represent can be 'hyperreal', editing in contents not normally found together in 'reality'. Voice-overs, as another example, inject a superego-like authority in the ad. With great flexibility the ad constructs a mini-reality in which things are set in juxtapositions that violate the rules of the everyday. In particular, TV ads associate meanings, connotations and moods that are inappropriate in reality, subject to objections in dialogic communications, but effective at the level of desire, the unconscious, the imaginary. TV ads constitute a language system that leaves out the referent, the symbolic and the real, working instead with chains of signifiers (words) and signifieds (mental images). The referent, the symbolic and the real are absent and only come into play if the viewer buys the product.

The meaning structure of the TV ad, strictly keeping itself to the levels of signifiers, meanings and images, powerfully invites the viewer to identify with the commodity. The ad stimulates not an object choice, a cognitive decision, a rational evaluation, but works at other linguistic levels to produce the effects of incorporation and attachment between the viewer and the product. The viewer is the absent hero or heroine of the ad. The viewer is solicited to displace him or herself into the ad and become one with the meanings associated with the product. In its monologue, in its construction of context and its association of non-connected meanings, the TV ad inscribes a new pattern of communication into the culture, one repeated *ad infinitum,* one extended to politics, religion and every conceivable aspect of social life.

Through these communications, the realist linguistic paradigm is shaken. The TV ad works with simulacra, with inventions and with imaginings. The modernist print-oriented communications associated with education, capitalism/socialism, bureaucracy and representative democracy— identities centred in Weber's instrumental reason— are displaced in favour of a postmodernist, electronic-oriented communication in which identity is destabilized and fragmented. This is accomplished not in the highly ritualized collective action of religion or other community function, but in the privacy, informality and isolation of the home. And it is accomplished not at special moments of the calender, but every day and for long hours. The population places itself in communication situations in which the TV ad is the norm of language construction, and the effects on the construction of subject positions are no doubt profound.

Jean Baudrillard, in *Consumer Society, The System of Objects* and *Toward a Critique of the Political Economy of the Sign,* began the line of thinking about contemporary culture which I am pursuing in relation to TV ads as part of the mode of information.[5] Baudrillard broke with the realist paradigms of social science at first by combining Roland Barthes's semiology with the neo-Marxism of Henri Lefebvre. In the late 1960s and early 1970s, he attempted to move social critique from the level of action to that of language. He began to look at consumer culture not as a process of Veblenesque mimesis, of 'keeping up with the Joneses' of conformist behaviour, but as a peculiar restructuring of signs. Structuralist linguists had shown that meaning was a result of relations of difference between words. The key to language was not so much a connection between a word and a thing but an arbitrary designation that depended on a differential mark. Language for them was composed of binary oppositions of signifiers—I/you, black/white, and so forth—whose ability to have meaning hinged on the stable relation between the terms or what they termed the 'structure'. Language was theorized as a vast machine for generating such differential relations. But in order to grasp this the theorist needed to shift his or her point of view away from the individual as a subject who produced and received meaning to language as an objective system of relations. In other words language became intelligible only from the standpoint of its structure; language then constituted the subject, not the reverse.

For Baudrillard the structuralists were too formalist, restricting themselves too closely to linguistic signs. He shifted the object of analysis to daily life, taking society itself as the field for interpretation. Consumer activity would then be seen as a circulation of signs in the structuralist sense. The commodity is thus extracted from the domain of economic theory or moral commentary and viewed as a complex code. The key to consumerism is not an irrational tendency to conspicuous display but the insertion of individuals into a communication relation in which they receive messages in the form of commodities. The consumer is not 'irrational' and the object is not a 'utility'. Between the poles of object and intention is the advertisement which disrupts the normal set of differential relations of signs. The ad presupposes language not as a reference to a 'real' but as an arbitrary connection of signifiers.

It simply rearranges those signifiers, violating their 'normal' references. The aim of the ad is to associate a chain of signifiers in a narrative of a desirable lifestyle: Pepsi = youth = sexiness = popularity = fun, for example.

The status of the ad as a linguistic and cultural phenomenon, Baudrillard argued in the 1980s, is that of a simulacrum, a copy that has no original, has no objective referent. For him today's culture increasingly is composed of these simulacra which taken together compose a new order of reality which he terms 'the hyperreal'. Culture consists of constructed realities, Disneylands, which are more real than the real they are supposed to refer back to. But in the end there is no reference back since once social life is presented as a theme park in one place, its constructed element emerges and tends to dominate over its presence as a fixed, natural order. Society becomes a collage of theme parks which one enters at will (and for a price). Baudrillard totalizes his view of the hyperreal, dismissing other modernist perspectives on politics and the economy as without value. By contextualizing his understanding of consumer culture in relation to the mode of information, by connecting it with specific communication technologies, I hope to extract the critical impulse of his position without acceding to his monolithic vision.

Computerized databases are another form of electronically mediated communication that have been studied from various perspectives. Liberal writers have rightly been concerned that the vast store of data accumulated in this form and its relative ease of transfer poses a threat to the privacy of the individual. With so much information about individuals now digitalized in databases, one's life becomes an open book for those who have access to the right computers. Agencies of all kinds—military, police, governmental, corporate—continuously gather data to be exchanged from one computer to another while the individuals to whom the data refer have little control over this flow or, in many cases, knowledge of its existence. In the eyes of liberals, society is indeed nearing the nightmare of 1984, only a few years behind Orwell's schedule.

Marxists for their part have shown how data-bases are a new form of information as commodity, one which has largely passed into the control of the largest corporations. Increasingly society becomes divided into the information rich and the information poor. Existing class divisions on a national and even a global scale are reinforced and further sedimented by the technology of computerized information. As the economy relies more and more upon information, access to databases is not at all a trivial matter. The fate of companies, even nations, hinges upon the timely procurement of information. In comparison with feudal regimes, capitalist societies once prided themselves on establishing the free flow of information, thinking of this feature of modernity as a touchstone of freedom. The digitization of information in the form of databases acts to facilitate its instantaneous, global availability, so the restraint of commodification flies in the face of the advance of the technology.

While these perspectives are valuable for a full understanding of the database as a communication technology, they neglect a fundamental aspect of the phenomenon: its ability to constitute and multiply the identity of the individual and thereby to promote his/her control. The social model implicit in the above positions is one of individuals/groups confronting institutions and social forces in a relation of struggle, contest and opposition. At the most general level, liberals and Marxists assume a world of discrete, stable entities. Hence the notion of privacy, for example, with its sense of a micro-world in which individuals are sequestered from others and about which no one has knowledge without the explicit agreement of those individuals. Without such privacy, liberals contend, resistance to the state is impossible because privacy is a sort of small cloud within which critical reason may safely function, the space of independent thought, distant from the influence of the phenomenal, perceptual world of the senses. Liberals value urbanism precisely for its tendency to lose the individual in the anonymity of the crowd in contrast with the rural village in which everyone knows everything

about everyone else. The city, for them, is the locus of freedom, paradoxically because its density of population is an obscuring mask behind which the atomized individual may secure independent thought.

The contemporary urban quotidian strips the mask away. Individual actions now leave trails of digitized information which are regularly accumulated in computer databases and, at the speed of light or sound, transmitted back and forth between computers. Previously anonymous actions like paying for a dinner, borrowing a book from a library, renting a videotape from a rental store, subscribing to a magazine, making a long distance telephone call—all by interacting with perfect strangers—now is wrapped in a clothing of information traces which are gathered and arranged into profiles, forming more and more detailed portraits of individuals. This postmodern daily life is not one of discrete individuals, hidden behind shields of anonymity in market interactions with strangers; nor is it a return to the village of familiar faces.[6] Instead it combines features of both without the advantages of either. In the credit card payment for dinner, the waiter is a stranger but the computer which receives the information 'knows' the customer very well. Urban life now consists of face to face interactions with strangers coupled by electronically mediated interactions with machines 'familiar' with us. The lines dividing individual from individual and individual from institution are consistently crossed by computer databases, cancelling privacy as a model of action or even as an issue.

Information flows today double the action of individuals and subvert theoretical models which presuppose either privacy or the class struggle. Society is now a double movement: one, of individuals and institutions; another, of information flows. A recent television drama, for example, depicted the fine grained level of current information retrieval. A murderer attempted to secure his alibi by leaving a message on the answering machine of the person he murdered, falsifying the time of the call. But he did so from his cellular car phone so that the police were able to find out the actual time of the call because all such calls are logged by the cellular phone company. The murderer took into account one aspect of the mode of information (answering machines) but forgot another, the traces left in databases by calls from car phones.

Databases are inherently limited and restricted structures of information. Unlike the subtlety of narratives, they rely upon severe restrictions of inputs. In database programs only certain marks may be made in certain 'fields' or areas. For instance, if after the name of the individual, a 'field' for magazine subscriptions follows, normally one cannot fill this field with the name of the magazine, but only by a code for certain groups of magazines. Thus the *New Republic* might be coded as 'l' for liberal and the *Guardian* as 'r' for radical. If video rentals are included in the database, *Deep Throat* and *Last Tango in Paris* might both be coded as 'X'. Such simplification of data, one might complain, drastically distorts particular experience, but it also vastly facilitates the speed with which information may be retrieved. In this way, databases configure reality, make composites of individual experience that could be characterized as caricatures. By contrast, databases may also include graphics, that is to say pictures or copies of fingerprints, for example. Information about individuals then becomes much more complex. The important consideration, however, is not the question of verisimilitude: would any individual be pleased by the accuracy of the information portrait contained in a database? But rather that databases constitute additional identities for individuals, identities which—in the interactions between computers and between institutions which rely upon them, on the one hand, and individuals on the other—take the place of those individuals. When a computer search is done for John Smith, the output from the machine is, from the point of view of the receiving computer or institution, John Smith himself. Just as actions in daily life are doubled by information traces, so identities are multiplied in the interactions of computer databases.

The theoretical problem of accounting for the social impact of databases is best assisted by

the work of Michel Foucault. This is so in three senses: first, Foucault theorized power in relation to a specific social formation, the Panopticon, which has direct application to databases; secondly, Foucault theorized the relation between social phenomena and the subject that is relevant to the case of databases; and thirdly, Foucault theorized the relation between discourse and practice, ideas and action, attitudes and behaviour in a way that permits the understanding of databases outside the limitations of the paradigms of liberal and Marxist theory.

In *Discipline and Punish* Foucault uses the term Panopticon to designate the control mechanism in prisons by which a guard, stationed in a central tower, could observe the inmates, arranged in cells around the tower with windows facing in towards the tower, without himself being seen by them.[7] Panopticon, literally 'all-seeing', denotes a form of power which attempts to orient the prisoners towards the authority system of the prison as a step in their reformation or normalization. For the process of reform, the Panopticon is a part of a broader set of mechanisms which included a minutely regulated schedule, a file-keeping system on each prisoner, and so forth. What interests Foucault in the system of discipline is not only its micrological detail but also its 'positive' inscription of power. Unlike the central government which uses power as a 'negative' principle of preventing or denying certain activities, the Panopticon shapes and moulds the behaviour of the criminals, producing, in a sense, a new person, the prison inmate. The key to the mechanism of discipline is the continuous, systematic, unobserved surveillance of a population. The criminal is coerced to follow a plan and to be aware that the slightest deviation on his part from the plan would be observed and would have consequences for him. Through the workings of the Panopticon, a norm is imposed on a population, on its practices and its attitudes, a norm that is a result not of the imposition of someone else's will, as in feudalism, but rather of an anonymous authority that is seemingly omnipresent. In the Panopticon Foucault locates a system of power at the level of the everyday as opposed to the level of the state which combines discourses and practices to instantiate the social character of the inmate. As a general feature of society, the Panopticon is an example of what Foucault calls a 'technology of power' or a 'microphysics of power'.

In a second way Foucault's theory of the Panopticon applies to databases. As a positive instantiation of power, the Panopticon constitutes the individual criminal as an inmate. The discourse/practice of discipline produces the behaviours and attitudes of the prison population, regardless of the degree to which the prisoners resist or subvert that imposition. Their identity becomes that of an inmate however enthusiastic they may or may not have been about such a fate. By the same token, databases in the super-Panopticon constitute identities for each individual and they do so regardless of whether the individual is even aware of it. Individuals are 'known' to computer databases, have distinct 'personalities' for them and in relation to which the computer 'treats' them in programmed ways. These identities also serve as a basis for the communication between computers, communications that occur routinely and without the knowledge of the 'real person'. Such identities are hardly innocent since they may seriously affect the individual's life, serving as the basis for a denial of credit, of an FBI investigation, or the termination of social assistance, or the denial of employment or residence. In each case the individual is acted upon in relation to his or her identity as it is constituted in the database. Simply because this identity has no intimate connection with the internal consciousness of the individual, with his or her self-defined attributes, in no way minimizes its force or effectiveness. With the dissemination of databases, a communication technology pervades the social space and multiplies the identity of individuals, regardless of their will, intention, feeling or cognition.

In order fully to comprehend the significance of the constitution of identities by databases, one must appreciate the epistemological break Foucault enacts with the commonplace sense of the distinction between action and language,

behaviour and intention, a distinction that is one of the hallmarks of modern social theory. In relation to the social import of databases, Marxists, for example, concern themselves with the use made of databases by the state and the corporations. They criticize the way these organizations use databases to enhance their control and power over subordinate classes. In their work they maintain a clear distinction between institutions and individuals, action and knowledge, behaviour and information. The state is a force external to individuals, an institution whose power increases by dint of the tool of databases. The vast information at the state's disposal constitutes another link in the chain of oppression. By contrast Foucault focuses on the way power is both action and knowledge and the way power implicates the individual. He looks for the connections between phenomena which others see as discrete oppositions. The science of criminology for him is simply another element in the mechanism of discipline, not a privileged locus of truth outside the play of power. Similarly the individual's identity is not outside power but constituted by its operations, linked to it inextricably. The super-Panopticon then emerges not as an imposition or restraint upon the individual but rather as part of the individual's identity. Foucault's ability is to specify the relation that a Panopticon inmate derives from his post-structuralist rejection of the separation of mind and body, language and action, ideology and institution in favour of their mutual imbrication. My analysis of databases, following Foucault, moves to a model of communication in which the level of the subject is not cut off from practice, the body, power, institutions.

Databases, I argue, operate as a super-Panopticon. Like the prison, databases work continuously, systematically and surreptitiously, accumulating information about individuals and composing it into profiles. Unlike the Panopticon, the "inmates" need not be housed in any architecture; they need only proceed with their regular daily life. The super-Panopticon is thereby more unobtrusive than its forebear, yet it is no less efficient at its task of normalization.

Each characteristic of an individual's profile in a database is easily distinguished for unusual qualities, from credit ratings and overdue book notices to excessive traffic violations. Another advantage of the newer power mechanism over the older one is its facility of communications, or transport of information. Computers easily exchange databases, the information in one being accessible to others. Instantaneously, across the globe, information from databases flows in cyberspace to keep tabs on people. Databases 'survey' us without the eyes of any prison guard and they do so more accurately and thoroughly than any human being. A major impact of the super-Panopticon is that the distinction between public and private loses its force since it depended on an individual's space of invisibility, of opaqueness to the state and the corporations. Yet these characteristics are cancelled by databases because where ever one is and whatever one is doing, traces are left behind, traces that are transformed into information for the grist of computers.

Electronic writing is the third example of the mode of information as a communication technology. It covers a wide variety of writing practices, including word processing and hypertext,[8] electronic mail and message services and computer conferencing. In each case, the computer mediates the relation of author and reader, altering the basic conditions of the enunciation and reception of meaning.[9] Electronic writing continues the tendency begun with handwriting and print: it permits the removal of the author from the text, increases the distance, both spatial and temporal, of author from the reader and augments the problem of the interpretation of texts. Compared with speech, writing is a way of storing language, fixing it so that it can be read by those not directly intended by the author. Writing thus promotes the transmission of culture from generation to generation, the transformation of cultural works into monuments and the elevation of authors into authorities. Writing also fosters the development of critical thinking on the part of the reader: with words stabilized on the page, the reader can reflect upon them, go back to earlier passages and re-examine links of argument, and accomplish all of this in isolation without the presence of the author or the community exerting any pressure on the act of interpretation. Printing is often credited with shaping the autonomous rational individual, a condition of modern democracy. Electronic writing furthers all these features of handwriting and print simply because it is a far more efficient system of storage. Compared with print, digitized writing requires less time to copy and less space to store.

But electronic writing also subverts the culture of print.[10] In the case of word processing, the ease of altering digital writing, the immateriality of signs on the screen compared with ink on the page, shifts the text out of a register of fixity and into one of volatility. Also digital texts lend themselves to multiple authorship. Files may be exchanged between people in several ways, each person working on the text, with the result, in its spatial configuration on a screen or printed on paper, of hiding any trace of signature. In addition, hypertext programs encourage the reader to treat the text as a field or network of signs in which to create his or her own linkages, linkages which may become part of the text and which other readers may follow or change at their will. These programs permit searches for words or phrases throughout a text or group of texts which may be added to the text or saved. The result is a new text which brings terms together that were not so associated by the author. The reader has substituted her own hierarchy of terms for that of the author. With electronic writing the distinction between author and reader collapses and a new form of text emerges that may challenge canonicity of works, even the boundaries of disciplines.

Computer message services establish a form of communication that also subverts the culture of handwriting and print. There are several forms of these electronic 'post offices'. In the case of electronic mail, the individual has an 'address' on a computer and anyone who knows it may send a message or letter to it from his or her own computer. In another instance, certain computers serve as 'bulletin boards' which allow many individuals to browse through messages and leave their own. These 'electronic cafes' encourage strangers, individuals who have never met face to face, to communicate to one another. Strangers here exchange messages without the extraneous presence of the body or the voice, only signs passing from one to another. What is more, these bulletin boards use pseudonyms or handles: individuals do not use their own names and may easily disguise any of their attributes, such as gender or ethnicity. As a form of writing, the message services foster not the autonomous, rational stable individual but the playful, imaginative multiple self. In countries that have experimented extensively with message services, such as France, they have proved enormously popular.[11] People seem to enjoy a communication technology in which they invent themselves in the process of exchanging signs.

Another form of communication made possible by computer writing is computer conferencing.[12] In this instance, digital writing substitutes not for print but for face-to-face meetings and oral communications. Computer conferences eliminate the need for gathering people in one place at one time. There exists now an alternative to synchronous meeting or community as we know it. A central computer reserves an area for the conference. Individuals, using their personal computers hooked up to telephones, call that computer and read the presentations and comments of others, responding as they see fit. Studies of computer conferences reveal that the gain is not simply efficiency: new qualities of community relations develop in this cyberspace. Without the cues of body language, status, force of personality, gender, clothing style—all present in face-to-face situations—conversation changes in character. Interventions are less conventional, less deferential, as social authority is cancelled through computer writing. Criteria for effective responses change to typing speed and terse expression. Some analysts argue that computer conferencing creates conditions for a form of democracy more vibrant and animated by unorthodox thought than the colonial town meeting.[13] While this form of computer writing

may never fully replace traditional community, it offers an alternative to synchronous meeting that meliorates the increasing isolation of the information age.

The theory of deconstruction of Jacques Derrida anticipates in many ways changes brought about by computer writing. He counters the traditional theory of writing as fixity of meaning, monumentality, the authority of the author by focusing on the material aspect of signs inscribed on pages. He argues that such inscription leaves language open to multiple meaning, that the spacing of traces differs and displaces meaning away from the author, that the linear form of the book, with its order of pagination, its margins, its diacritical markings, its chapters and paragraphs, imposes a hierarchy that the reader may subvert by taking it as a text, a stream of marks whose contradictions and impasses are open to a close reading. Western thought relies upon printed writing to support the author's stable meaning, to insist that the book signifies only what the author intended. This 'logocentrism', as Derrida terms it, works by exclusions, supplements and marginalizations which may be reintroduced in a subversive reading. Books establish oppositions of terms, binaries in which one term is subordinate to the other and often absent from text. In the American Declaration of Independence the phrase 'All men are created equal' omits women and suppresses the question of race, even as it inscribes these groups as inferior. Deconstruction attempts to destabilize the march of univocal meaning in written texts by unlocking the logic of difference that it hides.

Derrida's interpretive gesture is similar to my understanding of electronic writing. Both deconstruction and electronic writing understand the volatility of written language, its instability and uncertain authorship. Both see language as affecting a destabilization of the subject, a dispersal of the individual, a fracturing of the illusion of unity and fixity of the self. Derrida, however, understands these qualities of writing as applying to all of its forms and he differentiates only partially between handwriting, print and digital writing.[14] Deconstruction, then, is Derrida's interpretation of writing in all its forms. By contrast my effort is to distinguish between print and electronic forms of writing, to assess the significance of the difference enacted by a new communication technology. Derrida's strategy removes the task of interpretation from the context of contemporary changes in culture and society, repeating the gesture of earlier thinkers by producing a discourse as a reinterpretation. Ultimately, then, the force of deconstruction returns to see Derrida as a Western philosopher, defeating his own effort to subvert that position. Nonetheless the corpus of Derrida's writing provides powerful analytic tools to criticize the cultural and ideological patterns that have accompanied print writing. In that way and to a certain extent, deconstruction permits the reading of texts in a manner that suits electronic writing.

In the examples of TV ads, databases and computer writing, post-structuralist perspectives permit a comprehension of the linguistic features of new communication technologies and relate these to the cultural problem of the constitution of the subject. In particular they enable us to see the way electronically mediated communication promotes a new configuration of the subject that may be termed postmodern in the sense that it is structurally different from that of the modern era. Research on the mode of information has barely begun and much remains to extend these analyses to communication technologies not even mentioned here. I want now to raise some epistemological and political issues concerning the use of post-structuralist theory in the field of communication studies and point to additional areas for further research.

The theory of mode of information intersects with critical social theory's recognition of the stalled dialectic. As the Frankfurt School recognized long ago, in the course of the twentieth century, working-class movements have become attenuated, have been abated or have disappeared altogether, interrupting or permanently suspending the dialectic of the class struggle. The critical social theory of the Frankfurt School and more generally Western Marxism interpreted this situation as the deleterious effect of mass culture on

the proletariat. However, these theorists do not adequately conceptualize the role of electronically mediated communications in the cultural integration of the working class into modern society. A good part of their difficulty stems from a theoretical model that does not account, with regard to the phenomena of mass culture, for the constitution of the subject through language, more specifically through the language patterns of the mode of information. The theoretical tendency of Western Marxism has been to approach the question of a politically stabilized modernity from orientations themselves far too rooted in modernity and its communication technologies. Like modern thinkers since Descartes, they attempt to establish an atemporal or universal foundation for theory which usually takes the form of some definition of the human.

The grounding of theory in the human tends to dehistoricize one's position, making it invulnerable to temporal contingency but also to render it blind to its dependence on that contingency. In the twentieth century, for example, communication has been dramatically altered by electronic technologies, a situation, as I argue above, that urges social theorists to look anew at many of their fundamental assumptions. The widespread dissemination of radio, telephone, film, television, computer enhanced communication such as electronic mail and computer conferencing, telex and fax machines, satellite communication systems changes not only communication but basic features of social life. Whatever *theoretical* priority one wishes to place on the question of communication, when recent *historical* developments are taken into account, it must move from the periphery to the centre of social science. But this means that the problem of communication theory begins with a recognition of necessary self-reflexivity, of the dependence of knowledge on its context. It requires from the outset a frank acknowledgement of contingency: the 'truth' of communication theory is registered in relation to historical change and is in no sense 'absolute', offering no vantage point from which one can claim a purchase on universality. A continuing issue for communication theory, then, is to sustain this sense of contingency, to develop strategies to avoid at every level and turn becoming grounded, stabilized, founded, established in the Truth. Communication theory must produce a new kind of truth, one not linked to the modernist goal of universality.

Because communication theory is so obviously and directly responding to the world with its unpredictable shifts and turns, the temptation is strong for theorists, at the epistemological level, to flee that world, to reduce that contingency, to find some stable ground upon which to secure a firm knowledge. Norbert Wiener's 'cybernetic' theory of communication, to take one example, turned for a ground to mathematics, the traditional locus of pure theory, a theory that appears at least not to depend in any way on the vagaries of human time.[15] Communication knowledge for him becomes a precisely determinable ratio of information to noise. But an important lesson learned from the impact on social theory of the shift to electronically mediated communication is that theory must avoid the pretence that it is independent of the world, protect itself at every point against slipping into the assumption that it is somehow constructed on a foundation of self-generated certainty. The first principle of communication theory in the age of electronic technology, then, is that there is no first principle, only a recognition of an outside of theory, an Other to theory, a world that motivates theory.

The requirement that theoretical categories have built into them a certain contingency or self-limitation faces an equal difficulty from an opposite side, the side of history. The danger here is that history, once invoked to forestall abstract theorizing, itself becomes a stable, dogmatic ground. In this case the context provides the foundation for theory: a presumed certainty or closure within the context of theory 'guarantees' its truth. The pertinent example in this case is Marxist writing on communications which takes the mode of production as a fixed horizon, focusing on questions that refer back to it (such as what is the effect of the corporate structure on the information age and vice versa) and omitting

or repressing questions that do not appear to relate to the class structure. History in this perspective is already a given and the new ingredient, in this case electronic communication, poses no new questions, merely reinforces old ones. For communication theory, the turn to history must sustain a sense of an open field, not a closed totality, a sensitivity to the new, not a confirmation of the already given.

Post-structuralist interpretive strategies are germane to communication theory because they attempt to confront both of these theoretical dilemmas. They make problematic both the authorial position of the theorist and the categories he/she develops. By focusing on language and stressing the instability of meaning in language, post-structuralist theory undermines the effort to dissolve communication into a 'real' of action or into a universal definition of the human. At the same time it calls into question versions of the relation of theory and history/context that present the latter as a closed or totalized field that serves to turn theory into ideology, into a discourse whose assumptions are disavowed or made invisible.[16] For these reasons post-structuralist theory opens the field of electronically mediated communication in a way that locates its internal complexity and its relation to culture. It enables one to see what is new in the dissemination and emplacement of these technologies.

Post-structuralist theory is often accused of its own kind of totalization, linguistic reductionism. It is charged with never going beyond the text, of depoliticizing social action, of theorizing only an endless play of discourse analysis. While the practice of some post-structuralists may lend itself to this accusation, my effort, in theorizing the mode of information, has been to counteract the textualist tendency by linking post-structuralist theory with social change, by connecting it with electronic communication technology, by 'applying' its methods to the arena of everyday life, by insisting on communications as presenting a historical context which justifies the move to an emphasis on language. The 'linguistic turn' of post-structuralism is apposite not only for its ability to critique modernist theory but because of changes in the sociohistorical field. By the same token, I relate post-structuralist theory to the mode of information to underline the contingency of that theory, not to provide it with a false stability, a solid foundation in history. The political implications of the resort to post-structuralism, then, must be viewed in this light.

Post-structuralist theory invalidates modernist political positions, those that rely upon a view of humanity as in need of emancipation from forms of external oppression.[17] These views presuppose man as centred in rational autonomy but as prevented from attaining this centre by institutions that block its realization: arbitrary government, religious intolerance, private appropriation of the means of production. However, the focus on language rejects this position because language already configures the individual. Only after the individual has been constituted as centred in rational autonomy by Enlightenment discourse does it appear that monarchy, institutional religion and capitalism are external fetters to freedom. If language is seen as already implicating the individual, then the question of emancipation changes its character. The question becomes one of understanding the positioning of the individual in the given language pattern and the relative change of altering that pattern, rather than one of a search for an absolute, universal beyond the given order, one that would somehow allow an already defined human creature to emerge as if from its tutelage, or chains.

Contemporary society contains modernist institutions and discourses which privilege certain configurations of the subject, those that support autonomous rationality, and subordinate others (women, ethnic minorities, etc.). But contemporary society also contains 'postmodernist' institutions and discourses, such as electronically mediated communications, which support new configurations of the subject. To the extent that it is now appropriate to raise the issue of the restrictions of modernist forms of subject constitution, electronic communication, understood in a post-structuralist sense, provides a basis for critique. This does not mean that every emission

from such communication technology is automatically revolutionary; by far the preponderance of these communications work to solidify existing society and culture. But there is a way of understanding their impact that reveals its potential for structural change. In other words, there is a secular trend emanating from electronic communication that undermines the stability of the figure of the rational autonomous individual. Hence the outcry against these forms of communication, the warnings of their dangers by those adhering to modernist political positions.

The other tendency that amplifies the post-structuralist understanding of the political impact of electronic communication is the spread of protest movements from outside the modernist paradigm, certain feminist and ethnic positions, certain aspects of gay and lesbian politics, certain kinds of ecological and anti-nuclear concerns. To the extent that the politics of these groups challenges the privilege of the rational individual as the universal ground of human identity (the Western tradition), they affect changes that are parallel with those of electronic communication. The operation of hegemonic ideology is effective to the extent that it is unrecognized. When everyone assumes that human beings have a nature, centred in reason, that is violated by institutional chains, then those chains are exposed but that ideology is confirmed. Electronic communication and the social movements mentioned above sometimes tend to put modernist ideology into question thereby changing the terms of political discussion. When this is effective, as in the effort to abandon the required teaching of Western civilization as the exclusive introduction to culture, modernists of all stripes, from the Marxist Eugene Genovese to the conservative Lynn Chaney, recognize only a threat to freedom. To those not completely under the spell of this ideology, its operations become manifest and hence dissolved: 'man' cannot mean Western man, rationality is not the final ground of human experience.

Electronically mediated communication opens the prospect of understanding the subject as constituted in historically concrete configurations of discourse and practice. It clears the way to seeing the self as multiple, changeable, fragmented, in short as making a project of its own constitution. In turn such a prospect challenges all those discourses and practices that would restrict this process, would fix and stabilize identity, whether these be fascist ones which rely on essentialist theories of race, liberal ones which rely on reason, or socialist ones which rely on labour. A post-structuralist understanding of new communication technologies raises the possibility of a postmodern culture and society that threatens authority as the definition of reality by the author.

NOTES

1. Mark Poster, *The Mode of Information* (Chicago: University of Chicago Press, 1990).

2. Elizabeth Eisenstein, *The Printing Press as an Agent of Change: Communications and Cultural Transformations in Early Modern Europe* (Cambridge/New York: Cambridge University Press, 1979).

3. Jean-François Lyotard, *Inhuman,* trans. Geoff Bennington and Rachel Bowlby (Cambridge: Polity Press, 1991).

4. J. Hillis Miller, 'The work of cultural criticism in the age of digital reproduction', in *Illustration* (Cambridge, Mass.: Harvard University Press, 1992).

5. Jean Baudrillard, *Selected Writings,* ed. Mark Poster, trans. Jacques Mourrain (Stanford, Calif.: Stanford University Press, 1988).

6. Joshua Meyrowitz, *No Sense of Place: The Impact of Electronic Media on Social Behavior* (New York: Oxford University Press, 1985).

7. Michel Foucault, *Discipline and Punish: The Birth of the Prison,* trans. Alan Sheridan (New York: Pantheon, 1977).

8. Michael Heim, *Electric Language: A Philosophical Study of Word Processing* (New Haven, Conn.: Yale University Press, 1987); George Landow, *Hypertext: The Convergence of Contemporary Critical Theory and Technology* (Baltimore: Johns Hopkins University Press, 1992).

9. Jay Bolter, *Writing Space: The Computer, Hypertext, and the History of Writing* (Hillsdale, NJ: Erlbaum, 1991).

10. Richard Lanham, 'The electronic word: literary study and the digital revolution', *New Literary History, 20* (1989), pp. 265–90.

11. Marie Marchand, *La Grande Aventure du Minitel* (Paris: Larousse, 1987).

12. Andrew Feenberg, 'Computer conferencing and the humanities', *Instructional Science, 16* (1987), pp. 169–86.

13. Starr Roxanne Hiltz and Murray Turoff, *The Network Nation: Human Communication via Computer* (London: Addison-Wesley, 1978).

14. Jacques Derrida, *Postcard: From Socrates to Freud and Beyond,* trans. Alan Bass (Chicago: University of Chicago Press, 1987).

15. Norbert Wiener, *The Human Use of Human Beings* (New York: Anchor, 1954).

16. Louis Althusser, 'Ideology and ideological state apparatuses', in *Lenin and Philosophy and Other Essays,* trans. Ben Brewster (London: New Left Books, 1971).

17. John Hinkson, 'Marxism, postmodernism and politics today', *Arena, 94* (1991), pp. 138–66.

29

COMMUNICATION AS THE MODALITY OF STRUCTURATION

JAMES R. TAYLOR, CAROLE GROLEAU,
LORNA HEATON, AND ELIZABETH VAN EVERY

SITUATED COMMUNICATION: "A TALKING OUT OF TEXT IN THE CIRCUMSTANCES OF A CONVERSATION"

We begin by inviting you to join us in performing a thought experiment. We are going to consider the sequence that initiated the situation in Operations, as reported by Suchman (1996), in two different ways. The segment of dialogue as she described it goes like this (the pauses and other punctuation can be ignored for our purposes; they are there to attest to the scientific rigor of the research):

1. Radio: Operations::ah(.)
2. (pilot) Four seventy one?
3. Ops A: (4.0) Rrahhh. [struggling with radio]
4. (.2) Four seventy one.
5. Radio: Yessir would you send
6. somebody out here the::ah(.) [Ops A looks to video monitor]
7. agent working the *jetway* here
8. is running around with their
9. *hands* up in the air (.2)
10. Ops A: //[laugh]
11. Radio //obviously
12. doesn't know how to work
13. //the uh: (.8) stairways or
14. can't get it to work (one).
15. We need some help.
16. Ops B: //Must be Sarducci [looks to monitor]
17. Ops A: Will advise. [looks to PP, or passenger service planner]
18. (1.0)

SOURCE: Taylor, J. R., Groleau, C., Heaton, L., & Van Every, E. (2000). *The computerization of work: A communication perspective* (pp. 80–92, 96–101). Thousand Oaks, CA: Sage.

Our thought experiment has two parts. First, imagine that you are either physically present in the Operations Room as this exchange is going on or looking at a videotaped version of it. Suppose also that instead of it being a "mid-sized metropolitan airport in the United States," this is all taking place in Pakistan and you do not speak the language (the version shown previously is a later rendering into English, not a faithful transcription of the original transaction). The only parts of the exchange that will be accessible to you are the "offstage" comments such as "looks to monitor," "looks to PP," or "radio." You will understand something of what is going on, but only something. For example, you probably will guess that this is a work conversation. You will be able to arrive at this conclusion for two reasons. First, it is clear that the circumstances are those that typically characterize work (uniforms, equipment, disposition of the room, attitudes of people that connote concentration on something, absence of idle chit-chat, and so on). Second, the interaction between the people in the room and the disembodied voice to which they are responding has the form of to-and-fro talk that is one of the defining properties of conversation, as an impressive body of research stretching back now more than a quarter of a century has made clear (the work of the field known as *Conversation Analysis*).

So you, as the observer, will know it is collective work and that it is a conversation—what Goffman (1963) called a "focussed gathering"—but you will not know exactly what it is about (for example, you will not be able to tell that the voice is that of an airline captain, although you might guess). You would not be able to say with much accuracy, afterward, what the "situation" was.

Now let us take a second step in our mental experiment. Suppose that it occurred not in Pakistan but indeed in a mid-sized American city. However, you are not present, and you do not have immediate access to a videotape of the episode (which, for us readers, is in fact the case). You have to rely on Suchman's (1996) account for whatever you know about the situation.

Suppose in addition that, instead of this segment appearing in an article written by a well-known and respected ethnographer, supported by marks of typical ethnographic framing (such as the punctuation to indicate pauses), we were to tell you that this is an extract from a Hollywood script proposal—or it could be for a new television series, let us say a humorous take on aviation, a sort of *Ally McBeal* with a twist.

Now it is not a conversation at all, or at least not a "real" conversation, even if it should eventually get acted out. It is just a segment of script—a piece of text. There is no "real" situation, for the moment, other than the one dreamed up in the head of the author, even though you now understand perfectly well, unlike before, what the situation is! There are no pilots, no supervisors, no ramp crew, and you could not possibly be sitting in on the situation or (until it is actually produced as a film or TV show) be viewing it on videotape. And Lucy Suchman would be turned into what John Van Maanen (1988) said an ethnographer really is: a teller of tales.

How did you know, based on a script, what the situation was? Again, two factors supply the explanation. First, there are the words people were using: *operations, agent, jetway, hands up in the air, stairways* (as in "working the stairways"), *help, advise.* These communicate because you can link them with what linguists call a *common ground* or *frame knowledge* (Goldberg, 1995; Werth, 1993): You know about airports, and radio communication, and how stairways are used to get passengers off planes, and what throwing your hands up in the air means, and how impatient passengers get when there are delays. Scriptwriters count on your frame knowledge, even when they toss in a bit of jargon, such as "Four seventy-one," because it adds that little extra touch of authenticity (as long as you recognize it as technical talk, of course).

Second, the script unfolds in the way it should: following lines that you recognize as characteristic of stories, such as a dilemma, a call for help, some perplexity as to how to respond. You are ready for what follows because stories are supposed to work this way. It is your

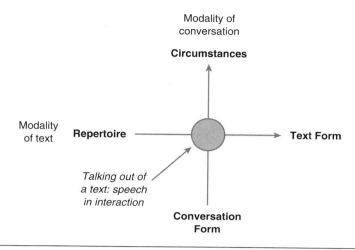

Figure 29.1   Communication as the Intersection of Axes of Conversation and Text

ability to recognize these kinds of sequencing patterns of turn-taking as meaningful that linguists claim calls on "construction knowledge" (Goldberg, 1995).

What are we trying to show by this little thought experiment? Our point is this: Human communication occurs at the intersection of two modalities—conversation and text. Deprived of access to its text (talking and other linguistic expressions, such as writing), conversation still has meaning—but not its usual meaning. This is the Pakistani airport illustration. Similarly for text: Taken out of conversational context, it is reduced to its essential textuality—a resource for communication, but not communication itself. This is the Hollywood script illustration.

Communication thus supposes a talking out of text in the circumstances of a conversation. The talking out supposes not just an actant (a speaker) but also at least one reactant (a listener). To illustrate, imagine communication as occurring at the intersection of two axes, one representing conversation, the other text (see Figure 29.1).

The sense of this figurative representation of communication is as follows. Conversation is framed by two parameters: (a) *circumstances* (of

time, place, occasion, persons, materiality, etc., the basis for the "situatedness" of which Suchman writes) and (b) *conversation form* (the need to maintain an orderly back-and-forth sequencing of speaking as part of the dynamics of interactive talk, in the absence of which conversational coherence becomes impossible). Text is similarly framed by two parameters: (a) the existence of a *repertoire* of basic frame knowledge that forms the common ground of the communicators (without which they have no shared basis for the interpretation of events) and (b) *text form* (the syntactic and other generative rules that must be respected for communicators to produce a comprehensible string of language and thus to speak intelligibly and be understood).

Sense-making, of the text-dependent kind we automatically do unless we find ourselves in the unusual circumstance of a Pakistani airport, involves two orders of mapping: (a) of circumstance onto *frame knowledge* and (b) of patterns of interaction (what conversation analysts call *adjacency pairs*) onto *construction knowledge* (see Figure 29.2). Frame knowledge is simply the sum of acquired understandings that makes it possible for us to recognize a situation and to formulate our interpretation in language (as

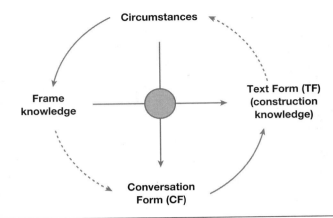

Figure 29.2   The Construction of Sense (Interpretation of Circumstances) and the Organization of Talk
(Creating a Basis for Collective Action)

the captain and the operations room crew were struggling to do in Suchman's 1996 case study). Construction knowledge is that branch of understanding that permits participants in a conversation to interact both by producing comprehensible strings of language ("agent . . . running around with their hands up in the air") and knowing how to address speech to someone else in such a way as to produce a desired effect on them ("Would you send somebody out here"). It is more than simply knowing how to formulate sentences; it means being able to frame explanations, give direction, argue a point, tell a story— all the forms of expression that language furnishes to structure the flow of interaction and lend it an intrinsic meaning.

When the mapping has been accomplished as a collective achievement mediated by interaction, two distinct but interrelated (and interdependent) features of communication will emerge:

1. *Cognitively,* a situation has been produced to which the participants are now cooriented, in that their understandings of the circumstances are sufficiently aligned to have established for themselves a basis of coherent conversation.

2. *Pragmatically,* a basis of collective action has been created, in which roles have been negotiated (or reinforced) and the aligning of an agent-to-agent relationship is under way (what we earlier called the formation of a head/ complement system of agency).

[. . .]

What initially had been a two-dimensional space or communication potential is now transformed into a one-dimensional vector, in which communication is seen to mediate the passage from a reading of a situation into a resolution of it (solving the problem of the malfunctioning stairways, for example), and thus a basis of collective action: *fact* to *conclusion,* mediated by *acts of speech.* It is this that Hutchins (1995) refers to as *distributed cognition.* A single collective agency—a power to act together—has been produced.

It is by such a mapping of one dimension– situated interaction—onto another—text—that circumstances are transformed into a "situation" and the conditions are created for the processes of distributed cognition necessary to deal with it (see Figure 29.3). Specifically, (a) the elements of circumstance are given a name and in this way

FACTS ⟶ ACTS OF SPEECH ⟶ CONCLUSION

Figure 29.3   The Transformation of Facts Into Conclusion Through Interaction

matched with available frame knowledge; and (b) the patterns of interaction that are characteristic of all species interaction—not just human—are interpreted semantically, and the meaning of behaviors, as well as the identity of those who generate them, is produced. In other words, a theory of situated communication is also a theory of distributed cognition, and vice versa.

Following the analytical scheme of Marr (1982) and Hutchins (1995), communication can be analyzed as (a) *mediation,* in the usual sense of that word—how information is physically displayed and exchanged (face-to-face, by phone, radio and television, in Suchman's example); (b) a representation of a situation in some code or language—verbal, graphic, or whatever (the *symbolic* function of communication);[1] and (c) entering into the problem-solving process itself and how it thus mediates (comes to direct) collective action in a situation (for example, it furnished the only means by which the personnel in the Operations Room could play an effective role in the minidrama unfolding on the ramp because they were connected to it only electronically, not physically). This is the *essential* function of communication.

The essential function of communication, in other words, is about speech as action. But action, as Giddens points out, involves the exercise of power. To explain why communicative action generates relations of domination, we introduce the concept of agency.

The Centrality of Agency in Communication Theory

A fundamental difference between our interpretation of the theory of structuration and that of Giddens . . . is in how we understand the terms "agent" and "agency." Giddens thinks of agency as individual action. We think of agency as acting-*for* someone or something. An agent is the actor-who-acts-*for.* It is in the acting-*for* that structuration occurs—how relationships of interdependence and domination form and are sustained. Acting-*for* is organization in the making.

Consider again the minidrama reported by Suchman (1996). The operations crew has been galvanized into action by a call from the arriving pilot, and their attention is now focused on getting the stairway reactivated. We describe this as an *A-B-X* unit. The object, repairing the stairs, is *X.* The agent whose activities are being described to us (the operations team) is *B.* But *B* is acting for a waiting airplane crew and their passengers. They are *A.* We could say that a communication unit has formed, for the duration of the crisis, based on acting and acting-for. Newcomb (1953) called this a *co-orientation system,* and we believe it to be the building block of organization (see Figure 29.4).

Let us consider some of the properties of the *A-B-X* unit.

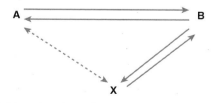

Figure 29.4   The Concept of a Co-Orientation System

Agents may be collective as well as individual. The components of an *A-B-X* unit are defined by the structure of relationships and not the other way around. Objects, for example, are defined by the purposes of agents. An object is something to which we do not attribute intention; it is the target of an intention. An agent, *A* or *B,* is defined both by the objects that are their preoccupation and for whom they act (or who acts for them). Whether *A* or *B* is a single individual, a collaborative team of workers, or a corporation is not fundamental.

To act, one must have the status of agent—acting for someone or something. Agency exists only in its *A-B-X* connections. Because the *A* and the *B* in any given relationship are both agents, it follows that the *A* in one relationship must be the *B* in another (otherwise *A* would not be an agent because he, she, or it would not be acting for). The pilot acts for his crew and passengers (his *B*-ness, because he acts for), but in his dealings with operations he is the one making a request (his *A*-ness, because he asks someone else to act for him). Similarly, the operations crew is responding to the call from the aircraft (*B*-ness) but initiates the call to ground crew (*A*-ness). This recursive transfer of agency explains a second property of co-orientation.

Co-orientation has characteristics of a fractal.[2] A fractal is a repetition of structure at finer and finer degrees of scale. We began by describing the situation as an aircraft making a request of operations. But it was in fact Ops A that the Captain spoke to—two individuals, each representing their community of discourse in that transaction. Then both Ops A and Sup got in touch with someone in ground crew. Now a new *A-B-X* unit forms: Operations-Ground crew—two communities of discourse linked by talk. Then Sup phones the other airline to request a loan of stairs. This produces another *A-B-X* co-orientation—two companies interrelated by the request for assistance. Then Sup has PP (passenger service) make a phone call for him. Here, the *A-B-X* unit is individual-to-individual, but it is embedded in a larger unit: Operations-Ground Crew.

Although some of these relationships may be interpreted as interpersonal—Sup and PP, for example—even there institutionally defined identities are involved. Some relationships involve whole work groups: the airplane crew, the operations team, ground crew. And some are corporate: one airline asking a favor of another. And there are virtual actors involved as well: the passengers, for example.

The *A-B-X* concept, in other words, is generic, a tool of analysis intended to point to the communicational characteristics of a situation. It describes the formation of an agency relationship, wherever that occurs, and whomever or whatever it involves. The importance of highlighting agency is that it is in the negotiation and renegotiation of the agency relationships that organizing occurs. From these considerations, a third principle follows.

Agency relationships tend to become imbricated. Imbrication means quite simply the arranging of units so as to overlap like the tiles on a roof. An *A-B-X* unit illustrates a form of layering, in that, for example, the aircraft crew cannot complete the unloading of their passengers without the contribution of ground crew in making sure the stairway is in place for the passengers to disembark—an imbrication of agency. Ground crew presumably mobilizes its own agencies. Some of those agencies are human; some are not. And so on. On the fractal principle, the imbrication of agencies can be as dense as one likes (or can design).

Co-orientation explains the constancies in organizational performance—why structures persist when they become imbricated. The principle of co-orientation thus appears to us to be a powerful tool in explicating the structurational principle of the propagation of structure in systems of interaction. We return to the issue of imbrication shortly.

Narrative Theory and the Structuring Role of Time

An important dimension of structuration theory . . . is the role of time in structuring activity. One way that time functions to structure events is by its narrativization. The sequencing of Suchman's (1996) episode, for example, can be seen as a trajectory. The failure of the stairs led the captain to contact Operations, and they in turn were led to communicate with the ramp crew, with maintenance, and with another airline. In this unfolding drama, the participants moved progressively from an assessment of the facts, to an exploration of possible solutions to the problem, to an eventual resolution of the situation, and—breathing a sigh of relief—back to routine. The event thus had a structure. It is, as embodied in Suchman's account, the structure of a *narrative*. She founds her analysis on the telling of a story.

Narrative structures are built around the core of a *transaction*. In its simplest form, a narrative unfolds in five steps (Greimas, 1987; Groleau & Cooren, 1999):

• A breakdown occurs, requiring constructive action.

• A principal engages an agent in the service of performing some task (this is the initiation of the transaction, and it may or may not imply negotiation of terms, persuasion, seduction, threats, promises, etc.; in effect, a head-complement relationship is established, aircraft/operations, for example).

• The principal's agent (Operations, in our example) assembles such skills, helpers, tools, and knowledge of the situation as may be necessary in the performing of the task (a phase of the narrative that frequently involves the formation of secondary principal-agent relationships—stories within stories).

• The agent (or perhaps the agent's agent, or the agent's agent's agent) carries through the action.

• The breakdown is resolved, or not, to the satisfaction of the requester, and the agent is compensated, rewarded, thanked, or otherwise acknowledged or punished (the sanction completes the transaction).

This is a structure that is endemic to narrative analysis. It applies straightforwardly to Suchman's incident: There is a breakdown; the skipper of the plane engages the intervention of airport operations; the latter, as agent, mobilizes a number of subagents; and the principal performance (repairing the stairs) is carried through, to the satisfaction of all. Suchman presumably chose this incident for analysis precisely because it had story characteristics. How to form a narrative is part of frame knowledge, part of how and why language serves as a modality of structuration (Giddens's "interpretive schemes").

What Is Meant by *Situation*?

What do we mean by the term *situation*? Consider again the Operations Room and the minicrisis that was occupying its attention in the episode Suchman (1996) analyzed. On the one hand, there were already what might be called *circumstances:* certain people with a certain history, the physical layout of the room and of the airport in which it is located, a range of sophisticated communication equipment, a set of activities that occur in a fairly regular pattern throughout the day and night, and so on. These we take to form the relatively constant background of the work group and its field of operations: a taken-as-given. On the other hand, there is a purpose that, to at least some degree, has temporarily galvanized everyone in the room and focused their attention on resolving a problem that has arisen: the breakdown of the stairs. It is the existence of this focus of attention that we take to be the motivation for speaking of circumstances as transformed into a situation.[3]

The components of a situation include (a) a focus of attention or "object," (b) resources to be mobilized, and (c) constraints to be respected.

The stairs, whose breakdown results in the upsetting of the usual uneventful unloading process, are normally a taken-as-given part of the infrastructure. They have become

a. A focus of attention and a locus of purpose precisely because they have ceased to be what they usually are—a resource to be automatically called up in the accomplishment of a task, unloading the passengers. They have been transformed from an out-of-awareness part of a given technology into a goal, and other resources will now need to be called into play. By their having become a goal, they in turn determine

b. which other circumstantial elements will be relevant to the situation (maintenance, ground crew, another airline).

All those elements are "downstream," potential instrumentalities to resolve the situation. The passengers impatiently waiting to get off the plane and the aircraft crew dealing with them constitute a third element of the unfolding situation. That is the "upstream" part of the equation:

c. That part of the organization for whom it is the operations room that is seen as a resource to be mobilized.

So although all these different elements are part of the situation, we can distinguish between (a) what is to be accomplished—the goal; (b) that which may be called on to accomplish it—resources; and (c) other constraints in the situation, such as the need to disembark the passengers, assist them in making connections, clear the ramp for the next flight, and so on. (It is because there is an upstream and a downstream that we know the system is imbricated.)

When the stairs stopped working—broke down—they then became an object of conscious care with properties that needed to be addressed. Now they had become *present-at-hand*. As Winograd and Flores (1986) wrote, "Objects and properties are not inherent in the world, but arise only in an event of breaking down in which they become present-at-hand" (p. 36). The stairs became "stairs" (for purposes of communication) only when, to again cite Winograd and Flores, they "presented themselves" as stairs in a breaking down or, to put it another way, in a state of *unreadiness-to-hand*.

It is in this sense that Engeström (1990) speaks of an "object," that part of the situation on which attention is focused because it needs attention. But note, however, that as the stairs became present-at-hand, they simultaneously made salient some otherwise *ready-to-hand* parts of the Operations team's physical and social environment, including maintenance crews, impatient passengers and pilots, and other airlines. These elements of the situation were normally also transparent—for purposes of ordinary work, invisible—but they now had to be consciously addressed by those in the team. Because these had also become present-at-hand objects that could be activated instrumentally, they were now a focus of attention. Similarly, such secondary considerations as passenger irritation, missed line connections, and delayed landing schedules now became salient.

Finally, we have to take account of one other element in the situation (and which contributes to defining it as a situation), namely, the Operations crew itself. This is what Engeström designates as "subject," but because sometimes that which acts is both human and nonhuman, we prefer to use the neutral term *actant*. So these are the elements: a problem resulting from a breakdown, an operation to repair the source of the breakdown (which implies the mobilization of resources, a goal on which attention is focused), an actant, and an instrumentality by means of which the resources can be put to effect).[4]

We can now define what is meant by the *situatedness* of communication: Communication is that process by which objects and their properties (things to be consciously addressed) are made present-at-hand in a system of distributed cognition.

This definition makes it clear that communication occurs in a situation but is not the situation itself. Instead, communication is that process by which what had previously been ready-to-hand (imbricated agency) is transformed into present-at-hand for those whose attention is being focused on a common goal-object.

Imbrication as a Principle of Structuration

Giddens always has been clear on the relation of practical to discursive knowledge. Most of what occurs as activity is routine, not requiring much in the way of active discussion or even conscious attention. One of the challenges that presents itself to a communication theory of structuration is how to represent the structuring effect of routine work in a manner that is consistent with other elements of the theory. We address this problem by introducing the concept of imbrication.

To be imbricated, as we have said, means to be arranged so as to overlap like roof tiles or shingles, the scales of a fish, or the leaves of a tree. In such a structure, each tile has its own integrity, but it is the interdependence between tiles—each of which both supports and is supported by others—that explains the capacity of the roof, or skin (of a fish), or foliage (of a tree), to form a shield of protection against the elements—to provide shade from the sun, for example, or protect against the rain. Applied to organizational analysis, we understand this to be the way that interagency relationships are interweaved to form a durable organizational infrastructure.

Nobody (or no thing), we have been saying, would be able to do their job in an organization if there were not many others doing theirs. A single flight of any large modern airliner supposes the ongoing actions of thousands of agents—probably millions, if all the working parts of the aircraft and airport and rental agencies and ticket offices, and so forth, are counted. But all these agency relationships quickly become, as Suchman (1995) puts it, "invisible" in ordinary circumstances of work, a taken-for-granted background of "infrastructure." This is the indispensable grounding of tiled agencies quietly functioning away, out of sight and mind, that nevertheless makes the organization work. All this imbrication is, in Heidegger's (1959) term for it, *ready-to-hand,* becoming visible only when there is what he calls a *breakdown (Geworfenheit)*—a failure of one of the indispensable tiles.

Our use of the term *imbrication* is intended to emphasize the tendency in organizations to proceduralize agency by making its operation automatic. Installing machinery is a way to imbricate agency because, once in place and working, it performs reliably on demand.

System designers are currently preoccupied with development of agents who can perform the multiple tasks that are required to make Internet communication a reality. A major objective of technology, typically, is to imbricate agency. But once imbricated, one generation's technology becomes an impediment to the acceptance of the next (Star & Ruhleder, 1996). Imbricated structures are resistant to change. That is the natural strength of this form of organizing—but also its weakness.

[. . .]

"Enactment" and the "Dance of Agency": The Outward Reach of Collaborative Groups

Pickering (1995) imagines scientific research as a "dance" of agency: scientists act and nature reacts, to produce an ongoing dialogue of scientific investigation, or what he calls a *dialectic of resistance and accommodation.* Weick (1979) developed a similar idea in his organizational theory of enactment: He sees action and cognition as a coupled system of act/learn in which people's actions produce the environment to which they subsequently orient. The communication that links a working group to its environing organizational context may similarly be thought of as "enactment," or as part of a continuing dance of agency, even though the "environment" in question is the rest of the organization—mostly other conversations (Figure 29.5).

Figure 29.5 shows two additional effects of the communication sequence that we have not mentioned before: (a) the circumstances have been affected by the actions of the group; and (b) the form of the conversation, including the identity and position of interactants within it, has been reiterated. By *dance of agency,* then, Pickering (1995) means the cyclic character of action. In one phase, knowing precedes acting; in the other, it follows.

For Pickering (1995), what scientists or system designers discover or design depends on what they have learned already and how they now set up the conditions for further inquiry. . . .

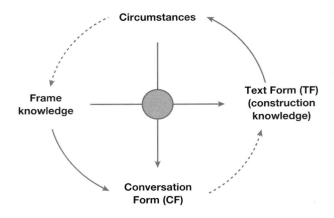

Figure 29.5   The Consequentiality of Communication

Of course, it is true that the circumstances to which people respond are already framed by the ongoing involvement of people in the activity in which the circumstances arise. A breakdown in passenger unloading is already framed by airport operations. But it is equally the case that, as Weick (1979) pointed out, circumstances are selected by managers and organizations through their proactive interventions (the supervisor's call to another airline, for example). Groups have an outward reach because they affect circumstance, and this same circumstance may link them to others in the organization.

Similarly the "form" of the conversation is dictated in good part by circumstances. There are, as Bakhtin (1986) was among the first to observe, "speech genres." The conversational patterns of an operations room in an airport, the navigation on a naval vessel, or the crew of a commercial airliner are specific to the kind of circumstances those different organizations encounter. Out of the fund of potentially relevant understandings possessed by some working community, circumstances serve to highlight—bring to the foreground of attention—some parts of their frame knowledge, whereas others remain virtual. Frame knowledge includes awareness of what the conversation is about, who participates in it, and what identities they

are expected to assume. The roles that people are called on to play there are part of their established frame knowledge. Identities, in other words, have a contextual dimension and are sensitive to circumstance.

What we now explore is the communicational implications of a group's tie to its larger organizational context, mediated by circumstances. An organization, after all, is composed of more than any one unit of situated activity or ongoing conversation. It is an interlinking of conversations, joined to each other through shared circumstances. The result is the construction of units of co-orientation and collective action involving, not just individuals, but groups and the organization itself. Because of the larger context, interfaces are created between groups, each locally situated, and between the local and the global—the trans-situational.

[. . .]

ORGANIZATION AS A METACONVERSATION, OR "CONVERSATION OF CONVERSATIONS"

An organization can be thought of as a dense overlay of many conversations, each oriented to some phase of activity. Boden (1994) used the expression a *lamination of conversations*. Krippendorff (1998) employed the term *an ecology of conversations*. Whatever the nomenclature, the concept is the same: a flowing, constantly evolving intersection of universes of talk in which people are caught up. It would be hard to contradict Boden's contention that the basic material out of which organizational reality is fabricated is situated talk, or conversation. It is where the meaning of events is negotiated and collective action engendered. The question of how such discursive universes link to each other, however, is what we now address. We do not want to focus on the conversations any longer but on the structural connections that link them. We are not so much interested in the processes by which conversations take form and become interrelated as in the structuring effect that follows as they do.

The Organization Considered as Itself a Unit of Action

Consider organizational communication in the context of our model (Figure 29.5). First, the "circumstances" that apply are those that confront the organization as a whole, no longer any particular subset of it (e.g., competition from other firms or countries, government law and regulation, or sweeping technological change). Second, the "conversation" must be conceived as a conversation of conversation—a metaconversation (typically, involving levels of management and policy-making). "Conversation form" can no longer be assumed to function only according to the rules of face-to-face interaction. The participants in this larger "conversation" speak for conversations (represent them), and much of the interaction is mediated by textual characterizations of groups and their work (e.g., statistics, reports, or projects). "Frame knowledge" here relates to corporate identities and issues (the nature of the organization, the structure of the hierarchy, corporate policies, etc.). Similarly, "construction knowledge" incorporates assumptions about the interaction appropriate to corporate actors (e.g., how to deal with

other departments). Institutional constraints enter the picture; rules and procedures become important.

Nevertheless, in spite of these significant differences, the organization confronts the same basic challenge as the small work group: how to transform a situation into a result ("fact" into "conclusion") and itself into a coordinated collaborative actor. The corporation-wide system of discourse also can be conceptualized as a form of distributed cognition. It too needs to reflexively monitor the flow of events and, using its accumulated frame knowledge, generate a rationalized interpretation of its own actions. It too needs to mobilize the actions of its members to produce a collective response to circumstances. As in the smaller group, the mobilization of action generates a hierarchy, or system of domination, with this difference: It is not just individuals, but groups as well, that are being structured. The organization too achieves a mobilization of action by the formation of co-orientation (*A-B-X*) units and depends for much of its routine performance of activities on the imbrication of head-complement relations. It too comes to be accorded the status of agent: The organization becomes an actor and can position its community in interaction with other actor-networks in the larger society. Finally, its processes too are subject to the principle of a dialectic of control, a dynamic of "resistance and accommodation."

An interface between two levels of communication is created, each with its special self-organizing properties. At one level, communication occurs in the way we have been describing in the first part of this chapter: as a critical enabler in the performance of tasks, in a situated world of local circumstances. At the second level, communication occurs as a linking-up of all these locally situated discursive universes into one enveloping metaconversation. We visualize as a cycle the interface that this embedding of one level of discourse within another produces, a cycle in which the local is successively translated into the global and the global into the local (Figure 29.6).

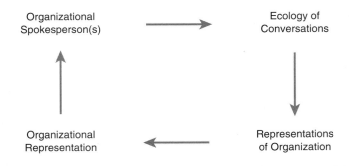

Figure 29.6   The Embedding of Levels of Discourse to Form an Organization

Because the cycle is an unbroken system of interlevel translations from one domain of communication to another, we can in principle take any of the elements of Figure 29.6 as our starting point and read the cycle either clockwise or counterclockwise. Suppose we begin from the multiple conversations of locally situated work and proceed clockwise. In one way or another, those conversations must be translated into "representations" if they are to figure in the global metaconversation, either as objects of attention (what other people talk about, manage, plan, or design) or as subjects (corporate actors who make their influence felt through the intermediary of spokespersons who assume the role of agents). The effect is analogous to the dynamic we discussed earlier: There are interactants (domains of work represented either cognitively, pragmatically, or both) who confront a situation (that of the organization) but have yet to organize themselves into a collective system of action to deal with it. For the organization to emerge as an actor, therefore, these disparate representations must resolve themselves into a single representation of the situation, which is that of the organization-as-a-whole. Here, the notion of distributed cognition again applies: Only when, through whatever interactive means, the organization has cognitively recognized its circumstances and transformed them into a situation can we say that the organization has a view. And if it has no view, it is not yet an actor capable of

being attributed an intention. One further step remains: the alignment of organizational actors into a system of action, which expresses itself as a single voice (the cognitive representation transformed into a pragmatic representation).

When the communicative process is complete, the organization is enabled to perform as an agent, or actor-network (i.e., one that speaks for and to the multiple interactants that compose it).

The other "interface" of local and global is represented by the upper line of Figure 29.6. It is an interface because, from the perspective of the organization-as-an-agent, the conversations of its multiple component-situated universes of discourse constitute part of its circumstances (and not just its composition). Similarly, for those caught up in the situated world of work, the discourse of the larger organization is part of their circumstances—an exterior influence to which they have to pay attention along with others, such as those emanating from other actors, including other parts of the organizational complex.

We could equally well read Figure 29.6 counterclockwise. The situated universes of discourse of an organization assume a background of corporate resources and a shared infrastructure. The "organization," as a socially constructed entity, assumes an ideological basis in the frame knowledge of its society. The modern corporation or government department is an invention of the last century and a half, an idea that has emerged in parallel with its pragmatic realization as a system of people and technology. That idea is nurtured by an ongoing dialogue involving both theoreticians and practitioners (basically the domain of management and administration science and of the sociology of organizations). And, of course, none of this would have any meaning in the absence of the reconstruction of the basis of organization in the day-to-day activities of its members.

Figure 29.6 thus describes a system with deep cultural roots. It is, as much as any technology, a historically situated artifact, a product of the collective enterprise of a particular society. That it is an artifact constructed out of communication constitutes its singularity, but in other respects it is merely one more development in an unbroken chain that links us back to *homo faber*— humankind as indefatigable craftsperson. It is still being designed, computerization being no more than an instrumentality being put to work toward that end.

NOTES

1. In systems development, as in communication research, this has sometimes been taken to be the principal function of communication: messaging, or information transmission

2. For a quite different interpretation of the company as fractal, see Warnecke (1993).

3. The distinction we are making between "circumstances" and "situation" is motivated by an insight of Heidegger (1959), the difference between ready-to-hand and present-at-hand (*zuhanden, vorhanden*). In the normal course of events, as Suchman (1996) emphasized, the circumstantial world that framed the activities of the people in Operations was largely transparent. As long as the stairs functioned properly, they were just there—part of a system that could safely be left out of consciousness, because they automatically came into play when they were needed, the object of somebody else's attention, perhaps, but not of the Operations personnel. For the latter, they were, by Heidegger's definition, ready-to-hand.

4. Note that the goal already figures in the definition of the situation, as well as the operation (and the

technology) that intervenes to realize the goal. This is a logical consequence of the structurational principle that activities become meaningful through monitoring and rationalization.

REFERENCES

Bakhtin, M. M. (1986). *Speech genres and other late essays.* Austin: University of Texas Press.

Boden, D. (1994). *The business of talk: Organizations in action.* Cambridge, MA: Polity.

Engeström, Y. (1990). *Learning, working and imagining.* Helsinki, Finland: Orienta-Konsultit Oy.

Goffman, E. (1963). *Behavior in public places.* New York: Free Press.

Goldberg, A. E. (1995). *Constructions: A construction grammar approach to argument structure.* Chicago: University of Chicago Press.

Greimas, A. J. (1987). *On meaning: Selected writings in semiotic theory.* Minneapolis: University of Minnesota Press.

Groleau, C., & Cooren, F. (1999). A socio-semiotic approach to computerization: Bridging the gap between ethnographers and systems analysts. *Communication Review, 3*(1–2), 125–164.

Heidegger, M. (1959). *An introduction to metaphysics* (R. Mannheim, Trans.). New Haven, CT: Yale University Press.

Hutchins, E. (1995). *Cognition in the wild.* Cambridge, MA: MIT Press.

Krippendorff, K. (1998). *Ecological narratives: Reclaiming the voice of theorized others.* Unpublished manuscript, University of Pennsylvania.

Marr, D. (1982). *A computational investigation into the human representation and processing of visual information.* New York: Freeman.

Newcomb, T. (1953). An approach to the study of communicative acts. *Psychological Review, 60,* 393–404.

Pickering, A. (1995). *The mangle of practice.* Chicago: University of Chicago Press.

Star, S. L., & Ruhleder, K. (1996). Steps toward an ecology of infrastructure: Design and access for large information spaces. *Information Systems Research, 7*(1), 111–134.

Suchman, L. (1995). Making work visible. *Communications of the ACM, 39*(9), 56–68.

Suchman, L. (1996). Constituting shared workspaces. In Y. Engeström & D. Middleton (Eds.),

Cognition and communication at work (pp. 35–60). Cambridge, UK: Cambridge University Press.

Van Maanen, J. (1988). *Tales of the field: On writing ethnography.* Chicago: University of Chicago Press.

Warnecke, H. J. (1993). *The fractal company, a revolution in corporate culture.* Berlin: Springer-Verlag.

Weick, K. (1979). *The social psychology of organizing.* Reading, MA: Addison-Wesley

Werth, P. (1993). Accommodation and the myth of presupposition: The view from discourse. *Lingua, 89,* 39–95.

Winograd, T., & Flores, F. (1986). *Understanding computers and cognition: A new foundation for design.* Norwood, NJ: Ablex.

GOOD TO TALK?

DEBORAH CAMERON

I think a lot of people tend to take communication for granted in some way . . . it's something they don't have to think about . . . if they perhaps learned to do it better it would improve everything else—all other aspects of their life.

—Anonymous respondent, *National Communication Survey,* 1996

Throughout the 1990s, 'it's good to talk' was the advertising slogan used by the phone company British Telecom (BT).[1] I imagine the advertising agency chose it for much the same reason that I am recycling it: not because it is original or witty, but because it is a truism—indeed, it is one of the great clichés of our time.

In its advertising, BT uses the everyday word, 'talk'. Elsewhere, it prefers the more formal and technical term 'communication'. In 1996, the BT Forum (a BT-funded body that sponsors research on 'the role of communication in society') commissioned the first in a promised series of National Communication Surveys, Listening to the Nation. Researchers interviewed a random sample of almost 1000 people. Among the 'head-line findings' they reported were that 83% of respondents agreed with the statement 'good communicators lead happier lives', and 73% agreed that 'making the effort to communicate is the key to happy relationships with people'. At the same time, only half considered themselves to be good communicators, and 60% expressed a desire to be better. One respondent commented: 'I think a lot of people take communication for granted in some way . . . it's something they don't have to think about . . . if they perhaps learned to do it better, it would improve everything else—all other aspects of their life'.[2]

It seems then that people attach considerable importance to 'communication'. Good communication is said to be the key to a better and

SOURCE: Cameron, D. (2000). *Good to talk? Living and working in a communication culture*. London, UK: Sage. (Pages 1–23). Reprinted by permission of Sage Publications Ltd from Deborah Cameron, *Good to Talk* (© Deborah Cameron, 2000).

happier life; improving communication 'would improve everything else'. But that in itself surely casts doubt on the idea that communication is something people 'take for granted' and 'don't have to think about'. The very fact that it is apparently so important might suggest that, on the contrary, we think about it a great deal. There is certainly no shortage of people exhorting us to think about it: employers and the various consultants they bring into our workplaces, experts who write self-help books and appear on TV talk shows, bodies that commission and publicize surveys like *Listening to the Nation*. When these people remind us how important communication is, the idea that we should 'learn to do it better' is seldom far away.

It is significant that people like the survey respondent quoted above use the term 'communication' when what they actually mean is 'talking' (*Listening to the Nation* found that 86% of all reported communication was face-to-face, while a further 12% was on the telephone). A commonplace social activity has been transformed into a technical skill, with its own professional experts and its own technical jargon. It is because I am interested in this transformation that I have chosen to focus on spoken interaction in this book. Equating 'communication' with 'talk' may seem perverse or naive; this after all is the much-hyped 'information age', and we are constantly reminded that the global citizen of the 21st century will need not merely to be literate, but to be literate in a range of media. Yet in a great deal of current rhetoric about 'communication' it is clear that the object of concern is spoken language used for interactive purposes. Where 'communication' refers to writing, or to the use of electronic media, or even to very formal modes of public speaking, that will usually be spelt out. In the unmarked case, 'communication' means *talk:* it means the spoken interactions we engage in routinely at home, at work or school, and in the course of our other everyday activities. This covers a range of social settings and relationships, and encompasses a spectrum from very casual to fairly formal talk, but still it is basically 'ordinary' talk: spontaneous as opposed to planned,

interactive rather than monologic. And what interests me is precisely the novelty of approaching this sort of talk in the way we have traditionally approached writing, and more recently other 'literacies'. The norms of written language have been codified and taught for centuries; literacy has always been an acquired skill—albeit in modern times one that is expected of almost everyone. In the case of spoken language, by contrast, only the most formal and ritualized instances have been extensively codified and their rules explicitly taught. Judgements of skill have undoubtedly been made, but the criteria have been variable and largely implicit. Now it seems that things are changing.

Changing attitudes to and practices of talk are the subject of this book, and I will ask two main questions about them. One is, *how* are people being exhorted or required to talk in contemporary society? What linguistic and social norms define 'good' and 'bad' communication? By whom, and for whom, are the norms constructed, and how are they enforced? The other question is *why*. Why is there a perceived need to regulate, codify and make judgements on even the most banal forms of spoken communication? What motivates the contemporary belief that communication is both the cause of all problems and the cure for all ills? Detailed answers to these questions must wait until later chapters. Here, though, I want to sketch out the broader context in which I have found it useful to locate my questions.

I have found it enlightening to think about the phenomenon of 'communication' (by which I mean not 'the phenomenon of people talking' but 'the phenomenon of widespread concern about the skills people bring to the activity of talking') in connection with the economic and social developments of the historical period that is sometimes termed 'high' or 'late' modernity. In particular, I find it pertinent to locate 'communication' in relation to recent shifts which are often put under the heading of 'enterprise culture'. These developments affect language, and our ways of thinking about language; in many cases they also work at least partly *through* language, which is an instrument as well as an object of cultural change.

REFLEXIVE MODERNITY

In his book *Modernity and Self-Identity,* the social theorist Anthony Giddens is concerned with the way people in the conditions of late modernity create what he calls 'self-identity', which he glosses as 'the self as reflexively understood by the individual in terms of his or her biography' (Giddens, 1991: 244). The concept of 'reflexivity' is central to Giddens's understanding of modernity in general. Modern societies continuously generate knowledge and information about the world, which then informs the way people act in the world: as a result the world itself changes. It is also characteristic of modern societies that knowledge and information are ordered into what Giddens calls 'expert systems': 'modes of technical knowledge which have validity independent of the practitioners and clients who make use of them' (1991: 18). Pre-modern or 'traditional' cultures recognize expert knowledge, of course, but Giddens argues this is usually dependent on procedures that cannot be codified and used indifferently by anyone. (Penicillin should work no matter who prescribes it for whom, but the efficacy of a traditional healing ritual may depend crucially on who performs it and in what circumstances.)

Modernity's 'modes of technical knowledge' are not only about things like medicine and engineering. There are also acknowledged 'experts' deploying recognized 'technical knowledge' about social identity and social relationships. These experts offer specialist knowledge and guidance on sex, marriage, divorce, bringing up children, and so on, all subjects where in the past people would have acquired knowledge and skill through more informal modes of instruction and through direct initiation. As Giddens says, the way people in contemporary societies both understand and actually 'do' sex, or parenthood, is affected significantly by their exposure to authoritative technical knowledge about it. In this book I will explore the idea that 'communication' is another area in which expert systems are asserting themselves over more traditional,

informal and diffuse ways of organizing knowledge and practice; and that this has implications for the way we experience, understand and conduct spoken interaction.

The increasing systematization of knowledge and the codification of procedures for talking to other people can plausibly be linked to the developments Giddens associates with the creation of 'self-identity' in late modernity. He suggests that 'in the context of a post-traditional order, the self becomes a *reflexive project*' (1991: 32, italics in original). People no longer make pre-ordained transitions from one life-stage to another in a cultural milieu that stays the same over generations. Instead they must constantly make and remake themselves (their 'selves'), connecting their personal histories to a larger social history in which change is rapid and continual. Giddens argues that people do this by reflexively constructing autobiographical narratives: 'A person's identity is not to be found in behaviour, nor—important though this is—in the reactions of others, but in *the capacity to keep a particular narrative going.* The individual's biography . . . must continually integrate events that occur in the external world and sort them into the ongoing "story" about the self' (1991: 54). This account throws up the possibility—one which, again, I will explore further in the chapters that follow—that at least some current anxieties about 'communication' are anxieties about the ability to tell that 'ongoing story about the self', either to oneself or to others. If identity depends on 'keeping a narrative going', and if narrative is essentially a verbal construct, then language and communication are implicated in the success or failure of identity, and will be foregrounded in relation to anxiety about identity.

One very obvious contemporary manifestation of this sort of anxiety is the pervasiveness of therapy and self-help (much of which is therapy minus the therapist). Therapy is an institution with its own particular procedures for constructing a narrative of the self. Anthony Giddens argues that in contemporary conditions it should be understood not, as some commentators have suggested, as a secular substitute for religion or as a compensation for the alienation and dislocation of life in consumer capitalist societies, but rather as a 'methodology of life-planning' (1991: 180). In therapy the individual pursues her or his 'reflexive project of the self', striving to integrate the inherited past and the present into a coherent ongoing narrative which leads to a 'better' future. While I agree that this is one of the things therapy is for, I will suggest that it also has the function—a moral, even if not specifically religious one—of disseminating ideas about what it means to be a 'good person', and more concretely, of providing models for the behaviour of such a person towards other people. 'Communication' is significant in relation to both functions.

Giddens makes the assumption that it is reasonable to talk about individuals having a *single* 'self-identity'. It is an assumption that might be disputed, as he himself notes: for some theorists, 'an individual has as many selves as there are divergent contexts of interaction' (1991: 190). He is alluding here to certain followers of Erving Goffman, but he also remarks on the resemblance of this view to poststructuralist/postmodernist ideas about the 'fragmentation' of identity. His own view is rather different. Given that modern societies are complex, and do demand that their members participate in 'divergent contexts of interaction', the construction of identity may involve the integration of diverse experiences and different roles; but in general there will, precisely, be *integration*, or at least an attempt at integration. Individuals do not simply treat their varied experiences as a series of disconnected fragments, but actively try to weave them into a single coherent narrative, whose protagonist is felt to be 'a *continuous* self and body' (1991: 55, my italics). 'A person with a reasonably stable sense of self-identity', Giddens maintains, 'has a feeling of biographical continuity which she is able to grasp reflexively, and, to a greater or lesser degree, communicate to other people' (1991: 54).

The demands made on their members by complex modern societies, and the resulting tensions between fragmentation and integration, have reflexes in linguistic or communicative behaviour, and in the regimes of verbal hygiene which seek to regulate, standardize or 'improve' that behaviour. Some regimes of communication training, for instance (particularly in the workplace and in vocationally oriented forms of education) are prompted by a perceived need to prepare individuals for the 'divergent contexts of interaction' they will encounter, and for which their previous experiences have not prepared them, because the contexts are either new or involve significantly reshaped expectations. For instance, as I will explain in more detail below, many regimes of workplace communication training are part of a managerial project whose overall aim is to produce an 'enterprising' or 'empowered' worker. The context—work—is not new or unfamiliar, but the expectation of enterprise/empowerment is a novel one, and people need guidance on how to meet it. Training and disciplinary regimes associated with 'empowerment' aim to change, not merely the way people behave in the context of work, but who they feel themselves to be in that context (Gee et al., 1996).

Other regimes of verbal hygiene, particularly those found in therapy and self-help, are more concerned with helping people 'make sense of their lives'—that is, to integrate the diversity of their experience into a satisfying narrative, and (crucially in the context of 'communication') to verbalize that experience more effectively and more 'authentically'. Although this might well be seen theoretically as a process of self-*construction*, it is more commonly represented by those engaged in it as a process of self-*expression*. It does not change who people 'are' or feel themselves to be, but gives them new tools for making intelligible—to themselves as well as others–who they are. A topic that receives systematic attention in some regimes of communication training is 'talking about feelings'—the assumption being that the feelings themselves are 'there', the established property of an already-existing self, and what is lacking is only the level of communication skill needed to do them justice.

Theoretically, I understand regimes of both types as constitutive rather than merely expressive: I would not argue that one is about creating 'inauthentic' selves and the other about expressing 'authentic' ones. Nevertheless, one reason

I prefer Giddens's account of self-identity to the postmodernist postulate of endlessly fragmented selves is that 'authenticity' appears to be a key issue in understanding the way people respond to regimes that seek to regulate their spoken interaction. Giddens observes (1991: 54) that 'The individual's biography, if she is to maintain regular interaction with others in the day-to-day world, cannot be wholly fictive'. He is talking about the need for an individual's story to integrate things that happen in the outside world, as opposed to being completely inward-looking and solipsistic; but in the context of 'communication' the comment takes on an additional resonance. The individual's ways of talking are part of the whole biographical package; indeed I will argue that they are commonly understood as rather direct products of innate 'character' combined with individual life experience (the sort of person someone is together with the sorts of things they have done). Consequently, people often display resistance to being made to interact with others in a linguistic persona they regard as 'wholly fictive'. Such resistance is one of the most significant problems facing those who wish to build new and comprehensive expert systems around the everyday activity of talking. Expert systems are general and impersonal: they apply without regard to the particularities of persons or contexts. In this case, they detach the skills and techniques of 'communication' from the personal histories and qualities of those engaged in it. But this approach does not meet with universal or complete acceptance, largely because it conflicts with ideas about individual 'authenticity', and about speech as an important reflex of that, which continue to have wide currency. If most people today really inhabited the multiple and fragmented subjectivities suggested by some poststructuralist and postmodernist theory, this would be difficult to account for.

In sum, then, current concerns about 'communication' provide a good example of modernity's 'reflexivity'. They exemplify the way every aspect of modern life is liable to be put under the microscope, both by experts and by laypeople. They are part of the general reflexive project of knowing how things are or should be done in order to control them and do them better. They are also part of the more specific 'reflexive project of the self', since the construction of a biographical narrative is a discursive and linguistic accomplishment. At the same time, the kind of biographical narrative that constitutes self-identity has continuity and 'authenticity' (see Giddens, 1991: 78–9) among its central concerns. The overall effect is somewhat paradoxical. As spoken interaction comes increasingly to be treated as a set of 'skills', and colonized by expert systems with their decontextualized, transferable procedures, there is a risk that its capacity to signify 'authentically' who an individual is and what s/he thinks or feels will be compromized.

ENTERPRISE CULTURE

The colonization of spoken interaction by expert systems has been accelerated and intensified by the recent social and economic shifts which are often glossed in the phrase 'enterprise culture'. Later I will make specific connections between 'communication' and enterprise culture, but first it is necessary to say something more about the phenomenon of enterprise culture itself. While the phrase may call to mind specific political projects, such as the propaganda initiative launched during the 1980s by Margaret Thatcher's government to encourage people to set up businesses and invest in the stock market, here it is intended to mean something much broader. It encompasses developments which have outlasted the Thatcher era (in some cases they post-date that era), which are not peculiar to Britain, and which cannot be seen as the sole preserve of the ideological Right. 'Enterprise culture' should not be taken as synonymous with 'business culture' either. It is possible to do business in ways that are not 'enterprising', and to conduct other activities (such as family life) in ways that *are* 'enterprising'.

If you look up *enterprise* in the *Concise Oxford Dictionary,* you find three senses listed: 1. An undertaking, especially a bold and difficult one. 2. (As a personal attribute) Readiness to engage in such undertakings. 3. A business firm.

The 'enterprise' in 'enterprise culture' means a set of attributes, values and behaviours—such as resourcefulness, self-discipline, openness to risk and change—that enable people to succeed in bold and difficult undertakings. These are prototypically of the business variety, but not exclusively so. As Graham Burchell notes (1993: 275), the hallmark of enterprise culture is to make business undertakings the model for all undertakings, so that there is a 'generalization of an "enterprise form" to all forms of conduct—to the conduct of organizations hitherto seen as non-economic, to the conduct of government and to the conduct of individuals themselves'.

Many illustrative examples of this 'generalization' come to mind (I will take mine mostly from the British context, but I have no doubt they will resonate with the experiences of readers located elsewhere). To begin with 'organizations hitherto seen as non-economic', the most obvious example of 'enterprise' in this context is the 'marketization' of public services since the 1980s. Some services that were state-run monopolies (such as the utilities and the railway network in Britain) were sold into private ownership, and are now enterprises in the 'business firm' sense. Others remained public institutions run on a non-profit basis, but were required to adopt the disciplines of business and the trappings of its culture. Schools and universities were encouraged to write mission statements and compelled to undergo quality auditing. The running of some public institutions, such as prisons, was 'outsourced' to private contractors. In the British National Health Service (NHS), an 'internal market' was created in medical services—which continued, however, to be paid for by tax revenue—in a deliberate effort to simulate features of market capitalism that were thought to make it more efficient than the welfare state.

Moving on to 'the conduct of government', it is notable that politicians now routinely compare the activity of democratic governance to managing a business. The US Vice-President Al Gore once declared: 'We have customers: the American people'. Shortly after the election that brought his 'new' Labour Party to power in 1997, the British Prime Minister Tony Blair told a BBC interviewer: 'If you are running a company nowadays, suppose you are running Marks & Spencer [a major clothing and food retailer] or Sainsbury [one of Britain's 'big four' high-street supermarkets], you will be constantly trying to work out whether your customers are satisfied with the product they are getting. . . . I don't think there is anything wrong with government trying to do that'. The grounds for the analogy between politics and retailing have always been there, but it is only recently that politicians have found it appropriate to incorporate it into their rhetoric. (To see what difference that makes, we only have to put Al Gore's 'we have customers' soundbite alongside something that was said by one of his most illustrious predecessors: 'Ask not what your country can do for you . . . '). The comparison is not only rhetorical, either; government departments are increasingly run on business lines, and new policies, like new product lines, are tested using market research methods like focus-group discussions. It has become fashionable to discuss the nation itself—quintessentially a political entity—in terms more usually associated with marketing consumer goods. One project to which Tony Blair gave a high profile in the early days of his administration was 'rebranding Britain'—modernizing its image so it would be seen less as a heritage theme park and more as 'Cool Britannia'. It was widely reported that this project had been inspired by a report produced for the think-tank Demos, which argued that a clear national identity, like a distinctive brand image, was an economic asset that helped to sell a country's products. The Demos report was titled $Britain^{TM}$ (Leonard, 1997).

When Graham Burchell asserts that enterprise values govern 'the conduct of individuals themselves', he does not mean only individuals' conduct in the public sphere of industry, commerce and politics, but also in their private lives as community and family members. For example, bringing up children has emerged as a 'bold and difficult undertaking' requiring the acquisition and exercise of quasi-managerial skills (this enterprise is now known as 'parenting'). Advice on all kinds of personal relationships urges us to treat them as if they were business projects: we are told we should 'set goals' or 'negotiate contracts' with family members and friends. We are also urged to 'work on' our individual selves with a view to becoming healthier, happier, better-adjusted and more successful. This philosophy of self-improvement is not new, of course, but it has never been more pervasive than it is now. It also acquires a certain edge as other developments within enterprise culture shift responsibilities from the state to the individual or household.

As I noted in passing earlier, though, enterprise culture is not just a matter of imposing the values and practices of one sphere, business, on other spheres like politics and family life. The values and practices in question are drawn from a particular approach to business, which is relatively recent (and not yet universal) in the business sphere itself. The new approach goes under various names, among them 'enterprise' or 'entrepreneurial' management, management for 'empowerment' or for 'excellence' (a reference to the work of the management 'guru' Tom Peters), or simply 'new wave' management. Whatever it is called, though, the important point to bear in mind about it is that it represents a culture change *within business*. Business has always been a privileged locus for enterprise, but the message of the 'new wave' is that practices which served business well enough in the past are not sufficiently enterprising to meet the particular challenges of the present and future.

If one asks what challenges those might be, the standard response focuses on economic globalization. Financial deregulation together with technological developments (such as better and faster telecommunications and computerized record-keeping) has enabled capital to move more freely across the globe. This intensifies competition: businesses can shift investment to wherever in the world they can produce goods to the necessary standard at the lowest cost. Developing economies, like the so-called Asian tigers, offer modern technology and skilled workers who do not however demand 'first world' wages. To compete, therefore, companies operating in the more affluent parts of the world must attempt both to lower their costs and to improve their standards of quality and service. It is this imperative that has been seen to require a new way of managing business organizations.[3]

Proponents of 'enterprise' usually contrast it with 'bureaucracy', a system that depends on elaborate hierarchies and rigid procedures. In a bureaucratic organization, management is a matter of 'command and control', that is, telling your subordinates what to do and making sure they do it. The 'enterprise' philosophy is different. Instead of setting tasks, the new manager sets goals, and motivates subordinates to meet those goals. The new manager is less concerned with the performance of particular actions than with the achievement of specified, measurable outcomes. Employees have more freedom to decide for themselves how best to achieve those outcomes: the expectation is that they will be 'flexible'—able to pick up new skills as the need arises. It is also assumed that employees at every level already have skills that were untapped, and so wasted, under the traditional 'command and control' regime. With the demise of that regime, their own 'enterprise' is liberated from bureaucratic constraints. This liberation is known as 'empowerment', and in theory it goes along with a flattening of the bureaucratic hierarchy (also known as 'de-layering'). The enterprising organization does not require as many layers as the command and control model did; nor does it want them, for one of its aims is to cut costs, and this is achieved by, among other things, 'downsizing'. 'Enterprise', then, is the key to achieving what on the face of it seems impossible: higher standards at lower cost. Fewer people making freer use of their entrepreneurial talents are supposed to be able to do more for less.

Another pervasive feature of 'enterprising' business is a relentless focus on serving the needs of the customer. Globalization and the associated intensification of competition can be invoked to explain this too. If you cannot compete on the price or the basic quality of the product (because it can be made just as well, and cheaper, in Mexico or Thailand) then you have to compete on service: giving the customer what s/he wants, when s/he wants it, and distinguishing yourself from your competitors through 'intangibles', such as helpfulness and friendliness. It is also notable that the most advanced economies have moved towards being 'post-industrial': the manufacturing sector contracts while the service sector expands. More and more people are working in the kinds of businesses where customer service is not just one consideration among others, but the defining purpose of the organization. And it is businesses of this service-oriented kind—companies like McDonald's or the Disney Corporation—that now tend to be held up as models for successful business in general.

If much of this sounds familiar even to readers who do not work in private businesses, that is partly because we have all encountered some of the manifestations of 'enterprise' when we are the customer, but also because the same philosophy now underpins the management of many public sector and non-profit institutions. Here, obviously, enterprise is not a response to the intensification of global competition. British schools and hospitals do not face the prospect of being undercut by rivals in Malaysia, and British government departments are not going to be subject to a hostile takeover by Germany. There *is* an economic motivation, in as much as most contemporary governments wish to reduce levels of public expenditure. But there are also ideological motives. These are not necessarily straightforward expressions of the 'business is best' philosophy that animated right-wing radicals in the Thatcher/Reagan years. One important motivation for importing elements of enterprise management into the public sector is the idea that state and local government institutions ought to be more responsive and more accountable to the people they supposedly serve. Institutions whose values are liberal or socialist (like universities and Labour councils) have proved as susceptible to this argument as capitalist organizations. But the 'customer care' approach to public service does implicitly take

market relationships as paradigmatic, and this requires a change of attitude, from service users as well as providers. Many novel features of public service culture—mission statements, user charters, quality auditing accompanied by published league tables for institutions like hospitals, universities and schools—are intended not only to make public servants shape up, but also to encourage a more enterprising, consumerist approach on the part of the public itself. School league tables, for instance, are published so that parents can make informed choices about where to educate their children; charters for rail passengers or post-office users incorporate complaints procedures and promises of compensation for those who exert themselves to take under-performing institutions to task. To reap the full benefits of 'better service' it is necessary to become a 'better customer'.

[. . .]

ENTERPRISE, LANGUAGE AND COMMUNICATION

At the heart of the new management philosophy is a change in the relationship between organizations and the individuals who work in them. Instead of just doing what they are told, 'enterprising' employees are made responsible for motivating, disciplining and directing themselves. At the same time, the organization must ensure that the self-directing worker is moving in step with institutional policy. Empowering people to use their creative abilities is all very well but their creativity could be directed to some very undesirable ends (embezzlement, sabotage and union organizing, for instance). As Paul du Gay points out (1996: 62–3), the aim is not to liberate workers unconditionally, but rather to organize things in such a way that 'all employees make the goals and objectives of their employing organization their own personal goals and objectives, thus ensuring they will deploy their "autonomy" and "creativity" correctly from the organization's point of view'. And as he also notes, this approach will depend for its success on 'the construction and promulgation of a "strong corporate culture"'. Persuading people to adopt the organization's goals as their own is an ambitious aim, especially if you are talking about the whole range of employees, and not just those with interesting jobs and relatively high status (or the prospect of attaining it). To achieve that aim, the company must endeavour to create a culture in which its goals and values are both made apparent to the workforce and presented in a way that encourages positive identification with them.

In this project, the language of internal communication will play a major part. Du Gay's informants said as much to him; he quotes many references to the idea that culture change involves, or even boils down to, linguistic change, and many more in which language is used metaphorically or metonymically to stand for organizational culture as a whole. For instance:

'You really have to learn a new language' (Regional controller, p. 128).

'You have to win hearts and minds, and it's jargon, I know, but hearts and minds, energies of every member of our staff . . . so that all 40,000 odd people in [company] would eventually be singing from the same hymn sheet' (Controller, p. 131).

'I don't underestimate the difficulties we have in making sure . . . that our managers get the right message every time and communicate the message consistently' (Personnel director, p. 132).

'[The success of staff training depends on how far] it becomes part of their everyday language . . . if they don't take it on board then it won't be successful' (Training manager, p. 147n).

Internal communication may be used simply as a way of 'cheerleading' for particular goals and values (this is the main purpose of the 'vision' and 'mission' statements displayed on office walls across the capitalist world). A more interventionist strategy, however, involves creating new communicative events in which employees are compelled to use a new linguistic register

actively. The QT meeting at which sales assistants in one of the companies studied by Paul du Gay had to come up with 'three hows' [that is, three possible solutions to a particular problem] is an example. The format of the meeting itself obliged participants to orient to certain norms of interaction and play particular communicational roles (in theory, anyway: in practice, [. . .] the staff refused to adopt their prescribed roles as initiators of talk). In addition, the subject matter and purpose of the meeting obliged participants to make use of a new terminology—it does not seem likely that anyone previously possessed the concept of 'a how', still less that they used the expression. Another increasingly common 'new' workplace speech event is the 'appraisal interview', where the goal of assessing an employee's performance is realized using interactive conventions that resemble those of a therapy or counselling session (some organizations actually call appraisal 'counselling'). Employees maybe invited to discuss their strengths and weaknesses, reflect on their past achievements and future goals, and set their own targets for improvement. Since appraisal is typically compulsory, and often consequential in terms of pay and promotion, everyone has an interest in mastering the quasi-therapeutic register associated with it.

Regulating the use of language for purposes of communication within the organization, then, is an important tool in the creation of a 'strong corporate culture'. New values, practices and implicit expectations are signalled by the adoption of new ways of talking—new genres like the mission statement, new speech events like the QT meeting and the appraisal interview, new terminologies which encode important new concepts such as the 'how' (or, to take some notorious examples from the recent history of British university teaching, the 'aim', the 'objective' and the 'learning outcome'). But language use is also regulated—often even more intensively—at the interface between the organization and the outside world, which is to say, in interactions with clients, customers, users and suppliers. This is another locale where enterprise culture requires its members to communicate differently, and to become more conscious of what they are doing when they talk.

As I noted above, the enterprising organization is likely to stress the importance of what is often labelled 'customer care'. After globalization, advanced capitalist economies are dominated by service industries, and even in the manufacturing sector it is often through its service that a company gains its competitive edge. This has implications for language and communication, because 'service' is to a significant extent accomplished by interacting with people. *How* staff interact with others when they represent the organization has become a matter of intense concern. Paul du Gay recounts a conversation with a retail manager who had been impressed, during his training, with an anecdote about the Disney Corporation firing a trainee sales assistant at one of its stores, not because she was dishonest, incompetent or slow, but because she did not make appropriate eye-contact with customers. This story had been told to the manager, and then repeated by him to Paul du Gay, as a tale about the Disney Corporation's legendary attention to detail. An acknowledged world leader in the customer-service game, Disney expected excellent communication skills, verbal and non-verbal, to be displayed by everyone from the CEO to the lowliest checkout clerk.

In the story, Disney fired the unsatisfactory employee; in other companies, or in a case judged less hopeless, an alternative solution might have been to try and fix her 'faulty' eye contact. Employees in many occupations are now routinely given training in various aspects of communication, from 'active listening' to body language. In later chapters I will discuss in more detail what they are being taught, and what they think of it. In quite a few occupations, too, the approach has been adopted of trying to *standardise* interaction between employees and customers. Rather than being trained in general strategies, staff are trained to use standard formulas, and at the extreme, to perform to a uniform script. This is one salient aspect of the phenomenon which the neo-Weberian sociologist George Ritzer calls 'McDonaldization', whereby

organizations try to maximise efficiency, calculability, predictability and control in all aspects of their operating routines (Ritzer, 1996).

In relation to customer care, language is once again an instrument of cultural change—new linguistic norms are intended to function as the outward and audible sign of a new inner commitment to the interests of the customer—and at the same time, language is a key target for attitudinal and behavioural change. If it achieves nothing else, communication training impresses on people that they have to think about the way they talk, and not take for granted that their ordinary communicative competence will be adequate for the particular purposes of the workplace. Often, it is intended to achieve rather more than this. It is intended to eradicate, or at least reduce, the variation people exhibit in their ways of interacting, and to bring the communicational behaviour of individuals into conformity with norms defined by the organization.

As we saw early on in this discussion, it is a feature of enterprise culture that norms and practices elaborated first in business are subsequently diffused into other spheres. Norms and practices relating to 'communication' are no exception to this rule; and there is a particularly strong link between the sphere of work and that of education. This is not surprising: from the point of view of employers, and of many politicians, parents and students, schools and colleges are there in large part to provide an appropriately skilled workforce. Educators themselves may take a somewhat different view, but few would deny entirely that it is part of their mission to prepare students for future employment. In any case, they are subject to both political and financial pressure to take notice of what employers want. Increasingly, employers are emphasizing that they want 'communication skills'. This is not, of course, a novel demand, but it is becoming more insistent, more explicit and more systematic.

One reason for that is that more and more jobs actually require workers to communicate. This is partly because of the growth of the service sector. Service work and selling have always involved talking to people; today significant numbers of workers are employed in occupations that consist of little else but spoken interaction (one recent and rapidly spreading development of this kind, which I will consider in detail later, is working in a 'call centre'). Traditionally, manufacturing jobs made fewer demands on workers' linguistic abilities; but the advent of new managerial approaches has changed this to some extent. Even factory assembly-line workers may nowadays find themselves in an appraisal interview, a team meeting or a 'quality circle', which means that talking has become part of what is expected of them.

Another change is that job descriptions, appraisal criteria and so on now foreground the status of communication *as a skill*—not just something workers are expected to do, but something they are expected to be, or become, 'good at'. The interpersonal and linguistic aspects of many jobs often used to be mentioned in job descriptions, if they were mentioned at all, as a vague afterthought ('must enjoy working with people'). Consider, by contrast, the following 'person specification', which defined the ideal recruit for the job being advertised as someone who could

> demonstrate sound interpersonal relationships and an awareness of the individual clients' psychological and emotional needs;
>
> understand the need for effective verbal and non-verbal communication;
>
> support clients and relatives in the care environment by demonstrating empathy and understanding. (source: *Medical Monitor*, 1994)

The language used in this specification might suggest that it is describing a skilled caring professional—a psychologist or social worker, for instance—whose job is centrally about talking to 'clients'. In fact, though, the job on offer is that of a ward orderly in an NHS hospital. Orderlies are 'ancillary' workers (the *COD* gives 'cleaner, esp. male, in a hospital' as a definition of *orderly*); the interactions they have with patients and visitors occur in the course of performing other duties, and are not part of the official clinical regime. In the past it is unlikely the routine but incidental 'communication' element of the job would have been considered worth remarking on. But in the new-style specification, the talking that orderlies do has been formalized as a professional responsibility that calls for specific skills.

The source from which I took this example cited it as a case of 'political correctness' (an attempt to be sensitive to the feelings of unskilled workers by representing hospital cleaning as a more elevated calling than it really is). Arguably however it has more to do with 'new visions of work', to use Nikolas Rose's phrase, according to which there is no such thing as an unskilled job or an unskilled worker—even the most menial job demands the exercise of multiple skills. This point is insisted on, not to spare the feelings of people who do menial jobs, but to make it easier to subject them to new kinds of discipline, such as training and appraisal. When talking to people on the job becomes a formal 'skill' instead of merely an incidental accompaniment to other activities, it becomes legitimate to regulate and assess the way employees talk. It also becomes legitimate to use people's 'communication skills' as a gatekeeping device in recruitment—a criterion for deciding whether or not to offer them employment.

It is at this point that employers' increasingly explicit and exacting requirements become a relevant consideration for the education system which prepares people to enter or re-enter the labour market. Oral communication is regarded as one of the so-called 'key skills' without which a job applicant has little hope of success in today's economy (other 'key skills' include literacy, numeracy, 'teamwork', information technology and problem-solving). In surveys, employers regularly rank communication as the single most important key skill; and they express considerable dissatisfaction with the oral communication skills of their recruits, whether they be school leavers or university graduates. One survey reported in *People Management* journal in 1997 found that 'oral communication was cited as the most important soft skill but was perceived to be sorely lacking in recruits coming straight from further or higher education. While 91% of respondents believed that this was an essential skill, only 32% said it was present among this group' (Mullen, 1997).

Surveys like this one report perceptions rather than hard facts, of course, and even when there is consensus on them it is difficult to gauge whether the employers' beliefs that their recruits are 'sorely lacking' in oral communication skills are well founded. Nevertheless, one reason why these skills might be lacking is that educational institutions have traditionally given them far less attention than the 'basics' of literacy and numeracy. In particular, oral communication has not been the object of standardized assessment and the explicit instruction that goes with it—or at least, not until recently. Schools, further education colleges and some higher education institutions are increasingly adopting a 'teach and test' approach to spoken language, either as part of the subject curriculum (oral skills are one component in the school English syllabus, for example) or as part of an initiative to equip students with a broad range of 'key', 'core' or 'transferable' skills (this approach is set to be adopted in education after the age of 16 in both England and Scotland). Communication has also become an element in courses that lead to what in Britain are called National Vocational Qualifications (NVQs). These courses are designed to be directly relevant to working life, and in some cases they teach oral skills that are specifically demanded by employers—one example is telephone communication.

Educators have not turned to teaching and assessing talk only because of pressure from employers. There has been, and still is, an independent educational agenda which advocates 'oracy'—a term coined as far back as the 1960s—as a means to help students learn more effectively and as part of their personal development. This agenda was at least as influential as the more utilitarian one in getting oral skills into the 'official' school curriculum in Britain in the first instance. But as business has discovered the key nature of these skills in the process of changing its own culture, its perspective on what communication means and why it matters has begun to exert more influence on educational practice.

Education is not only supposed to equip future workers with the skills and competencies their jobs will require, but also to socialize them in particular ways—to inculcate certain social habits, dispositions and values. This is explicitly recognized in the national curriculum for schools in England and Wales, with 'personal, social, health and citizenship education' forming a recognized part of the educational regime. According to the National Curriculum Council, 'the education system . . . has a duty to educate individuals to be able to think and act for themselves, with an acceptable range of personal abilities and values which must also meet the wider social demands of adult life'. I take this quotation from a report produced for the BT Forum, *Communication: A Key Skill for Education* (Phillips, 1998), which suggests that communication training could play a vital part in the process of socializing the young. Many forms of anti-social behaviour, whether directed against others (like bullying) or against oneself (like drug taking), arise, the report claims, because those who engage in them have not learned to use language to express their feelings and build good relationships with other people. Communication skills teaching offers a way to address these problems: even when remedial intervention is not called for, 'all children benefit from learning skills that will make them better friends, better employees, better life partners and better human beings' (Phillips, 1998: 7).

This sort of rhetoric may seem less obviously connected to the concerns of business than the discourse of vocational skills, but in fact businesses that have adopted new management philosophies and practices have a direct interest in the values and dispositions of the workers they recruit. 'Empowerment' calls for individuals who 'think and act for themselves', while increased emphasis on team building and customer care calls for people who have a certain ease in expressing themselves and relating to other people. The ideal recruit to an enterprising business is self-motivating, but also able and willing to fit in with the corporate culture. As the BT education report puts it (Phillips, 1998: 6), 'Management de-layering, and the need for a flexible workforce able to pick up new skills and competencies, means that businesses can no longer accommodate the genius in the corner . . . Employees today need to be able to pick up new skills and pass them on. They need to listen carefully and motivate themselves and others'.

But in any case, work itself is not the only domain in which 'enterprise' can be displayed. Calls to raise standards of communication in order to make 'better human beings' are part of the more general trend whereby every aspect of life becomes potentially a self-improvement project. This in turn reflects perceptions of the self as a tradable asset. Andrew Wernick argues in his book *Promotional Culture* that 'social life in every dimension has increasingly come to assume a commodity or quasi-commodity form' (1991: 185): not only jobs but social and sexual relationships have their 'markets', in which individuals must advertise themselves as desirable commodities. Language is both a medium for this kind of advertisement and one of the commodities being advertised (something that becomes overt in personal ads, which commonly specify conversational facility and a 'good sense of humour' as attributes of the desired/desirable person).

When incorporated into the school curriculum, the self-improvement project effectively becomes compulsory for people of a certain age; but there are plenty of other social locations where adults may (and do) engage in it by choice. Guidance on better communication is available even without making an institutional commitment (like signing up for therapy or counselling, or taking a course). Initiatives like the BT Forum and its 'practical' arm, TalkWorks, make some forms of communication skills training readily accessible to people in their own homes. Bookshops and libraries devote acres of shelf-space to self-help texts with titles like *Confident Conversation, Difficult Conversations, I See What You Mean, That's Not What I Meant, Words That Hurt, Words That Heal,* and so on. Entertainment media, too, especially talk radio

and television, now disseminate to a mass audience the idea that being able and willing to talk about problems, feelings and relationships is inherently desirable. Some popular media formats—notably the confessional talk-show—not only provide continual reinforcement for the basic idea that 'it's good to talk', but also model the 'correct' way of talking about personal experience in some detail.

Hybridity and Technologization

The . . . three major social domains discussed in the previous section [work, education, social/personal life] . . . are interconnected. For example, as we saw above, communication skills teaching in schools and colleges is advocated not only for its specific value in educational contexts ('oracy' enhances learning), but also on the grounds that employers demand the skills in question (a 'work' consideration) and that possessing those skills makes people 'better friends . . . better life-partners and better human beings' (a 'personal life' consideration).

Work is also, perhaps surprisingly, a 'mixed' domain. It might seem logical to treat business as a privileged source of ideas relating to 'enterprise', but in the case of ideas about language and communication that would be an oversimplification. Earlier I remarked on the tendency to compare the enterprises of private or personal life, like 'parenting' and 'relationships', to business projects. The analogy also works the other way, as people are advised to solve business problems using approaches developed by therapists and counsellors to sort out troubled marriages and dysfunctional families. This cross-fertilization between the corporate and the clinical is in fact much older than 'new wave' management. Communication is among the 'human factors' which were and are the province of occupational psychology—a discipline that had already established itself well before World War II (Hollway, 1991).

Workplace training frequently claims educational and personal development objectives as well as more narrowly instrumental ones to do with on-the-job performance. Many workplace training initiatives now involve close collaboration with educational institutions, and result in trainees acquiring nationally recognized credentials. It is not only at the point of entry to the labour market that workers need to acquire knowledge, skills and credentials—'lifelong learning' and 'continuing professional development' are buzz-phrases for politicians as well as businesses. Employers are encouraged to regard themselves as 'Investors in People' (the name of a (British) national scheme recognizing organizations that institute high-quality programmes of staff development through training and appraisal). The rhetoric of 'new age' management is full of claims about caring for the whole person, as in the following extract from a financial services company's 'vision statement':

> Our work environment will value our ideas and entire life experience. We will be treated with fairness and dignity, and recognized for excellence. We will be challenged to learn, to continuously improve, and to aspire to the highest standards. We will draw on the broadest base of expertise to ensure that we achieve our goals. Our work and personal lives will complement and enrich one another.[4]

I am suggesting, then, that the notions of 'communication' found in each of the three domains this book will consider are not 'pure' but 'hybrid', products of cross-fertilization. Ideas, theoretical frameworks and even specific pieces of practical advice on language-use circulate freely from one domain to another. This movement of ideas across different social and linguistic domains is characteristic of the process that the linguist Norman Fairclough dubs 'discourse technologization'. Fairclough explains:

> We can usefully refer to 'discourse technologies' and to a 'technologization of discourse' . . . Examples of discourse technologies are interviewing, teaching, counselling and advertising. . . . [I]n modern society they have taken on, and are taking on, the character of transcontextual techniques,

which are seen as resources or toolkits that can be used to pursue a wide variety of strategies in many diverse contexts. Discourse technologies . . . are coming to have their own specialist technologists: researchers who look into their efficiency, designers who work out refinements in the light of research and changing institutional requirements, and trainers who pass on the techniques. (1992: 215)

'Communication' is, admittedly, less well-defined and specific than Fairclough's examples of 'discourse technologies': it could perhaps be considered a higher-level discourse whose subject is discourse technologies in general. But teaching or discussing 'communication skills' surely qualifies as a 'transcontextual technique', with the skills themselves seen as appropriate, not to say indispensable, for all kinds of purposes in all kinds of situations. It is also the case that 'communication' has acquired its own 'technologists'—its specialist researchers, consultants and trainers. From these people's activities emerges a body of expert knowledge and practice. But this new body of knowledge and practice does not emerge fully formed out of nothing. In the next chapter I consider its sources and its antecedents.

NOTES

1. British Telecom was originally part of Britain's General Post Office (GPO), and as such was a publicly-owned monopoly. It was separated from other GPO functions such as the Royal Mail, and eventually privatized, since when it has become a major player in the global telecommunications industry (for that reason it now prefers to be known by the acronym 'BT').

2. Statistics are taken from *Listening to the Nation: Executive Summary;* the quote is taken from *Communication at the Heart of the Nation: Implications for Building a Communicating Society.* These documents, available from BT, are unattributed, undated and unpaginated. The full report on the National Communication Survey is Smith and Turner, 1997.

3. At this point, a caveat is necessary. Anyone familiar with recent management theory will recognize the account offered below of 'new ways of managing' as one in which differing approaches, originated by different people at different times, and in some cases contradicting one another, are blended together and presented under the umbrella of 'new managerial approaches' or simply 'enterprise', as if they were a single thing. This theoretical simplification may not be good scholarly practice, but it does reflect the way the ideas in question are often used in real organizations. As Micklethwait and Wooldridge (1997) point out, the most important change in managerial approaches over the last decade is not the adoption of any one model, but the more general willingness of organizations to continually remake themselves using new 'management tools' developed by theorists and applied by consultants. However, according to Micklethwait and Wooldridge, organizations' response to management theory tends to be *ad hoc* and uncritical. This produces 'contradictory organizations', committed simultaneously to ideas that do not go together (for instance, that a successful organization streamlines its workforce to minimize costs, and at the same time seeks to maximize the loyalty and trust of its employees). What follows, then, is a brief account of some key ideas that have influenced many organizations today, but it should not be taken as a rigorous account of management theory itself (on the history and status of this discourse, see Micklethwait and Wooldridge (1997), also Jacques (1996)).

4. This vision statement is written as if it were a collective utterance by all the company's employees: the pronoun in 'our work environment will value our ideas and our entire life experience' can only mean 'the workforce's'. My source confirmed that the statement was in fact written by senior managers with some assistance from an outside consultant; employees were not consulted.

REFERENCES

Burchell, Graham (1993) 'Liberal government and the techniques of the self', *Economy and Society,* 22(3): 266–82.

Fairclough, Norman (1992) *Discourse and Social Change.* Cambridge: Polity.

Gay, Paul du (1996) *Consumption and Identity at Work.* London: Sage.

Gee, James Paul, Hull, Glynda and Lankshear, Colin (1996) *The New Work Order.* St. Leonards, NSW: Allen & Unwin.

Giddens, Anthony (1991) *Modernity and Self Identity: Self and Society in the Late Modern Age.* Cambridge: Polity.

Hollway, Wendy (1991) *Work Psychology and Organizational Behaviour: Managing the Individual at Work.* London: Sage.

Jacques, Roy (1996) *Manufacturing the Employee: Management Knowledge from the 19th to the 21st Centuries.* London and Thousand Oaks: Sage.

Leonard, Mark (1997) *Britain™: Renewing Our Identity.* London: Demos.

Micklethwait, John and Wooldridge, Addrian (1997) *The Witch Doctors: What the Management Gurus Are Saying, Why It Matters, and How to Make Sense of It.* London: Mandarin Books.

Mullen, John (1997) 'Graduates deficient in soft skills', *People Management,* November.

Phillips, Angela (1998) *Communication: A Key Skill for Education.* London: BT Forum.

Ritzer, George (1996) *The McDonaldization of Society: An Investigation into the Changing Character of Contemporary Social Life.* Revised edn. Thousand Oaks, CA: Pine Forge Press.

Smith, Patten and Turner, Rachel (1997) *Listening to the Nation.* London: BT Forum.

Wernick, Andrew (1991) *Promotional Culture: Advertising, Ideology and Symbolic Expression.* London and Newbury Park, CA: Sage Publications.

PROJECTS FOR SOCIOCULTURAL THEORIZING

ADDITIONAL READINGS ON THE SOCIOCULTURAL TRADITION

A. To learn more about sociocultural theory in general: Baldwin, Faulkner, Hecht, and Lindsley (2005); Collins (1985); Ellis (1999); Grant (2003); Peters and Simonson (2004); Ritzer and Smart (2001).

B. To learn more about functionalism: Lasswell (1948); Burrowes (1996); Merton (1957); Wright (1960, 1986); and about structuralism: Lévi-Strauss (1963).

C. To learn more about structuration theory: DeSanctis and Poole (1994); Giddens (1984, 1991).

D. To learn more about postmodernist and poststructuralist approaches: Baudrillard (1981/1995); Bourdieu (1992); Foucault (2003); Lyon (1999); Lyotard (1984); Mumby (1997); Poster (1990).

E. To learn more about theories of ritual communication and American cultural studies: Carey (1989); Munson and Warren (1997); Rothenbuhler (1998).

F. To learn more about the theory of organizing and related theories: Cooren (2000); Taylor, Groleau, and Van Every (2000); Taylor and Van Every (1999); Weick (1995).

G. To learn more about other micro-social approaches:

1. Interactionism: Blumer (1968); Goffman (1974); Leeds-Hurwitz (1995, 1999); Mead (1934).

2. Ethnography of communication: Carbaugh (2005); Hymes (1974); Katriel (2004); Katriel and Philipsen (1981); Philipsen (1992).

3. Ethnomethodology: Garfinkel (1967/1987); Francis and Hester (2004); Heritage (1984).

4. Social phenomenology: Berger and Luckmann (1967); Schutz (1932/1967).

APPLICATION EXERCISE

An *iconic figure* is an image, object, or person that becomes an easily recognizable, meaningful symbol in popular culture. Napoleon Bonaparte became an iconic figure in the 19th century, as did the Titanic, Adolf Hitler, and the Beatles in the 20th. Think of an iconic figure, either past or present. If it is a past figure, also find a present version. If it is a present figure, also find a past version. What cultural meaning or meanings do these figures represent? What has changed in these meanings over time, and what has stayed the same?

PROJECTS

1. Functionalism has been a dominant theoretical approach in mass communication studies and continues to play an important role. Functionalist communication theory explains how communication performs certain essential functions for society. Burrowes (1996) wrote a

useful overview and critique of the approach. Wright's (1960, 1986) revision of Lasswell's (1948) general functional analysis added a fourth function (entertainment) to the three identified by Lasswell (surveillance of the environment, correlation among the parts of society, and transmission of the social heritage across generations). The two-step flow (Katz & Lazarsfeld, 1955), agenda setting (McCombs & Shaw, 1972), and media dependency (Ball-Rokeach & DeFleur, 1976) are prominent examples of functionalist mass communication theories. Read some of this literature along with recent general reviews of mass communication theory (e.g., Bryant & Miron, 2004) and assess the current and potential contributions of functionalism.

2. Compare several sociocultural theories of communication with regard to how they address the macro-micro split in the tradition. What exactly is this split? What seem to be the most promising approaches to integrating macro and micro perspectives?

3. Many scholars in this tradition conceptualize communication as a kind of work or pragmatic activity. Mead identified community with cooperative activity and argued that cross-community communication cannot occur apart from such activities. Lasswell (1948) analyzed vital societal functions that communication performs. Katriel and Philipsen (1981) described an American cultural pattern in which communication is seen as something we need to work at to build healthy selves and relationships. Taylor (Taylor & Van Every, 1999; Taylor et al., 2000) theorized communication as a process that produces the co-orientation needed to get things done together. Do these theories all conceptualize the work of communication similarly, or are there important differences among them? Does Poster (1990) also identify communication with work? Are we always doing work when we *really* communicate, even if we think we are only having fun? What are the alternatives to a pragmatic conception of communication as work?

4. Cameron (reading 30) notes that many people now believe that good communication

leads to a better life. Look at today's TV talk shows, such as Jerry Springer, current reality TV, and radio talk shows including Howard Stern and Rush Limbaugh. How is communication enacted in these shows? Also, look at practices such as therapy for depression and attention deficit/hyperactivity disorder. Does a biological or pharmaceutical fix for these kinds of personal problems seem to be replacing the fix of communication? What is the value placed on communication today? In their ethnographic research, Katriel and Philipsen (1981) identified two different categories of talk: communication, and mere talk (or small talk). Is communication still differentiated from mere talk or small talk? What other cultural categories of talk seem to exist today? What about the cultural category or categories of political talk? Is there a cultural category of rhetoric? What about the idea of "spin"; is that a cultural category of talk?

5. After reading several postmodernist theories (additional readings D), identify common themes of the postmodern condition as well as themes that differ among theorists. The social construction of reality is one prominent theme across postmodernism, social phenomenology, and other threads of sociocultural theory. Compare several of these theories to conceptions of social construction in popular culture. What are the popular notions of social construction as seen in various media? For example, movies like *The Matrix* have a sense of a false world that has been constructed. Is this notion of a false reality what is meant by social construction in sociocultural theories? How about the idea of politically correct talk? What would sociocultural theorists of communication have to say about this practice? What, by comparison, would semiotic, phenomenological, or rhetorical theorists have to say about this practice?

REFERENCES

Baldwin, J. R., Faulkner, S. L., Hecht, M. L., & Lindsley, S. L. (Eds.). (2005). *Redefining culture: Perspectives across the disciplines*. Mahwah, NJ: Lawrence Erlbaum.

Ball-Rokeach, S., & DeFleur, M. L. (1976). A dependency model of mass media effects. *Communication Research, 3*, 3–21.

Baudrillard, J. (1995). *Simulacra and simulation* (S. F. Glaser, Trans.). Ann Arbor: University of Michigan Press. (Original work published 1981)

Berger, P. L., & Luckmann, T. (1967). *The social construction of reality: A treatise in the sociology of knowledge.* Garden City, NY: Doubleday/Anchor Books.

Blumer, H. (1968). *Symbolic interactionism: Perspective and method.* Englewood Cliffs, NJ: Prentice-Hall.

Bourdieu, P. (1992). *The logic of practice.* Stanford, CA: Stanford University Press.

Bryant, J., & Miron, D. (2004). Theory and research in mass communication. *Journal of Communication, 54*(4), 662–704.

Burrowes, C. P. (1996). From functionalism to cultural studies: Manifest ruptures and latent continuities. *Communication Theory, 6*, 88–103.

Carbaugh, D. (2005). *Cultures in conversation.* Mahwah, NJ: Lawrence Erlbaum.

Carey, J. W. (1989). *Communication as culture: Essays on media and society.* Winchester, MA: Unwin Hyman.

Collins, R. (1985). *Three sociological traditions.* New York: Oxford University Press.

Cooren, F. (2000). *The organizing property of communication.* Amsterdam: John Benjamins.

DeSanctis, G., & Poole, M. S. (1994). Capturing the complexity in advanced technology use: Adaptive structuration theory. *Organization Science, 5*, 121–147.

Ellis, D. G. (1999). *Crafting society: Ethnicity, class, and communication theory.* Mahwah, NJ: Lawrence Erlbaum.

Foucault, M. (2003). *The essential Foucault* (P. Rabinow & N. Rose, Eds.). New York: The New Press.

Francis, D., & Hester, S. (2004). *An invitation to ethnomethodology: Language, society and interaction.* London: Sage.

Garfinkel, H. (1987). *Studies in ethnomethodology.* Cambridge, UK: Polity Press. (Original work published 1967)

Giddens, A. (1984). *The constitution of society: Outline of the theory of structuration.* Berkeley: University of California Press.

Giddens, A. (1991). *Modernity and self-identity: Self and society in the late modern age.* Stanford, CA: Stanford University Press.

Goffman, E. (1974). *Frame analysis: An essay on the organization of experience.* New York: Harper & Row.

Grant, C. B. (2003). Destabilizing social communication theory. *Theory, Culture & Society, 20*(6), 95–119.

Heritage, J. (1984). *Garfinkel and ethnomethodology.* Cambridge, UK: Polity Press.

Hymes, D. (1974). *Foundations in sociolinguistics: An ethnographic approach.* Philadelphia: University of Pennsylvania Press.

Katriel, T. (2004). *Dialogic moments: From soul talks to talk radio in Israeli culture.* Detroit, MI: Wayne State University Press.

Katriel, T., & Philipsen, G. (1981). "What we need is communication": "Communication" as a cultural category in some American speech. *Communication Monographs, 48*, 301–317.

Katz, E., & Lazarsfeld, P. F. (1955). *Personal influence: The part played by people in the flow of mass communications.* New York: The Free Press.

Lasswell, H. D. (1948). The structure and function of communication in society. In L. Bryson (Ed.), *The communication of ideas: A series of addresses* (pp. 37–51). New York: Harper and Brothers

Leeds-Hurwitz, W. (Ed.). (1995). *Social approaches to communication.* New York: Guilford.

Leeds-Hurwitz, W. (1999). *Communication in everyday life: A social interpretation.* Norwood, NJ: Ablex.

Lévi-Strauss, C. (1963). *Structural anthropology* (C. Jacobson & B. C. Schoepf, Trans.). New York: Basic Books.

Lyon, D. (1999). *Postmodernity* (2nd ed.). Minneapolis: University of Minnesota Press.

Lyotard, J.-F. (1984). *The postmodern condition: A report on knowledge* (G. Bennington & B. Massumi, Trans.). Minneapolis: University of Minnesota Press. (Original work published 1979)

McCombs, M. E., & Shaw, D. L. (1972). The agenda-setting function of mass media. *Public Opinion Quarterly, 36*, 176–187.

Mead, G. H. (1934). *Mind, self, and society from the standpoint of a social behaviorist* (C. W. Morris, Ed.). Chicago: University of Chicago Press.

Merton, R. K. (1957). *Social theory and social structure.* Glencoe, IL: The Free Press.

Mumby, D. K. (1997). Modernism, postmodernism, and communication studies: A rereading of an ongoing debate. *Communication Theory, 7*, 1–28.

Munson, E. S., & Warren, C. A. (Eds.). (1997). *James Carey: A critical reader*. Minneapolis: University of Minnesota Press.

Peters, J. D., & Simonson, P. (Eds.). (2004). *Mass communication and American social thought: Key texts, 1919–1968*. Lanham, MD: Rowman & Littlefield.

Philipsen, G. (1992). *Speaking culturally: Explorations in social communication*. Albany: State University of New York Press.

Poster, M. (1990). *The mode of information: Post-structuralism and social context*. Chicago: University of Chicago Press.

Ritzer, G., & Smart, B. (Eds.). (2001). *Handbook of social theory*. Thousand Oaks, CA: Sage.

Rothenbuhler, E. W. (1998). *Ritual communication: From everyday conversation to mediated ceremony*. Thousand Oaks, CA: Sage.

Schutz, A. (1967). *Phenomenology of the social world* (G. Walsh & F. Lehnert, Trans.). Evanston, IL: Northwestern University Press. (Original work published 1932)

Taylor, J. R., Groleau, C. H. L., & Van Every, E. (2000). *The computerization of work: A communication perspective*. Thousand Oaks, CA: Sage.

Taylor, J. R., & Van Every, E. J. (1999). *The emergent organization: Communication as its site and surface*. Mahwah, NJ: Lawrence Erlbaum.

Weick, K. E. (1995). *Sensemaking in organizations*. Thousand Oaks, CA: Sage.

Wright, C. R. (1960). Functional analysis of mass communication. *Public Opinion Quarterly, 24*, 605–620.

Wright, C. R. (1986). *Mass communication: A sociological perspective* (3rd ed.). New York: Random House.

UNIT IX   INTRODUCTION

THE CRITICAL TRADITION

Whether starting with Plato or Marx—whether we are in a cave seeing only the shadows or are distracted from the reality of our material conditions by ideology—that we are out of touch and need to be awoken to certain aspects of our actuality is a practical attitude at the heart of the critical tradition. The critical tradition conceptualizes communication as *discursive reflection*—that is, discourse that freely reflects on assumptions that may be distorted by unexamined habits, ideological beliefs, and relations of power. Communication without critical reflection is inherently defective, for example when it blindly reproduces social conditions that privilege some groups (for example, with regard to social class, race, or gender) over others. Critical theory exposes hidden social mechanisms that distort communication and supports political efforts to resist the power of those mechanisms. Ideology, truth, deception, power, resistance, liberation, democracy, identity, and participation are a few of the terms commonly used for thinking and talking about communication in the critical tradition. However, in keeping with the critical tradition, these critical ideas about truth and power are as open to critique as any others.

Before proceeding with the discussion of the readings in this unit, we want to propose a framework for entering this tradition. While there is no Plato reading in this unit, it is appropriate to discuss him here because he coined the term dialectic, the art of inquiry through questioning, which is a helpful framework for reading the works in this tradition. Thinking of a Platonic (Socratic) dialogue as a model for how the critical tradition develops and grows, each theorist is engaged in a dialectical questioning of previous theorists across time. Each theory in the tradition responds, explicitly or implicitly, to previous theories in a way that builds toward the presentation of a transformed idea. Each piece reads like what can be experienced as a somewhat dense pyramid where the foundation work is necessary to reach the point. However, the point is not always located at the end of a work; and as with any act of interpretation, what one thinker culls from an earlier thinker could be very different than what another thinker does. Keeping this framework in mind may help in navigating the pieces in this unit.

As we discussed in the introduction to unit III, Plato's theorizing *the problem of rhetoric* and its accompanying distortion of actuality led not only to a critique of rhetoric but also to putting the dialectical pursuit of truth at the center of philosophy, which was upheld as the most worthy human pursuit. The critical theorist revealing the distortion of reality can be seen in the *Gorgias* (reading 6), where Plato exposes rhetoric as a mere knack for flattery masquerading as an art. Plato shows how dialectical communication can overcome the distortion of truth by rhetoric. Although engaging in rhetoric may allow one to persuade others and even move them to action, in Plato's philosophy such discourse only maintains the veil that blinds us to a higher reality. It is only through dialectic that we are able to penetrate the illusions and see the truth.

In the mid-19th century, Karl Marx and Frederick Engels (reading 31) theorized another distortion, *the problem of ideology.* Dialectically questioning the idealist philosophy of Hegel, and influenced in part by Feuerbach's materialist critique of religion, they proposed that only the material world and the material conditions of our lives are real. Our physical action—our production, our labor—is real. It is ideology that keeps us from knowing the actuality of production—from seeing clearly the material conditions of our lives. In the history of humanity, it is only at that point in the development of the division of labor when material and mental labor become separated that ideologists arise. Ideologists, the first of whom were priests, make it seem as though there is life separated from the material processes of production. In stark contrast to Plato, who believed that ideas are the only true reality, Marx and Engels asserted that ideas have no reality of their own; rather they are produced by humans and depend completely on underlying economic relations of production that prevail at a particular time in history. The ruling social class of any given time makes its own ideas seem like the only possible, universally true, rational ideas, but in actuality those ideas are intellectual constructions that uphold the power of that ruling class to control the means of production. When ideals like honor, loyalty, equality, or freedom become detached from the conditions of their production, they become illusions that hide the actuality of our existence.

Marx and Engels prod historians for their lack of attention to the material production of ideas. Ruling classes use ideology to keep lower classes unaware of their unjust economic situation. In the bourgeois capitalist society of the 19th century, the ruling ideology keeps workers from knowing that they (the workers) are the true foundation of the society. Since physical labor and the consequent ability to produce and transform nature is a natural capacity of humans, when the system of production forces workers to give up ownership of their own labor, they give up an essential aspect of their nature, thus experiencing a spiritual loss. Workers in a capitalist society are alienated from the products of their labor and caught up in what Marx later called *commodity fetishism*—money and consumer products seem to have mysterious powers of their own, unrelated to their actual use-value and the labor that produced them. The economic class system seems like a necessary reality to which people simply must adapt. When the ruling ideology that supports these illusions is unmasked and workers realize their true position in the process of production, they will form a revolutionary class that will ultimately lead the way to a communist society in which workers will once again own their own labor and social relations of production will not be distorted.

Jumping forward in time about a century, Max Horkheimer and Theodor W. Adorno's essay on the "Culture Industry" (reading 32) addressed a world in which capitalist ideology, contrary to the optimistic revolutionary expectations of Marx and Engels, was still deeply entrenched in the West. Horkheimer and Adorno were members of the Frankfurt School, a group of radical social theorists who formed the Institute for Social Research in Frankfurt, Germany, in 1929 and migrated to America during the Nazi period. They are often read (see Jansen in this unit for an example of such a reading of these theorists) as pessimistic and not articulating a way out of the ideological distortions that they unmasked. In the piece included here, originally written in the 1940s during World War II and a decade before television became a widespread medium, Horkheimer and Adorno theorize *the problem of inauthentic culture and the acceptance of deception.*

Horkheimer and Adorno point out that culture is now mass-produced like other goods and services. They claim that mass media, movies and radio in particular, do not even need to pretend to be art any longer. No one cares that all the parts of industry (movies, electric goods, banks, etc.) are interwoven and economically dependent on each other. Culture has become an industry and the slight variations from one mass-produced version of something (a Chevy) to another (a Pontiac) are treated as if they were important and relevant distinctions. Pseudo-individuality via mass-marketed fads and fashions has taken the place of real individuality. People gleefully pay a few pennies to see a show that cost millions to make and accept the poor quality because, well, it is free or almost so. Art has become a mere commodity. What has been called enlightenment is really a relapse into magic where the unmasking of the arbitrary connection between word and meaning (the semiotic sign and object) has led to some connections becoming inexorably fused. The reduction of meaning associated with positivism is part of what has led to people using words not because they understand them but because they bring about a conditioned reflex, like trademarks. Mass-produced culture has led to the triumph of advertising where people buy products despite their low quality or needlessness. People do not mind being deceived, and companies and the media do not even need to pretend they are not

being deceptive. In fact, the more deceptive it is, the more successful a trademark may be. Ideology has become total, distortion is rampant, but does anyone care?

As a second-generation thinker of the Frankfurt School, Jürgen Habermas has both carried forward and transformed many of Horkheimer and Adorno's ideas as he has theorized *the problem of communicative hope.* Rather than a litany of the many ways in which communication in society is distorted by power and ideology, Habermas (reading 33) provides a critical standard for communication that would not be systematically distorted and argues that the hopeful anticipation of undistorted communication is built into the very structure of human interaction. In effect, we have no choice but to hope for a society in which genuine and unconstrained discursive reflection will someday be possible. Any honest attempt to communicate (achieve mutual understanding with others) involves acting as if that hope could be realized.

In the piece excerpted in this unit, Habermas discusses his consensus theory of truth, validity claims that are implicit in the communicative use of language, and the ideal speech situation. First presented as a lecture in 1971, this is an early and relatively readable formulation of Habermas's communication theory, which was elaborated and revised in many subsequent works (see especially Habermas, 1981/1984, 1981/1987). Building on his theory of universal pragmatics presented earlier, he argues that the rational validity of any act of communication (speech act) is based on four implicit claims that can potentially be challenged: that the act has an intelligible meaning, that it is true, that the communicator has a moral right to perform it (normative rightness), and that the communicator is truthful or sincere in performing it. For example, in explaining Habermas's theory (our communicative act), we implicitly claim that our account of his theory has a clear meaning (comprehensibility), that it is accurate (truth), that we have a right to express our interpretation (rightness), and that we are doing so in a sincere effort to achieve an understanding with readers (sincerity). Communication runs smoothly as long as these implicit claims are unquestioned. When someone does question an implicit validity claim, the participants must engage in discourse (rational argumentation) to redeem the validity claim and thus reestablish the necessary background consensus for communication to continue. To the extent that direct discourse is difficult to achieve with readers who might want to question one or more of our implicit validity claims (a disadvantage of the book as a communication medium), our communication with readers is thereby distorted. Completely undistorted communication can only occur in an *ideal speech situation* in which validity claims can be freely questioned and discussed by all participants on an equal basis.

Because Habermas endorses a consensus theory of truth (which holds that a proposition is true if every competent person rationally agrees that it is true), we could easily be led into an endless circle, where consensus depends upon discourse and discourse depends upon consensus. This would make communication impossible unless we were able to appeal to an ontological (objective) theory of truth. However, as Habermas notes, we do have discourse, and we do this without necessarily appealing to ontological claims. So how do we avoid this endless circle in practice? In short, his response to this problem is that in essence we pretend that communication is possible based on our confidence in discerning a rational consensus from an illusory one. We are able to communicate linguistically because we hopefully anticipate the possibility of an ideal speech situation. At the same time, however, we need to realize—and this is where a critical theory of society enters the picture—that the

real conditions in which we engage in discourse never completely meet the requirements of an ideal speech situation. The ideological and other distortions of communication identified by critics like Horkheimer and Adorno severely limit the potential for discursive reflection. (Can there be genuine discourse in a society where people are happily deceived in so many ways?) Although the ideal speech situation provides a counterfactual standard by which to measure how far our actual communication falls short of the ideal, the communicative hope built into the structure of interaction—our unavoidable anticipation of a more rational world in which genuine communication would be possible—constitutes a practical hypothesis that critical theory can work to realize.

Habermas's work exemplifies a common practice in the critical tradition (and other theoretical traditions), which is the building of a comprehensive framework through integrating the work of many other thinkers in various traditions. This pulling together of strands of thought can be seen in Marx and Engels if one parses their ideas and traces them back to potential roots. It can also very clearly be seen in the final two readings of this unit, for both Deetz and Jansen integrate the ideas of many others in their theorizing. The way that critical scholars build on each other is interesting to compare with other traditions, such as the sociopsychological and rhetorical, in which building directly upon past ideas is also a common practice highlighted by our selection of readings. Just as sociopsychological theories become more complex as theorists build on existing theory and research, critical theory becomes more complex as theorists accept some parts of earlier theories while rejecting other parts and mix together ideas to better theorize experienced problems. Habermas's writings pull together the ideas of Marx and the early Frankfurt School; the psychoanalyst Freud; the phenomenologists Husserl and

Gadamer; Mead and other sociocultural theorists including functionalists such as Parsons; the speech act theorists Wittgenstein, Searle, and Austin (a branch of the semiotic tradition unfortunately not included among the readings in this book); and the sociopsychological moral development theorists Piaget and Kohlberg, among many others.

In reading 34, Stanley A. Deetz builds on Habermas's idea of systematically distorted communication as he theorizes *the problem of discursive closure*. Stating this problem closer to the practice end of the theory-practice continuum, it could be termed the problem of nonresponsive corporate decision making. Deetz incorporates ideas from critical theory and several other traditions including phenomenological, cybernetic, and sociocultural theories. According to Deetz, all communication is distorted to some degree; and this becomes problematic when the distortion is systematic and meaning is strategically and latently reproduced rather than being produced through free and open participation in an ideal speech situation. This reproduction takes place in micropractices when in interaction certain identities are privileged or allowed while other equally possible identities are disallowed. This reproduction is latently (not necessarily consciously) strategic because it is done in order to maintain smooth operations. However, the guise of smoothness cloaks the productive possibility of conflict and becomes pathological when, linking now to cybernetic theory, an organization becomes closed and responsive only to itself rather than the environment (the system property of autopoiesis described by Luhmann in unit VI). In keeping with Gadamer's phenomenological thought, if there is open discourse, the inherent partiality of all descriptions is counteracted through the advancement of other descriptions that reveal some of that partiality. It is thus through genuine conversation that the possibility of

growth and change emerges. However, when open discourse is replaced by information repetition, the system is discursively closed. When closed, the organization continually reproduces itself in response to shadows of itself rather than producing itself in response to the environment. This piece ends with a discussion of the common communicative processes or forms of discursive closure that suppress conflict and disable participation.

The remedy for discursive closure is participatory democracy, which, in keeping with the dialectical growth of the critical tradition, is an idea taken up again in the last reading in this unit. Sue Curry Jansen theorizes *the problem of technocratic structure*. Stated another way, she theorizes the problem of the distortion of language through its use in the modes of management, public relations, and spin—ideology in the guise of technical expertise. How we use words matters. That language and culture have been dominated by instrumental reason (technological means-ends thinking) needs to be readdressed, as do the potential escape routes from this technocratically dominated landscape. In this readdressing, Jansen reviews and critiques the contributions of the Frankfurt School theorists as well as some readings of them by other theorists and draws together Habermas's ideal speech situation and Herbert Marcuse's notion of linguistic therapy as well as the American legal theorist Bruce Ackerman's concept of neutral dialogue.

As part of her questioning of the emancipatory potential of critical inquiry and democracy, Jansen recommends "eutopian" thinking (eutopian referring to building a better place in contrast to utopia, which means literally "no place") for its potential to build as well as distort just communities. According to Jansen, through a version of Marcuse's linguistic therapy, words like liberation and emancipation can regain their critical nature. However, media critics as well as critical theorists have to practice what they preach by following the dictates of neutral dialogue themselves; and though talk is important, so is action. Acting as vanguards and talking for the people is not appropriate. Rather, since research has shown that participatory democracy has retained its potential in small groups, coalition formation is appropriate.

A final key aspect of Jansen's theorizing is her reading of Peters (1999, and readings 2 and 14 in this volume) and his concepts of dialogue, dissemination, and the democracy of reception. Jansen concludes there is still much potential for emancipation in the critical project as long as the power-talk within the tradition proceeds in an open-ended fashion. In the continuing dialectical fashion of the critical tradition and heeding her own call, Jansen proposes the idea, since most people live in a mediated world, of Internet-based mediated technologies where talk embodying the values and following the requirements of reflexive power-talk occurs as a possible technological response to the questions posed and left unanswered by the Frankfurt School.

As reflected by the readings in this unit, critical communication theorists variably unmask distortions of communication by power and ideology and/or provide techniques for resisting or overcoming distortions. The tradition develops and grows in a dialectical fashion such that theorists propose new ideas in dialogue with previous theorists. As one considers this tradition (and especially the readings we have selected for this unit), one may be drawn to ask: Is all critical theorizing as Frankfurt School-centric as this group of readings? Indeed, this is a good question. In keeping with the dialectical nature of the tradition, it makes sense to include readings that build and transform a set of ideas from one to the next, yet even in these readings other important strands of the tradition are intimated. Feminism and postcolonial theory are two strands that Jansen mentions. What additional strands of thought should be included in the critical tradition? Is feminist communication theory essentially a form of critical theory? Or, a possibility mentioned elsewhere in this book, should feminism be regarded as a distinct tradition of communication theorizing in its own right? Is any theorist who addresses power and/or ideology a critical theorist? Are postmodernists and post-structuralists and even postpositivists critical theorists?

Some would argue there is a worldview or mind-set difference between critical theorists and theorists in other traditions such as the sociopsychological and sociocultural: Is this the case? What about rhetoricians and critical theorists? Do they have clearly distinct worldviews? Could the feminist rhetorical theorists Foss and Griffin (reading 9) have been placed in this unit? What about a post-structuralist phenomenologist like Chang (reading 18) or a post-structuralist sociocultural theorist like Poster (reading 28)? Can a thinker legitimately be both a critical theorist and in one or more other traditions as well? Is anyone who uses a dialectical approach a critical theorist? Burke (reading 8)? Or, again, Plato (reading 6)? On the other hand, can a theorist take a dialectical approach and yet be entirely outside of the critical tradition? Looking across the previous units of this book, does there seem to be a general trend toward more critical communication theorizing? Just as empiricist social psychology took on questions that had once been in the domain of rhetoric (in experimental studies of persuasion), is the critical tradition now taking on questions that used to be examined in other traditions?

The generally leftist political stance of these readings can bring other questions to mind. Is it appropriate for a communication theory to have political goals? Should theories be objective and therefore nonpolitical? On the other hand, is it true, as critical theorists tend to argue, that all theories have ideological implications that serve some political interests rather than others, if only implicitly? Are some traditions of communication theory more compatible than others with political conservatism? Is conservative ideology essentially a form of systematically distorted communication that is inherently incompatible with critical theory?

A final set of questions to contemplate while reading the pieces in this unit are ones that arise from the general project of theorizing: How do these theories inform your own interpretation of communication? Do you see the distortions pointed out by these theorists? Are there other distortions that you have seen or personally experienced (perhaps distortions related to race, gender, or sexual orientation) that are not directly addressed in these readings? Do you see another direction critical theory could take? Are the techniques for overcoming distortions proposed by these

theorists feasible, and would they make a difference? Are there other techniques that you can propose? Are there other readings that could have been included in this unit to better represent the critical tradition?

REFERENCES

Habermas, J. (1984). *The theory of communicative action: Vol. 1. Reason and the rationalization of society* (T. McCarthy, Trans.). Boston: Beacon Press. (Original work published 1981)

Habermas, J. (1987). *The theory of communicative action: Vol. 2. Lifeworld and system: A critique of functionalist reason* (T. McCarthy, Trans.). Boston: Beacon Press. (Original work published 1981)

Peters, J. D. (1999). *Speaking into the air: A history of the idea of communication.* Chicago: University of Chicago Press.

31

THE GERMAN IDEOLOGY

KARL MARX AND FREDERICK ENGELS

The production of ideas, of conceptions, of consciousness, is at first directly interwoven with the material activity and the material intercourse of men, the language of real life. Conceiving, thinking, the mental intercourse of men, appear at this stage as the direct efflux of their material behaviour. The same applies to mental production as expressed in the language of politics, laws, morality, religion, metaphysics, etc., of a people. Men are the producers of their conceptions, ideas, etc.—real, active men, as they are conditioned by a definite development of their productive forces and of the intercourse corresponding to these, up to its furthest forms. Consciousness can never be anything else than conscious existence, and the existence of men is their actual life-process. If in all ideology men and their circumstances appear upside-down as in a camera obscura, this phenomenon arises just as much from their historical life-process as the inversion of objects on the retina does from their physical life-process.

In direct contrast to German philosophy which descends from heaven to earth, here we ascend from earth to heaven. That is to say, we do not set out from what men say, imagine, conceive, nor from men as narrated, thought of, imagined, conceived, in order to arrive at men in the flesh. We set out from real, active men, and on the basis of their real life-process we demonstrate the development of the ideological reflexes and echoes of this life-process. The phantoms formed in the human brain are also, necessarily, sublimates of their material life-process, which is empirically verifiable and bound to material premises. Morality, religion, metaphysics, all the rest of ideology and their corresponding forms of consciousness, thus no longer retain the semblance of independence. They have no history, no development; but men, developing their material production and their material intercourse, alter, along with this their real existence, their thinking and the products of their thinking. Life is not determined by consciousness, but

SOURCE: Marx, K., & Engels, F. (1845–46/1968). *The German ideology* (excerpts). Marx/Engels Internet Archive (Marxists.org) 2000. Transcription by Tim Delaney, Bob Schwartz, and Brian Basgen. Retrieved June 9, 2005, from http://www.marxists.org/archive/marx/works/1845/german-ideology/ch01a.htm.

consciousness by life. In the first method of approach the starting-point is consciousness taken as the living individual; in the second method, which conforms to real life, it is the real living individuals themselves, and consciousness is considered solely as their consciousness.

[. . .]

Only now, after having considered four moments, four aspects of the primary historical relationships, do we find that man also possesses "consciousness," but, even so, not inherent, not "pure" consciousness. From the start the "spirit" is afflicted with the curse of being "burdened" with matter, which here makes its appearance in the form of agitated layers of air, sounds, in short, of language. Language is as old as consciousness, language is practical consciousness that exists also for other men, and for that reason alone it really exists for me personally as well; language, like consciousness, only arises from the need, the necessity, of intercourse with other men. Where there exists a relationship, it exists for me: the animal does not enter into "relations" with anything, it does not enter into any relation at all. For the animal, its relation to others does not exist as a relation. Consciousness is, therefore, from the very beginning a social product, and remains so as long as men exist at all. Consciousness is at first, of course, merely consciousness concerning the immediate sensuous environment and consciousness of the limited connection with other persons and things outside the individual who is growing self-conscious. At the same time it is consciousness of nature, which first appears to men as a completely alien, all-powerful and unassailable force, with which men's relations are purely animal and by which they are overawed like beasts; it is thus a purely animal consciousness of nature (natural religion) just because nature is as yet hardly modified historically. (We see here immediately: this natural religion or this particular relation of men to nature is determined by the form of society and vice versa. Here, as everywhere, the identity of nature and man appears in such a way that the restricted relation of men to nature determines their restricted relation to one another, and their restricted relation to one another determines men's restricted relation to nature.) On the other hand, man's consciousness of the necessity of associating with the individuals around him is the beginning of the consciousness that he is living in society at all. This beginning is as animal as social life itself at this stage. It is mere herd-consciousness, and at this point man is only distinguished from sheep by the fact that with him consciousness takes the place of instinct or that his instinct is a conscious one. This sheep-like or tribal consciousness receives its further development and extension through increased productivity, the increase of needs, and, what is fundamental to both of these, the increase of population. With these there develops the division of labour, which was originally nothing but the division of labour in the sexual act, then that division of labour which develops spontaneously or "naturally" by virtue of natural predisposition (e.g. physical strength), needs, accidents, etc. etc. Division of labour only becomes truly such from the moment when a division of material and mental labour appears. (The first form of ideologists, priests, is concurrent.) From this moment onwards consciousness can really flatter itself that it is something other than consciousness of existing practice, that it really represents something without representing something real; from now on consciousness is in a position to emancipate itself from the world and to proceed to the formation of "pure" theory, theology, philosophy, ethics, etc. But even if this theory, theology, philosophy, ethics, etc. comes into contradiction with the existing relations, this can only occur because existing social relations have come into contradiction with existing forces of production; this, moreover, can also occur in a particular national sphere of relations through the appearance of the contradiction, not within the national orbit, but between this national consciousness and the practice of other nations, i.e. between the national and the general consciousness of a nation (as we see it now in Germany).

[. . .]

The ideas of the ruling class are in every epoch the ruling ideas, i.e. the class which is the ruling material force of society, is at the same time its ruling intellectual force. The class which has the means of material production at its disposal, has control at the same time over the means of mental production, so that thereby, generally speaking, the ideas of those who lack the means of mental production are subject to it. The ruling ideas are nothing more than the ideal expression of the dominant material relationships, the dominant material relationships grasped as ideas; hence of the relationships which make the one class the ruling one, therefore, the ideas of its dominance. The individuals composing the ruling class possess among other things consciousness, and therefore think. Insofar, therefore, as they rule as a class and determine the extent and compass of an epoch, it is self-evident that they do this in its whole range, hence among other things rule also as thinkers, as producers of ideas, and regulate the production and distribution of the ideas of their age: thus their ideas are the ruling ideas of the epoch. For instance, in an age and in a country where royal power, aristocracy, and bourgeoisie are contending for mastery and where, therefore, mastery is shared, the doctrine of the separation of powers proves to be the dominant idea and is expressed as an "eternal law."

The division of labour, which we already saw above as one of the chief forces of history up till now, manifests itself also in the ruling class as the division of mental and material labour, so that inside this class one part appears as the thinkers of the class (its active, conceptive ideologists, who make the perfecting of the illusion of the class about itself their chief source of livelihood), while the others' attitude to these ideas and illusions is more passive and receptive, because they are in reality the active members of this class and have less time to make up illusions and ideas about themselves. Within this class this cleavage can even develop into a certain opposition and hostility between the two parts, which,

however, in the case of a practical collision, in which the class itself is endangered, automatically comes to nothing, in which case there also vanishes the semblance that the ruling ideas were not the ideas of the ruling class and had a power distinct from the power of this class. The existence of revolutionary ideas in a particular period presupposes the existence of a revolutionary class; about the premises for the latter sufficient has already been said above.

If now in considering the course of history we detach the ideas of the ruling class from the ruling class itself and attribute to them an independent existence, if we confine ourselves to saying that these or those ideas were dominant at a given time, without bothering ourselves about the conditions of production and the producers of these ideas, if we thus ignore the individuals and world conditions which are the source of the ideas, we can say, for instance, that during the time that the aristocracy was dominant, the concepts honour, loyalty, etc. were dominant, during the dominance of the bourgeoisie the concepts freedom, equality, etc. The ruling class itself on the whole imagines this to be so. This conception of history, which is common to all historians, particularly since the eighteenth century, will necessarily come up against the phenomenon that increasingly abstract ideas hold sway, i.e. ideas which increasingly take on the form of universality. For each new class which puts itself in the place of one ruling before it, is compelled, merely in order to carry through its aim, to represent its interest as the common interest of all the members of society, that is, expressed in ideal form: it has to give its ideas the form of universality, and represent them as the only rational, universally valid ones.

[. . .]

Whilst in ordinary life every shopkeeper is very well able to distinguish between what somebody professes to be and what he really is, our historians have not yet won even this trivial insight. They take every epoch at its word and believe that everything it says and imagines about itself is true.

32

THE CULTURE INDUSTRY

Enlightenment as Mass Deception

MAX HORKHEIMER AND THEODOR W. ADORNO

The sociological theory that the loss of the support of objectively established religion, the dissolution of the last remnants of precapitalism, together with technological and social differentiation or specialization, have led to cultural chaos is disproved every day; for culture now impresses the same stamp on everything. Films, radio and magazines make up a system which is uniform as a whole and in every part. Even the aesthetic activities of political opposites are one in their enthusiastic obedience to the rhythm of the iron system. The decorative industrial management buildings and exhibition centers in authoritarian countries are much the same as anywhere else. The huge gleaming towers that shoot up everywhere are outward signs of the ingenious planning of international concerns, toward which the unleashed entrepreneurial system (whose monuments are a mass of gloomy houses and business premises in grimy, spiritless cities) was already hastening. Even now the older houses just outside the concrete city centers look like slums, and the new bungalows on the outskirts are at one with the flimsy structures of world fairs in their praise of technical progress and their built-in demand to be discarded after a short while like empty food cans. Yet the city housing projects designed to perpetuate the individual as a supposedly independent unit in a small hygienic dwelling make him all the more subservient to his adversary—the absolute power of capitalism. Because the inhabitants, as producers and as consumers, are drawn into the center in search of work and pleasure, all the living units crystallize into well-organized complexes. The striking unity of

SOURCE: Horkheimer, M., & Adorno, T. W. (1976). The culture industry. In *Dialectic of enlightenment* (J. Cumming, Trans.; excerpts: pp. 120–124, 154–167): Continuum International Publishing Group. Excerpts from *Dialectic of Enlightenment* by Max Horkheimer and Theodor W. Adorno, Translated by John Cumming. English translation © 1972 by Herder & Herder. Reprinted with the permission of the publisher, The Continuum International Publishing Group.

microcosm and macrocosm presents men with a model of their culture: the false identity of the general and the particular. Under monopoly all mass culture is identical, and the lines of its artificial framework begin to show through. The people at the top are no longer so interested in concealing monopoly: as its violence becomes more open, so its power grows. Movies and radio need no longer pretend to be art. The truth that they are just business is made into an ideology in order to justify the rubbish they deliberately produce. They call themselves industries; and when their directors' incomes are published, any doubt about the social utility of the finished products is removed.

Interested parties explain the culture industry in technological terms. It is alleged that because millions participate in it, certain reproduction processes are necessary that inevitably require identical needs in innumerable places to be satisfied with identical goods. The technical contrast between the few production centers and the large number of widely dispersed consumption points is said to demand organization and planning by management. Furthermore, it is claimed that standards were based in the first place on consumers' needs, and for that reason were accepted with so little resistance. The result is the circle of manipulation and retroactive need in which the unity of the system grows ever stronger. No mention is made of the fact that the basis on which technology acquires power over society is the power of those whose economic hold over society is greatest. A technological rationale is the rationale of domination itself. It is the coercive nature of society alienated from itself. Automobiles, bombs, and movies keep the whole thing together until their leveling element shows its strength in the very wrong which it furthered. It has made the technology of the culture industry no more than the achievement of standardization and mass production, sacrificing whatever involved a distinction between the logic of the work and that of the social system. This is the result not of a law of movement in technology as such but of its function in today's economy. The need which might resist central control has already been suppressed by the control of the individual consciousness. The step from the telephone to the radio has clearly distinguished the roles. The former still allowed the subscriber to play the role of subject, and was liberal. The latter is democratic: it turns all participants into listeners and authoritatively subjects them to broadcast programs which are all exactly the same. No machinery of rejoinder has been devised, and private broadcasters are denied any freedom. They are confined to the apocryphal field of the "amateur," and also have to accept organization from above. But any trace of spontaneity from the public in official broadcasting is controlled and absorbed by talent scouts, studio competitions and official programs of every kind selected by professionals. Talented performers belong to the industry long before it displays them; otherwise they would not be so eager to fit in. The attitude of the public, which ostensibly and actually favors the system of the culture industry, is a part of the system and not an excuse for it. If one branch of art follows the same formula as one with a very different medium and content; if the dramatic intrigue of broadcast soap operas becomes no more than useful material for showing how to master technical problems at both ends of the scale of musical experience—real jazz or a cheap imitation; or if a movement from a Beethoven symphony is crudely "adapted" for a film sound-track in the same way as a Tolstoy novel is garbled in a film script: then the claim that this is done to satisfy the spontaneous wishes of the public is no more than hot air. We are closer to the facts if we explain these phenomena as inherent in the technical and personnel apparatus which, down to its last cog, itself forms part of the economic mechanism of selection. In addition there is the agreement—or at least the determination—of all executive authorities not to produce or sanction anything that in any way differs from their own rules, their own ideas about consumers, or above all themselves.

In our age the objective social tendency is incarnate in the hidden subjective purposes of company directors, the foremost among whom are in the most powerful sectors of industry: steel, petroleum, electricity, and chemicals. Culture monopolies are weak and dependent in comparison. They cannot afford to neglect their appeasement of the real holders of power if their sphere of activity in mass society (a sphere producing a specific type of commodity which anyhow is still too closely bound up with easygoing liberalism and Jewish intellectuals) is not to undergo a series of purges. The dependence of the most powerful broadcasting company on the electrical industry, or of the motion picture industry on the banks, is characteristic of the whole sphere, whose individual branches are themselves economically interwoven. All are in such close contact that the extreme concentration of mental forces allows demarcation lines between different firms and technical branches to be ignored. The ruthless unity in the culture industry is evidence of what will happen in politics. Marked differentiations such as those of A and B films, or of stories in magazines in different price ranges, depend not so much on subject matter as on classifying, organizing, and labeling consumers. Something is provided for all so that none may escape; the distinctions are emphasized and extended. The public is catered for with a hierarchical range of mass-produced products of varying quality, thus advancing the rule of complete quantification. Everybody must behave (as if spontaneously) in accordance with his previously determined and indexed level, and choose the category of mass product turned out for his type. Consumers appear as statistics on research organization charts, and are divided by income groups into red, green, and blue areas; the technique is that used for any type of propaganda.

How formalized the procedure is can be seen when the mechanically differentiated products prove to be all alike in the end. That the difference between the Chrysler range and General Motors products is basically illusory strikes every child with a keen interest in varieties. What connoisseurs discuss as good or bad points serve only to perpetuate the semblance of competition and range of choice. The same applies to the Warner Brothers and Metro Goldwyn Mayer productions. But even the differences between

the more expensive and cheaper models put out by the same firm steadily diminish: for automobiles, there are such differences as the number of cylinders, cubic capacity, details of patented gadgets; and for films there are the number of stars, the extravagant use of technology, labor, and equipment, and the introduction of the latest psychological formulas. The universal criterion of merit is the amount of "conspicuous production," of blatant cash investment. The varying budgets in the culture industry do not bear the slightest relation to factual values, to the meaning of the products themselves. Even the technical media are relentlessly forced into uniformity. Television aims at a synthesis of radio and film, and is held up only because the interested parties have not yet reached agreement, but its consequences will be quite enormous and promise to intensify the impoverishment of aesthetic matter so drastically, that by tomorrow the thinly veiled identity of all industrial culture products can come triumphantly out into the open, derisively fulfilling the Wagnerian dream of the *Gesamtkunstwerk*— the fusion of all the arts in one work. The alliance of word, image, and music is all the more perfect than in *Tristan* because the sensuous elements which all approvingly reflect the surface of social reality are in principle embodied in the same technical process, the unity of which becomes its distinctive content. This process integrates all the elements of the production, from the novel (shaped with an eye to the film) to the last sound effect. It is the triumph of invested capital, whose title as absolute master is etched deep into the hearts of the dispossessed in the employment line; it is the meaningful content of every film, whatever plot the production team may have selected.

[. . .]

In the culture industry the individual is an illusion not merely because of the standardization of the means of production. He is tolerated only so long as his complete identification with the generality is unquestioned. Pseudo individuality is rife: from the standardized jazz improvization to the exceptional film star whose hair curls over her eye to demonstrate her originality. What is individual is no more than the generality's power to stamp the accidental detail so firmly that it is accepted as such. The defiant reserve or elegant appearance of the individual on show is mass-produced like Yale locks, whose only difference can be measured in fractions of millimeters. The peculiarity of the self is a monopoly commodity determined by society; it is falsely represented as natural. It is no more than the moustache, the French accent, the deep voice of the woman of the world, the Lubitsch touch: finger prints on identity cards which are otherwise exactly the same, and into which the lives and faces of every single person are transformed by the power of the generality. Pseudo individuality is the prerequisite for comprehending tragedy and removing its poison: only because individuals have ceased to be themselves and are now merely centers where the general tendencies meet, is it possible to receive them again, whole and entire, into the generality. In this way mass culture discloses the fictitious character of the "individual" in the bourgeois era, and is merely unjust in boasting on account of this dreary harmony of general and particular. The principle of individuality was always full of contradiction. Individuation has never really been achieved. Self-preservation in the shape of class has kept everyone at the stage of a mere species being. Every bourgeois characteristic, in spite of its deviation and indeed because of it, expressed the same thing: the harshness of the competitive society. The individual who supported society bore its disfiguring mark; seemingly free, he was actually the product of its economic and social apparatus. Power based itself on the prevailing conditions of power when it sought the approval of persons affected by it. As it progressed, bourgeois society did also develop the individual. Against the will of its leaders, technology has changed human beings from children into persons. However, every advance in individuation of this kind took place at the expense of the individuality in whose name it occurred, so that nothing was left but the resolve to pursue one's own particular purpose. The bourgeois whose existence is split into a business and a private life, whose private life is split into keeping up his public image and intimacy, whose intimacy is split into the surly partnership of marriage and the bitter comfort of being quite alone, at odds with himself and everybody else, is already virtually a Nazi, replete both with enthusiasm and abuse; or a modern city-dweller who can now only imagine friendship as a "social contact": that is, as being in social contact with others with whom he has no inward contact. The only reason why the culture industry can deal so successfully with individuality is that the latter has always reproduced the fragility of society. On the faces of private individuals and movie heroes put together according to the patterns on magazine covers vanishes a pretense in which no one now believes; the popularity of the hero models comes partly from a secret satisfaction that the effort to achieve individuation has at last been replaced by the effort to imitate, which is admittedly more breathless. It is idle to hope that this self-contradictory, disintegrating "person" will not last for generations, that the system must collapse because of such a psychological split, or that the deceitful substitution of the stereotype for the individual will of itself become unbearable for mankind. Since Shakespeare's *Hamlet,* the unity of the personality has been seen through as a pretense. Synthetically produced physiognomies show that the people of today have already forgotten that there was ever a notion of what human life was. For centuries society has been preparing for Victor Mature and Mickey Rooney. By destroying they come to fulfill.

The idolization of the cheap involves making the average the heroic. The highest-paid stars resemble pictures advertising unspecified proprietary articles. Not without good purpose are they often selected from the host of commercial models. The prevailing taste takes its ideal from advertising, the beauty in consumption. Hence the Socratic saying that the beautiful is the useful has now been fulfilled—ironically. The cinema makes propaganda for the culture combine as a whole; on radio, goods for whose sake the cultural commodity exists are also recommended individually. For a few coins one can see the film which cost millions, for even less one can buy the chewing gum whose manufacture involved immense riches—a hoard increased still further by sales. *In absentia,* but by universal suffrage, the treasure of armies is revealed, but prostitution is not allowed inside the country. The best orchestras in the world—clearly not so—are brought into your living room free of charge. It is all a parody of the never-never land, just as the national society is a parody of the human society. You name it, we supply it. A man up from the country remarked at the old Berlin Metropol theater that it was astonishing what they could do for the money; his comment has long since been adopted by the culture industry and made the very substance of production. This is always coupled with the triumph that it is possible; but this, in large measure, is the very triumph. Putting on a show means showing everybody what there is, and what can be achieved. Even today it is still a fair, but incurably sick with culture. Just as the people who had been attracted by the fairground barkers overcame their disappointment in the booths with a brave smile, because they really knew in advance what would happen, so the movie-goer sticks knowingly to the institution. With the cheapness of mass-produced luxury goods and its complement, the universal swindle, a change in the character of the art commodity itself is coming about. What is new is not that it is a commodity, but that today it deliberately admits it is one; that art renounces its own autonomy and proudly takes its place among consumption goods constitutes the charm of novelty. Art as a separate sphere was always possible only in a bourgeois society. Even as a negation of that social purposiveness which is spreading through the market, its freedom remains essentially bound up with the premise of a commodity economy. Pure works of art which deny the commodity society by the very fact that they obey their own law were always wares all the same. In so far as, until the eighteenth century, the buyer's patronage shielded the artist from the market, they were dependent on the buyer and his objectives. The purposelessness of the great modern work of art depends on the

anonymity of the market. Its demands pass through so many intermediaries that the artist is exempt from any definite requirements—though admittedly only to a certain degree, for throughout the whole history of the bourgeoisie his autonomy was only tolerated, and thus contained an element of untruth which ultimately led to the social liquidation of art. When mortally sick, Beethoven hurled away a novel by Sir Walter Scott with the cry: "Why, the fellow writes for money," and yet proved a most experienced and stubborn businessman in disposing of the last quartets, which were a most extreme renunciation of the market; he is the most outstanding example of the unity of those opposites, market and independence, in bourgeois art. Those who succumb to the ideology are precisely those who cover up the contradiction instead of taking it into the consciousness of their own production as Beethoven did: he went on to express in music his anger at losing a few pence, and derived the metaphysical *Es Muss Sein* (which attempts an aesthetic banishment of the pressure of the world by taking it into itself) from the housekeeper's demand for her monthly wages. The principle of idealistic aesthetics—purposefulness without a purpose—reverses the scheme of things to which bourgeois art conforms socially: purposelessness for the purposes declared by the market. At last, in the demand for entertainment and relaxation, purpose has absorbed the realm of purposelessness. But as the insistence that art should be disposable in terms of money becomes absolute, a shift in the internal structure of cultural commodities begins to show itself. The use which men in this antagonistic society promise themselves from the work of art is itself, to a great extent, that very existence of the useless which is abolished by complete inclusion under use. The work of art, by completely assimilating itself to need, deceitfully deprives men of precisely that liberation from the principle of utility which it should inaugurate. What might be called use value in the reception of cultural commodities is replaced by exchange value; in place of enjoyment there are gallery-visiting and factual knowledge: the prestige seeker replaces the connoisseur. The consumer becomes the ideology of the pleasure industry, whose institutions he cannot escape. One simply "has to" have seen *Mrs. Miniver,* just as one "has to" subscribe to *Life* and *Time.* Everything is looked at from only one aspect: that it can be used for something else, however vague the notion of this use may be. No object has an inherent value; it is valuable only to the extent that it can be exchanged. The use value of art, its mode of being, is treated as a fetish; and the fetish, the work's social rating (misinterpreted as its artistic status) becomes its use value—the only quality which is enjoyed. The commodity function of art disappears only to be wholly realized when art becomes a species of commodity instead, marketable and interchangeable like an industrial product. But art as a type of product which existed to be sold and yet to be unsaleable is wholly and hypocritically converted into "unsaleability" as soon as the transaction ceases to be the mere intention and becomes its sole principle. No tickets could be bought when Toscanini conducted over the radio; he was heard without charge, and every sound of the symphony was accompanied, as it were, by the sublime puff that the symphony was not interrupted by any advertising: "This concert is brought to you as a public service." The illusion was made possible by the profits of the united automobile and soap manufacturers, whose payments keep the radio stations going—and, of course, by the increased sales of the electrical industry, which manufactures the radio sets. Radio, the progressive latecomer of mass culture, draws all the consequences at present denied the film by its pseudo-market. The technical structure of the commercial radio system makes it immune from liberal deviations such as those the movie industrialists can still permit themselves in their own sphere. It is a private enterprise which really does represent the sovereign whole and is therefore some distance ahead of the other individual combines. Chesterfield is merely the nation's cigarette, but the radio is the voice of the nation. In bringing cultural products wholly into the sphere of commodities, radio does not try to dispose of its culture goods themselves as commodities straight to the consumer. In America it collects no fees from the public, and so has acquired the illusory form of disinterested, unbiased authority which suits Fascism admirably. The radio becomes the universal mouthpiece of the Führer; his voice rises from street loud-speakers to resemble the howling of sirens announcing panic—from which modern propaganda can scarcely be distinguished anyway. The National Socialists knew that the wireless gave shape to their cause just as the printing press did to the Reformation. The metaphysical charisma of the Führer invented by the sociology of religion has finally turned out to be no more than the omnipresence of his speeches on the radio, which are a demoniacal parody of the omnipresence of the divine spirit. The gigantic fact that the speech penetrates everywhere replaces its content, just as the benefaction of the Toscanini broadcast takes the place of the symphony. No listener can grasp its true meaning any longer, while the Führer's speech is lies anyway. The inherent tendency of radio is to make the speaker's word, the false commandment, absolute. A recommendation becomes an order. The recommendation of the same commodities under different proprietary names, the scientifically based praise of the laxative in the announcer's smooth voice between the overture from *La Traviata* and that from *Rienzi* is the only thing that no longer works, because of its silliness. One day the edict of production, the actual advertisement (whose actuality is at present concealed by the pretense of a choice) can turn into the open command of the Führer. In a society of huge Fascist rackets which agree among themselves what part of the social product should be allotted to the nation's needs, it would eventually seem anachronistic to recommend the use of a particular soap powder. The Führer is more up-to-date in unceremoniously giving direct orders for both the holocaust and the supply of rubbish.

Even today the culture industry dresses works of art like political slogans and forces them upon a resistant public at reduced prices; they are as accessible for public enjoyment as a park. But the disappearance of their genuine commodity character does not mean that they have been abolished in the life of a free society, but that the last defense against their reduction to culture goods has fallen. The abolition of educational privilege by the device of clearance sales does not open for the masses the spheres from which they were formerly excluded, but, given existing social conditions, contributes directly to the decay of education and the progress of barbaric meaninglessness. Those who spent their money in the nineteenth or the early twentieth century to see a play or to go to a concert respected the performance as much as the money they spent. The bourgeois who wanted to get something out of it tried occasionally to establish some rapport with the work. Evidence for this is to be found in the literary "introductions" to works, or in the commentaries on *Faust*. These were the first steps toward the biographical coating and other practices to which a work of art is subjected today. Even in the early, prosperous days of business, exchange value did carry use value as a mere appendix but had developed it as a prerequisite for its own existence; this was socially helpful for works of art. Art exercised some restraint on the bourgeois as long as it cost money. That is now a thing of the past. Now that it has lost every restraint and there is no need to pay any money, the proximity of art to those who are exposed to it completes the alienation and assimilates one to the other under the banner of triumphant objectivity. Criticism and respect disappear in the culture industry; the former becomes a mechanical expertise, the latter is succeeded by a shallow cult of leading personalities. Consumers now find nothing expensive. Nevertheless, they suspect that the less anything costs, the less it is being given them. The double mistrust of traditional culture as ideology is combined with mistrust of industrialized culture as a swindle. When thrown in free, the now debased works of art, together with the rubbish to which the medium assimilates them, are secretly rejected by the fortunate recipients, who are supposed to be satisfied by the mere fact that there is so much to be seen and

heard. Everything can be obtained. The screenos and vaudevilles in the movie theater, the competitions for guessing music, the free books, rewards and gifts offered on certain radio programs, are not mere accidents but a continuation of the practice obtaining with culture products. The symphony becomes a reward for listening to the radio, and—if technology had its way—the film would be delivered to people's homes as happens with the radio. It is moving toward the commercial system. Television points the way to a development which might easily enough force the Warner Brothers into what would certainly be the unwelcome position of serious musicians and cultural conservatives. But the gift system has already taken hold among consumers. As culture is represented as a bonus with undoubted private and social advantages, they have to seize the chance. They rush in lest they miss something. Exactly what, is not clear, but in any case the only ones with a chance are the participants. Fascism, however, hopes to use the training the culture industry has given these recipients of gifts, in order to organize them into its own forced battalions.

Culture is a paradoxical commodity. So completely is it subject to the law of exchange that it is no longer exchanged; it is so blindly consumed in use that it can no longer be used. Therefore it amalgamates with advertising. The more meaningless the latter seems to be under a monopoly, the more omnipotent it becomes. The motives are markedly economic. One could certainly live without the culture industry, therefore it necessarily creates too much satiation and apathy. In itself, it has few resources itself to correct this. Advertising is its elixir of life. But as its product never fails to reduce to a mere promise the enjoyment which it promises as a commodity, it eventually coincides with publicity, which it needs because it cannot be enjoyed. In a competitive society, advertising performed the social service of informing the buyer about the market; it made choice easier and helped the unknown but more efficient supplier to dispose of his goods. Far from costing time, it saved it. Today, when the free market is coming to an end, those who control the system are entrenching themselves in it. It strengthens the firm bond between the consumers and the big combines. Only those who can pay the exorbitant rates charged by the advertising agencies, chief of which are the radio networks themselves; that is, only those who are already in a position to do so, or are co-opted by the decision of the banks and industrial capital, can enter the pseudo-market as sellers. The costs of advertising, which finally flow back into the pockets of the combines, make it unnecessary to defeat unwelcome outsiders by laborious competition. They guarantee that power will remain in the same hands—not unlike those economic decisions by which the establishment and running of undertakings is controlled in a totalitarian state. Advertising today is a negative principle, a blocking device: everything that does not bear its stamp is economically suspect. Universal publicity is in no way necessary for people to get to know the kinds of goods—whose supply is restricted anyway. It helps sales only indirectly. For a particular firm, to phase out a current advertising practice constitutes a loss of prestige, and a breach of the discipline imposed by the influential clique on its members. In wartime, goods which are unobtainable are still advertised, merely to keep industrial power in view. Subsidizing ideological media is more important than the repetition of the name. Because the system obliges every product to use advertising, it has permeated the idiom—the "style"—of the culture industry. Its victory is so complete that it is no longer evident in the key positions: the huge buildings of the top men, floodlit stone advertisements, are free of advertising; at most they exhibit on the rooftops, in monumental brilliance and without any self-glorification, the firm's initials. But, in contrast, the nineteenth-century houses, whose architecture still shamefully indicates that they can be used as a consumption commodity and are intended to be lived in, are covered with posters and inscriptions from the ground right up to and beyond the roof: until they become no more than backgrounds for bills and sign-boards. Advertising becomes art and nothing else, just as Goebbels—with foresight—combines them: *l'art pour l'art,*

advertising for its own sake, a pure representation of social power. In the most influential American magazines, *Life* and *Fortune,* a quick glance can now scarcely distinguish advertising from editorial picture and text. The latter features an enthusiastic and gratuitous account of the great man (with illustrations of his life and grooming habits) which will bring him new fans, while the advertisement pages use so many factual photographs and details that they represent the ideal of information which the editorial part has only begun to try to achieve. The assembly-line character of the culture industry, the synthetic, planned method of turning out its products (factory-like not only in the studio but, more or less, in the compilation of cheap biographies, pseudodocumentary novels, and hit songs) is very suited to advertising: the important individual points, by becoming detachable, interchangeable, and even technically alienated from any connected meaning, lend themselves to ends external to the work. The effect, the trick, the isolated repeatable device, have always been used to exhibit goods for advertising purposes, and today every monster close-up of a star is an advertisement for her name, and every hit song a plug for its tune. Advertising and the culture industry merge technically as well as economically. In both cases the same thing can be seen in innumerable places, and the mechanical repetition of the same culture product has come to be the same as that of the propaganda slogan. In both cases the insistent demand for effectiveness makes technology into psycho-technology, into a procedure for manipulating men. In both cases the standards are the striking yet familiar, the easy yet catchy, the skillful yet simple; the object is to overpower the customer, who is conceived as absent-minded or resistant.

By the language he speaks, he makes his own contribution to culture as publicity. The more completely language is lost in the announcement, the more words are debased as substantial vehicles of meaning and become signs devoid of quality; the more purely and transparently words communicate what is intended, the more impenetrable they become. The demythologization of language, taken as an element of the whole process of enlightenment, is a relapse into magic. Word and essential content were distinct yet inseparable from one another. Concepts like melancholy and history, even life, were recognized in the word, which separated them out and preserved them. Its form simultaneously constituted and reflected them. The absolute separation, which makes the moving accidental and its relation to the object arbitrary, puts an end to the superstitious fusion of word and thing. Anything in a determined literal sequence which goes beyond the correlation to the event is rejected as unclear and as verbal metaphysics. But the result is that the word, which can now be only a sign without any meaning, becomes so fixed to the thing that it is just a petrified formula. This affects language and object alike. Instead of making the object experiential, the purified word treats it as an abstract instance, and everything else (now excluded by the demand for ruthless clarity from expression—itself now banished) fades away in reality. A left-half at football, a black-shirt, a member of the Hitler Youth, and so on, are no more than names. If before its rationalization the word had given rise to lies as well as to longing, now, after its rationalization, it is a straitjacket for longing more even than for lies. The blindness and dumbness of the data to which positivism reduces the world pass over into language itself, which restricts itself to recording those data. Terms themselves become impenetrable; they obtain a striking force, a power of adhesion and repulsion which makes them like their extreme opposite, incantations. They come to be a kind of trick, because the name of the prima donna is cooked up in the studio on a statistical basis, or because a welfare state is anathematized by using taboo terms such as "bureaucrats" or "intellectuals," or because base practice uses the name of the country as a charm. In general, the name—to which magic most easily attaches—is undergoing a chemical change: a metamorphosis into capricious, manipulable designations, whose effect is admittedly now calculable, but which for that very reason is just as despotic as that of the archaic name. First names, those

archaic remnants, have been brought up to date either by stylization as advertising trade-marks (film stars' surnames have become first names), or by collective standardization. In comparison, the bourgeois family name which, instead of being a trade-mark, once individualized its bearer by relating him to his own past history, seems antiquated. It arouses a strange embarrassment in Americans. In order to hide the awkward distance between individuals, they call one another "Bob" and "Harry," as interchangeable team members. This practice reduces relations between human beings to the good fellowship of the sporting community and is a defense against the true kind of relationship. Signification, which is the only function of a word admitted by semantics, reaches perfection in the sign. Whether folksongs were rightly or wrongly called upper-class culture in decay, their elements have only acquired their popular form through a long process of repeated transmission. The spread of popular songs, on the other hand, takes place at lightning speed. The American expression "fad," used for fashions which appear like epidemics—that is, inflamed by highly-concentrated economic forces—designated this phenomenon long before totalitarian advertising bosses enforced the general lines of culture. When the German Fascists decide one day to launch a word—say, "intolerable"—over the loudspeakers the next day the whole nation is saying "intolerable." By the same pattern, the nations against whom the weight of the German "blitzkrieg" was thrown took the word into their own jargon. The general repetition of names for measures to be taken by the authorities makes them, so to speak, familiar, just as the brand name on everybody's lips increased sales in the era of the free market. The blind and rapidly spreading repetition of words with special designations links advertising with the totalitarian watchword. The layer of experience which created the words for their speakers has been removed; in this swift appropriation language acquires the coldness which until now it had only on billboards and in the advertisement columns of newspapers. Innumerable people use words and expressions which they have either ceased to understand or employ only because they trigger off conditioned reflexes; in this sense, words are trade-marks which are finally all the more firmly linked to the things they denote, the less their linguistic sense is grasped. The minister for mass education talks incomprehendingly of "dynamic forces," and the hit songs unceasingly celebrate "reverie" and "rhapsody," yet base their popularity precisely on the magic of the unintelligible as creating the thrill of a more exalted life. Other stereotypes, such as memory, are still partly comprehended, but escape from the experience which might allow them content. They appear like enclaves in the spoken language. On the radio of Flesch and Hitler they may be recognized from the affected pronunciation of the announcer when he says to the nation, "Good night, everybody!" or "This is the Hitler Youth," and even intones "the Führer" in a way imitated by millions. In such clichés the last bond between sedimentary experience and language is severed which still had a reconciling effect in dialect in the nineteenth century. But in the prose of the journalist whose adaptable attitude led to his appointment as an all-German editor, the German words become petrified, alien terms. Every word shows how far it has been debased by the Fascist pseudo-folk community. By now, of course, this kind of language is already universal, totalitarian. All the violence done to words is so vile that one can hardly bear to hear them any longer. The announcer does not need to speak pompously; he would indeed be impossible if his inflection were different from that of his particular audience. But, as against that, the language and gestures of the audience and spectators are colored more strongly than ever before by the culture industry, even in fine nuances which cannot yet be explained experimentally. Today the culture industry has taken over the civilizing inheritance of the entrepreneurial and frontier democracy—whose appreciation of intellectual deviations was never very finely attuned. All are free to dance and enjoy themselves, just as they have been free, since the historical neutralization of religion, to join any of the innumerable sects. But freedom to choose an ideology—since ideology always reflects economic coercion—everywhere proves to be freedom to choose what is always the same. The way in which a girl accepts and keeps the obligatory date, the inflection on the telephone or in the most intimate situation, the choice of words in conversation, and the whole inner life as classified by the now somewhat devalued depth psychology, bear witness to man's attempt to make himself a proficient apparatus, similar (even in emotions) to the model served up by the culture industry. The most intimate reactions of human beings have been so thoroughly reified that the idea of anything specific to themselves now persists only as an utterly abstract notion: personality scarcely signifies anything more than shining white teeth and freedom from body odor and emotions. The triumph of advertising in the culture industry is that consumers feel compelled to buy and use its products even though they see through them.

33

TRUTH AND SOCIETY

The Discursive Redemption of Factual Claims to Validity

JÜRGEN HABERMAS

Having provided a preliminary clarification of the cognitive and communicative uses of language, I should like to examine the claims to validity that are contained in speech acts. The communicative theory of society whose development I am advocating conceives of the life process of society as a generative process mediated by speech acts. The social reality that emerges from this rests on the facticity of the claims to validity implicit in symbolic objects such as sentences, actions, gestures, traditions, institutions, worldviews, and so on. This nimble facticity of meaning that lays claim to validity conceals as much as it expresses the ultimately physical force of strategic influences and the material force of functional constraints; they can gain permanency only through the medium of acknowledged interpretations. In the third lecture I distinguished four classes of claims to validity: intelligibility, truth, normative rightness, and sincerity. These converge in the single claim to rationality. I am introducing these concepts at the level of universal pragmatics and linking them to the strong assertion that the idealizations contained in the possibility of linguistic communication itself by no means express merely a particular historical form of reason. Rather, the idea of reason, which is differentiated in the various claims to validity, is necessarily built into the way in which the species of talking animals reproduces itself. Insofar as we perform any speech acts at all, we are subject to the inherent imperative of "reason," to use an honorific for the power that I should like to derive from the

SOURCE: Habermas, J. (2001). Truth and society: The discursive redemption of factual claims to validity. In *On the pragmatics of social interaction: Preliminary studies in the theory of communicative action* (B. Fultner, Trans.; pp. 85–103, omitting pp. 86 line 3 to 89 line 7). Cambridge, MA: MIT Press.

structure of possible speech. This is the sense in which I take it to be meaningful to talk of the social life process as having an immanent relation to truth.

[. . .]

The validity claim of constative speech acts, that is, the truth that we claim propositions to have by asserting them, depends on two conditions. First, it must be grounded in experience; that is, the statement may not conflict with dissonant experience. Second, it must be discursively redeemable; that is, the statement must be able to hold up against all counterarguments and command the assent of all potential participants in a discourse. The first condition must be satisfied to make credible that the second condition *could* be satisfied as required. The meaning of truth implicit in the pragmatics of assertions can be explicated if we specify what is meant by the "discursive redemption" of claims to validity. This is the task of the *consensus theory of truth.* According to this theory, I can attribute a predicate to an object if and only if everyone else who could enter into discourse with me would also attribute the same predicate to the same object. To distinguish true propositions from false ones, I take recourse to the judgment of others—that is, of all others with whom I could ever enter into discourse (including counterfactually all discursive partners I could encounter if my life history were coextensive with the history of human kind). The truth condition of propositions is the potential consent of *all* others. Everyone else should be able to convince him-or herself that I am justified in predicating the attribute *p* of object *x* and should then be able to agree with me. The universal-pragmatic meaning of truth, therefore, is determined in terms of the demand of reaching a rational consensus. The concept of the discursive redemption of validity claims leads to the concept of rational consensus. Before discussing the aporias that arise from this, I would like to examine the types of validity claims other than truth claims that occur in ordinary language games.

A functioning language game, in which speech acts are coordinated and exchanged, is accompanied by a "background consensus." This consensus rests on the recognition of at least four claims to validity that competent speakers must raise reciprocally for each of their speech acts: the *intelligibility* of the utterance, the *truth* of its propositional component, the *normative rightness* of its performative component, and the *sincerity* of the intention expressed by the speaker. The course of a communication runs smoothly (on the basis of a socially learned [*eingespielt*] consensus) if speaking and acting subjects

(a) render intelligible the pragmatic meaning of the intersubjective relation (which can be expressed in the form of a performative clause) as well as the meaning of the propositional component of their utterances;

(b) recognize the truth of the proposition stated with the speech act (or the existential presuppositions of the propositional content mentioned therein);

(c) acknowledge the normative rightness of the norm that the given speech act may be regarded as fulfilling; and

(d) do not cast doubt on the sincerity of the subjects involved.

Particular validity claims are thematized only if the functioning of a language game is disturbed and the working background consensus is undermined. This then gives rise to typical questions and answers, which are a normal part of communicative practice. If the intelligibility of an utterance becomes problematic, we ask such questions as, "What do you mean by that?" "How am I to understand that?" "What does that mean?" We call the answers to such questions *interpretations.* If the truth of the propositional content of an utterance becomes problematic, we ask such questions as "Are things as you say?" "Why are they that way and not some other way?" We reply to such questions with *assertions* and *explanations.* If the normative rightness of a speech act or its normative context becomes problematic, we ask such questions as,

"Why did you do that?" "Why didn't you behave differently?" To these questions we respond with *justifications.* Finally, if in the context of an interaction we call into doubt another's sincerity, we ask questions such as, "Is he deceiving me?" or "Is she deceiving herself about herself?" These questions, however, are addressed not to the untrustworthy person himself, but rather to third parties. A speaker suspected of being insincere can at best be cross-examined in court or may perhaps "brought to his senses" in analysis.

These four claims to validity are fundamental in that they cannot be reduced to a common denominator. The meaning of intelligibility, normative rightness, and sincerity cannot be reduced to the meaning of truth. We understand what truth is when we grasp the meaning of the claims to validity contained in constative speech acts: The pragmatics of assertion is the key to the concept of truth, whereas the appeal of models such as the correspondence theory, which are located in a different sphere, namely, that of iconic representation, is misleading. Truth is not a relation of resemblance. The same holds for the other classes of validity claims. The intelligibility of an utterance is not a truth relation. Intelligibility is a validity claim that signifies that I have mastery of a specific rule-competence, namely, that I know a natural language. An utterance is intelligible if it is grammatically and pragmatically well formed, so that everyone who has mastered the appropriate rule systems is able to generate the same utterance. Thus what we call "analytic truth" could be understood as a special case of intelligibility, namely, the intelligibility of sentences in formal languages. But intelligibility has nothing to do with "truth." Truth is a relation between sentences and the reality about which we make statements. By contrast, intelligibility is an internal relation between symbolic expressions and the relevant system of rules, according to which we can produce these expressions.

Sincerity is no more a truth relation than is intelligibility. Sincerity is a validity claim connected with speech acts belonging to the class of representatives. It signifies that I sincerely mean the intentions that I express exactly as I have expressed them. A speaker is sincere if she deceives neither herself nor others. Just as "truth" refers to the sense in which I can put forth a proposition, "sincerity" refers to the sense in which I disclose or manifest in front of others a subjective experience to which I have privileged access. As soon as we conceive of sincerity as a relation between the expression of an experience and an inner state qua entity, we have already misunderstood it on analogy with truth. In acts of self-representation, I assert nothing about inner episodes—I make no assertions at all; rather I express something subjective. The complementary misunderstanding, which underlies *disclosure theories of truth,* is no less serious. In these theories (of which Heidegger's is a good example) truth is conceived on the model of sincerity as manifestation or unconcealment. This conception does not do justice to the fact that the cognitive use of language refers to reality.[1]

Compared to intelligibility and sincerity, the claim to normative rightness has received greater attention in philosophical discussions—albeit usually under the title of moral truth. Rightness is a validity claim connected with the class of regulatives. It signifies that it is right to recognize a prevailing norm and that this norm "ought" to have validity. This normative validity has nothing to do with the validity of truth. This is indicated by the fact that normative sentences cannot be derived from descriptive sentences. The oft-repeated objections to the naturalistic fallacy in ethics apply to the difference between rightness and truth. As soon as we conceive of rightness as a relation between a commendation or admonition and an inner entity such as a desire or aversion, we have already misunderstood it on analogy with truth. In acts of motivated choice I no more make assertions about inner episodes than I do in acts of self-representation. Rather I do something right or wrong. Nevertheless, to infer from this that there can be no truth in practical matters would equally be to misconstrue the meaning of normative validity. By expressing that one norm ought to be preferred to another, I want precisely to exclude the element of arbitrariness: Normative rightness coincides with truth in that both claims can be redeemed only discursively through argumentation and the attainment of rational consensus. Consensus, however, does not mean the same thing in the two cases. The criterion of the truth of propositions is the possibility of universal assent [*Zustimmung*] *to* an opinion, whereas the criterion of the rightness of a commendation or admonition is the possibility of universal agreement [*Übereinstimmung*] *in* an opinion.[2]

Not all of the claims to validity that we have elucidated by way of universal pragmatics with reference to the four classes of speech acts imply that they can be redeemed discursively. The consensus theory of truth, which has to rely on the concept of a discursively attained consensus, is relevant only for claims to truth and to rightness. Claims to sincerity can be redeemed only through actions. Neither interrogations nor analytic conversations between doctor and patient may be considered to be discourses. The case of claims to intelligibility is different. If the background consensus is upset to the point that ad hoc interpretations are no longer adequate, it is advisable to resort to hermeneutic discourse in which different interpretations can be tested and the one that is taken to be correct can be justified. Here too the difference is unmistakable. Claims to truth and to normative rightness function in everyday practice *as claims* that are accepted in light of the possibility that they *could* be discursively redeemed if necessary. Intelligibility, by contrast, is a claim that is in fact redeemed as long as the course of communication proceeds undisturbed; it is not merely an accepted premise; communication that is unintelligible breaks down.

The consensus theory of truth, to which I now return having distinguished the different types of validity claims, picks up on the fact that reaching mutual understanding [*Verständigung*] is a normative concept. Wittgenstein remarks that the concept of reaching understanding is contained in the concept of language. Hence the claim that the purpose of linguistic communication is to reach mutual understanding is analytic. Every act of reaching mutual understanding is confirmed by a rational consensus; otherwise it is not a "real" act of reaching understanding, as we say. Competent speakers know that any de facto consensus attained can be illusory; but their basis for the concept of an illusory (or simply forced) consensus is the concept of a rational consensus. They know that an illusory consensus must be replaced with an actual one if communication is to lead to mutual understanding. As soon as we start communicating, we implicitly declare our desire to reach an understanding with one another about something. If consensus—even about a difference of opinion—can no longer be reasonably expected, communication breaks down. Yet, if reaching understanding is not a descriptive concept, what is the criterion for a rational consensus, as opposed to a contingently established consensus that is not "sound"? A rational consensus, as we have said, is attained through discourse. What do we mean by discourse?

Discourses are events with the goal of justifying cognitive utterances. Cognitive elements such as interpretations, assertions, explanations, and justifications are normal components of everyday lived practice. They fill information gaps. However, as soon as their claims to validity are explicitly called into question, the procuring of further information is no longer simply a problem of dissemination but a problem of epistemic gain. In the case of fundamental problematizations, equalizing information deficits is of no help. Rather, we ask for convincing reasons, and in discourse, we try to reach a shared conviction [*Überzeugung*].

Interpretations, assertions, explanations, and justifications, whose claim to validity was initially naively accepted and then problematized, are transformed through discursively attained justifications. Casuistic interpretations are integrated into interpretive contexts, singular assertions are connected with theoretical statements, explanations are justified with reference to natural laws or norms, and singular justifications of actions are derived from the general justifications of the norms underlying the actions. We engage in *hermeneutic discourse* when contesting the validity of how to interpret expressions within a given linguistic system. We engage in *theoretico-emprical discourse* when verifying the validity of empirically meaningful assertions and of explanations. We engage in *practical discourse* when accounting for the validity of commendations (or admonitions), which refer to the acceptance (or rejection) of certain standards. If what is at issue is determining which linguistic system to select in order to be able to describe a preliminarily identified phenomenon adequately, to capture an existing problem exactly and render it manageable, or even to pick out a knowledge-guiding interest, then we have a special case of a practical discourse at the metalevel.

Substantive arguments have the power rationally to motivate the recognition of a validity claim, though they cannot *force* this recognition simply by way of deduction (or by a methodological appeal to experience). That is, they cannot do so analytically (or empirically).[3] The logic of discourse can give an account of what "rational motivation" means only by contrasting it with "logical necessity." This explanation will have to appeal in a circular fashion to the characteristic unforced force of the better argument—better because it is more convincing. But is it then possible to define the meaning of truth—which differs from mere certainty precisely in its claim to be absolute—by reference to the wobbly foundation of the endeavor to reach consensus discursively? How are we to distinguish a rational from a merely contingently established consensus?

Let us return to the question of the *truth of propositions*. Constative speech acts allow us to claim that propositions are true. They enable us to draw the fundamental distinction between reality and appearance. According to the consensus theory of truth, the condition for redeeming the truth of propositions is the potential assent of *all* other persons. Now, as a matter of fact, there are always only a few persons against whose assent I can check my assertion's claim to validity. The actual assent that I can possibly obtain from a few others is more likely to be endorsed by further judges, the less we and others see any reason to

doubt their competence to judge. Therefore we shall restrict the truth condition that has been introduced counterfactually as follows: I may assert *p* if every other *competent* judge would agree with me in this assertion. But what can competence in judgment mean in this context?

Kamlah and Lorenzen have proposed that competent judges must be capable of performing appropriate verification procedures. They must have expert knowledge. But how can we determine what sort of verification procedure is to count as appropriate in a given case and who may claim to be an expert? These questions, too, must be subject to discourse the outcome of which in turn depends on a consensus among the participants. Expertise is no doubt a condition that must be satisfied by a competent judge. But we cannot specify any independent criteria for what counts as "expertise"; deciding on the choice of these criteria itself depends on the outcome of a discourse. That is why, if the assent of a judge is to be the test of my own judgment, I should not like to make his competence depend on his expertise, but simply on whether he is "rational." We cannot escape this dilemma even if we assume that verification procedures appropriate for compelling consensus about the validity of empirically meaningful assertions could be derived from the universal-pragmatic features of descriptive language—or even if we could term "rational" all judges who, for example, are capable of methodical observation and inquiry. For how could we ascertain this competence with any certainty? It is by no means sufficient for someone to act as though she is making an observation or engaging in inquiry. We also expect her to be, for lack of a better word, in possession of her senses—that is, to be accountable for her actions. She must live in the public world of a speech community and must not be an "idiot," that is, incapable of distinguishing between reality and appearance. To be sure, we can tell whether someone is indeed rational only if we speak with her and can count on her in contexts of interaction.

In cases of doubt, whether a consensus is true or false must be decided through discourse. But the outcome of discourse depends in turn on the attainment of a sound consensus. The consensus theory of truth makes us aware that it is not possible to decide on the truth of propositions without reference to the competence of possible judges. This in turn cannot be determined without evaluating the sincerity of their utterances and the rightness of their actions. The idea of true consensus requires that the participants in discourse be able to distinguish reliably between reality and appearance, essence and accident, and is and ought; for only then can they be competent to judge the truth of propositions, the veracity of utterances, and the legitimacy of actions. Yet in none of these three dimensions can we specify a criterion that would allow for an independent assessment of the competence of possible judges or participants in deliberation. Rather, it seems as though the competence to judge itself must be judged on the basis of the very same kind of consensus for whose evaluation criteria are to be found.[4] This circle could be broken only by an ontological theory of truth, but none of these copy or correspondence theories has yet held up under scrutiny.

Were this the case, however, it would be hard to understand why we nonetheless assume in every conversation that we can reach a mutual understanding. In fact we are always confident that we know how to tell a rational consensus from an illusory one. Otherwise we could not tacitly presuppose the sense of speech that is always already accepted at the metacommunicative level and without which ordinary language communication would be meaningless—namely, its rational character. This phenomenon requires explanation.

I would argue that what explains it is that the participants in argumentation mutually *presuppose* something like an ideal speech situation. The defining feature of the ideal speech situation is that any consensus attainable under its conditions can count per se as a rational consensus. My thesis is that only the *anticipation [Vorgriff] of an ideal speech situation* warrants attaching to any consensus that is in fact attained the claim that it is a rational consensus. At the same time,

this anticipation is a critical standard that can also be used to call into question any factually attained consensus and to examine whether it is a sufficient indicator of real mutual understanding. The consensus theory of truth is, it seems to me, superior to all other theories of truth. But even it can break out of the circular movement of argument only if we assume that in every discourse we are mutually required to presuppose an ideal speech situation. Obviously this or a similar anticipation is *necessary* in order to avoid making the discursive redemption of a validity claim depend on a contingently attained consensus. The question remains of whether it is possible to design [*entwerfen*] an ideal speech situation. If, first of all, all speech requires that at least two subjects reach an understanding about something or, if necessary, discursively arrive at mutual understanding about disputed validity claims; if, second, mutual understanding means bringing about a rational consensus; and if, third, a true consensus can be distinguished from [a] false one only by reference to an ideal speech situation—that is, through recourse to an agreement that is conceived counterfactually as though it had come about under ideal conditions—then this idealization must involve an anticipation that we *must* make every time we want to engage in argumentation and that we are also able to make by means of the tools that every speaker has at her disposal by virtue of her communicative competence.

How is it possible to design an ideal speech situation by means of the speech acts that every competent speaker knows how to perform? In terms of distinguishing between a true and a false consensus, we call a speech situation ideal if communication is impeded neither by external contingent forces nor, more importantly, by constraints arising from the structure of communication itself. The ideal speech situation excludes systematic distortion of communication. Only then is the sole prevailing force the characteristic unforced force of the better argument, which allows assertions to be methodically verified in an expert manner and decisions about practical issues to be rationally motivated.

Only if there is a symmetrical distribution of the opportunities for all possible participants to choose and perform speech acts does the structure of communication itself produce no constraints. Not only are dialogue roles then universally interchangeable, but there is in effect also an equality of opportunities to take on these roles, that is, to perform speech acts. From this general assumption of symmetry we can derive special rules for each of the four classes of speech acts that we have introduced. If all participants in dialogue have the same opportunity to employ communicatives, that is, to initiate communication and continue it through speaking and responding or asking questions and giving answers, then equally distributing opportunities for employing constatives (as well as the subset of regulatives relevant for commending and admonishing)—that is, equally distributing the opportunities to put forth interpretations, assertions, explanations, and justifications and to establish or refute their claims to validity—can be a way of creating a basis on which no prejudice or unexamined belief will remain exempt from thematization and critique in the long run. These determinations are what ideally govern the speech acts that we employ in discourses. However, they do not fully specify the conditions of an ideal speech situation that ensures not only unrestricted, but also nonhegemonic discussion solely in virtue of its situational characteristics—that is, its structure. For the previous definitions do not by themselves guarantee that interlocutors not merely imagine themselves to be engaged in a discourse while they are in fact trapped in communication subject to coercion. We must assume in addition that speakers deceive neither themselves nor others about their intentions. Interestingly enough, therefore, the ideal speech situation requires determinations that refer directly to how contexts of interaction are organized, and only indirectly to discourses. The freeing of discourse from coercive structures of action and interaction, which is required for the ideal speech situation, is apparently conceivable only under conditions of pure communicative action. Therefore, the two other special assumptions

refer to rules governing speech acts that we use in interactions.

The ideal speech situation admits only speakers who *as actors* have the same opportunities to use representatives. For only a harmonious reciprocity as to the scope of utterances, which are always individual, and the complementary oscillation between proximity and distance ensure that subjects are transparent to themselves and others in what they actually do and believe and, if necessary, can translate their nonverbal expressions into linguistic utterances. To this reciprocity of unimpaired self-representation there corresponds a complementary reciprocity of expectations about behavior, which rules out privileges in the sense of norms of action that are only unilaterally binding. In turn, this symmetry of entitlements and obligations is guaranteed if interlocutors have equal opportunities to employ regulatives, that is, if the opportunities to command and resist, to allow and forbid, to make and extract promises, and to answer for one's actions and demand that others do so, are equally distributed. Together with the equal opportunity to use communicatives, this ensures the possibility of withdrawing at any time from contexts of interaction and entering into discourses that thematize claims to validity.

The counterfactual conditions of the ideal speech situation can also be conceived of as necessary conditions of an emancipated form of life. For to determine the symmetrical distribution of opportunities to choose and perform speech acts in terms of (a) propositions qua propositions, (b) the speaker's relation to his utterances, and (c) compliance with norms is to recast in linguistic terms what we have traditionally sought to capture in the ideas of truth, freedom, and justice. These terms mutually interpret one another. Taken together, they define a form of life that follows the maxim that all publicly relevant issues are to be dealt with by entering into discourse and that in doing so, we must presuppose that if we were to engage in communication with this intention and persist long enough, we would necessarily arrive at a consensus that would count as a rational consensus.[5]

The idealization of the speech situation is interlocked in a characteristic way with an idealization of the action situation. The concept of "pure communicative action," which I have introduced without justifying it, requires explanation.

Up to now we have distinguished between two forms of communication (or "speech"): *communicative action* (interaction) and *discourse*. In communicative action, the validity of utterances is naively presupposed in order to exchange information (experiences related to action). In discourse, validity claims that have been problematized become explicit topics of discussion, but no information is exchanged. In discourses we attempt to reestablish or replace an agreement that had existed in communicative action and became problematized. This is the sense in which I spoke of reaching a mutual understanding discursively. The goal of argumentation is to work through a situation that arises through the persistent problematization of validity claims that are naively presupposed in communicative action. This reflexive form of communication leads to a discursively produced, justified agreement (which of course can settle once again into a traditionally pregiven, secondarily habitual agreement).[6]

Communicative action takes place in habitualized and normatively maintained language games. They comprise expressions [*Äusserungen*] from all three categories (sentences, expressions [*Expressionen*], actions), which are not only formed according to rules, but are also connected with one another according to complementarity and substitution rules. Discourse, on the other hand, requires *suspending constraints on action*. This is meant to bracket all motives save that of a cooperative search for truth, and to separate questions of the validity of knowledge from questions of its origins. Second, discourse requires *suspending claims to validity*. This is to make us reserve our judgment regarding the existence of the objects of communicative action (that is, things and events, people and their expressions) and to remain skeptical with regard to states of affairs and norms. In discourse, to use Husserlian terms, we bracket the general thesis of the natural attitude. Thus facts turn into *states of affairs* that may or may not obtain, while norms become *suggestions* that may or may not be right.

In conclusion, I want to elucidate the meaning of normative validity, which is a fundamental concept of the communicative theory of society. The naive validity of norms of action contains a very far-reaching claim. This claim is the source of the counterfactual power that allows prevailing norms to sustain without violence their immunity against continual violations. Let me take as my starting point a phenomenon of which every subject capable of action has an intuitive awareness. If we encounter an other as a subject and not as an opponent, let alone as an object that we can manipulate, we (inevitably) take her to be accountable for her actions. We can only interact with her or, as I have put it, encounter her at the level of intersubjectivity, if we presuppose that under appropriate questioning she could account for her actions. Insofar as we *want* to relate to her as to a subject, we *must* proceed on the assumption that the other *could* tell us why in a given situation she behaved as she did and not otherwise. Thus we perform an idealization, and one that affects us as well, since we see the other subject with the eyes with which we look at ourselves. We suppose that the other, were we to ask her, can give us reasons for her actions just as we believe that we can account for our own actions if asked by another subject. This intuitive knowledge, which in the course of action conceals from itself the status of a supposition (or anticipation), can be broken down into two counterfactual expectations: (a) We expect that actors intentionally obey the norms that they follow. Thus we are incapable of imputing unconscious motives to the other in the course of an interaction.[7] As soon as we make such an imputation we leave the level of intersubjectivity and treat the other as an object *about* which we can communicate *with* third parties but with whom communication has broken down. In addition, this *expectation of intentionality* includes the assumption that all nonverbal expressions can if necessary be transformed into linguistic utterances. (b) We expect that acting subjects obey only those norms that they take to be justified. Thus we are incapable in the course of interaction to expect the other to obey a norm that she would not also recognize as legitimate (if she is obeying it intentionally). Even if a subject is obviously only bowing to an empirically imposed constraint, we impute to her general principles according to which she would justify this behavior, too. This *expectation of legitimacy* also includes the assumption that the only norms (or general principles) that are considered justified in the eyes of acting subjects are those that they are convinced would hold up if necessary under unrestricted and uncoercive discussion.

These two counterfactual expectations contained in the idealization of reciprocally imputed accountability, which is inevitable for actors, refer to a mutual understanding that is in principle attainable in practical discourses. The meaning of the claim to validity of norms of action consists therefore in the promise that the norm-governed behavior of subjects, which is in fact habitual, can be understood as the responsible action of accountable subjects. We presuppose that subjects can say what norm they are obeying *and why* they accept this norm as justified. In so doing, we also suppose that subjects to whom we can discursively demonstrate that they do not meet the two above conditions would abandon the norm in question and change their behavior. We know that institutionalized actions as a rule do not correspond to this *model of pure communicative action,* although we cannot help but always act counterfactually as though this model were realized. On this inevitable fiction rests the humanity of social intercourse among people who are still human, that is, who have not yet become completely alienated from themselves in their self objectifications.

The status of the unavoidable anticipation of an ideal speech situation (in discourse) and of a model of pure communicative action (in interaction), however, remains unclear. I want to conclude by cautioning against two obvious misunderstandings. The conditions under which arguments actually occur are clearly not the same as those of the ideal speech situation—at least not often or usually. Nevertheless, it is part of the structure of possible speech that in performing speech acts (and actions) we act counterfactually as though the ideal speech situation (or the model of pure communicative action) were not merely fictitious but real—precisely this is what we call a presupposition. Thus the normative foundation of linguistic communication is both anticipated and yet, as an anticipated basis, operative. The formal anticipation of idealized conversation (perhaps as a form of life to be realized in the future?) guarantees the "ultimate" underlying counterfactual mutual agreement, which does not first have to be created, but which must connect potential speaker-hearers a priori. Moreover, reaching a mutual understanding regarding this agreement must not be required if communication is to be at all possible. Thus the concept of the ideal speech situation is not merely a regulative principle in the Kantian sense. For with our first act of linguistic communication we must in fact always already be making this presupposition. On the other hand, the concept of the ideal speech situation is not an existing concept [*existierender Begriff*] in the Hegelian sense. For there is no historical society that corresponds to the form of life that we anticipate in the concept of the ideal speech situation. The ideal situation could best be compared with a transcendental illusion [*Schein*] were it not at the same time a constitutive condition of possible speech instead of an impermissible projection (as in the nonempirical employment of the categories of the understanding). For every possible communication, the anticipation of the ideal speech situation has the significance of a constitutive illusion that is at the same time the prefiguration [*Vorschein*] of a form of life.[8] Of course, we cannot know a priori whether that prefiguration is a mere delusion (subreption)—no matter how unavoidable the presuppositions that give rise to it—or whether the empirical conditions of an even approximate realization of this supposed form of life can be brought about in practice. From this point of view the fundamental norms of possible speech that are built into universal pragmatics contain a practical hypothesis. This hypothesis, which must first be developed and justified in a theory of communicative competence, is the point of departure for a critical theory of society.

NOTES

1. For a recent discussion of world disclosure, see *Thesis 11,* vol. 37 (1994), especially for the articles by Kompridis, Lafont, Seel, and Bohmann. Trans.

2. This difference may be connected with the fact that empirical beliefs must be grounded in experience whereas the acceptance or rejection of norms need not have an immediate experiential connection to external reality. The claim of a norm to be right may be based on the reflexive experience of the participating subjects of themselves. This experience indicates whether one "really wants" to accept the norm and whether the interpretation of needs and desires that it expresses "really" picks out what can be understood as "one's own" needs and desires.

3. S. Toulmin, *The Uses of Argument* (Cambridge: Cambridge University Press, 1964), pp. 146ff.

4. This goal cannot be attained because we cannot go behind a discourse; that is, we cannot engage in "metadiscourse." In a metadiscourse, we act as if—and this has been our attitude until now—we could ascertain that the participants in this discourse satisfy the conditions that allow them to participate in discourse. Yet strictly speaking, discourse and metadiscourse are at the same level. *All* discourses are intersubjective events. The appearance of the arbitrary iteration of the self-reflection of isolated subjects does not so much as get off the ground; see A. Kulenkampff, *Antinomie und Dialektik* (Stuttgart: Metzler, 1970). Even the self-reflection whereby interlocutors ascertain that they have indeed stepped out of contexts of communicative action and have suspended the forces of the reality of making risky decisions—even this is an intersubjective event; cf. my *Knowledge and Human Interests,* trans. J. Shapiro (Boston: Beacon Press, 1971), ch. 10. We cannot engage in discourse without *presupposing* that the conditions for entering into discourse have already been met. After having made this presupposition, however, discourse about whether we were right to do so is meaningless. At the level of discourse, there can be no separation of discourse and the external point of view of observing discourse.

5. I have sought to characterize the ideal speech situation not in terms of the features of the personality of ideal speakers, but in terms of the structural features of a context of possible speech, specifically the symmetric distribution of opportunities to take on dialogue roles and to perform speech acts. This construction is meant to demonstrate that we are indeed *capable* of anticipating an ideal speech situation, which a competent speaker must be able to do if she wants to participate in discourse, by means of the four mentioned classes of speech acts—and only those four. Hence my suggestion for giving a systematic account of speech acts can be justified in retrospect from the point of view that speech acts can only function as pragmatic universals—that is, as means of producing universal structures of possible speech—if they can simultaneously serve for designing an ideal speech situation.

6. Even a discursively justified validity claim regains the status of being "naively" presupposed as soon as the result of the discourse reenters contexts of action.

7. This also holds in the special case of therapeutic discourse, which both interlocutors enter with the intention of raising unconscious motives to the level of consciousness.

8. I have since retracted this formulation. See J. Habermas, "A Reply to My Critics," in J. B. Thompson and D. Held, eds., *Habermas: Critical Debates* (Cambridge, MA: The MIT Press, 1982), pp. 261ff.

34

SYSTEMATICALLY DISTORTED COMMUNICATION AND DISCURSIVE CLOSURE

STANLEY A. DEETZ

Meaning is polysemic in its intrinsic nature; it remains inextricably context bound. It is caught in and constituted by the struggle to "pre-fer" one among many meanings as the dominant. That dominance is not already inscribed in structures and events but is constructed through the continuous struggle over a specific type of practice—representational practices.

—Stuart Hall (1989, 47)

Communication is distorted whenever genuine conversation is precluded or, more specifically, any of the conditions of the ideal speech situation are not upheld. In a general sense, all communication is distorted to some degree. Symmetry conditions are partially violated, because at each moment there is a primary speaker, and every expression is inevitably one-sided and imaginary. Many of these distortions are overcome in the to-and-fro character of interaction. And following a participatory motive, structural conditions and individual ability differences could be overcome to a large extent. In many everyday settings, common distortions could give way to expanded and conflictual meanings in the pursuit of common understanding. Some distortions, however, are systematic. In these cases there is a latent strategic reproduction of meaning rather than participatory production of it. Systematically distorted communication operates like strategic manipulation, but without overt awareness. The latent

SOURCE: Deetz, S. A. (1992). *Democracy in an age of corporate colonization: Developments in communication and the politics of everyday life*. Albany, NY: SUNY Press. (Pages 173–198).

prejudice, preconception, predefined personal identity, or object production precludes open formation. The one-sidedness becomes reproduced rather than opened by conflicting representations.

The most familiar cases of this exist when the interactant is self-deceived. The psychoanalytic analogue of this describes when an individual has repressed certain experience and consequently the psychological experience and the expression of it become displaced or projected. In this sense an individual is out of touch with self-interests, needs and feelings and may well substitute other socially derived experiences and expressions for his or her own—an ideological expression or false consciousness. Strategic social forms dominate the individual or group consciousness. In the extreme model, only through a "talking cure" can the code be broken so that the disguised expression of the repressed state can be read and the individual can reconnect with self-experience. In this view, society and organizations can be seen as filled with "social neurosis." While instances of such distortion are at times present and the analysis is useful, such an analysis is too simple and creates difficulties. With the simple view, the role of social therapist, which can be attributed to the theorist, is elitist, and leads to everybody and everything being viewed with suspicion. The search for "real" motives, needs, and interests creates a new domination and another privileged discourse. And the implicit assumption that linguistic expression should represent a fixed, knowable interior provides a weak understanding of language and experience. But we can learn from the intuitive conception.

We know that we respond to unknown socially derived elements of experience, if only in using a particular historical language. We see people unwittingly act in opposition to their own values and needs. And we hear and participate in discourses that feel restrictive, like trying to express a sunset on canvas when you don't know how to paint. These are significant to the communication process. Here, systematic distortion is based not on a simple mismatch of fixed interests with a fixed expression, but on an interactionally determined reduction of certain experiences to

other ones outside the intentional awareness of the interactant. The core issue is the way certain experiences and identities are preemptively preferred over equally plausible ones.

A simple example may help display the important complexities. Young boys and girls often tease each other a lot and often profess and probably feel a degree of animosity. Yet an adult watching a young boy tell a young girl that she is "fat and ugly" would understand the expression to mean that he likes her and wants her attention. If confronted, the boy would probably deny it. I doubt that most of us would consider the adult egocentric if he or she thought that the male was only partly in touch with his feelings and that his most explicit expression was a distortion. We seem to accept this because we know that sorting out feelings at transitional points in life is difficult, that what are considered appropriate, even thinkable, feelings are socially developed, and that expression is constrained by group norms and expectations. If we pay careful attention, we will see that the early adolescent male is not experiencing false consciousness, but rather is actually making a fairly clear expression of confusion and mixed feelings, but ones that are "forgotten" or "misrecognized" by both speaker and recipient. The explicit message conceals the full variety of messages, affects both the speaker and listeners, and can elicit responses and counterresponses that perpetuate the one-sided development of feelings and expression rather than foster perceptual and expressive options. The distortion is not the tease (though some freeze that as a response option to the demise of later work relations) but the centering of the variety of experiences in one discourse. If the explicit message changed but was still singular, the distortion would still be present—for example, if in the wake of the television show "The Wonder Years," a twelve-year old male were to say to the female, "I want to go to bed with you," we could determine how such a discourse arose as privileged over other potentially competing relational statements—what it includes and what it leaves out, what kind of imaginary relation it is.

In a more technical sense, what is happening here is one type of self-deception. In this deception the individuals believe that they are engaging in communication action—pursuing mutual understanding—but are actually engaged in a concealed strategic action, even concealed from themselves. As Habermas (1984) described it: "Such communication pathologies [systematic distortion] can be conceived of as the result of a confusion between actions oriented to reaching understanding [communicative action] and actions oriented to success [strategic action]. In situations of concealed strategic action [manipulation], at least one of the parties operates with an orientation to success, but leaves others to believe that all the presuppositions of communicative action are satisfied. On the other hand, [in systematically distorted communication] at least one of the parties is deceiving himself *[sic]* about the fact that he is acting with an attitude oriented toward success and is only keeping up the appearance of communicative action" (332). When the people acting strategically know they are, we have a clear case of morally reprehensible manipulation. But in the case of systematically distorted communication the individual is self-deceived. A moral violation of participation is present but hidden. The conditions of discourse in pursuit of a legitimate consensus cannot proceed, since an unknown false consensus is already in place. Manipulation is clearly present in organizations, but systematically distorted communication is of more interest. Methods of corporate control perpetuate a false consensus without the members understanding them as a violation of basic moral rights or misrepresentation of interests. Understanding the latent strategic character of the apparently transparent is a step toward reopening the exploration of the private, social, and external world.

I believe that Habermas (1984, 70ff) is right in his analysis of the nature of this reformation. What is involved is a learning process rather than therapy. We can participate in the development of distinctions and articulation. This involvement is certainly not neutral, for our involvement partially determines the direction of development.

But we can determine when we participate with the other in development, versus when we try to teach them how to think and express. And we can become aware of when even subtle authority relations change enabling power relations into disqualification and discursive privilege. Such a learning process, however, is not one of putting people in touch with themselves or learning to articulate their insides clearly (hidden effectiveness issues) but one that reopens engagement in the development of differentiated feelings and discursive possibilities, to participate in the affective and expressive development of self and other.

Systematic distortion is a common property of human communication rather than something that occasionally arises during periods of transition. Human thought, feelings, actions, and expressions are often skewed. Certain dominant forms of reasoning and articulations stand in the stead of other valuational schemes. If career development exhausts the expression of personal development, if control drives the forms of human association, or if statements about the external world preclude those about affective states, we have a certain one-sidedness or systematic distortion. Such expressions can and should be examined for possible suppressions of alternative voices, not to implement alternative values, but as part of ongoing community development.

THE PATHOLOGIES OF SYSTEMATIC DISTORTION

Processes of systematically distorted communication can be said to be pathological. Following the normative foundation presented in the last chapter, we can say that communication is pathological to the extent that it (1) endangers the survival of the human and other species by limiting important adaptation to a changing environment, (2) violates normative standards already freely shared by members of a community, and (3) poses arbitrary limits on the development of individualization and the realization of collective good.

Clearly each of these is true of most instances of systematically distorted communication: To the extent that the communication system precludes responsiveness to an exterior, adaptation is limited; to the extent that the ideal speech situation is denied, freely shared normative standards are violated; and to the extent that the self and experience are reproduced, concept formation cannot occur in regard to otherness. Although the details of this need to be clearly specified, the modern corporation is filled with pathological interaction in each of these senses.

We already know a fair amount about pathological interpersonal systems. Interaction process analysis (Watzlawick, Beavin, and Jackson 1967; Pearce and Cronen 1980) initiated careful research into the way family systems can develop internal logics and rules, which structure frozen identities for the participants, which preclude the meeting of critical needs in their production of other needs, and finally strip participants of responsibility and responsiveness (see Laing 1971 for the most extreme examples). Such systems, because of their closure and fixed interpretive processes, properly have no outside, no natural checks and balances, and few moments of escape to see the system as it works. Yet they grow; they become supported by external structures and engulf others in their peculiar logics. The theoretical base of these studies, particularly in regard to the social structure of identity and reality, is too weak to show their political character or to demonstrate the workings of the modern organization, but their descriptions are useful in showing how pathological systems work. Corporate images and career paths, dependent and codependent processes internal to corporations, and reality production operate in organizations much like these interpersonal systems, and thus, provide for particular corporate pathologies.

Systematic Distortion in Decision Making

From a participatory communication perspective, many of the issues of good decision making look much the same as those from an effectiveness perspective. Good decisions require appropriately distributed information, openness to alternative perspectives, and reasoning based on personal insights and data rather than on authority relations. Implicit in these analyses, however, is the acceptance of priorities, goals, and authority relations that are not necessarily warranted or freely selected. When difficulties arise, then, the appeal is rarely to *discourse* along the model of the ideal speech situation. In most decisional effectiveness analyses, problems in the process are often conceptualized as individual or technical, thus requiring technical structural adjustments or personnel training. In cases of conflict, rather than reinvolving the community, higher order privilege is evoked, backed by symbolic control and expertise. The problem is "solved" rather than addressed. Based on the privileged situation, better information is gotten to the "right" people rather than asking who the right people are (based on the full variety of community needs) or what is the nature of the information presumptively included or excluded.

Forester (1989) provided a typology both of inevitable distortions that arise in communication processes and of systematic distortion related to decision making.

[. . .]

Self-Referential Systems

Forester's work is instructive but only takes us part of the way. Forester, like Habermas, operated primarily from a linear model of communication and focused on the speech act within a structural context. Communication researchers are and have been concerned with these relations, but we also know that human interaction takes place within multimessage, multilevel systems that are more complex than the segmented and largely intentional (even if hidden) communicative context described here. Communication systems as suggested by interaction process analysis and in chapter 5 are multitextual and produce the intentions of the participants. Rationality and intentionality are only partially descriptive of operating systems, and not only because they are sometimes distorted. Rather than taking an overtly intentional direction, both an orientation to reaching mutual understanding and strategic interaction can be defined in non-personal terms as systemic outcomes owing to internal system logics. The ideal speech situation must be understood in systemic as well as structural and intentional terms.

In organizations the most important systemic forms of systematic distortion can exist in "self-producing," "self-referential" systems. Many recent organizational theorists (Faucheux and Makridakis 1979; Ulrich and Probst 1984; Morgan 1986; Mingers 1989) have used Maturana and Varela's (1980) conception of *autopoietic systems* to describe the *self producing, self-referential* character of corporate systems. The intent here is to avoid many of the systems' assumptions and terminology, but to use their descriptions to draw attention to practices by which organizations can become distorted in their self-production, cut off from anything other than their own products (be they workers, consumers or the environment), and thus unknowingly engage in systematically distorted communication as they try to operate rationally.

In saying that organizations are self-producing and self-referential, attention is drawn to the way in which corporations, like all human systems, produce themselves in an environment (as signified) that they have enacted from their own internal signifying system, and evaluate their success through the use of criteria developed internal to the processes being evaluated. They do not simply adapt to an external environment, they enact the environment to which they react. The environment in which the corporation exists is "autobiographic" as well as an external reality to which it shapes itself. Maturana and Varela's (1980) work thus denies a simple distinction between the system and environment in much the same way that Althusser denied a person/world separation. There can be no open system, nor fixed external environment to get right or adjust to. The identity of the subject and world arise imaginarily in a chain of signifiers. Parallel to the "subjected subject," systems attempt to reproduce themselves by subordinating all changes into a maintenance of their own set of imaginary relations. Corporations attempt to recreate and maintain their imaginary identity by projecting themselves outward, producing a boundary between themselves and an environment, and monitoring that environment for things that reflect their interest and concerns. The corporation and environment are enacted as the same imaginary move. The relations within this large complex "closed" system are central to the analysis here.

The patterns of relations are thus of more interest than the particular substantive character, for substantive elements are products of the system itself. The process, rather than either the initial structure or the "external" conditions, produces the outcome. No action or structure can be good in itself. In Weick's (1979) work, the various relations internal and external to the system can thus be mapped by a series of causal lines and loops. Some of these produce systems that are "charmed." In a "charmed" loop the enacted environment is produced in regard to a relatively full set of needs and interests facilitating an internal development that enacts a richer environment and increased system differentiation and autonomy (see Pearce and Cronen 1980; Morgan 1986). Others map what Morgan (1986) called "egocentric" organizations, where the attempt to maintain and reproduce existing identities and world relations drive a vicious deviation amplifying loop. Charmed loops thus describe the systems equivalent of democratic participation, where one-sidedness is overcome as differentiation and autonomy drive enlarged produced identities, whereas "ego- (or any-) centric" forms are latent strategic systems of control. The choice is between a dynamic relation between a self-producing system and an open world, and a system that struggles to reproduce itself by control of the insides and outsides.

A couple of examples may clarify. Recall that identities are always imaginary in the sense of their inevitable partiality and one-sided representation. They momentarily provide a unity, temporarily suppressing conflict among alternative identities and objective relations. In nonpathological systems the illusion of completion and objectivity is temporary and gives way in process to the perpetual antagonisms and resolutions in response to successive life events. In the pathological version the individuals in the system maintain particular identities and object relations as they are reproduced in continued action within the system. Self-fulfilling prophecies are the best examples of this at the individual level, though such systems become quite complex in social organizations.

Control-oriented, self-referential systems exist in many aspects of everyday life. In a system of assumed equality, one individual perceives a control move on the part of the other and thus responds with defensiveness and control, which evokes a countermove of defensiveness and control from the other which evokes a greater move to control by the first, and so on. No one has to desire control for the cycle to work. If the logic of the system demands reciprocity, even a mistaken initial perception sets into play a cycle that feeds on itself. Once in motion, even claims that one or the other does not desire control can be interpreted as a more sophisticated control strategy. And ultimately both may regretfully assume that control is a central part of dealing with others. A relation to the excess of the outside over existing conceptions is lacking, hence the cycle cannot be put in perspective (i.e., Gadamer's "demand" of the subject matter).

Within work life and between work and nonwork life, similar cycles can develop for individuals. Weick has provided a clear example of such self-referentiality when an individual develops a system of reasoning that follows Linder's (1970) rule that people try to equalize the yield of their work and nonwork time. Quoting Weick (1979):

> Suppose that in my work one hour of writing produces one-third of an article. Now suppose that by using a dictating machine I increase my production to one-half of an article per hour. Each of those hours has increased in value. Linder argues that two hours of recreation have to count for more. To accomplish this I add expensive consumer goods to amplify the yield from my consumption time. I trade in my Instamatic for a Hasselblad so that I'll get more return from my two hours of photography. But I have to pay a great deal for the Hasselblad, which tightens the screws on me to become more productive and to earn even more, which in turn makes me try to squeeze even more out of my photography. I then become one more member of the "harried leisure class." (31)

Such deviation amplification often happens within organizations. Most agree that organizations demonstrate bounded rationality whereby members attempt to maximize certain utilities in ways limited by available information, costs, and capacities. In the clearest cases of systematic distortion and system pathology, the normally bounded rationality takes on strange forms. Schulman (1989) demonstrated such processes in a variety of organizational "blunders" owing to a kind of decisional "tunneling" or "traps." Watergate is perhaps the most widely known. In these cases member decisions "interact progressively to circumscribe one another—distorting processes of search and calculation, and narrowing the scope of available options. Under such circumstances, the pursuit of rational self-interest can actually be displaced by 'pathology,' that is, by behavior that is logically self-defeating, both from an individual stand point and from the stand point of the organization as a whole" (32). The primary logic of such systems is fairly common. Individuals overweigh the certainty of winning, hence they will accept assured small successes over more risky but potentially larger gains, and conversely they will attempt to avoid a sure loss even when they have to risk an even larger loss. To worsen the effect, most technical design features account for the successful functioning of a system but not its failure. Often the same features that assure integration in complex working processes create a geometrically expanding system collapse once a portion of the system breaks down. Consequently, there is an unavoidable trade-off between designs for effective functioning and those preventing and containing error. The one-sided emphasis on effectiveness aligns with individual logics in creating pathology in these cases. These are often visible pathologies, because they affect the narrow, but defined as significant, context of self-interest and organizational (read managerial) goals.

Bounded rationality—or in terms of the language here, a *delimited appropriation of discourse*—itself is already political and potentially pathological in a broader sense. The defense industry has grown to great magnitudes through a more complex and invisible, but similar, cycle. Defense is needed, which creates jobs; jobs are needed or feared lost, which creates a need for a claim of outside threat to increase defense, which creates a threatening situation, which creates an environment where defense is needed, which creates greater job dependency. . . . And some of the clearest examples of egocentric corporations come from the defense industries. Kurtz (1988) provided a useful description of how complex weapons systems become a goal in themselves, threatening world order rather than being a means to the goal of security:

> Because of the way bureaucratic institutions are structured, individuals who work in the military-industrial complex expand the arms race by simply pursuing their own careers. In the day-to-day decision making, in order to justify their job responsibilities, they must provide reports and strategies of action that enhance their work status as well as that of their superiors and the institutions for which they work. . . . Cooperation in these tasks leads to a final hard-to-resist outcome—career security and organizational expansion. (866–67)

Of course the system has a larger sway than just the internal reports and action. Major media organizations have their own layer of career-minded individuals as well as local communities wanting jobs and congressional representatives wanting to assure them. In the course of events of 1990 prior to the Iraq "crisis," the demise of the "Soviet block" presence was quickly offset in the media with promotion of the fear of a unified Germany. But the self-referential defense system is only the more obvious. The example would run much the same if we substituted in the pharmaceutical, cosmetic, fashion, or auto industries.

In the terms of this volume, the imaginary image is reproduced by the system that it both initiated and is a response to. A communicational analysis of self-referential systems draws attention to the textual nature of the interplay of various produced identities and events. Every linguistic description is a distortion, in that it is partial and imaginary. In open discourse, partiality becomes displayed and partly overcome as further descriptions are advanced. In the continued interplay the outside (the "otherness") initiates concept formation and enrichment of the natural language. Distortion becomes systematic when the process becomes one of *in-formational* repetition rather than conversation. The manner by which this works in larger social systems has been described by Baudrillard (1975). He refers to this as *the monopoly of the code*. In such a situation the signifier changes. Rather than signifying an outside, it becomes signified itself. As Baudrillard (1975) described the relation:

> The form-sign [present in a monopolistic code] describes an entirely different organization: the signified and the referent are now abolished to the sole profit of the play of signifiers, of a generalized formalization in which the code no longer refers back to any subjective or objective "reality," but to its own logic. The signifier becomes its own referent and the use value of the sign disappears to the benefit of its commutation and exchange value alone. The sign no longer designates anything at all. It approaches its true structural limit which is to refer back only to other signs. All reality then becomes the place of semi-urgical manipulation, of a structural simulation. (127–28)

As will be developed in detail later, corporations today operate more and more as systems of *simulations* in Baudrillard's sense. Despite their claim to "real" worldliness, they operate as images reflected upon each other, developing a thickness of images that appears grounded on something solid but that is simply another layer of production. Or as Lefebvre (1968) showed, "There is *nothing*—whether object, individual or social group—that is *valued* apart from its double, the image that advertises and sanctifies it . . .

imparting an ideological theme to the object . . . endowing it with a dual real and make believe existence" (105–6). Such simulations run with strange constructed rules, strategically designed to assure power-laden reproductions.

Systematically distorted communication, then, is an ongoing process within particular systems as they strategically (though latently) work to reproduce, rather than produce, themselves. It is shown in systems that respond to themselves and are unable to form a relation to the outside on the outside's own terms; they respond to shadows of themselves cast on the events around them. In this form they translate all back to their own conceptual relations, thus precluding alternative discourses or conflicts with contrary institutional interpretive schemes. Such systems largely fool themselves in presuming themselves to be referential and purposively directed to an actual outside. In order for this to happen and be sustained, active processes of discursive closure occur in the internal discourses.

DISCURSIVE CLOSURE

Discursive closure exists whenever potential conflict is suppressed. This might derive from several processes, several of which will be discussed below. One of the most common is the disqualification of certain groups or participants. Disqualification can occur through the denial of the right of expression, denying access to speaking forums, the assertion of the need for certain expertise in order to speak, or through rendering the other unable to speak adequately, including through processes of deskilling. Closure is also possible through the privileging of certain discourses and the marginalization of others. For example, Habermas (1984) and other critical theorists have extensively detailed the domination of technical-instrumental reasoning over other forms in the Western world (see Fischer 1990). Foucault in his many works has shown how certain discourses historically arise as normal and preferred. Organizational studies clearly show how managerial groups and technical reasoning

become privileged. Further, closure is present in each move to determine origins and demonstrate unity. In each case the multiple motivations and conflict-filled nature of experience become suppressed by a dominant aspect. Later this will be shown in analyses of organizational narratives, language, and standard practices. With unity the continued production of experience is constrained, since the tension of difference is lost.

Chapter 5 describes the processes of construction of knowledge and identity. Each individual is "subjected" in a variety of competing discourses. The basic political questions concern the interrelation of these competing discourses. In a purely participatory context, the conflict among the alternatives would undermine the necessity felt of any particular concept and open a measure of freedom to choose. In this way particular imaginary relations would be given up in the practical demands of the events and expression of others—in Gadamer's sense, the demand of the subject matter. If this were the case, the particular forms of distorted communication extending from the imaginary relation would be replaced in dialogue with a move toward concept formation and individuation in Habermas's sense. This is of course not to say that the perception would be freed from its imaginary quality or suddenly become a truthful discourse. Rather the formation of experience would be less routinized, less dominated by subjectivity or at least a particular fixed historical subjectivity, and while still socially constrained, it would be more responsible to events and others outside of the socially produced self-centered totality of which each particular experience is a part. In short, the formation of self and experience would more closely match the participative ideal.

Discursive practices, however, can either lead to such open formation by further exploration of the subject matter or divert, distort, or block the open development of understanding. When discussion is thwarted, a particular view of reality is maintained at the expense of equally plausible ones, usually to someone's advantage. It should not be surprising that systems of domination are protected from careful exploration and political advantage is protected and extended. Their continuation provides both security and advantage. The particular alignment between various systems of subject and world production, along with the discursive means by which the politics of production are concealed, will be discussed later as the "strategic power apparatus." Here I only wish to introduce basic discursive moves that conceal the production of subjects and world that we have discussed (see also Pateman 1980).

The primary effect of these moves is to suppress insight into the conflictual nature of experience and preclude careful discussion of and decision making regarding the values implicit in experience, identity, and representation. These are not themselves major value claims or organized strategies. Rarely are they seen in regard to dominating ideologies or the politics of identity and experience. They are rather quiet, repetitive micro-practices, done for innumerable reasons, which function to maintain normalized, conflict-free experience and social relations. Allow me to review a few of the more common processes of discursive closure.

Disqualification

As we have discussed, Habermas demonstrated that central to every communication community is an assumption (though not always fulfilled) of equal opportunity to select and employ different speech acts for the representation of one's interests. Many have discussed this principle in regard to access to various forums and media, but it applies fundamentally to the determination of who has a right to have a genuine say. Disqualification is the discursive process by which individuals are excluded (Bavelas 1983; Bavelas and Chovil 1986). For example, statements such as "You're just saying that because you are a woman [manager, lover, angry . . .]" function within certain systems to exclude the expressed view from the discussion. Such an activity skews the development of mutual understanding.

Socially produced notions of expertise, professional qualification, and specialization are

central to qualification and to the imposition of the opposite, the disqualification process. Specialization has always fostered control, whether through deskilling or through loss of understanding of the function and effects of one's own actions. Although such effects can be overcome by integrative activities, they are often precluded. As Jehenson (1984) argued, expertise clearly functions as an ideological fiction, an imaginary relation, but further it reproduces itself by proclaiming who has the capacity to determine and question it. As will be described, the creation of managerial expertise (and management science to certify, institutionalize, and finally signify it) centers management capacity in certain locations and outside certain groups. Such a placement is, even if diffused in more participatory management, retained as a prerogative by its own assertion of placement. The often subtle processes of deferring, calling in, and studying for, operate like the more explicit forms of dismissal and ignorance in protecting powerful groups' inserted realities and denying the implicit values on which they are based.

Naturalization

One [of] the most compelling observations of Marx, and perhaps one of the most shared outside the various Marxists groups, is that of reification. Lukács (1971) in particular has developed how social relationships and subjective constructions become made into objects that are treated as fixed and external, that is, reified. Rather than introducing the commodity theory on which this is based, I wish to focus on one aspect of it—the treatment of the socially-produced as given in nature. I call this naturalization. In a naturalizing discourse, the social historical processes (whether in the actual production of objects and institutions or in the production of the subject and structures of experience) are removed from view. Not only is this an occurrence in everyday life of communities, but it is fostered by the operating philosophy of the social sciences. In treating their perceptions as transparent renderings of the external world, the concepts, methods, and practices of perception production are made invisible, especially as abstracted and presented in manuals, textbooks, and training sessions. The constituting subjectivity of science is thus hidden behind the claim of objectivity. Social scientists, news reporters, and other experts help institutionalize a discourse through "the projection of an 'imaginary community' by means of which 'real' distinctions are portrayed as 'natural', the particular is disguised in the universal, the historical is effaced in the atemporality of essence" (Thompson 1984, 25).

In open discourse, the subject matter is a constituted/constituting object in relation to interactants. Every perception has a social historical dimension. In naturalization, one view of the subject matter is frozen as the way the thing is. In this process, the constitution process is closed to inspection and discussion. In a sense, the subject matter has been "silenced" by the claim that someone's conception is what it is. As will be developed, the corporation itself is often treated as a simple existing relational form. On reflection, most know that modern organizations are particular historical constructions, constructed toward certain ends. But in everyday talk, in the naming of the corporation as an object, and in the research treatment of it as an entity, its production is forgotten. Naturalization frequently stops discussion—at the determination of what is—at precisely the place where it should be started— how is it that.

Naturalism always plays in the privileging and marginalizing of discourses. For example, perceived differences between female and male emotional reactions in organizations are frequently treated as naturally occurring, as if women and men were different in some fixed manner. In such a claim, such reactions are depicted as natural and self-evident, thus justifying the necessity of their presence to the advantage or disadvantage of either group. When male aggressiveness or female tears are treated as natural and necessary, we can either adjust to them or use emotional expression to exclude one or the other from certain jobs. But quite apart from the descriptive adequacy of such differences, the claim of being natural often places the value of emotional expression beyond discussion. Aristotle's ancient view of natural laws is overlooked (the fact that people are usually "naturally" right-handed does not keep the left from being developed as well). And the presentation of the perceived differences as a truth claim obscures how the claim of truth works politically to preclude discussion and development.

Neutralization

Neutralization refers to the process by which value positions become hidden and value-laden activities are treated as if they were value-free. Not only are socially constructed objects and processes treated as natural objects, but the values in the construction process are forgotten as arbitrary and chosen as well. Such a process is significant because it is key to the universalization of sectional interests (Giddens 1979). Different groups in a society perceive and interpret events using different values. In Saussure's sense every linguistic distinction is an attention, a valuing. In the neutralization of language, language does not lose its valuing, rather one system of valuing is treated as the only possible one. A possible world is treated as *the* world. Weedon (1987) developed this position as one of the presumptions of representational transparency, a presumption that hides the need for examining the arbitrary nature of distinction. The transparency presumption suggests that language, research methods, and other constitutive activities can be seen through to a world as it *really* is. This is neutralization.

Presumed "objective" claims hide both the activities that produced the claim and the values carried with them. For example, just giving the "data" or the "facts" hides the criteria used to choose certain observations rather than others and the conceptual frame that produced the "facts" and "data" in the first place. In the same sense that the documentary film is often the most difficult film to critique since the politics in it are hidden by the proclamation of the "real," judgments disguised as descriptions often effectively block the open construction of the "facts." Recent works in accounting (Ansari and Euske 1987; Hopwood 1987) and data collection forms (Sless 1988) have reclaimed corporate data production from presumed neutrality, showing not only the existence and use of value claims in accounting but also their relation to systems of advantage (see chapter 10). Technologies are often granted the same type of transparency granted to other constitutive activities. As I have argued, technologies as institutions carry a point of view, a way of being in contact with particular aspects of the world. Neutralizing practices hide and forget constitution and thus suppress potential conflict between different constitutive practices.

Topical Avoidance

Every social group prohibits or discourages the discussion of some events and feelings. Often these surround significant areas of potential conflict, such as prohibitions against discussing religion or politics at family gatherings. These prohibitions may be motivated to enhance propriety and order, but they often function to preclude a discussion of the values that define propriety and order and the benefits that certain groups acquire from them. Foucault (1980, 1977) demonstrated this well in terms of sexual discourse and the hiding away of the insane. Gilligan (Gilligan, Ward, and Taylor 1988) documents much of the same in her treatment of adolescent girls' struggles with their relational attachments and the forces against these attachments in contemporary society, a tension that renders them mute. Males can be muted in a different way. In the most bold way that Wolfe (1987) described, *"masters of the universe* don't cry." From teamsterville to *he-man,* places of expression and topics of talk are highly constrained and constrained to certain ends (Philipsen 1975). The corporate prohibition against expression of personal doubts and problems at home essentially hides the home and removes the corporation from having to change or account for

these problems. Their hidden quality makes them the employee's problem even if they result from work-related experiences.

All topical avoidance leads to systematically distorted communication and not only because the interaction must be structured to go around and leave out. The internal state of the person can already experience the exclusion. Bodily states are fundamentally ambiguous. The focus and channeling of physiological excitation is socially constructed (see Harré 1986). Males in a corporate environment may not "feel" betrayal or hurt but may directly feel anger or the drive to control. Only in reflection can the same state in the same context be seen as feeling "betrayal" or "hurt," feelings that more "spontaneously" arise in some females. Who has or does not have certain feelings is a political question. The systematic exclusion of humanly experienceable emotions avoids certain "topics" and thus the concealment of conflict—the conflict over what this physiological state "is."

Organizational researchers have understood the power of omission. Bachrach and Baratz's (1962) familiar work is an example in point. As they argued, pluralist conceptions of power emphasize "the importance of initiating, deciding, and voting and, as a result, take no account of the fact that power may be, and often is, exercised by confining the scope of decision making to relatively 'safe' issues" (948). This point is made even more clearly by Wolfinger (1971) in his study of how routines produce nondecisions. What cannot be talked about and what cannot be brought to decision making are significant in organizations. Their analysis, however, is only a surface reading of the larger issue in the politics of experience and how this politics is concealed.

Subjectification of Experience

A focus on personal experience and the embracing of relativism are common features of today's society (Adorno 1973; MacIntyre 1984). Many communication writings still begin with the claim that meaning is in people, even though the theories on which such an idea were based have been largely dismissed as inadequate and misleading. More sophisticated reader-response theories that focus on subjective interpretation processes might on the surface appear to be concerned with alternative value systems but often have the opposite effect. Private decisionalism and relativism often appear as being open to others but usually function to preclude questioning of normal routines and assure closure of experience. The produced identity is taken as a given rather than a social formation, and the acceptance of the privilege of the personal precludes the examination of that social formation. The proclamation in interaction that the issue is "a matter of opinion" is a frequent casual move used to end the discussion. From the standpoint of participation, this proclamation is where discussion should begin. The difference between different people's opinions represents the opportunity to escape from self-blinders (from opinion) and indicates that more is to be learned about the issue. In fact it represents a major reason to seriously talk at all.

The micropolitics of opinion protection is important. When meaning is personalized, difference of opinion can be resolved only in power politics rather than in examining the politics of opinion formation—an activity that forms opinion as something to be had and a particular opinion. When democracy becomes opinion polls, participative interaction has no place. It is always too late and precluded. Further, the individual is blamed for effects of social institutions. In the same sense that televised violence could be excused since viewing prohibition is a family issue and interpretations of violent acts are individual, both the television production of meaning and responsibility can be precluded at once. Democracy falls to a false assumption of private interpretive processes.

Meaning Denial and Plausible Deniability

Every expression has several possible meanings; such is inevitable in the structure of interaction. Meaning denial happens when one possible interpretation of a statement is both placed in the interaction and denied as meant. The most obvious interpersonal example of this is when someone shouts at you and then proclaims that they are not angry. A similar process is nearly always present with inappropriate sexual innuendo in corporate talk. A message is present and disclaimed, said and not said. The effect is to shift meaning production to a positioned listener, thus enabling the produced speaker control without responsibility and precluding the critical examination of what was said (because it was not said). The listeners respond to the "message" based only on their own produced meanings, but in a context where, if they do not respond to it, the message can be re-evoked as if it were clearly said (i.e., "I don't care what I said, you knew I was angry"). Consent and unowned control are built into such practices.

Eisenberg (1984) affirmed the significance of multiple meaning in corporations in his treatment of the strategic use of ambiguity. He argued that ambiguous messages and the deniability of formal messages are extremely effective means of control. Especially since he intended this positively, his evidence is particularly useful in exemplifying the possibilities of conflict suppression and discursive closure. Eisenberg did not miss the ethical issues involved, but his treatment of them is clearly worth quoting:

> It is easy to imagine the ethical problems that might result from the misuse of ambiguity. In the final analysis, however, both the effectiveness and ethics of any particular communication strategy are relative to the goals and values of the communicators in the situation. The use of more or less ambiguity is in itself not good or bad, effective or ineffective; whether a strategy is ethical depends upon the ends to which it is used, and whether it is effective depends upon the goals of the individual communicators. (239)

Obviously Eisenberg does not see open participation as a value in itself, nor strategy itself as a concern. Clearly his own study had values including the preservation of privileged positions. One wonders how to read his position if strategic ambiguity advances some ends and goals over others, and these same goals are the sole remaining ones used to determine ethics and effectiveness. The neutralization of means is significant and will be discussed later as an important part in the maintenance of managerial advantage.

The logic of ambiguity and meaning denial is institutionalized with new legal rules creating a defense of plausible deniability. Here the test of product liability or plant safety is determined not by critical investigation of adequate testing and appropriate participation in decisions, but rather by the claim that one might not have reasonably known of such a danger. Such a position produces hidden talk, avoidance of exploration, disowned expression and knowledge, and sets in motion a web of concealments. We have orders without orders, knowledge without knowing, practice without intention. The responsible subject disappears but not in the sense of pluralistic subjectivity. Rather the subject hides behind its own shadow.

Legitimation

Legitimation appears in the rationalization of decisions and practices through the invocation of higher order explanatory devices. Such devices make sense out of difficult-to-interpret activities and conceal contradictions and conflict. They attach a higher order value where one's own values might lead to different choices. Habermas (1975), following Weber, has shown that motivation and relatively high productivity have been sustained in the Western world more by the supportive existence of the Protestant work ethic than by intrinsic qualities of the work experience. The invocation of values of hard work, long hours and stress as evidence of salvation covers up inadequacies in the reward structure and qualities of the work experience. A largely irrational work experience is rationalized through discursively reproduced value principles based on a nearly forgotten and rarely critically examined religious doctrine. As the power of these principles wane[s], motivation and productivity appear more directly related to the actual work relations.

The same analysis could of course be applied to the Japanese. Here concepts of authority, tradition, and honor perform much the same function.

As these grander master values and historical narratives lose their command, newer and more specific ones take their place. Jehenson (1984) demonstrated how effectiveness, excellence, and expertise become new "moral fictions" used in much the same way as the older ones to stop value clarification and lead to commitments and actions that are beneficial to certain dominant groups. Even more specifically, Hannan and Freeman (1977, 128), among others, have concurred that corporate goal statements are more often used to make decisions appear acceptable and legitimate than to guide decisions and action. The reasons for decisions are often different from the reasons given for them. Obviously this gap is political. Here we are interested not simply in how the person giving the reason may gain, but in its effects on the construction of meaning and open choice making.

Pacification

Democracy in the participative sense requires the capacity to mutually solve problems through exploration of different points of view and alternative actions. Pacification describes the process by which conflictual discussion is diverted or subverted through an apparently reasonable attempt to engage in it. In this sense it is a fooler like a pacifier. Messages that pacify tend to discount the significance of the issue, the solvability of the issue, or the ability of the participant to do anything about the issue. Thus discussion is made either trivial, implying that "the issues are not worth the effort," or futile, implying that the magnitude of the issue exceeds the limits of capacity. We can all recall how effective such a strategy was in initially avoiding the problems of gender-linked job-classification labels. The jokes said that gender-linked terms were trivial, the opposition said that they were too pervasive. The same is of course occurring with the campaigns for equal pay for equivalent work. The process is not limited to major issues, but is a significant daily practice—what will be called a "micro-practice" of power. For example, if an employee requests a raise because of personal need and quality of work, the supervisor could potentially pacify at least temporarily by talking about how many people are out of work and the poor salaries others are receiving. While the employee's claim may now seem trivial in contrast, the minimization has subverted the conflict conception and discussion. Or on the contrary, the supervisor can expand the issue by discussing the company's financial situation, uncertainties in the economy, and effects of the matrix of other salaries. These of course are not irrelevant issues. They work precisely because they are relevant, but they divert attention away from the things that the interactants can change (e.g., the allocation of resources within a unit) to the things that cannot be changed (the state of the general economy).

In complex social settings, both types of claims have a plausible appeal—what is "really so bad" and how could we possibly deal with the size and complexity of most problems confronting us? The debilitating effect of recurring pacification is great. The development and strength of the individual are stripped away along with the possibility of mutual decision making—that is, in the loss of democracy and individual freedom.

Argyris (1986) demonstrated how this type of conflict and solution avoidance can become systemic in corporations in what he called a *defensive routine*. His analysis utilizes concepts similar to the topical avoidance and meaning denial discussed earlier, now placed in a "skilled" strategy of "chaos" production. He suggests four steps in this routine: (1) Design an obviously ambiguous statement that the receiver recognizes as ambiguous but does not question, (2) ignore any inconsistencies in the message, (3) make the ambiguity and inconsistencies undiscussable, and (4) make the undiscussability undiscussable. The culture of chaos and inability to deal with significant problems can become routinized. Systems are then created so that members confront chaos production as the norm for appropriate behavior;

in fact, they become practiced and skilled at it. The strategic quality thus becomes doubled. The unowned, routinized strategy of chaos production protects the corporation from examination, discussion, and possible change. And the individual use of the strategy becomes part of the individual's strategy for advancement. In the logic of the distorted system, the individual must produce chaos to be advanced as he or she works hard to solve problems.

REFERENCES

Adorno, T. 1973. *The jargon of authenticity.* Translated by K. Tarnowski and F. Will. Evanston, Ill.: Northwestern University Press.

Ansari, S., and K. Euske. 1987. Rational, rationalizing, and reifying uses of accounting data in organizations. *Accounting, Organizations, and Society* 12:549–70.

Argyris, C. 1986. Skilled incompetence. *Harvard Business Review,* Sept.–Oct., 74–79.

Bachrach, P., and M. S. Baratz. 1962. Two faces of power. *American Political Science Review* 56:947–52.

Baudrillard, J. 1975. *The mirror of production.* Translated by M. Poster. St. Louis: Telos Press.

Bavelas, J. 1983. Situations that lead to disqualification. *Human Communication Research* 9:130–45.

Bavelas, J., and N. Chovil. 1986. How people disqualify: Experimental studies of spontaneous written disqualification. *Communication Monographs* 53:70–74.

Eisenberg, E. 1984. Ambiguity as strategy in organizational communication. *Communication Monographs* 51:227–42.

Faucheux, C., and S. Makridakis. 1979. Automation or autonomy in organizational design. *International Journal of General Systems* 5:213–20.

Fischer, F. 1990. *Technocracy and the politics of expertise.* Newbury Park, Calif.: Sage.

Forester, J. 1989. *Planning in the face of power.* Berkeley: University of California Press.

Foucault, M. 1977. *Discipline and punish: The birth of the prison.* Translated by A. Sheridan Smith. New York: Random House.

Foucault, M. 1980. *The history of sexuality.* Translated by R. Hurley. New York: Vintage.

Giddens, A. 1979. *Central problems in social theory.* Berkeley: University of California Press.

Gilligan, C., J. V. Ward, and J. M. Taylor. 1988. *Mapping the moral domain: A contribution of women's thinking to psychological theory and education.* Cambridge: Center for the Study of Gender, Education, and Human Development (distributed by Harvard University Press).

Habermas, J. 1975. *Legitimation crisis.* Translated by T. McCarthy. Boston: Beacon Press.

Habermas, J. 1984. *The theory of communicative action, volume 1: Reason and the rationalization of society.* Translated by T. McCarthy. Boston: Beacon Press.

Hall, S. 1989. Ideology and communication theory. In *Rethinking communication 1: Paradigm dialogues,* ed. B. Dervin, L. Grossberg, B. O'Keefe, and E. Wartella. Newbury Park, Calif.: Sage.

Hannan, M. T., and F. Freeman. 1977. Obstacles to comparative studies. In *New perspectives in organizational effectiveness,* ed. P. S. Goodman, J. M. Penning, and Associates, 106–31. San Francisco: Jossey-Bass.

Harré, R. 1986. *The social construction of emotions.* Oxford: Basil Blackwell.

Hopwood, A. 1987. The archaeology of accounting systems. *Accounting, Organizations, and Society* 12:207–34.

Jehenson, R. 1984. Effectiveness, expertise, and excellence as ideological fictions: A contribution to a critical phenomenology of the formal organization. *Human Studies* 7:3–21.

Kurtz, L. R. 1988. Military organizations. In *Handbook of organizations,* ed. James G. March, 838–78. Chicago: Rand McNally.

Laing, R. D. 1971. *The politics of the family.* New York: Vintage.

Lefebvre, H. 1968. *Everyday life in the modern world.* New York: Harper & Row.

Linder, S. B. 1970. *The harried leisure class.* New York: Columbia University Press.

Lukács, G. 1971. *History and class consciousness.* Translated by R. Livingstone. Cambridge: MIT Press.

MacIntyre, A. 1984. *After virtue: A study in moral theory.* 2d ed. Notre Dame, Ind.: University of Notre Dame Press.

Maturana, H., and F. Varela. 1980. *Autopoiesis and cognition: The realization of the living.* London: Reidl.

Mingers, J. 1989. An introduction to autopoiesis—implications and applications. *Systems Practice* 2:159–80.

Morgan, G. 1986. *Images of organization.* Newbury Park, Calif.: Sage.

Pateman, T. 1980. *Language, truth, and politics,* rev. ed. Newton Poppleford, Great Britain: Trevor Pateman and Jean Stroud.

Pearce, W. B., and V. Cronen. 1980. *Communication, action, and meaning.* New York: Praeger.

Philipsen, G. 1975. Speaking 'like a man' in Teamsterville: Culture patterns of role enactment in an urban community. *Quarterly Journal of Speech* 61:13–22.

Schulman, P. 1989. The 'logic' of organizational irrationality. *Administration and Society* 21:31–53.

Sless, D. 1988. Forms of control. *Australian Journal of Communication* 14:57–69.

Thompson, J. 1984. *Studies in the theory of ideology.* Berkeley: University of California Press.

Ulrich, H., and G. J. B. Probst, eds. 1984. *Self-organization and management of social systems.* New York: Springer-Verlag.

Watzlawick, P., J. Beavin, and D. Jackson. 1967. *Pragmatics of human communication.* New York: Norton.

Weedon, C. 1987. *Feminist practice and poststructuralist theory.* Oxford: Basil Blackwell.

Weick, K. 1979. *The social psychology of organizing.* 2d ed. Reading, Mass.: Addison-Wesley.

Wolfe, T. 1987. *The bonfire of the vanities.* New York: Bantam.

Wolfinger, R. E. 1971. Nondecisions and the study of local politics. *American Political Science Review* 65:1063–80.

35

PARIS IS ALWAYS
MORE THAN PARIS

SUE CURRY JANSEN

Pascal's assertion that "there is a time to call Paris Paris and a time to call it the capitol of the Kingdom" implicitly recognizes the knot that binds power and knowledge. But the legacy of Western rationalism encourages us to deny or ignore its epistemological implications. Thus, for example, formalism directs us to regard synonymous expressions as equivalencies: interchangeable "markers" that can be represented by a common symbol in the manipulations of machine languages. Only rhetoric has consistently applied the Pascalian insight. Following the precedent set by Aristotle, however, philosophers have generally dismissed rhetoric as a secondary art, at best a form of salesmanship, so that even the work of a great rhetorician like Kenneth Burke has remained at the margins of contemporary thought about thought.

During the past two decades, however, the ranks of those who recognize that Paris is not just Paris have swollen. Crisis within the philosophy of science as well as growing political cynicism among the general population have led to widespread questioning of established modes of legitimating both knowledge and power. During the 1970s and 1980s, this questioning generated a renewal of interest in the Frankfurt School of critical social theory. Initially articulated by Max Horkheimer, Friedrich Pollock, Theodor Adorno, and their associates at the *Institut für Sozialforschung* in the 1930s, the approach was subsequently enriched by Herbert Marcuse and Jürgen Habermas in their respective attempts to secure a basis for emancipatory communication (and politics) in industrial (or postindustrial) societies.

The two waves of critical theory explicitly recognized the bond that unites power and knowledge. They affirmed the familiar dictum that "power is knowledge and knowledge, power." They did so, however, through the lens

SOURCE: Jansen, S. C. (2002). *Critical communication theory: Power, media, gender, and technology* (pp. 43–68). Lanham, MD: Rowman & Littlefield.

473

of a radical critique of Enlightenment-based epistemology. Frankfurt School critical theory does not merely acknowledge that power uses and corrupts knowledge, but also recognizes that it sets the conditions for knowledge: that power-relations provide the auspices for knowledge and cultural production, and establish the rules of permission and proscription that endow them with coherence. The resulting theory of knowledge is realistic but also deeply pessimistic. With Nietzsche, apologists of the first wave of critical theory recognize the impossibility of "immaculate perception." They acknowledge that "we all harbor hidden gardens and plantings." But, with Marx, they also realize that capital usually determines how those gardens are planted.

The German Ideology of 1846 was, of course, the immediate textual precedent for critical theory's perspective on repressed or distorted communication. In the relevant passages, Marx and Engels contend that the abstract (formal) language of philosophers that creates the impression that thought is free of practical interests is only "the distorted language of the actual world": a language that reflects and secures the prevailing form of the division of labor.[1] They point out that, under capitalism, even the categories that lie behind our semantic conventions are skewed by property relations, so that "in language [as in life] the relations of buying and selling have been the basis of all others."[2]

Taking up their charge nearly a century after these fathers of world revolution had completed their mischief, critical theorists chose their prefix and defined their theoretical enterprise deliberately, reflexively. Critical theorists sought to distance their perspective from vulgar (mechanical) Marxism and to establish kinship with the Hegelian and philological roots of Marx's conceptions of alienation, consciousness, and ideology. They were students of Dilthey, von Humboldt, Schiller, Heine, Grimm, Nietzsche, Weber, and Freud, as well as Marx. But they were also contemporaries of Hitler, Mussolini, and Stalin.

Contra positivism, including the positivistic strains in Marxism, they regarded the Enlightenment as a betrayal of reason rather than an extension of it, a betrayal that established the hegemony of instrumental reason and thereby prepared the way for the emergence of monopoly capitalism.[3] Moreover, they rejected the prevailing liberal view, which regarded fascism as a singular historical aberration. Rather, they saw it as a logical extension of the structures of crisis-ridden advanced capitalism. Consequently, the Frankfurt School tried to outline a perspective on capitalist social institutions that was both "scientific" (amenable to documentary validation) and at the same time "critical" (committed to the creation of a more robustly rational and just social order).[4]

Their theory of personality and culture was also radically revisionist. Consistent with the German philological tradition and the then-emergent Freudian perspective, they maintained that we are captives of culture trapped in "the hermeneutic circle" of language. They were far less optimistic than Marx regarding prospects for breaking out of that captivity, believing instead that, in the twentieth century, mass media and mass entertainments (what Adorno would later call "the culture industry") had so thoroughly colonized the consciousness of the industrialized masses that they were no longer able to even conceive of resistance, let alone articulate a platform for emancipatory social change. Indeed, Horkheimer and Adorno contended that the culture industry had actually invaded the collective unconscious, so that even the hopes, dreams, desires, and utopian fantasies of the masses had come to bear the imprimatur of Hollywood, the world headquarters of the culture industry.[5] As students of Freud and residents of Nazi Germany (until their self-imposed exile after 1933), Horkheimer and Adorno were keenly aware of the roles mythic thought and storytelling play in human motivation, even in a scientific age. They believed that apologists of capital not only control the institutions of popular culture through ownership, but also exercise dominion over the popular imagination.

Horkheimer and Adorno could see no way out. The first wave of critical theory offered no practical plans for resistance, no program for translating criticism into collective action; at best, it invested some limited hope in the generative powers of critical knowledge. Consequently it is generally regarded, even by sympathetic interpreters, as deeply pessimistic despite its emancipatory commitments.

Reread today, in the wake of a virtual flood of postmodern critiques of the Enlightenment, the sweep and originality of Horkheimer and Adorno's work remains striking. Their heavy-handed wielding of the dialectical hammer is, however, also striking. It forces evidence into the either/or of the binary logics of the dualistic (cum dialectic) patterns of Western thought that they sought to implode. The net effect of this conceptual overkill is to underestimate the historical vitality of the lost or betrayed democratic potential of French and American Enlightenment thought. That is, the dialectical structure of the argument itself combined with the brutal realities of the dire historical moment in which Horkheimer and Adorno wrote to prevent them from fully grasping the resilience of democratic impulses: a resilience that is nicely, if perhaps a bit too optimistically, evoked by Charles Douglas Loomis, who writes,

> The word democracy has been . . . used and betrayed by state, party, sect, and interest. Yet it still has honest lovers, who detect in it something that has mysteriously remained immaculate and true.[6]

Despite its egalitarian goals, the first wave of Frankfurt critical theory is nevertheless pockmarked with elitism.[7] Horkheimer's and Adorno's arguments imply that only critical theorists and other trained dialecticians possess the conceptual resources necessary to see through the trickery of the culture industry. Whether this apparently elitist assumption is evidence of an endemic arrogance (and implicit vanguardism) within the perspective or a testament to the power and cogency of critical theory in illuminating the hidden mechanics of the culture industry—or both—is for the reader to decide.

Failure to effectively resolve these issues combined with the hostile political climate of the Cold War to lead many postwar Anglo-American social scientists to dismiss much of the work of those associated with the first wave of critical theory as irrationalist and nihilist. Some associates of the original Frankfurt School (e.g., Erich Fromm, Franz Neumann, Karl Mannheim, and Paul Lazarsfeld) established reputations in philosophy, political theory, sociology, and communication scholarship independent of their earlier affiliations with the Frankfurt Institute. Others, like Horkheimer, Adorno, Leo Lowenthal, and Herbert Marcuse, worked throughout their lives to resolve the impasse of the first wave of critical theory.

A second generation of critical theorists, led by Jürgen Habermas, subsequently took up the challenge. Marcuse's analysis of linguistic domination and its dialectical counterpart, his proposal for "linguistic therapy," as well as Habermas's theory of "communicative competence" and his attempt to specify the conditions of an "ideal speech situation," are of special interest to students of political linguistics. Both of these thinkers try to chart escape routes out of a language and culture dominated by instrumental reason.

In this chapter I describe the topography of the proposed escape routes, note their limitations, and review some related explorations in critical theory that suggest new possibilities for countering the antidemocratic effects of linguistic domination. What the thinkers examined in this chapter have in common is the conviction that "just communication is an index of the good society."[8]

A ROAD NOT TAKEN

A few prefatory remarks are, however, in order. The revival of interest in the Frankfurt School in communication and sociology was relatively short-lived. By the late 1980s, it became fashionable in many circles to dismiss the entire project because its progenitors were not able to bring it to full fruition. The readily identifiable flaws in some of the work were treated as synecdoche for the entire corpus. Adorno and Horkheimer were tagged as elitist, cultural mandarins: the passages in their work that displayed shallow or erroneous understandings of specific contents of American popular culture were repeatedly cited. Marcuse was framed, in Cold War terms, as a quasi-totalitarian; and the argument of his most popular and, from the perspective of 2002, prescient book, *One-Dimensional Man* (1964), was widely faulted as overdetermined. Similarly Habermas's early explorations of the communicative constituents of participatory democracy were variously labeled as "naive," "idealistic," "utopian," and packed away among the relics of a more buoyant moment in history. To be sure, the cultural terrain identified by the Frankfurt School has continued to productively engage serious thinkers who do not ride the tides of intellectual trends.[9] Such work is, however, a continuance of a resistant tradition of research, which John Lent aptly characterizes as "a different road taken" and a road I would describe as still sparsely traveled, especially in the United States.[10]

This book aligns itself with that resistance. It distances itself from the easy glamour of the intellectual fashion shows that too often privilege the new over the profound or the difficult. That is, I argue that the bold and trenchant questions posed by the Frankfurt School, not its incomplete answers, are what continue to make this work relevant and instructive. The agenda these thinkers set is an agenda that those who still believe in the ideal of participatory democracy cannot ignore. Their questions retain their relevance precisely because they resist definitive answers. The point of participatory democracy is to continuously struggle with such questions, not to settle them. As Goethe pointed out long ago, freedom can only be earned by daily conquering it anew.[11]

The conundrums in Habermas's work were already apparent by the late 1970s: its idealism, which fails to contend with the formidable powers of mass media; the problematic role psycho-analytic concepts play in his work; the liberal bias of his approach to democracy and the state; and his gendered blindspots. Yet, few living thinkers have struggled as long or as hard as Habermas

has to find ways to regenerate the public sphere and to energize the democratic discourse that can sustain it. To paper over that struggle with cynicism is to play into the hands of the enemy. As James Carey points out, the public sphere exists as "desire" in our life world, not simply as nostalgia for what never was or might be in the future.[12] We feel its presence as desire. We know something is missing from our collective life. Habermas may not have found the way, but he points the way to a democratic quest for something better. Habermas's "ideal speech situation" is indeed, as his critics repeatedly charge, a utopian construct; but I would argue that this utopianism is a strength as well as a limitation of Habermas's work. It proposes a normative standard or democratic ideal, which helps us identify and assess what is missing in actual power talk and in the tightly scripted spin that passes as political communication today. Marcuse's concept of "linguistic therapy" is also utopian, as is much of his later work, which overcorrects the determinism of some of his earlier work.

Within the current cultural climate of postmodern cool, to call a piece of work utopian is to call in the gravediggers. Yet, democracy itself is a utopian formation: an ideal that always falls short, even in its best moments, of its promises. Utopian thought—the desire for something better—is a necessary precondition to improvements in the human condition: the theory that gives birth to practice. Practice, alas, like all human endeavors, is always imperfect. Rejecting postmodern paralysis, Jacques Barzun uses the term "eutopian" to suggest that writers like More, Campanella, Bacon, and Rabelais were not writing about "no place" but about a "good place," and that they contributed much to social thought in doing so.[13] The same could be said of Erasmus, Diderot, Voltaire, Jefferson, Madison, Sojourner Truth, Susan B. Anthony, Gandhi, Martin Luther King Jr., Lech Walesa, Nelson Mandela, and many others. Without the capacity to identify what is missing and to articulate the desire for something better, we resign ourselves to current antidemocratic trends and thereby invite something worse.

EMANCIPATORY COMMUNICATION

The concept of emancipatory communication is an eutopian idea: its users sensed that something was missing in the age of administered public discourse. They tried to imagine something better: a good place where the link between community and communication could be affirmed—I am even tempted to say "consecrated." I use the past tense here because emancipatory communication, like its sister term "liberation," has fallen out of fashion: a casualty of the end of the Cold War and the triumph of globalization.

Critical resources have been redirected toward resisting cultural homogenization and preserving local cultures. These worthy pursuits have underwritten some of the best recent work in cultural studies; nevertheless, a just world cannot be constructed within a museum of cultural diversity. Politics is still necessary. The goal of critical theory is to expand participatory democracy at the local as well as national and international levels. Therefore local cultures are not protected from critical scrutiny.

To interrogate local cultures is, however, to court charges of Western imperialism; such charges need to be given a full and fair hearing in fora that are sensitive to local traditions. Western cultural imperialism has never been more pervasive than it is today. Moreover, it must be acknowledged that the human rights charters that provide the legally recognized transnational platforms for interrogating local practices do reflect Western values.

This is not, however, an excuse for romanticizing local traditions. Some local traditions, such as torture and slavery, are now considered inhumane and illegal by most of the world's governments.[14] Recent human rights discourses on female infanticide, female circumcision, child prostitution, and child labor are instructive. Locals who benefit from these practices defend them against human rights monitoring groups by framing them as practices that are integral to local cultural traditions and economies. In short, emancipatory politics in non-Western nations, as in Western nations, are often sites of conflict between traditional, patrimonial forms of authority and more broadly based, inclusive, and participatory forms.

Democracy is an emancipatory project. To retreat from the word is to retreat from the quest. To tread cautiously in unfamiliar terrain is sensible; to listen before one speaks is prudent; to interrogate one's own positions before others is the beginning of wisdom; but to remain silent in the presence of brutality is to become complicit in it.

For these reasons, I continue to swim against the cynical, anti-utopian current. I argue that terms like liberation and emancipation do what Virginia Woolf once said good words should do: they soak up a lot of truth. These particular good words also galvanize action. The neoliberal globalizers, who denounce them as polemical, are right. They are polemical! This is an argument for their recuperation by friends of democracy, not an argument for their censure.

Fixing damaged words is, of course, not enough. Systematic research in the political economy of communication, media institutions, and propaganda analysis is imperative. Moreover, this work needs to be combined with political activism dedicated to reforming social practices. Without these efforts, wordsmithing is an idle pursuit.

POLITICAL LINGUISTICS

Building upon the foundations crafted by Adorno and Horkheimer, Herbert Marcuse forged his classic statement on political linguistics in 1955.[15] Because he framed his argument within the context of his longstanding debate with "revisionary neo-Freudians," especially Jungians, these ideas remain relatively unfamiliar to most communication theorists. One need not share Marcuse's Freudian sympathies to find his perspective on language and communication compelling. In essence, Marcuse tried to preserve the liberating message in Freud's theory of repression. He saw it as the essential subtext of the Freudian breakthrough. Thus, he maintained that, at its inception, "psychoanalysis was a radically critical theory" because it provided a method for demystifying repression and nurturing desires for real autonomy.[16] Marcuse contended, however, that the neo-Freudians had transformed psychoanalysis into an ideology that justifies repression as the price that must be paid for civilization.

Contra this "ideological" reading of Freud that reifies repression, Marcuse offered a "sociological" reading. That is, he insisted on viewing every collective form of repression in relative and historical terms. Thus, he maintained that, in our time, domination is based upon (a) "surplus repression," which supports a complex hierarchical division of labor, and (b) "the performance principle," which subordinates all life-affirming energies to the demands of work. He contended that this system of domination has made a sham of participatory democracy, and that even science—once the cutting edge for human freedom—is now implicated in legitimating and maintaining the sham. Marcuse's *One-Dimensional Man*, published in 1964, was intended as an extension of this sociological analysis.[17] He conceived it as an empirical case study of the increasingly invisible structures of social control in advanced capitalist societies: control effected by subordinating all human needs to the imperatives of the instrumental reason of the market. Marcuse's description of the dehumanization of American language and culture in *One-Dimensional Man* rivals the most desolate passages in the writings of Horkheimer, Adorno, and Walter Benjamin.

But the work of the dialectician does not end with critique. Unlike many of his followers in the New Left of the 1960s and 1970s who were too often content to sloganize and vulgarize Marcuse—cry "cooptation" and retreat to a comfortable narcissism—Marcuse himself combined critical rigor with an unwavering commitment to a "new sensibility" that could transcend instrumental domination. He continued to pursue all paths that might lead those who had been socialized into silence and subservience to discover new vocabularies that could prepare the way for "a return of the repressed." Marcuse's somber

testaments, like Freud's, contain promises of transcendence, promises that could be realized through "linguistic therapy."

To describe the way those in power are able systematically to skew semantic conventions, linguistic rules, and epistemological criteria, to deny dissent and preserve their own interests in the maintenance of the status quo, Marcuse used the term "political linguistics." He characterizes political linguistics as the "armor of the Establishment" and points out that "one of the most effective rights of the Sovereign is the right to establish enforceable definitions of words."[18] So, for example, "in the established vocabulary, 'violence' is a term which one does not apply to the action of the police, the National Guard, the Marshals, the Marines, the bombers."[19] Conversely, "terrorism" is never used to describe the actions of friendly governments, no matter how abhorrent. In contemporary pseudo-liberal societies, "censorship" has become a pejorative code word reserved for those who posit constructions of reality different from the established one. For example, in current debates in the United States about the separation of church and state, those who seek to remove displays of the Ten Commandments from courthouses or the words "under God" from the Pledge of Allegiance are frequently dismissed as censors. However, many of these activists see themselves as defenders of the First Amendment and advocates of religious diversity and intellectual freedom.

Politically engaged rhetoricians like Kenneth Burke and Murray Edelman have provided invaluable tools for decoding political linguistics.[20] However, Marcuse's approach to linguistic therapy is far more radical. He contends that development of a new sensibility and a new consciousness requires a new language to create and communicate new values: "the rupture with the continuum of domination must also be a rupture with the vocabulary of domination."[21] Linguistic therapy, then, is an attempt to liberate words (and thereby concepts) from distortion of their meanings by established systems of domination. Marcuse acknowledged that this may be a utopian quest. He admitted that the process of linguistic domination has been with us throughout history and that no revolution has transcended it: no revolution has severed the hierarchical scaffolding of language and power. Yet, he expressed the hope that, when humankind is released from the most demeaning forms of labor by advanced technology, a new, humanistic reality principle will displace the imperatives of "surplus repression" and "the performance principle."

Marcuse regarded linguistic therapy as prologue to, and building block of, an enlarged concept of rationality in which "the aesthetic dimension" of human sensibility is no longer repressed.[22] He maintained that, so far, black Americans have been the most effective agents of linguistic therapy. He cites their refusal and aesthetic reversal of the language of oppression as expressed in words and phrases like "soul," "black power," and "black is beautiful." Similar claims have, of course, been made in recent years for rap and hiphop.[23] The mandate of linguistic therapy, then, is to restore the dialogic powers of the people by rescuing language from the control of the dominators. Marcuse did not assume that words were free of history in the precapitalist era. But he did contend that it is possible to strip away the veneer of surplus distortion acquired by language under the rule of instrumental reason. So, for example, it would be possible to recover and restore the critical edge that words like "freedom," "equality," and "justice" had during the seventeenth and eighteenth centuries, when they were essential terms in the language of the repressed rather than in the vocabulary of ideological control.

There are, of course, problems with Marcuse's formulation. Despite his acute awareness of capitalism's power to absorb and domesticate criticism, Marcuse failed to come to terms effectively with the pervasive role mass media, especially television, play in colonizing consciousness and extending linguistic domination. Today, more than ever, technovisions and techno-toys cultivate the values, priorities, and interests of cultural hegemony. Moreover, the apostles of postmodernism have convincingly demonstrated that the aesthetic dimension itself

has now been captured and rather thoroughly colonized by the marketplace.[24] Marcuse's belief—hope, really—hat technology could liberate humankind from surplus repression appears, from the perspective of 2002, as a both/and prospect at best. Some lives have been dramatically enhanced by technological prosthetics: these technologies have given speech to the mute, hearing to the profoundly deaf, sight to the blind, mobility to the paralyzed, and more. Ordinary people in technologically advanced societies now enjoy some of the lifestyle comforts that were once the exclusive preserves of princes and robber barons. Yet, these advances carry significant material and social costs: adding to the ecological strain on an increasingly fragile planet, exacerbating inequalities in the international division of labor and resources, and constraining as well enabling their beneficiaries. So that, for example, globalization has undermined unionization and [workers'] rights in developed countries by exporting jobs and repression to developing nations where slave wages are the norm. Labor-saving technologies have not produced more leisure; to the contrary, workers in the United States are working longer hours than they did before the computer revolution. According to the Bureau of Labor Statistics, for example, an average married couple now works 26 percent longer than comparable working married couples did thirty years ago.[25]

As Dallas Smythe demonstrated in *Dependency Road,* more time away from the factory or office does not necessarily mean greater freedom from instrumental relations; for, under advanced capitalism, productive labor includes consumption.[26] Mass media and, more recently, the Internet keep people "working" by marketing consumer products to themselves, even during their so-called leisure time. So most Americans spend their hours away from paid work with the National Football League, General Mills, Burger King, home shopping networks, and commercial websites rather than in liberative play, creative craftsmanship, or emancipatory dialogue. Until critical theory devises adequate strategies for countering the effects of hierarchically dominated media systems and the passive consumerist approaches to citizenship they cultivate, the return of the repressed will be delayed, and linguistic therapy will remain an interesting but esoteric idea.

MONOLOGIC INSTITUTIONS

At once more encompassing and less radical than Marcuse's view, Habermas's version of critical theory focuses directly on the problem of linguistic domination and the question of communicative competence. Thus, he maintains, "Today the problem of language has replaced the traditional problem of consciousness."[27] Like Marcuse, Habermas is concerned with the way science has been used to extend the hold of linguistic domination. Specifically, he is interested in the way expert technical and managerial knowledge is used by those in power to disenfranchise citizen participation in political debates by fostering the impression that many issues are inherently too complex for a layperson to comprehend or debate competently. According to Habermas, this disenfranchisement has led to the collapse of "the public sphere" and passive acceptance of technocratic elitism. Thus, he claims, all modern governments, whether capitalist or socialist, violate the terms of classic social contract theories of state power. None are legitimated by dialogic consensus.

Rejecting Chomsky's pursuit of linguistic universals as ill-conceived, Habermas's early work on emancipatory communication arrives at a theory of knowledge that bears striking resemblance to Burke's rhetoric.[28] Both thinkers, for example, propose pragmatic definitions of truth founded in dialogue.[29] Habermas maintains that truth can only be secured pragmatically: it is founded upon consensus that is realized in discourse. For Habermas, truth means "warranted assertability." He contends that a "model of pure communicative action (interaction)" presupposes that all parties involved in an interaction are accountable: that their behaviors are

intentional and that they are capable of justifying their beliefs and norms. But he points out that the monologic actions of contemporary institutions do not fit this model. Therefore, Habermas maintains, these institutional acts are embedded in systematically distorted communication:

> The barriers to communication which make a fiction of the reciprocal imputation of accountability support at the same time the belief in legitimacy which sustains the fiction and prevents it being found out. That is the paradoxical achievement of ideologies, whose individual prototype is the neurotic disturbance.[30]

Ideological legitimations of ideas and states are secured in monologic fictions. They are based upon false or forced consensus: hence the Orwellian deformations of the vocabulary of modern politics. Habermas argues that a genuine, rationally motivated consensus can be reached only if the conditions of an "ideal speech situation" can be anticipated during legitimating discourses. He regards the semantic analysis of the classic (Freudian) psychoanalytic dialogues of patient and therapist as prototypes of the ideal, reflexive speech situation. In an ideal speech situation, Habermas contends, all potential participants must have equal chances to initiate and perpetuate discourses; all participants must have equal opportunities to criticize, ground, or refute all statements, explanations, interpretations, and justifications; and discourse must be free from the external constraints of domination, for example, violence, threats, and sanctions. If these conditions prevail, the preconditions for a rational order will be met. If these conditions are also realized *within* the actual course of the dialogue, the resulting consensus will be free of internal and external constraints. It will be based upon the *power of the best argument*.

Habermas does not bar instrumental arguments from the arena of debate; he merely tries to ensure that other arguments can be heard. The ideal speech situation is both the means and the end—double objectives—of Habermas's emancipatory project. In Marcuse's critical theory, linguistic therapy and exploration of the aesthetic dimensions of dialogue were merely prologue: means whereby more humane visions of social organization might be articulated. Habermas's work is an apology for more rationality and more democracy in interactions between dominators and the dominated. It does not promise an end to domination. It offers no strategies for countering the massive agenda-setting machinery of today's culture industry. Moreover, his conception of rationality is quite narrowly, one might even say parochially, framed when viewed from the perspectives of postcolonial, feminist, or postmodern positions. Habermas successfully demonstrates the importance of language and communication in legitimating knowledge and power. He does not successfully transcend positivism and instrumentalism. Therefore, he has been correctly labeled a "right-wing Marxist" or a "radical Liberal."[31] Habermas has, however, clarified the issues and demonstrated that the impasse in the emancipatory project of his critical theory is not an impasse in critical theory per se. Moreover, his extended engagement with the problems of deliberative democracy has set an agenda for a robust transdisciplinary conversation that continues to resonate with partisans of participatory democracy.

DEMOCRATIC POWER-TALK

Ben Agger has offered a provocative synthesis of the ideas of Habermas, Marcuse, and the liberal American legal theorist Bruce Ackerman.[32] In Agger's critical theory, dialogue is regarded as both a means to discrediting and overcoming repressive institutional arrangements and as "an imaginative model—a telos—of free human activity."[33] Like Habermas, Agger contends that technocratic capitalism is supported by a scientization of ideology that not only discourages dialogues between laypeople and experts, but also encourages a "socially structured silence" among citizens. He contends that "the monopoly of capital goes hand in hand with the monopoly both of information and of dialogue-chances."[34]

Agger's synthesis has three essential components: (a) a conversational basis for delegitimating a repressive social order, through which the powerless can engage the powerful in justificatory dialogues, (b) a critique of the ideology of technocratically induced silence that *uses* the public experience of delegitimation as a means of generating more sophisticated political dialogues, and (c) an outline of concrete social and political action in which the human capacity for competent involvement in person-nature, person-symbol, and person-person dialogues is affirmed. Ackerman's "neutral dialogue" provides the first component, Habermas's critical theory the second, and Agger's conception of dialogue as an exemplar of free human activity the third.

Ackerman's neutral dialogue provides an independent criterion for identifying illegitimate, nonrational, "constrained power talk." Constrained power talk entails failure to engage in dialogue or, once engaged, failure to offer rational justifications for one's advantaged position. According to Ackerman:

> A power structure is illegitimate if it can be justified only through a conversation in which some person (or group) must assert that he is (or they are) the privileged moral authority: Neutrality. No reason is a good reason if it requires the power holder to assert:
> (a) that his conception of the good is better than that asserted by any of his fellow citizens, or
> (b) that regardless of his conception of the good, he is intrinsically superior to one or more of his fellow citizens.[35]

Pulling rank, citing credentials instead of reasons, using technical data to obfuscate, and invoking procedural rules to mute or deflect justificatory dialogues are, by definition, illegitimate, repressive communications, violations of democratically grounded free speech. As Ackerman puts it, "A sustained silence or a stream of self-contradictory noises are decisive signs that something very wrong is going on."[36]

Ackerman is not a critical theorist. He posits his conception of neutral dialogue in an attempt to breathe new life into liberalism. However, he demonstrates that, by virtue of their monologic stances, most existing liberal institutions are illegitimate. He provides a perspective for principled recognition of corruption, but no program for purging corruption. He is interested in the ground rules of free speech, not in the sociology of communicative competence. Thus, he has nothing to say about socially stratified inequalities in educational and linguistic opportunities which, according to sociologists like Basil Bernstein, cause the disadvantaged to abstain from participation in public forums.[37] Habermas's perspective, however, criticizes technocratically induced silence and encourages the powerless to respond to failed justificatory dialogues by developing communicative competence and thereby renewing political dialogues and actions.

Agger, like Marcuse, sees the first step—identifying illegitimate power relations—and the second step—developing communicative competence—as prologue to the third step—articulating a new sensibility that replaces instrumental control with humanistic productive and organizational relations grounded in dialogue liberated from repression. Thus, Agger contends: "Communicative competence in this sense is nothing less than a competence to manage all the facets of our lives, in transcendence of an ideology that robs us both of our political voices and our substantive social and economic freedom of self creation."[38] It is not just the power to generate fluent reports or warranted assertions; it is the power to transform ourselves and the world. This power does not necessarily preclude hierarchy. But it does require such hierarchical moves to be secured in egalitarian dialogues. Thus, in contrast to historical (Marxist-Leninist) socialism, for example, it insists that the processes and the product of socialism cannot be divorced. If the ends are social democracy or communitarianism, these ends can only be justified if they can be secured by democratic means: egalitarian dialogic processes. To Dag Hammarskjöld's wise prescript, "Only he [or she] deserves power who everyday justifies it," might be added the caveat that he or she must justify it in both theory and practice.[39] In short, Agger's robust concept of communication competence is unapologetically eutopian.

POLICY IMPLICATIONS

What Paulo Freire tried to do to create conditions that would develop critical consciousness and articulation among those repressed by neocolonial structures of oppression, Agger's work attempts to do for those disenfranchised by technocratic structures.[40] He provides them/us with a dialogic warrant for recovering their voices and discovering their competencies. Agger's synthesis transcends the praxeological impasse of the first wave of critical theory. The standard of neutral dialogue, as radicalized by Agger, advances critical theory beyond ideological critique. It provides a practical interactional test of the symmetry (and democracy) of dialogic relationships: not just political relationships, but also the organization of work and of social and domestic relationships. Moreover, it provides a prophylaxis against vanguardism: the perennial problem of the left whereby the emancipatory vision is distorted and betrayed by leaders who predicate their claims to speak for the people on a refusal to listen to the people. Agger's approach is interested in encouraging the repressed to speak for themselves, to make policy. Therefore, he does not examine in a concrete way the policy implications of institutionalizing neutrality, although he does suggest that it would revolutionize the division of labor in society.

As I interpret these policy implications, they would seem to suggest, at a minimum, that in a truly democratic state, all institutional spokespersons would be instructed in the rules of neutral dialogue rather than in the principles of technocratic management, advertising, public relations, and spin control. The institutions of such a state would be structured to maximize opportunities for generating justificatory dialogues. Racism, sexism, classism, and ageism would be outlawed as violations of the terms of neutral dialogue. A primary responsibility of the press would be to report breaches of the rules of neutral dialogue by those in positions of power as violations of their trust. The press itself would have to rethink its covenant because, by definition, the hierarchical concentration of control of mass media that prevails in technocratic societies is an abrogation of neutrality.

Similarly, claims by the press to the superior moral authority of "journalistic objectivity" would have to be abandoned. Copyrights, royalties, patents, and other reified concepts of information ownership would also have to be thoroughly rethought. Present trends toward privatization of information resources would be reversed. A new international information order would be established that would bear little resemblance to that presently envisioned by either its proponents or opponents. The culture industry as we know it, with its monologic programming, would talk itself out of existence, and the knowledge industry would manufacture a new warrant through which scientists would invent less manipulative relationships with nature, objects, and people, and thereby articulate more nurturing vocabularies of motive and expression. Clearly, this simple and eminently reasonable paradigm for free speech is a very radical idea—perhaps as radical as ideas like "freedom," "equality," "justice," and "liberalism" were in the seventeenth and eighteenth centuries.

FLIES IN THE OINTMENT

Neutral dialogue, as it is conceived by Ackerman and Agger, is not just a good place. It is also a distant place. It will remain an unreachable place (or value) unless critical theory recovers its political will, its commitments to participatory democracy, and its investment in the future. The odds against its realization are great, even monumental.

Media Industries

The most obvious, pernicious, and intractable obstacles are, of course, the established powers of mass media and the culture industry more generally. Given the present organization of media and the corporate economic stranglehold on national politics, at least in the United States, it is pie in the sky to contemplate reforming national politics from the top-down through neutral dialogue. New media mergers are constantly shifting the alignments and increasing the conglomeration, integration, and synergy within the handful of global communication companies that now control most of the world's media.

Moreover new, user-friendly media technologies, post-Fordian modes of production (flexible, stratified, and targeted), and personalized marketing techniques threaten to dismantle remaining vestiges of the public sphere by erasing the shared universe of discourse upon which an informed citizenry depends. Technovisionaries tell us that Internet-mediated infobots, which allow users to design personalized newspapers and other information resources by filtering out entire categories or genres of messages in advance, are the wave of the future. So, for example, Consumer A can bypass political news entirely and immerse himself in sports media, while Consumer B tunes into political news but filters out all viewpoints that challenges her ideological presuppositions, and so on. Personalized media—so inviting from an efficiency standpoint in an age of information overload—may in fact create "technological echo chambers," which preclude encounters with people and perspectives that are unfamiliar or challenging to their users.[41] Yet, as Cass Sunstein points out, free expression and deliberative democracy depend upon: (a) unplanned and unanticipated exchanges of diverse viewpoints that people do not seek, frequently find disturbing, and must struggle to integrate into their understandings of the world; and (b) a citizenry that has a range of shared experiences. He maintains that these requirements hold in any large nation, but that

[t]hey are especially important in a heterogeneous nation, which is bound to face an occasional risk of fragmentation. They have all the more importance as each nation becomes increasingly global, and each citizen becomes to a greater or lesser degree, a "citizen of the world."[42]

Computer-enabled target marketing and consumer tracking further erode these democratic requirements. Intended to use advertising dollars more efficiently, these practices not only respond to self-selecting taste cultures and lifestyle differences, they cultivate them. Segmenting markets and media audiences, these profit-maximizing strategies also divide consumer/citizens based upon age, gender, race, class, and other variables. That is, they create echo chambers as well as reinforce and amplify the filtering mechanisms that insulate these chambers.[43]

Failures of Critical Theories and Politics

The logical counter to both new and old forms of media hegemony is, of course, broadly based democratic media activism. Recent attempts to create coalitions of media scholars, media activists, and media workers have, however, been notorious for their own forms of fragmentation and factionalism, infighting, and identity politics. As neutral dialogue, most of these efforts fail.

Would-be media reformers need to get their own houses in order. Some of the fault lines in failed efforts at critical media coalition politics are readily transparent. None is perhaps more crucial than the absence of coherent vision (or amalgamation of visions).

From its inception, critical social theory has been committed to recovering the unity of theory and practice: to discovering what is missing and imagining something better. That is, it has been eutopian. Since the collapse of the Soviet dystopia, neoliberalism, the anti-ideological ideology of globalization, has succeeded in censoring all utopian visions except the technovisions upon which its own future depends.[44] Framing

itself as the "end of history"—as both the telos and terminus of historical evolution—neoliberalism thereby positions itself to reject all challenges to its hegemony as regressive, ahistorical, irrational, reductive, and potentially totalitarian.[45] This alchemy has worked relatively well, at least within neoliberal states where the left, with some exceptions, has largely surrendered (if only by default) to the "end of ideology" thesis that it once roundly rejected.[46] Yet, without some shared vision, some bridging of ideals, coalition politics are impossible.

The current intellectual fashion of blaming the Enlightenment for all of the errors of modernism misses the point. As the conservative economist Friedrich Hayek pointed out long ago, it was the marriage of scientism and Marxist-Leninism that led to totalitarianism: a universalistic, reductive, unitary, and ultimately closed vision.[47] A similar and similarly dangerous but unacknowledged scientism, rooted in social evolutionary assumptions, lies at the core of current neoliberal apologetics for globalization.

Eutopian ideals, unfettered by scientism and articulated on more modest, even local, scales, are still needed to build just communities and viable coalitions. The Golden Rule is such an ideal, one that can be found in some form as a normative standard in all enduring societies: never fully realized, but as a perennial dream. Those who find something missing in the current subordination of all values to market values need to dare to dream again; to recover the eutopian impulse and to exercise it wisely, reflexively, with a clear-eyed realism. They need to once again find the courage to speak truth to those in power: to take risks, including risking the possibility of once again making humiliating errors.[48]

Feminist Questions

Then, there is "the feminist question." Gestures that are friendly to feminism can be found or read into all of the theories of emancipatory communication explored in these pages; however, none of their authors engages directly with the feminist critique of patriarchal language, structures of thought or discursive practices. None considers what recent feminist epistemological critiques of rationalism and empiricism would mean for a theory of dialogue; how the feminist project would reconstruct models of rationality and discursive rules or how it has deconstructed social contract theory; how the gendering of public and private spheres and conceptions of good arguments can be reconciled in comprehensive theories of dialogue; or how Cartesian mind-body dualism conditions contemporary concepts of communication, information, and mediation. Indeed, all of these theories of emancipatory communication appear to import unstated and nonreflexive images of imaginary dialogic partners who already share some fundamental agreements about how public issues, rationality, and warranted assertability should be defined. Yet, these elements are the problem of the feminist epistemological critique. In sum, feminism poses some profound, though not necessarily insurmountable, problems for critical theory and for dialogic theories of democracy. Some of these challenges are more fully explored in part II of this book.

Elitism and Moral Tyranny of Dialogic Models

The most daunting challenges to dialogic models of emancipatory communication cut to their logical core. In his thoughtful and imaginative book, *Speaking into the Air* (1999), John Durham Peters radically questions both the desirability and tenability of using dialogue as a "normative model for the extended, even distended, kinds of talk and discourse necessary to large-scale democracy."[49] He points to the simple and obvious, but frequently glossed over, fact that dialogic relations are dyadic, person-to-person, reciprocal interactions involving "the marriage of true minds." Dialogic couplings are both exclusionary and very rare; moreover, they sometimes involve tyranny and exploitation.

Socrates, the Socratic method of questioning, and the dyadic relationship of mentor and student are the prototypes for romanticizing dialogue as

an idealized model for communication in Western culture. Socratic dialogues are elitist, in Peters's view, because the reciprocity they offer requires (a) orientation through education; and (b) the junior partner to successfully negotiate intellectual contests to achieve relative equality. They are not open to all; in historical fact, they were open only to an elite few within the limited franchises of Athenian democracy.

In place of the Socratic ideal of dialogue, Peters proposes "dissemination" as a more accurate, and in his view, more democratic model for mass communication. Here, he offers Jesus and the Gospels as prototypes of dissemination. Peters locates democracy in reception rather than in transmission; that is, receivers are free to accept, reject, ignore, or reconfigure messages.

More specifically, for our purposes, Peters criticizes the "moral tyranny" that he believes is implicit in Ackerman's apparently congenial invitation to dialog because it does not leave potential dialogic partners free to refuse the invitation.[50] Peters's moral objection is justified if neutral dialogue is taken as a model for all forms of dialogue. However, Ackerman is a political theorist, not a social psychologist. He intends neutral dialogue as a means whereby citizens can take back (or create) democracy by making corrupt monologic institutions accountable for their actions by, in effect, making them more dialogic. That is, Ackerman intends neutral dialogue as a model for legitimating dialogues in which the governed ask governors to justify their exercises of power. In this context, institutional structures and procedures are already heavily stacked in favor of the powerful, giving them many ways of preemptively opting out of dialogues. Within Ackerman's liberal schema, then, the refusal of representatives of monologic institutions to justify their actions to the people is a violation of the democratic social contract of liberalism. This refusal is tyranny. Conversely, the threat of the people to engage in violence if the representatives of monologic institutions refuse their invitation to dialogue, which Peters objects to, is not tyranny—at least not to a Jeffersonian or Ackermanian liberal. It is entirely consistent with the democratic premises of the liberal social contract, which originated in both [the] United States and France in violent revolutions against the monologic regimes of monarchies. In short, the threat of violent resistance by the people is part of the bargain of liberalism.

Nonetheless Peters's larger point about the inappropriateness of dialogue as a model for public communication does identify serious conundrums in communication theory and liberalism. Dissemination is a far more accurate description of how mass media and public communication work today; however, I am not persuaded by his advocacy for the democracy of reception. To be sure, receivers are not the passive puppets that many theories, especially Marxist theories, of communications have assumed, but without a diverse media and a viable public sphere, even actively resistant receivers are poorly positioned to do the work of democracy.

Peters's conception of communication is, however, far richer and, in my judgment, truer than the theories of communication he critiques. Peters recognizes that there is a kind of "permanent kink" in the human condition, which makes perfect communicative reciprocity impossible; our efforts to "reconcile self and other" always involve some "strangeness."[51] There are always gaps that are filled with contradictions, ironies, wit, word play, logical inversions, and awkwardness; yet, he claims, these gaps are the sources of love and justice. In negotiating them, we become fully human.

Peters is surely right in claiming that the liberal dialogic models of Habermas and Ackerman are much too sober to take into account the strangeness and wonder of human communication. These models only tap our highest cerebral functions: the upper attic of our minds where formal logic eliminates all of the noise of life and engages in the simplistic reductions of rationalism. These models ignore the fact that we all live in bodies, bring different gendered, racialized, class experiences, life histories, educational backgrounds, semantic resources, and creative cunning to legitimating conversations.

If we accept Peters's enriched conception of communicative processes, must we surrender our dialogic dreams? Must we settle instead into the congregations of nay-sayers or yeah-sayers that his "dissemination" model appears to offer?

Not necessarily! Within Peters's work, there is a loophole that saves dialogue from extinction in communicative ethics and in developing rules for engaging in power talk. In a move that is less slick than it initially seems, he turns the demands of reflective dialogue inside out, or more precisely "outside in." That is, Peters imposes the rules of dialogue on the self rather than on the other:

> The motto of communication theory ought to be: Dialogue with the self, dissemination with the other. This is another way of stating the ethical maxim: Treat yourself like an other and the other like a self.[52]

He makes explicit what has always been implicit, but not always honored in practice, in theories of emancipatory communication: theorists need to practice what they preach.

RETURNING TO PARIS: LINGUISTIC THERAPY FOR DAMAGED THEORIES OF DIALOG

Was the communication-turn in critical theory a wrong turn? Should we abandon dialogues about dialogue, repress our "desire" for more satisfying forms of collective life, and return to just calling Paris Paris?

I think not. To be sure, we need to do much more than talk about talk. Studies in political economy and institutional analysis, which examine the material and social conditions in which public communications take place in contemporary societies, need to be reinvigorated and recentered within communication research.[53] But talk about talk remains an essential part of critical theory's emancipatory mission. The thinkers profiled in this chapter have contributed much to the advancement of that talk even when (and sometimes especially when) they have talked themselves into comers. The dream of full reciprocity in communication may be a romantic fiction. But the desire for reciprocity is not only what makes us human, it is what makes society possible. Conversational rules or etiquettes, which are designed to bring a wider range of voices into democratic debates, may not work. Or, if they do, the conversations they produce may end in stalemates. But to give up on the possibility of such conversations is to give up on democracy.

A first step toward opening up richer dialogues about dialogic theory might be to abandon the abstractions of the armchair and engage in real conversations that test and amend the rules of neutral dialogue in practice. This is because ultimately the rules for such dialogues, if they really are to be open and just, must be articulated contextually by committed participants. A vast research literature is now available on the ways gender, race, class, heterosexism, and other positionings intersect and condition actual and perceived communication competence in a wide range of intercultural contexts. There is, in short, an ample knowledge base to put theory into practice if participants are committed to coalition building. Moreover, liberal models for coalition building, which often impose rather than achieve consensus, have been extensively critiqued; and alternative, equity based models, which can accommodate irreducible differences, have been developed and successfully deployed by activists, for example, by some antiglobalization groups.

Testing communication models in micropractice—in the palpable, participatory presence of real talking, gesturing, and touching people—should also short-circuit some of the abstract logorrhea that has led so much high theory astray in the last two decades. Or, as Peters bluntly notes, in an otherwise mixed assessment of Jacques Derrida's work, "[T]o think of the longing for the presence of other people as a kind of metaphysical mistake is nuts."[54]

Putting the house of critical theory in order also requires fidelity to what Ackerman calls consistency in practice as well as in dialogic claims. That is, it requires consistency within the micropolitics of critical theory whether those politics function in theory groups, academic gatekeeping, or in political organizing. If critical theorists are genuinely committed to participatory democracy, then they must submit their own practices to its frequently inefficient, usually time-consuming, sometimes irresolute, often frustrating and disorderly, but self-reflexive, litmus test.

Consistency is always a heavy burden for humans: our flawed souls are battlefields of conflicting desires. Yet, perhaps in no scholarly endeavor is the mandate clearer: in theorizing emancipatory communication, we are obligated, both logically and morally, to strive for consistency. Ultimately the most valuable outcome of this striving may be the ethic it imposes on the theorist/activist (as in Peters's redeployment of dialogue). Taken seriously, the norm of consistency can serve as a self-reflexive ethic for modeling and monitoring our own contributions to justificatory dialogues. That is, those who claim to be seriously committed to communicative and community justice could begin their reformation by interrogating their own dialogic motives and practices. In *Doing Documentary Work* (1998), Robert Coles provides an insightful, if inescapably tension-laden, model for conducting such self-interrogations in research settings that involve communications across class, race, and status. The reflexive, personal, and social ethic that Coles advocates in the research process can also serve as a useful, self-imposed normative standard for guiding participation by intellectuals in justificatory dialogues and community activism.[55]

Today, much, perhaps even most, of our discursive space is technologically mediated. Practicing what I preach in a milieu in which most of my potential conversational partners are engaged in mediated experiences most of their waking hours may be morally uplifting, however, except in very rare instances, it is likely to be politically irrelevant. Yet, counter-hegemonic, Internet-based mediating technologies could be designed to facilitate political dialogues that embody the values of and conform to the rules of reflexive power-talk.[56] A long shot? Yes indeed! But a long shot is better than cashing in one's chips and resigning oneself to the "end of history."

The clock is ticking. While media reformers have been factionalizing, the media monoliths have been conglomerating, consolidating, and integrating. They have been using their increased financial clout to "reform" communication law, to dismantle the mandates of regulatory agencies like the Federal Communication Commission, and to foreclose public debate about international trade agreements that further advance their global hegemony. As Herbert Schiller pointed out more than two decades ago, globalization, the convergence of "new electronic industries, the changing sites of industrial production, and instantaneous international communication are imposing a new form of hierarchical organization on much of the world."[57]

The Agger-Ackerman critique of "monopolies of both information and of dialogue chances" is incomplete; and neutral dialogue is a preliminary and flawed formulation, perhaps at best a provocative hypothesis. It may not prove viable in practice even in the micropolitics of organizations dedicated to democratic social change. Nevertheless, the questions it addresses—questions posed so long ago by the Frankfurt School when the specters of earlier totalitarian ambitions were at their heels—are still salient questions.

There is now considerable research that shows that participatory democracy is still possible in small groups.[58] Powerful arguments have also been made for the indispensability of coalition politics of resistance under present political arrangements.[59] Critical scholars have a role to play in coalition building, not as vanguards or authoritative experts, but as collaborators in genuinely democratic processes. Within these collaborations, consistency, with democratic principles,

may often require scholars to consume salutary servings of humble pie by assuming secondary roles as research associates.

Realization of neutral dialogue and self-reflexive dialogic ethics will not sever the knot that binds power and knowledge. Struggles to identify and reduce surplus repression cannot undo the "kink" in human communication processes. But revised, historicized, and contextualized, struggles for norms of emancipatory communication are still worth pursuing.

Many critical theorists are, in my judgment, too eager to declare this pursuit a dead end and move on to the next game. Yet, this declaration comes at exactly the moment in history when feminism and other subaltern perspectives are actively interrogating the power talk of critical theory, seeking to reverse its exclusionary clauses, hold it to norms of reflexivity and consistency, and effect transformative syntheses. Changing the subject before everyone has her say is, of course, also a breach of the rules of reflexive power-talk, as well as a familiar move in the politics of gendered conversation.

NOTES

1. Karl Marx and Friedrich Engels, *The German Ideology* (New York: International Publishers, 1970, original 1846), 119.

2. Marx and Engels, *The German Ideology,* 102.

3. Max Horkheimer, *Eclipse of Reason* (New York: Seabury Press, 1974); and Max Horkheimer and Theodore W. Adorno, *Dialectics of Enlightenment* (New York: Herder and Herder, 1972).

4. Max Horkheimer, *Critical Theory: Selected Essays* (New York: Seabury Press, 1972); Martin Jay, *The Dialectical Imagination: A History of the Frankfurt School and the Institute of Social Research 1923–1950* (Boston: Little, Brown, 1973); Trent Schroyer, *The Critique of Domination* (New York: Braziller, 1973); and Jules Sensat, *Habermas and Marxism: An Appraisal* (Beverly Hills, Calif.: Sage, 1979).

5. Horkheimer and Adorno, *Dialects of Enlightenment.*

6. Charles Loomis quoted by John Gastil, *Democracy in Small Groups: Participation, Decision Making and Communication* (Philadelphia: New Society Publishers, 1993), vii.

7. Ben Agger, "Work and Authority in Marcuse and Habermas," *Human Studies* 2 (1979): 191–208; and Paulo Freire, *Pedagogy of the Oppressed* (New York: Seabury Press, 1970).

8. John Durham Peters, *Speaking Into the Air: A History of the Idea of Communication* (Chicago: University of Chicago Press, 1999), 269.

9. Douglas Kellner, *Television and the Crisis of Democracy* (Boulder: Westview Press, 1990); Vincent Mosco, *The Political Economy of Communication* (London: Sage, 1996); and Dan Schiller, *Theorizing Communication: A History* (New York: Oxford University Press, 1996).

10. John A. Lent, ed., *A Different Road Taken: Profiles in Critical Communication* (Boulder: Westview Press, 1995).

11. Paul Carus, *Goethe* (Chicago: Open Court, 1915).

12. James W. Carey, "Public Sphere," plenary address presented at the annual meeting of the International Communication Association, Chicago, May 23, 1996.

13. Jacques Barzun, *From Dawn to Decadence: 500 Years of Western Cultural Life, 1500 to the Present* (New York: HarperCollins, 2000); and Roger Shattuck, "Decline and Fall?" *The New York Times Review of Books,* 29 June 2000, 55–58.

14. This is at least formally true for all members of the United Nations although, of course, subscription to human rights charters produces, at best, imperfect results.

15. Herbert Marcuse, *Eros: A Philosophical Inquiry into Freud* (Boston: Beacon Press, 1955).

16. Marcuse, *Eros,* 217.

17. Herbert Marcuse, *One-Dimensional Man* (Boston: Beacon Press, 1964), 217.

18. Herbert Marcuse, *An Essay on Liberation* (Boston: Beacon Press, 1969), 73.

19. Marcuse, *An Essay on Liberation,* 72.

20. Kenneth Burke, *A Grammar of Motives and Rhetoric of Motives* (Cleveland, Ohio: Meridian, 1962); and Murray Edelman, *Political Language: Words that Succeed and Politics that Fail* (New York: Academic Press, 1977).

21. Marcuse, *An Essay on Liberation,* 33.

22. Herbert Marcuse, *The Aesthetic Dimension: Toward a Critique of Marxist Aesthetics* (Boston: Beacon Press, 1978).

23. Michael Eric Dyson, *Between God and Gangsta Rap: Bearing Witness to Black Culture* (New York: Oxford University Press, 1997).

24. Andreas Huyssen, "The Hidden Dialectic: The Avant Garde-Technology-Mass Culture," in *The Myths of Information: Technology and Postindustrial Culture,* ed. Kathleen Woodward (Sun Prairie, Wisc.: Baumgartner Publications and the University of Wisconsin, 1980), 151–64; and Thomas Frank, *The Conquest of Cool: Business Culture, Counterculture and the Rise of Hip Consumerism* (Chicago: University of Chicago Press, 1998).

25. From *Parks and Recreation* (October 2000), cited in "Time Out," UTNE Reader (April 2001): 62.

26. Dallas Smythe, *Dependency Road: Communications, Capitalism, Consciousness and Canada* (Norwood, N.J.: Ablex, 1981).

27. Jürgen Habermas, *Knowledge and Human Interests* (Boston: Beacon Press, 1971), 220.

28. Burke, *A Grammar of Motives.*

29. In this regard, they share common, if not always acknowledged, roots in the American pragmatism of Dewey and James who, like their current apologist Richard Rorty, also valorize the conversational grounding of truth-making.

30. Quoted in Thomas A. McCarthy, "A Theory of Communicative Competence," *Philosophy of Social Science* 3 (1973): 135–56.

31. Ben Agger, "A Critical Theory of Dialogue," *Humanities in Society* 4, no. 1 (Winter 1981): 201.

32. Agger, "Work and Authority."

33. Agger, "Work and Authority," 7.

34. Agger, "Work and Authority," 9.

35. Bruce A. Ackerman, *Social Justice in the Liberal State* (New Haven, Conn., and London: Yale University Press, 1980), 10–11.

36. Ackerman, *Social Justice,* 8.

37. Basil Bernstein, *Class Codes and Control* (London: Routledge & Kegan Paul, 1971).

38. Agger, "Work and Authority," 28.

39. Dag Hammarskjöld, *Markings* (New York: Knopf, 1964), 138.

40. Paulo Freire, *Pedagogy of the Oppressed* (New York: Seabury Press, 1970); Agger, "Work and Authority"; and Agger, "A Critical Theory of Dialogue."

41. Cass Sunstein, "Exposure to Other Viewpoints Is Vital to Democracy," *The Chronicle of Higher Education* (March 16, 2001): 10(B)–11(B). See also Sunstein, *Republic.com* (Princeton: Princeton University Press, 2001).

42. Sunstein, "Exposure to Other Viewpoints," 10(B)–11(B); and Sunstein, *Republic.com.*

43. Joseph Throw, *Breaking Up America: Advertisers and the New Media World* (Chicago: University of Chicago Press, 1997).

44. Gunter Grass and Pierre Bourdieu, "A Literature from Below," *The Nation* (July 3, 2000): 25–28.

45. Grass and Bourdieu, "A Literature from Below." The end of history thesis was articulated (or rearticulated within the post-Cold War context) by Francis Fukuyama, "The End of History?" *National Interest* (Summer 1989): 3–18, and expanded in a book, *The End of History and The Last Man* (New York: The Free Press, 1992).

46. Russell Jaccoby, *The End of Utopia: Politics and Culture in an Age of Apathy* (New York: Basic Books, 1999).

47. Friedrich Hayek, *The Road to Serfdom* (Chicago: University of Chicago Press, 1996, original 1942).

48. Edward Said, *Representations of the Intellectual* (New York: Random House, 1996).

49. Peters, *Speaking into the Air,* 34

50. Peters, *Speaking into the Air,* 159.

51. Peters, *Speaking into the Air,* 9 and 29.

52. Peters, *Speaking into the Air,* 57.

53. On this point, I strongly agree with Vincent Mosco and Dan Schiller who stress the [importance] of reemphasizing the study of the material and social relations of cultural production in the wake of the ascendancy of cultural studies and postmodernism. See Vincent Mosco, *The Political Economy of Communication* (London: Sage, 1996); and Dan Schiller, *Theorizing Communication: A History* (New York: Oxford University Press, 1996).

54. Peters, *Speaking into the Air,* 270.

55. Robert Coles, *Doing Documentary Work* (New York: Oxford University Press, 1998).

56. Benjamin Barber is exploring development of such software. Benjamin Barber, presentation to Faculty Humanities Seminar, Muhlenberg College, February 13, 2001. See also Brenda Dervin's ongoing experimentations with computer mediated dialogic designs. For a recent installment, see Brenda Dervin et al., "Freedom Is Another Word for Nothing Left to Lose: The Inextricable Necessity of Theorizing! Philosophizing in Disciplined Communication Policy/Practice," paper presented at annual meetings of the International Communication Association, May 26, 2001.

57. Herbert Schiller, *Who Knows: Information in the Age of the Fortune 500* (Norwood, N.J.: Ablex, 1981), 2.

58. Gastil, *Democracy in Small Groups.*

59. William Julius Wilson, *The Bridge over the Racial Divide: Rising Inequality and Coalition Politics* (Berkeley: University of California Press, 1999).

PROJECTS FOR CRITICAL THEORIZING

ADDITIONAL READINGS ON THE CRITICAL TRADITION

A. To learn more about critical communication theory: Deetz (1992, 2005); Hardt (1992); Jansen (2002); Schiller (1996).

B. To learn more about Marxism, the Frankfurt School, and Habermas: Agger (1998); Aune (1994); Cooren (2000); Gramsci (1971); Habermas (1981/1984, 1981/1987); Horkheimer and Adorno (1944/1976); Rasmussen (1996); Rush (2004). *The Marxist Internet Archive* (http://www.marxists.org) is an excellent online resource for classic Marxist theory.

C. To learn more about feminist and gender theory: Ashcraft and Mumby (2004); Bobo (2001); Butler (1990); Collins (2000); Donovan (2000); Dow and Condit (2005); Kramarae (1989); Rakow and Wackwitz (2004); Speer (2005).

D. To learn more about critical cultural studies: Bennett, Grossberg, Morris, and Williams (2005); Grossberg (1997); Grossberg, Nelson, and Treichler (1992); Hall (1997); Miller (2001); Morley and Chen (1996).

E. To learn more about postcolonial theory: Ashcroft, Griffiths, and Tiffins (2005); Bhabha (2004); Fanon (1961/1963, 1952/1967); Kavoori (1998); Mohanty (2003); Said (1979); Shome (1998); Spivak (1999); Young (2001).

F. To learn more about critical race theory: Ashcraft and Allen (2003); Clark and O'Donnell (1999); Crenshaw, Gotanda, Peller, and Thomas (1996); Delgado and Stefancic (2001); Gandy (1998); Nakayama and Martin (1999).

APPLICATION EXERCISE

Find a story in a newspaper or newsmagazine that you think might be of interest to critical theorists. Although critical theorists look at both controversial and everyday topics, for this exercise choose a controversial topic such as immigration, marriage, equality, affirmative action, foreign intervention, or government surveillance. After reading this story, think of two perspectives that might interpret the story differently than how it was presented in this article. In what ways would the stories be different? Rewrite this story from these two perspectives. Then show the original article to someone who you think might hold one of these perspectives, and see what they actually have to say about the article.

PROJECTS

1. After reading in several strands of critical theory (A–F in the additional readings), consider this question: How well does this tradition fit together? Mohanty (2003) provides one integration of feminism and postcolonialism. How might other theorists respond to this proposal? Are there unifying themes across all (A–F) critical approaches? Is discursive reflection an

implicit ideal of communication that underlies all of them? Do they all examine different forms of systematic distortion? On the other hand, have we distorted some of these approaches by placing them under the critical tradition? Are some of them distinct traditions of communication theory in their own right? If so, how do their ways of conceptualizing communication differ from those of critical theory and other traditions?

2. Building on Horkheimer and Adorno's critique of inauthentic culture and the acceptance of deception, some have thought that the Internet and expanding media channels would usher in new modes of democratic and/or undistorted communication. However, this has not necessarily occurred (Andrejevic, 2003; Gutstein, 1999; McChesney, 2000). Does today's media environment still resemble the "culture industry" described by Horkheimer and Adorno? What has changed—for better and/or worse? Jansen prods media reformers to "get their houses in order" (reading 35). What are the best strategies to overcome the acceptance of deception? Where does change have to occur? What kinds of forums may be able to overcome this distortion? Again, taking a note from Jansen, what is the job of critical theorists in a technological-information culture, and where do the Internet and other continually developing media fit into this job?

3. There are many interpretations of identity in the critical tradition. Gendered identity, colonizer-colonized identity, supervisor-employee identity, and racial identity are some specific identities addressed. What are the ramifications of different enactments, embodiments, or ways of communicating an identity? One way to explore this would be to examine different communication of similar identities. Begin, for example, with a recent book by Marjorie Williams (2005), a *Washington Post* columnist. Comparing her essays to those of other female newspaper columnists such as Anna Quindlen, Maureen Dowd, Anne Applebaum, Ellen Goodman, and Susan Estrich, one can see an array of enactments of a similar public identity.

What topics or issues does each of these women choose to write about? What styles do they use? What are the pros and cons of each of these enactments? What would Butler (1990) or other theorists say about these performances of identity? This project could be done with any other category of identity as well, such as Christian, African American, parent, or businessperson.

4. Processes of economic and cultural globalization are often said to be bringing the world closer together. Reflect on this claim in light of postcolonial theory (additional readings under E above) and critical cultural writings such as the chapters on globalization in Bennett et al. (2005) and Miller (2001). What light do these ideas shed on current debates about free trade, intellectual property, cultural imperialism, and democracy?

5. Building on Deetz's analysis of discursive closure and Jansen's review of dialogic models in critical theory, consider how undistorted communication ultimately must be enacted in the micropractices of everyday interaction. How can we talk to each other in order to produce nondomination? What kinds of talk (including nonverbal gestures, etc.) are appropriate in a culturally diverse world? Is the ideal speech situation an appropriate model for these needed forms of communication? In addition to critical comments on Habermas by Deetz and Jansen, consider Cooren's (2000) argument that Habermas relies on a false distinction between strategic and communicative action. What would undistorted communication actually look like in practice? Can microanalysis of conversation (for example, Speer, 2005) discover the needed evidence?

REFERENCES

Agger, B. (1998). *Critical social theories: An introduction.* Boulder, CO: Westview Press.

Andrejevic, M. (2003). *Reality TV: The work of being watched.* Lanham, MD: Rowman & Littlefield.

Ashcraft, K. L., & Allen, B. J. (2003). The racial foundation of organizational communication. *Communication Theory, 13*(1), 5–38.

Ashcraft, K. L., & Mumby, D. K. (2004). *Reworking gender: A feminist communicology of organization.* Thousand Oaks, CA: Sage.

Ashcroft, B., Griffiths, G., & Tiffin, H. (Eds.). (2005). *The post-colonial studies reader* (2nd ed.). New York: Routledge.

Aune, J. A. (1994). *Rhetoric and Marxism.* Boulder, CO: Westview Press.

Bennett, T., Grossberg, L., Morris, M., & Williams, R. (2005). *New keywords: A revised vocabulary of culture and society.* Malden, MA: Blackwell.

Bhabha, H. K. (2004). *The location of culture.* London: Routledge.

Bobo, J. (Ed.). (2001). *Black feminist cultural criticism.* Malden, MA: Blackwell.

Butler, J. P. (1990). *Gender trouble and the subversion of identity.* New York: Routledge.

Clark, C., & O'Donnell, J. (Eds.). (1999). *Becoming and unbecoming white: Owning and disowning a racial identity.* Westport, CT: Bergin & Garvey.

Collins, P. H. (2000). *Black feminist thought: Knowledge, consciousness, and the politics of empowerment* (2nd ed.). New York: Routledge.

Cooren, F. (2000). Toward another ideal speech situation: A critique of Habermas' reinterpretation of speech act theory. *Quarterly Journal of Speech, 86,* 295–317.

Crenshaw, K., Gotanda, N., Peller, G., & Thomas, K. (Eds.). (1996). *Critical race theory: The key writings that formed the movement.* New York: New Press.

Deetz, S. A. (1992). *Democracy in an age of corporate colonization: Developments in communication and the politics of everyday life.* Albany: State University of New York Press.

Deetz, S. (2005). Critical theory. In S. May & D. K. Mumby (Eds.), *Engaging organizational communication theory and research: Multiple perspectives* (pp. 85–111). Thousand Oaks, CA: Sage.

Delgado, R., & Stefancic, J. (2001). *Critical race theory: An introduction.* New York: New York University Press.

Donovan, J. (2000). *Feminist theory: The intellectual traditions of American feminism* (3rd ed.). New York: Continuum.

Dow, B. J., & Condit, C. M. (2005). The state of the art in feminist scholarship in communication. *Journal of Communication, 55*(3), 448–478.

Fanon, F. (1963). *The wretched of the earth* (C. Farrington, Trans.). New York: Grove Weidenfeld. (Original work published 1961)

Fanon, F. (1967). *Black skin, white masks* (C. L. Markmann, Trans.). New York: Grove Press. (Original work published 1952)

Gandy, O. H., Jr. (1998). *Communication and race: A structural perspective.* New York: Oxford University Press.

Gramsci, A. (1971). *Selections from the prison notebooks* (Q. Hoare & G. N. Smith, Trans.). New York: International Publishers.

Grossberg, L. (1997). *Bringing it all back home: Essays on cultural studies.* Durham, NC: Duke University Press.

Grossberg, L., Nelson, C., & Treichler, P. A. (Eds.). (1992) *Cultural studies.* New York: Routledge.

Gutstein, D. (1999). *E.con: How the internet undermines democracy.* Buffalo, NY: Stoddart.

Habermas, J. (1984). *The theory of communicative action: Vol. 1. Reason and the rationalization of society* (T. McCarthy, Trans.). Boston: Beacon Press. (Original work published 1981)

Habermas, J. (1987). *The theory of communicative action: Vol. 2. Lifeworld and system: A critique of functionalist reason* (T. McCarthy, Trans.). Boston: Beacon Press. (Original work published 1981)

Hall, S. (1997). *Representation: Cultural representations and signifying practices.* Thousand Oaks, CA: Sage.

Hardt, H. (1992). *Critical communication studies: Communication, history, and theory in America.* London: Routledge.

Horkheimer, M., & Adorno, T. W. (1976). *Dialectic of enlightenment* (J. Cumming, Trans.). New York: Continuum International. (Original work published 1944)

Jansen, S. C. (2002). *Critical communication theory: Power, media, gender, and technology.* Lanham, MD: Rowman & Littlefield.

Kavoori, A. P. (1998). Getting past the latest "post": Assessing the term "post-colonial." *Critical Studies in Mass Communication, 15,* 195–203.

Kramarae, C. (1989). Feminist theories of communication. In E. Barnouw, G. Gerbner, W. Schramm, T. L. Worth, & L. Gross (Eds.), *International encyclopedia of communications* (Vol. 2, pp. 157–160). New York: Oxford University Press.

McChesney, R. W. (2000). *Rich media, poor democracy: Communication politics in dubious times.* New York: New Press.

Miller, T. (Ed.). (2001). *A companion to cultural studies.* Malden, MA: Blackwell.

Mohanty, C. T. (2003). *Feminism without borders: Decolonizing theory, practicing solidarity*. Durham, NC: Duke University Press.

Morley, D., & Chen, K.-H. (Eds.). (1996). *Stuart Hall: Critical dialogues in cultural studies*. London: Routledge.

Nakayama, T. K., & Martin, J. N. (Eds.). (1999). *Whiteness: The communication of social identity*. Thousand Oaks, CA: Sage.

Rakow, L. F., & Wackwitz, L. A. (Eds.). (2004). *Feminist communication theory: Selections in context*. Thousand Oaks, CA: Sage.

Rasmussen, D. M. (Ed.). (1996). *The handbook of critical theory*. Malden, MA: Blackwell.

Rush, F. (Ed.). (2004). *The Cambridge companion to critical theory*. Cambridge: Cambridge University Press.

Said, E. (1979). *Orientalism*. New York: Vintage.

Schiller, D. (1996). *Theorizing communication: A history*. New York: Oxford University Press.

Shome, R. (1998). Caught in the term "post-colonial": Why the "post-colonial" still matters. *Critical Studies in Mass Communication, 15*, 203–212.

Speer, S. (2005). *Gender talk: Feminism, discourse, and conversation analysis*. New York: Routledge.

Spivak, G. C. (1999). *A critique of postcolonial reason: Toward a history of a vanishing present*. Cambridge, MA: Harvard University Press.

Williams, M. (2005). *The woman at the Washington zoo: Writings on politics, family, and fate*. New York: Public Affairs Books.

Young, R. J. C. (2001). *Postcolonialism: An historical introduction*. Malden, MA: Blackwell.

CONCLUDING REFLECTIONS

ROBERT T. CRAIG AND HEIDI L. MULLER

Having surveyed seven traditions of communication theory, we now step back to reflect on the state of the field and the communication problems that seem especially ripe for theorizing at the present time. The field of communication theory faces interesting questions concerning the blending or hybridization of traditions and the polarization between discursive and behavioral theories of communication. Several new or previously unrecognized traditions may also be emerging in response to current communication problems. We reflect on each of these topics in the following sections.

HOMOGENIZATION, POLARIZATION, OR FRAGMENTATION?

One question is whether progressive cross influences and converging trends among the seven traditions are making the distinctions among them less relevant. Is the field becoming more homogeneous? Or, to the contrary, will constant innovation and debate continue the proliferation of communication theories, progressively fragmenting the field? Is there an optimal balance that we should be seeking between these opposite tendencies toward homogenization and fragmentation? Is the debate about communication beginning to organize itself around a new set of distinctions that require a different model for the field?

Blending, hybridization, and innovation are all inevitable and all potentially good things from our point of view. We would be more than delighted for the next edition of *Theorizing Communication: Readings Across Traditions* to demonstrate that the ongoing conversation in the field has reconfigured the main positions. Conversation across the traditions of communication theory is a chief goal of the project of theorizing, for the very reason that conversation sparks new insights and the potential for adaptive change. If we can agree that cultivating the practice of communication, addressing communication problems in society, is a common project that makes the conversation worthwhile, there is no reason to worry that the field will become either totally homogenized or hopelessly fragmented. The distinctions among traditions of theorizing communication that we have explored in this book—communication as a practical art (rhetoric), communication as experience of the other (phenomenology), and so on—will continue to be available as resources for thought even as the traditions themselves evolve. Intellectual debate in the human sciences seldom leads to homogeneity. Instead, intellectual debate typically leads to finer distinctions among more clearly delineated, better thought-out views, an outcome that should be valued in our field for its potential to increase the sophistication and critical reflectiveness of communication theory and practice.

Nevertheless, it is true that cross-tradition influences and general intellectual trends can blur distinctions among existing traditions of thought. A trend toward postmodern (discursive, radically reflexive, dialogical, social constructionist) thinking is evident in the more recent readings across several traditions, with sociopsychological theory a notable exception to this trend. Foss and Griffin (reading 9) push the rhetorical tradition "beyond persuasion" while Peters (reading 14) leads semiotic thought toward a "democracy" of universal communication that would be "transspecies, transgender, transrace, transregion, transclass, transage, transhuman." Chang (reading 18) "deconstructs" communication in the phenomenological tradition, concluding that communication is "undecidable." Luhmann (reading 22) takes the postmodern turn in cybernetics with his seemingly paradoxical claim that "only communication communicates," whereas Poster (reading 28) brings post-structuralist thought to sociocultural theory. The newer readings in sociocultural and critical theory similarly follow a broad trend toward theorizing communication and society in terms of discourse. Is this apparent postmodern trend across traditions merely an artifact of our bias in selecting readings, or is the field now becoming polarized between a somewhat homogenized *postmodern tradition* in which communication is defined as *discourse* and a *sociopsychological tradition* in which it continues to be defined as *behavioral interaction*?

On the other hand, does a postmodernist tilt in our selection of readings confirm Myers's (2001) criticism that our constitutive metamodel is really a way of smuggling relativistic, social constructionist assumptions into the field as a grand theory, thereby eviscerating all other traditions?

Our model of the field indeed is based on a discursive, postmodern metatheory, which puts it in line with discursive approaches in contrast to the behavioral interaction approach of social psychology. However, keeping in mind that there are different levels of theorization, as Craig (2001) argued in reply to Myers, a discursive metatheory does not rule out nondiscursive conceptions of the field in particular traditions. Rather, this metamodel highlights the variety of ways of theorizing communication and hopefully facilitates productive discourse among those varying conceptions. All communication theorists can engage in discourse with other theorists without necessarily conceding that communication should be theorized exclusively as discourse. Myers's criticism is therefore disputed. Whether theorists in different traditions will actually engage with the practical implications of each other's theories in the way that our model of the field calls for is a different question altogether. We remain hopeful.

EMERGING TRADITIONS?

The trend toward postmodern theory across traditions is interesting. Other critiques suggest, however, that more, not fewer, traditions of communication theory need to be recognized. Maybe postmodernism, with its central notions of discourse and discursive formations, should be parsed out as a distinct tradition of communication theory. Craig (reading 5) envisioned the possibility of traditions based on feminist, aesthetic, economic, and spiritual conceptions of communication while he questioned the idea of a biological tradition. As we have suggested in the unit II projects and elsewhere, theorizing these or other traditions within the framework of the constitutive metamodel (the matrix of traditions) could be a useful contribution. To illustrate further what this would involve in particular cases, let us briefly consider the current status of four candidate traditions: feminism, biology, pragmatism, and, for want of a better term, non-Western thought.

Feminism

A *feminist tradition* seems to us particularly ripe for theorization, although no consensus has yet crystallized on a distinct feminist way of conceptualizing communication problems. Feminist thought has become an important influence across several traditions of communication theory and takes on different colorations as it appears in different traditions: feminist rhetoric, gender studies in social psychology, and so on. It can be argued that feminism's critical posture toward gender ideologies and its social change commitments place it primarily in the critical tradition. However, as we noted in the unit II introduction, some aspects of feminist thought seem inconsistent with the theme of discursive reflection that we find at the center of critical theory. The rationalistic tendencies of some forms of critical theory, its elevation of theory as a normative standard for practice, its drive to unmask distortions, perhaps sometimes at the expense of failing to listen to the voices of others, all strike us as valid criticisms of critical theory from what might be considered a typically feminist point of view. Behind that point of view may be a distinct, feminist way of theorizing communication that has not yet been fully articulated to our model of the field.

Note that the question is not whether feminism is a coherent (though highly diverse) tradition of thought and practice that addresses important social problems. It clearly is and does. The question is whether that tradition has developed a distinct way of understanding communication and communication problems, a distinct metadiscursive vocabulary, and so on—that is, a tradition of communication theory parallel to the other seven traditions presented in this book yet clearly different from all of them. Although we are not yet prepared to add a feminist row and column to our matrix of theoretical traditions (see Tables 5.1 and 5.2, reading 5), we do find some intriguing suggestions in the recent literature. Kramarae (1989) stated that feminist theories of communication "welcome a plurality of perspectives" and "focus on the importance and

usefulness of talk, connectedness, and relationships" (p. 157). Feminist theories also highlight women's experiences and are critical of traditional gender-based language and the public-private distinction, according to Kramarae. Foss, Foss, and Griffin (1999) emphasized their commitment to specific feminist values and principles such as "self-determination, immanent value, affirmation, mutuality, and care" and against "oppression, domination, and hierarchy" (p. 5) as a basis for transforming the theory and practice of communication.

Rakow and Wackwitz (2004), while maintaining that feminist communication theory "does not begin with an assumption about or definition of communication" (p. 5), used three emergent themes—difference, voice, and representation—to build a conceptual framework for presenting feminist theories. In this view, communication is a process in which socially constructed distinctions (of gender, race, etc.) cast people into certain relationships, grant or deny them opportunities to speak and be heard, and are reinforced or undermined by media representations. Ashcraft (2005), finally, has proposed an explicit feminist definition of communication: "the dynamic, situated, embodied, and contested process of creating systems of gendered meanings and identities by invoking, articulating, and/or altering available discourses" (p. 154). Do these feminist writings converge toward a common, distinctive way of theorizing communication? If so, then the task of conceptualizing that tradition more fully and engaging it in dialogue with other traditions in the field cries out for attention.

Biology

Although Craig (reading 5) argued against a *biological tradition* of communication theory, prepublication reviewers of this book suggested we should reconsider that stance. Their concern is understandable in light of the growing evidence that many aspects of human behavior are genetically influenced. Biological explanations of human communication have been extensively discussed in recent years (Ayers, 2000; Beatty, McCroskey, & Valencic, 2001; Cappella, 1996; Teboul & Cole, 2005; Sherry, 2004). As with feminism, the question is not whether biology will continue to have a prominent role in communication theory. Current trends certainly indicate that it will. The question is whether biological communication theories cohere around a distinct conceptualization of communication per se, one that needs to be articulated as a new row and column in the matrix of theoretical traditions. Of this, we are skeptical. Rather than contributing a distinct way of theorizing communication, biological thinking contributes to several traditions already included in our model of the field, especially the sociopsychological, semiotic, cybernetic, and sociocultural traditions.

Recall that the sociopsychological tradition theorizes communication as a process of interaction and influence. Communication problems are discussed in terms of how to influence human behavior and manage interactions effectively. What biology contributes to this tradition is not a new concept of communication but a different way of explaining human behavior that changes how we think about practical problems of interaction and influence. For example, if personality traits like extraversion and self-monitoring are strongly influenced by genetics (Beatty et al., 2001; Yamagata et al., 2006), they are likely to affect communication behavior in ways that are both practically consequential and highly resistant to change. Does this mean that in the future we will be using drugs and gene therapy to solve our communication problems? This is a question to be pondered from many points of view (e.g., Silva, 2005). What sociopsychological communication theory can contribute to the debate is a clearer understanding of the complex ways that biological factors affect communication processes and outcomes along with many other individual, relational, and social factors (Condit, 2000; Sherry, 2004).

Another quite different biological approach to communication contributes primarily to semiotic theory. Recall that the semiotic tradition theorizes communication as an intersubjective process mediated by systems of signs. Communication problems are discussed in terms of signs, codes, and meanings. Biology contributes to this tradition through studies of signaling systems in animal communication and evolutionary explanations of sign systems in general (Hauser, 1996; Liska, 1993). The underlying concept of communication still comes from the semiotic tradition, but biology can enrich our understanding of semiotic systems and processes.

Yet another strand of biological theory relies on cybernetic concepts of communication, sometimes in combination with semiotic or sociopsychological concepts. Recall that cybernetics theorizes communication as information processing. Biological organisms are, of course, cybernetic systems and have often been used as a model for understanding complex systems in general. Maturana and Varela's (1980) theory of *autopoiesis* is currently a very influential example in this genre of cybernetic theorizing (see Luhmann's application of autopoiesis, reading 22). With the discovery of the genetic code, basic biological processes have been retheorized in terms of information processing. Biotechnology and information technology seem to be merging in a new metatechnology of biological and digital information (Braman, 2004). Because genetic codes can also be analyzed as semiotic systems, theorizing at the intersection of cybernetics and semiotics has been stimulated by these developments (e.g., Barbieri, 2006; Brier, 2006).

Finally, biology also contributes to the sociocultural tradition in which communication is theorized as shared social and cultural patterns that enable coordinated interaction. As Mattelart illustrates (reading 3), metaphors from biology have long been used as a way of understanding society. Societies grow, develop, and evolve like organisms. The flow of people, goods, and information through transportation and communication channels is like the flow of blood bringing oxygen and nutrients to all parts of the body. Here, the underlying metaphor of communication is actually biological in origin, but it is used as a way of understanding communication as a sociocultural process. This biological metaphor of communication is not the basis of a coherent biological tradition of communication theory. For example, it plays no role at all in sociopsychological theory (except tangentially, perhaps, in discussions of personal or relational growth), and cybernetics replaces it with the more abstract, nonbiological terminology of information processing and systems.

We conclude, then, that biology contributes to our understanding of communication in many ways, but biology has not yet produced a distinct, coherent tradition of communication theory in its own right. To us, this is an important distinction.

Pragmatism

A *pragmatist tradition* of communication theory recently has been proposed by Russill (2004, 2005) and further elaborated by Craig (in press). As Russill points out, our model of the field is strongly influenced by philosophical pragmatism—a philosophy that espouses pluralism (the idea that many different perspectives on truth can all be valid in different ways), orients to practical problems, and evaluates ideas according to their usefulness rather than by an absolute standard of truth (for more on pragmatism, see Perry, 2001). Our model of the field is clearly based on those pragmatist principles: seven (or more!) traditions, all of them valid in different ways; a field that is unified by its common orientation to practical communication problems; and a metatheory that posits usefulness as the essential standard for evaluating theories. Why, then, did Craig neglect to mention pragmatism in his original analysis of communication theory as a field (reading 5)? Why did he not recognize it as one of the main traditions of communication theory? Probably, he did not think of doing so because pragmatism has never, until now, been explicitly articulated as a theory of communication in its own right, despite the widespread influence of pragmatist ideas across much of the field.

Russill (2004, 2005), however, finds a distinct conceptualization of communication at the heart of pragmatist thought, especially in the work of

William James, George H. Mead, and John Dewey. Craig (in press) goes on to elaborate this tradition as a new row and column of our theoretical matrix. In this tradition, communication is the practice of pluralistic community, and problems of communication arise from *incommensurability*—the impossibility of translating between different points of view or measuring them by a common standard. If different people and social groups have different perspectives on reality and if those different perspectives cannot be fully expressed in each other's terms, then how is it possible to form an inclusive, cooperative community based on mutual understanding? This is the problem that Dewey addressed in *The Public and Its Problems* (1927), arguing that a vibrant democratic public "will have its consummation [only] when free social inquiry is indissolubly wedded to the art of full and moving communication" (p. 184).

Although it is only now being articulated explicitly as a distinct tradition of communication theory, this pragmatist ideal of pluralistic community has been an important thread running through much of the communication theory of the last century. One task for the project of theorizing that now needs attention is to follow that thread as it weaves through various other traditions to develop a more comprehensive picture of the history of pragmatist communication theory. Carey's ritual model (reading 4), with its emphasis on the community-building function of communication, contributes to this tradition. Coordinated Management of Meaning (CMM) is another important theory in this tradition, a theory that was hard to place in this book because it falls through the cracks—that is, it does not very well illustrate any of the seven traditions although it relates to several. Initially developed by Pearce and Cronen (1980), CMM is best understood as a pragmatist theory that responds to the problem of incommensurability: how people with different perspectives on reality are able to cooperate. In subsequent writings, Pearce has focused on the pluralistic community-building side of CMM (Pearce, 1989; Pearce & Littlejohn, 1997), while Cronen (2001; Cronen &

Chetro-Szivos, 2001) has deepened its roots in pragmatist philosophy. One great advantage of recognizing a pragmatist tradition of communication theory is that it allows us to see the ritual model, CMM, and probably many other communication theories in a clearer light.

At the same time, conceptualizing a pragmatist tradition poses an interesting challenge to our model of communication theory as a field. As Russill (2004) points out, our model itself is a communication theory in the pragmatist tradition, explicitly intended to construct a pluralistic community and to promote better communication and cooperation among diverse theoretical perspectives across the field. Is pragmatism one tradition in the field or is it a metatradition that defines the entire field? Can it be both? Craig (in press) has presented some initial thoughts on these questions.

Non-Western Traditions

Finally, let us return briefly to an issue that was broached early in this book (unit I projects, 2): the Western cultural bias of communication theory. Every tradition of communication theory we have examined, including each of the three candidate traditions just discussed, derives primarily from traditions of European thought and civilization, some perhaps even going back to the archaic Greek culture described by Wiseman (reading 1). Most of our current theories of communication have been written in Europe and North America by scholars of European heritage and reflect in some ways, as all theories do, the sociocultural backgrounds of those theorists. Critics have argued not only that these Western theories do not necessarily apply to people of non-Western cultures, but also that the intellectual range of communication theory and its potential for universal relevance are limited by the field's current inattention to non-Western traditions of thought, even among non-Western scholars themselves.

Miike (2006), for example, has proposed that Asian communication studies should pursue an Asiacentric agenda "that insists on placing Asian values and ideals at the center of inquiry in order to see Asian phenomena from the standpoint of Asians as subjects and agents" (p. 5). One component of this Asiacentric project of theorizing communication is to derive theoretical insights by studying concepts indigenous to Asian cultures "in order to consider and reconceptualize the nature of human communication" (p. 14). Among many other examples, Miike mentions "Thai concepts such as *bhunkun* (reciprocation of favors) and *kreng jai* (consideration, familiarity, and comfort)," which, he suggests, "have profound implications for theorizing about the psychology of the Asian communicator and the practices of Asian communication" (p. 15).

Clearly, we should not now consider adding a non-Western row and column to our matrix of traditions. Even if we (or better qualified scholars) could come up with a credible formulation, the reduction of non-Western thought to a single tradition among seven (or eight, or nine, . . .) Western traditions would only reify the field's ethnocentrism. As Miike points out (2006, pp. 20–22), non-Western traditions challenge the field at a metatheoretical level. Not only our theories but also our definitions of theory may turn out to be Eurocentric. If our model of the field as a whole is culturally biased, then simply adding any number of non-Western or other ethnically based traditions will not solve the problem. Every encounter with a different way of theorizing and practicing communication potentially challenges our own thought and practice on all levels. The best advice to communication theorists at present is "to be diligent students of non-Western learning and abandon the role of being teachers at all times" (Miike, 2006, p. 23). How this learning will ultimately reshape the field of communication theory cannot be known in advance.

Miike's (2006) particular version of Asiacentrism is controversial. For example, he criticizes Kim's (2002) theory of interdependent self-construals because it continues to apply standard sociopsychological methods of theory construction even while it challenges the individualistic assumptions of current (Western) theories. Recalling the trend toward biological explanations in social psychology (e.g., Yamagata et al., 2006), we can anticipate a long argument about the potential for universal versus culturally specific theories of communication. Ito (1989) advocated using indigenous Asian concepts to construct new communication theories but also saw a role for more universal theories. The project of theorizing non-Western traditions of communication faces many issues. On one point, however, we cannot but agree with Miike: "Without a shadow of a doubt, theorizing about non-Western communication philosophies and practices is a compelling academic undertaking in the 21st century" (2006, p. 23).

ADVANCING THE FIELD

Note that these four candidate traditions all raise different kinds of questions for the field and illustrate different ways that new traditions can possibly contribute. Feminism potentially contributes a unique conceptualization of communication and a new set of distinctions between the feminist approach and other traditions: in effect, a new row and column in our matrix of the field. Biology, in contrast, does not seem to warrant a new row and column of its own but still contributes to several existing traditions of communication theory. Pragmatism and non-Western theory, like the polarization of postmodern versus sociopsychological theory discussed earlier, raise even more complex questions, each having implications not only for the base level of communication theorizing (the possible addition of new rows and columns to our matrix) but for the metalevel structure of the field as a whole.

Also note that these various questions and new possibilities would never occur to someone who worked exclusively in one tradition of communication theory. Only by reading and thinking across traditions, as we have done in this book, can we advance the field as a whole while conducting specialized work on particular topics.

All of these emerging themes and traditions reflect efforts by theorists to address practical communication problems in our current sociohistorical situation. Changing gender roles, the need for pluralistic community in an increasingly interdependent world, advances in biotechnology, and the ongoing emergence of a global culture and economy are among the pressing social concerns that currently challenge the field of communication theory.

The countless questions and possibilities discussed here and throughout the book also make clear in a positive spirit that the field of communication theory is dynamic and constantly changing, a process we hope this new introduction to the field will encourage. This anthology of readings across traditions does not propose a fixed model or a set of canonical texts for communication theory. Instead, we hope it will open new avenues for innovation and entice readers to join in the vital project of theorizing communication for the 21st century.

REFERENCES

Ashcraft, K. L. (2005). Feminist organizational communication studies: Engaging gender in public and private. In S. May & D. K. Mumby (Eds.), *Engaging organizational communication theory and research: Multiple perspectives* (pp. 141–169). Thousand Oaks, CA: Sage.

Ayers, J. (Ed.). (2000). Special focus: The nature/nurture balance. *Communication Education, 49*(1), vii–98.

Barbieri, M. (2006). Life and semiosis: The real nature of information and meaning. *Semiotica, 158,* 233–254.

Beatty, M. J., McCroskey, J. C., & Valencic, K. M. (2001). *The biology of communication: A communibiological perspective.* Cresskill, NJ: Hampton Press.

Braman, S. (Ed.). (2004). *Biotechnology and communication: The meta-technologies of information.* New York: Lawrence Erlbaum.

Brier, S. (2006). The cybersemiotic model of communication: An evolutionary model of the threshold between semiosis and informational exchange. *Semiotica, 158,* 255–296.

Cappella, J. N. (Ed.). (1996). Symposium: Biology and communication. *Journal of Communication, 46*(3), 4–84.

Chen, G.-M., & Miike, Y. (Eds.). (2003). Asian approaches to human communication [Special issue]. *Intercultural Communication Studies, 12*(4), 1–218.

Condit, C. M. (2000). Culture and biology in human communication: Toward a multi-causal model. *Communication Education, 49*(1), 7–24.

Craig, R. T. (2001). Minding my metamodel, mending Myers. *Communication Theory, 11,* 231–240.

Craig, R. T. (in press). Pragmatism in the field of communication theory. *Communication Theory, 17*(2).

Cronen, V. E. (2001). Practical theory, practical art, and the pragmatic-systemic account of inquiry. *Communication Theory, 11,* 14–35.

Cronen, V. E., & Chetro-Szivos, J. (2001). Pragmatism as a way of inquiring with special reference to a theory of communication and the general form of pragmatic social theory. In D. K. Perry (Ed.), *American pragmatism and communication research* (pp. 27–65). Mahwah, NJ: Lawrence Erlbaum.

Dewey, J. (1927). *The public and its problems.* Chicago: Swallow Press.

Foss, K. A., Foss, S. K., & Griffin, C. L. (1999). *Feminist rhetorical theories.* Thousand Oaks, CA: Sage.

Hauser, M. D. (1996). *The evolution of communication.* Cambridge, MA: MIT Press.

Ito, Y. (1989). A non-Western view of the paradigm dialogues. In B. Dervin, L. Grossberg, B. J. O'Keefe, & E. Wartella (Eds.), *Rethinking communication: Vol. 1. Paradigm issues* (pp. 173–177). Newbury Park, CA: Sage.

Kim, M.-S. (2002). *Non-Western perspectives on human communication.* Thousand Oaks, CA: Sage.

Kramarae, C. (1989). Feminist theories of communication. In E. Barnouw, G. Gerbner, W. Schramm, T. L. Worth, & L. Gross (Eds.), *International encyclopedia of communications* (Vol. 2, pp. 157–160). New York: Oxford University Press.

Liska, J. (1993). Bee dances, bird songs, monkey calls, and cetacean sonar: Is speech unique? *Western Journal of Communication, 57,* 1–26.

Maturana, H. R., & Varela, F. J. (1980). *Autopoiesis and cognition: The realization of the living* (Vol. 42). Dordecht, Holland: Reidel.

Miike, Y. (2006). Non-Western theory in Western research? An Asiacentric agenda for Asian communication studies. *Review of Communication, 6*(1–2), 4–31.

Myers, D. (2001). A pox on all compromises: Reply to Craig (1999). *Communication Theory, 11,* 218–230.

Pearce, W. B. (1989). *Communication and the human condition.* Carbondale: Southern Illinois University Press.

Pearce, W. B., & Cronen, V. E. (1980). *Communication, action, and meaning: The creation of social realities.* New York: Praeger.

Pearce, W. B., & Littlejohn, S. W. (1997). *Moral conflict: When social worlds collide.* Thousand Oaks, CA: Sage.

Perry, D. K. (Ed.). (2001). *American pragmatism and communication research.* Mahwah, NJ: Lawrence Erlbaum.

Rakow, L. F., & Wackwitz, L. A. (2004). *Feminist communication theory: Selections in context.* Thousand Oaks, CA: Sage.

Russill, C. (2004). *Toward a pragmatist theory of communication.* Unpublished doctoral dissertation, Pennsylvania State University, University Park, PA.

Russill, C. (2005). The road not taken: William James's radical empiricism and communication theory. *The Communication Review, 8*(3), 277–305.

Sherry, J. L. (2004). Media effects theory and the nature/nurture debate: A historical overview and directions for future research. *Media Psychology, 6*(1), 83–109.

Silva, V. T. (2005). In the beginning was the gene: The hegemony of genetic thinking in contemporary culture. *Communication Theory, 15*(1), 100–123.

Teboul, J. C. B., & Cole, T. (2005). Relationship development and workplace integration: An evolutionary perspective. *Communication Theory, 15*(4), 389–413.

Yamagata, S., Suzuki, A., Ando, J., Ono, Y., Kijima, N., Yoshimura, K., et al. (2006). Is the genetic structure of human personality universal? A cross-cultural twin study from North America, Europe, and Asia. *Journal of Personality and Social Psychology, 90*(6), 987–998.

AUTHOR INDEX

SUBJECT INDEX

ABOUT THE EDITORS

Robert T. Craig is a Professor of Communication, University of Colorado at Boulder, where he has been on the faculty since 1990 and served as chair of the Department of Communication for 2001–2004. His academic degrees are from the University of Wisconsin–Madison (BA, 1969) and Michigan State University (MA, 1970, and PhD, 1976). Craig's teaching and many scholarly publications have addressed topics in communication theory and philosophy, discourse analysis, and argumentation. His article "Communication Theory as a Field" (included in this volume) received both the International Communication Association's Best Article Award and the National Communication Association's Golden Anniversary Monograph Award in 2000. He is a Past President (2003–2004) of the International Communication Association and was founding editor of the ICA journal, *Communication Theory*.

Heidi L. Muller (PhD, Communication, University of Colorado at Boulder; EdM, Harvard Graduate School of Education; BA, Psychology, Carleton College) is currently a Lecturer for the Communication Studies Program in the School of Communication at the University of Northern Colorado. She researches and theorizes in discussion as a discourse form, developmentally based interactive pedagogy, and symbolic structural foundations of communicative practices. She is the recipient of numerous teaching awards as well as the Award for Communication Excellence from the Rocky Mountain Communication Association (2006).